PENGUIN MODERN CLASSICS

My Happy Days in Hell

György Faludy was born in Budapest in 1910 and died there in 2006. he was educated at the universities of Vienna, Berlin and Graz and left Hungary in 1938 to live in Paris. He served with the US Army during the Second World War and returned to Hungary in 1946. As dramatized in his famous book *My Happy Days in Hell*, he was sent to a labour camp on trumped-up charges for three years. After the failure of the 1956 revolution Faludy left Hungary, living first in London and then in Toronto, before returning to Hungary for the final eighteen years of his immensely long life. He was a poet, editor and translator.

GYÖRGY FALUDY

My Happy Days in Hell

Translated by Kathleen Szasz

PENGUIN BOOKS

To Suzanne

PENGUIN CLASSICS

Published by the Penguin Group
Penguin Books Ltd, 80 Strand, London WC2R ORL, England
Penguin Group (USA), Inc., 375 Hudson Street, New York, New York 10014, USA
Penguin Group (Canada), 90 Eglinton Avenue East, Suite 700, Toronto, Ontario, Canada M4P 2Y3
(a division of Pearson Penguin Canada Inc.)
Penguin Ireland, 25 St Stephen's Green, Dublin 2, Ireland (a division of Penguin Books Ltd)
Penguin Group (Australia), 250 Camberwell Road, Camberwell, Victoria 3124, Australia
(a division of Pearson Australia Group Pty Ltd)
Penguin Books India Pvt Ltd, 11 Community Centre, Panchsheel Park, New Delhi – 110 017, India
Penguin Group (NZ), 67 Apollo Drive, Rosedale, North Shore 0632, New Zealand
(a division of Pearson New Zealand Ltd)
Penguin Books (South Africa) (Pty) Ltd, 24 Sturdee Avenue, Rosebank, Johannesburg 2196, South Africa

Penguin Books Ltd, Registered Offices: 80 Strand, London WC2R ORL, England

www.penguin.com

First published by André Deutsch 1962
Published in Penguin Classics 2010
1

Set in 10.5/13 pt Dante MT
Typeset by Ellipsis Books Limited, Glasgow
Printed in England by Clays Ltd, St Ives plc

ISBN: 978-0-141-19320-5

www.greenpenguin.co.uk

Contents

PART ONE

France

In November, 1938, in Budapest, I was invited to a party at which the guest of honour was a British MP. There was also a fat, very conservative and melancholy baron at the party, as well as a few skinny, radical and cheerful colleagues of mine from the left-wing periodical financed by the above-mentioned right-wing baron. The principal subject of conversation was Munich and its consequences. We argued, shouted, gesticulated and finally came to the conclusion that Hitler could do in Europe exactly as he pleased. Everyone was excited, only the features of the British Member of Parliament preserved their somewhat waxy, statue-like calm as he explained quietly why Chamberlain's policy was correct. When we reached this point, our hostess, a serene and terribly rich lady, no longer young, who made no secret of it that she spent a month or two every year in a lunatic asylum, declared that the topic and mood of our conversation reminded her strongly of the first pages of *War and Peace*.

Our polite British guest hastily changed the subject and began to question us concerning our plans for the future. Béla Horvath, a young Catholic poet who, regardless of the time of the year and the occasion was wearing a bright, checked jacket, black trousers and a Michaelmas daisy in his buttonhole, declared that he would fight against Hitler even if he had to give his life for Christianity, for social justice and for Hungary's independence. He spoke cheerfully, without tragic pose, and in a low voice so as not to disturb the intimate atmosphere of the silk-lined, box-like little salon. He quoted a great deal from the Fathers of the Church, but even more from Chesterton. At the end of his address he joined his hands as if in prayer, raised large, round eyes to the ceiling and thanked the Holy Virgin and his pet saint, St Catherine of Siena, for blessing him with such virility: a virility proved whenever his sense of duty made him speak at mass meetings, whenever his rebelliousness brought him into court, and whenever his pleasure led him into the bed of a peasant girl.

Horvath's impassioned speech seemed to have further saddened the honourable Member, who said in his reply that he had not come to Budapest to interfere with our affairs, yet now begged us to allow him to express his modest and honest opinion. We were all young, some of us – I for instance – almost children. He did not wholeheartedly share our radical views, at least not here (by which he probably meant that only Westerners were worthy of freedom; for us even Horthy's semi-fascist squirearchy was far too good), but he was afraid that should the Germans march into Hungary we would no longer be in a position to express our beliefs. Our periodicals would be confiscated, our books seized and we would be arrested and hanged in secret. The best advice he could give us, he said, was to leave Hungary. It was not impossible that there would soon be a war in spite of Chamberlain's efforts. After the war, however, we could return and serve the ideals for which, today, we would sacrifice ourselves in vain.

We paid no heed to his words because we were too intent upon venting our anger against Chamberlain on the poor man. Two months later all the guests at the party, with the exception of the Catholic poet, had left Hungary. The good baron didn't stop until he reached India. Some had gone to America, others to England.

It was not the honourable Member who made up my mind for me. All he did was to sever the last tie still holding me back – my fear that I would be called a coward for running away. Yet I had good reasons to leave. I knew that if I remained I would have to fight in the Hungarian Army as an ally of the Germans. I knew that if Hitler won the war Hungary would disappear from the map and a few decades hence only the Hungarian serfs of the German landowners would still speak Hungarian when, after a long day's work, they stretched out their aching bones in the darkness of the stable. Only if Hitler lost the war was there a chance of survival for my country, but even that was not certain. It seemed clear to me that in case of war my place was on the side of the so-called enemy.

I, too, had participated in the tragi-comic dress-rehearsal. I, too, had been called up when the Hungarian Army was mobilized in the days before Munich. We had marched through the streets of Budapest to the railway station, accompanied by a military band. At the back exit of the station, however, we were loaded on lorries and driven back to the barracks. In the afternoon we repeated the performance and in the evening we marched through town for the third time. When, at last, we climbed into the train, we had to take off our new uniforms issued by the government and change into old, ragged ones. At the same time we had to hand in our new repeating rifles in exchange for old carbines into which shells had to be fed one by one.

A few hours later I – then commander of one of the signal platoons of the 11th Infantry Regiment – lay with my men on the southern shore of the River Ipoly, two hundred yards from the Czechs. To the left I could hear one of the battalions of the regiment wandering purposeless in the under-brush, until they gradually dispersed to lie down in the shelter of hollows or among the maize. They had no guns and most of their officers had remained behind in the villages because they were afraid of an attack. On our right the fields were deserted. The poplars on the shore, high above the Czechs' concrete shelters, stood in the moonlight like old actors wrapped in dressing gowns, peering barefoot in the door of the larder to see whether there was any wine left. The thick, russet foliage of the autumnal bushes never stirred, as if it were painted; the stage was set for the great moment of ultimate destruction. While the clatter of the Czech tanks echoed across the water I thought that if they attacked now the Hungarian Army would be routed in two hours and the Czechs would march into Budapest by dawn.

When, the next day, we received neither supplies nor reinforcement, neither ammunition nor orders, I contacted the Czechs by radio. The troops facing us came from Pozsony and spoke Hungarian. They invited me to dinner that evening, and I went. When I was filling my rucksack with tins for our soldiers before I left the Czechs, the staff sergeant asked me with friendly directness how long it would be before we attacked. We shouldn't pay attention to their concrete shelters nor to their hand grenades, he said, they all had their white handkerchiefs and towels ready. It was high time someone liquidated that rotten Czechoslovak democracy.

Next day I was summoned to battalion headquarters in the village. A young, tall and nervous colonel hauled me over the coals and declared that he would have me court-martialled for treason. The next minute, however, after he had sent his adjutant from the room, he recited one of my anti-Nazi poems and congratulated me warmly. He begged me to forgive him for arresting me and particularly for not being able to provide a jail befitting my rank, but he couldn't help it. Thereupon he accompanied me to a pigsty which had been thoroughly cleaned out and furnished with a large, wine-coloured couch and a huge, poison-green, betasselled armchair. He made up for this lack of comfort by sending me wine, cigarettes and books.

The colonel profited by the chaos following upon Munich to send me back to my detachment which had, in the meantime, plundered all the orchards of the region and fed itself by throwing hand grenades into a nearby fishpond. Shortly after that we marched into Southern Slovakia, re-annexed to Hungary by the Vienna Resolution. In the territories inhabited by the Slovaks we were watched with fear and mute bitterness, in the Hungarian-inhabited regions we were received with cheers and flowers. We put up in a Hungarian village where, on the second day, my windows were broken by stones during the night and two of my men were knifed in a pub. This occurred after the peasants had found out that henceforth they would receive half as much for their wheat but would have to pay nearly twice as much for industrial products as they had done under the Czechoslovak Republic. A few days later a special company, the so-called *ragged-guardists*, arrived in the neighbourhood. These differed from partisans only in that they carried on their activities not behind the enemy's back but behind that of their own armies. One of their characteristic feats of heroism was to emasculate a Jewish jeweller in front of his wife and children and place the few gold watches he had in his store in a Budapest pawn-shop – presumably for patriotic purposes. As the Ministry of Defence had ordered the regular army not to interfere with the affairs of the special companies, my battalion commander was helpless. Soon we were ordered back to Budapest and only the special company and the gendarmes remained behind to complete the work of liberation. It was then that I decided never to participate again in the military operations of the Hungarian Army, however patriotic I might feel.

The second reason for my emigration was even more pressing. I had written a few satirical poems about the Hungarian fascist leaders. One of them, a deputy by the name of Andras Csilléry, had a heart attack when his malicious secretary showed him my poem after dinner; a poem the social-democratic party disseminated in the form of a leaflet. I had always considered this the greatest achievement of my life. However, until March, 1938, none of my victims had conceived the idea of starting legal proceedings against me. The day following Hitler's entry into Vienna a great many leading officials, judges, prosecutors and intellectuals queued up before the arrow-cross party headquarters at 60 Andrassy Street, to be received into the party. They stood there for hours, many of them red with shame, for few of them truly sympathized with the Nazis. Still, they waited patiently and found comfort in the thought that there was nothing else for them to do since the West would leave Hungary in the lurch as it had done Austria. The atmosphere of the entire country changed from one minute to the next. A series of actions for slander was brought against me and the Public Prosecutor started proceedings because of my anti-Nazi poems. In one case I was sentenced to two years' imprisonment and it seemed probable that the Supreme Court would increase the sentence. In December, 1938, one of the department heads of the Ministry of Justice – Béla Csank – whom I had never met, summoned me to his office and urged me to leave the country as soon as possible because my arrest was impending. I received the same message from the head of the Budapest Police and from Istvan Antal, Minister of Justice. I was deeply moved by their solicitude, mainly because I had considered both my determined enemies. Istvan Antal asked me to let him have a dedicated copy of my poems before I left.

The third reason for my emigration was the mad urge to run away not from the army, not from prison, but from my beautiful wife whom I had married barely a year before.

I had met her three years earlier in the dusty reception room of the liberal newspaper for which I worked. I was sitting there correcting the proofs of some poems of mine when a tall, lovely girl walked in with a provocative, insolent and silly arrogance that immediately repelled me. Outside, heavy snowflakes were falling from a yellow-grey sky; not the first snow of the year.

She excused herself for the intrusion and explained that she had come to copy out a poem from one of the paper's back numbers.

'Take off your coat,' I said and watched her peeling off her fur coat. From the way she did it it was evident that she was used to men helping her off with it.

'The Faludy poems,' I said, 'are always cut out from the office copies and taken home. You won't find a single one . . .'

At first she refused to believe that I was the author of the poem in question. She had imagined me much older, much more dignified. However, she was glad to have been wrong and began to praise my work to high heaven. I cut her short by declaring that I was busy at the moment but would give her a ring very soon and bring her the poem in person. A week later I called on her and asked her to meet me at the indoor swimming pool so as to make my intentions quite clear. She came but I was again disappointed by the way she moved. She walked towards me in her two-piece white swim-suit exactly like a small-town *prima donna* who knows – and knows nothing else – that she is the belle of the town and that all men, from the grocer to the mayor, are crazy about her. Yet her beauty soon made me forget her movements and the excessive make-up on her face. She had a low, rounded forehead, large brown eyes, a short, straight nose, long, exciting lips and a lovely figure. We sat under the sun lamps and I entertained her with a number of amusing stories. She bent forward to listen and involuntarily showed me her small, boyish, pink-tipped breasts. Never before had I seen breasts so beautiful, neither in the Paris music-halls nor in museums: not even on Titian's Venus or the headless Aphrodite of Cyrene. My voice betrayed my excitement and, becoming aware of the reason, she straightened up.

'Back!' I snapped at her, 'back as you were before!'

Obediently she bent her shoulders, then burst into tears. Suddenly I was sorry for her and assured her that I was not the kind of man her mother had undoubtedly warned her against, who seduced girls and then threw them out. She was surprised that I knew her mother's way of thinking so well, but my reassurance comforted her. Ten days later we were sitting in a pastry-shop when I thoughtlessly declared that I would gladly marry her. She blushed with pleasure but made no reply. Later we walked to the ruins of an ancient Roman amphitheatre on the outskirts of town and sat down on thick snow. We kissed until we sank deep into the snow and found ourselves on a wet marble bench, at the bottom of a funnel-shaped well. This is where I woke up. My love for Valy had lasted from the swimming pool to the amphitheatre.

On the way home, I suddenly remembered what I had said to her at the pastry-shop and a wild panic took hold of me. I would gladly have walked the ten miles to her home on my bare feet in the snow to entreat her to forget and forgive, like Henry IV under the walls of Canossa. But it was very late and I knew that her father – a venerable cabinet-maker – retired early. I tossed and turned all night, helpless and desperate, exactly as I was to toss one and a half years later when I was to meet Valy on the following morning at the Register office. I knew beyond a shadow of a doubt that I was insane to keep our date because our marriage was doomed in advance; yet I also knew that I would go because I had promised it to her that afternoon at the pastry-shop and because once or twice she had reminded me of that promise.

Valy was a faithful, honest, loving and selfless wife; she was an excellent housekeeper and she adored me. Or rather, not me, but a gigantic bronze bust of the Platonic idea of the poet as seen by a blue-stocking. When I worked she retired to the kitchen so as not to disturb me by moving about in her room next to mine, and sat motionless on a kitchen stool until daybreak. When we went out together she praised me so loudly and so long that I fled into the darkest corner to hide my shame. She imagined herself my Muse and believed that should she leave me I would perish on the roadside.

Thus it was in my own interest that she protected me and bossed me. As time passed she froze out all my friends and acquaintances. Once, when someone gave me a pot of tulips and she noticed that I looked at the flowers three times in succession, she threw the pot out of the window. She was jealous, hysterical and touchy and because she believed that all poets were solemn and pompous she tried to cure me of my easy-going indolence and irreverence. She loved quarrels, the noisier the better. Whenever we quarrelled she enumerated all the crimes I had committed against her, from the oldest to the most recent, sobbing and screaming until all our neighbours woke. If I fell asleep during these scenes, she shook me awake and reproached me for being a wash-out, good for nothing, not even for a quarrel, and if I still slept on she resumed the quarrel in the morning.

On the afternoon of the day when we moved into our new apartment I went out on to the balcony and made a vow that I would take the first opportunity to get rid of her. I waited a whole year for such an opportunity. In the meantime relations between my parents and my wife became worse and worse. My parents' objection was that Valy came from a relatively insignificant family and had received no dowry – to which I was absolutely indifferent. Their objections, however, compelled me to take my wife's side and the more they ranted the more gallantly I had to defend her. My journey to France offered the long-awaited opportunity to leave her behind. Because of the foreign currency restrictions I could take no more than a few hundred francs with me and my future in Paris seemed absolutely insecure.

Apart from these three negative reasons, my emigration had two positive ones. The first I shall call the yearning for adventure. My life had become too dull, a simple matter of routine, and I hadn't been in Western Europe for over three years. The second reason was Paris itself. Not French democracy, not French military power (which I believed would be able to rout Hitler in no time) and not the city itself, much as I loved it – but the culture of Paris which to my generation was the centre of the world and the shrine of our ideals. It was in the garden of this shrine – we thought – that the antidote to the German poison grew.

We loathed German culture not because of its content but because of its monopolistic influence. When Hungary was founded one thousand years ago the state order of the Holy Roman Empire was adopted. Our Kings' advisers, our craftsmen and our artisans had all come from Germany. Up to the middle of the nineteenth century our urban *bourgeoisie* was almost exclusively German. All our intellectual trends came from Germany ready-made, like bread from the baker: the Reformation from Worms and Wittenberg, the Counter-Reformation from Melk, even the ideals of enlightenment by way of Vienna and the German translations of Voltaire's and Diderot's works printed in Vienna. Our school system was like that of the Prussians, German elements prevailed in our aesthetics and philosophy, our encyclopaedias were translated from the German. In our grammar schools Lessing figured with one, Schiller with three and Goethe with two plays in the obligatory reading, but there was no Shakespeare, no Molière.

We protected ourselves against this Niagara of German culture in two ways. The more atavistic and instinctive protection was a vulgar chauvinism which, though it was in many ways ridiculous, still seemed, with its impassivity and cocky humour, less ridiculous than the tragic and hopeless pathos of the adorers of the West. The trouble with this trend was that, together with German culture, it also rejected the rest of European thought and technical civilization. In summer, particularly in the eastern part of the country, passengers in the Orient Express often wondered why the girls and women working in the fields near the railway lines turned their backs on the train, lifted their skirts and displayed their bare, white behinds. The passengers may have believed that this gesture of peasant contempt was directed against the rich and idle travelling in the train, but in fact it was directed against the railway itself, built by German engineers eighty years before. When anaesthesia was first introduced in Hungary the famous Professor Magyar denounced this decadent and harmful western method and insisted that his own method, the so-called Hungarian narcosis, be used. He made his assistants strap the patient to the operating table and hit him over the head. When one of the country's foremost newspapers sent one of our best writers to

Rome to see the world and write reports on the election of the new Pope, he dispatched a few articles on the difference between stables and cow-sheds he saw in the villages near Rome and stables and cowsheds in Hungary. The rest held no interest for him.

The lowest category of West-lovers consisted of the dandies and old gentlemen dressed in cloth from Manchester who sat at the small tables of the Danube cafés, reading *The Times* even if, as it sometimes happened, they understood not a word of it. *The Times* was their letter-patent of nobility. The other extreme was embodied in Sandor Petöfi, one of the greatest poets of the nineteenth century, who called Goethe an ice-cold, heartless German, despised his work and considered the 'divine Béranger' his unique, brilliant paragon. I adopted more or less the same attitude. My father read Schopenhauer's aphorisms – I read La Rochefoucauld; he read Nietzsche – I read Pascal. The favourites of my fledgling days – Anatole France and Ernest Renan – were conspicuously absent from my father's bookshelves, which were loaded with German classics and German philosophers. My father believed that only a German university could make a man out of a man; I, on the other hand, knew all the Paris metro stations by heart and the order in which the sidestreets opened from the Boulevard St Germain. I set out for Paris as a medieval pilgrim set out for Rome: with humility written all over his face but pride in his heart, because he knew that salvation was awaiting him at the end of his journey.

Finally, the sixth and seventh reasons for my emigration were that two of my acquaintances were already there. One of them was a young Austrian actress with whom I had spent my student years and whom I had not seen for three years; the other was an old politician and publicist, Laszlo Fényes, whom I had met but once, in my childhood. In those days he had appeared to me as a supernatural being. I had often thought of him since; his legend lived on in me as it lived on in the entire country which he had left over fifteen years before.

I had met Laszlo Fényes twenty years before in a small town in northern Hungary, called Zsolna, where my grandparents lived. We used to go there regularly, twice a year, in the autumn and in the Christmas holidays.

My grandfather lived in a large, L-shaped, one-storey house opposite the railway station, looking out towards the mountains. Once upon a time it had been a guest-house and it was so old that every part of it and every piece of furniture it contained was bound to every other by sacred ties of friendship as if they had lived together for centuries. When someone knocked on the front door towards evening, the tall-stemmed wineglasses in the cupboard at the other end of the corridor began to dance like young girls waiting in the twilight to be taken to their first ball; and when a cart turned in to the back gate, the small kitchen window flew open by itself, remembering the servants of yore who used to stick their heads out when the mail-coach arrived, asking the coachmen to tell them the latest news.

Two rooms at the front of the house made up my grandfather's pub – the same two rooms that had once served as public bar and dining-room. Slovaks in white trousers and black boots stood around in them, their slow movements stirring the pipe-smoke and the smell of their mouldy sheepskins into the penetrating aroma of marc-brandy. Dead flies lay between the panes of the double windows on stiffly extended wings, with their legs pulled in like oars.

The roof of the old house was flat and small with a wild vegetation sprouting from it. This I found all the more wonderful as no one in the capital possessed such a roof garden. In wintertime only the tiny red carnations remained, like patches of clotted blood at the end of dry, straw-coloured stems. The huge loft, however, with its window in the roof, where the most diverse mysteries awaited me and where no one but the draught and I knew our way around the heaps of discarded furniture, broken plates, cracked kettles and various odd pieces, was more interesting even than the roof garden. Great big wooden barrels stood in the corners in which I liked to squat for hours like a Robinson Crusoe waiting for his Man Friday. At other times I contemplated the blue and violet glass flowers, moved to tears by their melancholy fate, or played with old jars that had once held mercurial ointment. I found queer-shaped, opalescent bottles haunted by the ghost of ancient perfumes: perfumes used by sutlers and itinerant whores following the armies of Oxenstierna and Wallenstein at the time of the Thirty Years War.

I was happiest, however, when I was allowed to go to the mill and sit on the flour sacks. The mill stood at the bottom of the garden. My grandfather performed his daily chores with slow, familiar movements but sometimes he would stop before me and talk. He would fix his protruding eyes on my face, bend his neck – strong as a bull's – and his beard, white with age and flour, fluttered in the draught. He waved his long-stemmed pipe like a fishing rod. He did not tell me fairy tales, neither did he explain his work. There were but two subjects that aroused his passionate interest: the secrets of the universe and United Europe. He talked simply yet excitingly, the way children should be talked to. Although I understood little of what he said, I remembered every word of it, and years later discovered what he had meant. While he spoke he watched me with tender, appreciative eyes. At the time I thought that his glance expressed only love for his grandson, but later I knew that his joy in me was partly due to the knowledge that when he died there would be someone left to witness the creation of the United States of Europe.

At times visitors looked in at the mill, acquaintances, neighbours, who sat on the flour sacks and gossiped. During these visits my grandfather did not light his pipe but went on with his chores barely listening, asking a question or two out of politeness for his guests. I, however, listened with the greatest attention. The men told of embezzlements and revelries, abductions and secret love affairs; they told malicious anecdotes about the king and the dukes, blackguarded the Prime Minister, Count Istvan Tisza, and called the generals of the monarchy a bunch of idiots. I felt as if I had fallen among conspirators. At home my parents never talked politics and – though with mute disgust – were resigned to the existence of the Austro-Hungarian monarchy. The human race living here seemed to me entirely different from that which I knew in the capital. The people who came to visit my parents did so to fulfil their duty as relatives, acquaintances or friends. They had no worries, no adventures, no love affairs and, what is more, they knew of no such weaknesses in other people.

My favourite among the guests at the mill was Mr Remy, owner of the little town's only hotel. He was an ugly, fat little man who never betrayed the secret of his Christian name. According to my grandfather, when he came into this world fifty years earlier as a healthy male child, his parents, partly because they were Anglophile, partly to save him from military service, registered him as Victoria.

Mr Remy belonged to the rare category of angry fat men. He walked slowly, with great dignity, pushing his protruding belly through the door with care and circumspection as if it were new-born twins in a pram. His speech was loud, excited and breathless; he knew everything about everyone, or rather, he knew everything that was to their discredit. He never praised anyone, but when he spoke of himself his voice softened and tears of self-adulation flooded his eyes.

I listened with rapture while he told of dissolute officers who could not pay their bills, of duels following the terrible quarrels that took place in his restaurant. The fights were divided into two categories: fights between two men started by some drunken guest usually because of a woman; and free-for-all fights started usually by the circumstance that a Czech did not get to his feet quickly enough when the Hungarian national anthem was played. The names of certain county officials and elderly army officers frequently recurred in Mr Remy's stories, but the name of Simon Pan, district administrator of Hatarujfalu, appeared in every single one of them. He was the bogeyman of the region and although I had never met him he loomed so large in my imagination that I often saw him in my dreams.

Every Saturday the district administrator drove into town from his country residence and set up quarters in Mr Remy's hotel. He came down to dinner, sometimes only to listen devoutly to the music, and then retired to sleep. At other times, however, he would rise, walk over to one of the tables and with his long arm – according to Mr Remy it unfurled like the arm of a polyp – would push his selected victim in the chest. Then he would pick the man up and take him on his lap. When he was in a good mood he would stroke and pet the unfortunate fellow, beg his forgiveness, ply him with champagne and entertain him until late in the morning. When he was in a bad mood, however, he would grasp the victim's chin, force open his mouth and spit in it. Then he would wait for the other's Adam's apple to move to make sure he swallowed the spittle. He would repeat this performance several times, then chase the poor thing from the pub with kicks in the pants. There were Saturdays when he skylarked with his friends, broke the mirrors, kicked the furniture to pieces, shot every electric bulb in the chandelier and stood drinks for all those present. In the morning he would drive everyone home in his coach. Then he would dictate to the head-waiter everything he had consumed: 'I had sixteen dinners, thirty-five bottles of champagne, two mirrors, three chairs, seven window-panes and two cracked ribs at twenty forints each.' Because, as Mr Remy declared with awe, Simon Pan was a real gentleman.

Sunday mornings, when the weather was good, Simon Pan would take up his place on the promenade next to the little town's only litter-bin in which the fallen leaves and horse-droppings were collected, and watch the people returning from church. He would select a few – usually Hungarians of the opposition because the Slovaks were all loyal to the government – pick them up by the scruff of the neck and fling them into the litter-bin. He never took more than six. When the bin was full he would close the lid, climb on top and from there smilingly greet his acquaintances, friends and enemies alike.

Mr Remy told in detail about all of Simon Pan's doings – but omitted one. One Saturday – as the barber living nearby recounted – the district administrator and his friends stayed on in the restaurant after closing time. Mr Remy served the guests himself behind closed shutters. By dawn everyone was drunk and Mr Remy thought it was safe to put three unconsumed bottles of champagne on the bill. However, Simon Pan was never drunk enough to overlook such a trick. He declared that he would deprive Mr Remy of his licence unless he pledged himself to fulfil certain conditions. Mr Remy agreed. The following Saturday Simon Pan dined at the hotel. The restaurant was crowded. The district administrator ate in silence with a face as innocent as if he had never in his life harboured an indecent thought. When he had finished he climbed on to the table. Mr Remy, whose head was as red as a beetroot, climbed up behind him, and knelt down. The orchestra played a flourish, Simon Pan lowered his trousers and Mr Remy placed three smacking kisses on the district administrator's bare behind. One of Simon Pan's conditions was that the kisses must be smacking or the whole performance would have to be repeated.

After that little event Mr Remy's face lost some of its cheerfulness. He lost several pounds but continued to speak of Simon Pan with the same reverence as before and seemingly without resentment. Like the others, he too cursed the monarchy and its institutions but he accepted the representatives of those institutions as they were. He hoped that one day the monarchy would disappear but considered Simon Pan eternal and immovable like the mountain on the other shore of the River Vag.

One afternoon, between Christmas and New Year, I was sitting in my grandfather's mill waiting for him to fulfil his promise and take me sledging. We were alone and the old man spoke to me as he usually did about the miracles of the universe. This time it was about the light which flies at a speed of three hundred thousand kilometres per second in space. Whatever happens on earth – he explained – disappears without a trace, but the reflection of the event flies along on the wings of light. 'Imagine to yourself,' he said, 'a gigantic soap-bubble which grows and expands but never bursts. Well, that is the screen on which the history of mankind is projected. The creatures who live on the fixed stars, two thousand light years from us, are now watching the battles of Caesar or Alexander the Great and in two thousand years our life will be running on their screen.'

His hour would come soon, the old man continued, and he too would disappear, leaving no trace except the beam of light he would be sitting on. He wished me a long time on earth before I followed him but regretted we would never meet again, unless, he said doubtfully, Einstein were right and the fourth dimension of curved space turned back his light-beam. When he said that, he gave me a long restless glance. I was about to ask the old man to take me with him when he stepped on that beam of light, when suddenly I heard my grandmother's voice:

'Come in quickly, Father, we have company!'

My grandfather straightened up and made ready to go. Only on rare occasions did he go into his own pub.

'I hope it is not some general,' he murmured on the way.

A middle-aged, bearded man stood at the counter in yellow boots and green knickerbockers. He was drinking gin out of a beer glass.

The horizontal figure-of-eight frame of his spectacles and his plain, country clothes clashed strangely with his belligerent, high shirt-collar and his stiff, rattling cuffs. His jaw-bone and his right hand were covered with scars that looked like notches on a yardstick – obviously souvenirs from various duels. His pink, protruding chin had also been cleft exactly in the middle by a sword, so that it resembled the plucked behind of a turkey. Anyone else would have seemed ridiculous in this get-up, with this exterior.

'Friend,' he turned to my grandfather, speaking in a sharp, jarring voice. Then he made a deep stiff bow. To my surprise, my grandfather took off his cap.

'Sir,' he replied. For a while the two men eyed each other tenderly, deeply moved.

'I came about Simon Pan,' the stranger said. 'I want to finish him.'

He told my grandfather that he had taken the train the same morning in Budapest and had alighted at Zsolna because he wanted to reach Hatarujfalu unnoticed. He had hired a coach but they had been forced to turn back because of the snow. He asked grandfather to lend him his sledge. The coachman would drive it.

My grandfather immediately declared himself ready to oblige the stranger, the only difficulty being that he had promised his grandson to take him sledging. To which the stranger replied that children should never be cheated and that, therefore, he would take me along. Before we set off he gave me a small glass of gin because, he said, he would not take even a baby out into this biting cold without giving him a drink.

Soon we were sitting side by side in the sledge, wrapped in heavy blankets. On the seat, next to the stranger, I noticed a military haversack with the neck of a bottle sticking out of it. When we left the town behind the horses gathered speed, the icy wind hit our faces and we flew on and on like time.

I cast a sly glance at my neighbour. From the side, his face lost much of its bullying quality; with his long, straight, pointed nose he reminded me of the sad-faced knight, Don Quixote, as I knew him from a children's edition of Cervantes, going to battle against the windmills.

When we reached the wooden bridge of Budetin and the coachman raised his whip to egg on the horses, the stranger jumped up and grasped the coachman by the shoulder.

'You scoundrel!' he shouted, 'Leave those horses alone! I told you, didn't I? Or are you deaf?'

'We shall be late, your excellency,' the coachman pleaded. 'At this pace we shall never reach Hatarujfalu by nightfall.'

'If we are late, we are late. I don't care.'

In the meantime the clouds had dispersed and the sky was deep blue as on a May morning. Under the blanket we shared I felt the friendly, animal warmth radiating from my neighbour. His argument with the coachman had filled me with a glowing friendship for him.

An hour later, at the foot of a hill, the coachman again reached for his whip. My friend emitted a deep, inarticulate growl and his hand went to his right hip as if for a gun. The coachman must have sensed the movement because he turned a frightened face towards us.

'Forgive me, your excellency, but it is in my wrist.'

'What is in your wrist?'

'The whipping of horses, your excellency.'

'And do you know what is in my wrist? The slapping of your face!'

The coachman sighed with relief. The passenger was not quite the monster he pretended to be. A few minutes later, on a straight section of the road, he turned back with an insolent grin:

'Has your excellency ever been to Battonya? Has your excellency ever met the squire Janosfalvy? No? I was in his service until 1904. He was a fine gentleman too, like your excellency. And he too loved horses, and every kind of animal. He forbade me to whip the horses. Because I was his coachman. Not even the cows could be prodded on his estate. It took his peasants a week to plough an acre of land. He would allow neither meat nor fish in his kitchen. He was the chairman of the society for the prevention of cruelty to animals. He lived on salad, like a rabbit. And he stuffed himself with raw tomatoes, like a pig. And eggs. And what a beautiful dining-room he had!

Panelled walls and a chandelier as big as a piano. One spring the swallows built their nests in that chandelier. From then until late September the windows of the dining-room had to be left open. And the juice of the fledglings ran down the squire's face as he sat eating his dinner, and the droppings landed on his bald head but he said nothing. He loved animals. But he knew no mercy when it came to his fellow men. Four families lived in every room of the servants' quarters and he beat his own wife with a rope soaked in salt water. She was a sickly woman and soon died of it. His son, disgusted with his father's carryings-on, moved to the capital.'

'Have you finished?'

'There is only the end to come. I mean the squire's end. He died in the summer of 1904, early one morning. It took him a long time to die although he had two doctors attending him. But he had a difficult nature, he had. As soon as he had closed his eyes the bailiff entered from the yard, his boots shining, his gun on his shoulder. He went into the sick-room to make sure the squire was really dead. Then he opened the window. The chickens were scratching about among the dahlias. A large white cock, not less than thirty years old, sat on top of a rose tree. As usual. The bailiff took his gun from his shoulder, shot the cock, then shot the hens, one after the other. When he was through he jumped over the windowsill and ran into the orchard. He shot the jackdaws and crows sitting on the fruit trees. The shooting brought the whole farm alive, the gardener began chasing the ducks from the salad beds. You should have seen them, your excellency, how indignant they were! The footman kicked the dogs from the armchairs in the house and two of the maids threw the cats from the window in dustpans. The grooms reached for their cudgels and gave the donkeys a good beating. There was a lot to make up for. In the evening, when the young squire arrived from the capital, everything was ready for the funeral meal. The pheasants were plucked, the pigs killed and two cows were turning on the spit in front of the manor house. The house, the fields and even the village were drenched in the smell.'

'What smell?'

'The smell of blood, your excellency. Blood.'

My neighbour smiled but made no reply. Half an hour later the coachman halted the horses on the hillside, just before the top, and jumped off his seat.

'The star.' He pointed to the evening star pale in the blue sky.

'Well?'

'*Shabes*, your excellency. I cannot drive on. I am a Jew, your excellency.'

'Are we to spend the night in the open because you are a Jew?'

'I will go into the village and send a *goy* to drive your excellency. If I can find one.'

When we were alone we got down into the fresh snow. Now at last I could ask the question that had been turning in my head all afternoon.

'Uncle, who are you?'

'Difficult question,' the stranger smiled. 'I have been asking myself that question for the last fifty years but I still haven't found the answer. Let's turn the question around. Who do you think I am?'

'Somebody who cuts people's throats.'

'Who told you that?'

'You said so to my grandfather at the pub. You said you wanted to finish Simon Pan.'

'True, I did say that, but I meant it figuratively. However, if we come down to it, you are right,' he added pensively. 'I do cut people's throats. But only bad people's throats. And not with a knife. I travel around in the country, visit the bad people, and then I write up what they are doing. And then they are sacked from their jobs. I have finished four hundred scoundrels to this day but there are many more left. I still have to travel a great deal.'

'And what does your wife say that you travel so much and are never at home?'

'I have no wife,' replied the sad-faced knight. 'But I have a dog.'

It had turned completely dark when a limping young coachman arrived from the village, wearing felt boots. Half an hour later we stopped before the house of the district administrator.

'Why do you stop, you idiot!' my neighbour shouted. 'Take us to the pub, you goof, the pub!'

But he was too late. The tinkling of the sledge's bells had warned those inside of our arrival, the large French windows flew open, and in a second the three steps leading to the road were overrun with laughing, shouting men streaming out of the brightly lit house. I immediately recognized Simon Pan among them. His body, from his Adam's apple to his loins, was shaped like a huge, regular ellipsis, as if his short legs were carrying the petrified, giant egg of a dinosaur. In one hand he waved a long cigar, in the other he held a hand of cards.

'Here you are at last! We thought you would never arrive! Your dinner has gone stone-cold . . .' the men shouted.

My friend stood up in the sledge.

'Gentlemen,' he said in a humble voice, 'you are mistaking me for someone else. I am a poor travelling salesman, selling good liquor at low prices.' With this he raised his haversack with the bottle in it.

'Don't talk rubbish!' Simon Pan exclaimed. 'You are Laszlo Fényes. You have come to write me up in your paper. I got word from Budapest as soon as you took the train. You thought you were very smart getting out at Zsolna. But I was even smarter. My Jew was there waiting for you at the station. The famous Laszlo Fényes walked straight into my trap. Well, walk into my house now.'

'Very kind of you. But, as I have decided to reveal the truth about you I cannot accept your hospitality. I shall spend the night at the inn.'

'No, you won't. I gave orders to close down every public place. And the town crier announced to the villagers that I strictly forbade anyone to talk to you. So, if you won't accept my hospitality you can spend the night outside in this beastly cold with the boy. Come in, man. I'll tell you everything you want to know, all the shady deals, all the lousy tricks, everything my peasants would never dare tell you because they fear me more than God. Come in, man, come in!'

We alighted and the men returned to the dining-room where they continued to drink over the ruins of the finished dinner. Our host took us into the smoking-room where a table, laid for two, was waiting for us. Then he excused himself and returned to his card game in the corner of the room.

Perhaps a hundred candles were burning in the golden candelabra on walls covered with cherry-coloured silk. There were oil prints between the candelabra, one a portrait of the young Franz-Joseph, one of Queen Elizabeth. The third represented the poet, Sandor Petöfi, wounded in the left breast and writing 'Fatherlan' in blood in the dust of the battlefield. The missing letter was meant to signify that he died the hero's death before completing the word. In the dining room gipsies stood behind the drinkers, softly playing their favourite melodies.

First we were given boiled beef and horseradish, then soup, then fried carp, fried chicken and pancakes. My friend was served marc-brandy with the boiled beef, beer with the fish and champagne with the pancakes while I received only wine from the bottle brought in with the chicken. Our host joined us for a moment and drank a toast in champagne to Laszlo Fényes.

'Now come the more substantial dishes,' he reassured us.

And indeed, after a five-minute pause, we were served roast pork and sausages, then roast duck, curd noodles and finally a cream cake. When we had consumed it all the footman asked my friend whether he wanted black coffee boiled in rum or in cognac.

'In water, son.'

'His excellency the district administrator will not allow us to use water for the coffee. He says that is a stinking Jewish custom.'

'It is a Turkish custom, son, but never mind. I'll do without coffee.'

Seeing that we had finished, our host rose from the card table and pulled up a chair between us.

'I am at your service,' he smiled at my friend winningly. 'But before we start on the facts permit me to ask you a question. Are you a descendant of the great statistician Elek Fényes?'

'He was my great-grandfather.'

'I thought so,' the district administrator nodded. 'That makes us distant relatives. The mother of my deceased brother-in-law, Pal Janosfalvy, who chewed grass while he lived, was a Fényes girl. I know your family chronicle pretty well.'

'Very flattering,' Fényes replied icily.

The district administrator was all sweetness and light. He poured champagne, drank to his guest and watched him with shining, almost devout eyes. He spoke so beautifully that I began to doubt the veracity of the stories circulating about him. The journalist, however, remained stiff and unfriendly and every time his host bent closer to him as if about to make a confession, he drew back almost angrily. At such times the muscles above the corners of his mouth tautened and twitched. I resented his unfriendliness. It seemed to me that of the two the district administrator was the more attractive figure, although Fényes treated him like a leper.

I had drunk three glasses of wine and felt dazed; the panelled wall with its cherry-red silk was rocking gently like a Roman galley covered with purple carpets.

'I have often compared the histories of our two families. We are certainly the two poles of the Hungarian globe. Your departed grandfather, Laszlo Fényes, owned five thousand acres in County Bihar. He was a true gentleman and drank like a fish. God bless his memory. Your father, Laszlo II, was left but two thousand acres of the fat Bihar soil. He sat in the House behind Prime Minister Kalman Tisza for fifteen years without opening his mouth once, except when he cheered. He too was a real gentleman. He lost his two thousand acres at the card table, God bless his memory. And here you are, Laszlo III, without land, without wealth, and in addition, a rebel. And yet, you got into Parliament without buying drinks or distributing bribes. I can't imagine how you did it, but you are a man after my heart. I like you even if you come here to wring my neck for me. Your health! Bottoms up!

'But let me get down to brass tacks. My departed grandfather, Simon I, had nothing he could call his own except an old letter of nobility and whatever he saw when he looked behind him in the tub every Christmas, when he took a bath. For twenty-five years he was county recorder of Trencsén. He drank like a fish and yet he acquired nine hundred acres of land, every handful of it by cheating on the land-register, by crooked railroad deals and bribery. God bless his memory. My predecessor in office, my departed father, Simon II, was called the scourge of the Slovaks. He increased the family estate by five hundred acres, God bless his memory. In his youth, he chased skirts. When I was a child – but why don't you drink? You too, child! – I remember him coming home from Zsolna early one morning. As usual, he was bringing an old whore with him who had to sit in front, with the coachman. At the door he ordered her to get off and climb into bed next to his wife, then he lay down between them with his clothes and boots on. Because to him women weren't even worth undressing for.

'In his old age he turned to cards. Sixteen years ago he was lying sick in the next room, in his widower's bed, with his card partners around him. They had been playing for two weeks, from noon till midnight. It was his custom to send the coach for his three favourite partners every year when the first snow fell and not to let them go until the thaw set in. On that particular afternoon my father won every single game. After dinner his partners asked him for a return game. "Why not?" he said. "Of course I shall give you a return game, but you will have to wait until we meet in hell." With that he turned his face to the wall. The partners thought he was joking. They shuffled the cards and waited. But the old man didn't move. They thought he had fallen asleep and waited another half hour. Then they prodded him. He was already cold. He died like a true Hungarian gentleman, God bless his memory.

'And here I am, Simon III,' the district administrator continued with a mild smile. 'I play cards, chase skirts and drink. And still, I doubled the family estate. How? You know it as well as I,' and he laughed at the journalist.

'If you look out of your window before going to sleep you will see in the moonlight the alpine pasture extending behind the house. When I took over my father's heritage I looked at this piece of land and decided that it had been created by God to be an alpine pasture. Only, there was no water. The nearest stream ran across my neighbour's estate, from the hillside to his stables. Not for long, though. One night, I commandeered the village population to perform an urgent and unpaid public job with shovel and spade. I myself led the procession to the top of the hill. By the morning the stream was running behind my house.

'My neighbour, Kazmér, sent word that there were still judges in Hungary! Nevertheless he sold one hundred and fifty head of cattle to the dealer I sent to his door. Why should the poor beasts perish of thirst when I had plenty of water? The judges did their best. Three times they passed judgement against me but somehow the enforcement order never arrived. I had friends in the Ministry of the Interior. More than one. I had almost forgotten the whole affair when, in 1905, the government fell. Two weeks later I received orders from the county sheriff: the Brezina must be returned within two weeks to its rightful owner, Kazmér Prokovszky. I read it over and over again, wondering what to do. In the end I returned the order to the county sheriff but not before I had written on its back: "Your Excellency, my dear old Steve! If you want your orders enforced, send an entire army battalion because, if I know Simon Pan, he will not easily let go of what he considers his own. Yours obediently, Simon Pan."

'Over twelve years have gone by since,' the district administrator continued, 'but the stream is still running behind my house.'

'Aren't you afraid that I shall make this public?' the journalist asked with flashing eyes.

'Go ahead, friend, tell your readers what a bastard I am,' Simon Pan said resignedly. 'I promised to tell you everything and you must use my story the way you see fit. That's your profession.'

'I'll use it not for the sake of my profession but to serve public interest.'

'That is as may be,' the district administrator replied sadly. 'But would you prefer a Slovak to sit in my place? Does it never occur to you that you are fighting your own class? Gentry against gentry? However, let me continue. It does me no good to argue with you . . .'

And Simon Pan went on to tell us with apparent gusto about his election experiences. Once, at election time, a branch line was being laid in his district. He arranged with the contractor that the foundations of the station buildings should be put down exactly two weeks before election day: in the loyal villages the station should be sited in the village itself; in the opposition villages it should be five miles away. Should the opposition villages change their minds, all right, let them have their station building in the village. If not, not. Nagybiccse resisted; its station is still standing five miles outside the village in the middle of nowhere.

One of the election districts consisted of one small loyal village and two large opposition ones. The only voting booth was set up in the loyal village. The problem now was to prevent the inhabitants of the other two villages from voting. Simon Pan surrounded one of the villages with gendarmes who told the villagers that plague had broken out in the area. He planned to deal with the other village in the same way but he discovered that there weren't enough gendarmes. Thereupon he sent an old Jewish commercial traveller to the second village with strict instructions. The traveller announced with the help of the town crier that the same evening, shortly before the train was due to leave, he would buy up hens' droppings for two crowns fifty a pushcartful. Who would have been fool enough to go voting when they could make so much money! The train left but there were still hundreds of pushcarts standing in line before the station building. The traveller walked up and down along the line in his long, black jacket. He pushed his walking-stick into every cartful, pulled it out, smelled the dirty end and shook his head. 'There's cocks' droppings mixed in with it,' he said. 'Didn't you hear me, men? I said hens' droppings, didn't I?'

The peasants naturally beat the Jew within an inch of his life, but the government party won the elections in the district.

I listened to the stories but grew sleepier and sleepier. The district administrator filled my glass, then got down to his more slippery stories. Dazed with sleep I heard him tell about a pale widow in a lilac dress and a large hat who opened a prosperous brothel with her two young daughters – and the financial help offered by Simon Pan. This story demonstrated the district administrator's kind-heartedness and, reassured, I fell asleep.

I woke lying on a bed with Simon Pan taking off my shoes. My friend lay in the other bed of the guest room in a nightshirt, his pipe between his teeth. At the foot of the bed stood a squat, dark-skinned gipsy with a shy, embarrassed smile on his lips. He held his violin to his chin but his right hand with the bow hung by his side.

The district administrator covered me to the neck, stroked my head and told me to sleep on. Then he went up to the gipsy, spat on his forehead, took a ten-crown note from his vest pocket, tore it in two and stuck half to the gipsy's forehead.

'You will play for his excellency and the young master until morning, but quietly, to give them beautiful dreams. If you stop even a moment I shoot you dead. If you obey you shall have the other half of the banknote in the morning.'

With that, he retired to the other room but left the connecting door slightly ajar. I heard him undress and throw his gun on the marble top of the bedside table. When I woke the next morning the gipsy was still there, pale with exhaustion, but playing valiantly.

Twenty years later when the Paris express crossed the Hungarian frontier and I watched the snowy fields slip by with a strange sadness in my heart, I again remembered that scene. Or, to be exact, I had never forgotten it. But it took time until I had fully understood the meaning of that evening and in the meantime the two protagonists had often changed places in my mind. Immediately after the event I saw Simon Pan like some wonderful being straight out of a fairy tale; compared to him Laszlo Fényes seemed a drab, ordinary, almost insignificant person.

One year later revolution broke out in Hungary and the former Prime Minister, Count Istvan Tisza, was shot. In those days I frequently heard Laszlo Fényes's name mentioned. He was appointed commander of the national guard and later, in the young Republic, Governor of Transylvania.

According to the terms of the 1920 peace treaty, Zsolna was annexed to Czechoslovakia. Only a year later could my parents and I visit my grandparents. From my grandfather we learned that Simon Pan had turned into a great Slovak patriot, pretended that he didn't speak a word of Hungarian, and was occupying a very important post in the state administration. Laszlo Fényes, on the other hand, was in prison accused of the murder of Istivan Tisza. My grandfather declared that he was undoubtedly innocent and just because of his innocence would certainly be hanged.

I did not fully grasp the situation, but somehow Simon Pan and Laszlo Fényes changed places in my imagination. The journalist suddenly seemed interesting, moving, heroic, and the district administrator a disgusting monster. I saw him with a bloated face, hair standing on end, roaring like a boar, while a soft halo drew itself around Laszlo Fényes's undistinguished, angry face. Not even the fact that the judges found him innocent on every point of the accusation altered my admiration.

As soon as I reached Paris I inquired as to his whereabouts and on the second morning I went to see him. None of my compatriots knew his address but I was advised to get out of the metro at Clignancourt and look around. Where I saw a jar of fat on the windowsill, wreaths of red pepper hanging from the latch and chives and dill in flowerpots, I would find Laszlo Fényes.

In the small hotel room – in no way less depressing than my own – soup and vegetables were boiling, meat was roasting on four or five spirit stoves. A pair of shoes stood on a shelf, in one a bag of flour, in the other a bunch of carrots. A pot of geraniums, with pale, anaemic leaves, was standing on the floor under the window.

Laszlo Fényes threw me a suspicious look but when I told him my name he put another plate on the table.

'I cannot offer you a dinner like the one Simon Pan once gave us,' he said. 'Besides, I have had to give up heavy foods. Six years ago, in Vienna, I had a stomach haemorrhage. I was admitted at the Allgemeines Krankenhaus for observation. The next morning, however, when I woke in the common ward I noticed a priest standing in the open door, saying mass. Have you ever heard of such insolence? I got out of bed, took my things and left without seeing a doctor. Since then I have been curing myself.'

Only his side-whiskers were missing, for the rest he looked exactly the same. During dinner he questioned me about Hungary, but he seemed fully informed, knew even the gossip. He then told me why he had to leave Hungary. In the socialist newspaper for which he worked he had published a detailed account of the murders committed by the white terrorists. He reported that these murders had been aided and abetted, and in at least two cases – those of the social democratic journalists Béla Somogyi and Béla Basco – inspired by the regent: Miklos Horthy. But his enemies grew even more incensed when they found out that, dressed as a beggar, he had knocked at the door of Gyula Gömbös, later prime minister, and had listened quietly while Gömbös's silly and good-hearted old mother, who had given him a glass of milk and a piece of bread, boasted of the two German patriots hidden in their loft whom she provided with food. These were the men Fényes was looking for: the escaped murderers of the German chancellor, Matthias Erzberger.

Fényes had to emigrate and in 1934 he participated in the February fights in Vienna on the side of the socialists. He was wounded, escaped to Pozsony, from Pozsony to Prague, from Prague to Paris.

'Do you speak French?' he asked me suddenly.

'Yes.'

'Of course. You translated Villon into Hungarian. When I was young I had a French governess but I remember nothing of what she taught me. I asked you because, not knowing the language, I move about with difficulty, at least in the streets. This is one of those cold, foggy; winter afternoons when one should visit cemeteries. Would you like to accompany me to the Père Lachaise?'

Chopin's grave was the first he wanted to see. Then came Ludwig Börne, the great liberal German journalist who died in exile in Louis-Philippe's days. Then we visited the grave of Otto Bauer, leader of the Austrian social democratic party, and the neighbouring grave, that of an unknown Spanish loyalist. Opposite stood the Mur des Fédérés, a sinister, bullet-scarred wall. On it hung a few wreaths with five-pointed red stars and wind and rain-torn strawberry-coloured ribbons with the inscription: 'To the memory of the Communards.'

'Shall we go closer?' I asked politely when I noticed my companion looking in that direction.

'No,' he replied curtly.

We entered an ugly little bistro opposite the cemetery wall. The old gentleman asked for red wine. When he put down his glass, his stiff cuff emitted the same rattling cough I remembered from our first meeting at my grandfather's inn. We sat side by side on the leather seat running the length of the bistro. The weather had brightened and the evening star shone bright in the evening sky. I glanced at my friend: he wore the same determined but resigned Don Quixote expression he had worn that time on our way to Hatarujfalu.

I am not thirty yet, and already life is a succession of memories, I thought. What does this emigration still hold in store for me?

My neighbour's thoughts must have coincided with mine. He brought out a thick, black pocketbook and extracted a few snapshots.

'This,' he handed me one, 'was taken in 1919, during the Commune, when they wanted to execute me. The rope was already around my neck when the reprieve arrived.'

The picture must have been taken a few minutes before the arrival of the reprieve. It showed Fényes walking between two Red Army men across the cobbled yard. In his left hand he held a large piece of bread and bacon, in his right a pocket knife and he was eating with obvious enjoyment. In the right corner of the snapshot I could discern the scaffold with the loop.

Another picture showed his mother at the window of their manor house, watering the flowers on the sill, and his father, riding to the hunt at the head of a large party. On the side of the road stood a group of peasants, their heads bent, the brims of their hats touching the dust – the light, flour-like dust of the Hungarian lowlands.

In the meantime the bistro had filled with people from the neighbourhood, men on their way home from work, skinny, faded women. They spoke loudly, drank greedily and though individually they seemed cheerful enough, collectively they created an almost hysterical atmosphere in the worn, ugly, yet friendly little place. I looked at my neighbour who seemed to guess my thoughts.

'You want to know what drove me from that manor in County Bihar out among plebeians, revolutionaries and socialists? And finally here? I know you want to ask me but lack the courage,' he added musingly and lighted his pipe. He waited until the glowing spots merged and the top of the tobacco blazed up at every draw like the disc of the setting sun.

'My story is brief and very simple.' He leaned back in his seat, making himself comfortable, as he always did when preparing to tell a story, and his face broke into a smile.

'It happened at the 1883 elections, back home at Ércsoklya. A little platform was raised in the middle of the village from where my father, my brother and I could watch the procession of voters. These processions were a kind of test-match: the contending parties showed their strength. First came my father's followers in carts, on horse-back and on foot. Then came the opposition carrying national banners and cheering Lajos Kossuth. There were relatively few of them, mostly independent farmers owning fifteen to twenty acres, who didn't mind whether the state did or did not give them tobacco-growing contracts or raised their taxes. They were led by three tall, handsome peasants with long moustaches, the principal canvassers of the opposition. When they noticed us, the landowner and his children, they shook their fists at us.

'The next morning I was playing in the garden when I saw them again. They came in through the main gate, side by side, with six gendarmes behind them. Only when they came closer did I notice that they were handcuffed. I followed them into the corridor from where the fireplaces were fed in the winter, and climbed into the fireplace in my father's room. My father was standing by his desk, pulling on a white glove. He wore that glove, always only the right one, when he inspected the work in the fields or was called by the steward when one of the farm-hands was causing trouble.

'The three peasants stood in front of the desk, behind them the gendarmes. My father slapped each in turn, but they never said anything and never stopped bowing from the hip, like poplars in the wind. When my father had finished, he pulled off his glove and threw it on the table.

'"You can go," he said. He looked after them from the window until they disappeared from sight. Then he sat down to his desk, and yawned. He covered the yawn with his hand although he was alone in the room. Well, he too had been brought up by a French governess.'

He fell silent, then motioned to the waiter.

'This is why I am here,' he concluded. 'And now have the kindness to tell the waiter that I have never drunk wine as bad as this in France.'

He counted out the seven francs of our bill in small coins, then threw a ten-franc banknote on the table for a tip. With his greyish-green, old and somewhat rheumy eyes he blinked out of the window to where the light of the street-lamp danced uncertainly on the damp cemetery wall and lit up the small, white, almost decorative cross on top of a tall monument, like an obelisk.

'No, don't tell him anything,' he said and shivered with the light and passing shiver of a man who – unlike myself – was not afraid of death but was only annoyed by it.

From then on we met twice every week, not counting the Monday nights which we spent with our fellow-emigrants at the Café Napolitaine. I was inordinately proud of Fényes's friendship, not only because he was a suspicious and unapproachable man who confided only in his contemporaries, friends of long standing, men at least forty years older than I, but also because of his extraordinary moral strength. Moral strength radiated from every pore of his body, invisibly but almost tangibly. It reached out from behind his uninteresting features, from under his worn jacket, and permeated the entire room in which he was. Once one of our fellow-emigrants brought along a man who looked like a professional fighter and had – some ten years earlier – been an intimate friend of Miklos Horthy. Fényes looked at the man, lifted his hand and pointed at the door. We thought that we would now witness a fight. 'Get out!' Fényes said quietly when the man showed no inclination to move. The man rose and slunk from the café with his tail between his legs.

A few weeks later my wife showed up in Paris without informing me of her impending arrival. I was scared to death. I had always known that sooner or later she would join me and though I considered every day spent without her a gift of God, I did not particularly mind her coming, especially since I feared that she would be persecuted because of me in Hungary. To be perfectly candid it was not her fate that caused me anxiety; what worried me was that future Hungarian lexicographers or historians of literature might accuse me of infamy for having abandoned my wife and having cared only for my own security.

When she entered my hotel room her face reflected surprise and disappointment. She expected to fall into a den of iniquity and to find me in the arms of the actress from Vienna. She had probably worked out in great detail how she would react to the situation, how she would subsequently forgive me and save me from the moral mire in which I wallowed. Instead she found herself in an ugly, five-cornered room among the standard furniture of all cheap Paris hotel rooms, permeated with a constant composition of smells created by time, by the indifference of the guests, the spirit stoves smuggled in behind the landlady's back and by frequent, over-hasty love-makings. Mice gambolled in the waste-paper basket while I lay on my huge bed, decorated with greenish brass knobs, reading Robert Herrick's poems. The unexpectedness of this peaceful and by no means immoral scene scared my wife. Her preparations had been in vain, here she could play neither the Muse nor the angel of mercy.

I too was surprised – surprised by her extreme beauty which I had completely forgotten in the last few weeks. Strangely enough my first thought was of what Fényes would think of her. Valy was a communist in theory but all the more vociferously, and there was nothing Fényes hated more passionately than devout bolshevik mysticism. When I told her about my friendship with Fényes she immediately declared that I must keep away from such old, reactionary idiots and make contact, instead, with the communist emigration that was expecting me with open arms.

In spite of these not very promising preliminaries, the first meeting went off very well indeed. The old gentleman was completely charmed by Valy. Her beauty enchanted him and so did the excellent dinner she prepared for him on the small spirit cooker, guessing the old man's taste in food. She knew by instinct that he liked his lettuce with lard and paprika instead of oil and vinegar, as prescribed by Hungarian baroque custom, and that in the case of spices he insisted on the Renaissance court cuisine, demanding that they be sharp and that they be plentiful. Fényes never paid much attention to female prattle and Valy tactfully refrained from praising Stalin though not from abusing Chamberlain and Daladier, a sentiment we warmly applauded. During those months to come Fényes appeared at our hotel every single Thursday for dinner, spruced up for the occasion, a flower in his button-hole and a bunch of flowers in his hand.

We were too poor to visit the theatre, the movies or other places of amusement. According to French law foreigners had no right to seek employment, and illegal employment was punished by expulsion which was, in our case, equivalent to a death sentence.

We paid our hotel bill with the price of the jewels we had brought with us from home and except for the two evenings a week when Fényes was our guest or we his, we lived mainly on porridge cooked for the whole week in a huge pot. We received our meat, or rather our bacon and sausages, from our parents who regularly sent us parcels of food. Not once during the year and six months spent in Paris did I have sufficient money to go to the barber's; Valy put a pot on my head, and cut off the hair showing underneath the rim with tiny nail scissors. But even if we had to go hungry, we always saved enough for cigarettes and the café.

Our landlady, a small old woman always in black whose heavy body odour filled the corridors for hours after she had sailed through them, stopped us every evening as we were coming down from our room to go to the café. She was usually in her porter's cubicle, sitting before a small table laid for one. Her husband, killed in the First World War, stared from the widow's glazed, oval brooch into her onion soup: a shining white-skinned Frenchman with uncouth features, a straight nose and a huge black moustache who looked annoyingly like Guy de Maupassant. Madame Freynault complained daily that we were using too much water to wash ourselves, quarrelled because we were cooking in our room and spoiling her furniture with the fumes, or declared that we pulled the chain of the WC twice, although once would have been enough. After the outbreak of the war she added political threats to her financial ones: she threatened to denounce us to the authorities if we remained in our room during the alert, imparted her suspicion that we were signalling to German aeroplanes from our window and reminded us that while we were spending pleasant evenings at the café the poor French soldiers were suffering in the Maginot Line. Yet it did not even occur to us to move. We had already pawned our suitcases and besides, as our acquaintances informed us, other hotels were not much better than Madame Freynault's.

The greatest problem of all was our permit of residence. As I did not possess the two to three thousand francs, for which some fixer could have obtained the permit, I had to have our temporary permit extended from month to month. This involved at every single occasion a two- or three-day wait in the yard of the Préfecture. The extension of the permit depended entirely on the goodwill of the clerks. True, they generally granted it, and it was not so much the waiting I minded but the rudeness and intentional humiliation that went with it. When the war broke out I volunteered for the French Army and was found fit for service. I fervently hoped that now at last we would be permitted to remain in France until I was called up.

One day Valy and I were caught by an alert in the street. We went into a nearby hotel where we were known, but when we descended to the huge, vaulted cellar where the guests had taken refuge the landlady complained that we were breathing away their air and would have to go. She led us up the stairs, pushed, us out into the street and locked the front door in our faces. A few seconds later we were picked up by a patrol, conducted to the police station and the next day I received my expulsion order. Only I and not my wife, which showed that gallantry had not died in French hearts.

The expulsion order meant that my permit of residence had to be extended every eight days, so that now I spent half of every week at the Préfecture. I was always careful to be interviewed not by a male clerk but, if possible, by an elderly, slightly withered though not aggressively ugly female. And I was always lucky. Had I not been I would have been deported back to Hungary where there was a warrant out against me for desertion to the enemy and treason.

Still, the villainy of the authorities and the unbearable atmosphere at the Préfecture failed to drive me to despair. My old friends who were more experienced in emigration than I was had warned me in good time that only communists and – to a certain extent – Catholics were loyal to their own kind, democrats never. I knew what to expect. I had sought asylum in France, not loyalty, and, though in the most heartless form possible, that asylum had been granted.

When, after the outbreak of the war, the general loathing for foreigners increased, it found me and my fellow-emigrants utterly indifferent to it. The continuous insults drove us out on the margin of society and we knew it was useless to remind the French that we were all in the same boat.

Thus conditions threw us together and our double exile – from Hungary and from French society – lent our friendships and conversations extraordinary intensity. We felt like a bunch of roving knights hopelessly in love with the same woman, but whether that woman's name was Hungaria or Marianne was a secret we kept from each other and often from ourselves as well. Though we stopped wooing the lady we preserved our love for her, and remained haughtily true to that love, because love is one's private affair and in no way concerns its object.

Our abstract adoration, however, was often sorely tried. We had to separate ideas from phenomena, the principles of French democracy from the institutions of the French state. We had to forget – like the knight his lady – the French Parliament in which both the right and the left wished for the victory of the enemy, and the French Government which, by its very helplessness, helped to fulfil that wish. We had to forget the Prime Minister of France who forbade the press to write against Goering because he believed that Goering would one day seize power from Hitler and would offer the French peace. We had to forget the general staff looking at us from the pages of the illustrated papers like a bunch of impotent old fogies interested in nothing but their bowel movements or, at best, their intrigues; the air defence, unable to scare off even a single enemy aircraft but sounding the alert when the balloons of the meteorological institute appeared above the Seine; the police which could not catch a single Nazi spy but arrested German anti-fascist emigrants to the last man. We had to forget their military plan to win the war without tanks, without planes, sitting in the Maginot Line and leaving their allies in the lurch. What we missed was the very character of France: logic, rational thinking, political sharpsightedness, the merciless analysis of facts and the inherited military virtues. In our compulsory retirement we believed that, though latent, these virtues were still there and therefore, ignored by and ignoring the inhabitants of the town, we found ourselves in a dead city like Pompeii in which only the Louvre, Notre-Dame, the Bibliothèque Nationale, the public buildings, bridges and statues were real. We clung to them like romanists cling to the stones of Pompeii, its inscriptions and charred parchments, because they know that outside of their imagination these are the only evidences of antique town life.

We had nothing to do but to talk and to think. Our permanent hunger – not the rumbling, acute hunger which makes men's eyes bulge out of their sockets, but the imperative need for more and better food – made our souls susceptible and our bodies light. We felt that we could easily rise up and levitate five feet above the ground if we wanted to. Spiritual acrobatics seemed even easier, whether they involved childhood memories, the hitherto unregistered phenomena of our emotional life or simple games of logic. This silent hunger devoured our inhibitions as it did the superfluous fat on our bodies and while it liberated our imaginations it compelled us to dream. Added to exile and hunger there was also a third component which began to transform our ways of thinking – or mine, at least: time. Not the passing of time but the almost unlimited amount of time I had at my disposal. Until then I had rarely thought about everyday problems and never about what I was writing, for in my work thinking was a hindrance rather than a help. Now I began to think intensively, if not about my work, at least about my life. Until this time my thinking had resembled a stream carrying fallen leaves, dead branches, all kinds of objects, without, however, changing them. Now it resembled a stream of vitriolic acid in which everything dissolved. This difference, I found, was simply and exclusively a question of intensity; that is, a question of the time at my disposal. It had often occurred in the past that I discussed a subject for several hours, but now I had sixteen, eighteen hours a day at my disposal and if we did not solve a problem until four in the morning we could go on arguing the next day and the next and the next.

My constant partners in these conversations were Ernö Lorsy, the historian, and Bandi Havas, a young, red-headed poet from Hungary. It would be inexact to call them *friends* because only Laszlo Fényes was my friend. He and I talked the same language. When he recounted stories from his life, his experiences, these stories contained his moral attitude, his political and philosophical views, as a glass of sugar-water contains sugar, invisible but potent. Bandi was different, he loved arguments about social issues or discussing his emotional life bashfully but with gusto, as if he were making a confession. He was my antithesis, or at least my reciprocal value, like the integral to the differential or four plus to four minus. Lorsy, on the other hand, was a being who could in no way be compared to me. He offered his incredible erudition to be scanned like a lexicon but was as indifferent to emotional ties as the *Encyclopaedia Britannica* which expects, at the most, to be kept at hand and often used. Not so Havas who offered me his eternal, flaming friendship. For years we lived in close proximity, often in the same flat, shared a table and repeatedly saved each other's life (together with our own and, in the given circumstance, we had no choice); I even came to like him to a certain extent, as one would a four-legged pet, but my basic attitude towards him remained contemplative, critical, non-friendly and merciless. This attitude; moreover, was not one that had evolved gradually: I had chosen it in the first moment of our meeting and maintained it to the end.

I adopted this – to me – surprisingly ruthless attitude because Bandi was unlike any of my former friends and close acquaintances. It was usually strong characters which attracted me, knights *sans peur et sans reproche* like Laszlo Fényes, or rationalists, witty and erudite and liberal, leftovers from the past century, who lived virtuously although they did not believe in virtue. Apart from these two categories I liked cultured men of wide learning, men who could discuss every aspect of human knowledge without forming a definite opinion. Yes, I preferred men who lived in the past, in the days of antiquity, the Renaissance or the nineteenth century, because I too, being unable to resign myself to the most important phenomena of the present, would have preferred to live in those days rather than in my own. I deplored that the role of fate had been taken over by politics, that technical civilization was leading mankind into a blind alley, that man's time was taken up by cars, the radio and the monomania of politics. There was nothing to make up for the annoyance of having to live in the twentieth century except the slight comfort offered by the amazing discoveries of astrophysics.

When twenty-four hours after our first meeting, I inquired among my acquaintances about Bandi Havas, two of them said he was the 'hero of our age'. I, whose relations with the twentieth century were far less intimate than those of my acquaintances, saw in Havas only a caricature of the hero of our age, a most original and yet a most typical caricature. I immediately resolved to put aside my strong antipathy, to observe him with impersonal curiosity and to use him in a novel. Although at the time I was interested in poetry alone and was not even planning to write prose, I thought that had Bandi Havas not walked into my room that morning I should one day have had to combine the 'hero of our age' from ten or twelve different people, while now the most perfect specimen was there ready before my eyes; I felt the way Flaubert would have felt had Madame Bovary rung his bell one day and walked in with her two lovers before he had even begun to work on his novel.

Bandi knocked at my door one morning at about eight, in the days before my wife's arrival in Paris. He introduced himself through the keyhole but his name meant nothing to me. I was angry because I never liked to be woken early and this prejudiced me against him. From his excited, weak and rather high voice I immediately concluded that he must be ugly, and the fact that he rose at dawn threw a doubtful light on his character. I didn't know at the time that it was not selfish ambition that drove Bandi from his bed at six in the morning but his ridiculous though sincere concern about the fate of mankind. Every morning he woke filled with hope that the affairs of the world would certainly be settled by nightfall.

When at last I opened the door I was indeed dumbfounded by his ugliness. This was more than I had expected. I made him sit down in the only armchair in the centre of the room and climbed back on to the bed, sitting with my legs crossed.

There he sat before me with his stiff red hair standing on end, his large, shovel-like front teeth protruding from between pale lips. Tiny drops of perspiration covered his forehead and his long, hooked nose, although a dirty yellow mist was hovering outside the half-open window. His face and hands were bestrewn with rhomboid-shaped freckles as if he had taken a sunbath under a sieve. He held a large cardboard box under his arm from which he immediately offered me some crumbly cakes which, he said, had been made and packed for him three days ago in Budapest. I felt certain that he had never let go of the box since he left Budapest, sleeping with it under his head in the train.

He spoke rapidly and although my armchair was solid enough his violent gesticulation repeatedly threatened to overthrow it. He was young and thin, he chortled with laughter, and his long skinny legs wriggled and danced as if they were attached to his body by wire and not by tendons, joints, muscles and cartilage. Crumbs from the cakes fell from his fingers, from his lips, so that he hardly swallowed anything. He praised my last volume of verse with great understanding and with such passionate enthusiasm that he jumped from his chair, ran into the wall and backed into the mirror.

I must find a way to get rid of this fellow, I thought to myself.

'Are you a communist?' he asked suddenly and without transition.

'No.'

'And have you never been one?'

'Oh, yes. At the university, but only for a few weeks. Never really.'

When I noticed that he was waiting for an explanation I added: 'It is not obligatory to err. It is frequent, but not obligatory. Perhaps it is instructive, but it is not obligatory.'

'Neither is suffering?'

'Suffering is,' I replied quickly. 'But why do you believe suffering is the privilege of the communists?'

'That is my experience. Pity that you de-personalize the question and refuse to give me a straight answer.'

I examined my bare ankles, still tanned from last summer's sunbathing. I felt that I ought to blush because my opponent had unmasked me: his arrow had wounded my Achilles heel. I had practically no vulnerable spot but for my strange inability to suffer.

I was not yet twenty when my poems, written with relative ease, had made me famous throughout the country. While I was doing my military service the editor of a large liberal daily 'discovered' me and reprinted my poems from a small, insignificant periodical. I made no particular demands on life, was not interested in money, and the women I liked but was too shy to woo soon grew tired of my helplessness and came to my room to lie across my bed. I was a good deal happier than others thought. The wishdreams of my youth (I wanted to be a famous poet and nothing else) had come true to a degree and nothing had prevented me from remaining loyal to the ideals of my boyhood. But I was happy in the first place because existence, the bare fact of being alive, was sufficient to make me happy. The more I feared death during the night the happier I was during the daytime. The details of my profession, a four-syllable rhyme, for instance, had always been more important to me than outside events, people, material worries, the future. The luminous circles I saw when closing my eyes, a kaleidoscope, the coloured pebbles of the river-bank, the passers-by watched from the window of a café, a flowering cactus or the bloom on fresh fruit amused me and obliterated everything else from my mind for hours at a time. I felt that even if all this were taken from me, if I were thrown into a dark hole, I should remain untouched because I could, like a projector, unroll the images of the world for my entertainment.

During my university days the problem whether or not I would become a poet often tormented me, but I knew no other mental crisis. This circumstance was due to the realization that my categorical imperative was incomparably stronger than either my will or my passions and could always be relied on, trusted like the automatic pilot steering an aircraft.

My mother had brought me up with extraordinary severity. When, as a child, I pushed the horn of an automobile in the street she threatened me that I would have to pay the price of the entire car. This is why, as an adult, I married my wife. I married her because

I had promised to do so; that is, I submitted to my categorical imperative, or rather, identified myself with it. This identification, however, extended only to my actions, not to my thoughts, for I knew that the marriage would bring unhappiness to both of us. I was like an aeroplane steered in a certain direction by the automatic pilot while the passengers inside see that they are running into a storm. I chose the storm because I hoped to get out of it sooner or later; I chose the storm without thinking – because it was the task of my automatic pilot, my categorical imperative, to save me unnecessary worrying.

In the territories that do not come under the jurisdiction of the categorical imperative my iron nerves and my nature protected me against serious emotional upheavals. As I thought in images, not in ideas, I obeyed my instinct and not my logic to which I denied not only the vote but also the right to free speech. I honoured rationalism only in the great men of the nineteenth century: Renan, France, Berthelot, and in my old friends. In my own profession I found it little if any use.

The red-headed visitor sitting opposite me in the armchair had good eyes and took precise aim. I did not know suffering and with my playfulness, my dreaminess, unpretentiousness, and self-confidence, my successes and my disposition that conceived *life* the true, unique, wonderful, royal gift of nature there was very little chance of my becoming lastingly unhappy. I had fled Hungary to escape prison, suffering, perhaps even death, and would return there, after a period of privations, a champion of justice, the exile with the martyr's halo around his head. Sooner or later I would get rid of my wife and if not I could always find comfort in other women. Thus, suffering was nowhere in sight and it was questionable if, with a nature like mine, it was possible to suffer at all. I realized, of course, that it was not to be happy, but to write good poems that I was brought into this world. And, because literary works are improved by suffering, I acknowledged its value and never ceased yearning for it. But only for this reason. I considered suffering an instrument, not a virtue as did my red-headed visitor in the armchair.

He dropped the subject and turned the conversation to his acquaintances, in Paris. He spoke of Roger Martin du Gard who was fond of him, and would sometimes compare him to one of his heroes, Jacques Thibault, which made Havas inordinately proud. He mentioned Gide (who, he confessed, had received him coldly when he approached him at the Café Dôme), one of whose poems he had translated into Hungarian. Bandi, being what he was, could not refrain from reciting the entire poem. It dealt with the coming cataclysm, after which some would wake in the swamps of the Congo, others in the jungle or on some oceanic island, but there would be some who never woke again.

A few days later Bandi visited me a second time, during the afternoon. I received him with bad grace, although all the information I had got about him was excellent. He was known to be a selfless, loyal friend, *un homme chaste*, and everyone reassured me that I would soon get used to his ugliness and forgive him for it, as others had done before me. We went out for a walk and sat on a bench by the river in the lukewarm, almost stifling evening mist. There he told me, in a nutshell, the story of his life. He had lost his parents early, and while still very young had joined the underground communist party. He distributed leaflets at gates of factories, painted communist slogans on walls in the middle of the night, organized, agitated and enthused. Later the party used him as a messenger between Budapest and Vienna. He did not mention that to a man of his conspicuous appearance, this appointment was highly dangerous. However, he spoke at great length about his break with the communist party. He still believed in the ideals but had become disgusted with the leaders who jeopardized the lives of party members without turning a hair, even when it was utterly unnecessary. He was disappointed in them because they co-operated with the fascists as soon as Moscow ordered them to do so and he had also quarrelled with them ideologically, because they disqualified Freud's teachings which he admired, and held political morality to be a petty *bourgeois* deception.

Finally, he was expelled from the party. After his expulsion his best friends turned away in the street when they saw him, his girl-friend spat in his face and two weeks later he was arrested by the police.

The judge knew every detail of his activities as a messenger, details which according to Bandi only the party leaders themselves could have known. He was sentenced to two years' imprisonment. While he was in prison his former comrades accused him of being an informer and persecuted him more cruelly than the guards. When he came out of jail the party relented towards him and he too forgot his resentment, although he refused to join again. His yearning for the party – he added at this point – was still considerably stronger than his disgust with its leaders.

He explained that he realized he had been driven to the communist party by his ugliness, his loneliness and his yearning for a family; by the ideology only in so far as he could not exist without some universal ideal that imposes order on the affairs of the world.

'Something that settles the affairs of the world once and for all?' I asked.

'Once and for all,' Havas said and looked around. He held a cigarette clamped between his protruding upper teeth and his lower lip and drew on it with an application as comic as if this were the first cigarette of his life. 'He is looking around for some conspicuous example of social injustice,' I thought maliciously, but there were neither beggars nor even *clochards* about. Between the bookstalls lovers were leaning over the parapet and although their bottoms thus exposed looked thin enough under their worn overcoats I hoped Bandi would not cite them as examples of capitalist exploitation.

'I didn't care much about the poor,' Bandi intruded on my thoughts. 'I joined the underground movement in search of love. Perhaps it is my mother I was seeking, mother-love, but at the same time I, too, felt like a mother separated from her child whose breasts grow unbearably heavy with accumulated milk until she is compelled to distribute it to the needy. I distributed it, at last, among the members of the great communist family. It was not out of idle curiosity that I asked you whether you were a communist. I asked you because then and there I had begun to like you and until then I had considered only communists as members of the family. But when you replied that you had never really been one I immediately decided to extend the family to all intellectuals sympathizing with the movement.'

When he came to the end of his sentence I raised my hand in protest but, carried away by his own eloquence, he failed to notice my gesture.

'Let me go on,' he said, 'because if we let it go at this my confession will be but half true. It was not only love that led me into the communist party but also hate. Not hate against the rich. It is the disorderliness, the haphazardness, the incalculableness of the world that I hate. I have always had an irresistible desire to settle the affairs of the world, outside as well as inside, in my soul. I searched for a direction to follow, for a light that would lead me out of the chaos of my own thoughts and emotions. Because basically I am a religious man, you know, who must believe in something. Faith is the only satisfaction I yearn for and this yearning arose much earlier than my acquaintance with the Communist Manifesto. My primary passion and need was the search for an ideal and this passion is as old as my power to think.'

'I am afraid it is even older,' I said curtly and rose from the bench.

'You are right,' Bandi replied with resignation. 'It is older.'

I felt a huge wave of antipathy, almost loathing, sweep over me and decided to prevent him from going on with his subject. At the next street corner, however, I asked him with unforgivable stupidity, what had given him the idea that I could be a communist.

'The fact that you wrote against the fascists. In one of your poems you compare the communists to the primitive Christians, don't you?' he asked triumphantly.

'Do you believe that every anti-fascist must necessarily be a communist? On the contrary! He who denies fascism must *a priori* deny also communism and if he hasn't found that out yet he will find it out in time . . . And as far as metaphor is concerned: I compared the communists not to the primitive Christians but to the heretics of the fourth century. Don't ask me to go into detail.'

'Don't give me any of your humanistic indulgence, please,' Bandi begged, resting his back against the corner of the Rue du Seine. 'Every Settembrini must sooner or later lose patience with me. A moment ago I confessed, quite truthfully, but with slightly provocative intent, that I was a fanatic by nature. My attitude to the party is that of a faithful Catholic to his church and although I am ready to admit that the party is a prison to my intellect I must add that it is at the same time the horizon of my heart. The party and the church attract the same conflicting attributes: they are at the same time bogged down and soaring, cruel and mild, petty and generous, compromising and unbending, stinking and fragrant. I will also add that my attitude to the communist ideal is that of a believer to the deity: a mixture of adoration and doubt. Yet, however conspicuous the similarity, it is a comparison that does not touch the heart of the matter, namely: that communist man is a typical phenomenon of the twentieth century and represents a much higher degree of development than the Christian who has his future behind him. You can suggest many more analogies but you cannot convince me.'

'I have no intention whatsoever of convincing you,' I laughed. 'Heretics like you can be cured only with the smoke of the stake. Therefore I refuse to take our differences too much to heart. Not only because, unlike you, I want to change neither the world nor your opinions but also because already on the bench you tried to draw me into an argument and compel me to contradict myself. I know what you mean by humanistic indulgence. But if – and I am aware of the honour – you compare me to a Thomas Mann figure and identify yourself with Settembrini's opponent, the Jesuit-communist Naphta – because this is what you did, didn't you? – suggesting that we continue the great debate of *The Magic Mountain*, let me inform you that this is out of the question. It is you who are outside of Time, not I; it is you who have remained behind the twentieth century. In *The Magic Mountain* the two men argue on and on until both discover that their argument can be resolved only by a duel. Yet in principle both disapprove of duels. However, twenty-five years have gone by since then. It has become evident that such preliminary arguments are utterly useless. Thus, if we took our differences seriously we should have to stand face to face on the river-bank with pistols in our hands and shoot until one of us dropped dead into the water. Am I right?'

'You are,' Bandi replied moodily.

'Let me suggest therefore,' I continued, 'that we stop analysing each other's and our own *Weltanschauung* and stick to ordinary human relations, all the more so as relations between two natures as conflicting as ours can never be ordinary anyway.

'But, though I am disinclined to argue,' I went on more mildly as we walked towards my hotel, 'I should like to impart to you an impression. On one point you divorce the Christians from the communists and refuse to allow a comparison. And yet this is the point where, in my opinion, you are at one with the once-triumphant church.

'While we were sitting on that bench you told me the story of your life. I closed my eyes to see what you were telling me in images. There you stood before me, in the classroom, your hair a flaming red and your Adam's apple moving up and down like the hammers of a concert piano, busy organizing a band of your classmates to paint communist slogans on the house walls.

'I saw not only you but also the others. For instance, that little fat boy in the window recess with pouches under his eyes and an old, worried expression. He permitted himself to be persuaded by you because he was afraid that should you win, you would liquidate him along with the other members of the former ruling class. Driven by cowardice he volunteered for the boldest ventures. Then there was that tall, elegant, melancholy youth in his white leather sandals. How it hurt him to watch the suffering of the poor from the beautiful carriage that brought him to school every morning! You, however, despised him because he joined the movement for sentimental reasons . . . The third stands behind you, with the shadow of your head on his knee: only thus does he feel secure. You prefer him to the others because he truly admires you, yet you know that he is silly and ungifted. He has never been able to learn the four obligatory Sappho poems by heart, however hard he tried. He joined the movement because he wants a secure future.'

'I protest against the four Sappho poems,' Bandi interrupted. 'Only one of her poems survived.'

'Yes, but at the time you stood there in the schoolroom there were still hundreds of them . . . Perhaps there was also a fourth boy in your group who hated his father, a fifth who told happily of the good beating he had received the night before when he was caught distributing leaflets, a sixth who was driven to you by his desire for adventure, and whose older sister oppressed him at home – I can only see types and I know this is a rough generalization. However, I feel certain that not one of your classmates had your fanaticism, your courage and your will to act and thus you were the most mature among the adolescents – probably to remain an adolescent in maturity.'

'And what is all this to convey, if I might ask?'

'You shall see. Let me go on. The next moment I saw you leading your classmates on a midnight outing. The others consider these excursions boyish antics, but you know that they scare your enemies and have a deep, psychological effect. You take the gang into a residential district. You stop before a house. One holds the paint-bucket, you dip in your brush and wipe it on the rim. You don't like the letters to be smeared. You are always very careful to make no mistake in the wording. Then without haste you paint the symbols of the underground movement under the words.'

'Why do you express yourself in such a roundabout way? I wrote: DOWN WITH THE BOURGEOISIE! LONG LIVE THE COMMUNIST PARTY! and then painted the hammer and the sickle.'

'I am not repeating to you your own story, what would be the point in that? I am only telling you what I saw while listening to you. There are certain differences between your memories and my image of them as far as your clothing, the time, the place, and other such unimportant items are concerned. Instead of the rough tweed worn by adolescents I saw you and your friends wearing something like a nightgown; and when you left there remained on the wall a fish, the sign of the cross and a sentence in ancient Greek: Ιησος Χρνστος Οει 'γιος Σωτηρ – Jesus Christ, Son of God, the Saviour.'

'I see,' Bandi said and swallowed noisily. 'You mean to say that I should have acted in a similar way had I lived under Nero . . .'

'I never determined the time. A while ago, when you spoke about Settembrini, you were twenty-five years behind in time. I can well understand why you should want to smuggle yourself back from Constantine the Great's days into the heroic age of Nero, two hundred and fifty years earlier. Unfortunately, conditions have changed in those two hundred and fifty years. The pagans liberated the slaves. Perhaps under the influence of Christianity, perhaps not. The plan to overthrow the state had been dropped from the agenda; in Byzantium a central power, much more horrible, much more uninhibited and hypocritical than the former, had come into being. Classical literature is condemned as decadent, the works of the philosophers are burned and the creations of Greco-Roman sculpture hacked to pieces. Soon the distributed land is taken back from the peasants to form large church estates and the paying of wages is left to the Heavenly Bridegroom.

'Why do you look as if you had bitten into a sour apple? This is your world where you thrive like a fish. The social problems that have never really interested you are gradually forgotten and men kill each other for a notion that does not exist, a word that has no meaning. Here you can wriggle and writhe in one uninterrupted St Vitus dance from cradle to grave. I am not in the least surprised that in your exultation you should consider every attitude that differs from yours vain and rigid, but mainly obsolete and old-fashioned. This is why I dared suggest that you may not be as modern as you believe and that you too had your historical predecessors among the heretics.'

'Why do you say heretics and not believers?' Bandi asked nervously as we stopped in front of my hotel.

He looked at me with ravenous, grovelling eyes. I wondered whether I should tell him a merciful lie, but I met his glance and blurted out my thoughts.

'You are far too honest to be a believer,' I said almost pityingly. 'They will burn you at the stake, Bandi.'

Suddenly my nose was full of the horrible smell of burning human flesh. Bandi receded by twenty yards and stood straight, tied to an imaginary stake. His rigid, tousled red hair was the tip of the flame that covered his entire body.

'And yet, you not I are the hero of our age,' I said with a shudder.

Running up the stairs to my room I saw the grin with which he registered my last words. It was exactly like him: simultaneously benign and devilish.

*

I had met Lorsy, the historian, in Budapest. When Havas brought him to visit me I threw a disapproving glance at his paunch which had, in the meantime, grown out of all proportion.

'Forgive me my appearance, George,' he said with an expression of worried helplessness on his face. 'I was compelled to commit this act of tastelessness by my instinct of self-preservation. This was the only way to smuggle out of Hungary twenty extra kilogrammes of lard, twenty kilogrammes of lard that I could neither pawn nor give away. Just think of it: over one hundred thousand calories . . . Two months' food supply,' he added with disgust.

Apart from his mother tongue, Lorsy spoke perfect French, English and German. In any of these languages he could deliver first-class, improvised lectures on world politics, historical subjects or any literary event. His lectures were far superior to anything published in the international press on the given subject. His gifts and his erudition predestined Lorsy to live not on his own fat, but on caviare, lobster, pheasant or whatever he liked. But ever since he had left the university, thirty years earlier, his character had completely paralysed his gifts. How often we begged him to write down what he had just finished telling us at the café! How often Bandi offered to take the manuscript immediately to the editor of a large daily! But no. Lorsy would promise to write it down himself during the night, but he never did. When asked for an explanation he declared that any subject already discussed bored him so much that he could not think about it again.

Immediately upon his arrival in Paris a well-known publisher had written to Lorsy asking him to come to his office, because he wanted to commission a book on the history of the French fortresses, a book that would have been entitled: *From Vauban to Maginot*. After several letters and telephone calls Lorsy set out resignedly towards the Boulevard St Germain where the publisher was waiting for him at his office. He never got there. The resistance of the medium – as Lorsy liked to describe it – intervened. He met an acquaintance, asked him for a small loan and entered a café where he conversed with various people until late in the evening. Another time he walked down to the river to browse among the books, woodcuts, reproductions, until the bookstalls were locked up. Then he walked home, peaceful and contented, and never noticed that he hadn't eaten all day.

Bandi, who realized Lorsy's weaknesses but was unable to resign himself to them, offered the historian his services as a secretary. Free of charge, naturally. Lorsy refused, but the day after the publication of the Stalin–Hitler pact, when Bandi was running from friend to friend to find comfort in his terrible despair, Lorsy took pity on him and graciously accepted his services. Bandi's first task as a secretary was to obtain a little money from somewhere, get Lorsy drunk and drag him to the publisher's office where, in his dazed condition, he signed a contract. It was from Lorsy that I learned this story; Bandi was so ashamed of himself because of the Stalin–Hitler pact that he dared not show his face.

Only towards the end of September did I see him again. I was sitting in my room, reading how the Soviet Union and Germany were gobbling up Poland between them, when I heard Bandi's voice calling me from the street.

'Come to the window, George. I have sad news for you. Uncle Sigmund is dead.'

He was standing in the middle of the road and his face, raised to the window, was bathed in sunshine and pathos, but to tell the truth it was not really sad. The fact that he was the first to impart the news to his friends greatly mitigated his pain. He said he was on his way to Lorsy, who had often visited Uncle Sigmund at his flat in the Lange Gasse, to make him write an article on the dear departed and sell it to the papers.

I wished him good luck although I had my doubts about Lorsy's willingness to comply with Bandi's wishes, and went back to my desk. Valy was away visiting one of her communist girl-friends whom I had thrown out a few days ago when she declared that the war was the affair of the French *bourgeoisie*, and I was profiting by her absence to write a poem. I wrote that Europe was disappearing from the face of the world like Atlantis and that in this situation there was nothing left for me but to take refuge in the subconscious layers of my soul or to flee to the continent where the subconscious past was still alive and for which I longed: Africa. For a moment it occurred to me that

I should, perhaps, write about Freud but I realized that he was just as present in the mythical poem I was writing as he was in the one I had written three years earlier on the occasion of his eightieth birthday which, though it dealt with my own emotional problems and never mentioned him by name, was still a tribute to him. By the time I finished Valy was back and I had completely forgotten about Bandi when I heard a taxi stop before the hotel.

'Get dressed, you two!' Bandi shouted from below. 'Ernö is waiting in the cab, he is taking us out to dinner!'

At first Valy protested, but I dispelled her doubts by reminding her that we had not eaten a bite that day. Thereupon she began, slowly and circumstantially, to rub cream into her face. It never took her less than an hour to get dressed and though I was sorry for Lorsy waiting below in the cab, there was nothing I could do about it.

For several months now, on my way home from the Café Napolitaine, I would drop in on a former mistress, the Viennese actress, who lived in the Rue de Névers exactly half-way between the café and my hotel. My wife was incomparably more beautiful, more attractive and more intelligent than Eva; the only thing they had in common was their hysteria. The real reason for my visits was not the erotic one, although after some obligatory yet sincere preliminary conversation they always ended in love-making.

In my student days Eva had been a famous actress in Vienna. Although I was only an unknown young student she remained faithful to me for years. She often came to fetch me in the evening at the University Library – usually, because she loved to cause a sensation, in her stage costume. Once she arrived in full armour with her long, dark hair streaming over her shoulders from under her helmet. She was playing Jeanne d'Arc that night. If, after the show was over, she noticed me standing on the other side of the Josefstädter Strasse under the gas-lamp, she would leave a world-famous director without saying goodbye and run across the road between automobiles and streetcars to join me. At such times Max Reinhardt gazed after her with a melancholy expression, thinking, no doubt, about the ruthlessness of youth. Now she was living in exile, poor and almost friendless. In the last four years, since she had left Reinhardt, she had aged unbelievably.

I felt that by climbing up six flights to her room I was repaying at least some of her past kindnesses to me. On the way down again there was no smile of self-satisfaction on my lips; I sighed a deep sigh and repeated mechanically: *Salvavi animam meam. . .*

Apart from the gratitude I owed her I was led also by the consideration that this relationship gave me sexual independence from my wife, though the delights awaiting me at the top of those flights of stairs in no way vied with those awaiting me at home. My poverty, which prevented me from taking a woman to a café or seeing her home in a taxi, made new conquests impossible, or rather, it deprived me of the opportunity to create a situation in which a woman could seduce me. Thus, I had to make do with those who knew me from the past, with whom I still had intellectual credit.

One day when, contrary to my custom, I visited Eva before lunch, she informed me that she was pregnant. She added however, that to the best of her knowledge I was innocent. The blond young man who was responsible for this state of affairs had been called up on the first day of the war and was now in the Maginot Line. She begged me, seeing that she had no one in the world to turn to, to help her get rid of the child or, should that be impossible, to provide for it after its birth. This problem, to which I saw no solution, preoccupied me day and night so that I was somewhat reconciled to my wife and thus watched her patiently, regardless of the ticking of the taxi-meter, until fifty-five minutes later she was at last ready to go. She was beautiful in her simple black frock, almost perfect. Throwing a last glance at the mirror reflecting her bare shoulders, shining like sixty-watt, frosted-glass electric bulbs, she caught sight of me standing behind her, green with hunger. Going down the stairs she took my arm because, on such occasions, she always behaved ceremoniously even when we were alone.

A large, black, coffin-shaped taxi stood before the door. The darkness inside was so dense that I found my way to my seat only by sounds, smell and the electromagnetic repulsion of three bodies. Only when we had left behind the Porte d'Orléans on our way to Fontainebleau was I able to distinguish in a corner of the taxi Lorsy's immense, sprawling body, looming in the twilight like some pulpy and formless monster in the subconscious regions of the soul. As always, he was in black from top to bottom, holding in his hand his huge, soft hat that, according to Bandi's testimony, he put down on the bedside table before going to sleep and put on again first thing in the morning before shaving. He was holding a bottle of cognac between his knees which he offered first to Valy, who refused indignantly, then to me.

The drink put me immediately on the same level with Lorsy and Bandi. The facts that had been imparted to me before, namely that Lorsy had dictated an article on Freud to Bandi, that Bandi had immediately sold it to a weekly for three thousand francs, that Lorsy had ordered a dinner by telephone in one of Fontainebleau's finest restaurants – explained the situation but somehow failed to penetrate my mind. The slow drive without headlights through the blacked-out city, then along the inky highway increased the mail-coach atmosphere I had felt when climbing into the taxi. In this completely secluded world Lorsy and Bandi were quarrelling passionately and intimately. I had joined them like a kindly stranger but now, at one stroke, I understood it all.

My first coherent thought was that at last, after months of semi-starvation, I would eat a complete, multi-course dinner. The prospect, however, rather repelled than attracted me. I felt my bowels contract before the merciless, triumphant onrush of food, like citizens in the cellars of a besieged fortress before the final attack of the enemy, of which the outcome is certain. The habitual and almost chronic melancholy of hunger would now – I thought bitterly – be replaced for a few weeks by acute pangs of starvation.

Suddenly the towers of Warsaw appeared before me with painful sharpness and a map from my history textbook showing how Poland was dissected three times in the eighteenth century. Behind the towers of Warsaw I saw the smoking ruins of Budapest and German tank divisions, not in Polish territory but between the draw-wells of the Hungarian lowlands, advancing with geometrical precision like a long column of figures; from which I deduced the mathematical thesis that the occupation of Poland involved, necessarily, the occupation of Hungary.

Then came Freud. According to my habit I tried to recall his features, gestures and actions with the sentimental and magical idea that a dead man is a little less dead or may even come back to life if someone thinks of him intensively. But Freud's face escaped my memory. Instead I remembered old dreams and the sexual experiences of my childhood while with half my attention I was listening to Bandi's and Lorsy's conversation, thinking with satisfaction that they were in the same boat with me. Columbus was dead, and the subject of conversation was not Columbus but America.

'Continue with the dreams of your childhood,' Lorsy urged Bandi.

Bandi refused, though I knew that there was no living man who loved to confess as much as he did. He considered public confession a spiritual need and a duty to himself. Now, however, he was angry with Lorsy. The fact that he had succeeded in forcing Lorsy to write an article and thereby earn some money deprived Lorsy of his greatest attraction: his poverty, his helplessness, his need for others. With a few thousand francs in his pocket Lorsy felt rich and made careful plans to enjoy this Sancho Panza's kingdom to the full for a night. The circumstance that for once he was the host added arrogance to his natural conceit. But, strangely enough, Lorsy was also angry with Bandi. For him the only natural way to live was to live on advances and to cheat his editors and publishers. And now he had worked and was still deeply shaken. He felt that he had enriched himself on Freud's death and was now driving over his grave as he took us to dinner. Yet, it was not really himself that he blamed but Bandi who had made him sell the Master for thirty gold pieces to the editor of *Candide*.

'Bandi promised,' Lorsy turned to me, 'that he would deliver a lecture on the animals of his childhood dreams. Everyone has his own individual animals. Leonardo da Vinci, for instance, had vultures in his head . . .'

'First we should like to hear about *your* vultures!' cried Bandi angrily. 'Isn't it revolting that someone should know everything there is to know about mankind's childhood, the childhood of Freud, of Charles XII and Henry IV, but nothing at all about his own? When you were still in your cradle you must have reached for the *New York*

Times instead of your mother's teats! I am afraid you have never been young!'

'All right, I wasn't,' Lorsy replied sadly.

'Of course you were,' I broke in consolingly. 'You sat there with the peasant kids, on the side of the ditch baking sand-cakes and tasting them when nobody was looking . . .'

'He tasted them but he never baked them,' Bandi insisted. 'Ernö watched while the others were doing the work. Ernö doesn't know that he once wanted to kill his father and sleep with his mother, but he knows who else has tried to kill his father and sleep with his mother, when and where, from the founding of Troy to yesterday midnight . . .'

'When I last talked to Freud,' Lorsy said musingly, 'I asked him why he had not psycho-analysed psycho-analysis out of his system. What was the psychological cause that had made him and nobody else discover the jungle of depth psychology? Was it because he himself was full of inhibitions, frustrations and over-compensations? Or was it because these things were completely missing from his psychological make-up? What do you think he replied?'

'He said: "Go to hell, my good Mr Lorsy, go to hell!"' I suggested.

'Essentially you are right. That's what he said, only in a more polite form. He said that he was far too old to ask himself such far-reaching, complex questions . . . True enough. He was nearly eighty at the time.'

'Lorsy, on the other hand, is only fifty,' Bandi insisted. 'There is no reason why he should not ask himself why he isn't working on his book. The contract was signed six weeks ago but so far he has written nothing but the first six lines of the foreword.'

We were approaching Fontainebleau but the further we got from Paris the more uncertain our driver became. Only at long intervals did we notice a pale, cobalt-blue light seeping out from behind the blacked-out windows of roadside bistros or little houses; it seemed to me as if we were advancing between the obsolete trenches forgotten here from the 1914 war, an abandoned, crumbly front line filled with the fetid smell of thick, invisible layers of fallen autumn leaves.

'Do you refuse to answer?' Bandi cried belligerently.

The huge body moved.

'I could give you a number of answers,' Lorsy said. 'For instance, that such is my nature. I am lazy, phlegmatic, indolent. I could also say that you made me drunk and dragged me by brute force to the publisher's office to make me sign the contract. But let us leave recriminations aside and examine the essence of the question. After having left fifty-seven good books unwritten I, as an historian, cannot take it upon my conscience to write one that tries to convince my contemporaries of the impregnability of the Maginot Line. The Maginot Line is beset with cowardly soldiers led by a moronic general staff. Experience teaches us that such fortresses can be blown away by the farting of a cow. What I wish to say cannot be said – namely that the Maginot Line could protect France only if there were Frenchmen to protect the Maginot Line. Under such conditions the only ethical thing is to write nothing.'

For a moment we fell silent.

'Dear friends,' he continued and his voice softened, 'Carthage fell and so did Athens. Corinth fell and Alesia, Rome and Granada. Why should Paris not fall too?'

The restaurant, when we at last arrived, was elegant and warm, as if we had suddenly entered the gates of heaven. I looked up at the large, funnel-shaped chandelier with its innumerable candle-holders, then I closed my eyes tight and imagined that the chandelier was a Christmas tree held by an angel hovering above the room. A moment later I had thrown off the depression that had held me in its throes in the infernal darkness of the taxi, listening to Lorsy's sinister prophecies. I shared his views on conditions in France yet considered his conclusions too pessimistic. Observed so closely, every war looks the same and the fact that people have no desire to die does not necessarily mean that they are going to lose the war. The same phenomena existed among the enemy.

To whet our appetites Lorsy had ordered dark Malaga wine. Then came the first course: wine soup with black mussels, then saddle of venison with cranberries, accompanied by a dark red wine. I found the idea of serving black foods to fit the occasion – an idea of which

Lorsy was very proud – somewhat ridiculous. But at least it taught me something about our host's, the polyhistor's psychology that must have run to ground somewhere between Baudelaire and the *fin de siècle.*

Valy, although she obviously enjoyed the good dinner and the elegant environment, was preoccupied, as usual, with her own beauty. She turned her waist a little to the left towards the large Venetian mirror in its crystal frame, and everything she did, her chewing, her smiles, her wriggles, was all directed at her own reflection. Only from time to time did she swing her hip or her shoulder for our sake, or for that of the waiter or the guests.

Bandi's face was the very symbol of misery. Here, in the brightly lit room, he became victim of a breathtaking, perspiring, almost convulsive soberness. I knew what was bothering him and although I realized that it had needed the Stalin–Hitler pact to drive him into a crisis of conscience, I was sorry for him.

'To Poland and resurrection!' Lorsy raised his glass.

'And to Freud's memory,' Bandi added, somewhat comforted. As was his habit he did not raise his glass to his lips but dipped his face into it, and, pursing his lips, sucked up the wine noisily.

'I shall drink to your recovery, Bandi, to your slow reconvalescence,' I said. 'I admit that for some people it is difficult to live without an ideology. Therefore I suggest a slow and quiet transition; I should not have mentioned this had not, simultaneously with the outbreak of war, a struggle broken out between your conscience and a hostile ideology.'

I fell silent, knowing that I had said more than necessary. Bandi filled his glass, drank and gazed rigidly before him. I followed his glance. His iris, resting on the crescent moon of his bloodshot eyelid, was glued to the slender red candle standing in the middle of the table.

Then murmuring as if he were talking to himself, or perhaps to the chocolate cake on the plate before him, he said:

'My mummy has left me. My mummy is dead.'

'What does he mean?' Valy turned to me. 'I thought his mother died five years ago . . .'

'I had two mothers,' Bandi said. 'One came into my room and brought me fresh underwear when she knew I was going to a woman although I never told her. While I stole her money from her purse she pretended not to notice. Sometimes, when I was rude to her or indifferent, and turned away because her skirt smelled of cabbage, she would say: "You will want to dig me up with your bare hands when I am gone, Bandi, my boy . . ." This mother of mine died five years ago to rest her back against the bottom of her coffin. My other mummy was the communist party. People were always gossiping about her but I never would listen. And now I have caught my mummy in bed with Hitler, wriggling her shameless, bare behind. I think the best thing for me to do is to pretend she is dead.'

Valy broke into a sharp, hooting laughter.

'You are a silly goose,' Bandi said, wrinkling his nose. 'One doesn't laugh beside a grave. But why do you look so frightened, George?'

'What you said frightened me.' I hesitated for a moment and resolved to be as tactful as possible. 'I find your words too hasty . . . However estimable such outbursts of fury may be, I believe that they are merely emotional and of a temporary validity . . . The day after tomorrow you may again identify yourself with the communist practices of the day before yesterday . . . It would have been more reassuring had you not rejected communism so summarily but had only given voice to a few severe doubts . . .'

My words sounded as strange to me as if I were listening to a recording made several years before. At every beat of my heart I felt the alcohol mount to the frontal lobes of my brain, between my temples, driving me towards a superficial and irresponsible sincerity that I usually held in check even when drunk. However, my fury about the division of Poland was stronger than my customary sober drunkenness. I could have taken Bandi's head between my two hands and knocked it against the mirror next to Valy's reflection.

'If someone,' I continued, 'enters a room and there finds his mother in bed with a stranger he will be shocked and indignant, disgusted and ashamed. He will be even more disgusted if he finds out that not human frailty, but business has made his mother act this way. But ever since 1917 everyone knows that in every world-historical procession, every carnival masquerade, it is mummy who leads the guild of whores with a red lamp raised high in her hand. I am sorry that you had to find this out at the most disagreeable moment and discover mummy making love with Hitler while a roast chicken is waiting for them on the bedside table. From time to time they reach out, tear off a leg and stuff it into their mouths, never stopping their acrobatics.

'Still, I hope you will soon find comfort. Tomorrow you may already tell yourself that what you saw was but an optical illusion. Later you will reassure yourself that she did it for love. Jean-Jacques and Marx bequeathed to mankind a very useful method. With the help of this method you can forget about moral norms, you can ignore individual responsibility and you can trace back everything there is to social and historical causes. My mummy – you will say to yourself – was forced into prostitution by the historical situation and social conditions of the era, without prostituting herself she could never have raised her sons. And your heart will flow over with love and gratitude every time you see her standing on the street corner. As you are bound to your mummy by strong emotional ties you must at all costs find a way to justify your most sincere feelings by applying the falsest possible logic. The trouble is not that you discovered your mother was a prostitute. The trouble is that the prostitute is not your mother!'

I stopped talking. Bandi had listened with interest but without visible emotion and sat staring at the damask table-cloth. This time I swallowed two glasses of wine in quick succession: the worst was still to come.

'Quite recently you formulated your attitude beautifully. You said that communist ideology was the prison of your mind but the horizon of your heart. Yet, I must contradict you. I should compare the Marxist–Leninist ideology not to a massive prison building but to a wobbly pillar left over from the past century. It could be brought down by a single kick but what would be the use? You are chained to it with the twenty-four-carat gold chain of Freudism. There could be nothing stranger than the situation in which you involved yourself. You are bound to an exclusive, conspiratorial, underground brotherhood by the very fact that you belong to an even more exclusive one. It would be a vain effort to apply the Freudian outlook to communism and reject its vulgar and mechanical materialism. And it would also be vain to look at Marx's obsolete political economy through Freud's eyes, because you would still remain chained to bolshevism by your mother-complex, your herd instinct, your frustrated sexuality and suppressed thirst for power – the very emotions that communism so passionately denies and to which it owes its best followers. Not even if you proved to yourself that the communist ideology is all wrong could you break with bolshevism. You could break with it only if Freudism failed. But Uncle Sigmund died only last night and I am afraid a psychological theory like his might live for decades and may survive all of us.'

Bandi nodded. Somehow, I had the impression that he considered my entire lecture rather as a compliment than as an attack.

'I am convinced that you will never free yourself from communism,' I concluded with resignation. 'And that may be just as well. If I subtract from you your communist creed and your Freudian complexes that generate the high tension of your life, the remainder would probably be a very average, honest but entirely uninteresting person. The most striking feature of your psychological make-up is your reaction to this filthy political brass-band, the St Vitus dance you dance to the music of our modern age. Only by this reaction do you become what you are: the hero and martyr of our age.'

'But why only I?' Bandi asked, a little shaken. 'If Ernö is right in his cowardly defeatism and the Germans invade us, all anti-fascists in France will be beaten to death. And in that case you will all be heroes and martyrs of our age along with me.'

'No,' I replied decidedly. 'Martyrdom implies the rarity of martyrs. As in the early days of Christianity. When, under Diocletian the Christians were massacred, nobody paid any attention. Each of the early martyrs, on the other hand, rated a day of the year named after him or her. Those massacred under Diocletian had to make do with a collective name-day . . . At the time of the Inquisition, or today, when hundreds of thousands are massacred, one cannot attain martyrdom by simply sacrificing one's life for an ideal; such things are regarded as elemental disasters or mass accidents. The things we expect from the heroes and martyrs of our days are increasingly severe and perverted; it isn't the girondists and the social-revolutionaries who are the heroes of the French and Russian revolutions, but those who achieved a much less glorious and yet apparently much more exciting martyrdom through devious political and psychological labyrinths: the Dantons and Robespierres, the Zinovievs and Bucharins. If you are the hero of our age – of which I am certain – it logically follows that you cannot be beaten to death by the Germans.'

'Who then will beat me to death?'

'Ask the historian. He can give you exact and reliable information on this subject,' I said, pointing at Ernö. Ernö looked back at me with frightened eyes, for he had understood my meaning. But, to extricate himself from a very uncomfortable situation, he called for the waiter and asked for the bill.

I was wakened from a deep, coma-like sleep by the pressure of a hand on my shoulder.

'Wake up! We must leave. The Germans have taken Pontoise. They will be here by morning.'

Even in my sleep I recognized the over-dramatic touch of Bandi's weak hand. I heard his words but their meaning escaped me. Only when he and Valy overturned the bed and I rolled from the mattress on to the cold floor did I fully realize what he had been saying. The dirty yellow gleam of the weak electric bulb stung my eyes like sliced onions. I began to dress with the slowness of a snail. Bandi and Valy stood by the fireplace watching me anxiously and with hostility. There is no hurry, I thought. Hundreds of thousands are waiting at the railway stations . . . the trains will be bombed by the Germans . . . he who runs too fast towards Damascus to escape death is intercepted by it along the road.

A few weeks before, Laszlo Fényes had brought us the news that the socialist mayor of Montauban had invited all of us, leaders of both the Hungarian and the Austrian emigration, to come to his town. In his letter he had warned us with charming *naïveté* not to remain in Paris because should the French capital fall, even if only temporarily, into Hitler's hands, the Germans would without doubt hand us over to our respective governments. I persuaded Fényes, who had a forty-four-year sentence hanging over his head in Hungary, to accept the invitation as soon as possible, but when he asked Valy and me, and even Bandi whom he often violently abused for his former communist convictions but still loved, to accompany him, I refused. Both Bandi and I had decided to help in the defence of Paris and, apart from that, I did not consider the matter urgent.

After Fényes's departure I went straight to the Ministry of Information where I submitted my poems to the censor several times a month before sending them home to Hungary: an act always considered purely formal but which permitted us to conduct interesting conversations and exchange gossip. One of the heads of department assured me that the Germans were still two hundred kilometres from Paris and that the capital would be defended from house to house. But, he said, should anything unexpected occur, he would immediately send word and have me evacuated with the Ministry.

Next morning thousands of refugees flooded the streets; cars, horse-drawn carts, bicycles rolled towards the Porte d'Orléans, and those who had nothing to drive, walked. I hastened to the Ministry of Information but found the doors locked. From the bistro opposite the building the porter shouted to me that the entire staff had been evacuated to Tours early in the morning. By the time I got home I found Lorsy waiting for me. He had walked along the Champs-Élysées watching the black smoke rising from the chimneys of the various embassies. From the smoke of those archives, he said, he had learned more than if he had been permitted to read the documents themselves.

Lorsy decided to take the train to Montauban and Bandi accompanied him to the railway station. I, however, made up my mind that the best way to avoid the dreadful stampede at the stations was to set out on foot with my wife towards the south. I would wait for the very last moment, when the worst of the panic was over, and steal out by the southern gate while the Germans were marching in by the northern. Until then I decided to forget the whole matter and sat down to write my poem to the Hungarian language that had been bothering me for weeks. Strangely enough the endless crowds billowing below in the street, the smoke from the burning oil reservoirs that hung above the Jardin des Plantes like a low storm-cloud and the music of the windows set rattling by the distant, irregular gunfire, rather elated than disturbed me in my work. I became more and more absorbed in my task: this language was the only language I would never lose.

Late in the afternoon Bandi dropped in on us completely exhausted. Patches of perspiration, shaped like sugar-beet torn from the ground, showed under the arms of his greenish-yellow shirt. He told us that hundreds of thousands had thronged the Gare d'Austerlitz when he and Lorsy got there at dawn. By about three in the afternoon they had advanced to the entrance to the platform. This relatively rapid progress was due to the determination of Lorsy, who pushed forward like a tank. When Bandi had warned him indignantly to keep his head, the historian replied that his head was in the right place: whatever Bandi might think, it was the duty of every humanist to proceed with the maximal brutality in order to save himself, because in saving himself he was saving the ideal of humanism.

On the platform Lorsy penetrated the ranks of a girls' school. When people around him began to shout and ask him what business he had there, Lorsy turned to them and with a sweeping movement of his arm replied: '*Je suis l'instituteur!*' He stroked the girls' hair, gave instructions, shouted and cajoled and in the meantime pushed steadily forward, treading down the frightened children like young grass. Bandi had remained standing at the entrance, watching his friend shamefacedly. The last he saw of Lorsy was that the latter had taken hold of a fat girl's two pigtails and was sledging into the train in her wake. He was so disgusted with his friend's behaviour that he left the railway station forgetting his luggage which contained fifty kilogrammes of newspaper cuttings. He found the loss tragic because it was from these that he had hoped to write the history of the Second World War following the pattern of Roger Martin du Gard's *The Thibaults*. I reassured him by saying that the rules of the First World

War were no longer valid for the Second: the newspaper cuttings would have been nothing but a burden to him both in his flight and in his literary work.

It was our own flight I was picturing to myself, in my sleep, when Bandi woke me. I saw ourselves hiding in cool forests under hazel bushes where nothing but a few delicate mushrooms grew in the smooth, black earth; I saw ourselves asleep in the loft of a peasant house with the moonlight weaving labyrinths of black and silver bars on the straw; I saw ourselves sitting in the park of a French castle where slender fountains flashed in the sunshine like raised swords, and we soaked our feet in the basin, sharing the water with silly, fat goldfish.

My despair when Bandi and Valy tipped me out of bed was caused by the sudden, cold realization that I would have to give up the somewhat obsolete Odyssey I had dreamed about for an ordinary train ride, on which the only variation offering itself would be whether or not we would reach our destination alive. This was the only, truly the only cause of my disgust. The knowledge that in a few minutes, when I left the hotel, I would have no home, no bed of my own, no possessions for a long time to come and that I was going towards absolute insecurity – that made me rather happy. I shouldered my rucksack and indicated that I was ready to go. Bandi and Valy were still standing motionless by the fireplace. Bandi was gazing longingly at the classics lined up on the mantelpiece and Valy was staring with a haughty but pained expression at her dresses hanging behind the open door of the wardrobe.

Two women were waiting for us in the corridor outside our room. I had completely forgotten about them in my bemused state, although the evening before they had knocked at our door and begged us to take them along. The older of the two was a fox-faced old procuress made up like a movie star, the younger, allegedly the former's daughter, danced at the *Folies Bergère* and had always sent us free tickets for the opening of a new programme. It was Valy who had made their acquaintance a few months earlier. They had heard that I was unable to obtain my royalties from Budapest because of the currency embargo and, as they wanted to help relatives in Hungary, we agreed that they would give us the cash and my publisher would pay it out to their relatives.

Lilian's body was milk-white, so blindingly white that it reflected the light like porcelain. But whenever I tried to recall her face it was her lovely, snowy bottom that appeared before my eyes. It seemed to me as if some crazy art student had drawn two eyes, a mouth and a straight nose on this bottom, changing it into a face for his own amusement. When, at regular intervals, she came to see us with her mother, she sat quietly, with a silly, haughty smile on her lips and when our eyes met she looked quickly away. Paupers like myself held no interest for her.

Aunt Marfa, as her alleged mother liked to be called, always wore black, held herself like a lady but made up for her daughter's silence with an endless flow of chatter. She had lived in Paris for thirty years and her trade gave her an admirable knowledge of human nature. Her gossip was usually rather vulgar but at times she would deliver a truly inspired dissertation on the art of procuring. She was both ashamed of, and deeply interested in, her profession. While she talked she would sink into the depths of the armchair, but from time to time she straightened up with a sudden, violent jerk of her body. Bandi and I often wondered about this frequent but always unexpected change of position. I suggested that it indicated her struggle against old age but Bandi insisted that it denoted a moral itch: the procuress was trying to rise, at least to the waist, above the moral quagmire she knew and described so well.

When, the evening before, they had knocked on our door the old woman's face betrayed utter desperation. Her usual garrulity was replaced by a solemn, affected pride. She told us that Lilian was a Yugoslav citizen and that, according to her information, all foreign girls were taken to Nazi brothels. All Lilian's gentlemen friends were in the front lines or had already escaped; her colleagues at the *Folies* would do nothing for her because they were all homosexuals and didn't give a damn about women. As always when they were in trouble the women had turned to the spirits for advice. They had drawn the letters of the alphabet on the bedside table in lipstick and the spirit Léon had spelled out my name. This is why they had taken the liberty to come to me for assistance.

When we came out of our room (which I instantly forgot as if I had never lived in it), the two women were standing outside modestly and humbly. Their appearance filled me with pity and sympathy. Both were wearing pretty afternoon frocks – it was obvious that they possessed nothing else. They moved around in a cloud of scent and carried on their backs bundles made up of multi-coloured silk pyjamas. To complete this get-up the old woman held between her purple-nailed fingers a heavy, knobby, walking stick. The stick almost moved me to tears. There had always been wandering bards, itinerant students and actors, travelling whores, but procuresses were always anchored to one place by their profession. Here, in Paris, she was queen among her fellow-procurers but what would she do in Montauban? She must have been struggling with the same doubts, for her forehead was covered with perspiration. Solemnly and tenderly I kissed her hand and rearranged the shoulder-straps of her bundle.

'Thank you, Mr Faludy,' Aunt Marfa said in a grating voice. 'We shall not be ungrateful.'

'Come on,' Valy cut the scene short, 'and let me warn you, ladies, that I shall not tolerate any show of gratitude towards my husband.'

The large hall of the Gare d'Austerlitz was deserted. We thought we were too late but we were soon reassured that we had arrived at the most auspicious moment because, though the trains were still running, there were almost no more passengers left. We walked along the train in the pitch-dark railway station until we found an empty, obsolete compartment divided in two. The three women occupied one side of it, Bandi and I the other. Aunt Marfa offered us a bottle of cognac and the next second the train began to move soundlessly, almost on velvet feet.

The cheerful chatter of the women increased my anxiety. I drank slowly, remembering the effect cognac had on me on our way to Fontainebleau, but I soon grew numbed and dazed, while a million ants were running up and down my ankles and elbows. Then Warsaw fell, now it was the turn of Paris. Suddenly ants climbed to my head, my entire body was crawling with them and even the cognac bottle seemed to itch in my hand. A rain of sparks fell outside the windows on both sides of the carriage: red ants, ants everywhere.

'Let's talk,' I said to Bandi. He accepted with enthusiasm. I was a little afraid that he would repeat the prophecies he had voiced during the last few days, namely that the Soviet Union would never permit sweet France to be destroyed and would sooner declare war on Hitler, but fortunately he spoke of his childhood and its nightmares. While listening to him I pursued my own thoughts. Perhaps it was a grave error to have taken the train instead of sticking to my original idea of walking to the southern border. Now I was bound helplessly to a merciless course without being able to swerve to the right or to the left before the oncoming danger, as I would have done on the open highway. I was caught in a narrow, square, steel-lined tunnel cut by the train into the darkness of the night, there was no escape and at the end of this mad course I should run into a wall, invisible and impenetrable like the pressure of an explosion.

I looked out of the window. Towards the east the horizon was alight with gunfire, as if storm-clouds were lying low above the ground with their behinds in the air like a row of dead soldiers, emitting flashes of lightning. With half an ear I listened to Aunt Marfa who was explaining something to my wife in gay, excited tones:

'. . . by the same token you could say that you owned a public swimming pool but would admit only one customer. One guest wouldn't even pay for the scrubbing of the basin, my dear. To maintain a swimming pool you need many customers, the more the better. It is the same with women. Is it worth while to spend all that money on massage, rouge, powder, perfume, hairdresser, good clothes, a charming apartment, and so on, for the sake of a single man? Where is the profit? To maintain a beautiful woman it takes the joint efforts of many men . . . the more the better . . .'

I felt that I was advancing on the rails of determination towards doom. But was this determination valid only for the present? In a second I reviewed my entire past which appeared to me like a deep shaft, exactly like the one into which I had now plunged. I swallowed to shut out Bandi's voice telling me in detail about the cat he had shaved with his father's safety razor, and was back in my childhood.

As always when I remembered those days – which was not very often – I recalled my grandfather, the miller, standing before me in the mill with his long-stemmed pipe in his hand, and I heard him telling me that once he was dead nothing would remain of him except the reels of his life carried into space on a light-beam at a speed of three hundred thousand kilometres per second, straight as an arrow on the constantly widening girth of a gigantic soap-bubble. Nobody would ever catch up with it unless by chance, or by an act of mercy, the fourth dimension about which he had read in Einstein's works, wound it back again. Suddenly I saw him as clearly as if he were there before me in the white cloud of flour, but there was a light-beam under his feet and he was flying in the flour-dust of the nebulae in the gigantic mill of the Lord. By the time I reach Sirius he will have reached Aldebaran; I shall never catch up with him.

I sipped some cognac and shivered.

Havas fell silent. I turned my head and looked out into the night through the window on the other side. Suddenly I noticed the flickering of gunfire on that side as well. The Germans were approaching from both directions.

Try and get back to the mouth of the tunnel, I advised myself. I had always been more interested in the genesis of memories than in the memories themselves, more interested in the limits of consciousness and the border-clashes between conscious and unconscious than in the topography of the conscious. I had often played this game but now I was driving myself into it with a hysterical, furious frenzy. How far back in that tunnel could I remember? Around the age of five my memories became scarcer, they lost their sharpness and interdependence; half a year back it was no longer I who decided what I wanted to recollect and what I didn't want. The important events of those days escaped me but I remembered the bronze statue standing in the corner of the room next to my bedroom, sparkling in the darkness, or the time when I locked myself into the bathroom and was afraid of starving because I couldn't unlock the door.

I made a desperate effort to recall my early childhood: the shape of my mother's breast; the scene when they taught me to walk and I hung on the nurse's arm like drying clothes on a clothes-line; the blinding first ray of light – but in vain. Many of the things I thought I remembered were things I had invented or heard from my parents, observed in others or read in books. At the mouth of the tunnel I hit my head against a rock. What was behind that rock? A mountain? Or another tunnel?

Suddenly the train slowed down with its brakes screaming. We were standing in a fully illuminated station, Juvissy.

The station was deserted, as if the railway staff had been evacuated together with the population of the town. The open door of the station-master's office creaked on its hinges. Somewhere a telephone rang but nobody picked up the receiver.

'Do you hear it?' Bandi whispered in my ear.

An aeroplane was circling above us, humming mildly like a bee above a summer garden. As there were no French aeroplanes it could only have been a German one.

'And love, is that nothing?' Valy asked in the next compartment.

'A man must pay,' Aunt Marfa declared. 'He must learn to put down the money on the bedside table before he takes off his pants. Afterwards he would give only half as much. And the woman should count the money twice, slowly, before putting it away. He must learn that she is doing it for money, not for lust. There is nothing worse for a woman than to be known as passionate. Men will flock to her like bees to honey but they won't pay – why should they if she enjoys it! – and behind her back they will call her a . . .'

The plane came down in a nose-dive, screaming. Bandi jumped up and yelled at the top of his voice:

'Put out the lights, morons! The lights, you scoundrels! The lights.'

The roaring of the plane swallowed his voice. I felt as if it were flying straight at my forehead. 'It will cut off the top of my skull,' I thought. Exactly the top, and from that moment everything will be upside-down. The saucer on top and the cup on the bottom. Bandi stopped shouting. The aeroplane seemed to have spared us this time. I was almost reassured when suddenly I heard a noise like the slamming of the door. Compared to my anxiety the sound was insignificant. The bomb must have dropped somewhere outside, in the fields.

When Bandi and I climbed out of the train we were surprised to find that approximately thirty carriages ahead of us a shapeless mass was hanging from the smooth, black wall of the coach. There was complete silence but for the running feet of the stretcher bearers. Suddenly all the lights went out, only the carbon filaments glowed red for another second or two in the darkness.

'What happened?' Aunt Marfa asked anxiously, leaning out of the window.

'Nothing,' Bandi replied.

We climbed back and a second later the train started moving, gathering speed as if it wanted to get away from there without delay.

Bandi drew back into the corner of the compartment. The women too had fallen silent. Only I didn't feel like sleeping. I experienced a sharp, almost erotic thrill at the thought that once again my tipper was allowed to run on unchecked in the shaft. But I was even more pleased by the circumstances that in the meantime I had recalled what was to be found behind that rock at the mouth of the tunnel. Not a mountain, but a relatively thin layer of earth beyond which two shafts opened. Further on each shaft forked out, then each of the two new shafts again forked out, until, around 1800 I counted sixteen shafts and at the time of the Renaissance I had one thousand six hundred ancestors, unless some of the shafts had joined in the meantime. Further back, in the days of Adam and Eve, there were again only two shafts and there my research ran into a new wall or rather into the terrible explosion of creation.

I opened my eyes to see Lilian standing before me. She had come so noiselessly that I hadn't heard her at all.

'I brought you some chocolate,' she whispered, offering me a bar of the ribbed Swiss chocolate I liked so much. She was so close to me that when I lifted the chocolate to my lips the back of my hand brushed against that part of her abdomen which, on the stage, she covered with a silver shield. In my nose and mouth the smell of the chocolate mixed with the strong perfume of lilies she always poured into her palm and rubbed into her hips and loins with a vulgar but very attractive movement. I felt as if I were sitting in the first row of the *Folies Bergère*, but it was not Lilian's body I saw behind my closed lids but that of her partner, a charming, fair boy who had remained in Paris to await the German officers. Lilian backed into the other compartment but on the way ran three fingers through my hair.

At dawn we crossed the bridge over the yellowish and absolutely motionless water of the River Loire. Later, at Vierzon, the train was overrun by refugees. I sat in my corner and tried to sleep, but my ears continued to register the stories told by the new arrivals about French troops chasing the refugees who held them up in their flight with gun-butts, about a concrete fortress on the Belgian border where the troops retreating from near Brussels could not take refuge because their officers had run off with the keys to the steel doors; about General George who had been taken prisoner with his entire staff and the military plans the very moment he arrived at the front. Yet all this left me so completely untouched that I might have been listening to insignificant episodes of the Peloponnesian war.

The next day, early in the afternoon, I was walking with Lorsy in the market place of Montauban. From the railway station we had gone directly to the mayor, who had received us with joy except for Aunt Marfa and Lilian whose appearance did not fit in with his ideas as to how a social democratic, political exile should look. He entrusted us to the care of a municipal councillor. As Montauban was already crowded with refugees, Bandi, Valy and I were billeted with a peasant family a few kilometres outside the town. The next day I walked into the town to find Fényes and Lorsy. I found the latter in a café, in company with Aunt Marfa and Lilian. The dancer and her alleged mother had been placed by the elderly municipal councillor in the town's best hotel where Léon Blum had been unable to obtain a room on the same day and where, by the way, Lorsy lived.

'I have every reason to be optimistic,' he explained, when I asked him why in hell he was so cheerful. We left Lilian and the procuress at the café with the old town-councillor who had found them their hotel room and was hanging round their table in order to make love to Lilian. We walked up and down under the arcades of the market-place in the sticky afternoon heat, among fat fruit vendors, giant heads of lettuce, stalls loaded with snails and fish: a true, peace-time atmosphere of calm and plenty.

'You must not believe that my optimism springs from the base consideration that the mayor of this old and noble town named after the Mons Alba takes care of my food and lodgings and will do so for a long time to come. I derive my optimism not from selfish and petty considerations but from historical-philosophical contemplations. I thought of this yesterday while sitting at the café with the charming Madame Marfa who told me in confidence that she was carrying fifty thousand francs in her handbag. This, as we immediately swore eternal friendship, was more reassuring to me than if the money had been in my own pocket. Her charming conversation, however, did not prevent me from following my own thoughts and I came to the conclusion that the Germans cannot win this war.'

He stopped and turned to me, still deep in thought. Only then did I notice the bottle of wine sitting in the pocket of his black alpaca coat. Red burgundy.

'I am not crazy,' he continued, 'and I do not believe that the Germans will be held up at the Seine, the Loire or the Garonne after having crossed the Meuse, the Somme and the Marne. These things are not decided by rivers.

'But still, Hitler will lose the war. Not for reasons of strategy or ideology, but because the general current of modern history never allows the worst, the most frightful, to happen. The thing that happens is never the worst but always the most disgusting. Remember the sixteenth century. When Soliman II got going in the Balkans it was to be feared that he would occupy all of Europe. That would have been the worst. The best would have been had Charles V, Francis I and the Pope formed an alliance and kicked out the Turk at one stroke. However, neither the worst nor the best happened, but the most disgusting: Francis I and the Pope allied themselves with Soliman whereupon, instead of occupying Europe, the Turks took only Hungary and exploited her for one hundred and fifty years. Then think of the First World War. It would have been a terrible catastrophe had William II defeated the West and it would have been ideal, had the West, after defeating William II, created lasting peace.

However, here again the most disgusting prevailed: the West won the war but the limping peace treaty it imposed on the defeated enemy caused the same war to be fought a second time twenty years later. Now I cannot imagine anything worse than Hitler winning this war nor can I imagine anything more ideal than the West winning the war and democratizing the entire world, including the Soviet Union. But this would be too good, therefore the most revolting remains: the West will ally itself with Hitler against Stalin or . . .'

He could not finish the sentence. For some time already we had been disturbed by the continuous mad screeching coming from the direction of the café where we had sat with Marfa and Lilian. A coarse, excited female voice screeched without pause and without punctuation as if its owner were declaiming a ten-thousand-syllable word. It was going strong when Lilian appeared round the corner with Aunt Marfa at her heels. When they noticed us their faces brightened.

'How fortunate we are to find you! Save us, poor helpless creatures!' the procuress cried, taking Lorsy's arm. Lilian held on to me, though it was obvious that she was amused by the scandal. Her pale yellow silk skirt was drenched in dishwater from her navel to her knee. As she stood there in the strong sunshine an exciting, leek-smelling cloud of steam rose from her humid lap. Aunt Marfa's lips were trembling and her eyes were full of tears, although she had received but little of the dishwater. Slivers of lettuce and bay-leaves hung in the hair round her forehead like a wreath.

The councillor, she related, had talked to them from the next table, mainly to Lilian, of course. The innocent conversation, however, was soon interrupted by the gentleman's wife who had suddenly appeared with a bucketful of dishwater and had thrown it at them, without cause or reason, of course.

'Oh, why did we ever leave Paris!' she wailed. 'We could have got along with the Germans somehow, but in this dreadful little town we shall perish, Monsieur Lorsy!'

Taking advantage of the opportunity Lilian pressed her body to mine, which did not prevent her from following with her eyes the tall lieutenant who passed us for the third time.

The procuress immediately forgot her troubles.

'Don't you make eyes at that scoundrel, you silly goose!' she chided the dancer. 'He couldn't even buy you that cheap, thousand-franc ring, don't you remember? Does he think we shall accept his services for nothing? Come on home and change. Will you see us home, gentlemen?'

Lorsy gave the procuress his arm as if she were a queen requiring his services. He winked at the market women who had been watching the scene avidly with open eyes and mouths.

'You love me, don't you, George?' Lilian whispered.

The plane appearing directly before us above the trees saved me from having to reply. The deafening roaring of its engine made us all stop. I thought it was going to hit us when, making a somersault above our heads, it flew on. I turned back and established that it was a German plane. But I also noticed that Lilian's skirt was drenched at the back too, and stuck to her bottom like the skin of an onion, revealing not only the two hillocks but also the narrow valley between them that greeted me with a friendly smile.

She proposed that I visit her at her hotel the next afternoon, at three. I was depicting to myself the details of that meeting when we sat down to lunch with our hosts the following day. The windows of the large, dark dining-room were almost completely overgrown with wild vine and yet it was so hot inside that my shirt stuck to my chest as we spooned up our thick onion soup. There was dance music on the wireless and Bandi talked ceaselessly and enthusiastically to entertain us. Our host, a dignified peasant with flashing eyes and a goose-neck, listened attentively and kept nodding his small, round head in assent. His wife, a large, beautiful peasant woman whose white, hard, fat nape looked as if it were pulled tight over flexible fish-bone, reminded me of the great ladies of the Renaissance: Elisabeth Gonzaga or Beatrice d'Este. She was obviously bored by our conversation and kept her eyes haughtily averted from Bandi's ugly face.

I was wondering how to ask for a barrelful of hot water after lunch so that I could take a bath before going to Lilian. In my daze I failed at first to notice that the dance music had stopped and that the company round the table was tensely listening to an announcement.

The voice of the announcer was excited, wavering, quite obviously he was not at all certain whether to mourn or to celebrate. He informed us that Pétain had asked the Germans for an armistice which would come into force the next day at noon. He added that the Germans would occupy part of France, but didn't say which part. Our hostess rose, turned off the radio with an energetic flick of her wrist and fled into the kitchen.

The first thought that occurred to me was that for me this armistice had come at the right moment; at least I would have a peaceful afternoon with Lilian. The next moment, however, I felt a sharp stab of pain. The Third Republic was dead. The mournful silence in the room was disturbed only by the cackling of a hen under the rose-tree outside the window. The sound became more and more unbearable. We listened to it helplessly and humbly, as to the words of a supreme ruler who held us in his power. Suddenly the peasant jumped up from his chair, picked up an overripe apricot from the table, ran to the window and flung the fruit at the hen with such force that the thick, yellow juice ran all over her feathers.

After lunch I sat in the arbour with Bandi and Valy discussing plans. I suggested we start the next morning, we were certain to find a ship in the Bay of Biscay that would take us to England. Bandi agreed and said he would come into town with me that afternoon. He was impatient to discuss our affairs with Lorsy and Fényes but the real attraction was Léon Blum who was in town. Bandi adored to talk to great men and he would have hated to miss this opportunity.

In the meantime our host had again turned on the wireless. The same excited voice was warning the population to remain calm, there was no cause for anxiety. He told them to remain where they were but added that this advice was not valid for foreigners who would do better, in their own interest, to leave France as soon as possible.

The announcer was still speaking when the garden gate flew open to admit a dust-covered Aunt Marfa and behind her Lilian.

'Thank God you are here,' the procuress cried, collapsing into a garden chair. 'Léon says Mr Faludy's life is in danger, he must leave immediately.'

'Léon?' I stammered. 'Have you been talking to Léon Blum?'

'No, the message is not from Léon Blum but from Léon the spirit,' the old woman said with awe. 'After lunch we asked the table what to do. Léon said: "Faludy's life is in danger. He must start immediately." We asked him where he was to go. Léeon told us that too. Here it is, I wrote it down . . .'

She brought out a piece of creased pink tissue-paper from her deep bag on which she had noted down the spirit's message in lipstick. Bandi winked at me and grinned.

'Perpina,' Aunt Marfa read. 'You must go to Perpina. This is what Léon said.'

'Perpignan, on the Spanish frontier,' I corrected the message, amazed.

'I wouldn't know. I have never heard of that town,' replied Aunt Marfa.

'Well?' Bandi said looking at me questioningly. 'What do we do?'

'We are going,' I said, and rose. 'And what are you going to do?' I turned to the procuress while from the corner of my eye I watched Lilian who was sitting there unmoved, crushing pale green vine leaves between her fingers. 'Are you coming with us?'

'With the greatest pleasure!' Aunt Marfa answered enthusiastically. 'We are fed up with this hole!'

In ten minutes we were ready, said goodbye to our hosts and set out towards the town. I was surprised how glad everybody had been to do something instead of waiting for things to happen. This sudden decision had shaken all of us alive. The transformation from small-town citizens into hobos seemed unbelievable and, perhaps because of that, rather amusing. We were soon overtaken by an ox-cart but it could take only three, Aunt Marfa, Valy and Bandi whose feet were badly blistered from his innumerable excursions into town. Lilian and I remained alone but a few minutes later we too were picked up by an ox-cart taking new potatoes to market. We lay down on top of the potatoes and immediately began to kiss furiously. While she bloodied my lips with her sharp teeth, I thought to myself that I ought, instead, to be working on a poem bemoaning the fall of the Third Republic; though, fortunately, the circumstances of that fall had relieved me of my obligations.

Arrived in town Bandi and I went to see Fényes. We found the old man in the garden, sitting on a three-legged camp stool under the star-shaped foliage of an apple-tree. Next to him stood a bucket of cold water and in it a bottle of wine. Only his cold grey eyes betrayed his bitterness. He informed us that from midnight on the trains would travel only from Toulouse-Sète-Avignon southwards, therefore we had better start immediately. If we remained the Germans would make hash of us. We must get to England by ship, canoe or raft, there were probably British ships at Bayonne that would take us.

I begged him to come with us but he refused with a sharp movement of his head.

'If there is no other way out,' he said, 'I still have my old revolver. I am tired of retreating. I have retreated more often than befits a Hungarian gentleman . . . Don't gape at me! Have you never seen an old man before? Anyway, there is still plenty of time to finish this bottle.'

When the bottle was empty he took us to the garden gate. He made a brief, uncertain gesture as if he wanted to embrace me, then blushed and turned away.

The next day at noon we reached Bayonne. As we were walking into town from the railway station troops were marching parallel with us in the middle of the road, but before we came to the bridge on the Adour they scattered in all directions, paying no heed to the non-commissioned officers who were desperately shouting after them. In the market-place at least ten thousand men, women and cars lined the streets. Strangely enough we came upon acquaintance after acquaintance in this dense mass of people. From the windows of a café Franz Werfel greeted us with a melancholy wave of his hand, at the foot of a fruit-stall in the square the German playwright, Mehring, lay resting on the ground. He told us that his car had reached the middle of a bridge over the Loire when the French and the Germans began to shoot at each other from either side of the river. Fishermen had helped him off the bridge and he had walked the rest of the way to Bayonne.

We continued towards the harbour. When we approached the

Adour we caught sight of a mast and on top of the mast, to our great joy, a Swedish flag. However, we were soon stopped by a policeman who told us that civilians were not allowed in the harbour and besides, no ship was sailing. We turned back into town to look for a place where we could spend the night. In the market-place we ran into an acquaintance of Lorsy's, an angelically mild, grey-haired, pink-cheeked Hungarian who looked like a cardinal but was an anarchist, and had spent the last twenty years of his life in exile. He had just returned from St Jean de Luz where he had hoped to board a British ship, but the British were taking only their own fellow-citizens, Poles and Czechs. No Hungarians, no matter who they were.

We roamed the streets dismayed and helpless, there were no rooms to be had, the hotel porters laughed in our faces. Involuntarily we started back towards the railway station. Opposite the station we found an empty bistro. The patron, standing in the doorway in his shirtsleeves, looked us over carefully, then declared that he had nothing to offer except some Viandox. We gratefully accepted the hot soup.

We sat silent but suddenly I noticed that Bandi was staring with popping eyes at something behind my back. I turned round and saw that the patron was painting little red swastikas on the wall where the yellow oil-paint and the whitewash met in a ragged line. He was obviously unskilled in painting – as well as unfamiliar with the Nazi symbol – because he painted them the wrong way round, anticlockwise.

'Let's get out of here,' I suggested.

'But where shall we go?' Bandi asked.

'To Perpignan. We may still find a ship that will take us to Africa.'

At that moment a gigantic clap of thunder shook the earth and set the cups and glasses on the table tinkling. Then the rain came down in torrents.

'We are idiots,' Lorsy said meditatively. 'Why in heaven's name do we have to go to England where there is a war on. In Lisbon there is sunshine, in Lisbon there are rich Hungarians and their addresses are in my notebook. We are citizens of a neutral country, there is no reason why we shouldn't get visas to another neutral country. If we don't like it in Portugal we can still go to America. And apart from that,' he turned to Bandi, 'Portugal has been Britain's ally for centuries . . .'

'I have been told,' Aunt Marfa mused, 'that life is very gay in Lisbon. Very gay.'

'Except for those who have to work for a living,' Bandi remarked.

'A courageous little people,' Lorsy continued, 'already after the Tortesillas treaty . . .'

'. . . they were smart enough to organize a police force that is known today as the vest-pocket Gestapo,' Bandi continued with false melancholy.

'They have a pious government,' the procuress hastened to Lorsy's aid.

'As pious as Prince Alba and as Christian as the Inquisition,' Bandi agreed.

'In your place I shouldn't be so particular,' Lorsy said angrily.

'Be serious,' Valy chided, 'and tell me what kind of country Portugal really is?'

'It smells of mint.' I cut off the argument.

When the rain stopped we left the bistro to look for the Portuguese consulate. It stood in a dirty little back street and there was a queue many hundreds of yards long before the gate. We were a little surprised that Lorsy's brilliant idea had occurred to so many but we took our places at the end of the queue except for Lilian who – wearing a pale blue silk skirt – sat down on the edge of the wet and steaming pavement. The fierce sunshine beating down on us at an oblique angle burned my nape as if a dozen wasps were stinging it. A few minutes later the sky darkened again and large, violet clouds came rolling out from behind the roofs.

'Even God is a fascist!' Bandi shouted, shaking his fists at the sky.

When the shower was over a couple of policemen came walking along the line and asked everyone to hand over their identity papers. The French were made to leave the queue.

'Go home,' the policemen told them, 'the Germans won't do anything to you.'

Then they made Lilian get up from the pavement.

'If you are tired,' they told her, 'go to Biarritz and lie down in the sand . . .' Soon Lorsy made friends with a squat gentleman wearing horn-rimmed glasses who turned out to be a Hungarian though he had lived in France for thirty years. Before me an old woman with terribly swollen legs and an inch-thick layer of powder on her face sat in a barber's chair. She informed the people around her in a voice that carried for miles that she was a British citizen and lived in Lourenço Marques, but her weak heart had prevented her from moving fast enough and therefore she had missed the British ship. In the past, she wailed, when a British citizen got into difficulties in China or South America, a British man-of-war appeared in the harbour and woe to the town if even a hair on the Britisher's head was damaged. But now? She had to pay two hundred francs a day for that barber's chair . . . God knows, the excitement might kill her . . .

She lit a long cigar and wriggling her huge behind to indicate that she was talking to me, she asked whether, if she sent him a cable, the First Lord of the Admiralty would send a man-of-war to Bayonne to fetch her.

An hour later, during which time we had not advanced an inch, ten soldiers arrived in close military formation led by a very young, very short and very cocky fair-haired sergeant. When he noticed that his appearance caused general laughter he mounted the steps leading to the entrance of the consulate, opened his small, narrow lips as wide as they would go and began to shout at us:

'You are laughing, are you? Well, I'll show you that I am not such a toy soldier! I shall have everyone who disturbs the peace put to the sword! Put – to – the – sword!' he screamed in his thin little voice. 'Don't be mistaken, it is not for cabbage that you are standing in line here but for your lives! For – your – lives!'

The line had lengthened behind us in the meantime. At the corner of the Dôme square, two or three hundred yards back, where a bearded Polish Jew in a black kaftan was standing, the line broke at right-angles. There was no noise, no pushing and shoving: we stood motionless, waiting. Only from the invisible vibrations of accumulated anxiety pressing down on my nape did I conclude that at least a thousand people were standing behind me.

My neighbours stood with their heads bent; Valy snuggled up close to me, even Lorsy and his crocodile-eyed friend were silent. I glanced at Lilian who stood with a dreamy smile on her lips as if she were completely unaware of the seriousness of our situation. Soon I lost count of time, forgot my environment and drew back into myself. The tumble in the new potatoes with Lilian seemed as distant as the days of Alexander the Great. I pressed my wife's hand tenderly and thought, with tears in my eyes, what a selfless, loyal wife she had been to me in spite of her hysterics and quarrels . . . Then I had to stop wool-gathering and concentrate my attention on a single phenomenon: the unbelievable hardness of the cobblestones beneath my feet. There were three possibilities: either the stone had grown harder or my feet softer or both. My body is deteriorating, I thought, objects are becoming my enemies, the earth no longer tolerates me on its back. I looked down at my shoes and observed that my once so beautiful black-and-white Oxfords were in a dreadful condition. Then, from under the point of my shoe, I heard a thin, sibilant, weeping voice. The nature of the sound was new and unusual; I established that I had never before heard a sound of exactly this frequency of vibration, since normally it would be inaudible to the human ear. Only then did I realize that I had been making treading movements with my feet, and quickly lifted one of them. Tiny ants were scurrying back and forth on the cobblestones, they had been crying for mercy. I pressed my chin on my chest and gazed down into semi-darkness – there was not enough room to bend down. Five little black ants were running in an excited, sinuous line. I had killed the sixth.

Suddenly I heard a loud, solemn voice behind me and turned to see whose it was. The bearded Polish Jew was speaking, beating the air with his stick. Under the big black shadow of his hat his long, straight, milk-white nose jutted out sharply against his beard, his hair and earlock.

'Open that door!' he shouted in German. 'Hundreds, thousands are standing beneath your windows, Mr Consul, hundreds and thousands whose lives are in danger! Where is your humanity, where is your mercy? Are God's commandments not valid in Portugal? If so, tell us! Open your window and spit on our heads!'

The door of the consulate remained closed so that from that point of view the speech was without result, but it awakened the waiting crowd and put an end to the apathy which had taken hold of all of us. People began to call the consul, demand to be let in, others criticized the attitude of all diplomats, their indifference, their inhumanity. Now everyone began to push and shove: as a result we were so tightly pressed together that even breathing became difficult. Taking advantage of this illusion of movement Lorsy pushed quickly forward. Very soon I could discern his large black hat some fifteen yards ahead of us, hovering high above the crowd, and the small grey locks on his nape, like white chrysanthemum petals. The voice of the Polish Jew behind me rose to a scream:

'What? Do you have the courage to pretend that you are in as much danger as I? Do you know who I am? Have you never heard of the limericks I wrote against Hitler in the Yiddish paper of Berdichev? Do you want to see them? Here, I can read them to you!'

'Oh, shut up!'

'Do you know what Adolf will do to you? He will send you all to work. And do you know what he will do to me? He will have me emasculated!' he cried triumphantly. 'But he will be too late! I won't be emasculated with an unconsecrated knife! Not on his life! I have a consecrated knife right here with me, I'll do it myself and the sooner the better!'

It needed three people to disarm the crazed Jew and the Tom Thumb sergeant shot three times into the air to frighten the crowd into silence. Then two of his soldiers took hold of the kicking, screaming man who was already foaming at the mouth and carried him away.

'This madman has spoiled our chances,' a red-cheeked man with a German accent remarked. 'The consul will never open the doors to such rabble!'

At that moment a short young man in black appeared on the balcony of the consulate. He had tremendous shoulders and a broad chest, and his legs were so long that it seemed as though the middle section of his body were missing. He looked exactly like a bronze bust on two legs.

'I am the Portuguese Consul,' he introduced himself. 'I am sorry to have kept you waiting but I had to get in touch with my government before granting so many visas. My government approved, so come back tomorrow, all of you, hand over your passports and two hundred and forty francs. We shall work all day tomorrow and the day after, and in the evening we shall distribute the passports with the visas. Don't worry and don't be impatient. Portugal is a small country but her heart is big. You will all be admitted without exception.'

'Long live Portugal! Long live the Consul! Long live Salazar!' people shouted at the top of their voices.

'Long live France!' the little sergeant screeched in his thin voice.

'Long live France,' the crowd repeated after him. 'Let us sing the Marseillaise!'

The sun was still high in the sky but the thousands of refugees in the Dôme square were already at supper or asleep on the cobblestones. There was no place left for us so we set out on the highway towards Biarritz. We knocked on many doors but no one would give us shelter. Finally we came to an A-shaped, yellow house covered in cobwebs and vines like some bewitched castle, that seemed deserted. We kicked in the garden gate, walked up to the house and there, at Lorsy's orders, made three deep bows to conciliate the spirits of the place. Then we threw ourselves into the worn garden chairs that stood in grass so tall that only the amethyst-blue candles of the delphiniums showed above it. Valy set out to reconnoitre and soon returned with two large loaves of bread, cheese, radishes and a paraffin lamp. After dinner Lorsy jumped up and informed us that he would now proceed to Biarritz and ask his publisher, who was on holiday there, for another advance on *The French Fortifications from Vauban to Maginot*. Should the publisher declare that those fortresses were no longer worth anything, he would reply that the same was true for the franc, so why not give him some.

After he left, Bandi and I discovered a smooth, protected place close to the wall of the villa where, under the eaves, we would be safe from the rain. We tore up armfuls of grass and carried it there to make beds. It was almost completely dark when Lorsy arrived with ten thousand francs in his pocket. He would not, however, stay with us because, being unable to sleep in the open, he had made arrangements with the greengrocer opposite to sleep in one of the huge spinach-baskets in the shop.

'I am sorry, my dear,' he turned to Aunt Marfa, 'but there is only one basket free.'

We lay down side by side with our heads against the wall: Bandi, I, Valy, the procuress and finally Lilian. When I knelt up to put out the lamp our eyes met for a moment. I listened to the sand trickling from the mouldy wall next to my ear, as though in an hour-glass, and then suddenly I was sound asleep.

At dawn we all woke at the same minute. Lorsy was still asleep huddled up in the huge vegetable basket like a boa constrictor. There was also a second basket there which Aunt Marfa eyed with a mournful expression; it was full of spinach and on top of the leaves, close to Lorsy, there lay an empty wine bottle.

'Get up, Ernö,' I nudged him.

'Leave me alone! But you can get me a cup of strong black coffee . . .'

'We must go to the Portuguese consulate.'

'Tell them to jump in the lake. I want peace . . .'

Finally Bandi succeeded in dragging him from the basket. In front of the consulate hundreds were sleeping on the pavement. An hour later thousands thronged in the narrow alley. We stood there without food or drink until late in the evening. Only a few dozen of the many thousands had been admitted. In the evening the crocodile-eyed friend of Lorsy's came to tell us that Tom Thumb was standing guard at the back door of the consulate and for ten one-hundred-franc notes opened it to anyone. The thousand-franc queue was running out and tomorrow we would be admitted free of charge. There was no cause to worry, the Germans were only at Bordeaux and it would take them at least another four days to get here.

The next day towards noon we were beginning to lose our nerve and sent Lorsy to the back door with our passports. No sooner had he gone than the doors of the consulate flew wide open and those waiting outside were let in in groups of a hundred. We went and sat on the steps of the Dôme, chewing the ten kilogrammes of cucumbers the greengrocer had given Lilian that morning. Hours later Lorsy joined us, saying that he had handed in our passports and we would all have our visas for six thousand francs, our last money.

Bandi departed to find out when the Spanish consulate would be open and how soon we could obtain our transit visas, and returned with two bottles of wine. He related that a wine merchant was standing in the middle of the road handing out wine to all passers-by. He had also visited the harbour; the police cordon had disappeared and it was whispered that ships would soon sail for North Africa. We were not interested. After midnight the Portuguese consulate began distributing the passports. Everything was fine.

In the morning we walked down to the Spanish consulate. Again the square was filled to capacity but this time the crowd was shouting, screaming, cursing, quarrelling. They had been told that the Spanish consulate would give a transit visa to anyone possessing a valid Portuguese visa. The Portuguese visas granted us were, however, invalid because the consul had forgotten to sign them. We raced to the Portuguese consulate but the doors were locked. The brief announcement tacked to it read:

CLOSED FOR THE SUMMER
IN URGENT MATTERS TURN TO
CONSULATE OF PORTUGAL IN BORDEAUX

We walked down to the harbour. Bandi told us everything he had learned the previous day. Passage on the ships to North Africa had to be bought in the customs building. The procedure was as follows: you paid a hundred thousand francs to a customs official. For this amount you were permitted to board a ship, without even giving your name. If you could not pay a hundred thousand francs, you had to wait by the fence of the customs building. Here tickets were distributed and if you were lucky you could get one. With this ticket you could enter the customs building and if you could prove that you were a distinguished democrat you were permitted to board a ship, free of charge. All ships were going to Casablanca.

The fence of the customs building was high and topped with iron lance-heads. Every twelfth lance was longer than and twice as thick as its neighbours. People were standing twenty deep along the entire length of the fence. On top of one of the lances sat the Polish Jew who had wanted to emasculate himself three days ago in front of the Portuguese consulate. Blood was dripping from under his long black kaftan but nobody was paying attention to him.

'I was the Polish eagle who was to be gored,' he cried when he caught sight of Valy and Lilian. 'Now I am the Gallic cock and I gore myself.'

I told our women to sit down on the other side of the embankment. There were so many people in front of us that I was afraid we would never reach the fence. Dazed with exhaustion I leaned against the man standing before me and a few minutes later I noticed that the law of gravity worked not only vertically but also horizontally. The unresisting mass opened before me and closed behind me like a block of ice when a steel wire is slowly cutting through it, exactly as we had been shown in the school laboratory. The reason was perhaps that most of these people were much older than I and they were certainly more exhausted. As my body leaned against theirs I felt as if my muscles were twice as hard. Half an hour later I reached the fence and fell to my knees. Ten minutes later Bandi joined me.

Towards noon a slender flight officer appeared in the door of the harbour building and advanced towards us with springy, dancing steps. He had a short, thick, crooked nose as if the tip had been cut off with a knife and large, cinnamon-red nostrils.

'The entrance tickets!' people sighed around me.

The flight officer came very close to the fence. He stopped about two yards from us, lifted the green book of tickets high as if to show it to us, then walked comfortably from one end of the fence to the other, so near that the outstretched hands almost touched him.

'Give one to me, lieutenant, to me!' some begged, but the majority waited in silence.

When the officer reached the end of the fence he turned round, shifted the book to his other hand and walked back. The fence between us had by then lost all meaning or at least its meaning had become meaningless. No one knew any more who was inside, who outside, whether we were prisoners behind bars or he a wild beast in a cage.

After having peered into our faces as he walked along, the officer sat down on a bench in the middle of the fenced-off area, put the green book of tickets down beside him, selected a cigarette from his gold case, opened his paper and began to read. He read quickly and avidly as if every printed line were dealing with him and him alone. From time to time he looked up, brushed us with a glance, then turned back to his paper, blowing smoke-rings into the air. Like a young man waiting for his beloved on a garden bench.

Then, when we had given up all hope, he jumped from the bench, ran to the fence and tearing a handful of tickets from the book pressed them at random into the extended hands, by fives and tens. In the confusion that followed the unfortunate men who snatched the tickets first usually lost them to a hundred grabbing fingers and had to wait patiently for the next distribution.

We stood there until late in the evening. In the meantime Valy had acquired a large tin of meat and some biscuits, and Lilian forty packets of cigarette tobacco which she slipped into my rucksack. We did not open the tin but decided to go back to our camping place, find Lorsy and dine together. Lorsy, however, was not in his vegetable basket. We ate, then lay down to sleep.

I dreamed that I was standing on top of a hill in the middle of the Great Flood, and that water was pouring down on me until I was knee-deep in it. A deafening clap of thunder woke me from my dream, and I found that my feet were indeed wet because the eaves protected us only down to our knees. I sat up and looked towards Lilian. A flash of lightning showed her staring into my face with wide-open, glassy eyes.

In the morning we went to look for Lorsy but his basket was empty except for three wine bottles. We set out towards the harbour. Seeing us approach with our rucksacks the passers-by turned away their eyes or lowered their heads in obvious embarrassment. From their behaviour we concluded that the Germans must be near indeed. In the market-place we ran into Lorsy's crocodile-eyed friend.

'What are you doing here? Have you missed the ship?' he asked, amazed.

'What ship?'

'The ship Monsieur Lorsy found for all of you yesterday. The one that took him to Casablanca at dawn!'

'The scoundrel! To have left us behind!' Aunt Marfa wailed.

'I just don't understand anything,' I said. 'Ernö hasn't said a word about any ship . . .'

'Yesterday,' Crocodile-eye explained, 'I accompanied Monsieur Lorsy to the harbour. We found a lovely 1,000-ton freighter. Hundreds of people were standing around on the shore begging the captain to let them come on board. He stood looking down on us but made no reply. From time to time he spat, but never far enough to hit us.

'Monsieur Lorsy got tired of waiting. He opened his arms wide and began to orate. He spoke about the French *gloire* and about seamen's honour. He spoke solemnly and convincingly, beautifully and movingly, believe me, it was better than Mark Antony's funeral oration! Finally he addressed the captain directly: "Let us suppose, Monsieur le Capitaine," he said, "that at this moment the Allies possess one thousand ships and the Germans also one thousand. If you take this ship to Africa the Allies will have one thousand and one ships and the Germans only nine hundred and ninety-nine. Therefore, in reality, this ship is not one ship but two ships . . ."

'In the end the captain was so completely bowled over by Monsieur Lorsy's avalanche of words that he promised to have the ship ready to sail by five in the morning and would admit as many as could find a place to sit on deck, in the only life-boat, in the engine-room, on the lower deck and in the lavatories.

'I,' Crocodile-eye concluded, 'lacked the courage to board that ship. Last night I heard over the radio that the Germans were dropping floating mines in the entrance of all French harbours to prevent the ships from leaving.'

'He left us here to face death,' Aunt Marfa cried. 'And yet all he had to do was to cross the street and he could have saved us all! The scoundrel!'

'Scoundrel? No. Simply lazy,' Bandi said meditatively. 'He did want to visit us last night but suddenly he felt too exhausted to move. And in the morning he was so excited that he simply forgot all about us. At this very minute he is standing at the railing of the ship, accusing himself and shedding large tears into the ocean.'

'Or vomiting into it,' Lilian remarked soberly.

'Whether he sobs or vomits, there isn't time to discuss his character now. Let's go to the customs building.'

We had plenty of cigarettes and this made waiting considerably easier. The air officer came out once every hour and by nightfall he had distributed two hundred tickets. Worn out as we were, we did not even think about sleeping in the magic garden but lay down beyond the embankment in the grass. I was not yet asleep when a terrible thunderstorm broke out, as if runaway elephants were dancing above us. We found shelter under a railway truck and spent the night mostly awake. Early in the morning Bandi and I stood again in the queue before the fence. Again we did not obtain tickets. Late in the afternoon I decided that it would be sheer madness to spend another night at Bayonne, the Germans were due any minute. I told Bandi that we would walk to the Spanish border and cross into Spain illegally. Compared to the Gestapo, Spanish prisons were Gardens of Eden.

The women were still asleep on the embankment, under railway trucks. Before waking them I looked down on the landscape that reminded me of a map spread out on a table. The River Adour was rolling across emerald-green fields, narrow dirt-paths dogging its steps all the way to the dunes blocking the horizon, beyond which lay the sea. Far away, perhaps half-way between myself and the sea, a ship was anchored in the river. Thick, white clouds of steam rose from its funnel.

'It is hooting!' Bandi cried.

My knees began to tremble with excitement. Indeed, a second later the sound of the hooting hit our ears.

'We can still catch her!' Bandi yelled. 'That was only the first!'

The women climbed out from under the freight cars, we picked up our rucksacks and began to run along the muddy road. We waded knee-deep in mud, fell on our faces, rose and ran on, until finally we decided to slow down. Valy and Lilian advanced side by side like two beautiful horses in a race. Bandi and I exchanged glances, then broke into wild laughter. Wasn't it exceedingly funny that we should pursue our lives with such zeal and determination? In front of us the setting sun was caught between two purple rain-clouds as in a pair of pincers or the lips of a mythical dragon. And then the ship's funnel hooted for a second time. The gathering storm-clouds loomed before us like an insurmountable wall, more and more forbidding as we came closer. God knows how long we had been running but there were only fifty yards between us and the ship when it hooted for the third time.

We ran up the landing stage but the gangway had already been pulled in. A bearded captain stood on the bridge with a fish-shaped pipe in his mouth. The bowl of the pipe had two little glass eyes that sparked and shone, and a sudden gust of wind brought down a shower of sparks upon us.

'Can we jump?' Bandi asked the captain.

The ship was moving away slowly from the shore. Fortunately the deck and even the rail were lower than the landing stage on which we stood.

'I have received strict orders,' the captain said in a quiet, friendly voice as if he were talking to someone sitting in an armchair opposite his – 'to shoot everyone whom I see boarding this ship. If I see them boarding it,' he added with emphasis. Then, with a regular, military about-face, he turned away and disappeared.

When we hit the deck it was so frighteningly dark that we saw no one and stumbled about half-blind between a multitude of tall iron barrels. We met no one, as if the captain with his devilishly glowing pipe were the only passenger on a vessel bound for hell.

Finally we discovered a door hidden behind heavy rain-soaked tarpaulin. We stepped into a completely dark room smelling like a hospital.

In front of me someone was counting slowly in Hungarian: 'One hundred and thirty-second victim . . . one hundred and thirty-third victim . . . one hundred and thirty-fourth victim . . . fifth, sixth, total: five new victims . . .'

I took the man by the arm and pulled him towards the door. He was a squat little man with a huge nose, wearing a French uniform with two rows of decorations on his chest.

'What the hell is the matter with you? What do you mean by victims?'

'I didn't know you were Hungarian,' he excused himself. 'My name is Rozgonyi.'

When I introduced myself his face brightened.

'A poet? Excellent. Then I shall tell you what I am afraid of. This ship is going to blow up. Look,' he said, pointing to the barrels upon which a heavy rain was beating down, 'do you see what is written on them? They contain explosives.'

'Have you never seen a ship that carried explosives?'

'This afternoon the passengers were cooking their food on the lids of these barrels. On open paraffin fires, of course. When I warned them they just laughed. And look at this crazy anarchist!'

The captain was approaching out of the darkness with a burning pipe in his mouth.

'We shall sink, captain!' Rozgonyi said.

'If it is written that we shall sink, sink we shall. Do you know how many ships have sunk since the Phoenicians first dared brave the seas? Just think of it: the riffs, the rocks, the storms, the battles! Salamis, Actium, Lepanto, Aboukir, Trafalgar, the last war and now this!'

'It is not the sinking I am afraid of, but the explosion!'

'To drown is a long and painful operation. Explosion is the best narcotic to make it bearable. Better than chloroform. It takes effect immediately, you don't have to count up to eighteen. And there is no unpleasant after-effect. In fact, there is no after-effect at all, sergeant.'

Valy and the procuress had, in the meantime, gone to sleep in the straw in the hold of the ship. Lilian had disappeared. Rozgonyi explained that though the ship was going to Casablanca it was, for the moment, sailing up and down the Adour waiting for high tide.

The captain did not want to drop anchor because he was afraid that should the Germans take the town they would requisition his ship, the *Château de Boncourt*.

We were all glad that the ship was going to Casablanca. Aunt Marfa confessed that she had already forgiven Lorsy for his desertion and could hardly wait to see him again. Bandi was happy because he had heard that a counter-government had been formed in Casablanca that wanted to go on with the war, and I was happy because I felt that my most secret wish was coming true: I would at last see Africa. Everyone was exhausted and we all lay down to sleep in the straw. Before falling asleep I suddenly remembered the ominous name of the ship and felt a strange anxiety. In 1789 the rabble had tried to set fire to the Château de Boncourt, ancient home of the Chamisseau family. When the round, Roman stone towers of the castle would not burn they put kegs of gunpowder in them and blew them up. The son of the squire who found refuge in Germany and became a famous poet and liberal wrote a poem about this event and asked God's blessing on the peasants ploughing the soil above the one-time castle.

Suddenly I was awakened by a subtle, tender caress.

'Quiet, be quiet,' Lilian whispered, 'and follow me . . .'

She was waiting for me outside the door, glued to the tarpaulin.

'I have made friends with the first mate,' she whispered. 'He is a fine gentleman, you must not think of anything indecent. He offered me his cabin while he is on duty. Come with me, but be careful that no one sees you from the bridge.'

The first mate's cabin was small but painfully clean like the morning room of a first-class hotel before the arrival of the guests. There was a well-filled straw mattress on the bed with corners as sharp as a match-box and covered with a red blanket. I was so deeply moved by the sight of this room that I just stood there, stupidly, as if I had entered a royal chamber for audience and the chamberlain had bade me stop. In the meantime Lilian had locked the door and stuck the corner of her handkerchief into the keyhole.

Towards dawn we were lying under the bed, and little blocks of wood kept falling on my head and shoulders. Only when Lilian stuck out her head from under the blanket that had slipped so that it was now hanging down to the floor did I discover that the small pieces of wood were African statuettes carved out of ebony.

'It is five-fifty,' Lilian said, 'the first mate is coming off duty at six. I shouldn't like him to find us here and I want to wash up before we get out. We have four minutes left.'

I drenched myself with the first mate's cologne so that my wife should not notice the strong perfume of lilies, then slipped from the cabin. I was happy that I should in a moment have the sea before my eyes. The boards of the deck and the steps of the ladder slid away beneath the soles of my feet like conveyor belts. A hot, strong wind and a vibrating blue sky received me. But the ship was standing close to the shore in the same place where we had boarded her the day before.

A minute later I ran into Rozgonyi. He was coming up from the hold fully dressed, carrying all his effects.

'I am getting off,' he said. 'The ship sails in an hour. I have no intention of being blown up with her.'

'Stop that idiocy!'

'It is not idiocy. Have you never heard that rats always leave a ship that is going to sink before she leaves harbour? Well, I watched all night. There isn't a single rat on this ship.'

'All right. See you again, sometime!'

'Sure. In the afterworld!' he replied with an insolent grin.

Valy and Bandi were sitting in the bow on a barrel. Above them three bottles of wine hung in a wire net.

'Well,' Valy began, 'did you spend a pleasurable night with your whore?'

'Stop that. We have something more important to discuss,' Bandi said. 'We have to get off this ship. It is going to explode.'

'Has that idiot Rozgonyi driven you out of your mind?' I asked.

'I never spoke to him. But I feel it in my bones that this ship is going to sink. Look at the people. Death is written in their faces. Their cheeks are covered with blue stubble as if it were growing in the grave. They stink like corpses. Some have only been living to fight against the Germans, others to sell rabbit-skins to Amsterdam. But now one can no longer fight against the Germans and Amsterdam has no need of rabbit-skins. They have accomplished that for which they were born. Consequently they must die. It is also quite likely that this is the seventeenth ship. According to reliable statistics every seventeenth ship goes down. I can assure you that this ship will sink if for no other than for statistical reasons. If it finds no floating mine to sink it, it will explode on the nose of a sardine . . .'

'George, darling,' Valy begged, 'why do you want to die so young?'

'He whom the Gods love dies young,' I replied, absent-mindedly watching the wine-bottles dance in the wind.

'If you come with us I shall forgive you all your sins. I shall even steal these three bottles of wine although I never stole anything in my entire life. Do you know why I shall steal them?'

'Why?'

'Because their owner will not be needing them. He will explode.'

'And what about your collected works?' Bandi wheedled. 'Are they finished?'

'Listen,' I said, 'if you feel certain that this ship will sink I have no objection to leaving. Let's go.'

Bandi ran off happily and a moment later returned with Aunt Marfa. The procuress had straw sticking in her hair and her face was half amused, half angry.

'You were so clever, so calm, so reasonable and now all of you have gone utterly mad. At last we have found a ship, she sails in half an hour and you are determined to go back to certain death. Do you want my little daughter to become the prey of German soldiers? But if you insist,' she added hesitantly, 'we can ask Léon . . . Léon, the spirit . . .'

'There is no table here and besides we have no time,' Bandi shouted. 'Are you coming or are you not?'

'No,' the procuress replied unhesitatingly.

I sped down the steps and began to hammer at the cabin door with my knuckles. An animal roar replied from inside. A moment later Lilian opened the door, but only a crack. She was barefoot and wore the red bedspread as her only garment.

'George, darling, you sweet madman, what do you want here?

This kind gentleman has lent us his cabin, I must show him some gratitude, mustn't I? Don't you understand?'

'Listen. We must leave this ship.'

'Stop it, darling. I told Étienne you were my brother. If you start a scene of jealousy Étienne will kill you. He is strong as an ox!'

The cabin door flew wide open with a threatening squeak. A middle-aged man stood on the threshold clad in a pair of trousers. His chest was covered with unkempt, rusty hair like dry seaweed. He looked at me out of tired, stupid eyes, then he closed the door gently.

'You misunderstand me, Lilian. I am not jealous. All I wanted is to tell you that we are getting off. This ship is going to blow up.'

'How do you know?'

'I feel it.'

'And Marfa? Is she getting off too?'

I stammered.

'Don't lie to me!'

'I never lie in important matters. Aunt Marfa does not want to get off.'

'In that case leave me alone and stop being an idiot!' she said and slipped past me back into the cabin.

Trotting back along the shore of the Adour all three of us were in a filthy mood indeed. All at once it seemed idiotic to have left the ship. When we got back to the customs building it was again besieged by hundreds. We climbed on to the embankment, put down the wine bottles in front of us and lay back. We were too tired to uncork them. Very soon I fell into a not exactly disagreeable apathy. I followed the flight of a bee circling above my head, tried dreamily to decipher the meaning of the various cloud formations and forgot all about the present. Bandi was in the same frame of mind, so Valy's entreaties that we go and line up for tickets fell on deaf ears. I declared that I was tired of standing around, we would now rest and then set out on foot towards the Spanish border.

Valy looked at us with unconcealed disgust, rose and hurried down to the customs building. Some ten minutes later she was back with three tickets for the *Cap Figalo*, sailing at noon for Casablanca. We drank the wine, put our rucksacks under our heads and went to sleep.

When, shortly before noon, we went down to the harbour, thousands were waiting to board the ship. Most of them had no tickets. Four soldiers stood at the foot of the gangway, their guns pointing at the crowd, and the captain informed us through a loudspeaker that anyone trying to board the ship without a ticket would be shot.

It was seven o'clock when the ship finally sailed. However, before going out to sea it had to turn round, which, as the Adour was narrower than the length of the ship, was a rather delicate operation. I stood at the rail between Bandi and a Dutch diamond merchant when suddenly complete, deadly silence descended on the ship. I looked towards the shore: at a distance of a few hundred yards the German flag with the swastika was fluttering gaily on the tower of the City Hall.

'This is the end,' Bandi said.

'Don't worry,' the Dutch diamond merchant reassured him. 'Nothing is lost yet. I have carefully studied the occupation tactics of the Germans lately. It is one of their fixed ideas to raise the flag the minute they arrive.'

'Every army has the same fixed idea,' I argued.

'Very true. But the Germans do it in a different way. They send ahead a car with two officers and a few soldiers armed to the teeth. And the flag, of course. They go straight to the City Hall, and tell the mayor that the town is occupied. The soldiers raise the flag and the officers sit down for a glass of beer. A few hours later advance patrols arrive, search the streets and houses, and only then does the bulk of the army march in to occupy the town. It is followed again, a few hours later, by the various technical units and finally by the civil administration that takes over the water, gas and electricity works, the railway station and the harbour. We are now at the point where the officers sit down to guzzle their beer.'

A few minutes later the ship accomplished the turn.

The estuary of the river was bounded on both sides by cliffs. The open sea before the bow was a greyish black with white-frilled waves, agitated but no longer stormy. Still, it seemed to me as if the sea were higher than the deck on which we stood and as if the *Cap Figalo* had to climb up the side of a huge cog-wheel revolving in front of her. Lead-grey clouds hung on the edge of the horizon and immediately above the water where shortly before the red disc of the sun had blazed, a long, narrow stripe of ivory-coloured cloud framed the landscape.

'Look,' Bandi pointed.

Close in front of us the poop of a ship rose from the water, wedged between the cliffs, white and elegant like the semi-circular balconies of Austrian resort hotels built in the past century, where a constant breeze set the tablecloths a-flutter. The poop had no continuation, as if it had been torn from the body of the ship by the explosion. A piece of the twisted blade of the propeller rested mildly and harmoniously against its side like a man's hand on a woman's thigh. In the centre of the balcony large black letters proclaimed the name of the ship:

CHÂTEAU DE BONCOURT

I shivered and Bandi touched my shoulder.

'Look,' he said.

He held out his hand and on the tip of his pointing finger, behind the no-man's-land of the blacked-out French shore I discerned the first bright lights of San Sebastian.

PART TWO

Africa

We arrived in the harbour of Casablanca after five days of semi-starvation during a very strenuous trip, and were moved on to the deck of the hospital-ship *Canada*. For a week we were kept under severe medical supervision and finally, after being disinfected once more, we and all the other passengers were transported to the indescribably filthy stables of the Ain Chok internment camp outside Casablanca where we had to sleep on rotting straw. The camp had been empty for only a few weeks since the last of the Spanish loyalist soldiers imprisoned there had died of cholera.

We were kept in complete isolation, were not permitted to write letters and were not even asked our names. As we knew that Morocco's governor, General Nogues, had given his allegiance to Pétain, our eventual liberation seemed at best doubtful. We were all the more surprised when, ten days after our arrival, two Hungarians who lived in Casablanca appeared in the camp: a tall and melancholy chemist called Fekete and a short, squat and lively haberdasher called Fortunatus. They had come to take us back with them to Casablanca, and when we thanked them they explained that they had been sent by someone called Ujvary, that it had been Ujvary who had bribed the authorities and that the car in which we travelled was his. When we inquired about opportunities to make a living they assured us that we had nothing to worry about, Ujvary would get us clothes, Ujvary would find us a place to live and would provide for all our needs. They spoke about this Ujvary as about some great, powerful and rather frightening institution, speaking his name with such awe that we dared ask no questions. Only when we were approaching our destination did they reveal that Ujvary had come here twenty years ago from Hungary, where he had played an important role in the proletarian dictatorship – and that he was today one of the richest industrialists of Morocco.

As we had no money to speak of, we took a single room for the three of us, where we hastened to wash off the filth of the camp. We would have liked nothing better than to go out, but Bandi's only pair of trousers had disintegrated while we were still on board ship so that he had left the camp in his pyjamas. Valy sat down on the only chair in the room, Bandi and I on the bed. Half an hour later a messenger brought a huge flower arrangement for Valy and a grass-green jacket with a pair of lemon-yellow trousers for Bandi.

'I wonder what happened to Lorsy,' Bandi mused while putting on the trousers in front of the mirror.

'Don't ever mention that scoundrel again!' Valy exclaimed, applying a thick coat of lipstick to her mouth.

'I have forgiven him,' Bandi declared magnanimously. 'And you, George?'

'So have I.'

Ten minutes later, leaving the hotel through the revolving glass door, we ran straight into Lorsy who was about to enter. He was wearing a beautifully cut black suit, a feather-weight silk shirt over the broad expanse of his chest and a delicately worked gold pin stuck in his heavy silk tie. When he caught sight of us he took off his spectacles and, with a smile of pure happiness on his face, opened his arms wide to embrace us.

'*Solamen miseris socios habuisse malorum!*'

'You can keep your quotations and your rotten sentimentalism, you base, soulless, cynical blackguard,' shouted Bandi, raising his arm in a gesture so threatening that Lorsy backed in terror against the wall of the hotel.

'How right you are, my dear Bandi. I am indeed a soulless, rotten old man. And it is also true that on the last evening in Bayonne I drank more than advisable at the house of Crocodile-eye. When I left he gave me two bottles of wine to take along for you but I must confess that I drank one on the way and that made me feel so ashamed of myself that I didn't go on to your place. Instead, I opened the second bottle, but of that I only took a sip. God be my witness, no more than a sip, and even that only to mitigate my sorrow over the fall of France. I thought I would tell you in the morning, if you hadn't found out in the meantime without me, that this ship was sailing. In the morning, however, I was badly under the weather . . . Anyway, it was a miserable little vessel, a three-hundred-and-eighty-ton row-boat with five hundred passengers on it. And what passengers! While I washed they stole my shirt. Imagine me, arriving here without a shirt! I must congratulate you for not having taken that stinking egg-crate!'

'You are obscuring the issue, you dirty scoundrel!' Bandi cried, raising his fist for a blow.

'Of course, I am,' Lorsy admitted humbly. 'I am terribly afraid of being slapped, Bandi dear, but I submit. Don't slap me once, slap me twenty times, thirty times! I deserve it. Go ahead, slap me, here, in the street, for everyone to see! I am a heartless old villain. I left you in the lurch. I left my family in the lurch. My wife and my two fatherless little children. They live in Geneva and I haven't written to them for a year. Nor to my eighty-year-old mother in Hungary. I am a pig, a lazy, dirty pig, a coward and a scoundrel . . .'

Tears were streaming from his eyes on to the sharp points of his patent leather shoes.

'You deprive me of the pleasure of hitting you,' Bandi complained bitterly and dropped his arm.

'Where have you left Aunt Marfa and her daughter?'

'At the bottom of the sea.'

Half an hour later a hired carriage with a white canopy took us along the serpentine road running up the hillside. Gay little bells jingled on the four corners of the canopy and on the necks of the horses. Although our rags contrasted sharply with the elegance of the Hotel Anfa, the waiters fell over themselves in their zeal to serve Lorsy.

Large rain-clouds obscured the sun, and although the night was still far off, the iridescent shades of the ocean were the same as they had been when we sailed from Bayonne harbour.

'Let the dead bury their dead,' said Lorsy fastening a napkin round his thick neck and throwing a glance at the sea. 'And let us imbibe this cocktail in their memory. Let our shame for having survived be alleviated by the knowledge, my friends, that a hundred years hence the order in which we perished will be utterly unimportant. Then let us remember that we could have perished in their place, and in that case they would now be drinking to our memory under similarly favourable circumstances . . . Yes, waiter, bring another round of Manhattans . . .

'Lately, at this hotel, I have often remembered our dear Marfa. Her greatness revealed itself to me in its full glory although I did not yet know that she had departed from the world of the living. It was Monsieur Durant, the chef, who brought her to my mind when we discussed together the secret of various dishes. Monsieur Durant is a disciple of the great Savarin but I believe that his knowledge exceeds that of his master. He explained to me that the taste of a dish is determined rather by the mode of preparation and a thousand other factors than by the raw materials it contains. Thus, for instance, if beans are cooked for two hours with some bacon and a little flour stirred in we obtain a thick, gooey, lardy mush known as boiled beans. The same beans and the same ingredients cooked not for two but for twenty-four hours in a covered pot on a low fire so that only tiny bubbles rising to the surface betray the boiling, produce a dish fit for kings in which every single bean preserves the tenderness of the freshly shelled vegetable, the fragrance of the bean-flower, while the aroma of the smoked bacon rises from it like the bluish smoke from a thirteenth-century Gothic fireplace.'

I listened enthralled to Lorsy's culinary lecture, although it occurred to me that we should perhaps discuss the origin of his sudden opulence, the provenance of the funds with which he would pay for our dinner, our prospects for tomorrow and the ways and means to get out of this country where we would, sooner or later, be arrested by Pétain's henchmen unless the Gestapo got in first. But the joy of having escaped from Europe, the pleasure of being alive, this unexpected encounter, the beauty of the African town, the hotel and the sea filled me with such delight that I closed my eyes and listened smiling to Lorsy's words.

'. . . But the most involved and truly responsible task, according to Monsieur Durant, is the proper combination of food and drink. He swears that for each dish there is but one appropriate kind of wine. Roast pork must be accompanied by Chablis, smoked spare-ribs by Tokay, pork chops by Liebfraumilch. Some wines, as for instance, the Béarn Rosé and the Chilean Riesling, have no counterpart in food, just as there is no appropriate wine for eel and calves-liver sauté. Monsieur Durant's explanation is that long before the advent of the Incas some wild Indian tribe must have exterminated the animal species created by God to be served with Chilean Riesling, while the hills producing the wine to go with calves-liver sauté must have been the hills of Atlantis. Seeing that most of his guests are totally ignorant of these secrets it is always he who suggests the wine to be consumed with the various dishes. Those who insist on some particularly repulsive combination are forever banned from his hotel.

'Listening to Monsieur Durant's lecture I could not get poor Marfa out of my mind. For if this excellent disciple of the divine Savarin rose to such heights of fame by matching food and wine, what shall I say about dear Marfa who was a past master in the matching of men and women, an art requiring infinitely more psychological insight, social knowledge, imagination and absorption . . .'

At this point Lorsy drew in his breath sharply: Bandi had kicked his shin under the table. Luckily the waiter was engaged in serving us with lobster mayonnaise, which gave our friend an opportunity to pull back his chair and find a safer place for his legs. His face reflected absolute determination: he would finish his funeral oration at whatever cost.

'When we roamed through the streets of Montauban, less than a month ago, the dear departed communicated to me a fraction of her abundant experience in life. I listened with awe, as if I were listening to the memoirs of the great procuresses of the Renaissance, the Putana Errante or Tullia d'Aragon. I am deeply convinced that it is my sacred duty to bequeath dear Marfa's method – naturally with suitable discretion – to posterity in one of the works I am going to write. If there is enough time left . . .'

'There won't be,' Bandi assured him with a sardonic grin.

'I felt, that night, as if I were reading a hitherto unknown work of the inimitable Ovid, or by Aretino or Stendhal,' Lorsy continued mildly. 'I have no intention of boring, or rather, titillating you with details from dear Marfa's life story. I shall not, as she did, draw a parallel between the affinity of certain men and women and the affinity of certain foods and wines. Neither shall I explain that just as beer should be consumed quickly and wine slowly, there are men and women made for brief and passionate, or for tender and long-drawn copulation; not to mention the resemblance of women to salads and *hors-d'œuvre*, the magic of which, as everyone knows, depends on the way they are dished up.

'I shall not enumerate to you the categories into which dear Marfa classified men, comparing some to male sparrows which, after a few seconds' fun, shake their feathers and disappear as if they had never been there; others to silk-moths that insist on endless, deadly love-making; others again to rabbits enjoying the pleasures of life without pretension or discrimination. She spoke of the type that selects mistresses not from an erotic but from a social point of view and regards them merely as objects of prestige; of the lovers of environment who can devote themselves to the delights of love only between damask curtains, surrounded by crystal vases with purple roses swimming in them, or, on the other hand, prefer rocky hillsides, lie among nettles, as close as possible to the footpath used by a host of tourists . . . I should like to call your attention to just one tiny point in illustration of dear Marfa's astounding finesse and wonderful instincts.

'We were talking about the colour of the female nipple. Dear Marfa told me that she had to ask only middle-aged men endowed with extraordinary intellectual capacities what colour of nipple they preferred. With the others she always knew, from their manners, their character, their occupation, their appearance; and men were always flabbergasted when she told them straight away whether they liked red, pink or brown nipples, small, medium or large. Here, dear Marfa gave me a few interesting pointers: according to her, high-class intellectuals and complex sensualists usually want women with small, pink nipples; strong male animals prefer brown nipples, while men who have once been orphan children or are sorrowing widowers, liked to rest in the shadow of large, red nipples. The real stags – those who don't care what kind of woman they embrace – have, of course, no preferences. Dear Marfa emphasized, however, that the problem of nipples was merely secondary, even the most sensual of men regard the physical-spiritual qualities of a woman as more important than the colour and size of her nipples. Yet the nipple of a woman is like the buffer of a train; when you run after a train it is the buffer you see, and when you recall one or the other of your mistresses it is, at least subconsciously, her nipple to which you react.

'Dear Marfa found that in the analysis of the highly complex relationship between man and woman the not so very important nipple supplies the only fixed point. Δὰ μὰ ποὺ στῶ χαὶ ℵινῆσω τὰν γὰν. Given this fulcrum, to use Archimedes' words, she lifted love out from its orbit and classified men into precise categories according to the nipple they preferred. To be exact – she explained with a very happy simile – all she had to do was to find the coat to go with the button. And this brilliant intellectual feat provided her with the perfect guide in the intricate trade of procuring.'

'Stop vomiting obscenities,' Bandi exclaimed impatiently. 'Get down to brass tacks and tell us how you got here from Bayonne.' Then he turned to the hovering waiter. 'Bring Mr Lorsy a triple espresso!'

Lorsy poured the coffee down his throat, then wiped the wet, somewhat reddened corners of his eyes with his handkerchief.

'You are quite right,' he said, 'I lost my way in the maze of nipples like Hafiz in the rose-garden. Let me, however, remind you of the alleviating circumstance that in this, as in so much else, I am like Gargantua and Pantagruel who were always discussing but never practising the art of love. What cognac? Courvoisier, naturally. Napoleon's brand! For aren't we after Waterloo? *Victrix causa Diis placuit, sed victa Catoni,*' he said and reached for his glass. But Bandi pushed it from his reach.

'No more guzzling! Talk!'

Lorsy spread his fat, white hands on the table and related the story of his sea voyage and the days spent in the harbour of Casablanca.

'Two weeks ago we were put on shore and herded into barracks erected on the pier. When I learned that the French state was providing us with living quarters I knew I was at the gates of Hell. As I told you before, my shirt was stolen from me on board ship with my last ten thousand francs in its pocket. I was on my way to an internment camp with a bare chest under my black jacket and a shoe-box under my arm. But these details did not deter me. The exit from the barracks was blocked by a big Senegalese sergeant with a gun. I pushed him aside with my elbow, simply flipped him off without even looking at him, stepped out into the street with the dignity of a Paris cardinal when he comes out of the Notre-Dame to bless the people, and cried loudly: "Taxi!"

'Fortunately there was one right in front of me. I ordered the driver to take me to the best hotel in town, whereupon he brought me here, to the Hotel Anfa. I walked up to the desk, my bare chest exposed. "A room!" I commanded. "We haven't any," the man at the desk replied indifferently. "Call the owner. Tell him State Councillor Lorsy wishes to see him!" I don't have to tell you that I was immediately shown to a room. I made the porter pay the taxi and sent him out to purchase six silk shirts for me. Then I walked into town. I couldn't enjoy my walk as I should have liked because I was tormented with petty anxieties. What if they should send up a bill? Thanks to my meditation I was nearly run down by an automobile on the corner of the Boulevard des Quatres Zouaves. "Ox!" I shouted at the bald-headed driver, and in my distrait condition I said it in Hungarian. He looked at me, got out of the car, threw his arms about me and called me his saviour. Then he asked me whether I had completely forgotten him: Sandor Ujvary?

'At the time of the Hungarian dictatorship of the proletariat, in 1919, this Ujvary had played a rather important role. I had known him ever since we were children. After the fall of the Commune he visited me one night at my flat, told me that the police were at his heels and that if they found him, they would hang him under martial law. I was then departmental head at the Ministry of Foreign Affairs. I hid him in my house, gave him money and helped him escape from the country. He came straight to Casablanca. Although he remained true to his convictions he rose, owing to hard work and intelligence, to be one of the wealthiest merchants of the country.'

'This sounds as if you were quoting from *The Arabian Nights*!' I said.

'A nabob,' Lorsy turned to me, 'that is what he is. He knows your name and he is eager to meet all of you, Tomorrow he will come to your hotel to pay his respects. He will then buy you clothes and footwear, furnish an apartment for you and surround you with every luxury. He regards this as his most pleasurable duty.

I live,' he continued, 'like an ancient Greek itinerant scholar in the house of a Latin nobleman in Cicero's days. I teach the Ujvary children but also advise their parents in all their dealings. They are extremely kind people but somewhat prudish, even the word "love" makes them blush. As old communists they are also teetotallers, believing that alcohol kills, besots and turns you into a pauper. And yet, the contrary is true: it is intellectual oppression, exploitation or stupidity that makes you an alcoholic. Like my forerunner, Philodemos the Epicurean at the Pompeii house of the Pisos, I am forced into a sort of play-acting. When sitting at the table of these blessed people I lecture on the repulsiveness of alcoholic beverages and dismiss from my mind the frivolous thoughts and off-colour jokes that flash through it. But after dinner I walk out into the garden, sit down under the fig-tree and bring out my bottle of red wine from under the myrtle bush. While I consume its contents I let my mind wander among the most hair-raisingly lewd ideas. Give me back my cognac, Bandi, old man. Now at last I have friends with whom to drink and talk smut!'

He lowered his lids and wetted his lips with the cognac.

'For the first time in my life I am happy,' he said piously. 'I have been roaming the world for over fifty years and, had I wanted to save myself from starving, I should have had to work. I always chose the lesser evil: starvation. But now I have found Eldorado. Never again shall I permit myself to be chased from this Garden of Eden. And let me advise you to do likewise. This is where I shall terminate my life. Amen . . .'

'And the Gestapo?' Bandi asked mildly. 'Has it arrived in your Eldorado yet?'

'You are crazy!' Lorsy exclaimed. 'It never will!'

'We are caught in a mouse-trap, no matter how loudly you squeak!' Bandi shouted, baring his huge teeth. 'But apparently the smell of cheese has deprived you of your reason.'

When Lorsy took us back to our hotel I felt that the night was still young and, as fortunately no one offered to come with me, I set out alone towards the Arab town.

Four hours later I came back exalted and perspiring, though the night was cool. I didn't understand myself what had impressed me so deeply. Perhaps it was the perfumes, the smells and odours. It began with the scent of the veiled Arab women walking in the alley-ways. The scent they used did not linger, hovering above the street long after the wearer was gone, like the perfumes used by European women. This scent was attached to the wearer and trailed behind her in an ethereal train three or four yards long; whenever I entered the rarefied gas-haze of one of these comets I discerned the aroma of musk, myrrh and attar of roses. These scents compared to French perfumes as oranges picked from the tree compare to orange-flavoured candy, or Dekobra's or Pittigrilli's erotics to those of Catullus. I knew beyond a doubt that these scents were the ancient, the authentic, the true, the only scents befitting the human animal; Europe's perfumes are but concoctions made by cunning but not really clever alchemists, a refined and sterile collection of distillates that do not even deserve the name of distillate because the very essence, the quintessence of things is missing.

In the alleys I ran up against veritable shock-troops of smells. It was all there: burnt oil, mint, thyme, familiar and unfamiliar herbs, fruits, the smell of camel and donkey dung; scattered and discreetly fetid goat-droppings shining black in the moonlight, the silky cavities of empty banana-skins like the beginning of the furrow between the buttocks immediately under the tail-bone of a tall, beautiful woman; but there was also a unique, particular smell to the white garden walls, the deep archways, the front doors carved of cedar-wood; what is more, to every single street: an individual smell independent of the sum total of smells invading everything.

There was a new, unknown component in these smells. This component transformed the basic smells and determined the atmosphere of the entire district. I had discerned this light, coquettish, almost obscene odour of putrefaction emitted by the town while I was still in the harbour. There was nothing disagreeable, nothing repulsive in it; rather it conjured up the fragrant, humid and mystical decomposition of autumn leaves, it was as if it were in some way related to the secret transubstantiation of fermenting grape-juice. Not a sickly sweet, nauseating, cadaverous smell, only its discreet forerunner, a stimulating spice placed by Death on the table of the living.

All this raced through my mind outside the window of a dirty little café where I stood watching two chess players inside. Never have champions bent over the chessboard with greater concentration. Suddenly one of them, a man with a beautiful white beard, clapped his hands for the waiter and made him reach into the clothes on his back to pick out a flea from somewhere between his shoulder-blades. As I turned away, a funeral procession carrying burning torches ran by me at a pace so fast that I hardly had time to take a look at the corpse or the bearers. Walking on, I was just a second too late to witness a knife-fight; the scene was deserted, as if all these usually idle people had hurried off to attend to some urgent business. Only a pool of blood remained, shrinking slowly in the middle of the concave road. As I was advancing along a narrow alley-way towards a distant gas-lamp, a crouching boy whom I had failed to notice threw his arms about my knees and pressed his face to my hip. I pushed him away, but as I continued on my way I heard him cry after me in broken French: 'Silly man, you don't know what you are missing!'

In this town – I thought to myself – Death sits among the guests at every feast and lies in bed with the lovers. He is present, always and everywhere, like in the woodcuts of Holbein's *Totentanz*, but not in the same capacity. In Holbein's works Death is the uninvited guest whose appearance causes terror and vain despair. Here, he is not regarded as a trap to be avoided by clever men. Here, they do not expect to live to be a hundred and hope to live to be five hundred.

Here, no one would dye his hair and beard at the age of fifty, do gymnastics with weights every morning to remain fit. Here they know that even health does not protect against death. Here, death is a welcome guest at the table of friends and when he sits on the edge of the lovers' bed he does so only to inspire them to even more passionate embraces.

Here, people have accepted the smell of decay and instead of holding their noses, they draw their conclusions and live more intensely, more greedily and yet more calmly. They do not struggle against death because they know that they are doomed to defeat. They need not make friends with death because they have never quarrelled with it, and they do not demand pious lies from their doctors because they are not afraid of dying. Young, they look death bravely in the eye; old, they walk slowly and with dignity towards the grave, as if it were a comfortable armchair in which to rest. It is very probable that their image of death is entirely different from ours. It is not an old, grinning skeleton with a scythe, because where there is no fear there is no terror, where there is no resistance there is no need for the scythe; death in this place must be a beautiful young boy like the Thanatos of the Greeks, who can be distinguished from Eros only because his torch points downwards instead of up.

I arrived back at the hotel completely exhausted and lay down on the floor next to Bandi. Long before, when I was still at the university, wrote execrable poems and feared the future, I had a recurring dream. In this dream I was walking along the broadest street of Budapest. Suddenly the houses began to swell, invaded the pavements, drove me into the middle of the road and continued advancing upon me until I was compelled to hold them apart with my extended elbows. I used to wake up panting, bathed in sweat, thinking that my elbows were indeed too weak and could never hold back the walls which were pressing in upon me. I dreamt the same dream now, but with a different beginning and new scenery. I was fleeing from pursuers who were circling above me in aeroplanes and on flapping bat-wings, shooting arrows at me – the Hungarian Nazis were called the arrow-cross party – until I took refuge in the Arab district. The houses joined roofs above my head but underneath there was a tunnel, a kind of shaft, where I could walk undisturbed as if I were walking in the secret corridors of a pyramid. The bat-wings and arrows were left behind, but my advance was blocked by a huge painting. There were two portraits in the picture against a dark green and blue-black background: the portrait of a veiled woman and that of a boy whose arms, however, reached out from the canvas and embraced my waist. The woman was wearing a dark blue veil, like most Arab women, but I, who like all Europeans was used to discerning the figure of a woman under her clothes, saw that her face under the veil was beautiful. The veil – I thought in my dream – is but a second, looser skin and these women wear it only to enhance their mystery and appear more exciting, more beautiful. The boy's face was also beautiful and bore a strong resemblance to the woman's. However, it was not his face I saw, but the skull under the skin, just as I guessed the woman's face under her veil. The skin – I thought in my dream – and the little flesh put on the bones by a miserly hand, serve only to veil the skull, and are worn only to make the skull underneath the more exciting.

I wanted to chase away the painting but it wouldn't move. Neither could I. I had reached the end of the blind corridor, as if I had descended into the pyramid on the ground floor of the Louvre, and it didn't occur to me to turn round. I just stood there, petrified, gazing at the picture which hovered before my eyes until dawn.

Next morning Bandi and I went to the post office to write to my parents and his brother in Budapest and let them know that we had crawled out from under the ruins of the French collapse and were now safe. Before the entrance to the post office, in the exact centre of the topmost step between two pillars, I noticed a tall, slender young man in a white burnous, white trousers and white leather slippers; only his tie was a pale blue and his fez scarlet. Although he was undoubtedly standing there by chance, without particular cause or motive, it seemed as if he were waiting for me. The scene was almost theatrical in the perfection of its staging.

There was something conspicuous and extraordinary in that young

Arab; at first glance I could not make out what it was. Only as I came nearer to him did I understand it. It had not been his beauty so much as the perfect proportions of his body that had caught my eye. His were not the sculptural proportions of a statue, recalling the works of the great masters of ancient Greece; as I looked at him I did not wonder in which museum I had seen his likeness. I felt that here was the original mould of man, the true first edition created by nature in its happiest mood. Since then, forms and proportions have deteriorated, degenerated and become distorted, like a cliché used too often. But even today, though very rarely, someone is born who looks like the original. His beauty was not that of a silly, vain young boy; his features awakened no memories and he seemed, not perhaps self-centred and cruel, but certainly autochthonous, introverted and spiritual.

I gazed at him, or rather I pushed my glance into his eyes like an electric plug into a wall-socket, until I neither could nor wanted to pull it out again, and would have run straight into his arms had Bandi not held me back at the last minute. While we were writing our letters the young Arab, who had followed us into the building, waited calmly at the end of the long hall. Whenever I raised my head he looked at me unsmiling and without curiosity, humbly waiting. He was standing under a window in the sharp sunlight, on a snow-white marble square, throwing a pale blue shadow on the floor: When we had mailed our letters he joined us, introduced himself politely and invited us to join him for a cup of coffee. Bandi, who believed him to be a procurer, a guide or something even worse, and in addition had a hysterical fear of and hatred for the Arabs – although he would never admit it even to himself because, as a communist, he had no right to such feelings, *ergo* he could not have them – left us with some flimsy excuse.

At the café Amar told me that he had studied philosophy at the Sorbonne, owned a small property in Southern Morocco and was now having a little holiday which he spent in idleness, enjoying the blessings of love and philosophy. During the days that followed we met at the swimming pool, sat on the stone wall dividing the sweet from the salt water, broke oysters from the rocks and ate them with the lemon we had brought with us while squatting in the hot sun we talked, mostly about historical or philosophical problems. Amar asked me to accompany him to his property which lay at a day's ride from Casablanca, on the edge of the desert, close to the border of Rio de Oro. I should have been happy to accept his invitation but, on the one hand, Europeans were forbidden by law – in the interest of their own security – to leave the so-called pacified belt along the sea-shore, and on the other hand I was a little afraid of going on such a long trip with someone who never divulged anything about himself.

I told Amar about the first problem. He said that he had thought of it but that it was easy to solve. He would lend me a djellaba and a fez, and then nobody would be able to tell me from a Moroccan. Even in my European clothes everyone thought I was an Arab. My curiosity and love of adventure outweighed my anxiety but, unexpectedly, I came up against the determined resistance of my friends. Bandi confessed his instinctive fear that my ultimate intention was to disappear in the desert and that this trip was to be a reconnaissance. He begged me to give up the idea and argued that I owed it nor only to myself and my friends but also to my fatherland, to Hungarian literature, to behave like a responsible human being. On the last evening before my departure Lorsy visited us at the five-room flat rented for us by Ujvary, and he, too, broached the subject. He said that I was facing a triple danger: first, that the Arabs would rape me, second, that they might hold me for ransom, thirdly, that they might even murder me. He warned me that my type always inspired Arabs to lust and murder. And even disregarding these extreme possibilities, there still remained the danger of kidnapping. A heavy ransom might be too much even for Ujvary, it would turn him against us and he might even discontinue financing us. Lorsy's passionate pleading affected him so deeply that he threw himself on his kness before me. How could I be so cruel as to deprive him of his livelihood in his old age, he asked me, with tears in his eyes. I brushed off these petty *bourgeois* arguments and tried to explain to them that my curiosity had always been stronger than my fear and that my profession demanded the pursuit of adventure regardless of the consequences.

To my joy Lorsy accepted my decision under the mellowing influence of a good dinner and a few bottles of wine and so, finally, did the others.

The next morning, at Amar's house, I put on a pair of embroidered linen trousers and a djellaba, pushed my feet into leather slippers and put a fez on my head. Amar taught me how to sit down on the ground with my feet crossed without using my hands, how to rise, how to look round me without turning my neck and how to move lightly and yet with dignity. Then he led me to a large, blue-tinged mirror.

'Now there is no longer any difference between you and us, who are all the sons of Ali,' he said contentedly.

What I saw surprised even me. The mirror showed two brothers. Our skin was of the same hue though I wore the tan borrowed from the sun only on the surface while he wore the colour inherited from his ancestors ingrained in his skin.

'What is smoke on you is stain on me,' he said.

This time it was not a servant girl but a slender young woman who brought us tea.

'Sit down and take off your veil, Bouthayna,' Amar commanded.

The woman expressed her protest with a wild movement of her waist, but then she sat down obediently and rested her hands, holding the blue veil, in her lap. She was a gipsyish, very beautiful woman with a surprising likeness to Valy. She had a blue star tattooed on her forehead and a vertical line on her chin. The tattooing was compact and shiny like new linoleum. Bouthayna was so embarrassed that I hardly dared look at her but even my fleeting glances confused her to such an extent that I blushed and began to scan the books on a shelf behind me.

'With a few exceptions,' Amar said when we were again in the street, 'all women and girls in Morocco are illiterate. As a result they are interested in nothing except gossip and love. It is impossible to talk to them and an intellectual relationship between a man and a woman is unimaginable. This may be why every woman deceives her husband at the first opportunity. Only during love-making can he be sure of her and even then she wonders and plots how to deceive him.'

On the corner of the market-place a canopied carriage passed close by us with Valy and Lorsy sitting in it. Neither recognized me. For a second Valy's glance alighted on my face, unaware that it was that of a man, while Lorsy's glance hit me between the brows like a bullet as, with haughty indifference, he leaned back against the black leather head-rest. For them an Arab is not a human being, I thought to myself, without a trace of anger.

'Be careful not to talk to me in the bus until we have left the town behind us,' Amar said. 'You need not fear that our fellow passengers will speak to you. Your clothes are too elegant for that.'

A very long, low vehicle was waiting for us in front of the garage. Two people sat with the driver, three crouched on the floor in the back and three squatted in the luggage rack on the roof. The driver greeted Amar with deep reverence. With a light movement of the hand my friend ordered the three on the roof to get down. They obeyed, grumbling, and lifted down the burning charcoal stove on which they had probably planned to cook their mutton or tea during the trip.

We took our places on the back seat. At the town limit we were stopped by soldiers who wore a piece of khaki cloth wound round their steel helmets.

'All brothers!' one of the soldiers called to the other and motioned to the driver to carry on.

We drove at a crazy speed between copper-red fields, along bumpy highways, uphill, downhill, through villages and gorges, always towards the butter-yellow sun-disc swinging before us like a pendulum. The landscape did not seem unfamiliar to me, neither did the houses or the people. It was as if I had already seen these flat-roofed little cubes with the one tiny window next to the front door, the water-carriers with their goatskin bags, their copper-coloured bare legs pillar-straight like young beech trees with root-shaped muscles streaming down around the ankles; the old men squatting with their backs against the long stone wall as if unable to move and waiting resignedly for someone to come and help them rise; the women, their date-stone eyes staring with wild curiosity from behind blue veils; the children in their coloured wraps running to and fro in front of the car, the only lock left on their shaved heads fluttering in the wind; the camels with their turtle-heads supported by long, sluggish necks; the hard-featured men sitting in mint-smelling tea-houses who pretended to ignore our arrival, turning their heads slowly with disdain after the car as if the seven deadly sins were travelling in it and the great Babylonian Whore were sitting at the wheel. I was overwhelmed by this feeling of familiarity and thought that I could have described this landscape precisely and faultlessly in a school composition many years ago. I could have described the flowers of the field though I had never seen them, the people sleeping in the shade of the roadside trees or of the houses, with a net on their faces to protect them against the clouds of flies hovering above them; the green, empty skins of the barbary figs scattered on the ground near the villages, the female donkeys wandering homewards with their heavy teats dangling, the lipless wells along the roadside opening into the red, arid soil like so many navels; the old but still virile wanderers walking with their chins stuck forward so that their white beards pointed straight towards the ground like unkempt icicles, the lapis-lazuli blue humming-top of the sky whipped into faster and faster revolutions by rebellious angels – I could have described all of this biblical, heroic landscape with its tumbling stone walls, windowless, apparently uninhabited huts; the scattered carcases of dead animals, the ram-horns and the traces of fires, some still smoking; things, which, had I seen them in Europe, would have reminded me of the Thirty Years War, but which here represented permanence, calm and peace. It was all as familiar to me as if I had seen it a hundred, nay, a thousand times. What I felt was not the timid and uncertain familiarity of the *déjà vu*, nor the slightly bored familiarity of the often seen and no longer interesting: this landscape was simply familiar, without any emotion, home-like and agreeably indifferent like something I had become used to but still loved.

Only one thing seemed unusual: the speed. From time to time the driver bit into a yellow, pie-shaped cake which he fished out from under his feet, or quarrelled with his neighbours or, turning back, carried on long conversations with the Arabs sitting behind him. He did this even on the sudden curves which he took without slowing down. I thought that he must have travelled along this road innumerable times but when, at a crossroads, he lost his way and then drove back at the same breakneck speed I began to wonder whether we would survive this day.

Late in the afternoon the driver put us off at a roadside café and turned back with his passengers towards the sea-shore which we had left at Agadir an hour earlier. We ordered dinner and after dinner set out towards the east, along a gully.

'We shall have to walk only two kilometres,' Amar reassured me. 'On top of the hill we shall wait for the caravan that is to take us to my kashba some forty kilometres from here.'

During the following fifteen minutes the landscape changed its physiognomy completely. It was still biblical and heroic but much more austere, rocky and bare like an Etruscan fresco, or the background of a Michelangelo painting. The tamarisk bushes disappeared, the gully narrowed to a kind of ditch coming up to our ankles, the fields covered with scanty grass tufts turned into stony wasteland. At last we reached the lonely hilltop.

'Here we shall wait for the caravan. But before you sit down turn this way and smell the breeze.'

For a moment Amar kept silent, then he continued:

'This breeze brings neither smoke nor the perfume of flowers, it brings neither the smell of the sea, nor vapour nor dust. It is tasteless, empty, odourless, but constant. Transcendent and constant. It has no strength. It is as if an ant tried to push you over with its tiny front legs; or as if ten ants tried to bowl you over with the help of a glass rod the thickness of a matchstick, quietly, invisibly, untiringly, stubbornly. If you pay no attention you hardly notice it. But once you have noticed it you will always be aware of it. Do you feel it now?'

We sat down side by side on the hilltop. Behind us we could see the inn and the last tamarisks, in front of us there was nothing but the desert. Already during the day I had felt as if, in possession of a time-machine, I were travelling backwards in time, into a feudal and theocratic past, the world of the Arabian Nights, across towns with bazaars and open markets resembling perhaps not Baghdad but Basra or other provincial towns of the Caliphate a thousand years ago. Now I was even further back in the past, as if I were observing the past at the time when light, the heavenly bodies and the earth were already created, but not yet plants, animals and humans; or, on the contrary, as if I were a witness of the last days of the world when the humans had already disappeared with their plants and animals. When we were leaving the tamarisk bushes behind us I had felt as if I were standing on a stage from which stage-hands were busy carrying out the pieces of scenery; only the bare stage-roof of the sky was still there above me while under my soles I felt the bare, rough boards of being.

After a while Amar took his lighter from his hood and offered me a cigarette. When he bent forward I discovered a silk rope running across his chest and when I followed it I saw the outlines of a yatagan at his hip. Although I knew that the Arabs usually carried a knife, this discovery disturbed me a little.

'When is the caravan coming?'

'It should have been here long ago.'

'Perhaps it won't come at all.'

'Perhaps,' he replied indifferently. 'The moon is full, I know the region pretty well, we shall have a nice walk of forty kilometres.'

'Couldn't we start right away?'

'Let's stay a little longer. I should like you to watch the sunset from here. There is a moment before it turns from scarlet to blue and purple when suddenly everything becomes green. For a second only. But you cannot see it from anywhere else as you can from this hilltop.'

Half an hour later the sun set and then the scarlet glow began to disappear under the edge of the horizon.

'Watch now,' Amar said.

At that very moment six figures appeared at the foot of the hill. They approached us in a scattered military formation, leaving a distance of thirty or forty yards between them. They were clad in rags but each carried a gun.

'Robbers,' Amar explained calmly. 'When they reach us we shall rise and greet them. It would be senseless to run or try to defend ourselves. If they answer *aleikum salem* to our *salem aleikum* we shall know that they have no intention of killing us.'

I was watching Amar's beautiful, noble profile: the straight and cruel outline of his nose, the compressed, merciless corners of his mouth. I felt a mad impulse rise in me to slap him hard so as to see blood spurt from that face, not only because he had led me into a trap and had sent for his bandits, but also because he was still trying to fool me. I thought of the civilized and secure shore-belt which I had so recklessly abandoned. Now I should have to write to Ujvary for the ransom. With the excellent espionage system these blackguards had they would ask for at least a hundred thousand francs for my release.

The bandits waited until all had reached the hilltop and then approached us in a group. For a few moments they and Amar yelled and screamed at each other like banshees, then suddenly all began to laugh.

'Do not be afraid,' Amar turned to me. 'These are peaceful people who invite us to dinner.'

I did not bother to reply but set out with one of the bandits behind Amar and the others who were gossiping loudly and gaily.

'Do you speak French?' I asked my companion. He was a fellow with limp, thick lips and a crooked nose, holding a telescope-gun, the butt of which was covered with mother-of-pearl squares. A heavy smell of mutton-fat emanated from his white and brown striped djellaba.

'A little. We could talk better in German or Spanish.'

'Where did you learn German?'

'I served with Abd el-Krim's general staff; for a while I was commander of the guard at his headquarters. You know,' he explained, 'there were many officers of Austrian and Hungarian extraction among Abd el-Krim's men. Many had run away from the Foreign Legion, but many had come straight from Europe, They were professional soldiers who could not find work in their countries after the First World War. It is from them that we learned German. Because we were all fighting in Abd el-Krim's army against the Spanish, *Verstehst du mich?*'

We were stumbling along in the twilight among huge, ragged rocks.

'For a while,' my companion continued, 'I was commander of the guard on the mountain-top above Tetuan. The town was in Spanish hands but the steep five-hundred-metre cliff was ours . . .

'I am a master marksman,' he went on, 'and I knew all the officers down there not only by name but also by their faces. There were a few who had committed atrocities in the Riff. For instance, there was this Captain Alcala. I knew that man from Ceuta. Because Ceuta is the town where I was born. Captain Alcala's son often played with my son on the sea-shore. The captain's son liked to build sand fortresses and mine gathered shells to cover the towers. One day Captain Alcala came down to the sea-shore and told his son not to play with that dirty Arab brat. At least, this is what my son told me.

'Do not believe that I swore vengeance or that the matter caused me much heartache. But when we were keeping watch on that mountain-top I recalled the incident. We had not cut the telephone lines and neither had the Spaniards; we used them to abuse each other in our time off. On Saturday evening I called up the Captain in Tetuan and reminded him of what he had said to my son two years before. Then I warned him that I was a master marksman and told him that I would shoot him like a dog if he went out on the broadwalk the next day after church. He laughed and replied that I could never hit him from that distance in a big crowd. Sunday morning I killed him. He came along with his wife and son, swaggering like a peacock. From time to time he glanced up to where we were. I shot him when he was looking up so that nobody could call me a sniper.

'However,' he said, 'I shall show you tonight what I can do.'

'You are very kind indeed,' I replied wryly.

We descended into a deep depression. In the background I noticed the shapes of sleeping camels and donkeys; in the centre of the clearing four men were sitting around a glowing charcoal fire. One of them, an old man with a shark face and a seven-day beard – obviously the leader of the gang – greeted us heartily and asked us to sit down on the mats.

I sat down sadly. The whole scene was more like an ordinary, cheap piece of trash than like reality. While Amar and the leader of the gang engaged in excited conversation in Arabic my eye was caught by a young boy in a burnous lying opposite me on the other side of the fire. In this absolutely unreal environment he was the most improbable feature, with his girlish face, light brown hair and blue eyes. Even his long leg stretched out on the mat was entirely different from the straight, pillar-like legs of the Arabs; he had beautiful, shapely shanks like the Indo-Europeans.

'Are you European?' I asked him.

He shook his head, then, resting his chin on his fist, looked curiously and provocatively into my eyes.

'Have you never heard about the Vandals and Visigoths who came to Africa two centuries before our era and mixed with the Riff-kabils?'

'You are right,' I said blushing. 'Your only error is that the Vandals came to Africa not before our era but in it. In the fourth or fifth century.'

'You have every right to reckon time from the birth of the Nazarene. But have the kindness to permit me to reckon it from the Flight!'

Our conversation was interrupted by the bandit leader who turned to me and delivered a short speech in excellent French. He explained that there had been a misunderstanding. They were neither highwaymen nor murderers. However, as according to their information a single caravan was expected to pass that way tonight they had become suspicious when they noticed us on the mountain-top. True, for the time being, they were on friendly terms with the authorities but who knew how long that truce would last. They had captured us to find out whether we had been sent by the police. They knew Amar, or rather, he had frequently given them permission to camp on his land around the well: as a sign of gratitude they would put two camels and a man at our disposal in the morning to take us to our destination. Until then, however, they would consider it an honour if we accepted their invitation to a modest dinner.

The marksman who was eager to show his prowess before we sat down to our meal took us up on the moonlit plateau. The Riffkabil had volunteered as a target. He took a twenty-five-franc silver coin between his thumb and middle finger and raised his hand with the coin to his temple. The old man took up his position at a distance of about thirty yards and, almost without taking aim, shot the coin from between the lad's fingers seven times in succession with a pistol. When he wanted to repeat the performance with his rifle from a distance of a hundred and fifty yards we were fortunately called to dinner.

Sidi Mohammed – this was the leader's name – sat with his back straight, his legs crossed, a solemn expression on his face and a beautifully adjusted white turban on his head. A large earthenware dish was placed in the centre of the mat, containing boiled chicken, baked lamb and rice. They probably considered the ceremony of eating from one dish a pledge of friendship. The conversation was slow and dull, turning around conventional subjects, spiced with flatteries and polite compliments. We had reached the sweet when our host turned to me and asked me about my origin, my profession and why I was going about in Arab clothes. He seemed to find great satisfaction in my replies, I could feel excitement rise in him, his beard seemed to bristle as if with electricity generated in his body. Finally he raised his hand like some deity calming the fury of the waves, though it was his own emotional storm he was trying to calm.

'It is a great honour that I am permitted to be your host. It is also a great honour that you have garbed yourself in djellaba and fez. But the circumstance that you happen to be a writer fills me with extraordinary joy. I have met many people in my lifetime but I have never yet encountered a writer. When I became paymaster in Abd el-Krim's army I often saw journalists, even Americans. They never stopped asking questions and put down our replies in fat, little notebooks with a Parker pen, in shorthand. It is difficult to give good answers but it is easier to ask good questions. Those people,' he snorted, 'did not even know how to ask.

'The way I see it, writers never ask questions,' he continued, gazing at me intently without moving his head. His pupil rose and sank almost imperceptibly as he observed me from my forehead to the point of my slippers,

For a while he remained silent; perhaps he was deliberating what to say and, at the same time, enjoying his power, for he, and be alone, having the right to speak, the others had to wait until he finished. There he sat like a Phoenician merchant-god: his hand, much softer and pudgier than one would have expected from his relatively narrow but very muscular arm, was extended in line with his chest and on each finger sparkled a heavy, gaudy, gold ring. The master marksman watched his leader with awe; Amar, on the other hand, delighted in the play of tensing and relaxing muscles in his own long, narrow feet, from which he had stripped the socks. In the light of the acetylene lamp that scattered the multiple shadows of the tall tea-glasses, the pitcher, our bodies and limbs in criss-crossing stripes over the bright mat on which we sat, his foot looked like a gracefully extended, nervous giraffe neck. The young Riffkabil eyed the moon as if she were a woman he wished to accost and take straight to bed. Only I observed them all conscientiously, as if this were my duty.

'It is getting late and you must be tired,' the chief said at last somewhat stiffly. 'I do not want to exhaust you with endless stories. I am afraid that were I to tell you stories like Sindbad the Sailor was wont to tell his listeners, you would be sorely disappointed. Everyone who has travelled in various countries has similar stories to tell. I do not even know whether or not you intend to remember me in your works. Perhaps, when one day you recall this evening it will be the physiognomy of the moon and not mine that will rise in your mind.

'A while ago, when you summed up your life-story in a few words I felt deeply moved. Willy-nilly, you have conjured up all the things I regard as the spurs of my actions and which, it seems, are common to us both. It was then that I decided to tell you something about myself. Not a story, but rather a train of thought.'

He raised his tall glass of mint tea to his lips and, with a flick of his hand, gave us permission to do likewise. He waited a few moments, rather for the sake of tension than to give himself time to think, then he began.

'I was born at Dar-es-Salaam and studied at the al-Azhar University in Cairo like my father and grandfather before me. Then I became head of the business inherited from my ancestors, We have always been importers of tea and spices but we also owned a large clothes shop in the Bazaar. We sold Moroccan fezes, burnouses from Manchester, djellabas from Rumburg and liks from Osaka. I had five assistants and two clerks, I knew the captains of the ships; in Sumatra it was my pepper they loaded last so as to unload it first back in Dar-es-Salaam. My caravans left and returned with exemplary punctuality carrying my tea to the Chad Lake arid to the southern regions of Fezzan.

'My private life was not unhappy. I had bought myself three wives, gave my first-born son an excellent education in preparation for his entering the University of Cairo. I was considered one of the worthiest citizens of the town and had numerous friends. I was on good terms with the British authorities and therefore had little trouble with my taxes. I did not have to cheat more than was usual.

'I liked my occupation. Late in the afternoon I used to go to the shop, supervise the accounts and look into the store-room to make sure my ginger wasn't getting mouldy or my tea too dry. After dinner I talked with my friends at the café and before supper I visited the brothel to have a little fun with one or another of the girls. In general I preferred them unformed and immature, between the age of ten and eleven. After supper I was wont to return to the shop, for that was always the busiest time. After midnight I locked up the shop myself, returned home and spent the night with the wife whose turn it was.

'You can sec that my happiness was complete, but even had it not been so I should not have complained because I never pretended that man was born to happiness. And yet, each night, after having sent my employees home but before locking up the shop, I used to walk up and down filled with despair and anxiety. I was in complete darkness as to the cause of my despair but it was becoming increasingly unbearable. The clock ticked on unceasingly, the years flew by with frightening speed. But it was not the mad flight of years that scared me. It was the thought that I should live in exactly the same way until the sand of my life had run out. When the son of my friend, a goldsmith from Zanzibar, was called up for military service by the Sultan, I was sick with envy. I thought: lo, this boy who was brought up from the day of his birth to be a goldsmith like his father, will now learn soldiering, become an outstanding horseman or a mediocre sergeant, but at any rate, he is on the threshold of a new life.

'Gradually I began to understand the cause of my despair. I, my father before me and my son after me, had all been born into a determined way of life, a sharply outlined mould, a finished pattern. We obtained everything ready-made, our occupation, our friends, our pastimes, our pleasures. I lived like a grain of wheat sown by a peasant in the soil at a certain spot. What can a grain of wheat do? Grow into an ear and wait for the scythe.

'I related my problem to a friend of mine, a captain who was always travelling to distant lands. He replied that though he loved his profession, he often thought of me, my peaceful life, my beautiful family and great happiness with envy when he was fighting the storms of the Indian Ocean or waiting for cargo in filthy harbours. He said he would gladly change places with me, and that I was lucky not to have been born in his skin. But such is man: on firm ground he yearns for the ocean, but spending his days on the sea he dreams of a quiet life on firm ground. He warned me not to rebel against Allah's will, then invited me to accompany him on a trip that would take several months, in order to regain my equanimity.

'I explained to him that he had misunderstood me. Had I been born in his skin I should feel just as miserable as I was feeling now. The only solution would be if he took over my business and I became captain of his ship. However, he knew nothing about business and I knew even less of navigation; besides, my family, social and other obligations made it impossible for me to free myself from what I had been born into. I was not rebelling against Allah's will; on the contrary, I felt convinced that Allah had given every man several lives to live in a single lifetime and only convention prevented us from doing so. My friend looked at me sadly, shook his head and departed.

'Two weeks later I was again in the throes of utter despair. This occurred at the time when the news of the Riff uprising reached us, though I must confess the event itself made little impression on me. I was so depressed that I did not even visit the brothel, although I knew that a new consignment had arrived. I sat on the sea-shore and wondered whether I had lost my reason, whether there was really no escape from this life of misery, this life without will or freedom. I mused for hours without finding an answer to my question. On the way back I noticed a blazing red light in the sky. At first I thought it was a figment of my imagination, a heavenly sign, a vision. But when I got closer I realized that the Bazaar was burning.

'I immediately started to figure out the value of my stores compared to the amount at which they were insured. The day before, a caravan had taken a thousand burnouses and almost my complete stock of cinnamon, cloves and nutmeg to be sold elsewhere: the fire brought me a profit of at least ten thousand pounds. Then I stopped calculating: it was not money I needed, but glory. My whole body trembled with joy because I knew the time had come, that here was the hour for which I had waited. I concealed myself in an archway and listened to the desperate cries of people running like madmen from one end of the Bazaar to the other. I learned from the talk that the fire had spread with terrific speed in the palm-leaf-covered alley and in the dry store-rooms, that panic had broken out in the Bazaar and several persons had lost their lives in the flames. Suddenly I distinguished the smell of burning tea-leaves. I had twenty-five tons of tea in my store-room. I don't know whether you have ever smelled burning tea but I can tell you that it is a divine perfume.

'The next second, however, I felt the smell of burning human flesh and, nauseated, ran to the harbour as fast as I could. By then I knew exactly what I would do, although I had not been conscious of making plans. I hired a fisherman from Zanzibar to sail me across the channel and then took a ship to Port Sudan. For years I had been carrying large sums of money on me, though I never quite knew why.

'My first idea was to open a brothel in Cairo. But my mother was of Persian descent and her brothers, who lived in Shiraz, often came to Cairo. Besides, I could easily run into a business friend and a few years hence my son would come to Cairo. But even apart from these considerations, this occupation was far too stationary and that was exactly what I wanted to avoid. This is how I came to the Riff, four thousand kilometres from my place of birth, and offered my services to Abd el-Krim.

'I lived in an ecstatic dream, like an adolescent boy, although the wrinkles under my eyes were deepening and when I sat alone in the afternoons I felt the skin on my cheeks crack like dry tree-bark. I had exchanged my old life, characterized by stability, for a life of perpetual movement and while, until then, I had always been led by utilitarian principles and regarded my servile humility towards the authorities as an irksome duty, I was now fighting for the freedom of the Arabs against the armies of Spain, selflessly, without hope for reward. Even my rules of sale and purchase had been turned upside down. Until then, my principal worry had been to sell my wares and empty my store-rooms. Now my dominant preoccupation was how to fill them. I found all this indescribably amusing.

'Believe me, friend, the rebels of the Riff would have been defeated within a few weeks had I not arrived on the scene. In a very short time I familiarized myself with the intricacies of European politics of which I had been entirely ignorant, and found out that only from the Germans could we expect to obtain arms, money and equipment. Because the Republic had held on to the claims of Imperial Germany in Morocco. Our weapons were smuggled to us across the desert and the desert bandits became our bitterest enemies because they attacked the caravans and stole our consignments. It was my task to thwart the intentions of the robbers. My activities were successful, our consignments arrived untouched even from the Bay of Guinea.

'I was the only person in Abd el-Krim's entourage who knew from the first that our cause was hopeless. But, just as I had enjoyed ridding myself of the rich, cautious and lazy merchant I had been and assuming the role of an enthusiastic, selfless and determined freedom fighter, I was glad that this life, too, would come to an end. I knew it in my bones that this stage of my life would go up in flames like my store-rooms in Dar-es-Salaam, and that I should again begin a new life.

'The alarm bell rang when the French promised the Spanish considerable military aid because they were afraid the rebellion might spread to French Morocco. We were, at the time, expecting a large consignment of arms from the south. With twenty hand-picked men I set out to meet the caravan in the valley of the Draa. One day, at dawn, we were attacked by bandits on the road between the Atlas and the Anti-Atlas. It was the same large band that had caused us so much trouble in the past. The battle lasted throughout the day. At sunset one of our cases of ammunition exploded and the stable in which we had spent the previous night was burned to the ground.

'After darkness fell I lay in the sand not far from the still smoking ruins of the stable, wondering whether it would not be best to retreat under cover of the night and abandon the battle of uncertain outcome. Suddenly a hand touched me on the shoulder. It was a messenger from the enemy camp who had come to tell me that their leader was gravely wounded and would not live to see the morning. The gang, unlike their leader, did not want to fight against the liberator of the Arabs. They hoped to be accepted as volunteers and asked me to lead them to the Riff as their commander so that they might fight on Abd el-Krim's side.

'With the stimulating smell of the burning stable in my nose I felt the same excitement I had felt at Dar-es-Salaam while watching the burning of the Bazaar. I told the messenger that I was ready to accept their offer, would merge our two teams and take command. There was but one condition: that instead of joining Abd el-Krim we should continue as bandits, with me as chief. It took some time before I could convince the messenger and then the bandits. It turned out that by the time they had, in the kindness of their hearts, put an end to the suffering of the wounded, only eight of them remained. Later it became obvious to me and my men that even these were utterly unsuited to being members of a well-organized gang and therefore we finished them off. Quickly,' he added with the smile of a merchant praising his wares, 'quickly and painlessly.

'However, it was not easy to convince my own men either. But when they heard that the rebellion had been defeated they realized how right I had been and repaid me for my wisdom in loyalty. Since then I have completely forgotten Abd el-Krim. Only recently did it occur to me that in his exile on the island of Reunion he is probably speaking of me as his most loyal follower who died a hero's death fighting for him against the bandits of the desert.

'I felt that the freedom I enjoyed in the months that followed was fuller, sweeter, than any freedom on earth. The moments when we held up a caravan were moments of pure delight. The men in the caravan were usually petrified with fear, they aged ten years in one second. Some of the camels bolted and the women, first to realize the seriousness of the situation, screamed with fright. This scream was their answer to everything they believed awaited them; this high-pitched scream was the synthesis of all screams, that of the fear of death, the terror of rape, of surprise, a prelude to desperate sobs and many other things, although I still hadn't made up my mind what to do with them. Should I have them killed? Should I have them raped? Should I treat them to a feast and let them go after giving them gifts? Should I rob them and release them? Should I hold them for ransom?

'There I stood and I could do whatever I pleased. More than once I refrained from attacking a rich caravan though we were starving and only rarely did I force a boy or a woman in a captured caravan to share my bed. This, too, was part of my freedom. I wanted to be free, fully and completely free, like a god who has neither greeds nor passions.

'Gradually I began to see that the road to freedom led from the outside towards the inside, from the sphere of action towards the sphere of thinking, from the rational pleasures of the world to the spiritual orgies of asceticism, more perverted than physical perversion. When travelling on camel-back or lying in ambush I had excellent opportunities, almost compelling opportunities to meditate. I recalled the books I had read in my childhood and adolescence, books that had lain yellowing and dusty in the lumber-room of my memory. Not that I had forgotten them, but I simply had no use for them. Now at last I understood the meaning of my readings, al-Maari's rationalism, Iraqi's mysticism, Saadi and al-Farid, the whole library that I had carried around in my head for decades without using it. I added my own thoughts to theirs and after that they filled my mind in the daytime as well as under the soft light of the moon.

'In Mauretania I resolved to turn to smuggling because banditry was a game of hazards, he who did not know when to stop always lost in the end. It seemed as if I had completed the circle and returned to my original occupation, commerce, and any superficial observer would have come to the conclusion that my paternal heritage, Arab rationalism, had at last come into its own. What did I care! My mother's heritage, the light of Persian mysticism kept my soul in a perpetual glow and made me utterly indifferent to all that went on outside the convolutions of my brain.

'However,' he went on after a moment, 'even this form of life is not the last. As I grow older the whip of lust stings more and more cruelly. I think that I shall part with my followers and return, as a hermit, into the caves of the Tibesti Mountains so that when, at the approach of death, I look back upon my life, I shall have enjoyed all the pleasures of the earth. It is also possible, however, that I shall open a brothel in one of the towns of the Guinea Bay and offer for sale the little girls of ten and eleven whom I once so zealously bought.

'The difference,' he sighed, 'is negligible. Al-Maari writes that we are sliding deeper and deeper into the death-ditch of life; thinking is senseless, despair pointless, and our horror is alleviated only by the illusion that we are holding on to another body; Rumi and Iraqi, on the other hand, allege that the universe is but the shadow of the Deity's shadow, that nothing exists except the thought in our head, because that is the Deity itself. Girls, naturally, do not exist at all.'

For a few moments he watched the effect of his story, ready to brush off any sign of appreciation.

'My story has no ending,' he said at last in a low voice. 'I told it to you because I see a certain similarity between your fate and mine, and I hope it has been of some use to you. Many have wanted to hear the story of my life and have loudly insisted that I tell it. You, however, asked no questions and perhaps this put me into the mood. When I began I felt that your soul was drawing closer and closer to mine, towards the end I felt that it was receding. I believe that we have now reached the proper distance.'

The last sentence was spoken with a calm finality and I knew that our conversation was now over. I rose, my teeth chattering, and bowed deeply to the old man without pronouncing a single word. The master marksman accompanied me to the edge of the depression where he spread a few mats and blankets on the ground. It was a cold night. According to my custom I undressed to the skin and slid under the blankets. Amar and the Riffkabil boy remained sitting near the fire. They had put out the lamp and sat there motionless face to face. Their white outlines stood out sharply from the greenish-blue, phosphorescent background of the rock wall.

I was almost asleep when a feeling of wild terror electrified me in to complete wakefulness. My fear had nothing to do with Sidi Mohammed's story or the events of the day; perhaps not even with my flight from Paris, the bombing of Juvissy or the waiting in Bayonne in the unbearable heat. It may be that not having allowed myself to be afraid at the time, the anxiety remained dormant in my nervous system. Even with my eyes closed I could clearly see the landscape around me: that cruel moon-landscape, with the icy moon like the breast of a naked woman leaning out of the window of a lunatic asylum. I sat up with a single bound, shaken with an almost epileptic attack of death-fear and beating the empty air with my elbows. I did not fear my hosts, nor was I scared of some real or imaginary danger. In those days I used to bite my blanker and cold sweat would break out over my entire body. Later, in my student years, I would get out of bed and run down into the street to be among people. My friends always reassured me that in time I would get used to the idea of death but I did not.

Now again I could have screamed with despair. One day, twenty or fifty years hence, what did it matter, I would have to die and from then on it would be as if I had never lived. Billions of new variations of man would be born, but my variation would never, never return. I would rather be sick and miserable, a cripple suffering the pains of hell than not be at all. Yet complete annihilation was inescapable. God willing I should one day be given a place of honour in the Kerepes Cemetery of Budapest, there would be a marble column with my name on it in gold – but who would care? By the year three thousand everyone would have forgotten my name, by the year five thousand the marble column would have turned to dust, the cemetery would have disappeared under a wheat field, a heap of ruins, an industrial plant or the jungle, the language in which I wrote would also have disappeared and the nation to which I belonged would have died out. Even this second annihilation would not be the end. Then the sun would lose its heat, the earth collide with another heavenly body or explode, and Michelangelo's statues and Beethoven's symphonies would be flung after me into Nirvana.

The men sitting in the centre of the depression noticed my movements. Sidi Mohammed threw me a brief glance over his shoulder and whispered to the others. I did not want my hosts to think that I was watching them, therefore I lay back quickly, turned on my side and observed them from under my arm laid across my eyes. They went on talking and from time to time glanced towards me. Finally, the Riffkabil rose and approached me like a cat with light, inaudible steps. I recalled that on his right hip, where his djellaba had a slit, he wore a pistol close to his skin. As he approached, the pistol stood out sharply under the white linen, like a boss on a column. Will this be the ending of Sidi Mohammed's story? – I wondered.

I glanced up from under my arm and watched the Riffkabil spread out a mat and blanket next to me on the ground. He stood so close that I could have touched his ankle. This is how they finish off their wounded – I thought – quickly and painlessly . . . The Riffkabil threw an inquisitive glance in my direction; then, with a quick movement, he reached for the slit of his djellaba. But it was only the linen he grasped, and with a light movement he slipped out of the wrap. He folded the djellaba into a regular square, put it on the mat, threw down his pistol and knife and, soundlessly as he had come, he ran away. Behind my back I heard the splashing of water but I dared not turn round. He was probably washing himself. His bone-hafted knife in its silver scabbard sparkled on the mat next to his blindingly white djellaba, the deep wrinkles and folds of which reminded me of an antique bust freshly dug up from the black earth.

He returned on tiptoe, entirely naked. Then he slipped under his blanket and turned towards me. The distance between us was less than a yard but I was still pressing my arm over my eyes and peering out from beneath it. The dagger lay in the middle, between our two arms. I watched his face, searching for the features of Gaiseric's or Gelimer's descendants, vandal cruelty, but I found that he resembled a German medical student examining his patient curiously, musingly and somehow uncertainly. Soundlessly, at a snail's pace, he slid towards me, pushing himself forward now with his hip, now with his elbow, until he slipped out from his blanket and under mine. His body was emanating a light but penetrating perfume, that of withered flowers in an arid field; I felt this perfume not only in my nostrils but in my throat and further down in the ramifications of the bronchia, right into the apex of the lungs.

We started early at dawn. The smugglers lent us a camel and the master marksman accompanied us on donkey-back to bring the camel back. Sidi Mohammed himself saw us off. He seemed much older than the night before, and also smaller than he did when, like a king, he throned it in the centre of the mat, pressing his back against the straight-backed armchair of the night. However, he moved with surprising agility, not the agility of a merchant behind his counter but that of a sportsman. Before I mounted the camel that lay before me with its legs folded as though it would never again rise on its feet, the chief took me aside.

'Last night,' he said in a low voice as if he were telling me a secret, 'you were afraid of death. During the night I wondered what drug to recommend to you apart from the one you took. The best antitoxin would be resurrection, of course, but to someone who refuses to believe that the filthy worms populating the earth will resurrect, I must suggest something better.

'In the past I, too, feared death. Now I no longer fear it. If I could, I should collect around my death-bed eyeless beggars, hydrocephalic children and mad old hags. I should order a feast and make them eat until they began to vomit, then I should command emaciated, hectic drummers and short-legged, fat-bellied fluters to play gay melodies and I should bid my guests dance, gambol, somersault and copulate around my bed to show me once more how vile and ridiculous this earthly fare really is.

'Once, when I, too, was sometimes visited by the terror of death, I behaved like a reckless merchant faced with ruin who continues to spend lavishly because he knows that he will die before he is declared bankrupt. To comfort myself I savoured the fact that others, too, have to die: Alexander the Great, Saladin, Caesar and even Mohammed himself. Let me give you as a farewell present a verse by Abu Ali Ibn Sina, which I often recite to myself:

The man of virtue, learning or of art
Explores two worlds and seems to stand apart
From idle fools; but like the fools he must
Come to a silent end in a pinch of dust.'

We had been carried a long way on the rhythm of the camel's gently-swaying minuet before we lost sight of him, still standing on the edge of the cliff, on a little hillock, the Riffkabil boy beside him and a head taller than he. They neither waved nor smiled, but gazed after us stiffly, immovably, like two slender rocks against a background of larger, more rugged boulders.

Amar's kashba stood on a flat hilltop a little below the peak: it was a rusty-pink tower, almost square. It was enclosed by walls of the same colour – or rather the walls zigzagged round it in wild disorder like the squares, diamonds and oblongs scribbled by a child. Two walls ran down the hillside to encircle a trench-shaped well, a grassy, muddy depression and the few hundred date-palms which grew in the valley. Another wall framed a rusty-pink square of stony clay on the hilltop: this was where, thirty years ago, they used to lock up the slaves for the night. Its heavy iron gate, torn symbolically from its hinges, lay on the ground: the former slaves and their children – eight families – still lived in the same yard, in their tents. Amar told me that he had often suggested that they should move to the upper floor of the kashba, but they had refused, saying that even a tent was too good for them. Special walls had been built round the animals' pens and another, oblong yard served to house the caravans. Outside these walls, and separate from them, ran several others of various thicknesses. In the valley, beyond the well, extended a poor pasture. From the hilltop one had a good view over the rusty-pink desert, the rusty-red foothills of the Atlas and Anti-Atlas Mountains; at sunset even the sky hovered like a rusty-pink bell over the glowing landscape and the moon rose rust-coloured from the torpid vapours whirling above the well.

The lower part of the tower was one solid block of stone with only a narrow, tortuous spiral staircase weaving its way upward to the house proper. On this pedestal stood a regular, two-storey Arab house with its interior yard where four palms grew in the corners. Of the five rooms of the lower floor three yawned empty behind carved door-frames and coloured windows. The room in which we spent the day was cool and agreeable even during the hottest hours. A narrow, cushioned seat ran right round the walls, which were hung with dark Persian carpets. Between the carpets hung two large, greyish-pink glass dishes; inside the glass there was a delicate black pattern, like lace. Judging from the almost invisible cracks in the glass they must have been hundreds of years old. According to Amar they had been made in Cordoba under Abd-ar-Rahman III, and their commanding, haughty beauty degraded the extremely valuable Persian carpets to ordinary wall decorations.

The unusual and agreeable perfume pervading the room came from the joint action of heat and dryness on the room itself. In this heat every object emitted a smell, the sandalwood pipes on the brass table no less than the Persian carpets on the walls. The window-frame and the cedar-wood door also had a smell – strangely enough the renascent aroma of freshly cut wood combined with the sweet smell of drying wood, although the cedar-wood had probably been cut centuries ago. Even the brass table and metal objects had a smell, neither borrowed nor acquired. I felt the smell of brass and silver in the air and, together with the smell, a metallic taste in my mouth, just as I could taste the cedar-wood when I was five yards from the door, as if I were bending over a freshly cut trunk and putting my tongue on the still humid, rough surface. Also Amar had a smell of his own, not a smell of perspiration, of body, but a smell of flesh, like a newly killed animal. I could taste this flesh-smell too, just as I could distinguish the fresh, jellied smell of his bones, particularly the shoulder and thigh joints, and the horny smell of his long, narrow nails. The smell of his body and the objects drove the strong, spicy smell of the kitchen out of the room to lie motionless over the deep yard outside the open door.

On the brass tables and about the room approximately eighty books lay scattered. The Arab translation of Aristotle's *Metaphysics* and *Poetica*, the *Canon of Medicine* by Ibn Sina, used as a textbook at European universities for five hundred years in the bungled translaion of Gerardus de Cremona; two volumes of al-Maari's poems: *Embers at the end of the Poker*, and *Superfluous Ambitions*, given this name by the blind poet because it was written in treble rhymes; Arab Shah's biography of Timur, in which at Timur's wish he recorded all his master's horrible atrocities and crimes because the purpose of that biography was not to whitewash Timur to posterity but to frighten his enemies. There were volumes by al-Mutanabbi, al-Farid, al-Israili, Abu Nuwas and the poems of the famous Akhtal who, though Christian, had been a court poet of the Omayads and used to break into the throne-room with a large golden cross on his chest, his beard dripping with red wine, to read his latest creation to the caliph.

We lived in solitude for about a week. Usually Amar would translate to me, or we walked down to the well to bathe and to talk. On the last afternoon he was reclining on the couch with al-Hacen's book in his hand explaining to me that the ancient theory of Arab scientists and that of Professor Lyell concerning the origin of mountains is almost identical – when one of the tenants entered, announcing that minstrels were arriving in the evening. Amar was so glad that he jumped up and explained to me, walking up and down in the room, how fortunate we were. The al-Abiyya brothers came up from Mauretania only rarely; they were the last surviving scions of a famous family of minstrels.

They arrived very late. Amar had the table laid in the yard and a few torches were lit in the background. The minstrels were middle-aged, yellow-skinned Berbers, probably twins. Like many Berbers, they had a thicker layer of flesh on their faces than other people, evenly distributed over their protruding cheekbones and chins, giving their faces a mild, genial expression. They were tired and sat modestly at the table and when, after dinner, Amar asked them not to sing as usual but rather to recite, they were obviously pleased.

'First,' Amar said, 'console the stranger with a few poems about the continent where he was born. Perhaps you could recite al-Andaluzi's *Farewell to Portugal*, King al-Mutamid's poem about Toledo, Ibn Zaydun's poem about Cordoba and Ibn Hamdis's poem about Palermo . . .'

The *ranis* rose and, their contours lit by the torches behind them, recited the poems alternately. While one recited the other helped out in whispers whenever necessary. They spoke in the classical language, different in both vocabulary and accent from the dialect in which they had been speaking a few minutes before, and in a sing-song rhythm so slow that it gave Amar time to interpret.

We were sitting comfortably on cushions while the minstrels stood, and I was afraid that this might create an uneasy atmosphere between us and them. Fortunately it did not seem to do so, perhaps because it was not a foreign master whom the minstrels were entertaining with creations of their own culture as Arab poets used to entertain, once upon a time, the Turkish pashas. These poems were written by Arab invaders, oppressors, and the Berbers acquired their culture as well as their language. At the same rime, Amar could not regard himself as the exclusive owner of these poems, all of which had been written over seven hundred years ago. Since then the invaders and the invaded had made friends, and they shared the melancholy knowledge that the culture they now jointly owned was a dead culture which neither could do anything to resuscitate. Perhaps Ibn Zaydun's poem about Cordoba was the most beautiful of all; yet, while they recited it, I felt a stange sensation rising in me, a slight feeling of *Unbehagen*, caused perhaps by some hitherto unrealized European nationalism in me that rebelled against the idea that the Moors had at one time been so much at home in the towns of Europe.

When they had finished I asked them to recite whatever they liked. They began with Arab poets who have lived in Spain and led me back in time to the days of Mohammed. The yard was bathed in the competing light of the torches and the rust-red moon, and I closed my eyes to devote myself completely to this long and dreamy journey. We set out from Seville's rose-arboured streets, a European atmosphere with love-poems of a European tone, to return to the

African towns of the Caliphate, the mystics of Fatimide Cairo and Arab Sicily which differed little from Theocritus's; to al-Mutannabi, who visited every court from that of Syria's governor, Saif ed-Daula, to the Egyptian eunuchs and grew rich on his poems. This poet, when he was on his way home with his load of gold, was attacked by bandits at the crossing of Shatt-al-Arab. He was about to spur his fast horse to flight when his servant suddenly began to recite the poet's famous lines on courage. The poet turned his horse, faced the bandits and was killed. Then we visited Baghdad, the great capital of a liberal world, where Haroun al-Raschid and his sons recreated the atmosphere of Marcus Aurelius's Rome, and where Muslims, Buddhists, Christians, Jews and unbelievers, mystics and rationalists, argued and debated in the shadow of the gigantic library. From there we went on to the nomad tribes of the Arab peninsula, into the days before Mohammed, into a world of primitive tribal warfare and vendetta. Finally, in the last long poem, the verses of which the brothers recited alternately, we journeyed to Byzantium. The poem told the story of the depraved young equestrienne, Theodora, and her marriage to the Emperor Justinian.

According to our custom, Amar and I went to sleep on the roof of the kashba, lying on a mat and covering ourselves with a light blanket. Amar fell asleep as soon as his head touched the mat. It seemed to me as if his head were resting not on the mat but on his long, dark-blue, resilient hair. I sat up quietly and looked round me in the bright moonlight, down into the valley where the greenish-blue shades of the oasis shone like the beryls, amethysts and lapis-lazuli in Theodora's crown, further to the east where the outlines of the mountains glowed rusty-brown in the distance. I felt a deep contentment, the kind of contentment Joseph must have felt after he had learned to like Potiphar's house and before the woman had begun to pester him with her love, as he lay at night on the roof of the palace in Thebes remembering how miserable he had been at the bottom of the well and how beautiful were the poems sung here in Africa.

In the course of the past week I had felt at home here, not at all like a guest. But would it be the same if I remained for ever? My conscience did not protest against accepting help from Ujvary but my relationship to Amar was much more delicate. I looked down upon the sleeper; moonbeams were playing chess on his face and in the black and white death-mask only the temples shone blue, like lakes in a map. The blanket had slipped down to his waist. The network of his muscles lay relexed and his nipples were like two fresh, red seals on a scroll of parchment. I looked at his ribs then closed my eyes, feeling as if, in a dream, I had sneaked along a golden-brown fence. We had been living side by side for a week, for a week we had talked from morning till night and sometimes through the night. More than once our thoughts had been frighteningly alike. He often guessed what was going on in my mind and divined my wishes long before I realized them myself. Yet, after all this time, I knew almost nothing about Amar.

Early in the morning we set out towards the bed of the Draa on mule-back, and from there to Agadir. After a good lunch at the hotel Amar asked me to accompany him to a Marabou. We walked for a few miles between sand-dunes until, down below; we sighted the scintillating, pale blue sheet-glass of the sea. Amar explained to me that a Marabou was a seer, a wise old man, but at the same time the word also meant the square, cupola-roofed white building in which the sorcerer lived. I should have liked to find out the purpose of our visit but as I knew that a direct question was impolite, I asked Amar whether he believed in the power of the sorcerer. Instead of replying he treated me to a lecture. He said that the Mohammedan religion was even more rational than the Protestant and that, therefore, he didn't believe a word of it. He observed the religious rules merely because he was obliged to do so unless he wished his neighbours to put fire to his house, not to speak of the circumstance that he was living in a theocratic state in which, even had he wanted to, he could buy himself neither ham nor wine. The mystics of Islam, who, by the way, had not been Arabs but Persians or newcomers from Andalusia, like Ibn al-Arabi, had been so disheartened by the rationalism of their religion that they went to the other extreme.

'I was at a crossroads,' he said, 'like a European born in the days of St Bernard of Clairvaux and Pierre Abelard. On one side, infinite, mystical devotion; on the other, pure rationalism, accepting the existence of God only because it finds in the Bible a hundred and twenty-three proofs of his existence and only seventy-one of his non-existence. I chose neither of the extremes.

'I believe I am a Platonist or, rather, a neo-Platonist. As we possess only astronomers, chemists, geologists and mathematicians who correspond, to a certain degree, to the Ionian philosophers, but no Socrates, no Plato, we can have no neo-Platonists to drive our theologians mad and bring upon us a wonderful hereticism like neo-Platonism did. Therefore, having no other choice, I am compelled to adhere to your Plato – or rather, to his disloyal disciples. But the sorcerer we are going to visit,' he added, 'has nothing to do with mysticism or neo-Platonism. He offers only practical advice.'

The Marabou was sitting on a small rug in the exact centre of a large and almost completely bare room, right under the cupola. He was a bony-faced, beturbaned, bearded old man. He nodded to Amar, laid his arms ceremoniously across his chest and gave me a fleeting glance from eyes brown, protruding and bright, like raisins soaked in water.

'Hail, o Amar ben Achmed ben Othman ben Jusef ben Muhammed Abu Bekr as-Salahiyal!' he uttered slowly and solemnly. 'Hail, and peace be with you.'

Then with a crooked smile that revealed his slightly protruding but faultless, snow-white teeth, he continued conventionally and condescendingly:

'I am glad to note that for the sake of a foreigner you have deserted the young boys of Morocco. The fez looks good on the stranger, his eyes are beautiful, his waist narrow as if a snake were rearing its body along the outline of his hips. But by the look of him I should say that he is at least as much of a rogue as yourself!'

He threw me a brief, sharp glance. I bent my head in shame.

'Whenever I see you, Amar,' the old man continued, 'I am always reminded of a physical culture appliance I once saw at a school in Mogador. This school, too, was imposed upon us by the cursed French . . . It was a short, thin, iron rod with two iron spheres attached to its ends. It was called a dumb-bell. Your awe-inspiring appearance reminds me of that dumb-bell. Your backbone is the iron rod and the two sphere-shaped parts of your body at the two extremities of your backbone are the two spheres of the dumb-bell. I am not being improper: I mean those parts of your body without which you could neither think, nor sire children – assuming, for the sake of argument, that this were your intention. Allow me to greet in you one of nature's miracles; contrary to all rules and laws your body swings towards the smaller sphere and is dominated by it. Perhaps because the smaller sphere is so compact and so heavy that it outweighs your head, and its virile juices prevail over the juices in your head for, as Ibn Sina said, our body is ruled by juices. Every time you come to me for advice, it is not your head that brings you here but the small spheres at the other extreme of your body. Let me hear your troubles, son, with the usual shamelessness for which I like you.'

I hoped that Amar would give the insolent old man a piece of his mind and leave. To my surprise he laughed and jested with him wittily and in filthy language. At long last he told the old man squarely that he wanted to get rid of his wife who was quarrelsome, boring and an absolute nuisance to him.

'Go to the Cadi tomorrow and tear up your marriage certificate,' the Marabou said lightly. 'How many sheep did you give for her?'

Amar shook his head and explained that since his father's death his mother held the purse-strings and his mother loved his wife. However strange this might sound, the two women were strongly allied against him. If he divorced his wife against his mother's wishes, she might even disinherit him.

'But why do I have to tell you all this?' he exclaimed angrily. 'You know it as well as I.'

'Of course I know it,' the old man said and raised his right hand almost imperceptibly from his lap.

Amar threw him a twenty-five-franc silver coin which he caught easily, then raised his hand again.

'I shall give you excellent advice,' he said almost entreatingly.

Amar threw him another twenty-five-franc piece. The Marabou closed his eyes and meditated. He was completely motionless, only his lips moved as if he were praying.

'One of the lorry drivers of the Vulcan Garage in Dar el-Beida,' he murmured monotonously as if he were an oracle obeying a higher command without understanding it, 'loves his profession so much that he loves only money more. He answers to the name of Larbi. Look for this young man at the garage, Show him your wife in the street. Show her to him repeatedly until he would know her among all the women of Dar el-Beida, even in a crowd. Show her to him until he would know her from behind among all the women of Maghreb. Offer this Larbi first two thousand francs, then come to terms at four thousand. Warn him that the most he would get for the accident would be eight months – after all, she is only a woman – but if he confessed why he did it, then they would hang him.

'On the road to Derb Sidna the French have not yet built a pavement. Let Larbi run over your wife in the early morning, when she is on her way to the market, because there isn't much traffic on the road then. Let him run her over from behind. Include this in your verbal agreement, tell him that you won't pay if he runs her over in any other way. When a woman sees a lorry approaching she begins to jump back and forth like a hen; she may lose an arm or a leg and keep you tied to her for the next fifty years.

'Until the unfortunate accident takes place be kind to your wife and put up with her moods without a murmur. If she reproaches you for running around with boys, promise that you will mend your ways, and, violating your nature, take her then and there. Let Allah lend you the strength for this undertaking and be comforted by the knowledge that you will never have to do it again. In this way everyone will be sorry for you for having lost your young wife at the peak of your married happiness. And send Larbi, when he is in prison, a few good dinners. Not too many, or he will think you are afraid of him and will begin to blackmail you. Send him his dinner once a week, every Friday, to show that you have not forgotten him. Let the inhabitants of the town praise you for your generosity in forgiving your wife's murderer.

'But the hour of prayer is approaching,' he said in his ordinary voice. He motioned to us to go and in this movement there was disdain. Not moral indignation, just disdain.

We hurried down to the sea-shore to bathe. I was utterly downcast. While we were standing before the Marabou, the brutality and vulgarity of the scene had surprised me but at the same time I had found it rather amusing, but as soon as we stepped out of the house, I felt the full weight of humiliation descending upon me. How different had been our return to the Middle Ages last night, when we sat listening to the minstrels! The shocking, disquieting and yet so attractive duality of Amar's character, which enabled him to carry on this vile and filthy conversation with the dirty old man after his lecture on neo-Platonism, left me dumbfounded. I blamed myself, too, for this visit. I was Amar's partner in crime and was not in a moral position to give vent to my indignation and disgust. Yet I could not keep silent, either. I decided that I would try to convince Amar by argument.

'Do you want to know that I think?' I asked him when we reached the sea-shore and began to undress.

'Of course,' he replied absent-mindedly, kicking off his slippers. 'I know what is coming,' he added with a sigh. When he had stripped off all his clothes he sat down next to me in the sand and stretched out his legs. An incoming wave drenched his foot and ankle and, as a gift of the sea, placed a shell beside him.

I explained that the only way one could commit murder was the way used by one of Gide's heroes, who pushed an unknown man out of the window of a train simply because he did not like the stranger's face. Only an *action gratuite* remains without consequences, both in the field of penal law and of psychology. Having read *Crime and Punishment* he must know that an intellectual cannot kill even a disgusting, useless old miser with premeditation without becoming in some way crippled. *You must not kill* is not only a social convention, a religious rule and one of the paragraphs of the penal code: it is a law inherent in man's being. The observation of the law involves practical benefits, its violation is ruinous even if the authorities fail to discover the murder.

'Why? A woman has no soul. Mohammed said so!'

'Why are you referring to Mohammed? Didn't you say yourself that you didn't believe a word of it?'

'We are talking about moral norms and not about what I do or do not believe. Bouthayna can neither read nor write, there is no intellectual relationship between us. This is something you cannot grasp because your women are educated. When embracing an illiterate woman I feel as if I were committing sodomy: What is sodomy, if not this?'

'Sodomy is a lesser crime than murder.'

'Let's bathe,' Amar suggested.'

When we were in the sea to our knees he turned to me.

'There is only one thing I should like to know. To what extent do you reject me because of the Marabou and everything I have said to you? I don't mind your logical protests. But I should like to know how much you rebel against me in your emotions?'

I considered for a moment.

'Not at all,' I confessed at last.

We remained on the beach until late in the evening. When we walked back to Agadir Amar promised, though not very convincingly, that he would postpone his plans and not contact the lorry driver for the time being.

The subtropical summer fled with vertiginous speed. I spent the mornings at the huge swimming pool on the sea-shore. I lay on my stomach on the stone wall dividing the sweet water from the sea and watched the sun flying in a wide arc above my head or the sea which was greyer and more monotonous that I expected it to be. My thoughts dwelt on the tragedy of Europe, the miseries of emigration and the uncertainty of the future. But in the afternoons, when, clad in a djellaba, I sat with Amar on the mats in Arab cafés, or we lay in the hot water under the cupola of the Turkish bath like two boiled fish, I forgot everything and abandoned myself completely to my new, picaresque and happy life. I felt as if I had rid myself of my old habits and ideas acquired by mere chance of birth on the European jumble-market, the way I threw off my clothes in the dressing-room of the Turkish bath, and, that at last I had found my real self.

The sunset reminded me of the colours and consistency of the Turkish delight which I had loved as a child and had often bought from the merchant near the entrance to the school. At that hour Amar and I used to go down to the sea, to the red rocks overgrown with bougainvillaea where we came face to face with the fresh breeze while, from the direction of the town, we were pursued by the smell of burnt oil, mutton and fermenting fruit. At night we used to sit in the palm-grove by the sea, as though in some domed cellar above which the huge cylinder-mill of the moon scattered its sparkling flour so that it rained down slowly, soundlessly, between the black feather-dusters of the palms. At other times I would wander alone at night in another part of the town, over bare, red, granite-hard ground dotted with lipless wells. I would sit down to rest under the date-palms whose still unripened fruit rattled in the breeze, and, before going home to sleep, would drink a glass of champagne in one of the cafés. I was not at all bothered by my parasitic way of life: the authorities forbade Europeans to take employment – this remained the only privilege of the Arabs – and Ujvary, who gave us uncounted sums of money, had repeatedly said that he wasn't giving it for bread alone.

When the Italian armistice commission arrived and it was rumoured that it would soon be followed by the Gestapo, Amar invited me to his kashba for the 'next seven times seven years'. He told me to throw my expired Hungarian passport into the sea, he would obtain an identification paper for me in an Arab name, a name I could choose myself. He made me a gift of a number of burnouses, djellabas, fezes and slippers and insisted that the whole thing was only a question of decision. Within five years I would forget my mother tongue and if I followed him, no news or messages or letters from Europe would ever find me again. I felt like agreeing to his proposal on the spot, but suspended my decision until I had considered all aspects of the problem. Bandi said that if the Gestapo arrived we couldn't stay, with which I wholeheartedly agreed; then he added that it was our duty to volunteer for the British Army to fight against Hitler. Lorsy believed that we had nothing to fear from the Gestapo, because of our excellent connections, and said that it was a crime to leave a place where one lived so well without doing a stitch of work for it. Then he added that for the last hundred and forty years the British had prevented the political and economic unification of Europe, though only such a union could have thwarted Hitler's ascent to power. He explained that the British were responsible for the equipping of Hitler's army; that it was the British who had permitted Mussolini's ships to pass through the Suez Canal when he attacked Ethiopia, that Baldwin had stayed Blum's hand when the latter wanted to come to the help of the Spanish Republic against Franco and that Chamberlain had sold Czechoslovakia to Hitler at Munich. He – he continued – felt a deep sympathy for the British people, but now the day had come when they had to eat what they had cooked. It would be ridiculous, he said, if we permitted ourselves to be fooled by the axiom that in case of war one should side with the less despicable of the two opponents, for the only thing we should do in case of war was to run from it.

After a long debate, in which I took Bandi's part, Lorsy gave in and went to see the nearest British Consul at Tangier. He took with him our passports and those of a few other Hungarian refugees who desired to fight in the British Army. We had to entrust this mission to Lorsy, not only because of his gift for diplomacy and his knowledge of languages but also because his was the only passport still valid. Lorsy spent two weeks in Tangier. When he got back he gave us a detailed account of his experiences. The British Consul had thanked him warmly for our zeal but had declared that Great Britain had all the solders she needed. Lorsy related that for our sakes he had made friends with the American Consul too, and had several times lunched with him at the Roma, an excellent Italian restaurant, under Mussolini's portrait, but in vain. The American Consul could promise us nothing. At that point the conversation degenerated into a quarrel, Bandi reproaching Lorsy for having dined at a fascist restaurant, and Lorsy declaring that this was the best restaurant in Tangier and his stomach had no political prejudices.

I was about to intervene when the postman arrived with a registered letter from Laszlo Fényes in Montauban, telling us that he had just received an invitation from President Roosevelt to come to America. To his knowledge our friends in America had obtained the same invitation for Valy, myself, Lorsy and Bandi, but as no one knew our address, it would take a little time before we received it. I hoped that this good news would put an end to Bandi's and Lorsy's perpetual squabbling, but I was wrong. Lorsy declared that for the sake of

America, that real Garden of Eden, he was ready to leave this Eldorado, while Bandi refused to put a foot in a country whose consul sat down to eat under Mussolini's portrait, not even if they beat him to death here in Casablanca. He remained firm, although Lorsy tried hard to persuade him to change his opinion. I, on the other hand, resolved there and then to accept Amar's invitation, but I said so neither to him nor to anyone else.

The American visas did not arrive, but the agents of the Gestapo, disguised as tourists and recognizable from a distance of two hundred yards by their swagger and their walking sticks, did. Very soon a few Frenchmen, known for their democratic convictions, disappeared and Europeans were stopped at every corner to identify themselves. I protected myself against this persecution by going about in Arab clothes. My only worry was my wife. I decided not to go away with Amar before the American visas arrived or until I had found some other way of getting Valy to a safe place and thus being rid of her. A few days later the Hungarian refugees in Casablanca – there were sixteen apart from us – met at our apartment at Bandi's initiative. We came to the conclusion that as they could not go to England, and as a trek through the desert to Egypt appeared a little too romantic, there remained but one solution; to go to Martinique. There was a chance that the authorities would not object to our sailing from one French colony to another, but permission had to be obtained at the French Government-House in Rabat. The mission was again entrusted to Lorsy, who departed to the capital with nineteen passports in his pocket. He promised to be back within forty-eight hours because it was impossible to circulate in the streets without a passport.

When eight days had gone by without news from Lorsy, one of our unfortunate companions, a Hungarian sailor who had served as a volunteer in the French Army, tried to kill himself. I decided to follow Lorsy to Rabat. Only late in the morning, when the bus entered the old town gate of Rabat, did I realize what a difficult task I had shouldered. Where was I to find Lorsy in this town of two hundred thousand inhabitants and teeming with refugees?

A shirt, broad street opened from the bus terminus, probably Rabat's main street. It was bordered on both sides by arcades, and under the arcades there were dozens of cafés. The terrace of the third café on the left was so crowded that people were sitting almost in each other's laps. In one corner of the terrace I noticed two hands holding an open copy of *The Times*, as if to suggest that the man sitting behind that *Times* was sacred and inviolable, at least the ambassador of a neutral power if not an active minister, for had an ordinary mortal dared to read that paper he would immediately have been arrested and taken to an internment camp. Those hands could belong to no one but Lorsy.

'Take a seat, George, my dear,' Lorsy said, as if we had parted an hour ago. 'I am happy to see you here . . . You want me to fold *The Times*? But why? However, for your sake . . .'

He took off his glasses and wiped them elaborately. Without his glasses the expression of his blue eyes was childlike and innocent.

'Oh, you want me to get down to brass tacks? All right, then. What are our friends in Casa doing? Are they worried about their passports? No reason to worry. The passports are in the safest possible place. After all, no one can expect me to run around with nineteen passports in my pocket in this heat . . . I keep them at the hostel, of course. In my wardrobe? By no means! I have no wardrobe. Nor do I have a room. I sleep in a bathtub, a beautiful, large tub . . . The passports are hidden behind the tub in the left-hand corner. You see, they have nothing to worry about . . . That they cannot go out in the street without their passports? Let them stay in. People pursued by the Gestapo should lie low . . . Why I haven't written for a week? Why didn't you write when you went off into the desert? Was there no mailbox? Or did the monkeys steal the letters from the box? Well, if there were no mailboxes there, there are no pens here. Last night I came down here to write, because I can write only at the café, with the café pen . . . but the pen wasn't soft enough, there were flies in the ink and I lost my inspiration . . . Don't grumble, George, dear . . . In an hour's time you shall see for yourself how much I have accomplished. Naturally, I cannot just enter the consulate and ask the consul to stamp visas on nineteen passports! There are at least a hundred thousand people waiting for visas. The first step is to find the right connections, the second, to use them to the best advantage. I have already made excellent contacts, another day or two and everything will be settled . . . What contacts, you ask? You shall see within the hour. I am going to take you along with me, I have already spoken of you, praised you as the world's best translator of Villon and Rabelais. They are expecting you.'

'Don't try to fool me. An hour ago you had no idea that I would show up here!'

'And yet, I announced your coming,' Lorsy said, unmoved. 'What would you say to a bottle of ice-cooled wine? Look,' he begged with a sheepish smile, 'let's forget for a while this disgusting business of passports . . .'

I resigned myself to my fate. An hour later Lorsy called for a cab.

'To the Governor's palace,' he instructed the driver.

We stopped before the largest of the administration buildings scattered all over the park. A dignified Arab commissionaire came down the stairs to meet us, greeted Lorsy by name and helped us alight from the cab. We waited for a moment in the tremendous lobby while the commissionaire spoke on the house telephone. Suddenly a door flew open on the first floor and a young man called down to us, bending over the banister:

'Mon cher, cher Monsieur Lorsy!'

'Who is that?' I asked my companion.

'That is Monsieur Grimaud, Governor Nogues's secretary.'

We mounted the stairs. The commissionaire hastened away to fetch refreshments while other servants held beautifully worked bamboo armchairs for us to sit down. Lorsy introduced me to the secretary.

'My friend Faludy is the greatest living Hungarian poet. Last year, on the occasion of Racine's three hundredth anniversary, he translated *Phèdre* into Hungarian . . . But we talked about Racine yesterday, didn't we?'

Monsieur Grimaud gazed at Lorsy with the adoration some people bestow on Mona Lisa's portrait. He paid no attention whatsoever to me. I was annoyed by Lorsy's silly lies but I soon found out that they served a certain purpose. Monsieur Grimaud declared that he would be charmed to hear more about Racine. Lorsy complied and continued where – as he said – he had left off the day before. Monsieur Grimaud listened enthralled, swallowing Lorsy's words greedily, his little Adam's apple sliding rapidly up and down like that of a zealous student.

Lorsy discussed Racine's vocabulary. He stated that this outstanding poet made do with two thousand and a few hundred words, one-tenth of the number Shakespeare used, while in Shakespeare's works every abstract word had also a particular significance depending on who used it, when, and with how much emphasis. With Racine the same word always covered the same notion.

But Racine had it easy in Louis XIV's century! He stood in a solidly built, heavy baroque colonnade: he believed that the laws of morality and the rules of the political game were exact and eternal, like the rules of conjugation. To our misfortune – Lorsy held out his arms helplessly, clutching a martini in one hand and a caviare sandwich in the other – our age is no longer a baroque colonnade but a swampy jungle with pythons strangling the breath out of us. Words have lost their meaning. What one man calls slavery, another calls freedom, what is sin to one is virtue to another. But, to be more exact, it is not that words have degenerated, for words are only labels stuck on to ideas, and machine-guns can harm neither ideas nor the concept of virtue. What has really happened is that a label bearing the word 'Cyanide' has been stuck on a bottle containing syrup, and a label bearing the word 'Syrup' on to a bottle containing cyanide.

'And who exchanged the labels?' asked Monsieur Grimaud provocatively.

Lorsy pretended not to have heard the question.

'The *Roi Soleil,'* he continued, swallowing his martini, 'said: *"L'état c'est moi."'*

He pronounced the word *'état'* quickly and without emphasis. I recalled that Pétain had introduced the use of *État Français* instead of *République Française.* The same thought occurred, without doubt, to Monsieur Grimaud.

'Louis XIV,' Lorsy continued, 'identified himself with the French State. When his dinner was brought in the steward of the royal household cried: "The King's dinner!" upon which everyone present had to make deep obeisance to the dishes, sweeping the floor with their hats. He burned Heidelberg to the ground and not only did he offend against all earthly and heavenly laws but he was completely unaware of offending against them. Yet, however unlimited his power, it never occurred to the *Roi Soleil* to change thousand-year-old ideas and to oblige all Frenchmen to call imprisonment in the Bastille a matter of honour and glory as certain heads of state are doing today.'

At these words Monsieur Grimaud began to show signs of nervousness. With a sly glance in his direction Lorsy made sure that his words had achieved the desired effect, then he returned to discussing Racine. A little later a young official by the name of de la Brouquière joined us to listen with bated breath to Lorsy's lecture, and shortly afterwards the excellent art historian, Funck-Brentano, came into the room. When all five of us rose to go out to dinner I whispered to Lorsy to bring up the matter of our visas. He replied that greed would only spoil our chances, the gentlemen not being, as yet, sufficiently softened up.

We dined at a restaurant called Kyrnos, sitting at the table until five in the afternoon, and talking. Then Lorsy and I drove out to Sale. Lorsy, who was afraid of growing fat and exceeding his hundred-and-ten-kilogramme average weight, suggested a ten-minute constitutional on the hilltop, along the streets of the small town built in the crater. Then he led me to a café built on the cliff-edge above the sea like a bird's nest. The deep blue, motionless surface of the sea was dotted with old-fashioned sailing boats with colourful sails. Conjuring up the spirit of the place, Lorsy talked about the pirates who had once preferred this shore to Tunisia, and had sailed out from here all the way to the St George Canal.

Before tasting his champagne he splashed a few drops on the ground – 'as an offering to the Gods of Antiquity,' he explained sentimentally.

'Sitting here and looking down on these multicoloured sails it is almost impossible to believe that the Emperor Tiberius is no longer among us. But even apart from that, I feel in Morocco like an ancient

Greek sophist among the practical, uneducated and crude Romans. The snobbism of our hosts vies with that of the Roman nobles. This is why we are more honoured among them than we should be were we to eke out our existence among refined, erudite people. You must trust me, George. I have conversed in this town only for a week, and already I have made the necessary contacts. You may rest assured that you shall obtain your visas. Our friends in Casablanca are convinced that I eat and drink and spend my time in brothels. They do not comprehend that to me eating and drinking mean nothing except in good company. And as far as love is concerned . . . I find the kinetics of love-making far too exhausting. To tell the truth, I am far too fat and far too lazy to turn on my belly for so little pleasure.'

After having thus reassured me, he took me to a restaurant and then back to the hotel where, after considerable bargaining, he obtained a bathtub for me too. Remembering our friends in Casablanca and ashamed of myself for having idled away the whole day, but also in order to sleep with a good conscience, I gathered up the passports from under Lorsy's tub. They were all there, all nineteen of them, but so wet that I had to dry them out on the flagstones of my bathroom in the warm night air. In the morning we breakfasted at the café where I had discovered Lorsy the day before.

We were getting ready to proceed to the Governor's palace when Bandi arrived, sweating and excited, from Casablanca. He was beet-red with fury, called Lorsy a blackguard and me an idiot. He was also clutching an unusually long and sharply-pointed nail-file in his hand, which Lorsy eyed with some apprehension although he said nothing about it.

When we reached the palace Lorsy declared that only I could come up with him, but Bandi stuck to us like a leech. When Monsieur Grimaud caught sight of us he swallowed and gave Lorsy a reproachful look. However, the atmosphere soon improved. Grimaud began to discuss relations between Vichy and Roosevelt, which gave Lorsy an opportunity to deliver a short lecture on the Hungarian policy for survival. Hungary – he said – had spent three hundred and seventy-seven years of the last four hundred under foreign occupation. He related how our rulers allied themselves with the head of the Holy Roman Empire against Byzantium, with the Pope against the Emperor and with Byzantium against both; then with the Germans against the Turks and with the Turks against the Germans . . .

Monsieur Grimaud seemed particularly grateful for the lecture. He himself was probably wondering how to serve Vichy in such a way as to remain acceptable to the next regime. In the meantime de la Brouquière had come in. This young man was a strange mixture of self-confidence, mannerisms, solemn curiosity, swagger and melancholia. The day before he had remained stubbornly silent, but now he appeared resolved to question the oracle, our good Lorsy, on his own affairs. Grimaud, however, who knew his colleague's problems by heart and was bored by them, plied Lorsy with new questions, preventing the other from speaking. When we rose to go to dinner at the Kyrnos, Bandi, who was still clutching his nail-file, stepped up to Lorsy and whispered in Hungarian.

'Ask him to get us our visas for Martinique. If you don't, I'll stick this nail-file into your behind up to the hilt!'

'Don't,' Lorsy whispered back, 'don't, for heaven's sake. This moment is particularly inauspicious both for the request and the stabbing: After dinner, when they are sufficiently mellowed by food and drink, I shall broach the subject. I swear by the life of my children that I shall. But don't use that thing.'

At the restaurant Bandi sat close to Lorsy and didn't take his eyes off him. De la Brouquière was also watching him, waiting for the moment when he could bring up his problem, but Grimaud was too quick for him. At first de la Brouquière did not notice that his colleague was blocking him on purpose, and when Grimaud at last told him rather rudely to shut up he was so amazed that he forgot to close his baby-lips, round with surprise. Yet, in spite of the slight tension in the atmosphere, we ate and drank abundantly so that by the time we had finished with the quince-stuffed pheasant Bandi and de la Brouquière were a little drunk and Lorsy had forgotten the nail-file.

When the waiter had carried away the cheese-tray I felt as if my waist were of lead and my bottom had grown roots in the chair. De la Brouquière took advantage of the momentary silence to pick up the two-beaked oil-and-vinegar bottle and, shaking it towards Grimaud, he began to shout:

'You won't prevent me from telling this gentleman, whom I trust, all my troubles and asking for his advice. You won't prevent it!' he yelled, and splashed some vinegar on Monsieur Grimaud's pale grey, tropical suit.

'I,' he turned to Lorsy, 'am a convinced, even stubborn, fascist. I hate liberals, socialists, but most of all the Jews. My colleague considers it shameful that someone should have convictions. What do you say, Monsieur Lorsy, is it a shame or isn't it that I hold principles?'

At Lorsy's encouraging but noncommittal reply he told us that his father, a county prefect, had been a convinced anti-Dreyfusard; he himself had, since his early childhood, admired Barrès, Léon Daudet and Maurras. A year ago he had prayed for his country to lose the war. This was the only chance for France to rid herself of her corrupt democratic politicians and raise the fascists to power. 'I know it was a tremendous price to pay,' he exclaimed, 'but I believe it was worth it!'

'When Pétain took power,' he continued, 'my friends here arranged a banquet. I got home blind drunk, vomited up my dinner and made myself a pot of strong black coffee. When I had drunk it I suddenly became quite sober. I meditated and came to the conclusion that in our days it was not principles, battles won or lost, or the size of the occupied territories that decided the outcome of a war but the industrial potential of the hostile parties. I realized that it was unavoidable that the United States and the Soviet Union should join in the war against Germany. The industrial potential of these countries, including England, being three times that of the Berlin–Rome axis, Hitler will without doubt lose the war. And then we, the fascists of France, will be lynched or executed. I don't know whether it will be my compatriots, the Arabs, the Americans or the Jews who beat us to death, but someone will. Is my analysis correct, Monsieur Lorsy?'

'Unfortunately, quite correct,' replied Lorsy with a contented sigh.

'There I sat in my armchair on the night of triumph,' de la Brouquière continued, 'and asked myself the question what to do in my desperate position. Am I to sacrifice my life for a lost cause? Or betray my principles, which are dearer to me than life itself?'

Lorsy took off his glasses and examined de la Brouquière's childish, insolent features, probably to determine the degree of the young man's drunkenness. Then he explained that man's ties to his principles are much looser than is generally believed. Our thoughts, our favourite expressions are not, usually, reflections of our character or of our mind. We learn them, hear them, or simply borrow them from others and they have little or nothing to do with our real being.

I felt the time had come for me to interfere.

'You, Monsieur de la Brouquière,' I began cautiously, 'were just telling us that it was your father's views, your reading, your environment and chance experiences that led you towards fascism. But had you been born one thousand and six hundred years earlier and were we now in Alexandria, at the time of Emperor Jovian, drinking wines no less tasty but mixed with honey, you would probably explain to us that a world in which the Son was consubstantial with the Father was not worth living in, and you would commit suicide or permit yourself to be beaten to death in the street for your Arian conviction.'

'Nothing could be further from my mind than materialism,' Lorsy interrupted me in a dreamy voice, 'but let me confirm the saddening fact that we have very little in common with the principles and ideals we so proudly call our own. We own a woman when she is lying in our arms, we own this wonderful cognac which is in the process of blending with our blood and we own the magnificent dinner proceeding from our stomachs to our intestines. We own these much more completely than the indigestible thoughts in our heads or than ideals that are fundamentally alien to us. Let us admit with Christian humility that we are much more closely related to the food in our stomach than to our thoughts, and that we have more right to call our bottom our own than our head.'

After pronouncing these words he hid his head in his cognac glass. Monsieur Grimaud smiled triumphantly and de la Brouquière digested Lorsy's words with a worried face. It was Bandi who interrupted the long silence by speaking to Lorsy in Hungarian.

'If you don't broach the subject of our visas immediately I shall push this nail-file up to the hilt into that part of your body you call your own.'

'Give me another five minutes, until I have progressed from Charles VII to the island beginning with an M.'

'Why Charles VII?'

'You shall see . . .'

And indeed, Lorsy began to speak about the French patriot who lived in British-occupied territory in about 1425. He was not in a position to join Jeanne d'Arc; but if he deposited a declaration of loyalty to Charles VII with a notary public he could even kiss the English king's horse's arse in the street without endangering his future. The situation was similar after the battle of Leipzig when nobody in France knew whether Napoleon or the Bourbons would win. One could place a bet on Napoleon or again one could place a bet on the Bourbons, but the most rational course was to place a bet on both; that is, to reserve a passage on the ship of the opponent who was preparing to sink the frigate on which one already was. From Napoleon Lorsy went on to Josephine, who was born on the island of Martinique. After discussing the beauties of Josephine and those of Fort-de-France he turned to Monsieur Grimaud, asking him to help his friends obtain visas for that island. Monsieur Grimaud replied that he would do what he could for us, but that the passports must be sent to Vichy with the recommendation of M. Nogues, the Governor, and if Vichy approved, they must be sent on to Martinique for the approval of the Governor of that island. This procedure would take at least one year.

'We don't have quite so much time at our disposal,' said Bandi, 'and therefore we shall no longer abuse the hospitality of these gentlemen. We have a great deal to do. Come on, Ernö!'

Monsieur Grimaud threw Bandi a surprised glance and Lorsy a conspiratorial smile, but Lorsy did not smile in return. His eyes caressed the bottle of cognac on the table before him, he filled his glass to the brim and downed it at one gulp.

'Let's go,' Bandi commanded. 'These gentlemen will take care of the bill.'

Lorsy rose from his chair with surprising agility and without paying the slightest attention to our hosts' unbelieving amazement, or even taking leave of them, he led us triumphantly from the restaurant. When we reached the door he smiled broadly.

'I am happy that you have not obtained your visas,' he said. 'At least we can remain together in this Garden of Eden until the end of the war.'

Lorsy was mistaken, however. We remained in Casablanca only for another two months, while the subtropical summer turned into autumn. I grew so accustomed to my way of life that I regarded it almost as a permanent summer holiday; a summer holiday from which there was no returning home, at the end of which no permanent occupation, no determined object of life awaited me. I was waiting for the arrival of the American visas: I thought I would put my wife on the ship and, before it sailed, disappear with Amar in the desert. On the morning of the last day of October we received the unexpected news that the Casablanca police were going to intern refugees in the smaller towns of Morocco: Agadir, Mogador and Mazagan. Valy, Bandi and I were ordered to proceed to Marrakesh the following morning. Of all the refugees only Lorsy was allowed to remain in Casablanca. This measure was not one inspired by the Gestapo; on the contrary, it was an attempt of the Moroccan police to hide us from the Gestapo.

While Bandi and Valy ran about, nervous and excited, to say goodbye to our friends, I went to the café where I was to meet Amar at eleven o'clock. There was no point in my going to Marrakesh to live under police supervision until the American visas arrived and I could see Valy safely off; thus I made up my mind to dissociate myself from this war and my past as quickly as possible and go off to the desert that same night. On the terrace of the café I wrote a brief letter to Lorsy, leaving my wife in his care, and drank absinthe. I observed contentedly that the leter completely lacked pathos and was rather cheerful. Then I turned my eyes towards the white skyscraper on the street corner from where Amar would appear. Not far from where I was sitting, along the garden wall, bushes were shedding coloured berries that were rolled by the breeze across the snow-white pavement towards the middle of the road; but the autumn gathered only a meagre harvest, the palms continued to raise their green swords towards the sky as if taking an oath, and the woolly clouds danced against the vibrating azure of the sky like cool, drying handkerchiefs. I stretched out both legs under the table: the happy tingling that I felt in my ankles and thighs rose until it reached my chest and made me shudder with joy.

It was a quarter past eleven, and Amar had still not shown up although he was usually very punctual. I pulled my feet under me and thought that in the valley of the Draa, in Amar's kashba, the autumn would be even more powerless than here and that I would sunbathe on the roof throughout the year until the brown films of the sun would accumulate, layer upon layer, under my skin as it did with the Arabs, and not only on the surface as it did now. I recalled the story told us by Sidi Mohammed, the bandit chief, and I established with contentment that I had now become the hero of the story. Then I thought that if my father walked by, he would certainly not recognize me as I sat there in burnous and fez. This saddened me a little, though not too much.

When Amar did not arrive by half past eleven I began to be a little anxious, wondering what could have happened to him. He often took Czechoslovak pilots or Gaullists in a motor-boat to Port Lyautey, from where they could easily cross to Tangier and Gibraltar, but he never told me about these excursions until after his return. If he were arrested it would be no more than annoying because, thanks to his connections, he would soon be released; but, knowing him and his protégés, I was certain that they would not surrender to the patrol boat without a fight, and besides, the sea had been pretty rough for days. I noticed that I was impatiently moving my toes in my slippers and tried to concentrate on my environment. First I drew arabesques on the marble table top with the few drops of water that had dripped down from the neck of the soda bottle, then I watched a fat pasha who had come into the café and was now walking up and down in the darkest corner on unsteady feet, green, inflated, purposeless, like a man drowned.

Towards a quarter to twelve I began to be anxious not only because of Amar but also for my own sake, since my fate was tied up with his. I began to count and decided that at a thousand I would rise and go home, but that until then I would keep my eyes away from the street corner. However, at my favourite number, sixty-six, I broke my pledge and when I reached six hundred and sixty-six, Amar appeared around the corner in his red fez and pale blue tie.

'Forgive me, something unexpected has happened,' he began, sitting down next to me.

'I am not interested in your unexpected something,' I said angrily, although I was not angry at all, and I closed my eyes, smiling happily. I took a deep breath and inhaled the perfume of his djellaba washed in herbs, not in soap, his perfume of withered flowers in an arid field. I felt this perfume not only in my nostrils but in my throat and further down in the ramifications of the bronchia, right into the apex of my lungs. I resolved to listen to his excuses and lies, and then to tell him about my decision to follow him into the desert. But Amar kept silent.

'Do you already know?' he asked in a frightened voice when I opened my eyes.

'I don't, I can only guess.'

'You guessed?' he asked and bent his head in shame. Two feverish red roses blossomed in his cheeks up to his long lashes. I was a little moved by his being so ashamed.

'If you have already guessed, then let me tell you the whole thing the way it happened,' he said in a relieved voice.

'I am not interested,' I repeated absentmindedly.

'But you forgive me?'

'Of course I forgive you.'

'In that case,' he said, 'let me confess the whole thing. I had a little family trouble, that is all . . . At eight o'clock in the morning, as she was going to the market, my poor wife was run over by a truck. At nine she was brought home, by ten she was laid out, by eleven buried, by twelve forgotten . . . That is why I was a little late. I hope you are not angry with me.'

An hour later, as we were wont, we walked down to the sea-shore.

It was too cool to bathe, so we kept walking up and down along the cliff-edge that felt harder than usual to me today. Amar said how pleased he would be if I could at last make up my mind to follow him to his kashba and I thought that if Amar had killed his wife himself, or if he had driven the lorry which ran her down, I should now admire him for his manliness. The source of the trouble was that he trusted me and had thus made me an accomplice.

I gave no reply to his renewed invitation, upon which he collected flat pebbles and began throwing them into the suddenly calm, frighteningly green sea. He had no luck: the majority of the pebbles sank right away. Even the best jumped only two or three times. I tried to beat him at the game, but without success, until, angrily, I threw my letter to Lorsy after the pebbles into the sea.

We alighted from the train at the station of Marrakesh in a very bad mood indeed. The night before, getting ready for the journey, we discovered that all our belongings filled no more than two rucksacks; Bandi and Valy were scared of the characteristically Arab town on the edge of the desert, and in addition, we were now poor. Ujvary, who had so generously provided for us in Casablanca, had given us no money for the journey; he probably thought that in this new place we should find someone else to look after us. At the station a disagreeable surprise awaited us: the colonial government had entrusted the Jewish community with the care of the refugees, although only a few of them were Jews. We were met by a squat young man of extreme enthusiasm and warm friendliness, a Jewish schoolmaster, Mr Bizbass. He told us that refugees who had no money of their own would be placed in Jewish families. The Jews here were generous but very religious people who regarded only a Jew as a human being. Therefore, he begged us to attend services in the Temple and to observe the Jewish religious laws and rites to our best ability. He regarded himself as a modern, enlightened man and was deeply sorry for this state of affairs, but his fellow-religionists were still living in the Middle Ages. Bandi and I looked at each other dumbfounded.

'I haven't got the faintest idea about Jewish rites,' I said.

The station-master, a fat, red-faced, freckled man wearing the uniform of the Foreign Legion, answered cheerfully, in Hungarian:

'Never mind, you'll soon learn!'

Some thirty soot-black, obsolete coaches were waiting for us in front of the station building with brilliantly polished copper lamps, grey horses, and an Arab lad on the box of each coach. Mr Bizbass, who looked much more like a Danish civil servant than a Jewish schoolmaster in Africa, arranged the procession. In the first coaches he put the refugees who had good leather suitcases, in the subsequent ones those who had fibre luggage and in the last few coaches those who, like ourselves, possessed nothing but a rucksack. He himself mounted his bicycle and rode at the head of the procession along several miles of road through the French and Arab sectors, then along an endless dirt road following the town wall between granaries and warehouses, until we reached a little square in front of the Rabbinical Tribunal. Here we were met by tall Jews clad in black kaftans and black skull-caps, wearing beards like the prophets, who embraced us, sobbing, and felt our shoulders and arms as if to make sure that we were really all there. In the background gipsy-looking women in colourful silk dresses and kerchiefs, with painted faces and heavy gold jewellery, watched this biblical scene motionless but with tears running down their cheeks.

A large table was laid in the middle of the square and we were served a heavy but excellent meal accompanied by sweet, sticky liqueurs, while from the more distant roofs Arab boys threw rotten eggs and horse-droppings into the dishes or at the speakers giving us a voluble welcome. They hit the mark every single time. Mr Bizbass hastened to reassure us that their relations with the Arabs were excellent though at times the Arabs were a little excitable. Not long ago the French soldiers from Marrakesh had returned from the war in Europe but there was no sign of the Arab soldiers. Besides, it was the twentieth day of the Ramadan and the long fast was beginning to tell. I asked Mr Bizbass to find us quarters in some public building – not a family – possibly in the school-house. Some fifteen refugees joined me in this request, the others had enough money to look after themselves.

After discussing the matter with the Jewish prophets, the schoolmaster returned and informed us joyfully that we could make ourselves at home on the top floor of the Tribunal. We could cook our own food over a charcoal fire on the marble floor of the central hall, and were provided with straw mattresses and blankets. In the afternoon Mr Bizbass, who was at least as conservative morally as he was liberal religiously, brought us screens to be set up between the married couples and the others, and between men and women. Unfortunately, he brought us neither a table nor chairs. He made us promise that if we wanted to smoke on the Sabbath or eat pork we would hide in the lavatory of the Tribunal to do so.

Every morning we were awakened by a dreadful row going on in the court-room below. Usually it was some woman arguing at the top of her voice, her arms akimbo, with the Rabbi. We assumed that the subject of the excitement was some family quarrel. The end of the matter was usually that the Rabbi had the woman thrown out by the court-room attendant, a huge Negro called Bentoto. By the time we were dressed the woman was throwing maledictions at the Rabbi from the square outside. The Rabbi was standing on the balcony, with his back to the street, listening to her absorbedly.

Although our quarters were far from comfortable, and we had to undress in the dark, eat on the floor, and our clothes were turning into rags, I felt happy and unable to share Bandi's despair. He considered Marrakesh the anteroom of Hell. There was indeed something frightening about this town. In the evenings, when we stood on the town wall looking out over the pink desert, from the multitude of rats gambolling at the foot of the wall like a black pattern on a pink carpet constantly changing its shape towards the even, snow-topped range of the Atlas Mountains bordering the horizon, it was indeed as if Horror itself were sitting enthroned on top of that mountain in the face of an emaciated young man with pointed shoulders, gazing down malevolently at Marrakesh. But what Bandi called the cataclysm of destruction within the town, I called life: real, earthy life, which my friend could neither see nor fathom. When we sat in the little Café Universel on the corner of the Djema el-Fnaa Place, where little boys sneaked up to us under the table to show us crickets imprisoned in match-boxes, snatching the cigarette butts from our hands and playing to us on tiny musical instruments audible only to us, Bandi dreamed aloud about a society in which there would be no beggars. The permanent and monotonous sound of the snake-charmers' flutes and the drums ceaselessly beaten in the square drove Bandi to distraction, while they relaxed the tension in my nerves until I sat as if enthralled and began to write a poem. And when one of the small boys ran out into the street to pull the tail of one of the donkeys loaded with bricks that were standing in the market-place to be ready should someone wish to build a house, Bandi delivered a long lecture in defence of the donkeys. When, one afternoon, two cyclists collided in front of the café and one, getting to his feet, stabbed the other in the belly, Bandi remarked that in a communist society such things would never occur.

Sometimes I walked around for hours in the huge market-place, the Djema el-Fnaa, listening to the story-tellers, watching the goldsmiths at work, loitering beside large heaps of spices, inhaling their fragrance; or I entered filthy little Arab tea-rooms to converse with my neighbours about the caravan-roads, the weather, or eternal life. But I preferred the room-sized premises of the Café Universel where, at times, a hundred people were sitting around thirty tiny tables. The café was owned by a former Legionnaire, a huge German fellow, who stood behind the counter; order was maintained by the Arab waiter, Ahmed. When a fight broke out, he separated the fighters while the Legionnaire looked on from among his bottles as if he were sitting in the control-tower of an airfield.

The whole town, the entire region walked by the windows of that café: veiled Tuareg men who stopped up their nostrils – with cotton-wool imported from England – to protect themselves against having to inhale the stench of the town-dwellers; healers who cleaned out the festering sores of their patients in the street with their tongues. Opposite, along the tall wall, squatted the visitors who came down from the mountain villages of Atlas; they remained there for a week or two observing life in the market-place, then rose and returned to their villages. At the table next to mine sat the professor of the Arab Lyceum with his two boy-lovers. Sometimes he played chess with me while the two boys watched with devotion until I beat him at the game. Outside, the square filled with donkeys carrying dates and vegetables; the teats of the she-asses hung down as if they had two cocks attached to their bellies. Caravans of spindly-legged camels arrived, walking with an almost transcendent stride, and in the early afternoon the Pasha's flat-footed soldiers came marching by. At the head of the detachment, in front of the sergeant, a sheep advanced with dancing steps, and when the sergeant shouted *right turn!* the sheep turned gracefully from the Djema el-Fnaa into the street on the corner of which the café stood, glancing back to make certain the troops were following. Every four hours I listened to the cries of the Muezzin of the Kotoubia Mosque, coming to me across the little garden that separated me from the Mosque.

Late afternoon was the period of angry quarrels and street-fights. In the café, however, the fighters did not attack straight away as they did in the street. They would sit in opposite corners, their long legs drawn under them, staring at each other. Ahmed, the waiter, would watch them sometimes for hours. Then suddenly, one would jump up and run towards the other, pulling out his dagger on the way. Yet he never reached his opponent, because the watchful Ahmed always caught him and with the help of the old Legionnaire threw him out through the window. The victim would sit on the roadside cursing and waiting for his enemy. He never bore a grudge against the waiter or the Legionnaire, however much he may have hurt himself falling. He knew that it was forbidden to wield a knife in the café and that if they threw him out they had a good right to do so.

The bus from Zagora arrived just before sunset, when the yellowish-pink light set the whole market-place ablaze. Seventy or eighty people were crowded into the small vehicle built to hold twenty-five. The children, carried on their mothers' backs like rucksacks, hung out of the windows. Thirty to thirty-five people sat on top of the bus in the baggage-rack. The bus stopped with a jolt. The passengers who had travelled on the top with their glowing charcoal burners jumped down, but no one from the inside got out. Arms, legs and waists formed a star-shaped hurdle in the narrow door. Finally, someone was catapulted out like a stone from the crater of an erupting volcano, then after a while another, then at last the bus seemed to vomit them out in a single stream until its belly was empty. Meanwhile wooden cases and pieces of luggage were thrown out of the windows. At times a basket would fly open to disgorge a cobra that wound itself around the still warm wheels of the bus or slithered across the square to disappear among the piles of oranges.

My deepest joy, however, was the evening. I sat in the open window of the café, directly by the street. The drums and the flutes of the snake-charmers had fallen silent and the night was alive with the monotonous voice of the story-tellers and the whisperings of the procurers. At times a hoarse-voiced boy or a veiled woman would call to me from the street to come to bed with them; opposite, from above the white stone wall the bluish branches of the magnolia trees would wave to me, sending out swarms of fire-flies like a procession of mute orphans carrying candles.

One afternoon we were invited to tea by our fellow-countryman, the former Legionnaire, now station-master in Marrakesh. He lived at the other end of town, in the European district. It was the last day of Ramadan. Valy, Bandi and I came back to the Djema el-Fnaa by bus. The market-place showed a picture entirely different from what we were used to. At this time of the day, just before sunset, people were usually sitting on the ground with fruit and bread on a mat before them, watching the sun and waiting for its disappearance so that they might begin to eat. Now, however, they were standing around in groups in the corners of the square, talking excitedly. Here and there a fez was thrown high into the air.

As we passed the Café Universel I noticed that there was a big, jagged hole in one of the windows as if someone had been thrown out through the pane. This was out of harmony with the café's tradition and also with the character of Ahmed the waiter. Advancing along the narrow street between the town wall and the row of shops I was beginning to feel anxious. Suddenly we heard pistol shots from around the next corner where the street broadened out a little.

The scene we witnessed when we got there was completely incomprehensible. A lieutenant of the Foreign Legion was standing in the middle of the road, with a revolver in his hand hanging dejectedly by his side; and before him in the dust lay three little Arab boys whom he had shot. For a moment I believed that the lieutenant had run amok, but I soon saw that he was not the attacker but the attacked. He was surrounded by some twenty boys, the same ragged little boys in their striped djellabas who were always crawling around our feet at the café, playing their tiny musical instruments or pulling the tails of the donkeys in the street. But now they had bricks and stones in their hands and were throwing them at the lieutenant, whose face and chest were covered in blood.

The shot we heard had been his last. There were no more bullets in his revolver. We were about ten feet from him when a brick hit him on the nape of his neck. He fell and in a second the children were upon him like a cloud of locusts. We walked on, in the narrow, dark space between the lieutenant's body and the town wall.

Because the walls were a continuation of the cliff on which the town stood, there was nothing to be seen through the holes in the wall but the vibrating blue of the sky. Suddenly I felt as if this blueness were already that of the Beyond. The children were kneeling on the lieutenant's chest, beating his head with bricks and with his own revolver until his skull cracked open and blood and brains bespattered the children's faces and the dust. They paid no attention to us.

A few yards further on a bicycle was lying in the road and beside it, a dead man: the son of the French store-keeper from whom we bought our soda water. We were in the very centre of a pogrom. The doors of the houses were locked, heavy shutters protected the shops and the Tribunal was still about five hundred yards away. It seemed certain that in a few minutes the children would have finished with the lieutenant and come after us in pursuit.

'What a miserable way to die after all our vicissitudes,' Valy sighed.

'Let us die with dignity,' I suggested. We walked on in the narrow alleyway with Valy between us. Had we begun to run we should certainly have attracted the attention of the children. Besides, who knew what was awaiting us around the next corner?

After a couple of seconds we heard the patter of the children's bare feet behind us.

'Don't look back,' I warned Bandi.

A shower of stones hit the dust around us. Then I was hit on the shoulder and Bandi probably between his shoulder-blades, because he tottered, his back sagged and he looked back towards the children.

'This is the end,' I thought.

Then suddenly I heard a little boy's voice shout in Arabic.

'They are English, not European! Leave them alone!'

Another brick fell at my feet. I stepped over it and glanced at Bandi, who had turned back again, gave the children a devilish, triumphant grin, showing his protruding gums, then, with a slight, arrogant flick of his wrist, shooed them away.

We covered the remaining four hundred yards in about two and a half minutes. Perspiration was running from my forehead into my eyes and at every step I felt as if only a frayed thread were still attaching my leg to my knee. At the gate of the Tribunal I turned to Bandi to thank him for saving our lives. He only laughed and pointed to his freckled face and red hair.

The heavy iron door was flung wide open at our approach: the huge Negro, Bentoto, got hold of Bandi with one hand, of me with the other, lifted us into the air and began to dance with joy. He told us that the anti-European pogrom had been started by Italian fascist agents. They took advantage of the discontent caused by a shortage of petrol and sugar, and of the excitability induced by the long fasting, and they harped on the fact that the Arab soldiers had not returned from Europe while the French had.

We climbed up on the roof where a fire had been laid under a huge cauldron of already boiling oil to be used, should the necessity arise, against the attackers. However, the Tribunal seemed safe, the children reappeared in the square a few times, once pursuing a young Italian who was freed from their hands by two elderly Arabs. Later a few older lads approached the building with burning torches in their hands but at the same moment a detachment of Legionnaires reached the square from the other side. The soldiers pursued the fleeing boys, caught a few, lifted them in the air by their feet and crushed their heads against the wall.

The next day we learned that six of the originators of the murders had been arrested and hanged the night before. These events convinced Bandi that it was indeed impossible to live among the Arabs, and he decided never again to leave the building of the Tribunal. A few days later I applied mild pressure to make him accompany me to the Café Universel where the former idyllic atmosphere was fully restored. The fat white-slaver who, on our first day here, had tried to buy Valy from me and was deeply offended that I wouldn't bargain, was back again in his corner doing business in whispers. The professor of the Arab Lyceum played chess with me. I beat him twice in succession, at which he ran out of the café across to the brothel for solace and when he returned we discussed Arab literature. The little boys who had missed, by a hair's breadth, turning me into the only poet in the history of literature to be stoned to death, crawled around my feet playing their tiny instruments and offering me crickets for sale while I was writing a poem.

A few days later our financial situation took an unexpected turn. Ujvary sent us a considerable sum of money and on the same day my good friend, Emil Szalai, copyright lawyer in Budapest, transferred my royalties to a Marrakesh bank in dollars. This was quite an achievement as I was an exile deprived of Hungarian citizenship and the Hungarian National Bank had never in its history granted hard currency to any Hungarian abroad. Although the sum itself was not large, in Marrakesh, where the dollar fetched five times its official rate, it made us suddenly rich. The monthly rent of a palace was somewhere between eight and twelve dollars. I commissioned a filthy little boy called Mohammed to find us a palace, saying that nine dollars was the highest rent I was ready to pay.

A few hours later we stood in the marble-floored patio of a large house in the short Derb Toubib alley, under hand-carved cedar-wood beams. At our feet a fountain, carved in porphyry, spurted a jet twenty yards high above our heads. We looked at each other. Our shoes had hardly any soles left, our trousers were patched, but at the thought that the same evening we would move into this ten-roomed palace and spend the night in canopied beds among heavy Persian carpets, we broke into peals of laughter, the echo of which circled round and round under the arcade supported by slender pillars.

The following day we employed an Arab maid called Aicha. Although our schedule changed but little and we acquired only the most necessary pieces of clothing, as if by magic the framework of a fairy world grew up around us. As the servant insisted on her right to give the master of the house his daily bath, I donned, on the first morning, a pair of black swimming trunks before stepping into the basin. When I climbed out and, on the highest step, waited for Aicha to throw the bathrobe on my shoulders, I became aware of loud sobs behind my back.

'Oh, my master, my poor master, most miserable among men, woe to you and woe to your unborn sons!' she wailed. Then she continued more calmly: 'I have never yet served a eunuch. At Agadir I worked for a very fine gentleman for five years. He covered his empty eye-socket with a black cloth. But no one has ever told me that the nobility are wont to cover their empty purse and cut-off genitals with black cloth. The colour black – I hope I am not offending you, Master, for asking – it is with you, Europeans, the colour of mourning, isn't it?'

I peeled off my trunks. The good soul began to clap and dance with joy, begging the Prophet to bless my grandsons, then rubbed me down thoroughly with the towel. When she reached the lowest part of my back she exclaimed:

'You are beautiful, Master, like the moon on the fourteenth day!'

Thereafter, she repeated the same exclamation every morning when reaching the above-mentioned part of my body. But all this was done with childish awe, without banter or any ulterior motive.

Each morning my mail was laid out for me in my stuccoed room with its coloured glass windows. A few days after we moved into our palace we received an invitation to dinner from the pasha, Ibn Glaoui, solemnly worded and written in green ink. He offered us a forty-nine-course dinner and afterwards the pasha took me by the arm and led me into the garden where rose-trees planted by the pasha's grandfather in the skulls of his enemies bordered the path. The teeth were still grinning among the roots, which had pushed their way through the bone. Some bore the names of their owners painted in green on the forehead.

Two weeks later two large, stiff envelopes lay on the marble table addressed to Bandi and to me. The paper on which the letters were written was shiny and uncreased: Franklin D. Roosevelt did us the honour to invite us to America where – he said – we could continue our valuable work in peace and security until the end of the war. Although the letter had been preceded by a cable from Cordell Hull, the whole thing seemed like a miracle. Yet, in spite of the pleasure the invitation gave me I was suddenly filled with uncertainty. Should I leave this country, which I had learned to love, to live in New York?

I was sitting there wondering when suddenly I was distracted by a light knock on the front door. Three Sudanese were standing outside in the street.

These so-called Sudanese who roam across Morocco are not Sudanese at all but the members of the Negro tribe who speak Tuareg. They are usually well-built, tall men who differ from other Negroes in that, though their faces are black, their features are Indo-European or, to be more exact, classical Greek in character. These three had beautiful straight noses, narrow lips and high, domed foreheads like the statue of Olympic Zeus.

They were identical not only in their dignified posture but also in their features. Probably brothers, I thought. The eldest was somewhat taller than the other two, the second was a little portlier than his brothers. Judged with European eyes, the eldest must have been at least seventy years of age, the youngest sixty-five, from which I deduced that in reality the oldest was around fifty-five and the youngest perhaps fifty.

Behind them stood a donkey. According to Moroccan custom they had tied the reins to the animal's feet, as a result of which its head and fetlocks were almost touching. It waited patiently in this humiliating posture.

'Peace be with you, illustrious Master,' they said in chorus, crossing their arms over their chests and bowing deeply.

'Peace be with you,' I replied. Then after some hesitation, I added, 'Please, enter.'

I had heard a great deal about these Sudanese. The most flattering of the stories circulating about them was that they would stab even their closest friends in the back; that they spread lice, the plague and syphilis; that their main occupation was the robbing of graves and highway hold-ups; that they began their love-life at the dawn of puberty with their mothers, continued it on the eve of their wedding with a he-goat, and concluded it on their death-beds with their male grandchildren.

I conducted my guests into the reception room. Aicha brought tea in tall glasses and an unbroken sugar-loaf with a small copper hammer. Then she went out in the patio and sat on the threshold to keep watch on the company.

The Sudanese sat enthroned on cushions with their legs crossed under them. They spoke with dignified gestures, in well-chosen words and with great circumspection. They began by inquiring about my health, that of my father, brothers, uncles, nephews, sons and all male relatives, then continued with my stallions, rams, billy-goats and cocks. When I replied that I kept no animals they exchanged sly glances.

After this introduction they turned our conversation to war.

'The Europeans,' the oldest among them said, 'are killing each other on the borders of Egypt. The desert sand covers their bones like camel dung. But our caravans come and go for ever.'

'Nothing is further from our thoughts than to offend your,' the squat one interposed. 'We know you are a follower of the Nazarene. But we have never before heard of a *nasrani* as illustrious as you are.'

'Until today,' the youngest said, 'we would have no more entered the house of an unbeliever than we would have entered a pigsty. With you we have made an exception.'

'To what do I owe this honour?' I asked them curiously.

'The Europeans live only to cheat and rob. This is why their merchants, excise-men, officials and Legionnaires come to Morocco. The Europeans are filthy, greedy worms. But you, you keep your eyes on more exalted things. And we know why. Because you have more money than you know what to do with.'

This made me smile.

'Each morning,' the oldest took the word, 'you proceed to the café. You carry a book under your arm. Because without books you cannot live. At the café you play a game of chess with the professor of the Lyceum. Then you read your book. You turn the pages like a whirlwind. Then you walk home along the hot, dusty, sun-drained road. After lunch you return to the café. You are a very fortunate man indeed that you have never slipped on a banana or orange skin and broken your neck. At the café you sit at a table writing and writing on large sheets of paper. What you write we do not know.'

'Perhaps a prayer-book for the unbelievers,' the youngest suggested.

'Or letters to your boy-lover,' guessed the second.

'At dinner time you walk home again. You advance along the Riad Zitoun Djedide where at times dishwater is thrown at you. You turn into the Derb Toubib where sheep-guts rot in the roadway. Rutting dogs joggle before your feet. After dinner, in the sooty darkness you work your way back to the café again. Harlots and male whores rub themselves against your thighs. When you return home at night they reach out for you from windows and doorways. A man like you should protect his dignity . . .'

'I can see you are thoroughly familiar with my way of life,' I replied. 'But now that we have come so far, would you betray the purpose of your visit?'

They exchanged smiles and kept their eyes above my head as if they had not heard my question.

'Six times each day you walk across the market square, along the main street and through the alleys. You walk between careless cyclists, in filth and refuse. Beggars pull at your sleeves, lousy camel-drivers touch you with their clothes. You must jump across opium-eaters and harlots writhing on the ground. A man like you must never walk on foot.'

'Particularly not at your age.'

'And with a dignified exterior like yours.'

It occurred to me that I must have grown a paunch in the bathtub or suddenly gone grey. A glance into the large mirror on the wall, however, reassured me. These three could easily be my grandfathers. Or even my great-grandfathers, considering how young they are when they start.

'You could do nothing wiser than to buy a donkey. Then you could enter the Café Universel three times a day the way the son of Miriam entered the town of Jerusalem.'

He must have meditated a great deal before hitting on this analogy because he looked at me triumphantly, watching for the effect. Then he continued:

'We want to help you. Therefore, we brought you a donkey. A she-ass. It pains us a great deal to part with her because she is the comfort of our old days. But for your sake we should be ready to sacrifice her. We offer her to you for a pittance: three thousand three hundred francs.'

I made an evasive gesture.

'The she-ass,' the squat brother took the word, 'lives on air and orange peels. Your servant can rub her down in the evening. But she will do even without the rubbing. Her skin is rough and tempered like shoe-leather. You can kick her and she won't feel it. Three thousand two hundred and fifty.'

'The café,' I said, 'is but a five-minute walk from here. I like to walk. I do not require a donkey.'

'This donkey,' the youngest explained, 'inherited modesty from her father and obedience from her mother. You climb on her back, dangle your feet down her rump, turn back and whisper in her ear: "Rrr-zid!" and she will fly like an eagle above the peaks of Atlas. Show her the way to the café but once and she will always find her way there and back, even in the darkness. Even if you fall asleep on her back. Even if an earthquake were to wipe out all the streets of Marrakesh . . . from which Allah protect us all. Three thousand and two hundred.'

'But I do not . . .'

'If, after eighty years are past and you lie on your death-bed,' the old man spoke with unshaken calm, 'remembering bygone days, you will recall this donkey. And then you will sit up on your death-bed and praise our memories. You will bless us, Sudanese merchants long ago turned to dust, for having given you this blessed donkey with the soul of a dove. Three thousand one hundred and fifty.'

'Dear friends,' I said, 'I have no intention whatsoever of buying this donkey. I shall not be here much longer.'

'No matter. The freight train will take her to Casablanca for one hundred francs. But if you hire a driver, he will drive her after you for fifty. We shall deduct it from the price. Three thousand one hundred.'

'But in Casablanca I shall board a ship. Passenger ships do not carry donkeys.'

'Speak with the captain. Every captain is open to suggestions. Three thousand and fifty.'

'But I am going to America where people ride in automobiles. There are no donkeys, camels, or horses there. What am I to do with a donkey in America?'

My guests whispered to each other in Tuareg and threw me insolent looks.

'Master,' the oldest said at last, 'you are wilfully trying to swindle us. The Americans use horses and donkeys for travelling. They no more ride automobiles than the inhabitants of the desert. The Americans live like mountain bandits on Atlas.'

'You are mistaken,' I said.

The old man shook his head.

'I am not mistaken. Three days ago we saw American actors in Uarzazate. That is how we know.'

'American actors on top of Atlas? Now? Impossible!'

'They jumped about on a white sheet like ghosts. There we saw that the Americans go to market on horseback, steal their brides on horseback and tie their horses to the fence before the house, as we do. After all, even Americans are human beings! Though they kill one another with great cruelty. Here in Marrakesh, for instance, stand fifty times one thousand houses yet yesterday, for instance, only three men were stabbed to death. There on the sheet in that American town there were perhaps fifty houses but some nineteen men were shot dead within two hours. I shall let you have this donkey for three thousand. I swear to you, only out of compassion because you have to go to America.'

'Listen to me,' I said seriously. 'I am going to a town called New York. That town is so large that there stand one thousand times one thousand houses if not more. What am I to do in so large a town with a donkey?'

'Tie her to the iron ring at your front door. Two thousand nine hundred and fifty.'

After a good hour, when we had finished our third glass of mint tea and had reached the figure of one thousand eight hundred, the oldest Sudanese turned to me.

'Tell me, Master, is it truly not your intention to buy the donkey?'

'Truly.'

'Do you swear?'

'I swear.'

'You are not making a fool of me in order to lower the price? Let me make a last experiment. I shall let you have her for one thousand five hundred, but only because you are so beautiful. Do you want her?'

'I don't.'

'I was afraid you might say yes. And if I offered her for one thousand four hundred?'

'I should still not want her.'

'The sun is standing high. We have lost the whole morning.'

He meditated for a while then turned back to me.

'You have offered us three glasses of tea. Politeness forbids us to accept a fourth glass. Allow me, therefore, to invite you this time. The bargaining was delightful. But it is not to bargain but to converse that we should like to invite you. Do not offend us with your disdain, ragged, miserable Sudanese merchants that we are, but accept our invitation.'

Aicha threw me a disapproving look as we made ready to go. At the front door I learned that the donkey's name was Zuleika. She trotted rapidly in front of us until we reached the main street of the Arab sector, the Riad Zitoun Djedide.

This main street bore little resemblance to the Champs-Élysées: it was at the most, three metres wide, in places only two and where broken by an archway, even less. A stream of sewage trickled along the runnel in its centre, with rotting fruit and vegetables on its two banks. I liked this street with its harlots reclining in the shady doorways, stretching their legs into the street, with its cyclists, riding at the speed of automobiles in novels depicting the coming century, with its open classrooms where little boys squatted on mats while a beturbaned teacher, holding a long cane, was writing beautiful, involved characters on the blackboard.

A caravan of about thirty camels was advancing towards us from the opposite direction. To make place for it – for each camel was carrying four bathtubs attached to its sides and thus took up the whole width of the street – we wanted to draw back into a doorway, when Zuleika suddenly decided to lie down across the street, barring the caravan's advance. It must have been that the monstrous sight filled her with indignation; that these ships of the desert which once brought silk from China along the Tarim and the African shore all the way up to Cordoba, silk of as many colours and patterns as there were bales, Damascus swords from Syria, each sword with a different hilt, should now be carrying bathtubs, all painted a nauseating grass-green and proclaiming that the days of lazy rests, long, friendly conversations, amusements of a social or erotic nature above and under the water in the ponds of the oases, the trenches before the town gates and the darkness of the Turkish baths were over: that the joyless days of solitary bathing had come and technical civilization – with all its beauties – was taking the place of culture.

At first my Sudanese companions encouraged their little donkey with mild words to rise, finally they showed her the cane and kicked her with their slippered feet. Thereupon Zuleika turned on her back and raised her four legs into the air. Traffic came to a complete stop, the camel-drivers and water-carriers cursed, the carters blew their horns, women coming home from the market loaded with merchandise screamed and the children jumped up and down with glee. The Sudanese gave their donkey a good beating but when she still refused to move, they lifted her with the help of a few strong camel-drivers, turned her around in the air, put her down on her four hooves and gave her a tremendous kick in the rump. Thereupon, as if nothing had happened, the donkey with the soul of a dove danced happily on.

The tea-room in the market square consisted of a single room; instead of a wall it was separated from the pavement by a raised threshold. Opposite stood the tents of the barbers with the clients sitting outside in the warm sunshine. As a result of the British blockade, soap had completely disappeared, the clients were shaved in their own perspiration. Whenever someone was cut we heard the sharp sound of a slap. Sitting with her back to the raised threshold of the café was a little girl of about eight or nine with her face veiled.

The waiter brought us our mint tea. I expected my Sudanese friends to start the conversation but they remained silent. The oldest, who, as I learned, bore the name of Ben Jusef, reached for his glass. But before touching it he pointed with his finger at the little girl sitting against the threshold.

'My daughter,' he said with awe. He fell silent for a moment to give me time to look at her. 'She must be ten or eleven. She was born the year when Abd el-Krim was captured.'

'That happened at least twelve years ago,' the squat one said. 'She is twelve. A mature virgin.'

'A beautiful virgin,' I replied politely but indifferently.

'Only her body is virgin,' Ben Jusef explained, 'her soul is not. Her mother has taught her the art of love to spare her future husband annoyance. It occurred to me recently that I might sell her to Glaoui, the pasha. But Glaoui already has three hundred wives and besides, he is seventy years old. I felt sorry for the girl and did not sell her to the pasha.'

'You were right,' the second brother said. 'Allah will reward you richly for your kindness of heart.'

'But I should be happy to sell her to you for thirty sheep,' Ben Jusef turned to me. 'Marry my little girl. I have always wanted a son-in-law like you.'

'You must know that . . .'

'Take her for twenty-five sheep. I would do anything for you.'

'You are wasting your time, I . . .'

'Should you find on the wedding night that she is no longer a virgin I shall return your twenty-five sheep and, as a consolation price, you shall have two additional ones.'

'You know very well that I am a married man and that the laws of my religion prohibit plural marriages.'

'Yes, I had thought of that,' Ben Jusef replied cheerfully. 'I know of a Cadi in the Arab sector who will give you a marriage certificate in secret. I shall keep it for you to save you trouble . . .'

'Now listen to me, old man. I already have a wife. Only one, that is true. But even one is more than I require.'

'Is that so? Then take my daughter as your concubine. For ten sheep. When you go to America you can send her back to me.'

'No, my friend, I don't want your daughter. Neither for a wife, nor for a concubine. And I want no girl, no woman, no harlot, neither for twenty sheep nor for two, not even as a gift. I don't want them, I don't, I don't.'

'I have suspected this for a long time,' the squat Sudanese smiled triumphantly. 'I knew that your taste is more delicate, more discriminating than that of my brother Ben Jusef who has pursued women all his life. Forgive him for it: he is a man of low tastes. He does not know what real pleasure means. Look at that long-legged boy in the square. Do you know which I mean?'

A tall, slender boy with his head shaved was crouching before a barber's tent. In his left ear hung a thick gold ring.

'I can see him,' I sighed, 'and of course he is your son and a virgin . . .'

'Not my son,' the squat Negro replied with feeling, 'but my boy-lover. Whenever someone looks at him I reach for my dagger. But I should lend him to you. Speak to Mustapha, the barber, and he will let you have his tent. You shall enjoy a delight so extraordinary that you will believe you are listening to the music of angels. Let me reveal to you that this boy has a certain part of his body so big that compared to it all the rest of his body seems but negligible appendage. And as far as . . .'

'There is no limit to your depravity, you Sudanese merchants,' I exclaimed loudly. 'You enticed me here with a low trick: you promised to tell me stories, and instead you are offering me dirty and dirtier bargains. Your minds are empty of thought not connected with lewdness and filth. But your villainy carries its own punishment. I sit at the café day after day to invent stories. Well, today's story will not have to be invented. I shall write about you and let the whole world know of your baseness. People will read about you even after the earth has caved in on your graves and scarlet weed will grow from your bones like burning torches.'

I looked from one to the other. They sat motionless, their backs straight, but they had drawn in their chins and huge tears ran down their shiny black faces.

'And Allah will have no mercy on you,' I continued. 'You know that the Koran condemns not even fornication with animals as severely as . . .'

'No, Allah be praised,' the youngest sniffled.

'. . . as an offence against guest-friendship. When the Prophet takes hold of you by your white beards to lift you into heaven, and looks into your eyes, he will fling you from him like rotten oranges. And do you know where he will throw you?'

'We know,' they replied in chorus, nodding their heads.

'But we can still atone for our sin,' Ben Jusef looked at me entreatingly. 'And we shall. Here and now. If you will listen, Master, I shall begin my first story. Shall I?'

'Do,' I agreed generously.

'At the time when the protector of the faithful was still Haroun al-Rashid Ibn Muhammed al-Mahdi – Allah bless his memory – there lived in Baghdad a poor dervish called Kamal . . .'

The squat brother told a second story, the youngest a third. Then it was my turn. When each of us had told his fourth story, the guests of the tea-house drew closer and even the boy with the gold ear-ring came in from the market square. He radiated a strong but not disagreeable perfume of roses.

Towards sunset I ran out of stories and began to tell them Hungarian folk-tales. By then sixty or seventy listeners had crowded around us. The audience sat silently, only when something seemed funny to them did they break into loud, unrestrained laughter. Behind them the pancake-maker made the rounds again and again and the waiter ran to and fro with new and new trays of tea.

I achieved my major success with a poem by the Hungarian poet, Janos Arany. The poem deals with two peasants who are neighbours. Both like to stand around in their garden listening to the song of a nightingale. The nightingale was wont to perch on the branch of a tree which stood in the garden of one of the peasants, but the branch itself extended over the fence into the other's garden. The two peasants quarrel about which of them the nightingale sings for, one says it perches on his tree, the other says that it is breathing his air. They agree to let the magistrate decide, but to be sure to win, both bribe the magistrate, who puts one peasant's gold in his right pocket, the other peasant's gold in his left. When the two peasants appear to hear the verdict, the magistrate slaps his right pocket and exclaims: 'It sings for me!' – then he slaps his left pocket and exclaims again: 'It sings for me!' – then he sends the peasants on their way.

'Ha – ha – ha!' Ben Jusef laughed, 'I met a Cadi in Timbuktu who was exactly like yours!'

'His name is Fadl,' someone in the audience cried. 'When I was in Timbuktu I met the scoundrel too!'

After nightfall our audience increased rapidly. There were perhaps a hundred people in the small café, not to speak of the crowds assembling in the square.

After midnight Bandi and Valy broke through to me.

'We have searched the whole town for you,' Bandi shouted. 'We have just come from the police because we believed you had been murdered. There we were told that you were staging a performance of *The Arabian Nights* in the market square.'

I resigned myself to my fate and rose. Ben Jusef followed me into the dark square.

'Just a word,' he begged, 'alone with you.'

'Now?' I asked suspiciously.

'You said you would put us in a story and deliver us to the contempt of the whole world to the day scarlet weed grew from our bones. I followed you to entreat you not to do this to us.'

'I cannot promise not to write about you at all, but when I do, I shall do it in a way that people may remember you without malice.'

'Which means that you will lie,' Ben Jusef stated with a radiant smile.

'No, I shall not lie.'

'Then how will you do it?'

'That is my business,' I replied haughtily as befits a young man living in a palace and writing about the affairs of men and gods.

PART THREE

The USA and the People's Democracy

I arrived in New York harbour on a sunny but already slightly misty afternoon in September, 1941. I had travelled on the *Navemar*, a rickety old Spanish freighter, with a thousand other refugees, and although we followed the route of the *Santa Maria*, from the jewel-box houses of Cadiz to the flat shores of the Bahamas, our journey took considerably longer than that of Christopher Columbus. The captain of our ship had to face many difficulties that the great Genoese, with his abundant but wholly retrospective imagination, could never have conceived. In addition to fighting the fury of the Atlantic and of his mutinous crew (most of them ran away in Havana), he was compelled by the RAF to steer his miserable ship into the most beautiful harbour of Bermuda, there to submit to a very thorough search and investigation. The *Navemar*'s slow progress was also held up several times by German submarines, far more dangerous than any sea monster of sailors' legends. The cunning Spaniard, however, by signals or by shouting in broken English while shaking his starched cuffs like a rattlesnake in his interlocutor's face, had always been able to convince him that it was for his side, and for his side alone, that the *Navemar* smuggled important war materials out of the United States. Neither side trusted him, but somehow they always let him go. It is probable that the captain smuggled for both, for this, in his opinion, was the most profitable and safe way to run the business. He was mistaken. On her way back from New York the *Navemar*, with her contraband, her new crew, her old captain, but no passengers, was overtaken by Fate.

Nobody knew exactly when we would arrive, so Dr Hollos, a member of the Hungarian Committee – a huge, walrus-moustached physician from New York, no longer young – had set up his headquarters in one of the taverns on the harbour. Although he had spent most of his life in America and had fully identified himself with the constitution, laws and customs of his adoptive fatherland, he completely ignored the existence of a hundred and thirty million Americans. He lived among Hungarians, his friends were Hungarians and he would accept no patient unless he were Hungarian. And even among Hungarians he was interested only in newcomers, in genuine and authentic Hungarians, who had brought with them all the quarrels and strife of their homeland, who had not yet rid themselves of their provincialism and who preserved, both figuratively and literally, the filth of Europe that he himself, in his dynamic Americanism, so deeply despised. Old Americans, like himself, bored him stiff and therefore he avoided them. The flat of this noble, selfless and hospitable old doctor served as a transit camp for every better-known Hungarian refugee, where he could rest until Dr Hollos considered him sufficiently prepared for the American way of life.

One of Laszlo Fényes's letters, filled with wry humour, had prepared me while still in Tangier for the fate awaiting me in New York. Dr Hollos was a great admirer, though perhaps not a connoisseur, of the arts, and even more of artists whose value to him increased a thousandfold as soon as he met them personally. Fényes had informed me that the doctor allowed newcomers very little rest and advised them to jump immediately into the American melting-pot. He would take them up into the torch of the Statue of Liberty, or on to the roof of the Empire State Building, and explain to them that their erudition or their skill was worthless here because the Americans knew everything better. Then he would comfort them by saying that the necessary knowledge could be acquired almost within minutes and without any effort whatsoever. After this he would conduct the victim into his surgery and inject him with an anti-tubercular vaccine invented by himself, which would plunge the cowardly hypochondriac who had rolled up his sleeve instead of extricating himself with a manly 'No', into two months of unspeakable torment, a terrible itching of his entire body.

The treatment would be followed by a dinner served by Mrs

Hollos: roast pork with a sweet gravy of sultanas, Coca-Cola and coffee boiled for at least half an hour until the last vestige of aroma was distilled into the walls of the kitchen. At dinner Dr Hollos would enlighten his guest concerning the Bill of Rights. Later, before leaving him to his own resources, he would help his protégé to find a flat, a job, and often a car, provided the hysterical anxiety and fear of America instilled into the newcomer by his protector had not, in the meantime, driven him to suicide – an event which had occurred twice before my arrival. Fényes declared that Hollos was the very embodiment of the rich American uncle, perhaps even Uncle Sam in person, for whom only two alternatives existed: either the newcomer learned to appreciate the materialistic happiness of the New World, or he did not deserve to remain alive.

When the *Navemar* dropped anchor in New York harbour I immediately recognized the old gentleman. As I rested my chin on the high railing in the bows of the ship I could see him standing just below me on the edge of the wharf, wearing a black morning coat, and holding a few typewritten quarto sheets in his hand. The sight was rather moving though I felt laughter prickling my throat. Next to Hollos stood, or rather fidgeted, a bow-legged, puny, salesman-type young man who I thought must be his secretary. Later I learned that Hollos had brought him along as representative of the working class, but treated him so condescendingly that the young man took offence and left. I called down to Hollos, who raised his palm to his forehead and peered up with a bright smile on his lips. When he caught sight of me, the smile froze, though Valy's beauty seemed to enthral him. He found me younger than he had expected and must have been afraid that in my youthful arrogance I would detract from the solemnity of the occasion. I concluded this from the fact that he kept shouting up to me, obviously without conviction but, it seemed, to encourage himself: 'I have always said genius is genius, no matter how old or how young!' Finally, he took up his post at the bottom of the gangway, put his spectacles on his nose and, grasping the typewritten sheets in both hands, made ready to begin his speech. When we were informed that I was not permitted to land but would be taken to Ellis Island, Hollos asked me whether he shouldn't deliver his speech anyway, while I was still at hand. 'Go ahead!' I shouted down to him. He raised his head, spread his arms wide, and began to speak in a beautiful, ringing voice. At the end of each paragraph, he pushed his glasses up on his forehead and looked to make sure I was still there. He must have heard a lot about me, because I think he was afraid I might crouch down behind the railing to laugh or to read the article about me in the *New York Post* that he had sent up by one of the sailors.

I did my best to behave. I had no intention of offending that decent fellow. Only when he was turning the pages of his manuscript did I sneak a glance at the opposite shore of which I didn't know whether it was Brooklyn or Staten Island, or at the luminous green valleys and dirty-yellow crests of the water on which low, squat tugs, furiously fast toy steamers and ferries were running back and forth carrying crowds of colourful people who kept shouting and waving to each other for no reason that I could see, since they had probably never met before and would never meet again. I found all this childish, amusing, but at the same time somehow moving, like a charity bazaar, and also a little obsolete; a nineteenth-century picture or even older, in sharp contrast with the modern – almost notoriously modern – sky-line of the city. I had the same impression of the men sitting on the edge of the wharf in their scarlet or pink braces and unbelievably colourful shirts, and of the other men running madly up and down in straw hats and stiff collars, with thick attaché cases under their arms as if they were hurrying to some meeting convened to settle the problems of the world once and for all.

After my calm and dignified Arabs these jerky, fidgeting, hurrying little figures reminded me of the early days of the film industry. Yet I discovered one likeness between Arabs and Americans: both are filled with the consciousness of their importance, but for the Arabs the importance lies in the thoughts preoccupying them or the subject of their conversation, while the Americans are moved, pushed, pulled, driven by the importance of their activities. To the right and left of Dr Hollos's morning coat I could look into the street through the two gates of the customs shed. I could see only the lower two-thirds of people's bodies, which created the impression of purposeful attaché cases flying back and forth on the long wings of trouser-legs. Listening to the kind old man, I sighed deeply, not because I was depressed but rather because this was exactly how I had pictured to myself my arrival in America.

The African euphoria, the picaresque life, was now over. My year of happiness in Morocco had fed on innumerable sources; the most important of which was that I had, at last, found my one and only, made-to-measure environment, the environment that fitted my character like a glove. This was true of the desert where, between the two concave lenses of heaven and earth, on a stage without scenery, I stood in the birthplace of dualist religions and was compelled to ponder at length, though without result, on the great questions of life and death, being and not being, good and evil – something I had always yearned for without having found the time for it amidst the duties, occupations and even pleasures of everyday life. But it was true also of the desert's opposite, the market-place of Marrakesh, the busy squares of Tangier, the tohu-bohu of the tea-houses after midnight where life was a medley of knifings, love-making, funerals, bargaining, quarrels, gossip, the strange exhibitionism of a world in which the beggars on the street corners conversed like philosophers and philosophers copulated in the streets like dogs. It was true of my Arab friends, first of all Amar but also of the robber prince Sidi Mohammed and the Sudanese merchants with the donkey, the storyteller in the market-place and the slipper-maker from whom, after hours of anecodotizing, I bought a pair of sandals. In all these I recognized myself, a more attractive, more uninhibited and more sincere incarnation of my being, reflections of myself – and this filled my intensely extroverted being with all the more happiness as at last, without the torment and discomfort of introversion, I encountered myself again and again, in a million shapes, in the scenery of the world outside, or in the actors and mutes wandering across the stage.

My pleasure in Morocco was enhanced to no little degree by the twofold discovery that I had escaped from the increasingly disciplined and unbearable workshop of technical civilization and, at the same time, rid myself of certain problems and dilemmas raised by my conscience. I had always borne everything without complaint although it had always pained me that I had landed – due to the place and time of my birth – in a technical civilization which not only determined my way of life but also limited my imagination, and which even censored and emasculated my thoughts and emotions. Ever since my early youth I had regretted – although I never talked about it lest I should be branded a reactionary or insane – that I had to live in a society in which I knew, long before undressing them, the colour, cut and price of every woman's underwear; in a society in which the lowest, the basic layers had discarded, or were in the process of discarding, their ancient culture and pleasures for the sake of the gas-oven, the sink, the bathtub and the monotonous drabness of industrial towns; where the progress of the food industry deprived foods of their taste and flavour; where mass-produced consumer goods were pushed down the throat of the consumer through the conditioning effect of advertising and the complete destruction of good taste, and where the walks and conversations of the Athenian philosophers and Faust, or even of two peasants of average intelligence, were replaced by the thoughtless tedium of automobile passengers stuck in the traffic of large towns. When listening to Hitler's or Stalin's speeches on the radio I wondered what would have happened to the Roman Empire had Nero's or Caracalla's nonsensical gabble been broadcast in the reading room of the great library of Alexandria or the market-place of Antioch

In Morocco, a few moments before the last, victorious onslaught of conquistador civilization, I had a glimpse of the world in which I should have liked to live. I could talk to artisans not yet compelled to spend their entire lives in the service of a machine and proud of never having carved the same pipe twice; I knew a world in which they were sorry for motor-car owners instead of envying them, because, at least symbolically, they had cut off their legs and thus left the world of the living, had wrapped themselves in a cloud of dust, isolating themselves from the titillating tempation of whores and lewd boys, the endless variations of chance encounters and conversations; where poems were recited by minstrels and where journalists were no more than the modest chroniclers of everyday events like authors of meteorological announcements and did not believe themselves to be lighthouses of history – and lighthouses which, moreover, guide ships in the wrong direction; where I met a more ancient, to me more familar form of story-telling which, instead of describing social reality or presenting flesh-and-bone people, was content to invent immortal fables.

My greatest joy, however, was that I was rid of all political and moral obligations. My upbringing, my timidity, but above all the extraordinarily disagreeable, yapping and pig-headed categorical imperative residing in my soul had unceasingly compelled me to fight against my instincts and the loud protests of my healthy egoism. Instead of just observing, pursuing my pleasures, writing poems or simply enjoying idleness, I was forced to serve certain humanitarian principles, to devote part of my time to the realization of a certain degree of social justice, and to struggle for democratic and patriotic aims. In Morocco I expended no zeal for my country, nor for the victory of the Allies, nor for any other cause, and in my state of helplessness I refused to make up for lack of action by listening devotedly to Western radio broadcasts or discussing politics at the café – my categorical imperative demanding either action or nothing. At last I could live the way I wanted: I observed the world, wrote poetry and spent my days in sweet idleness.

As I watched the flying attaché cases during Dr Hollos's address, in which, among other things, he enumerated the great political tasks awaiting me, I realized with deep melancholy that I had arrived not only in the Mecca of technical civilization, the Rome of the most efficient capitalism and the Babel of material prosperity, but also among friends, followers, compatriots and a political organization, into a predestined role, where the starved daemons of duty, political honour and ethics would throw themselves upon me like devils on the damned.

Five years later the thirty-thousand-ton luxury steamer that was to take me to Le Havre anchored in the very same harbour. The melancholy of my arrival was then replaced by a desperate anxiety, relieved only by a portion of untempered curiosity which I had not experienced at the moment of my arrival. Early in the morning I was taken to the harbour by about two dozen friends – among them Lorsy and his wife – in a solemn and depressed mood. They avoided talking to me and preferred joking with Valy. The whole thing reminded me of a funeral march, with everyone trying to give me the respect due to the corpse and speaking not to me, but about me. The tugboats, ferries and little steamers hurrying back and forth over the translucent green troughs and smoky yellow crests of the waves had, in the meantime, lost their strangeness; my shirt was as loud if not louder than those worn by the loiterers whom I had watched appalled five years before, and I knew not only the name of the Jersey shore opposite but also the cluster of towns behind it, and the cemetery on the marshy strip, near the shore, where we had buried Laszlo Fényes. All this, however, was only the skin of things, the thin layer on their surface, like the checked shirt on my body or the edge of the Hudson's estuary on America. Behind that thin layer I knew the entire continent, from the library at Harvard to the sandy beaches of Florida, or to wartime Detroit where, at night, freight trains loaded with tanks had rattled through the streets and where an aeroplane would rise in the direction of the Ford works as I lit my last cigarette after closing the Frigidaire, and the next one would rise as I stubbed it out; I knew the greyish-blue mud of the Big Snake River where in the sticky summer heat greyish-blue-bodied, slender Negro boys sunned themselves on the shore like alligators; I knew the beryl of the Green River, the blue of the Colorado, San Francisco's Golden Gate Bridge and, up north, Kodiak with its airfield covered with ice and steel netting, and Attu in the Aleutians where one's body and tommy-gun submerged in the light snow like a plummet in the waves of the sea. But it was not only the landscape I loved, with the enthusiasm and pathos of Walt Whitman, but also the people. I had drunk and revelled and travelled with them in cars, transcontinental railways, freighters, aeroplanes, jeeps and tanks; I had rejoiced and sorrowed with them, shared their fears and their boredom and had thrown musette-bags, beer-bottles and hand-grenades with them. I knew how they rose in the morning, I knew what they thought about before going to sleep, I even knew how they died.

Only when I was about to leave their country did I become conscious of how much I had become used to them, of how much I loved them, in spite of all my pretences, my objections and private opinions; of how much they meant to me with their chewing-gum, their drinking, their humour, and even their roast pork and sweet currant sauce, their undrinkable coffee, their historical amnesia and their conception of life as a race-track. I had to realize that my attachment to my own country was primarily a matter of language, since I could write poems only in Hungarian, but that I considered this people better, more honest and even in their simplicity more human than my own. I would gladly have remained among them if my remaining would not have broken my life in two. I felt as if I were leaving a party where the hosts were naïve but benevolent men who respected my intellectual capacities without, however, understanding them, who treated me with particular kindness and consideration and in whose company I would begin to be happier than ever now that the war was over and forgotten. And I was leaving it only to descend into an infernal cellar with dead bodies strewn over the floor, immured behind dripping walls; I was going among raving maniacs and bloodthirsty fanatics who tore, screamed, screeched, scratched at each others' purulent, never-healing wounds in deafening quarrels, the original reason for which everyone had long forgotten.

I felt that a funeral march was the best and most fitting description of the real situation; but subjectively I sensed only the approach of death. I was not like a sick man, concentrating his attention on his body and allowing his environment, the furniture around him, his friends and relatives to sink below the edge of his horizon; one who would have the trees under the window cut down, the flowers cut down, for why should they be there when he is gone? I felt more like a man condemned to death who looks around with absolute physical and mental alertness, to whom all the beauties of the world increase a thousandfold with the sparkling of the new stars, and who discovers new ties, new invisible tentacles binding him to hitherto unrecognized friends, to skyscrapers, to beefsteaks larger than the dish that holds them, to soldiers' graves, Coca-Cola automats, cheerful good-mornings, familiar newsvendors, striped socks, intellectual freedom and certain human rights – that is, to persons, objects, institutions, concepts, attitudes, situations and single English sentences alike.

In these circumstances it seemed a blessing that the ship should leave at three in the afternoon instead of at eleven o'clock, as scheduled. One of the men who came to see me off was Professor Rustem Vambéry, a slightly bent, bearded old gentleman with a face in which the features of a Greek sage, a wandering dervish and a naughty faun achieved perfect synthesis and about whom I cannot say that he hurried by my side with an alacrity belying his age, because alacrity was an inalienable attribute of his being and not only of his body. It was obvious that he belonged to that category of men who would immediately succumb to the absence or even decrease of physical and mental alertness, and thus it seemed natural to me that he would die of a heart-attack at an age reached by few – and to which he was getting perilously close – while squeezing himself into a subway carriage just as the doors began to close. Among ourselves we called him *delicium generis humani*, because his charm and wit were irresistible, although his wise courage, murderous humour and supremely idealistic and ethical actions – which were in flagrant and attractive contradiction with the cynicism of his way of thinking – reminded one rather of Marcus Aurelius. For ten years he had been my friend, mentor, admirer and even guardian angel, extending his long and invisible wings (invisible because he was always ashamed of sentiment) over me even while I was in Africa.

He had guessed, although I had never said anything about it in my letters, that I was planning to disappear in the desert. As a well-known expert on international law and a publicist, an adviser of the British government and a godson of Edward VII, he possessed contacts throughout the world, thus also among the Gaullists. It was he who arranged that President Roosevelt should invite me to America. When I received the invitation it was he who, from New York, persuaded the Gaullists in Morocco to send me to Tangier, and the Spanish-Moroccan authorities to expel me from Tangier and put me on a ship that would take me directly to New York. After my arrival there he and his friend Laszlo Fényes vied with each other with hardly concealed jealousy for a larger share in the role of foster-father. They never agreed, of course, because Vambéry's only ambition was that I should more or less follow his advice, and he minded not at all if I loved Fényes more; while Uncle Laszlo, on the other hand, alleged that if I followed Vambéry's political advice it would be equivalent to an emotional preference. When Fényes died before the fate of the war was decided and without having opened even one of the three bottles of wine which he had carried about for decades with the intention of celebrating Mussolini's, Hitler's and Horthy's fall, his role was taken over by Vambéry. When I learned from a letter forwarded to me by a member of the American mission in Budapest that my father had died immediately after the occupation of the town as a result of privations suffered during the siege and the lack of medicine, that my sister had been shot and thrown into the Danube three months before by the Hungarian Nazis, and that the majority of my friends had either been killed in the war, murdered by the Nazis or had disappeared in Soviet concentration camps, Vambéry assumed the role of my father readily, almost happily, though we never talked about it – never even gave a sign of this shared knowledge by so much as a tender word.

I persuaded my other friends to go home and not to wait until the ship sailed. Then Vambéry, Valy and I entered the smelly but popular sailors' pub where Hollos had once waited for me. When we sat down Vambéry's face reflected great inner joy – the kind of joy he always betrayed when speaking about his father, the famous Asian traveller who had spoken sixteen languages perfectly and who was the first European to visit Bokhara and Khiva on foot, disguised as a dervish, although he was lame. The professor still delighted in the beauty of women though he couldn't stand Valy, and was always shocked if women butted in when men talked, instead of simply looking after their needs. He devoted half an hour to softening up Valy, complimenting her, making her feel like a bewitched princess, in order to buy three hours of silence in which to talk to me in peace.

I made use of the time to order my thoughts and line up my arguments, or rather the premise and basis of my arguments: the five years in America. I had guessed rightly when I arrived here. The five years had gone by according to schedule, like a well organized political campaign. Soon after my arrival I had been elected secretary-general of the Free Hungary Movement and, at the same time, editor-in-chief of the movement's weekly, the *Harc* (Fight). As there were many exiled Hungarian politicians, journalists and scientists in America who were only too glad to work for us it was pretty easy to put out a good weekly. We could safely say that it produced itself almost without help, because the contributors in New York, Buenos Aires or Ottawa knew, without requiring instructions, exactly what to write, at what length and how. Only with Bandi Havas did I have difficulties from time to time. In the meantime he had gone to London where he became secretary to the head of the Free Hungary Movement, Count Michael Karolyi, the former President of the Hungarian Republic. The reason for our quarrels was the communist, or rather fellow-traveller, tone of his articles. Towards the end of the war we quarrelled for good because I refused to print his review of Koestler's *Darkness at Noon* which he described as an unfounded, unmitigated lie – in spite of the fact that he was very friendly with Koestler, adoring him and hating him, admiring him and wishing to destroy him at one and the same moment with all the fervour of his schizophrenic mind.

When, after Hungary's occupation by the Germans, the already radically censored Hungarian press was virtually liquidated, *Harc* remained the only worthwhile Hungarian paper in the whole world and thus, to a certain extent, it filled a historical role. Its circulation was pretty high but it was never a profitable enterprise. The contributors received no fees and neither did I. Every Thursday night the copies, fresh from the press, were brought to my flat, Valy wrapped and addressed them, and then I loaded the large packages on my shoulder and took them down to the huge mailbox which may still be there on the corner of 72nd Street and Broadway. Although I thought the weekly rather good, I found little pleasure in it. It gave me the same feeling that I experienced when talking to a meeting of American Hungarians, most of them over sixty, who did not bring their children because these no longer understood Hungarian and who, although they applauded my speeches, never handed on what they had heard but took it with them to their grave or crematorium. *Harc* never got into Hungary, neither its arguments nor its style ever entered the bloodstream of a people, as an inheritance for subsequent generations, but it withered like grain falling on rock. What bothered me most, however, was the fact that the paper, compelled by circumstances, was a political publication even though it discussed the social and historical events of the world on a very high level. I had, therefore, to realize that five years of my activity would figure only in a Hungarian history textbook dealing with the Second World War, or perhaps in a couple of paragraphs in my autobiography. It would not even get a line in the history of Hungarian literature.

At first I was rather reluctant to take part in the movement. I considered its leaders – Vambéry, Fényes and Karolyi – admirable idealists who were trying to make the allied governments accept and execute their untried political theories concerning Hungary. I persuaded myself that it was my duty to participate in such noble but unrealistic (and thus *a priori* condemned) schemes, but, to tell the truth, I was also greatly amused by the characters and ideas of the leading personalities present at the weekly meetings. A few months later, to my great surprise, I realized that I had been mistaken. The leaders of the movement, who had excellent diplomatic connections and enjoyed the support of the British and Free French governments, many outstanding American publicists and important dailies, as well as of Carlo Sforza, Jan Masaryk and others, planned not only to establish, after the war, a democratic Hungary on the Western pattern – which, we were certain, the Hungarian people would heartily approve – but to do this within the framework of a Danubian Confederation. The economic problems of Eastern Europe and the problems of the national minorities – my friends argued – could be solved only within the framework of such a confederation; only a federation of states with a population of seventy to a hundred million would be able to prevent the rebirth of German imperialism and the European advance of Soviet imperialism. The plan was supported by the former Czechoslovak Premier Milan Hodza and other leaders of the European emigration. Vambéry and his friends, it turned out, considered press-propaganda, the newspaper and our movement's meetings to be mere décor; far more important to them were the diplomatic negotiations prepared with great circumspection at which they tried, with weighty arguments, unbelievable patience and exemplary self-discipline, to convince the heads of the State Department of the correctness of their political views.

The heads of the State Department countered with various arguments based on a political realism that changed every month. Answers often depended on the room our friends happened to enter and the mood of the official occupying it. At first they tried to persuade us to collaborate with the emissaries of the feudal Horthy régime and the Hungarian Communists – a few almost illiterate Moscow agents – and when we refused, Under-Secretary Sumner Welles sent us a message that he would have us interned. We were saved from arrest only by the goodwill of Secretary of the Interior Ickes. A few months later they dropped Horthy's emissary like hot bricks and established at Camp Atterbury, in Indiana, a Habsburg Legion, the future of which was to serve as a guard of honour to the Emperor of the Habsburg Monarchy or the Holy Roman Empire; it was not yet decided which. When Otto Habsburg who, personally, is quite a nice fellow, arrived in America, the *New York Times* gave him a great deal of publicity and Roosevelt invited him to dinner. Quite naturally we were advised to toe the new line. When we replied that although we regarded the monarchists as a democratic political party, there was no denying the small number of its members, the antagonism of the Hungarians, the Roumanians, the Czechs, the Serbians and the Italians, the protest of the Czechoslovak and Polish governments in exile and the historical realities of the twentieth century, which factors led us to consider the restoration of the Holy Roman Empire, or even of the Habsburg monarchy, absolutely impossible, they looked upon us as upon raving lunatics. Another time they explained to us, very patiently, that our British and French connections were rather compromising, and argued, somewhat obscurely, that the Soviet Union was, in a way, democratic and Great Britain an imperialist power; or rather, that after the war America was going to democratize the Soviet Union with the help of a several-thousand-million-dollar loan and, hand in hand with a completely reformed Stalin, after putting an end to

England's role as a great power, would conduct the peoples of the world towards peace and prosperity.

For years I believed that Cordell Hull, Sumner Welles, A. A. Berle and the others were deliberately fooling us with these stories, so that they could go on elaborating their secret plans for the post-war period undisturbed. It was only after Roosevelt's death that it became obvious that it was he who inspired these naïve ideas, and that the members of the State Department had not deliberately been misleading us. They had been doing their best to serve the constantly fluctuating American line in foreign policy, to which only its hair-raising dilettantism gave a certain continuity. By the time we understood this the war was over, a democratic Hungarian Government had been formed, the Free Hungary Movement and its organ, *Harc*, had lost their purpose and I could at last return to a Hungary, the future of which was determined by the unpublished text of the Yalta agreement.

In addition to engaging in politics and editing the paper, I pursued a third profession in the United States. Immediately after Pearl Harbor I volunteered for military service. I was soon called up and was demobilized in 1945, at Fort Dix, without having performed any important feats of heroism. I always knew that my participation in the war would not decide its outcome and my reasons for volunteering were rather biographical than anything else. It would have been impossible that I, who regarded the struggle for democracy as a moral obligation, preached democratic principles in prose and verse, was a sworn enemy of Nazism and secretary-general of the Hungarian exile movement, should not take part in the defence of democracy and the liberation of my fatherland. I volunteered because I felt that it was up to me to represent my friends who were, without exception, twenty, thirty and forty years older than myself. I knew it would be more reasonable and infinitely wiser to remain in New York and write poems, but it was unthinkable that my biography should contain the sentence: 'During the Second World War, Faludy lived in New York and produced a few beautiful poems.' It would be bad enough even if my biographer refrained from adding: '. . . after he had so often and so enthusiastically encouraged others to risk their lives in the defence of liberty.'

I told my friends about my intention only after I had already signed up. I wanted to confront them with an accomplished fact and, at the same time, I was curious to hear their arguments. Laszlo Fényes remained silent but his eyes blazed with fury, particularly when he learned that any argument he would put forward against my joining up would come too late. Besides, there was nothing he could have said, because he too had always preached – and practised – that one must fight for one's convictions regardless of the risks involved. Vambéry, too, remained silent, but subsequently he did everything in his power to obtain a safe assignment for me. He tried first to have me transferred to the Office of Strategic Service and then to the Office of War Information. The first attempt foundered on my resistance, the second on that of a battalion commander who liked me a great deal. Only in the last year of the war did Vambéry succeed in having me recalled to New York, where I worked on military dictionaries in a department of the War Department and later in the editorial offices of the *Yank* newspaper. Freda Kirchwey, editor of the *Nation*, suggested that I volunteer as stretcher-bearer, in which case I would not have to bear arms, though the danger would be as great as if I served as an ordinary soldier. She was somewhat disappointed when I explained to her that I was no pacifist and that if I exposed myself to the risk of being shot at I should much rather be in a position to shoot back. Lorsy declared that a poet had but one single moral obligation: to run away from the shooting. Professor Oszkar Jaszi, whom, because of his beautiful, calm features that looked as if they were cut into pink marble, and his plain but frighteningly accurate logic we called, behind his back, the 'marble-headed ox', held that it was well worth dying for a great cause, Hungary's liberation or the unification of Europe. However, these would be accomplished only by the Third World War; the Second would do no more than liquidate one totalitarian power without solving the problems of either Hungary or Europe, so if I died in this war, my sacrifice would be just as senseless and useless as if I had been killed – as a volunteer, too – on a battlefield during the Spanish War of Succession, or the Seven Years War.

The opinion that affected me most was that of an extraordinarily erudite and sensitive old journalist friend of mine who was at the same time a woman-chaser and strategist, a man of the world and a scientist, a revolutionary and an aesthete: Pal Kéri. Had I asked him first, I am certain that I should never have volunteered. He explained that from a literary point of view – and let us here remember Thackeray, Tolstoy and Stendhal – only the Napoleonic Wars had proved fruitful. The First World War produced only reportage, and the Second, as I would see for myself, would produce not a single worthwhile work. Therefore, I had absolutely no business joining the American Army. Furthermore, there was a danger of my becoming so fond of the Yanks that after the peace treaty I would remain in the States and thus kill the poet in myself while, if I went home, the worst that could happen would be that I myself would be killed.

Behind Vambéry's shoulder, through the white lace curtain, I could look out upon the harbour. In the distance, between the Statue of Liberty and Staten Island, the sea swelled tautly like the weed-covered belly of a sleeping water-god. I was again overwhelmed with the fear of one condemned to death, but now this hitherto unknown sensation was coupled with an old, well known, indefinite anxiety. This anxiety had haunted me day and night throughout my childhood: sometimes it was caused by the wrinkles in a sheet, winding themselves around my legs like snakes; sometimes by the dim light emanating from the bronze naiad standing in a nest of bronze ferns in the darkest corner of the room next to mine; and sometimes, particularly in the twilight of winter afternoons, it came as I sat by myself, scared to distraction of the future, of the life waiting for me outside. Later, particularly in the seven years of my emigration, anxiety returned only in my dreams. One of the recurring dreams was that my enemies, the Hungarian Nazis, had tied me to the trunk of the famous five-hundred-year-old plane-tree on the top of a hill near Budapest and were sticking knitting needles between my vertebrae; at other times I dreamed that I was stealing into my father's house and was trying to reach the door to ring the bell, but my feet had turned to lead and I was unable to get to the door. I knew that I had 'come home too early', that our Nazi janitor had seen me and was going to hand me over to the police. At times I would have nightmares whenever I went to sleep. I begged Valy, and later my buddies in the army, to wake me should I toss around or scream in my dream. The mornings, when on waking I could look out upon the trees of Central Park or when my eyes fell on my machine-gun, were the happiest moments of my life. Lately, however, since the end of the war, my dreams had become hazier, although they were still far from enjoyable. In the morning I remembered only that I had been afraid but I couldn't remember of what. Now, for the first time, I felt that nightmarish anxiety in the middle of the day; and I had no doubts as to its cause. I was standing on firm ground, or rather the very edge of it, and in a few hours a ship would sail with me towards a half-submerged country of uncertain climate and poisoned atmosphere. For a while this journey into the dark would be accompanied by flashes from the last two lighthouses; this eloquent professor of law and the humanities, and that somewhat monstrous Statue of Liberty seen through the window.

In the meantime Vambéry had completely charmed Valy with a few compliments and witty anecdotes. Suddenly, however, my wife uttered a remark completely out of place and unconnected with anything we had been talking about. She declared how happy she was to be returning to Hungary to serve the Idea (meaning the teachings of communism), then complained indignantly at how unfair the capitalist powers were to the Soviet Union. Vambéry who, contrary to his custom, was sipping his second glass of wine after the oysters, did not, as he usually did, pretend not to have heard Valy's words. Instead, he inclined his small beard on the damask napkin tied around his throat, so that the flat, coin-shaped surface topping his long, vaulted and attractive bald head flashed bright for a moment, and then he nodded slowly. True, he said, the Anglo-Saxons were indeed unfair to the Soviet Union; they had already pursued the same wrong policies against Tsarist Russia. Valy was right – he said – one should indeed employ entirely different methods when dealing with an Asiatic despotism that interpreted the goodwill of its partners as stupidity, their tractability as cowardice, and their magnanimity as weakness. According to his habit he told a story to support his thesis. Towards the end of the 1870s, still a child, he had accompanied his father and Bishop Vilmos Fraknoi to Constantinople. As they were the Sultan's guests, the Monarchy put a special railway coach at their disposal. On the frontier of the Ottoman Empire a kindly, bearded Turk appeared in the door of their coach: the station-master. He told them, with many humble bows, that they would have to pay to remain in the coach, but he would make them a special price and refrain from giving a receipt. Should they refuse he would, to his deepest regret, disconnect the coach. Armin Vambéry jumped from his seat and slapped the station-master so hard that the latter rolled about on the red carpet. Oh! – the station-master exclaimed, getting to his feet – I didn't know, please accept my apologies. With this he picked up his red fez and backed away reverently. When the train moved out of the station the Bishop asked Vambéry senior what had given him the courage to slap the station-master. 'I know the Near East well,' the great traveller replied. 'Afraid though I was of slapping him, I was much more afraid of the consequences should I not slap him.'

'The Georgian Generalissimo,' Vambéry continued, but talking to me and watching Valy from the corner of his eye as she almost exploded with fury, 'speaks a little differently from the Turkish station-master in the last century, but they think alike. When my father slapped the Turk, my childish heart was filled with deep indignation. The childish public opinion of the Western world would probably be shaken with the same storm of moral indignation if the Anglo-Saxon powers, after winning the war, had given Soviet Russia a good kick in the behind. I, however, have, in the meantime, learned a great deal from my good father and this time I felt indignant when Roosevelt paid through the nose – and in advance – when Stalin presented his fantastic bill: presented it orally, and without giving a receipt. In addition it was not from his own pocket he paid, nor from other people's purses, but with other people's blood and freedom. I am afraid mankind will go on paying for a long time before the situation undergoes a fundamental change.'

'In your last book, and also in your article published in *Foreign Affairs,*' I interrupted, 'you spoke differently. You stated that after the war a more or less stable balance of power will develop between East and West. You also said that the new Hungarian constitution fulfilled the requirements of democracy. And so does Hungarian political life, as far as you can judge it from such a distance. You added that the Soviet Union obviously knows that its interests are best served if it is surrounded by benevolent, neutral neighbours rather than by rebellious communist vassals. And should this not be so, the Western powers, with the atom bomb in their exclusive possession, are strong enough to bring Stalin to his senses by threats alone. Finally, you quoted numerous examples from world history to show that it has never happened, not once since Chefren Pharaoh or the days of the Assyrian king, Tiglatpileser, that in a victorious coalition the weaker partner should get the larger share of the loot. These were your arguments, Professor, and they were very strong arguments which I, too, fully believe.'

I did not add that I did not, on the other hand, believe in formal logic and found it rather ridiculous when applied to future events, historical situations, people's actions or emotional lives. However, as I truly agreed with Vambéry's writings, and as the correctness or incorrectness of our political arguments had no bearing whatsover on my decision to go home, I dropped the subject. All the more so as I hadn't yet made up my mind whether to disclose the real motives of my return to Hungary or not. 'Politically,' the old gentleman bore down on me, 'the point is not to proclaim truth but to make it victorious. If I imagined that the world, *a priori*, agreed with my ideas I should not put them on paper. In my book I expressed, in my own modest way, my hopes for a rational Utopia. True, I called the spirit of the Hungarian constitution democratic, but I added that even the most ideally formulated constitution isn't worth a fig compared to a constitution the institutions of which live in the hearts and everyday habits of the people, even though they may not have been put into written words. I went on to say that to establish a democracy without democrats is just as risky an enterprise as to sell fans in Kamchatka, or to open a pork butcher's shop in Mecca. Consequently, I called attention to the necessity of supporting the new Hungarian democracy, which, up to date, exists only on paper. Its future fate depends on the alternative of developments, something which I tried to put across in the title of my book: *Hungary – To be or not to be*, and expounded in detail in the concluding chapter.'

The professor fell silent for a moment and sipped his wine. From behind the rim of his glass he gave me a long, friendly, almost loving glance.

'If,' he went on, 'my book led to your decision to go back to Hungary, I am sorry I ever wrote it.'

I made a movement of protest but he continued without waiting for my answer.

'The alternative I mentioned in my book will be decided within a few months. At present Hungary is in the throes of inflation. Your passport, handed to you at our Legation in Washington with such flattering solemnity, will be taken from you at the Hungarian border without any solemnity whatsoever. One should never voluntarily enter a room or a country the door of which cannot be opened from the inside. Wait until the situation has become consolidated, until the inflation is over and you can not only enter, but can also leave Hungary. I don't want to dissuade you from going home: that would be incompatible with my principles and the admiration I have for you. I don't quite know whether to ascribe it to my old and softening heart, to my delight in your poems or to the calcium particles accumulating in my brain-cells – but, silencing my own human dignity and offending yours, I have come here not to see you off but to beg you to delay your departure. Delay it, George, by at least six months.'

'But, Professor!' Valy interrupted excitedly, 'our luggage is on board ship, our flat . . .'

'That is beside the point,' I interrupted my wife. 'Our flat is probably still free and our luggage can be returned from Le Havre.'

Although I only wanted to show that I was not turning a deaf ear to Vambéry's request, it was obvious that my reply gave him much pleasure. Immediately he began to draw a very convincing picture of the second alternative, depicting the communist dictatorship so coolly and objectively that even Valy forgot to protest, and even I forgot to think him old-fashioned. He added that in a left-wing dictatorship I would start with all the odds against me. The trouble was not that I was not a Marxist, still less a Leninist, but that I fullfilled not a single one of the communist requirements, not even the very modest one of putting on an act and keeping my thoughts to myself. Secondly, I had visited many countries. Thirdly, I had received a classical education and was thus in the category of the unreliable. Lastly, I had no particular aspirations or passions; I would, in fact, embarrass even the most benevolent communist, because there was nothing with which I could be blackmailed or intimidated. Thus, from the bolshevik point of view, I was necessarily expendable. It was also important to remember that communists are interested neither in the value nor in the popularity of an artist. Their only consideration is his apparent usefulness to the totalitarian state. Vambéry mentioned Babel and Tarassov-Rodianov, whom the communists had murdered, and Jessenin, whom they drove to suicide.

While he was speaking, two completely contradictory trends of thought streamed through my mind. Jessenin's name scared me for a moment, but I quickly ascribed the parallel to the old gentleman's imagination, fired by anxiety and tenderness. As he had still made no allusion to the real motives of my return, which were absolutely independent of political eventualities, I wondered whether to mention them at all. He himself had retired to his room for an hour after the death of his first-born son, and never again, not even to his wife, had he mentioned his name; yet now, for my sake, he was transgressing the limits he had drawn with the precision of an international lawyer round his own and other people's emotional worlds, round man's individuality and the Semiramis-gardens of privacy: limits which he had always observed with a nineteenth-century modesty, not hypocritically, but with a noble, liberal ease. Still, I doubted that he was ignorant of my motives. Six years earlier, when I had intended to disappear in the desert, he had calculated my plans from a distance of four thousand kilometres. If now, at our last meeting, I kept silent, I should always feel guilty of spiritual disloyalty, even though he was aware that I, like himself, was reserved and modest.

The second train of thought was more a collection of impressions, underlining and colouring the foregoing but only loosely in contact with it. Without, of course, comparing myself to Columbus, I could not prevent my mind turning to the great Genoese. It was an *idée fixe*, consisting of several elements. There was the salty, tangy smell of the sea streaming in through the open windows and filling me with an irresistible desire for adventure; there were the large jetties on either side of the pier, reminding me of the slow, uncomfortable journey to this country five years earlier, on the deck of the *Navemar* which had set out from Cadiz with a crew of mutinous seamen and had taken seven weeks to reach the flat shores of the Bahamas. Then there was my wife's black velvet beret embroidered with semi-precious stones, copied from a portrait in the Louvre, attributed to Raphael, of Queen Joanna of Aragon, which suited Valy's beautiful face but clashed mercilessly with her bolshevik notions. Every time I looked at her I thought of her frightening resemblance to Raphael's model – though Mad Joanna was a melancholic, while Valy's attacks of screaming hysteria made her throw dishes and wake the entire neighbourhood at any time of night. It would have been difficult to draw a parallel between the professor and King Ferdinand of Spain, but I saw all the more similarity between Columbus's position and my own.

I too was setting out towards a continent in which, without confessing it, I hoped to find traces of an old world; and thus I too, like Columbus, had to count on the possibility that I might never know where I had landed. My journey, like his, was called madness and suicide. Everyone told me horror stories and foretold unknown dangers which frightened me even though I could not believe them. Like Columbus, I might, for all I knew, find myself among primitive savages instead of among cultured Asians – or among cruel Asians, instead of among simple but benevolent savages. But my closest bond with the great Genoese was that although I appeared to be setting out on this journey for the sake of symbolic treasure, the real motive was vanity, the desire for fame and glory: our different trades drove us both with the same imperatives, and both of us, while fully aware of dangers, still hoped for success.

This comparison so electrified me, and the immoderate quantities of French wine which I had drunk so loosened my tongue, that I plunged into my little speech, stumbling over my words and disregarding the order and importance of my arguments, although I had long ago worked them out.

I began with my feelings of guilt. Here in New York, and in the army too, I had lived in comparative safety, while at home people had been slaughtered, deported to concentration camps, gassed, or buried in their houses by the thousand. This was one of the reasons why I thought it essential to return home with the greatest possible humility *now*, and not like some unconcerned visitor, when inflation abated and things had settled down.

Then I spoke of the problem of the Hungarian language, which bound me to my fatherland with ties stronger than any other. I described how shocked I had been when, at the air-base at Kodiak, my fellow-soldiers told me one morning that I had been talking English in my sleep. At Fort Leonardwood, a military camp in the middle of a forest in Missouri, one of my buddies had stopped behind me when I was busy writing a poem in a PX, and had asked me why I wasn't writing in English. I had explained to him that when I pronounced the word *wood*, it meant to him the surrounding dense, dark-green forest of strangely-shaped, intertwining trees, a jungly undergrowth full of jiggers, an unfathomable, frightening darkness; when, on the other hand, I pronounced the Hungarian word for wood, *erdö*, I saw the thinly scattered, slender young trees of the Matra Mountains, with fragments of blue sky between their branches and wild strawberry plants and tussocks of grass at their feet. Even concrete words meant different things to us, not to mention abstractions such as *political party, ethics, way of life, religion* or *duty.*

When a Hungarian rhyme occurred to me I knew at once whether it had already been used by some other Hungarian poet; I knew whether it sounded modern or old-fashioned, solemn or comical, banal or affected. I knew whether it was slyly modest, refined, deliberately dim, artistically polished, or sham; whether its mere sound evoked melancholy, happiness, arrogance, despair, unexpressed rudeness, irony, boredom or nothing at all. In English I didn't even know for certain whether a rhyme was a rhyme on paper only, or also when pronounced. I had been born into the process of Hungarian literature, of Hungarian history: it was not Herrick whom I studied at school, but Balaasi, not Keats but Janos Arany. The word *victory* conjured up in me not the red brick wall of the Appomattox Court House but the green grass of the battlefield at Isaszeg; the word *democracy* took in my mind the shape of Lajos Kossuth's face, not that of Abraham Lincoln's. Hungarian literature and history were going through a phase different from that of American literature and history: it was a different river, with a different course, different currents, a different colour, on which one rowed with a different rhythm, in a different way. I knew everything about a Hungarian peasant: I knew what fairy-tales had given him bad dreams in childhood, how he moved, what grimaces he made when shaving in his kitchen on a Sunday morning; I knew just how distorted his notions and memories of Hungarian history would be. About the joys and worries of a farmer in Georgia I knew nothing.

And then there was vanity! In America, when I went into a restaurant, I might get good service by giving good tips – but what I got, I got for money. When I entered a restaurant at home the waiter would suggest the best and cheapest dishes not only because he would know who I was – for the sake, that is, of my fame as a poet – but because he could tell at once that I was an honest man, and poor. If I should want to win a woman, in America it would take me two weeks, in Hungary an afternoon. In Hungary I would have credit; in America I would be obliged to learn English perfectly and acquaint myself in detail with the country before I could even hope to open an intellectual bank account. This was valid not only in everyday life, but in making new friends and acquaintances, and among enthusiastic admirers from whom, at home, I did my shy and desperate best to escape, while in America I despaired because I had no one to escape from. It was even valid in death. Absurd I might be, but I felt that resting in the Kerepes Cemetery at home I would feel less dead than I would here, buried in that drained marsh, beside Lazlo Fényes.

How many arguments had I lined up? Six. For a seventh I would have to quote Dante, likening emigration to an endless spiral staircase; I would have to enumerate everything I had been through in seven years; describe how I had slept in the desert, in the hold of a ship, in a tank, on ice, in a jungle, at an air-base and in some two hundred beds, and explain that now, at last, I wanted to sleep in the same bed for decades, to collect a library, to plant a walnut tree for my grandchildren; that although my thirst for adventure was still alive, I felt that I could get all the adventure I wanted at home.

For an eighth argument I could put forward something which the professor knew as well as I did: the articles published day after day in Hungarian liberal and social democrat newspapers, calling me home; my books, once banned, burned and seized and now published again; my poems and songs, broadcast week after week over the Budapest radio. If I did not return home now, I should disown myself.

For a ninth argument I could say that my mother, my only living relative, was waiting for me. If I did not go I should have to forget my entire life, thirty years of it, and change my entire attitude. In the seven years of my exile I had lived in furnished flats and refused American citizenship when it was offered me, because it made no sense. Although my Hungarian passport had expired, to me it still seemed valid, and I hung on to it. Perhaps it was true that the door through which I should enter Hungary could not be opened from the inside, and perhaps my entering would close the door of America, and that door would prove impossible to open from the outside. But even so, the question outlined by Professor Vambéry – whether dictatorship or democracy would triumph in Hungary and Eastern Europe as a whole – was the most important problem in the next few decades. It pained me greatly that the most important problem of my day should be a political one, but that did not alter the fact that it was my duty to face it. I was trying to comfort myself with the hope that perhaps the difference between the two sides would not be so great as the professor supposed; I hoped that communism would be able to create some sort of social justice beyond the powers of capitalism to establish, but essentially it was not so much the outcome of the conflict which interested me, as the conflict itself – and that was no longer a merely political problem. It was the problem of the behaviour of people in battle as observed by Pierre in *War and Peace*, or of their actions behind the lines as described in *Vanity Fair*, or above all of their suffering as retreating armies as depicted by Stendhal. If I delayed my return I might well be left behind, and I had one duty and only one: to be on the scene from the beginning of the battle, no matter which side triumphed.

'Those are my arguments,' I concluded, watching Vambéry, whose face had gradually lost its brightness, even to the corners of his mild eyes which always seemed to smile, even when he was angry. 'I want to be honest, however, and I admit that I have a counter-argument which is almost as strong as all my arguments put together. I am afraid. Terribly afraid.'

Vambéry remained silent, offered me a liquorice – a sign of particular consideration – then declared that my arguments convinced him. Then he rose, saying that he must telephone his wife that he would not be back that afternoon. As he crossed the room his grey but still muscular nape and his arms, moving like slow paddles, betrayed the emotions he guarded so jealously. He considered his after-dinner nap as sacred – almost as sacred as human dignity or Roman Law.

When the ship left the harbour, he was standing on the exact spot where I had first seen Dr Hollos, five years ago. He looked tired, but was still holding out his arms towards me. Wearing the black cape he had inherited from Laszlo Fényes, with his little pointed beard, he became a few minutes later like one of those miniature statues of philosophers or fauns which the fifth-century Greeks liked to keep in their houses. Then he grew smaller and smaller until he was nothing but a black dot on the quay. 'And now he will begin to grow again,' I thought, as I turned to go down to my cabin.

Fear, which had attached itself to me the moment I boarded ship, remained my constant companion throughout the journey. There was, indeed, little opportunity to forget its presence: it seemed to me as if I were descending, ring after ring, into Dante's Hell. The ruins of Le Havre, the harbour improvised from old iron barrels, showed only the exterior signs of destruction; Paris looked like a provincial town at dawn with American jeeps whizzing along its broad, deserted streets. When one evening Valy and I visited one of our old haunts, the Café Flore, we were the only guests. I didn't see one of the old waiters and the new ones hovered round us with painful, utterly un-Parisian politeness. When we reached Germany I wore my

American uniform but this precaution turned out to be completely superfluous. When, with the ruins of Pforzheim in the background, the ticket-collector appeared in the door, my uniform made him too timid to ask for our tickets; he pulled his head between his shoulders and slunk away. The miserably dressed German civilians dared not come into the compartment where Valy and I were alone, and this made me feel so bad that I would have changed my clothes at once had I not registered all our luggage.

In Prague bitter diappointment was awaiting me. Before my emigration I belonged to that group of Hungarians who not only detested but openly opposed the chauvinism of the Horthy régime. I had repeatedly gone on lecture tours among the Hungarian minority in Czechoslovakia and it was always obvious to me that this minority enjoyed better living and greater liberty in this alien country than the majority in their own. I expressed this opinion in the Hungarian press, as well as my wish to see in Hungary a democratic system like that established in Czechoslovakia. For this opinion right-wing government circles called me a Czech agent and a traitor, and started various court proceedings against me. The sentence, still pending, was one of the reasons for my emigration. But even apart from the deep and intimate friendship between Professor Vambéry, the two Masaryks, Professor Jaszi, and the former Czechoslovak Premier Milan Hodza, we were, during the period of our emigration, in very close contact with the Czechoslovak government in London. We discussed all our actions with the Czech government and pledged ourselves in joint proclamations to promote, after the war, the co-operation, and if possible the federation, of our two countries.

In Prague I was received with icy coldness. The social democrat director of the Czech radio was very sorry not to be able to put me before the microphone, but he hoped I understood – after all, I was Hungarian. Minister Fierlinger who, a few months before, had offered to take my private letters personally from New York to Budapest, informed me through his secretary that he could not receive me. And when the director of the radio was showing us round we were almost beaten up in Venczel Square because, having no other common language, we were speaking in German. What was even more painful was the fact that the Czechs had succumbed to the same excessive chauvinism against which we had once so passionately fought in Hungary. The national minorities had been exchanged, but at the same time, allegedly for strategic reasons, the Czechoslovak government had annexed a small but densely populated part of Hungary. This annexation cut Hungary's most important artery of communication, the Budapest–Vienna highway, and created even more hatred between the two countries. I had to realize that the dreams we had cherished during the war would never come true, and that everything was going on from where it had been left off in 1939.

Jan Masaryk, Minister of Foreign Affairs, with whom I had spent an evening with Vambéry in New York, received me rather coolly. When we were alone, however, he complained bitterly that he was helpless against the chauvinism reigning throughout the country, but particularly among the Slovaks, although they, having served Hitler eagerly, had nothing with which to reproach the Hungarians. During dinner he drank more than usual, but without losing his gift for telling stories or his excellent humour. Then he expounded two sharply conflicting theories. The centuries of Austrian occupation and the years spent under Hitler's rule had taught both the Czechs and Hungarians every trick of the trade. We had learned how to serve the oppressor without putting ourselves in his hands. He referred to the Czech national heroes, to Tom Thumb and the good soldier Schweik who, while apparently submitting to it, had tricked brute force. The time had now come when we must listen with devoted expressions to Soviet orders, smiling only with the wrinkles in our bottoms, under our trousers, as did the lackeys of the Byzantine emperors. Heroic gestures would be of no avail; we would have to speak the language of flowers, be patient and cunning, as we had been under Hitler. The essential thing was to survive. It was his hope that the Western powers would in time discover that Stalin would have to be forced out of Central Europe by permanent political and economic pressure. Even the Russians themselves might realize that the exploitation of the Danube valley was not profitable and might, when the opportunity came – perhaps with the next palace revolution – clear out as the Tartars did in 1242, at the news of Genghis Khan's death. Then, at last, we could translate our dream of a Danubian Federation into reality.

His second theory was considerably more pessimistic. It was one of history's bitter jokes – he said – that Czechoslovakia, created by his father and Woodrow Wilson, should be annihilated twenty-five years later by another American president. We must discard our illusions, he warned me. Roosevelt had sold us to the Devil, bag and baggage. Now the Devil's commissars would roast us alive on the spit.

Masaryk told me all this with a plentiful seasoning of anecdotes and in a cheerful tone of voice. The table was loaded with bottles and bottles of the tart red wine made from vines brought from his fatherland and planted in the Moravian hills by the University-founding Czech king, Charles of Luxembourg. His words filled me with anxiety, but the more we drank the more ready I was to forget it. I lit one cigarette from the butt of another and watched the smoke caught by the draught and pulled out through the half-open window like a treble thread of blue wool. Whenever my eyes followed the smoke they fell on Russian soldiers walking impatiently back and forth on the hard, grey cobblestones under the window of the Palace.

The next day, in Pozsony, I found out that there was only one train a week from Pozsony to Budapest, which took twenty-four hours to cover a distance of two hundred kilometres. But what was even more annoying, I was told, was that the Soviet soldiers stripped everyone coming from the West of all their possessions. They also punished those coming from the East, who had nothing but their lives, for their poverty. A few days earlier the train from Budapest had arrived with three hundred completely naked passengers. The Russians had stripped everyone, including the engineer and the stoker. Only the very old and the children had been allowed to keep some of their clothes. Although I cherished no exaggerated illusions concerning the Soviet Union, had I heard this story two weeks earlier, in America, I should certainly have branded it as pure invention. But now, in addition to disappointment I was overwhelmed by the bitter realization of my helplessness.

When I was demobilized at Fort Dix and my buddies found out where I was going, they presented me with some fifty woollen shirts and trousers to distribute among the poor in Hungary. I had with me new medicines, still unknown at home, medicines and vitamins for my mother, chocolate, coffee, tea, a few thousand cigarettes – all the things I would not be able to buy in Hungary. I had with me clothing, gifts and various useful articles both for people I knew and for people I had never met; among them a hearing aid for a half-deaf communist ideologist who had only recently returned from Moscow. It had been handed to me by the ideologist's brother, a rich industrialist in New York, though he feared that he was sending his brother a treacherous gift, since only his deafness saved him from a bullet in the nape at the time of the Moscow purges.

The woollen shirts had already been stolen from my suitcase by French customs officials, together with a bundle of manuscripts wrapped in them; approximately a thousand poems translated into Hungarian from almost every language in the world. I had made them during the seven years of my emigration, whenever I had nothing better to do, partly to keep my hand in, partly so that when I got home I could publish the first anthology of world poetry in the language. After that robbery I decided to defend the rest of my luggage with my life. I was saved by the captain of the best Hungarian football team, the FTC, who embraced me enthusiastically in the lobby of a Pozsony hotel. His team had beaten the Pozsony team the day before. They had come in their own bus and though there were some fifty people ready to pay for the ten empty seats, he said that they would gladly take us along free of charge.

The next morning we made ready to go. The captain, Sarossy, laid on a festive reception, making his team stand in a half-circle in front of the bus and sing an anti-fascist poem of mine, written ten years before, which had in the meantime been put to music. We were made to sit in the place of honour, in the front seats of the bus. Sarossy sat behind us, but kept silent – in a few minutes we would reach the Hungarian border and he did not want to interfere in my thoughts at that solemn moment. Strangely enough I was not at all moved. While Valy stared greedily out of the window, her beautiful, long neck tense with excitement, I watched the hands of the driver.

I had already had plenty of time to delight in the landscape and the familiar environment during the week we had spent in Pozsony. This, the ancient Hungarian crowning-town, had become the capital of Slovakia twenty-seven years earlier. The people, the clothes, the manners of the waiters, the behaviour of the shop assistants, the shape and polish of the tumblers – all was as familiar to me as were the trees, the wild, deep blue of the April sky or the rounded, woolly clouds, white all over, without grey shadows, which conjured up the shapes of Ceylon, Sumatra or Tasmania, sometimes an Iceland but never a New Zealand or a Celebes. One shore of the Danube, as we crossed the pontoon-bridge, was as like the other shore as the two shores of the Mississippi below St Louis are alike. The approach of my country's border was heralded neither by a change in the landscape, nor by a change in the flora or the shape of the dwellings. When we stopped at it, it was with an entirely unexpected jolt, because we were in the Hungarian territory annexed to Czechoslovakia some weeks ago at the request of the Czech government, and while formerly the border had been marked by the Danube, now they had drawn it at random. Instead of the usual customs-shed we stopped in front of a villa-like building obviously requisitioned for the purpose. There was no barrier, only a telegraph pole laid across the road. A Soviet sergeant, two young men in civilian clothes and a Hungarian soldier stood before the building – the latter in an unbelievably ragged uniform, like a veteran reduced to begging.

Valy and I were the first to enter the building, accompanied by the Soviet sergeant and a civilian interpreter. The sergeant glanced at our passports, flung them into an open drawer and announced they would be returned to us in Budapest as soon as I had explained to the authorities why I had fled to the West with the fascists two years ago. I saw no point in arguing, but Valy could not resist explaining to the sergeant that I had been an American, not a fascist, soldier. The Russian, who could not take his eyes off my nylon shirt, replied that there was no difference: the Americans were no less fascist than the

Germans. He consistently addressed Valy as *Burzhujka* – which the interpreter omitted to translate into Hungarian.

As we were going out I noticed that the next passenger to go in, one of the paying guests in the bus – a squat and vivid Frenchman in striped trousers – showed neither his passport nor an identification card. Instead he pressed a pack of cigarettes into the sergeant's hand and this took care of all formalities. Sarossy applied the same method when the Hungarian soldier showed interest in the luggage; as a result, all he did was to climb into the bus, walk through it and get off at the other end. I stood despondently in the characteristically Hungarian, floury, white, light dust which lay as deep as puddles of rainwater. In the middle of my sole, under which, during the last seven years, air had been circulating, I felt the almost disagreeable pressure of Hungarian soil. When the bus rolled on I noticed that my pipe, which I had left in the ashtray, had disappeared.

That evening, while my mother and Valy were busy preparing supper, I walked up and down in my father's former study as he used to do, long ago, before meals. My mother, who had lost her husband, her daughter and her parents within six months, had taken up the organization of a new life with admirable energy. She had never worked before: now she earned her bread as a social worker and did her own housework as well. Her small body, topped by a disproportionately large head, like some ancient Chinese statuette, scurried tirelessly back and forth among the rather dilapidated furniture, knick-knacks and keepsakes of the overcrowded flat. But the source of her energy was not in herself. Her strength had come from the knowledge that I would come back. At the moment of my arrival she almost collapsed at the front door. Later she grew a little calmer. Before sitting down to tea I discovered, in one of her wardrobes, the chocolate, coffee and vitamin parcels I had sent her from America, almost untouched. My mother said she had saved them against my arrival, because I would probably be very hungry after seven years abroad.

Of our once very large flat she had been permitted to keep only two rooms; the second only because she had said she was preparing it for me. But in the drawing-room, where I now walked up and down, nothing had changed apart from the broken and still unreplaced window-panes and the bullet-holes. Only the palms were missing from the large Chinese vases; their place had been taken by pounds and pounds of beans. These had been saved before the siege to keep the family from starving, and my mother was still watching over them jealously, fearing that they might again be needed. In spite of the fact that a sharp wind was blowing in through the broken window-panes I was almost smothered under the heavy weight of conflicting emotions. I would have liked to go out for a short walk, but the house door was locked because of the early curfew. I could not even go up to the roof-garden, where I had so often sunbathed in my youth. My mother warned me that there was an unexploded bomb, and besides, the whole roof was covered by the excrement of the fifty Russians who had only recently moved out of the house and who had used it for that purpose.

On the desk I noticed my father's photograph in the uniform of a lieutenant. This was how he had looked twenty-eight years ago, when he returned from the First World War and was approximately the same age I was now, returning from the Second. His huge, gold-braided collar, stiff, waxed, coal-black moustache – all things imposed upon him by military regulations and the fashion of the day – contrasted strangely with the large and melancholy – even too large and too melancholy – eyes and the receding, frighteningly high forehead, not yet wrinkled but only furrowed. The sight of that high forehead reassured me, establishing at once that there was no likeness between us.

In the desk I discovered my sister's medical instruments, scalpels and syringes, in an almost completely new cedar-wood box. As I bent over it I could still catch the fragrance of the wood and the smell of the glue. Next to the box lay a few ancient, worn rulers, the Indian ink my father had used for his drawings, and a poem in German which he had written to me when I grew into a lad. As far as its form went it was not a very good poem; my father expressed in it his hope that I would grow not only into a unique phenomenon, an inimitable entity, like every human being, but into someone outstanding and unforgettable. Under the manuscript lay a bundle of clean, but now worthless, bank-notes. With this money my father, mother and sister could have spent the war years in one of the best hotels in Switzerland, and if they had done so they would undoubtedly all still have been alive.

From the desk I wandered over to the bookcase. Its glass doors were damaged by bullet-holes, like the old Dutch landscape hanging above the mantelpiece. I knew from my mother that they had not been hit by stray bullets from the streets, but by the bullets of the Russian soldiers camping in the room who had shot up the furniture for their amusement. In one wing of the bookcase stood German classics in an edition nearly a hundred years old: Schiller, Goethe, Lessing, Heine, Herder, Wieland. On the central shelves was the literature of our century – or what remained of it after I had carried off the pick. On the other side was my father's scientific library. I soon came to the conclusion that the works on physics and chemistry had all become obsolete. So had Ernst Haeckel, Herbert Spencer, Auguste Comte and Camille Flammarion's Astronomy, Muther's work on the history of painting and the illustrated chronicle of the First World War on the embossed title-page of which Emperor William and Franz-Joseph were holding hands above churning clouds while below them, in the battle-field, the German and Austro-Hungarian Armies were routing the enemy. Only in the middle of one of the central shelves, where a bullet had cut an irregular star-shaped hole in the glass, did I, to my pleasure, discover my father's favourite books: the Bible, Goethe's *Faust* bound in soft, blue leather, and Schopenhauer's aphorisms. Because of the crack in the glass the titles on the spines appeared double, and between the lines which hovered obliquely one above the other, a small rainbow played hide-and-seek, like a message from another world. 'Is that all that remains of a man?' I mused, trying to conjure up my father's picture: his black jacket; the thick, white, soft locks on his nape, like the petals of a chrysanthemum; his cheek-bones, on which the skin seemed to twitch with pleasure when, in his free time, he could put his violin under his chin. I was completely submerged in memories when my mother called me to dinner.

In the next few days I visited friends and collected information. The nauseating, sweetish smell of superficially buried corpses which pervaded the squares and parks of the capital; the sight of the bagmen climbing the emergency-ramp to the other bridge over the Danube, pushing and cursing, in a long, black line like a stovepipe; the almost motionless cloud of dust hovering above the rubble from which broken beams and iron girders stuck out like the skeletons of antediluvian animals; the old friends and acquaintances whom I met again after seven years; the innumerable stories about other old friends and acquaintances frozen to death on the Russian front, shot dead by Hungarian gendarmes for their gold wrist-watch or by Russian soldiers for trying to defend their wives from being raped before their eyes; all this filled me with an almost unbearable tension, as bad as if I were in the middle of a battle among exploding grenades, dying comrades, showering bullets. My tension was increased by the fact that I had left the side of the winners for that of the defeated although it was with the winners that I was in sympathy.

I found out that I could obtain a job on a newspaper, write articles, be allocated a flat or could even deliver a lecture only if I joined one of the parties: it did not matter which party of the coalition, I could make my choice. I was in no particular hurry to find a job, but it soon became clear that it was impossible to live on the income from my books. Soon after my return home, my publisher paid me 300,000,000,000 pengoes for a new edition of one of my volumes. I ran to the market, because by afternoon the money was worth only one-tenth of its morning value, and bought with the three hundred billion pengoes a chicken, two litres of oil and some vegetables. I had transferred one thousand five hundred dollars saved in America to the Hungarian National Bank because I thought it would be dishonest to deprive the Hungarian state of the hard currency and to traffic in dollars on the black market. Now I had to discover that everyone possessed dollars – the taxi-driver, the waiter, the market woman – everyone except me, who had just arrived from America. Small wonder that nobody believed me. Had I brought my money with me I could have purchased a five-storey house, which I had no intention of doing. Everything, from American cigarettes and coffee to penicillin, had to be paid for in dollars. When I collected my money from the National Bank it was just enough for key-money for a one-and-a-half-room flat. However, the flat was in the best part of town, at the top of Rose Hill, where I had always wanted to live, so I considered the problem as solved.

The first person I visited was a school-friend, Gabor Goda. When, seven years earlier, we had said goodbye, Goda was a well-known short story writer, and a typical golden youth, witty, cheerful, cynical and reckless. When my mother told me that he had been rewarded for joining the communist party with a high office in the municipal cultural department, I was surprised; but not very much surprised. He immediately suggested that I too should join the communist party. His first and most important argument was that the communist party, and only the communist party, disposed of funds. 'We hold the sack,' he said with some irony but also a little pride. His second argument was that though the country was governed by a coalition, and although within the coalition the smallholders' party held an absolute majority, the whole thing was no more than illusion. Real power, every key position, was in the hands of the communists; they were supported by the only real force, the Soviet Army. To rely upon the West might be a noble idea but in fact it meant suicide, he stated, and threw me from the corner of his blue eyes a quick, sharp glance. This glance of pity and irony was most familiar to me; it was the way my friend had always looked at stupid people whom, for one reason or another, he still liked.

Another friend of my youth was Sandor Szalai, the journalist and psychologist, who in the meantime had become head of the foreign affairs department of the social democratic party. Sandor Szalai gave me a detailed account of the political situation. He said that the programme of all four great parties was socialism and democracy; the difference was only that each had a different idea concerning the proportion of the two components. The smallholders' party, standing at the extreme right of the coalition, desired the largest possible proportion of democracy and the smallest possible proportion of socialism, while the communist party on the extreme left wanted much more socialism and much less democracy. The smallholders' party was led, on the whole, by very decent but slightly old-fashioned gentlemen who might not be exactly to my taste. The national peasant party had almost no members in Budapest except a few *narodnik* writers; and in the countryside, where the peasants loathed even the word 'communism', its organizations were simply used as cover organizations by the communists. There remained the alternative of the two workers' parties, and about them I should have to make up my own mind. It was not a philosophical, a political or an economic question, but simply a question of character. If I liked the bare-footed Franciscan brothers and preferred St Francis of Assisi to Ignatius Loyola, I must join the social democratic party; if I sympathized with the Jesuits, I must join the communist party.

Béla Zsolt, the most significant, most courageous liberal journalist of the country, received me with open arms in the editorial offices of his weekly *Haladas* (Progress). He asked me to work for his newspaper, then he outlined the situation. What the communists did in the Soviet Union was both economically and intellectually catastrophic. But their activities in Hungary had hitherto been praiseworthy. Had the Western armies marched into our country we should again have been saddled with Horthy and the Hungarian squirearchy, while as things now stood we had a parliamentary democracy and had even seen land-reform become reality – with a delay of a hundred and fifty years. The clearing away of the rubble, the restoration of public transport, the organization of the national food supply and the admirably rapid reconstruction of the country were also primarily the work of communists. If we had only non-communist parties, he said, the deputies would still be sitting before the ruins of parliament, debating the clauses of the election law. The West, as had happened so frequently in the course of our history, had left us in the lurch again, simply because it did not realize its own interests in Central Europe. We could at least hope that the Russians would be more reasonable: it would not even be in their interest to establish here the same infernal system as in the Soviet Union.

Then Valy and I went to visit Bandi Havas. Bandi had arrived immediately after me. He came from London with his wife and his little son, as secretary to Count Michael Karolyi, President of the 1918–19 Hungarian Republic – who was received with a nationwide ovation. Bandi had changed little since our days in Africa, although he was much more arrogant than before and spoke about Karolyi and himself in the first person plural. He embraced and kissed me enthusiastically, then, at vertiginous speed, he enumerated the current objects of his adoration. The first three among them were the heroism of the British people, Stalin, and my poems. He went on to expound various world-saving ideas but failed to notice that his ailing, skinny little wife had just walked up from the cellar to the fourth floor with a heavy basket of firewood, panting with exhaustion. To my great amazement he showed himself cautious in his political opinion; he declared that he would refrain from joining any party and suggested that I do the same.

The next morning I went to the headquarters of the communist party. At the gate I was surrounded by guards armed with revolvers who studied my identification papers very thoroughly. Then they asked me with whom I desired to speak. I replied that I wanted to see the head of the press department. They picked up the house telephone and from their conversation I learned that the head of the press department was called Laszlo Orban. Five people were waiting in his anteroom. When I entered, Orban, a smoothly shaved man with the look of a shop assistant, whose nostrils were extended in triumph, herded a guest from his room, then took me by the arm and led me into his office. It was crowded with huge armchairs, leather settees and a few monstrous dining-room chairs; collected, obviously, from several homes.

'We are glad, very glad, that you have come to see us, Comrade Faludy,' he said with a gesture more haughty than originally intended. 'We know that all roads lead to us. This is why we didn't take it amiss that you talked to your friend Goda first – who, by the way, is a good comrade – then to Sandor Szalai and Béla Zsolt. And finally with Havas,' he added significantly. 'He came to see us yesterday. You know, perhaps, that we are informed of everything —' I had turned my head away in disgust and was keeping my eyes on the thick red carpet. 'You must not be offended, Comrade Faludy,' the solemn voice explained. 'We must know what an important man like yourself is doing.'

I closed my eyes. I could hear the steady hammering, now almost familiar, which came from the Danube where workers were busy on the emergency bridge which had to be repaired all the time to prevent its collapse. It was the only bridge between the two sides of the city – and of the country. So they had been watching me since my return and this commercial traveller here was even proud of it. Perhaps he only wanted to impress me, or perhaps it was a manoeuvre of intimidation. What would be the next step?

There followed, as I expected, a nauseating, clumsy and to me almost physically painful glorification of my greatness as a writer. Then he said that the party would rebuild for me a damaged villa, on Rose Hill, which had belonged to the executed Prime Minister, Laszlo Bardossy. After the inflation – which would last only a few more weeks – they would give me, naturally in secret, a considerable monthly salary. He added that he fully understood my inner resistance, for I had been in opposition all my life, but I must realize that the situation was different now, because 'today the state is ours'. I wanted to interrupt, saying that the state was not identical with the communist party, nor the communist party with us, but I changed my mind. In the meantime he had reached the point where he declared that the party wanted nothing from me except that, after I had had sufficient time to think it over, I should sign an application to join; though, if I preferred it that way, we could keep my membership an absolute secret, like that of . . .

He swallowed the rest of the sentence and became suddenly so embarrassed that he rose from his chair, sat down again, opened the upper drawer of his desk in which I glimpsed an iron box, then blushed to the ears and closed the drawer. I had been listening to his speech with such rapt attention that at first I didn't grasp what had happened. This is probably what he hoped, because that 'like that of . . .' had undoubtedly been a slip of the tongue. I understood at a single glance that however much I might despise him, the man sitting opposite me was, in spite of his loquaciousness and vulgarity, highly discreet, at least in party matters: cautiously, painfully discreet, because he knew that his marriage with the personified party which had lifted him out of a complete obscurity, would immediately be dissolved if he betrayed any of his experiences on the bridal couch. The 'like that of . . .' was the introduction to a sentence the subject of which could be none other than Bandi Havas; it was he who had been here yesterday morning to sign the application of admission, which he had denied to me the same evening. His application lay in that iron box together, no doubt, with a large number of other such applications; that was why Orban pulled out the drawer, that was why he slammed it shut too quickly.

I felt my ears turning red and I wanted to rise, but Orban declared that he couldn't let me go yet. We had not finished with official business and he insisted that afterwards we should talk like friends. He picked up the telephone and ordered wine and biscuits. While he spoke he looked at me with shining eyes, he was obviously proud of his knowledge that I didn't like black coffee. Then he explained that he was too unimportant a man to discuss my affairs with me; therefore, upon learning that I had come, he had telephoned Zoltan Biro, who wanted to talk to me. He was no longer in the building but in the afternoon he would send a car to pick me up.

'Who is Zoltan Biro?'

'Head of the party's cultural department,' he replied, obviously surprised that I did not know. 'And,' he added, 'he is Comrade Rakosi's brother.'

'Half-brother?'

'No. Brother. Comrade Rakosi has several brothers, but all have different names.'

'Why?'

'Because there can be but one Comrade Rakosi.'

The door of the first-floor flat in the large apartment building opened the second my hand touched the bell. I stood before my host, a grey, tired, elderly man with a completely expressionless face. He did not resemble his brother, who, in his pictures, looked like a round-headed, genial, provincial shopkeeper. This man led me into the library, then excused himself and left me alone. On the bookshelves I noticed the collected works of Marx, Engels, Lenin and Stalin, all in Russian or German editions; a number of ideological works, all in Russian; a thick book on socialist realism, also in Russian, and a few Russian authors, naturally in Russian. There was not a single Hungarian book among them; I pulled out at random a German edition of Marx's *Das Kapital* published in Leningrad: the pages were uncut.

On the desk lay open a thin little brochure, also on socialist realism and also in Russian. There were marginal notes in Hungarian, underlinings, and here and there exclamation marks. Also on the desk was Stalin's portrait in a frame – not the photograph to be seen on posters and above the front doors of houses, nor the rarer one in which the Generalissimo was lighting his pipe; this picture was even smarter, and coloured into the bargain: Stalin, in a white jacket with all his war decorations, coming down a flight of marble stairs: a ballet dancer, a *maître d'hôtel*. Judging from the decorations it was taken during or after the war, but apart from a few silver hairs, Stalin's head was a shiny black – at the age of sixty-five. This is socialist realism, I thought. I was overwhelmed by a wild desire to make myself independent of the joyless atmosphere in this joyless room, and went to the window with its lace curtain. Night was falling: the sky shone a pearly blue and the setting sun painted the windows opposite a fiery red.

'What a beautiful sunset,' I said when Biro re-entered the room with the coffee. He threw me a frightened, helpless glance; it was obvious that in the circles in which he moved they never discussed such a subject. He placed the tray on the table and instead of joining me at the window, he sat down. It appeared to me as if he were thinking; thinking very intensely. He was probably trying to guess whether there was a trap in my question and how he should reply to it.

'Yes,' he uttered at long last. As if he were trying to calm down a madman or a naughty child. He spoke slowly and in a low voice, exactly like an actor playing Stalin in a film, and his words were accompanied by small, gentle gestures.

He was pretty well informed about my affairs. He inquired about my wife, my mother, my friends in America, Vambéry and others. Then I tried to find out how long he had lived in the Soviet Union, what he had done there, whether he had a family, what he had accomplished in the fifty or fifty-five years of his life, but he eluded my politely formulated questions or pretended not to hear them. What interested him most was what Laszlo Fényes and my other friends

– whom he had probably known though he did not say so – thought about the Hungarian communists. For the first time I seemed to detect some emotional undertone in his questions, the emotions of a man physically and spiritually crippled during the years of the Moscow terror, a man tormented by feelings of inferiority and yearning for the praise of his opponents. Had I stuck to the truth I should have repeated Fényes's own words: that he hated the Hungarian communists more than his own excrement. But I felt suddenly sorry for my host and selected a few sentences in which, as a rare exception, Fényes had something good to say about one individual communist or another. Biro was so pleased that he broke into a smile, but he craved more and more praise so that finally I was compelled to lie.

Then without any transition, he translated to me a paragraph from the brochure lying on the desk. It explained that socialist realism was the most advanced literary method, all the more so as it portrayed man in his social interdependences with scientific exactness, and therefore the central committee of the Soviet communist party advised writers, in their own interests, to apply this advanced method in their work. When Biro asked me what I thought about it I decided not to be so weak as I had been when I praised the communists in Fényes's name. I asked him whether the author of the brochure was a professional writer. When he replied that he wasn't I said that this was obvious. A writer writes books and not Orders of the Day for other writers. A writer knows that methods of writing cannot be made uniform, nor can they be prescribed. There are impressionist writers, surrealists, romantics, socialist realists – but most writers are several of these even in the same book. Only someone entirely divorced from literature can conceive the idea that a writer must follow a certain method. I granted that Zhdanov was not alone in his idea; there had been many theologians and Church Fathers in the past who had prescribed subjects, form, obligatory source-material and an optimistic ending. Thus, in the sixth, seventh and eighth centuries profane poetry was persecuted and only religious themes were tolerated. The poet was obliged to write his poems in iambic verses of four feet, grouped in four-line stanzas – that is, in Ambrosian verse – could choose his theme only from the Bible and had to stick to its words. And the optimistic ending was: Hail to the Father, hail to the Son and also to Thee, balsamic Holy Ghost, from century to century, from millennium to millennium!

'So Comrade Faludy believes that there is no socialist literature?'

'I didn't say that. There was also a Christian literature, and a very important one. Jacopone da Todi, Thomas of Celano, Hildebert de Lavardin, Pierre Abélard or Adam St Victor, for instance. But they wrote at a time when the Church no longer insisted upon determining the visions of the poets and, consequently, the poets were no longer obliged to put the resolutions of the Synods into rhyme . . .'

The names I mentioned made Biro blink; it was obvious that he had no idea what I was talking about. At any rate, he said, I would have to read and learn a great deal. Then, again without transition, he began to talk about the social democratic party. He explained how important the role of that party was in Hungarian democracy; but it could fill its role only if the left-wing elements were in the majority. Unfortunately, the social democratic party was teeming with deadly enemies of the communists, to mention only the right-wing Anna Kéthly and the Trotskyist Pal Justus . . .

'Approving of everything you and Orban agreed upon this morning,' he continued calmly, 'I think it would be best if you joined the social democratic party. Then you could report to Comrade Révai or to myself every week, in urgent cases more frequently, on what is going on in the headquarters of the party and in the editorial offices of *Népszava*.'

I felt that I was blushing furiously with excitement.

'You don't know me and you cannot know me,' I replied. 'You must have left Hungary when I was still a schoolboy. Since then I have lived in New York and you in Moscow, or I don't know where . . . For this reason I am not offended by your suggestion. Let us pretend I have not heard it, and let us forget about the whole thing. Perhaps we could speak about something else . . .'

Without betraying his discomfiture by the slightest sign, he turned the conversation to Hungarian literature, emphasizing the very large editions in which the communist publishing house could publish my works and what gigantic royalties I could obtain for them. Half an hour later he sent out for more coffee and then, while I was sipping mine, repeated his offer in identical words, except that I should have to report not to him but to Révai, or even to Rakosi himself. I rose and took my leave stiffly. In the hall he tried once more to make me change my mind but I gave him no reply. When I reached the street I noticed that Biro was just closing the window above my head; he had probably given instructions to his driver. When I approached the car, the chauffeur turned away his head. This was rather bad: the streetcars did not yet go so far out, it would have taken me an hour to walk home and there were only thirty minutes left to the curfew. Everyone seen in the streets after that hour was shot down by the Soviet patrols without warning.

As I didn't know anyone in the neighbourhood at whose house I could have spent the night I began to run as fast as I could. Ten minutes later I caught sight of the illuminated windows of the social democratic party headquarters. There were no guards at the entrance, as there were at communist party headquarters. The bespectacled porter was reading a book, he didn't even look up as I entered. A notice on the lift door announced that it was out of order. I ran up the steps. At the second floor I came upon a group of young people who recognized me from my picture in the newspaper. A red-headed, bespectacled boy of perhaps sixteen looked me over arrogantly from head to foot.

'Are you that George Faludy who came home from America to be hung by the communists?' he asked with a strange mixture of boyish insolence, curiosity and awe.

A few minutes later I sat in Anna Kéthly's room. While I was racing along the dirty, dusty streets between damaged houses, pictures of horror had been flashing through my mind. Now, suddenly, I was calm. Already the friendly, relaxed disorder of the party headquarters and the insolence of the red-headed boy had given me a feeling of ease, as if I had come from the barracks to a club, from an interrogation by the chief inquisitor into a pub; and the supreme calm of the lady minister sitting opposite me, her cool, hard beauty, completely restored my balance. She was almost sixty at the time, but still wore her beauty like an icy halo. Perhaps it was not so much an attribute of her femininity as the reflection of her moral conduct shining with nobility and even permanence from her incurious but observant eyes and her smooth, fresh complexion. It was a great joy to sit face to face with someone with whom, however different our views might be, I agreed on the most essential things, namely that honesty was more important than cleverness, character more important than success. When we met in the corridor she greeted me with cool friendliness, just as if we had last seen each other seven days, and not seven years, ago. She too was probably recalling the obituaries that bound us together. In 1943 it was rumoured in Budapest that I had been killed in Burma in the fight against the Japanese. Kéthly wrote a beautiful obituary in which she paid me homage. A year later, when the Germans invaded Hungary, Kéthly was put in a concentration camp but in New York it was believed that she had been shot. At that time it was I who wrote her obituary, in the weekly paper of the Hungarian emigration. Without mentioning these happenings we were now looking at each other with the resigned tenderness of those who had given each other the last rites.

On the wall opposite hung a few postcard-sized portraits. Kéthly began by telling me that the best thing for me to do would be to write poems and forget about politics. I had no need whatsoever of the social democratic party, though the party needed me. And not only the party but the whole country. They needed, in the first place, my lectures, my journalistic work, my educational activities, my erudition. After a thousand years, the question whether there should or should not be a Hungarian democracy was now in the balance. She wondered whether, for a few years, I should be willing to sacrifice my work as a writer and become a teacher. The main thing was that I should not judge by what I had seen in a hysterical capital, but should go to the countryside, look around, give lectures, hold seminars. And if I disagreed with the Marxist teachings, I could always talk about myself, about literature, about America, about whatever I pleased. And if, returning to the capital, I decided to make the sacrifice, the party would be glad if I joined *Népszava*. The party was poor, the cause important, the sacrifice great but, she hoped, not vain.

While she talked I looked absentmindedly at the pictures on the wall. Had anyone else made me a similar offer I should undoubtedly have rejected it, but Kéthly asked me with such sincere warmth that I was unable to do so. Nor did I feel like starting an argument on the vanity of the sacrifice, because we both held that one should serve the cause one considers just, or partly just, regardless of its chances of success.

The first picture on the wall represented Sandor Petöfi, the poet, struck down in one of the last battles of the 1848-49 War of Independence by some horseman of the Tsar who didn't permit himself to be influenced by the fact that the poet, unarmed, was watching the battle from the edge of the road. Then came a portrait of the scholarly-looking Béla Somogyi, one-time editor of *Népszava*, who was blinded with a penknife by Horthy's white terrorists in 1920, tied with barbed wire and thrown, still living, into the Danube. The subjects of the third and fourth photographs in the row, Illés Monus, former secretary of the social democratic party, and the round-headed, grey-haired Uncle Gyözö Gergely, former night-editor of *Népszava*, were well known to me. A year and a half before, when they were hiding from the Germans, a social-democrat turned Nazi recognized them in the street and shot them dead.

'Tomorrow, I'll leave for the country and start looking round Annuska,' I said, 'and when I come back I shall go to work at *Népszava*.' I was recalling all the others whose pictures were not on the wall, because all the walls of this little room and all the walls of the corridors of the social democratic headquarters, and all the walls of the houses along Rakoczi Street were still not long enough to hold them: the rebelling Hungarian peasants impaled by feudal landlords, the freedom fighters killed in battles against the Turks and the Austrians, the prisoners of the Seven Towers in Constantinople and the dungeons of Kufstein and Josefstadt; those executed by the German henchmen of Buda or hanged by Franz-Joseph after he had counted up to a hundred before signing their death-warrant, upon his mother's advice, lest history call him a cruel monarch; those murdered by the white terrorists and those tortured to death in the Svabhegy villas of the Gestapo, and those shot into the Danube by the arrow-cross party.

The nervousness and fear that had been my constant companions since I boarded the ship in the harbour of New York disappeared. I had become aware of and resigned myself to the situation: I was at home and had to submit to the customs of the country. To die for freedom or to end one's days in prison for liberty was not considered a very special feat in these parts; the view I had hitherto taken of the matter was indeed exaggerated.

More than three years later a car was taking me back to Budapest along the same Roman road on which I had driven into the countryside for the first time after my conversation with Kéthly. The road had since become very familiar to me. In the early days the old rattletrap lent me by the social democratic party had been stopped again and again by welcoming, kindly and curious peasants. Now, however, when the peasants caught sight of *Népszava*'s brand new British car, with its red flag and big, hulking driver at the wheel, they turned away or hid behind trees, bushes and corners.

In those vanished days I had gone swimming in cool rivers near blown-up bridges, where we sometimes had to wait an entire day for the ferry; when we had been out of funds, which often happened, my driver and I had lived on the fruit of mulberry trees bordering the highway, had baked run-over hares over a campfire and had slept on the top of haystacks with the cruel moonlight in our eyes. For two weeks I had taught history, democracy, but above all thinking, to the people of a small town, Dombovar, then had continued my lectures in another small town, Szekszard. I had talked with peasants on the crests of billowing hills, who, having no draught-animals, had harnessed themselves and their families to the plough and who had asked me whether the land, allocated to them at the time of the land-reform, would not be taken away again for *kolkhozes*. I had assured them, as I had hoped, that it would not be taken away. I had spoken at night meetings in harvest-time, in ducal stables by the light of a single paraffin lamp; there had been no tables, no chairs, nothing but the platinum inlays made by the moonlight in the chinks between the planks of which the walls were built. Most of the men had been barefoot, with pebbles or tufts of grass between their toes and although everyone had been dead tired, the atmosphere in those stables was that of a great first night. Until then, my listeners had had no opportunity to attend a meeting; they had done it now, after a thousand years of incredible misery and humiliation, in the hope that a new and better life would start for them, and when we ended by singing the National Anthem: '*These people have paid for their sins, past and future,*' tears had been running down all our faces. I had tried hard not to let my emotions get the upper hand, but the atmosphere of the audience, this vibrating and hypnotizing mixture of hope, happiness and fear, tiredness and excitement so familiar to me had been stronger than my resolution.

Three years later, where was the happiness, or even the hope? I never visited Dombovar or Szekszard after the local party organizations had merged with the communists and I avoided all the villages where I had held meetings. I felt, in a way, responsible and was deeply ashamed that in spite of my promises I had been unable to prevent seizure of power by the communists. Neither I nor anyone else had the opportunity to perform heroic deeds. Even heroic words could be pronounced but once; and he who pronounced them, disappeared without trace usually the same night; which did not mean that those preferring cowardly silence were safe from arrest.

Yet I often travelled in the country. I did it to escape the oppressive atmosphere of the capital, though I found peace not so much in the villages as during the six- to eight-hour drives between our destinations. On this particular occasion I set out, as usual, with the pretext that I was going to write a social survey for *Népszava*; but this time I had an additional and special reason to escape. I had read the indictment against Laszlo Rajk, the former Minister of the Interior: that he confessed that in the previous autumn he had met the Yugoslav Minister of the Interior, Rankovich, in a field guards' hut near mile post No. 116, to conspire with him concerning the overthrow of the Hungarian People's Republic. It was widely known that the Hungarian secret police, which was controlled directly from Moscow, watched and controlled all the Ministers day and night, so it seemed most unlikely that the Hungarian Minister would have got the chance to meet a Titoist Minister secretly, even had he dared to run such a risk. I happened to remember that the house of my old peasant friend, Janos Bulla, stood near that mile post No. 116. I decided to try to find out the truth on the spot.

To drive from Budapest directly to mile post No. 116 would have been suicide. Therefore I pretended to look at various archaeological finds in Transdanubia and stopped at my journey's destination only on the fifth evening, ostensibly casually. My friend Bulla was a self-educated man, who mixed Latin juridical expressions and Greek philosophical terms with his country dialect, always in their proper place but a little more frequently than necessary. In the course of his life he had collected a library of several thousand volumes which, in the old days, he used to keep in the loft, because Horthy's gendarmes disliked educated peasants. When I had visited him three years earlier, he had been planning to move his library to the ground floor, but in the meantime he had discovered that secret policemen did not like educated peasants either, and had changed his mind. We talked in the loft, among his books, under the pale pink grapes hanging from the beams. While we talked I stood by the window of the small attic room, and by bending my shoulders a little I could see the famous mile post. There was no field guards' hut there, nor had there ever been one, as my friend Bulla assured me.

I tossed and turned, sleepless under the hot eiderdowns in the bedroom smelling of apples. I was stupefied by what I had just learned. I had not believed there had been a meeting between Rajk and Rankovich in the field guards' hut, but I had never thought that there was not even a field guards' hut.

Then suddenly I started to think of Rajk. I had always loathed him and was only interested in his case, or, more precisely, in the implications of his case; that we were living in a country where innocent people could be arrested and hanged if and when the authorities so pleased. But now, for the first time, I felt something like sympathy towards the detestable victim, who in my opinion was guilty of all crimes but those he was charged with. I had only once met him personally, ten years before in a Paris café in Bandi Havas's company. Rajk had just returned from the Spanish Civil War, where he was said to have fought heroically. I found it rather unpleasant to converse with him. I would have been interested in his experiences in Spain; but instead of telling us about them he kept repeating over and over again that there were only two roads open to mankind, that of the *bourgeoisie* and that of the proletariat. He who did not follow the road of the proletariat belonged, in his passivity, to the other (this was addressed to me) and was consequently a traitor. While he repeated this wisdom, I gazed at the very beautiful Annamite girls sitting at the bar, and when the girls were just leaving and Rajk was still repeating his theory about the two roads, I replied that mankind could follow probably hundreds of roads and so could I, but now I wanted to follow the road of the Annamite girls. He may have taken my joke seriously, because he threw me a disdainful glance through the window of the café.

In Paris I found him only ridiculous, but at home I watched his activities as Minister of the Interior with hatred. He was the second man in the communist party, Rakosi's right hand, fanatical, cruel, incorruptible, reckless and boring. When some months earlier I learned that he was arrested my first thought was that murderers were murdering murderers. But when I read in the indictment that Rajk confessed to having been a spy of the Horthy police and had taken part in the Spanish Civil War as an agent of the fascists in order to demoralize the Loyalists, I was shocked. Antipathetic though the accused man was, the accusation in itself alarmed me; but even that, I found, did not alarm me so much as the non-existence of the field guards' hut. Thus I wondered why it was just this rather unimportant detail that changed my attitude towards the person of Rajk; why it was now, for the first time, that I could not deny a kind of pity for the hero of the Spanish Civil War, who was defeated by the friends he had served with so much loyalty instead of by his enemies. I drank again and again from the wine placed next to my bed by my peasant host so familiar with human emotions, until the dawn came.

The next morning I decided to return to the capital. Like most of my actions at that time, this return was inspired by two motives. One sprang from my tender feelings for Suzy Szegö. The second was a sort of compulsory concession to the unwritten laws of the people's democracy, which regulated my actions, my words and even, when I was in a public place, my movements, although I did my utmost to restrict its manifestations to the negative: to passivity, silence and stillness. The Rajk trial was nearing its end and I had to be in the capital when the sentence was announced. I could have heard the trial over the radio built into the car, but I knew that the editorial staff would listen collectively, as usual. These burnings of heretics were regarded as festive and joyful occasions, as in a certain sense they really were: they came as climaxes to long weeks of uncertainty, and put an end to campaigns of arrest so that everyone could feel safe for at least a few weeks until a new wave of arrests began. But if the heretic on the stake was widely known as a faithful believer, the audience – namely the whole country – felt involved in the same suspicion and thus it was advisable to be present at such collective radio-listenings and at the party meeting after them unless one wanted to be accused of complicity.

I have a weighty reason for describing my love for Suzy Szegö in such obsolete terms as 'tender feelings'. Compared to the two fundamental and extreme manifestations of sexual life in the people's democracy – over-rationalized sexual relationship and irrational love-making – our love seemed indeed to be old-fashioned. Marriages, and even the majority of love-affairs, were determined by what rating the partners had in the party. An intellectual who *had not* taken part in the underground movement and had come to the communist party from another party and was therefore suspected of heresy (of being a communist, that is, for logical considerations and not because of blind faith); or an intellectual who, on the contrary, *had* participated in the underground movement and was therefore even more suspected of heresy (of, in this case, nationalistic deviation from the Moscow line) – such people did best, if they wanted to keep their jobs, flats and party membership, to marry the daughters of the parry bureaucrats returned from Moscow. Nobody knew what kind of connections those former emigrants had in Moscow, or which of them was still a spy of the Soviet Secret Police, so the bare fact of being a Muscovite meant immunity for them and their families, regardless of whether they had spent their years of emigration in a Russian house or a Russian prison. A young girl, however, who joined the party in 1945 out of opportunism (which was considered officially as capitulation before the Red Army – a good mark), but whose father was a former manufacturer now living on parcels sent by his relatives from America (which was added to his daughter's crime-sheet), did best to leave her parents' home, meet them only secretly or not at all and marry an AVO officer or an engineer recognized as an expert (which did not necessarily mean that he was one). Such marriages, which were becoming more and more frequent, exempted the person in question from the persecution otherwise due to him or to her, and though mostly unhappy, were pretty stable.

The other extreme was represented by sexual intercourse performed with the speed of sparrows and discretion of dogs. People fell upon each other without discrimination, premeditation or prelude in parks, woods, state automobiles, on desks of offices, in party premises, party stairways, party lofts and party gardens; mainly because, owing to the scandalous housing conditions, and lack of hotels, they simply had no other opportunity. At such times both men and women were able, at last, to experience some real satisfaction, after being numbed or driven to furious despair by a working day increased to twelve, fourteen, sometimes twenty hours by collective newspaper reading or collective radio-listening, Marxist seminars, decoration, procession, wall-newspaper editing, women's and youths' days, house-to-house agitation, village propaganda, party meetings, trade-union meetings, workers' conferences, factory committee meetings, membership meetings, Hungarian-Soviet Society meetings and overtime. The satisfaction was not caused by physical delight but only by the knowledge that however overworked and tortured they were, they still had some energy left. Because of the twenty kinds of conference and party work, nothing was easier than to find a reason which would explain to parent, wife or husband why one had to stay out the whole night, so everyone made love happily and vengefully on the party's furniture, in the party's time, with the party's help and on the party's account, while the party bureaucrats shut their eyes, partly because they considered that kind of love-making as an innocent security-valve for all party members, and partly because it gave them one more handle for blackmail when the time came.

In such an environment my tender feelings for Suzy did indeed seem old-fashioned, although our love was neither more special, nor more romantic than the average; only – at most – stronger. Others, however, found it different and watched it either with benevolence or with envy, or foretold an early and bitter end to it, which made us carry it with some exhibitionism and pride. There was in fact no difference between us and any ordinary lovers of the twentieth century; the extraordinary was not in ourselves but in the society around us. This society was like that of a medieval town, which marched one day in a pious Lenten procession and on the next day performed orgies on the pavement of the same street. Suzy and I walked in those interchanging periods of procession and orgy, arm in arm, like simple lovers, and thus scandalized them.

I met Suzy for the first time a few days after my return home, when I went to see Béla Zsolt, the most courageous liberal journalist of the country, at the editorial offices of *Haladas*. At that time Suzy was not yet a communist and wrote excellent short stories and articles. She was deep in conversation with a woman friend, in a corner of a huge room with dirty windows which made it seem as though it were raining outside, although the streets were bathed in a lovely spring sunshine. She was leaning her hip against a desk, the top of which was strewn with the ashes of her cigarette; her red handbag, half open and revealing a purse, a flapjack, her documents and a handkerchief, lay in the middle of the desk. Her blonde hair fell in a single wave from the parting to her shoulder, like a stage curtain at the moment when it comes together, only to fall apart again for a fraction of a second. She had an oval face and greenish-grey eyes; not an impressionistic face put together from patches of colour, or from muscle and tissue, but a face put together of contours; she could have been painted – and indeed she was painted – by Botticelli and by Botticelli alone, perhaps in one of his lost pictures. She pressed her two long, spindle-shaped thighs slightly forward so that the shape of her knees was clearly visible through her tight, checked skirt. 'This woman and I will run away this very morning to San Francisco,' I decided and resolved to introduce myself. But then I became involved in a conversation with Béla Zsolt. Suzy left and I forgot her.

I met her again one and a half years later when, at the time of the liquidation of the social democratic party, she came to work for *Népszava* where I was employed. At that time the social democratic paper was being transformed into a trade-union journal, its editor was sacked and his place was taken by Zoltan Horvath, former foreign editor. Horvath was a short, squat, bald, intelligent, uneducated and uninhibited man with rolling eyes, a glib tongue and tufts of black hair protruding from his nostrils. He drank five or six litres of strong black coffee a day and gave proof of an unlimited capacity for work which, from the professional point of view, was of little value because he could not write at all. He was called the Judas of the social democratic party, not only because he had been one of the loudest propagandists for the merging of the two parties, but because he undertook the task offered me, as I have described, by Rakosi's brother. As a reward they promised him the job of Under-Secretary of Foreign Affairs, but when the merger went through they appointed him editor of *Népszava* and showed him no particular consideration.

Horvath, who had never let anyone stand in his way, defended not only Suzy (who was a daughter of a rich industrialist, although at that time she had turned with utter devotion to the system) and myself, but also our colleagues (who despised him) from the persecution of the communists. When someone fell ill, he took him to the best sanatorium in his car, he provided money, he looked after his family – in short, he behaved like a father to all of us.

Because of him I survived relatively easily the painful period while *Népszava* was transformed into a trade-union journal – which meant that its subscribers were raised from forty thousand to over a hundred thousand, but that nobody ever read it. Everything was fine until the party appointed as co-editor a one-time cloth-merchant by the name of Gacs. Gacs was a veteran communist and Révai's brother-in-law: a handsome, insolent, fairly young man, who wore suits made of cloth from Manchester, had owned a small weaving-mill with a few workers whom he exploited mercilessly up to the time of nationalization, and who spent at least as much time commenting on the fact that he wore only suits made of Manchester cloth as he did on abusing capitalist exploitation. Although he understood not a word of Russian his desk was always adorned with the latest issue of *Pravda*; when someone entered his room it was with the *Pravda* that he quickly covered his packet of Lucky Strike cigarettes, so as not to be obliged to offer one. A short time before, he had married the widow of a Hungarian communist leader – a friend of his – who was executed in 1944. Gacs used to assure us that the memory of his friend was still green. Whenever – he explained – after a long day's work he and his young wife went to bed, they always sat up on the pillow and rendered homage to his memory with one minute of silence, then – as he expressed himself – they had a little chat about the dear departed, before they got down to the brass tacks of love-making.

When Gacs took over his room in the editorial offices he brought with him a big, clumsy, red-headed worker with an asymetrical face. He introduced him as Bicsak, a communist hero, with whom he had worked in the underground movement, and he told us that from now on this young worker would read and judge every manuscript. A few days later I handed Bicsak a short article I had written on the three hundredth anniversary of the Treaty of Westphalia. I was standing at the window of my room, looking out at the dark grey drizzle. I had just learned that my old friend, Rustem Vambéry, had died of heart failure in the New York subway and I was remembering some of his words on human dignity and Roman Law when Gacs sent for me. Bicsak, with his asymetrical face, was sitting in a deep leather armchair opposite Gacs's desk; neither invited me to sit down. Gacs asked Bicsak whether he had read my article and what he thought of it, to which Bicsak replied with a single word: 'Shit'. He pronounced this word with extraordinary rapidity and cheerfulness, emphasizing only the first letter, upon which Gacs informed me with unconvincing sympathy that Bicsak personified the working class and that what he didn't understand, no other worker would understand. It was up to me to learn to write more plainly, in the language of the people. With this he dismissed me but first, so that I should harbour no illusions concerning the fate of my article, he tore it up and threw it into the wastepaper basket.

When, three days later, the same fate overtook my review of a performance of *Macbeth*, I asked one of my colleagues, a young worker, to intervene. This young man explained to Bicsak that I was one of the foremost poets in Hungary. Thereafter, to Gacs's disappointment, Bicsak described every one of my articles not as 'shit', but as 'a masterpiece', even if I wrote absolute rubbish. A few months later it became known that Bicsak had been an enthusiastic member of the Hungarian Nazi party, one of the bodyguards of the arrow-cross leader, Szalasi, and had a dozen thefts and probably even a few murders on his conscience. I expected Gacs to feel embarrassed at having introduced this man as his comrade from the underground movement, but he did not. After having fired Bicsak, Gacs often boasted of having saved us from this hooligan.

In the following months Gacs was forever inventing new tricks to exasperate me. Horvath was unable to come to my aid because Gacs's connections in the party were better than his, but I made him send me out of town as a reporter as often as possible – until Gacs was transferred to the trade union council.

On one of those trips I took Suzy with me.

We had become better acquainted by then, although our friendship had not gone very far. We used to go down to the espresso for a cup of coffee during or after office hours, and I kissed her when I arrived and left, but I was on the same footing with all female members of the staff, kissing the young because they were young, the old because they were old. I took her on this trip without any ulterior motive, just to have someone with whom to talk on the journey. I visited a few provincial museums; the director of one of them told me that a peasant had dug up the corner of a Bronze Age cemetery in the neighbourhood. I could take a look at it if I was interested. An hour later we were standing on a fragrant, breezy hillside. The short, skinny peasant was just opening up a new grave with extraordinary caution, inspired not so much by archaeology as by his respect for the dead however ancient they might be. He had put his greasy black hat on the ground, weighting it down with a stone so that the wind should not carry it away. We were gazing down into the open grave of a loving couple of the Bronze Age.

They were lying one close behind the other, with knees drawn up. Their skulls and their broad, butterfly-winged hip-bones had been full uncovered, but their vertebrae were still embedded in the earth, and their arm-bones were not yet visible. The pink paint that had once enhanced their complexions was now sticking to the bone: the man leaned his forehead against the woman's nape as if he wanted to kiss her neck, and the strawberry-ice-coloured bones in the grey grainy earth suggested not transience, but eroticism. Putting down his hoe the peasant stepped up to us. Suzy was standing close to me, and when, keeping my neck stiff, I glanced sideways at her, I was suddenly overwhelmed with the feeling that this was our wedding ceremony.

The next time I wanted to take her with me, Horvath protested. Suzy was a young girl, I a married man; he, as editor, could not condone such things. I didn't argue and didn't even tell him that I had left Valy some time ago and quite independently of Suzy. A few months earlier, while I was working hard on a play at about three o'clock in the morning, Valy had got out of bed, had come to stand before my desk and had begun to reproach me, apropos of nothing, because I had never bought her a hat. I had replied by enumerating the hats that I had not only bought her but had helped her to choose: a large straw hat with a red ribbon in Africa, a red velvet beret in New York, the grey pagoda-shaped one and the one she had copied from the portrait of Mad Joanna, Queen of Aragon. I had admitted that this was less than any woman had a right to, but still, they were hats. Facts did not alter Valy's opinion and she continued to shout at me and abuse me, saying the most offensive things, for an hour and a half. I didn't mind the abuse, I was used to it by then, but she screamed it at the top of her voice in a villa with walls as thin as paper. The next morning, on my way to *Népszava*, I took the same bus as the owner of the villa. He was standing next to me on the platform and said suddenly, very politely, without the slightest trace of irony: 'Look, Mr Faludy, buy your wife a hat. If you don't we shall never be able to sleep at night.'

I got off the bus, walked back to the top of Rose Hill and, with the excuse that I had forgotten to take something with me, threw my manuscripts, shaving things and toothbrush into an attaché case, left the house and never returned again.

Thus, after having visited the mile post, I wanted to see Suzy and I also felt that it would be proper to return and to attend the collective radio-listening. But I had other reasons for coming back. I was also interested in the fate of two of my colleagues who had been working with me on *Népszava*, had suddenly disappeared, and were now so-called witnesses in the Rajk trial (but under arrest, of course, as witnesses at a communist trial usually were). And I was further interested in the trial because of one of Rajk's fellow-accused, Pal Justus, whom I had known very well.

Justus had been one of the leaders of the social democratic party, Rajk's deadly enemy, and apart from that was a scholarly, honest man, though just as fanatical in his own way as his fellow defendant and enemy. Justus had always treated me with esteem and friendship – an attitude which I did not reciprocate – and often sent his poems to me at *Népszava*. I did not publish them because I did not find them good enough.

Justus had co-operated with his close friend Zoltan Horvath in bringing about the merging of the two parties, but his motives were entirely different. He believed that there was no point in sacrificing ourselves for the sake of the West in exchange for a few short obituaries in the *Daily Herald* and the *Populaire* in which our names would be misspelt. He believed that if we yielded to the communists it would save thousands of social democratic leaders and workers from the scaffold and prison – even if we were called cowards by our Western friends, who so valiantly emboldened us from abroad. After the merger Justus was appointed director of the Hungarian radio, in celebration of which he sent me another sheaf of poems.

On a warm, spring afternoon Zoltan Horvath knocked on my door. He came to ask me what I intended to do with his friend's poems, adding that the Saturday before he had heard Rakosi telling Justus that he intended to appoint him Minister of Public Culture. I should serve my own interest by having the poems printed. I looked up at him and Horvath blushed a fiery red; only then did it occur to him – although he was a clever man – that he had approached me with the clumsiest possible *captatio benevolentiae.* I replied that Justus's poems would never appear in the literary columns of the paper, but if he wanted to publish them in the political columns I could do nothing to stop him. He asked where they were and I pointed to the waste-paper basket. Without showing the slightest resentment, Horvath knelt down by the basket and picked out his friend's poems. Sitting there, looking down at my editor's bald head and at the tufts of black hair protruding from his mobile nostrils, I suddenly felt sorry for the fat, panting man. He put the manuscript in his pocket and ran down to the printing shop. Two hours later he came into my room again, his eyes popping, begging me in a whisper to go down to the printing shop and take Justus's poems out from the press. In the meantime he had learned that Justus had been arrested as Tito's fascist agent, and accused of high treason and conspiracy.

A few days later Justus's thin, ugly, blonde wife, who had once worked as a secretary at *Népszava*, appeared at the editorial offices to talk to her husband's best friend, Zoltan Horvath. She was turned away. She told me in the corridor, crying bitterly, that after her husband's arrest she had been fired from her job without a penny; that the AVO had seized the little cash they had at home and her husband's only treasure, his library; and that she had been forced to keep her little daughter at home because each morning her schoolmates had received her by shouting: 'They'll hang your daddy, they'll hang your daddy!'

I immediately began to make a collection for the unfortunate woman, with the help of Suzy and of the fat Ica, another member of the staff of *Népszava*, who had been secretary to Justus. A few hours later, at an editorial conference, Zoltan Horvath rose to speak. Without mentioning names and in a warning rather than an aggressive way, he said: 'There are among us certain comrades who interpret socialist humanism quite falsely. From sheer sentimentalism they have been collecting for the wife of a traitor. You must realize, comrades, that a traitor has no wife, a traitor has no daughter, a traitor has no family – a traitor should go to hell!' While he spoke, perspiration ran down his yellow-brown forehead – it was he who was the best friend of Justus and not we – and the tufts of black hair protruding from his nostrils were more lugubrious than ever.

Two days later Zoltan Horvath came again to my room. He looked worried and said he had learned that the fat Ica was being followed by secret police, which he considered natural, since she had been secretary to Justus. Nevertheless, in Horvath's opinion, it was easy for her to clear herself. In two days a party meeting would take place, where Ica should stand up and speak a few contemptuous words about Justus. As the widow of a communist martyr and the most stupid member of the social democratic party, she might justifiably expect some tolerance. But Ica refused to listen to Horvath's advice. So would I persuade her – he still felt concern for her – to behave in a reasonable way: she could do nothing to save Justus, but by denying him she might save herself.

I refused to comply with Horvath's wish, replying that I certainly would not persuade anybody to do anything against his conscience. Just before the membership meeting, however, he himself spoke to her and almost begged her to rise at the meeting and declare how grateful she was to the AVO for having unmasked the imperialist agent Justus who had misled her with his cunning practices, so that now she cursed his memory. Horvath even took the trouble to write it down on a piece of paper for Ica to learn by heart, because it would sound more sincere, more heartfelt if she recited it without notes. Ica declared that nobody yet knew the charges brought against Justus; if the hearing proved the charges true she might change her opinion, but she was not prepared to pass sentence on her best friend before the Court did so. After this statement she no longer struck me as stupid. At the party meeting a long speech was made by a well-known communist journalist, who called Rajk and Justus imperialist beasts. After this speech, which lasted for about two hours, the chairman of the meeting suddenly addressed Ica and asked her whether she had anything to say. Ica stood up with a glowing red face and a piece of paper in her hand, stammered something which nobody could understand, and quickly sat down again. She disappeared that same night, two weeks after the arrest of Justus.

Another two weeks later Mrs Justus was arrested for 'trying to win sympathy and talking too much'. Zoltan Horvath came again to my room and said that he had a presentiment of evil concerning another member of our staff, Györgyi Vandori, who had also been a close friend of Justus. Horvath did not believe that Györgyi Vandori could save herself with a statement against Justus. Thus he only asked me to persuade her to burn her diary before the AVO got hold of it.

At that moment I felt a cold shudder because it occurred to me that Horvath might be an *agent provocateur* of the secret police and that if he was I was lost. I always spoke to him frankly whenever we were alone. So I did not promise to talk with Györgyi Vandori about the ominous diary, although privately I decided to do so.

Györgyi Vandori was a blue-stocking with a musky smell, who constantly molested me with her love. By then nearly everyone on *Népszava* avoided her, since it was common belief that she would soon be arrested. One evening she came into my room and complained with tears in her eyes that everybody was afraid of her and she had no one to talk with. I saw her home and tried to cheer her up, although she bored me to death and on top of that we were followed by detectives. It was then that I tried to persuade her to burn her ominous diary. I knew that she recorded all the gossip, private conversation and confidential information that she could collect, and that she had been doing it for years. I was also afraid that, with her feverish imagination, she invented both events and conversations. I tried to make it clear to her that if the AVO got hold of this diary its contents would provide evidence against dozens of innocent people, who might well be arrested and even killed in consequence of her literary ambitions. After I had pleaded with her for nearly an hour, she at last promised to burn the diary. Then, thinking perhaps I had seen her home because I had fallen in love with her, she invited me up to her flat and I refused politely. The next day she did not come to the office; she had been arrested.

Nearly a fortnight passed, but Zoltan Horvath did not visit me in my room again. Finally I got nervous. I went to him and asked him who would be arrested next according to his presentiment of evil? For the first time in our acquaintance Horvath behaved brusquely, almost arrogantly, towards me. He assured me that the arrests had come to an end so that I could stop worrying and should mind my own business. He seemed very cheerful, as if he had fulfilled a difficult task and was expecting the praise to which his good work entitled him. The next day, early in the morning, Suzy and I left for our holidays on Lake Balaton. It was therefore only later that I learned that Horvath was arrested that very day on the charge of being 'one of Tito's most dangerous agents'.

Since their arrest I had heard nothing about any of my acquaintances. It was only from the indictment that I knew of Justus's role in the trial as an accomplice of Rajk (although they were deadly enemies and never spoke to each other), and that fat Ica would figure as a witness, that is to say as somebody who knew everything about the espionage relationship between Justus and the Yugoslavs. This seemed quite ridiculous. Allowing that Justus had such connections with the Yugoslavs, which was impossible, he certainly would not have told Ica a thing about them. I also learned that long passages from Györgyi Vandori's diary would be read out at the trial, providing a wide range of evidence against Rajk and his accomplices.

I was puzzled by this information, since the blue-stocking with the musky smell had promised me to burn her diary. I could not tell whether she had kept her promise or not. Perhaps she really had burned the diary, but the police had made her re-write it with a text that met their demands even better than the original one. But she might just as well not have burned it. And I remembered how I had tried to comfort her just before her arrest, saying in my zeal things I never truly believed: for instance that they would certainly arrest me before her. I had also agreed emphatically when she cursed and abused the system in terms which even I found exaggerated. On that last evening, when I had to turn down her invitation, I said politely that I had a terrible headache from correcting a proof of a speech by Stalin, and that I always got a headache and nausea, when I had to read anything pronounced by that Caucasian highwayman. The stupid goose had offered her mouth for a kiss, but her eyes had been sparkling with mental activity. At that moment I had thought: this idiot has promised to burn her damned diary, but she will not burn it; no, she will run straight upstairs in order to write down quickly what I have just said about the Caucasian highwayman. All this I remembered later, very precisely. I tried to comfort myself with the theory that if she had indeed recorded my words, I should already be in prison. But I could not get rid of the evil presentiment that she had written down what I had said, and that she had not burned the diary.

Because of all this I drove back to Budapest, passing the place where I usually stopped to dine: the Inn of Dunapentele. I had liked the inn-keeper's stories, loved his wines and simply adored the medieval Hungarian dishes he served, such as the meat soup cooked with germinated wheat that his dwarf-wife had stirred on the stove, standing on a footstool. I couldn't even picture the inn-keeper without the inn, which had been in his family for eleven generations, with its heavy smell of paraffin and pipe-smoke; and I had therefore been extremely surprised when, a few months before, he had come to visit the editorial offices and, catching sight of me, had drawn me aside.

Almost inarticulate with fury, wiping his purple forehead with his red-checked handkerchief, he had told me that the party wanted to take away his inn. He knew that one could not piss against the wind. He had not long ago offered the inn, the wine-cellars, the pigs, and everything else to the state, on condition that he could stay on as tapman and his wife as cook. He didn't even mind if they put a manager on his neck, so long as he was allowed to stay. But the local party secretary wanted to live in the inn himself, so he had been declared a *kulak* and he was told the inn would be requisitioned. He asked my help but I had to refuse; since he had been declared a *kulak*, not even a Minister could have saved him.

That night he killed his screeching dwarf-wife and his silent, tubercular daughter with a pole-axe, slaughtered his cattle and pigs, opened the taps of his wine-barrels, then hanged himself on the lovely wooden gate through which so many diligences and coaches had driven. I had learned all this from an article entitled *The Last Crime of a Bestial Kulak* written by one of the young members of our staff.

This article was never published. Imre Komor, the new editor-in-chief who had recently arrived from Moscow to occupy first Gacs's and now Zoltan Horvath's place, read the first few lines standing by the desk, as he always did, then returned it to its author. He raised his hand and smoothed his hair, all silver like a beautiful rococo wig. Then he spoke, briefly and succinctly, but with an amazing glibness, reminding one of the orators in the French National Convention of 1793, just as his handsome, noble, elegantly pink face, his straight, pointed nose and slightly bent back (that at times made him look like a hunchback, though he was not) reminded one of Maximilien de Robespierre. He explained that the purpose of a communist newspaper was not to disseminate information. 'The press,' he said, 'to quote Lenin's words, is a collective propagandist, a collective agitator. We do not write about murder, crime, traffic accidents. Except, of course, if they are reported from capitalist countries.'

Thus there was no restaurant on the two hundred kilometres of highway. Before starting I bought food for the journey, and at noon I made the driver stop on a friendly hilltop. It was a warm, early autumn day; fleecy clouds swam in the sky from which a raindrop would fall on us from time to time, as if we were sitting in a greenhouse. I looked at my driver, at his brutal, stubborn, but intelligent face, and suddenly I felt like laughing.

It was the same man, Kakuk, who had driven me three years before on my first tour. Before starting that morning, I had asked him to take me to the social democratic headquarters, where I had to talk to someone for a few minutes. When I came down and looked for the car I saw a skinny old bearded Jew standing on the pavement with Kakuk. 'You rotten fascist scoundrel, what did you do with my dining-room carpet?' he shouted and hit Kakuk with his stick. He repeated this performance several times and finally yelled for a policeman. At this Kakuk, who had until then been bearing the blows with patience, began to run away, followed by the old man.

The big, heavy driver and the Jew at least seventy years old raced like athletes at the Olympic Games. I climbed into the car. In those days it was not unusual for someone to recognize his wife's murderer in a tram, or his stolen treasures in the shop-window of a decent firm. Ten minutes later Kakuk reappeared panting, jumped in behind the wheel and drove off fast. I asked him whether he had indeed been a member of the arrow-cross party.

'Of course I was,' he replied.

'And what makes you a social democrat today?'

'The same thing. One must make a living.'

'Did you believe the Nazis?'

'Exactly as I believe the social democrats today and the bolsheviks tomorrow!' he replied, smiling at me.

True to his name, which means cuckoo, he kept a couple of girlfriends in every county. I was always careful to spend the night in or near towns where they lived, because in the morning Kakuk would show up sleepy, but always with a fat goose or a basketful of eggs in his arms. He was grateful for my consideration but our friendship was restricted to the duration of our trips. At the editorial offices he behaved as if he did not know me at all. Lately, however, he had begun to treat me with a certain gentleness and now, while he was stuffing chicken, green pepper and pickled cucumber into his mouth, I noticed him watching me with anxious eyes.

'They'll get you too, Comrade Faludy,' he said at long last. He spoke calmly, unemotionally, and swallowed down the food.

'They won't,' I said indifferently. 'I had nothing to do with Rajk.'

'And what had Justus to do with Rajk?'

'But I am not interested in politics.'

'Those on top all sit in the same sledge. The turn of each comes to be thrown to the wolves. They always throw out someone.'

'Nobody wants my job. My work cannot be accomplished by . . .'

'Don't say it! That's exactly what Comrade Justus said two days before he was arrested. As we were stopping at a street light.'

'What did he say?' I asked, reaching for the wine-bottle. Unfortunately the bad road had spoiled the good wine; it had no taste left, and it was warm into the bargain.

'Comrade Justus said that he was indispensable. And yet he did not write articles as beautiful as yours.'

'Do you read my articles, then? Do you understand them?'

'The hell I do! But they are beautiful,' he said with awe. 'It would be better for you if they were less beautiful.'

'Why?'

'Because they can see from those articles that you are not one of them.'

'All right,' I said, rising. 'Now I shall walk on a bit in the maize field. In ten minutes, when you have finished your cigarette, come after me.'

'I should like to ask you something if you don't mind.'

'Go ahead!'

'Why did you come back from America?'

'Because one doesn't like to live in a foreign land.'

'I see,' Kakuk said, digesting my answer. 'But when you saw that you had come to a pigsty, why didn't you go back? Why?'

His question was passionate, almost demanding.

'They guard the border. With dogs, machine-guns, barbed-wire fences. You know it.'

'I do. But why didn't you escape when the road was still open?'

I shrugged my shoulders. 'I missed the last train, I suppose,' I replied and walked away through the field towards the hilltop. I did not look back but I could feel the driver's sharp, suspicious and yet admiring glance between my shoulder-blades. He must have thought that I was an American spy, for what other reason could there be for my being in Hungary?

It was exactly three o'clock by the large clock in the editorial offices when I tried to sneak into Suzy's room but was intercepted by Annie, who stood watch in the corridor to catch as many members of the staff as possible for the collective radio-listening; She was a tiny, energetic, little middle-aged widow of good *bourgeoise* background, working at *Népszava* as a typist, and because she was terrified of being fired – she had a son of sixteen to bring up – she did her utmost to appear a good communist. Because of her zeal she was made the party group steward and was given a thousand little jobs to do. There was no membership meeting at which she didn't speak, though she never denounced anyone. The kind of thing she would say was: 'From this platform I call the attention of the women of the world . . .' or, 'I warn Mr Truman and suggest that he . . .' for which she was usually enthusiastically applauded. Imre Komor, our editor with the Robespierre face, used on these occasions to turn to me and say loudly, 'Oh, *sancta simplicitas . . .*' Of the fifty members of the editorial staff, we were the only two who understood even that much Latin.

In the course of a few months Annie had become completely transfigured; she walked on clouds, bathed in the transcendental happiness of a pious Catholic. She didn't understand a word of the communist dogma but identified herself with it completely. She regarded it as a privilege to work day and night for the party, was radiant with joy at having been given an opportunity to prove her importance from daybreak till midnight. She organized, managed, decorated, collected membership fees and chided those coming late to work, all without malice but with a frightening arrogance.

It was absolutely necessary to listen to the indictment against Rajk, she explained. However much I might know about everything, it would teach me how to recognize the cunningly masked imperialist spy who had penetrated the party and how to unmask him. In addition, the party would certainly appreciate my show of interest. She pronounced the word 'party' with panting emphasis and awe; to her it meant something like a combination of Orwell's televisor-network and of the omnipotent, omniscient deity. While she was lecturing me, Pal Gedeon, the foreign editor, came out of his room. Gedeon was a professional journalist, a tall, thin, quick and polite young man with a bird's head, a small moustache and thinning hair. He knew exactly what he was being paid for and therefore never omitted the *Great Stalin to whom we owe everything*, the *Glorious Soviet Union, leader of the peace camp*, or the *Tito, the lap-dog of the imperialists led on a dollar-leash* from any of his six fluent, garrulous, and wholly mendacious weekly articles. Less than a year earlier Gedeon had still been calling Tito *the partisan leader and freedom fighter of unequalled heroism*. I usually thought of my colleague as a waiter who served rotten fish to the guests with perfect manners and on a silver platter. As Gedeon was usually very busy and difficult to entice out of his room, Annie immediately concentrated her energies on him and I could slip unnoticed into Suzy's room.

I hitched myself on to the desk, pushing off, as if by accident, Stalin's brochure on nationality problems and shifting Suzy's red handbag from the middle of the desk. Some little time earlier I had criticized the party's agricultural policies in front of Suzy; when I had just about convinced her with my arguments she had suddenly declared that in spite of all, she agreed with the party. If the party said that her red handbag was white she would, henceforth, regard it as white. Since then I had persistently persecuted the handbag, pushed it, kicked it whenever I could. When I had turned my back to the portrait of the Caucasian and Suzy had put her handbag safely into the drawer of her desk so that all bad demons were dispelled, I took her hands in mine and began to play with her fingers.

She said she was glad that I had come back from the country so soon, or rather that I had come back at all, instead of roaming around or running away as was almost to be expected from someone not so much fickle, but rather dreamy and absent-minded, like myself. Then she looked me over carefully to see whether I was still as agreeable and handsome as she usually found me. Finally, she made sure with a quick glance that there was nothing in the corner of my eye that would lead her to suppose that I had been up to mischief. She also looked me over to make sure my permanent good mood was still in force, undisturbed by even a shadow of sorrow. She did this so that she could help and comfort me if necessary; assist me, whom, from the human point of view, she considered a unique phenomenon although from a political point of view I was an old-fashioned, mild, *bourgeois* democrat who was unable to understand the needs of our time.

I could not tell Suzy about my experiences on this trip, nor could I ask about the Rajk trial because that might have led to a quarrel. And as to the affairs of the newspaper: they held no interest whatsoever for me. When we were sitting like this I usually felt like a stupid country bumpkin who, having nothing to say, strokes his beloved's arm or plays with her hand. At other times, after a brief silence, we would begin to talk: I would tell Suzy about my African and American adventures, events that had no connection with the two of us nor with the present; or I would make love to her in extemporized verse, to which she listened with some surprise but great patience. When travelling in a bus together we sometimes pretended not to know each other; I would make passes at her like a practised woman-chaser and she would play the shocked and offended lady until, accepting my invitation to come and see my etchings, she got off the bus with me to the great indignation of the passengers. At other times we amused ourselves by discussing our financial affairs in public in a loud voice but not according to the decimal system, which completely mystified our listeners: 'You have four forints? Excellent. So have I. Four and four makes thirteen . . .'

Now, however, I remained silent, playing with Suzy's long fingers. I threw a suspicious glance towards the wooden case above the window that held the heavy iron shutters, to make sure that there were no new finger-marks or scratches on it, indicating that in my absence it had been opened and equipped with a microphone. A yellow, autumn sun was lighting up the narrow strip above the curtain. In the meantime they had switched on the wireless in the library opening from the corridor opposite Suzy's room. It was not the trial yet; a monotonous, nasal voice was reading something but the words became audible only when Almassi, the librarian, opened the door without knocking. He pushed his long, pale face obliquely through the opening, his greedy eyes darting around furtively like those of an animal in its lair. The librarian was a police spy. With the exception of Suzy, every member of the staff was aware of it. We also knew that he was being blackmailed because of his fascist past and that he could save himself from prison only by supplying other inmates in his stead. In the afternoons he went from room to room, asking everyone stupid and provocative questions, then ran back to the library to write his report. He had to hurry because he was very conscientious but possessed a bad memory.

'Aren't you coming to listen to the trial?'

I did not move but grasped Suzy's fingers strongly in mine. She looked up at me questioningly.

. . . *Rajk and his vile accomplices wanted to destroy our new, happy and free life* . . . I heard the bored, nasal voice of the radio-commentator. *These conspirators and spies, agents of the imperialists and Tito* . . .

'We are not coming,' I replied to the police spy.

'And why not?' Almassi asked sharply.

'No comment,' I replied and indicated with a flick of my wrist that he was dismissed.

For a while I listened for his receding step to make sure he was no longer at the door. Then I dropped Suzy's fingers. The monotonous nasal voice stopped and suddenly I heard Rajk – the voice which I remembered from the Paris café. He was replying to the presiding judge's questions, lengthily and fluently as if he were reciting long monologues from various plays; but I could not quite get what he was saying. I was thinking that now the police spy must be busily writing his report: 'While everyone was listening to the radio broadcast of the Rajk trial George Faludy and Suzy Szegö refused to join the collective,' or perhaps, 'Faludy and his mistress, afraid of being unmasked, hide in their room like cornered beasts.'

The door of the library opposite opened again and suddenly I could clearly hear Rajk's voice replying to one of the judge's questions:

'Yes. I recognize the photograph. This is the field guards' hut near Paks where I met Rankovich. And this is mile post No. 116.'

I bent forward a little and caressed Suzy's cheek with my face. My eyeballs, which for more than thirty years had functioned smoothly like the finest Swedish ball-bearings, suddenly felt like two dry clots of earth in their sockets. My toes, which at other times lay quietly side by side in my shoes, like sleeping horses in a stable, were curling up as they do with cramp. What caused these symptoms? Was I afraid that in a few days I would share the fate of Rajk, Justus, Zoltan Horvath; that I, too, would be forced to confess that I had regularly met the head of the American Secret Service in the middle of a maize-field in Transdanubia, to get orders for the preparation of Rakosi's assassination? Or was my nausea mainly the result of the circumstance that I could not confess my fears to anybody, not even to this girl whom I loved and with whose fingers I was now playing? Or had I been overwhelmed by moral indignation like some Frenchman at the beginning of the century, in Dreyfus's times, so that I longed to dash into the library, cut the radio to pieces, jump on the table and cry out the innocence of Rajk, until they sent me to join him in the box? For is it not easier to be hanged innocently than to witness the hanging of somebody else, who is innocent? I again touched Suzy's cheeks with my face, and sighed.

'What is bothering you?' she asked quietly.

'Me? Nothing,' I lied, jumping off the desk. I walked to the window; the yellow light was still shining above the curtain:

. . . Look, love, what envious streaks
Do lace the severing clouds in yonder east;
Cold light, and against it I would shut my eyes,
Sleeping in the shadow of your hair, blonde branches
In which the autumn weaves no spiders' webs,
For not a hundred thousand brethren
Can love with a love so strong as that between us.
So what would I care for our houses' opposition –
If it were not that I see your Capulets
Stab from behind, and stab with poisoned knives,
And if you did not call their evil good . . .

I was so deeply engrossed in my poem that I did not notice Imre Komor coming into the room on soundless rubber soles until he was standing by the desk. He had come into my room just as soundlessly a year ago, after his return from Moscow, where he had spent twenty years as an emigrant. At that time he had stayed in the office for no more than half an hour and the members of the staff had waited in crowds outside his door: each anxious to call Komor's attention to his own merits and the shortcomings of the others. Komor, however, had slipped out by a side door and come straight to my room in his elegant black suit, with his silver head, his compressed, haughty lips and Robespierre profile. We had talked for two and a half hours about Aeschylus, on whom he knew everything, even that he had hated the Athenian mob and people's courts, just as Komor knew that I hated the communist system and the communist people's courts. He had brought up the subject of Aeschylus in order to charm me with his knowledge, sweep me off my feet with his erudition and show me that not all communists were barbarians as I probably believed, at least not he. Before leaving he had pointed to a bilingual edition of

Poe on my desk, and had asked me what I was doing with that rotten, decadent book.

'I am reviewing it,' I replied.

'Consider it as expropriated,' he declared and, pocketing the book, returned to his room to let in the intriguers. That same evening, at the editorial meeting, he repeated every word they had said – indicating the source – and while the culprits hid their faces, he threw me a triumphant glance. Three weeks later, when I visited him at his home, I discovered the volume of Poe, read almost to shreds, on his night-table.

Komor belonged to the old, so-called great guard. Everyone knew that he had excelled in the international communist movement since his early youth not only with his burning idealism and intelligence but also with his personal courage. First, he became secretary to the Hungarian communist leader Béla Kun. When, in 1937, Béla Kun was arrested in Moscow, then killed, Komor was also imprisoned as a Trotskyist. He was released only seven years later. But this he never mentioned, not even in the form of an allusion. Owing to his merits and his talents he was a member of the highest party bureaucracy; but his attitude concerning his position was conspicuously ambivalent.

On the one hand, nothing was more important to him than that he should receive an invitation to the gala performance at the Opera every seventh of November, the anniversary of the Russian Revolution, and the question whether he would sit on the platform or in the stalls, and in which row. When, ten days after his arrival from Moscow, he had still received no invitation, he raged, wept and shouted at his colleagues – which conflicted strangely with his good manners and his pride. When he fell ill, which happened rather often because of his bad heart, he boasted to everyone that Rakosi had telephoned personally and that Révai had visited him. This boastfulness also conflicted with Komor's good taste, but still, it was understandable. The invitation to the Opera, and Rakosi's telephone call were indications of his privileged place in the hierarchy. The loss of these privileges was equivalent to the loss of his job, misery, prison, or even the scaffold.

On the other hand, however, Komor avoided the company of the

Muscovites, though this caste stuck together even when they hated each other bitterly – and in spite of the fact that only good connections ensured him the invitation to the Opera. At first I believed that Komor despised the practice of bootlicking because he trusted his own merits, although he must have known that no merits can survive in a people's democracy without bootlicking. Only later I realized that Komor, although he never disputed their leadership, must have hated the cynical Rakosi, the raving madman Révai, the stupid Farkas and the cunning racketeer Zoltan Vas. Komor was fanatical, cultured, an initially honest and pure partisan of the communist ideal and he must have known that his comrades had never been honest or pure partisans of communism, not even fanatics – with the exception of the madman Révai.

He looked up to power but he despised those in power; the only problem I did not understand was why Komor did not do anything to get hold of this power, although it was due to him, by virtue of his past, his knowledge, his ability and his talent. I did not find the answer until the afternoon when we were sitting in his room with Suzy, as usual, and while chatting Komor was informed by telephone of Rajk's arrest.

He turned to us. 'They have arrested Rajk.' He kept silent for some five or six seconds. Then he raised his hand as usual and smoothed his hair, that all-silver hair like a beautiful rococo wig. 'How fortunate that I never go anywhere,' he said at last, with some humiliation. This was his only comment on the Rajk affair.

Among the members of the editorial staff he was on friendly terms only with Suzy and myself. He despised the professional journalists as insignificant people or former social democrats; and he simply ignored the few dozen workers newly appointed to the paper by the party's cadre department. Not because they had as little chance of becoming journalists as a fifty-year-old fat lady of becoming a ballet dancer: this he did not care about. He merely felt disgusted by the unreliable proletarians whom – unlike other communist intellectuals who idealized the workers – he did not fear. He knew beyond a shadow of doubt that they were opportunists and cheats, not real communists like himself.

'All right, then,' he said when he came into Suzy's room on the day of Rajk's trial and closed the door, silently and softly so as not to offend the voice of the former Minister of the Interior as he shut it out of the room. I enjoyed his appearance, as I always did; and on this occasion I was also relieved in that I was now breathing the same air as someone who, like myself, was convinced of Rajk's innocence, although he never would mention it. And not only would he never mention it; he probably fully agreed that this man should be convicted on charges of which he was innocent. His intelligence, his erudition and his moral sense did not prevent Komor from accepting every measure taken by the people's democracy; what is more, to save his moral sense he used his intelligence and erudition to create false justifications for those measures.

He threw us a fugitive glance, not longer than a tenth of a second, while I registered malevolently that presumably he too was unable to stand the solitude in his room while Rajk was speaking. Then he smoothed his silver hair with the back of his hand. That meant that he had done his best, that he had struggled against our love as long as he could, mainly because, owing to my travels abroad, my political attitude and my way of thinking he did not consider my future in the people's democracy to be promising and had therefore repeatedly suggested that Suzy find herself another mate. Our stubborn resistance, however, had gradually made him yield; more than that, he was now helping us to get married, had promised to find us a place to live.

'All right, then,' he said again and placed two manuscripts on the desk: an article of mine on the two hundredth anniversary of Goethe's birth, handed in before I went on my trip, and one by Suzy on cosmopolitanism, which he had wanted me to write but which I had refused to.

'I congratulate you on your Goethe article,' he turned to me. 'It is a masterpiece. I haven't read so many interesting and original thoughts about Goethe for a long time. We shall not publish it.'

'Why not, if you find it so good?' Suzy exploded.

'This article has two faults,' said Komor, standing straight in a corner of the room as if he were addressing the Convention. 'George

Lukacs does not write for the papers, Révai knows nothing about Goethe. Consequently, the article on Goethe to be published in *Szabad Nép* will be much inferior to yours. Do you need that? Would it be good for you if the article on Goethe published in the party's official organ was much worse than the one we published under your name? That would only cause trouble. For all of us.

'The second difficulty is that you have original ideas on Goethe. Who can guarantee, how can you know in advance, that the party will approve *post-festa* of what you write? How do you know whether someone might not attack you, pick a fight with you? Why didn't you simply pick up George Lukacs's book on Goethe and copy out part of it? Something written by Lukacs can cause trouble only for Lukacs, not for you. You see,' he continued with a furtive smile, meaning that he wanted to defend me against his communist comrades, 'Suzy has written an excellent, articulate article on something you wouldn't even touch.'

'I hope you don't mean that I write better than George?' Suzy asked with indignation. 'Besides, I quoted the whole article from a brochure!'

'No,' Komor replied, 'that is not what I meant to say. You both write very well. But this article of Suzy's shows not only that she writes well. It shows more. It shows that Suzy knows what has to be written. It shows that she is on the road to becoming a true bolshevik.'

I looked at Komor, searching for a sign of irony in his face. There was none. He was gazing at Suzy happily, almost proudly.

'And how would you define a real bolshevik?' I asked him. 'Someone who believes in Marxism–Leninism . . .'

'To be a bolshevik is not a question of faith. Our Bible does not begin with the sentence: "In the beginning was the Word." We say: "In the beginning was the deed." What could you do for the party, Suzy?' he asked her.

Suzy blushed.

'I could die for it,' she said after a second's consideration.

'That is not enough,' Komor said with obvious disappointment. 'One must be able to kill for the party.'

'Kill innocent people?' I barred his way to prevent him from leaving the room on this highly effective curtain line.

'In the absolute sense, everyone is innocent,' Komor replied. 'And in the relative sense everyone is guilty whom the party declares to be guilty.'

He went out of the door, with the manifest intention of going back into his room, but he found himself opposite the door of the library, through which Rajk's voice was coming loudly. He remained rooted to the spot, but instead of consternation, he showed absent-mindedness, ennui, even some self-complacency, like someone who had witnessed hundreds and hundreds of trials. As soon as he noticed my scrutinizing glance, he smoothed his hair with the back of his hand and turned his beautiful profile away.

'I wanted to organize the armed forces with which I intended to overthrow the people's democracy from the Hungarian fascist émigrés living in Yugoslavia, Austria and Italy,' said the voice. *'In addition to this armed force Prime Minister Tito also offered me other armed forces . . .'*

'Did Prime Minister Tito also offer you other armed forces?' the judge cut in.

I cast a mischievous glance at Komor, who noticed my glance as well as the faulty timing. Then, with an apologetic and at the same time encouraging flick of his wrist, he hurried away. Suzy and I, contrary to our usual practice, had gone out into the corridor with him when he left the room, so that we too were opposite the open door of the library.

Some thirty members of the staff were sitting on chairs and on the green table listening to Rajk's confession. Of the fourteen original, social democratic members of the staff, only seven had kept their jobs; the rest were dismissed as soon as the communists took over. I was the only one of the seven now present. The others were writing the papers for the next day. The thirty people in the library did not write; they had been sent to the paper on orders of the cadre department of the party and spent their time chatting, sitting around, discussing politics; sometimes they wrote a news report or tried to rewrite the news bulletin, but it was never publishable. They could be classified in three very distinctive categories. Some of them were honest workers, ordered by the party to join the paper against their wishes. These longed to be back in their old jobs and felt ashamed of getting a salary for loafing. Others were dilettantes, who joined the paper by pulling party strings; these wanted to have their poems printed and felt humiliated when they were refused. The rest of them – the greatest part – were ragamuffins without inhibitions; these knew quite well that they need do no work while they could secure promotion by bragging, denunciation and police-connections. Almassi, the informer, was sitting at his desk with his back to the listeners, poring over his books; from time to time he turned sharply and measured everybody with his eyes.

Rajk spoke fluently for at least ten minutes about his meeting with Rankovich; as if he were speaking a monologue on the stage. Meanwhile I tried to discover the message hidden in the flick of Komor's wrist as he ran away. Probably he wanted to let me know with the apologizing part of the gesture that the staging of the trial was still somewhat inadequate. With the encouraging part of the gesture he was indicating that methods of communist propaganda would improve, and that I would gradually get used to them, as he had done.

I watched my thirty colleagues listening to Rajk. I found the view rather comforting. They all sat with downcast eyes or gazed at the corners of the room, at the bookshelves or at the wall, avoiding the picture of Lenin in the centre; some of them put their arms round the back of their chairs, as if they were clinging to them. A balding young man whose ears had turned purple sat directly behind the door, some two feet from me. Half a year ago he had changed his German surname to *Rajk*, which explained the present colour of his ears. He twisted and turned nervously on his chair. As soon as Rajk had finished his monologue, the presiding judge asked some questions and ordered a break.

'He is a terrible beast . . . that . . . that . . . that Laszlo Rajk,' muttered Rajk's namesake.

Seeking help, I took Suzy's arm. We were standing very close to each other and I thought: none of these thirty people believe in Rajk's guilt any more than I do – but I turn for help to the only person who does believe in it.

'Let us go down to the street,' I said.

While we walked down the stairs it occurred to me that I was doomed. Even if they do not kill me, it would not be worthwhile to stay alive. I felt only one sincere wish: to talk to a Westerner and tell him all about it.

My wish was fulfilled earlier than I had hoped. A few weeks after Rajk had been executed, Julien Benda came for a visit to Budapest. The author of *The Treason of Writers*, whom I knew from Paris, telephoned saying that he would like to see me and would gladly agree to an interview. We met in the hall of the Hotel Bristol, a hotel reserved mostly for foreign guests. He had aged a great deal since I had last seen him in Paris ten years before, but he seemed very happy and self-assured. An insignificant journalist sat next to him, and two men whom Benda believed to be interpreters – correct, in so far as they both spoke French, but they were also agents of the secret police. Benda told us what he had seen in town and then began to talk about the real purpose of his visit: the Rajk trial. He gave a pretty exact summary of what he had heard in France concerning Rajk's alleged innocence and said that he hadn't been quite sure what to believe. Then he went on to tell us that he had been talking to writers, lawyers, criminologists and politicians in Budapest, among whom there was not a single communist.

These men had openly admitted that on many questions they disagreed with the party. They went on to explain to him in great detail exactly what Rajk had done, and how conspiracy, espionage and treason had been proved beyond a shadow of doubt. On the basis of what he had heard he could, at last, make up his mind. The verdict passed upon Rajk was just; it was the duty of every state to protect itself against such criminals. He expressed his gratitude to the Hungarian government for having invited him. Returning to Paris, he would now write a book about it all to open the eyes of Western public opinion concerning the Rajk affair, and unmask those fascists who were spreading vile slander against the Hungarian people's democracy.

While he was talking he brought down his heavy stick again and again on the thick grey carpet under our feet as if to give added emphasis to his words. Several times I was sorely tempted to interrupt and tell him a few facts. For instance, that all the people he had talked with were *professional non-party members*, as we used to call them, and that before meeting him they had been briefed by the party's press department. I wanted to tell him that Professor Gyula Szekfü, whom he had seen, and who was the greatest living historian of the country, was blackmailed into obedience by the party. Should he disobey, they would deprive him of the expensive medicine with the help of which he prolonged his life from one day to the next. I wanted to beg him to write, not about Rajk but about us, who would sooner or later suffer the same monstrous fate, and who were being literally fried alive by these red devils steeped in inferiority complexes and ridiculous even in their terribleness, just as Jan Masaryk had foretold: Jan Masaryk, who had since been pushed out of the window of his palace. Even so – I should have told Benda – we could somehow put up with our fear and helplessness, our moral misery and the stench of our burning flesh and rotting souls, if we did not also have to put up, from time to time, with visits from the West of decent old nincompoops like himself, Andersen-Nexö or Eluard who refused to face facts or preferred to believe the propaganda and the Byzantine hospitality of the police state, then wrote a book on how happy, cheerful and healthy we were.

The detectives sat quietly sipping their coffee, offering American cigarettes and jumping from their seats to give us a light. At times they gave me a friendly, conspiratorial glance. That they regarded me as one of them, a cynical scroundrel, was the most unbearable of all. Had I been able to communicate my thoughts to Benda he might never have begun that apology for the Rajk trial left unfinished because of his death. The communists could never convince a visitor so thoroughly that a well-aimed kick in the small of his back could not bring him to his senses. I did not even have to fear that the detectives would drag me away with the excuse that I had gone out of my mind and was raving, although I was certain that they would have been convinced of it. My arrest could have taken place only after parting with Benda, in the door of the hotel. Next day they would no doubt force me to telephone him from the police HQ and tell him that I was recovering from my nervous breakdown somewhere in the countryside, naturally at government expense. But then, I would never see Suzy again and would now be drinking the last espresso coffee of my life. This sacrifice was neither subjectively nor objectively worth the effort of telling Benda the truth. And yet, I was filled with a burning desire to do so.

I thought I would try a few cautious allusions. I quoted from *Jean Barois* and *Histoire Contemporaine*, without mentioning the name of Captain Dreyfus. When this failed, I compared our French guest to Walafridus Strabo: I told him that his good health and vivacity contrasted with the physical condition of the Reichenau Abbot just as flagrantly as the book he was going to write on the Rajk affair and Hungary in general contrasted with Strabo's book – at least in so far as their reality or irreality were concerned. Benda certainly knew that during his grave illness Strabo had seen in his visions the hell which, after recovery, he described in a poem. Thus, the old man should have understood my allusion: that the Abbot of Reichenau had described Hell although he had never seen it, while he himself had visited Hell without realizing it. Unfortunately I failed again. I had to be so careful in my choice of words that the unsuspecting old man let them go by unnoticed. I was about to give up when Benda got up and limped away towards the WC. I hurried after him triumphantly: after all, truth remains truth even in a lavatory. However, a man in civilian clothes, obviously a detective, nipped through the door before we reached it and locked himself into one of the closets. Another one, who emerged from a corner of the hall, placed himself close to us.

'I can see you feel happy now that you are back home,' Benda said to me.

'Like Arius in Constantinople,' I replied.

The old gentleman seemed to deliberate; he must have remembered that Arius was murdered in a public lavatory by his political opponents in Constantinople.

'You still possess a sense of humour,' he said vaguely. I should have liked to go on talking, but as I had already finished the business which the old man hadn't even begun, and as the detectives were throwing suspicious glances at my trousers, I had to leave so as not to suffer the same fate as Arius.

Six months later, towards the middle of July, I set out on a hot Thursday afternoon from the *Népszava* office to visit Bandi Havas. A few days before, he had telephoned me, asking me to visit him at his office *in my own interest*. He added that he would be very glad to see me again. The invitation itself seemed no less enigmatic than the emphatic warning, so I had certain misgivings when at last I decided to go.

The previous autumn he had been Councillor at the Hungarian Legation in Paris. When the Ambassador, Count Michael Karolyi, had come to Budapest in an attempt to persuade Rakosi, in his grandiose and naïve way, to pardon Rajk who had confessed to crimes that, in Karolyi's opinion, he could never have committed, Bandi had sent a telegram to the Hungarian government in his own name and that of the Legation staff, in which he demanded that the *fascist beast Laszlo Rajk be punished with the utmost severity.* Had Bandi acted in the same way in Budapest, I should have paid no attention to it. But Bandi lived in Paris at that time, under the star of the categorical imperative. His wife and his little son were with him in Paris and Rajk was not only his superior but also an old friend. Bandi did not have to apply to himself the less severe moral standards imposed at home by circumstances and the will to survive. He should have resigned from his post and spoken up for Rajk on the Paris radio.

Karolyi, whom Rakosi dared not have arrested, resigned after his return to Paris. Bandi, however, remained in his job. Later, as a reward for his loyalty, he was given the task of organizing the Legation's espionage service in Paris. He approached this task with great zeal. He stuck a false red moustache on his upper lip from under which his huge teeth protruded, betraying his identity from half a mile away, put a beret on his head, donned a pair of dirty, frayed trousers and had himself driven into the suburbs of Paris to visit some dives. Of the first four men he tried to win for the Hungarian espionage service and to whom he immediately handed over large sums of money in the lavatories of the bistros, three were agents of the Deuxième Bureau, and the fourth – a Hungarian university student – gave him a good beating, on the spot. Thereupon the French government – which could not be expected to possess a sense of humour in such affairs – immediately expelled him as *persona non grata*.

When Bandi returned to Budapest he was given a good dressing-down by the Ministry of Foreign Affairs and dismissed on the spot. For two weeks everyone thought that he would be arrested, but instead he was appointed personal secretary to the Managing Director of our largest publishing house, the Athenaeum. After such preliminaries this was regarded as a favour. Although Bandi's office was only a hundred yards, as the crow flies, from my own – we were in the same block of buildings – I never saw him. I heard that he avoided his old friends, frequented only party officials, began every tenth sentence with 'we proletarians', was unbelievably arrogant with his subordinates including typists, janitors and chauffeurs, and that his hands were trembling. He had plenty of reason for the latter. As a one-time member of the communist underground, Rajk's friend, Tito's guest at Bled and a refugee to France and England, he could easily have been arrested and accused of having been Horthy's police spy and a French, British or Yugoslav agent.

The idea of meeting him made me shudder. As I walked slowly down the dark, cool staircase at the *Népszava* office I felt perspiration break out over my body although it was at least ten degrees colder here than in my room upstairs. The sweating was restricted to the triangle between my two armpits and my navel, although in more serious cases it had also extended to my neck. At such times my silk shirt felt like a concrete tube and my nipples pricked me as if their points were suddenly turned inwards. This time I perspired rather mildly: my thoughts concerning Bandi's fate had reminded me of my own future, but my excitement was counterbalanced to a certain extent by the safety and calm of the cool, dark staircase.

Our editorial offices were on the fifth floor of the building and the staff always went up and down in the lift. I too would use the lift when I arrived with Suzy, but when I arrived alone and someone else invited me into it, I would run up the stairs with youthful ardour, or pretend to have a phobia against lifts. In that way I could enjoy the calm of the staircase several times a day, and had spent the best moments of the last few months on it. The staircase held three main joys for me. Firstly, I could think there undisturbed, something I could do nowhere else. Secondly, I could not be arrested there. In my office or at the villa belonging to *Népszava* where I lived, I could have been picked up at any hour of the day or night. They could also arrest me in the street. Many of my acquaintances disappeared in AVO automobiles which stopped by the kerb, pulled in by an impersonal arm reaching out for them. They could have arrested me at the door of the office or at the door of the building, but while I was walking up or down the stairs I felt absolutely safe. Thirdly, I met no acquaintances there. Although I rarely intentionally met anyone apart from Suzy and my mother, I could nor help running into acquaintances in the doorways of cafés or restaurants, in the lobbies of theatres or cinemas. If they were party members or public functionaries our meeting threw them into such a state of panic that it was really embarrassing. They looked at me as though I were a ghost – sometimes a walking corpse, whose presence must be avoided at all costs, but sometimes a vampire who must be propitiated. There were some who, in the first interval of a play, approached me with open arms and stuck to me like leeches until we had to go back to our seats – but who in the next interval turned away their heads when they caught sight of me at the buffet.

Today, as usual, I was wandering down the stairs at a snail's pace, enjoying the situation. I stopped on every step, shifting the weight of my body from one foot to the other. Just below the fourth floor, a dirty little frosted-glass window high in the wall admitted some light; whenever I reached this point I would hold up my right hand to admire the length of my fingers, the suntanned smoothness of my skin and the regular, silky half-moons at the base of my nails. Sometimes I would stroke my thigh or grip my shoulder, shuddering with pleasure. My limbs were still hard and smooth, there was no middle-aged flabbiness about them and I was still whole.

As I wandered down I realized that not only my body but also my senses, my thoughts, my soul were still unharmed. Or rather that my entire being, my mode of thinking, my personality, had remained constant, not only during the last four years but ever since my university days: incapable of development but also incapable of degradation and adaptation, youthful and conservative, naïve and uninfluenceable, rebellious but stuck to one place for ever. I regarded the communist ideology as I did any other ideology, as a yoke, a thumb-screw which, even though imposed on millions and apparently greatly enjoyed by a few, still remained a yoke and a thumb-screw. I had rid myself even of the illusions I still cherished on my way home from America: that communism disagreed only with individualists like myself, but agreed with the large masses of the people; or that the realization of the second slogan of the French Revolution, even though on the lowest possible level, could hold some significance in a country where it was by no means advisable to remember the first.

My outlook, mode of thinking and personality were thus unaltered, but what good did it do me? I wrote very few poems and, when I did, I hurried to the Széchenyi Library, asked for one of the bound volumes of dailies of the 1848-49 War of Independence and, beginning with the last page and working backwards, I underlined in the hundred-year-old newspaper the letters that added up to my poem. On my way home I tore up my manuscript and, rolling up the slivers of paper, threw them one by one into manholes. As I was remembering this I passed the second floor and my thoughts returned to the staircase. From the darkness and safety I must inevitably continue down to the doorway blocked by huge bales of paper and guarded, since an attempt at sabotage, by a porter who looked me over suspiciously every time I left.

But even before the attempt at sabotage, whenever I saw the bales of paper in the doorway it always occurred to me how much I would enjoy throwing a petrol bottle into them. That would have prevented the publication of the mendacious and unreadable paper on which I worked, for at least three days. But the risk was too great and the result too insignificant. Three weeks earlier an unknown brother-in-arms threw a bottle of petrol and a burning rag into the doorway – at least that was what they had established in the course of the investigation. Unfortunately the fire had been put out before any serious damage was done. Although I had only left half an hour before the bottle was thrown, so that they would have been justified in suspecting me, to my great surprise the idea occurred to no one. In the evening, when I heard the news, I could hardly conceal my joy. In the following weeks I would pretend to myself that it had been I who had thrown the bottle, and that I had gone for a walk merely for the sake of having an alibi. I only regretted that I had been unable to obtain at least ten times as much petrol in order to blow up the entire building complete with editorial offices, printing shop and Stalin portraits. This fantasy was accompanied by the fixed idea that I had used my monogrammed handkerchief as a burning rag. So whenever I passed the doorway I had to fight down a treble anxiety: I saw the charred remains of my handkerchief everywhere, with the monogram still intact; I had to ignore the suspicious glances of the porter; and I had to forget the possibility that the AVO might be waiting in the street to arrest me.

Going down from the second floor, in fact, I came face to face with the most threatening elements in my situation. This part of the staircase was so dark that I could no longer see the yellowish-green walls from which paint peeled off in strips like wallpaper, covered with small, white protuberances which, if I pushed them with my finger, trickled an inexorable stream of lime particles, like sand in an hourglass. I gripped the smooth wooden rail and closed my eyes. In the American army, whenever we had to cross a forest at night, two of my comrades would take my arms. I would face our destination, close my eyes, and would lead my comrades towards the target, never missing it by more than five yards. The last six months had felt exactly like those blind wanderings in the jungle, except that now I could not hear the rumbling of enemy guns, and there was neither direction, nor plan, nor aim, nor anyone to guide me. Yet the enemy was there, all around, invisible and motionless in the clammy darkness.

A few weeks after the Rajk trial the situation had felt easier. I had begun to dream that I had been withdrawn from the spurting machine-gun fire and the land-mines which exploded like dirty-grey, sword-leaved bushes, looming above me as I crawled; that I had been sent back from the firing-line – the area of immediate, lethal danger – to the field hospital, where I lay among the gravely wounded, my condition not critical for the time being; only hopeless. I deduced this from various signs. When I received a letter it was obvious that the envelope had been steamed open. When I telephoned I seemed to detect that characteristic click betraying that the AVO was listening in. When I was walking in the forest I felt as if someone were following me. All these impressions, however, were superficial and uncertain; I could not decide whether they were only hallucinations or whether, on the contrary, they were a game played by the secret police, with a devilish knowledge of psychology, perhaps not even to collect information against me but only to destroy my nervous resistance by the most subtle means.

But there was no doubt in my mind that my file in the archives of the secret police was growing thicker and thicker. If, for instance, they had tortured Zoltan Horvath, they must have found out a great deal about me. There was also the diary of Györgyi Vandori, from which parts were quoted at the Rajk trial. There was no way to find out if she had written about me in other parts of it not read publicly, or if she had quoted me when I called Stalin a Caucasian highwayman. There was Almassi, *Népszava*'s librarian, with his sunken yet protruding eyes in a flat, motionless, mask-like face. With him I had always been on my guard. Yet, the fact that I never said anything compromising in his presence was not enough to save me; I should have reacted to his clumsy provocations, I should have defended the communist party, Rakosi and Stalin with a great show of passionate conviction. What is more, I should have denounced him for his subversive statements pretending, with moronic hypocrisy, that I didn't know them to be part of his job. But my fidelity to some memory of human dignity prevented me from playing this idiotic but obligatory game although I knew that every time I failed to denounce him, he denounced me.

By the time I had reached the first floor on the office staircase my anxiety had become even more acute. At this point I always tried to comfort myself by recalling agreeable things, most often my hiding place at Dunaharaszti on the Danube, near the island of Csepel, one of the country's oldest communities.

My trips to the country had become rare: I dared not visit old friends for fear of compromising them and there was no point in visiting strangers. The only place of refuge remaining was this inn, some twenty miles from Budapest. I went there when I wanted to see no one, not even Suzy. I usually left at midday and was back at the office the next afternoon. Sunday rowing parties approached the inn by river – few people knew that it could also be reached by a cross-country path. I never went on Sundays, but on a weekday I would take the local train to Dunaharaszti. I would turn on to a small footpath, and after descending a sharp slope and crossing a small wooden bridge, would find myself in a deserted, mysterious world. On every side, wherever I turned, horses and cows stood belly-deep in shallow ponds which looked like the pegged-out hides of giant animals, gone green and mouldy. Here and there a naked, sleepy peasant child would sit nodding on the back of a cow. After a while I left the animals and children behind: from that point I would be walking through small puddles which reflected, for a second, the open collar of my white shirt. Marsh-tits twittered in the rushes and sometimes a mosquito would zigzag across the path in front of me on an oblique course, like the twitching shoulder muscles of a naked, galloping horseman.

On my way to the inn I always experienced a sudden wave of happiness; the same happiness that I had felt four years before, when I had travelled through the country, drinking wine with the peasants in the cool of the vineyards and dreaming of Hungary's future. The hope was dead, but of the country this had survived: the naked peasant children with their high, yellow cheekbones on the backs of bathing cattle, the three shades of yellowish-green in the grass, the osier-beds and the rushes, the mosquitoes, the parching summer heat, and the writhing, living ponds changing their irregular shapes every hour, connected by secret underground channels with the water of the Danube. This was the Hungarian landscape, the original, the ancient, the genuine: not Horthy's, not Franz-Joseph's but the thousand-year-old, the Arpadian; the three-and-five-thousand-year-old, that of the Bronze Age, the Stone Age. This was the country's ground-plan, the original layout: the Hungarian Lowland, with its infinite flood areas, its marshes and distant woods flat on the rim of a far horizon. This yellowish-green was the basic colour of the painting framed by the dark green of the forests.

Perhaps I should have considered the things superimposed on the original picture as more important: the narrow tentacles of the Roman roads weaving their way slowly from the south-west towards the north-east, only to stop abruptly at the bank of the multi-branched cold current of the Danube; the parrot-cages of the railway lines, their double wires shining in the daytime with the silvery gleam of knitting needles, and at night eaten by rust; the telephone and telegraph wires, which I had lately come to see as a refined giant muzzle covering the country's face; the stripes, oblongs and deltoids of the cornfields which had undergone so many transformations in a thousand years, beginning with nothing but honey-yellow patches of wheat, then diversified with pale oats and reddish rye, then later again with blue-green vines, with the deep green bushes of potatoes and with the dwarf banana-palms of maize. How often these fields had been divided and joined together again since the common tribal estates were first split into as many plots as there were heads of families in the country! Between AD 1000 and 1400 they had been organized with frightening speed into latifundia, with a castle on top of the highest hill in the neighbourhood and in the castles petty monarchs, each busy digging away the earth from beneath the other's castle, until the Sultan arrived and put his pashas in their place. One hundred and fifty years later, after the Turks had been driven from the country, the fields were again divided, the smaller plots going to German settlers, the larger ones to the Hungarian gentry. In 1848 part of the larger estates were again split up; the rest of them were divided in 1945; and now, five years later, they joined together again by force, and the ancient system of serfdom was being restored under a modern Russian name.

But when I wandered in the marshes I was not interested in the present, nor in the recent past. I felt as if, after having searched through cheap prints and faulty reproductions, I had come at last on the real portrait of my country. As the ponds connected with the waters of the Danube, so was I bound to this land by mysterious underground channels and arteries. I too was no more than a writhing, living pool, feeding on Danube water until, at last, I too would dry out. Because it was not only I who had found a last refuge, like the almost extinct beaver and the lapwing, in this unchanging, primeval world which a thousand years ago had embraced half of the Lowlands and had now shrunk to a strip along the river only a few hundred yards wide. It was in these marshes that the men of the Bronze Age had buried lovers side by side in a squatting position, so that their ghosts should not return to haunt the living. It was here that people hid from the Tartar invasion, cutting dug-outs in the grey, clay soil like beavers; and these dug-outs were enlarged by other men, and connected by dykes cut through the reeds, so that they could live a free though confined life during the hundred and fifty year of the Turkish occupation. When the modern age dawned, it was in such haunted, wolf-infested marshes that the soldiers of many a lost struggle for liberty found safety; when their pursuers came to the end of paths leading straight into water, they stopped as if rooted to the ground, believing that the marsh would swallow them up at their next step. But the quarry had jumped into light craft and paddled to their reed huts, where they sucked raw lapwing eggs for breakfast and made their rush mats bridal couches for the prettiest girls from the neighbouring villages. When the rationalists of the nineteenth century drained the Hungarian marshes, they never dreamt that they were depriving descendants of a last refuge: descendants who, a hundred years later, would seek out what was left of those marshes as the only place where they could be free.

The inn at Dunaharaszti kept an excellent wine. If I wanted fish for dinner I walked down with the inn-keeper's daughter to the fish-trap, and picked out the best to be killed and grilled for me. I slept in a tiny guest-room, the only extra room in the inn, which they let to no one but me, with a straw mattress on the bed, a paraffin lamp on the whitewashed wall and a chair by the window. In the mornings I would row out into the middle of the reed-bank and lie naked in the sun. A red-tailed bird – I believe it was the same one every time –

would perch on a reed at my head and sing into my ear with boundless enthusiasm. I did not know its name but decided, out of gratitude, to look it up in an ornithological reference book.

The greatest joy came in the evening. When my hosts had gone to bed I would put out my lamp and watch the moonlit poplars opposite my window, the leaves of which turned little black mirrors towards me every time the breeze ruffled through them. Later I would climb out through the window. I was very careful that my hosts should not know of my nightly excursions, although there was really nothing secret about them. Reaching the river, I undressed and waded into the Danube. I let the current carry me down the middle of the moonlit expanse of water, going on with the tale of ancient Hungary that I had been telling myself as I came along the muddy path. Soon I would stop thinking altogether.

The once mighty stream of the Danube – a stream which could carry not only tree-trunks but whole masses of densely entangled forest and which could be forded only at the place called Horseferry, opposite the island – this stream once so wild and powerful, which found itself new beds year after year, divided the country from north to south into two essentially different and wholly incompatible Hungaries.

To the west lay Transdanubia with its gentle hills, its vineyards, wine-presses, beautiful gardens and great manor houses, where our liberal politicians, our scholars, our priests and our magistrates were born and lived; our teachers, too, who would put their pupils across their knees and give them a good beating with the long stems of their pipes when they slipped up in reciting the poet (Virgil, of course), but would reward them with a lovely red apple from the top of the cupboard if they recited him well. Transdanubia, in whose inns friends would meet round their usual table to talk and argue over their wine-glasses until morning, and where the chairs around that table had been handed down from father to son like the libraries in their heavy walnut bookcases, where Seneca stood on the shelves as well as de Tocqueville, Strabo's charming and instructive poem on gardening as well as St Augustine's *Confessions* and *The Spirit of Laws* by Montesquieu.

On the opposite, eastern bank of the Danube began the Asiatic and brutal Lowlands, flat, arid, treeless and gardenless, its villages atomized into small groups of cottages or lonely farms where only the telegraph poles following dusty, muddy by-ways indicated that we were in twentieth-century Hungary and not somewhere near Karakorum in the days of Genghis Khan. The Lowlands, from which came our prophets and tribunes, zealous to save and to change, but not to teach, humanity; the Lowlands where dawn and dusk do not paint the sky with slow, gentle brush-strokes as they do in Transdanubia, but where in the morning bonfires are lit in the sky, and in the evening the sun rolls down below the horizon like the severed head of a king. In the Lowlands the wines are rougher and more intoxicating than those of Transdanubia, and the guests in the inns break chairs over each other's heads and stick knives in each other's bellies instead of talking quietly. In the Lowlands there are no ancient buildings, no venerable orchards; instead of broad-crowned, mild chestnut trees, stunted acacias throw thin shadows on sweating heads, and no trees protect the houses: either they have been felled by the soldiers of plundering armies, or their owners have cut them down to keep themselves from freezing to death during the endless winters, or a neighbour has poisoned their roots. In the Lowlands there are no old and treasured libraries, no close circles of friends, no family vaults and no traditions. Driven by restlessness and misery, the people scatter like blown sand, and when they disappear nothing remains to perpetuate their names: no bench made by them, no tree planted by them, not even a cross on their graves, because those too will have been washed away by spring floods, or overgrown by weeds, or will have rotted for lack of anyone to tend them. The children will have gone off to America and will have forgotten the name of their fathers.

Of the mighty, medieval barrier which the Danube had once been between the two parts of the country, the effects remained long after the cause had disappeared. It was in vain that Count Széchenyi tried to remedy it, half-way through the last century; in vain that he built a suspension bridge to link the East with the West, so that British liberalism could cross its slightly swaying span together with world trade and industrialization. The two halves of the country remained hostile and incompatible, British liberalism never rolled across that swaying bridge, nor across later and more massive ones, and the country itself as a whole, instead of being the bridge between East and West intended by our first king when he founded it, became the springboard of the East towards the West. It was no use my breaking my head about it as I drifted on the Danube's current.

When I reached this point in my meditations I would stop swimming and would retreat into the ever blacker darkness of the entangled shadows stretched over the water by branches, bushes and roots. I walked along near the shore on tiptoe, up to my chin in water, stopping at times to spread my arms on the surface, then going on again. The round lips of fishes brushed my body and the soles of my feet were tickled by the sharp edges of open shells floating weightless on the soft mud. Out in the moonlight a silvery carp would arch above the water in a surprising feat of acrobatics, but I would hardly notice it. Under the low-hanging branches I felt as though I had left behind not only the present, but the Middle Ages, and was journeying back towards a more ancient world – the Bronze Age or even further – where, like the priest at some prehistoric and mystical ceremony, I was leading an invisible procession through the shadows of the various darknesses and depths of the night. Often I stayed there until the moon had set, and I could see myself as a naked primordial being, living half in the water and half on dry land, spying from under the concealing branches on the rake-shaped, beryl-green lights flashing on the edge of the horizon: messengers of the awful dawn, white as sour milk, before which I fled, trembling, my eyes half shut, into the darkness of my room.

For the last few months I had visited the inn among the reeds whenever I heard of a new arrest, whether or not I was indifferent to the person arrested: in each case I saw the promise of my own doom. I had gone there, for instance, when Arpad Szakasits, President of the Republic, was arrested and after him almost all the social democratic ministers and deputy ministers. A few days before I set out on my visit to Bandi Havas, the police spy Almassi had come into my room to tell me that now it was Anna Kéthly's turn. He did this in his role of spy: it was important that journalists should know who had been arrested, so that the person's name should never again be mentioned. I was so deeply shaken by Kéthly's arrest that I chased Almassi from my room, left a message for Komor that I was taking a day off, and caught the train for Dunaharaszti. When I came to the part of the flood area where even horses did not venture, I noticed that I was being followed. The man behind me was a short fat fellow, pushing a bicycle and panting in his hurry. He disappeared before I reached the inn.

Arriving there, I found a melancholy surprise awaiting me: two bulldozers, with dredgers, were at work nearby. The inn-keeper explained that they were digging a canal to connect the Danube with the River Tisza. They were going to drain the marshes and the whole flood area, so that inn, birds and boating parties were doomed.

That night I went for a long swim and hid under the branches at a place where I could not see the distant acetylene lamps shining into my eyes like death-rays. In the early morning I again walked down to the river. Among the reeds and the small, dancing boats, hundreds of white-bellied dead fish rode the ripples. The inn-keeper told me why. A communist cobbler's assistant had been appointed managing director of one of the chemical works on the outskirts of Budapest, and his first innovation had been to have waste chemicals containing nitric acid emptied into the river. It would be a hundred years, said the inn-keeper, before it would again be possible to catch the fat and ancient carp and the rapacious sheat-fish which had lived on the river-bottom in this place. As I was plodding back to the inn, the little man with the bicycle stepped out from the bushes. I looked him over carefully. He had a mottled face and was dumpy, self-assured, but at the same time melancholy – no doubt because he had been forced to spend a night in the reeds on my account.

All this had happened a week earlier, on a Thursday – but it was nothing compared to the Sunday. One of our staff, Kisban, was sent into the country on a story and Suzy and I decided to go with him for the trip. Soon after our car left Budapest an AVO Hudson showed up behind us. Its driver tried desperately to keep pace with us but our small British car was too fast for them even on those bad roads so that we soon lost them. We drove along the eastern shore of Lake Balaton and about half-way along the lake, at Szantod, we took a side road to the ferry in order to cross to the opposite shore. While waiting for the ferry Suzy and I swam far out into the lake: the rocky peninsula of Tihany with its deep green trees reached out to us like a large, black fist. By the time we got back the AVO car had caught up with us, and it crossed with us on the ferry. In Tihany we had lunch at a wonderful little restaurant which had not been expropriated and turned into a sort of soup-kitchen because it was the favourite eating place of Soviet party functionaries spending their holidays in a nearby hotel. I ordered fish, chicken, two kinds of wine, a brandy as an appetizer and chocolate cake and black coffee with whipped cream to end with. While I was talking to the waiter Suzy looked absent-mindedly at my American silk shirt of which the cuffs were slightly frayed. She was probably thinking that I would do better to buy myself a new shirt with the money I was spending on this dinner, while I was thinking that it didn't matter at all if they hung me in a ragged shirt, while it mattered a great deal that my last dinner should be all a last dinner should be. Instead of upsetting me, this thought increased my enjoyment a thousandfold. I had been particularly cheerful since morning and Suzy seemed to appreciate my stories though she would have preferred talking about emotional problems. I enjoyed the dinner like a noble Roman who knew that when he had finished he would step into his bath and, obeying the imperial command, cut an artery. I watched oily drops of the green local wine climbing the sides of my glass in narrow stripes, and the crumbs of the fried fish's crust lying on my plate like shipwrecked fragments of a miniature boat. I leaned my shoulder against the ivy-clad wall of the garden so that I felt the soft tentacles tickling my skin through the thin silk shirt, and the breeze blew Suzy's straight, blonde hair into my eyes. In the glowing, almost blinding sunshine it seemed to me as if the courses of stars, planetary systems and comets were flashing, shining, circling and sparkling before my eyes. The happiness that overwhelmed me, behind the stone walls of that old garden on top of the mountain of

Tihany was almost transcendent: the perspective of the horrors of the world began a good deal lower down, at the bottom of the sloping garden where in the flour-dusty road I could see the bonnet of the Hudson in which the AVO was waiting. In her utter innocence Suzy had not even noticed that we were being followed. Kisban thought that they were after him, for both his father and he were former social democrats; he threw nervous glances towards the road from time to time. Only Kakuk, the driver, paid no attention to the car.

Later in the afternoon, having a strong sporting spirit, he made a fool of the AVO driver who was unable to overtake us. That night, when we got back to the capital, I noticed another AVO car in the avenue leading to the *Népszava* villa, parked under the overhanging branches of huge trees. When I entered my room I had the feeling that it had been searched during my absence, although I could discover no traces of the search. Suzy was still down in the lounge talking to colleagues who had been listening to news of the Korean war. I put out the light and, retreating into the far corner of the room, I watched the garden through the open French window. It seemed to me as if under every one of the large, dense bushes a shiny black AVO car was hidden; huge, shiny, black dung-beetles; yet in the room, behind the balcony door, I felt perfectly safe.

I felt equally safe by the time I reached the bottom of the office stairs and stepped through a similar arched exit, emerging into the uncertain light of the yard and the sharp whiteness from the bales of paper. I arrived so quietly that the porter failed to notice me, and gave a jump when he caught sight of me. I felt as if I had caught him *in flagrante*; perhaps it was he who had thrown that petrol-bottle, to be promoted to porter from yard-sweeper and handyman. There was no car in the street except Komor's, only one or two lorries in front of the printing works. No one suspicious loitered in the proximity; I saw only two familiar paper-boys in the narrow Miksa alley, and a few housewives with shopping bags.

I was so relieved that I stopped in the doorway, lit a cigarette and urgently revised the trend of thought which had accompanied me down the stairs. Perhaps the general psychosis of the people's democracy had caught up with me too, as it had caught up with everyone since the days of the Rajk trial.

I thought it possible that last Sunday we had not been dogged by the AVO, that it had travelled the same road to Tihany quite by accident and that the car I had noticed opposite the *Népszava* villa, of which I felt so certain that it belonged to the AVO, was only the private vehicle of the party functionary living there who always kept late hours. Nor had my room been searched; these people were not so shy that they would perform a search so discreetly, in my absence. Last Thursday, when I had set out from the inn, no cyclist had emerged from the reeds; I had simply dreamed it all up in the terrible depression and anxiety following Anna Kéthly's arrest. I tried to conjure up the mottle-faced, dumpy little man with his bicycle and suddenly I saw him clearly, as I had seen him that morning emerging from the reeds and pushing his bicycle along the narrow path skirting the inn's dung-heap; and now I remembered, I recalled quite clearly that through his translucent body I could see dung-heap and the dried horse-droppings sprouting stalks of straw, and that I had smiled because he was wearing horse-droppings in the place of a heart. It had been a vision; a vision and nothing else.

Nor was the systematic arrest of the social democrats a cause for anxiety. Only politicians, ministers, under-secretaries, trade-union leaders and deputies had been arrested, they had not yet seized a single writer, nor any social democrat who, like myself, observed quietly and refrained from voicing his political opinions. Not a single social democrat had been arrested who . . .

'What's that? You are still running around free?' A tall, British-looking individual interrupted my thoughts, whom I noticed only after I had almost landed in his arms on the corner of the boulevard. Our meeting was so sudden and unexpected that it was seconds before I recognized Baron Gedeon Horvath.

'All the social democratic VIPs have been arrested. Now I know at last that you are not a VIP,' he added, smiling when he noticed how he had frightened me.

Baron Horvath had been a big landowner until the end of the war, but had acquired such merit in the anti-Nazi resistance that in 1945, by special decree, they left him his castle and three hundred acres of his estate. Two years ago the communists had tried to incite the peasants to chase him from his castle and divide his land, and when all attempts proved vain, they brought in several lorry-loads of arrow-cross men and former convicts from the next county, and these carried out the expropriation under police guard. The régime compensated Baron Horvath by granting him a lorry-driver's licence in Budapest and every time we met I felt deeply ashamed, as if I, too, had been responsible for these acts.

His words embarrassed me so much that I could hardly mumble a reply, and hurried on. I scuttled into the Athenaeum building, ran up the stairs and when, on one of the tall doors opening from the central hall I noticed Havas's name, I pushed aside the porter who wanted to announce me and entered Bandi's room without knocking. He was sitting behind his desk in his shirt-sleeves; opposite him a ventilator was revolving in the wall, causing a breeze that peeped indiscreetly into the papers lying on the desk and tousled Bandi's red and silver hair. The window was open and so was the door leading into the managing director's room. Coming up the stairs, I had thought that observing the etiquette of our old friendship, Bandi would embrace me, which – because of his attitude in the Rajk affair and for a thousand other reasons – would be extremely painful and out of place. However, when all I got was a rather friendly handshake, I felt it to be arrogant condescension.

Or was he simply afraid of me? I took a seat on the other side of his desk, facing him squarely. We asked each other polite questions and gave polite replies which affected me like some grotesque but in no way amusing ritual. But at least it gave me an opportunity to observe my surroundings. With the help of the ventilator I discovered on the desk a file, hidden under several sheets of paper, on which, in Bandi's hand, written in red ink, I saw the words, ANTI-CLERICAL ANTHOLOGY. Below, still in red ink: *Faludy* and three interrogation marks. Beyond the open door Sandor Haraszti, the managing director of the publishing house, was walking up and down in front of his huge desk in a brightly checked suit. From the fact that the draught made his soft, silver hair stand on end like a crown of feathers, I deduced that in his room too the window must be open and a ventilator revolving on the wall. His gentle lips were contracted into a straight line and he bore his beautiful, classic profile like the monstrance in a procession. Unlike him, Bandi was uglier than ever, but while his ugliness used to be mitigated by a sort of irresistibly grotesque charm – the comic quality of a punchinello handled by a clever puppeteer – it now gave him an acid, prematurely old look and his clownish gestures no longer made only his body ridiculous, but his entire being. At least that was how it seemed to me after having seen the interrogation marks after my name.

Sandor Haraszti had been one of the leading personalities among the Hungarian communists. Unlike his comrades, who in the 'twenties and 'thirties emigrated to Moscow, he had remained in Hungary and had worked in the underground movement. His principal activity was the teaching of Marxism–Leninism so that all communists, including the Muscovites, had at one time been his pupils. He remained a teacher, but without becoming an ideologist, which I considered a point in his favour. A few days after my return from America we had met in Michael Karolyi's salon and had immediately quarrelled. At the time he edited a communist boulevard-paper; and on that particular day he had published an editorial in which he made an extremely boorish attack on the founder of Hungarian sociological science, Oszkar Jaszi, for his liberal views. While we were sitting in deep armchairs waiting for Karolyi I mentioned that I didn't agree with his editorial; that it surprised me that while the country was lying in ruins and mass-murderers were walking among us, he found nothing else to worry about but the liberal views of Professor Jaszi, one of the great men in Hungarian science, and the apostle of the Danubian Confederation. Haraszti replied that since I had joined the social democratic party, I had better read the social democratic papers and stop sticking my nose in where it didn't belong. His tone was so offensive that I jumped up and we were about to fall upon each other when Karolyi entered the room. Since then we had hissed with hatred whenever we met.

Now, as Haraszti paced his room, he pretended not to notice me. But once, when he was facing me, I mercilessly caught his eye, whereupon instead of greeting each other we both stuck out our chins belligerently. By then I had given up my first idea that the two men wanted to laugh at me or provoke me. As soon as I had entered, Haraszti had turned on the radio without, however, trying to find a station. The singing of the radio and the humming of the two ventilator motors made it entirely impossible for the AVO to follow our conversation through the microphones fitted in the telephone receivers. I had to admit that this gesture was not only benevolent but friendly. During the last year, every time friends met at somebody's house the first act of the host was to turn on the radio or pick up the telephone and carry it out of the room. Haraszti – like Komor – was the sort of idealistic communist who would never denounce anyone for opinions voiced in private. Had they done so they would have had to admit to themselves that there was no intellectual freedom; something they always stubbornly denied.

'We have great plans for you,' said Bandi, turning to me excitedly. While he talked he stabbed the wooden arms of his chair with his pointed elbows and stuck out his long legs until his thick soles dangled to the right and left of me from under the desk. I sat there on a plain chair, with my hands on my knees.

'We know that you are not interested in money, but apart from the money you could also earn glory. There is no one in the entire country better fitted than you to do this job. What we want from you is an anthology . . .'

'Are you speaking in the name of your publishing house or of the party?' I interrupted. 'Or do you use the royal "we" even when speaking only in your own name?'

Bandi blushed a deep crimson.

'Gyurka,' he said, 'the idea is Comrade Rakosi's. But it was my idea that we should ask you to carry it out. Sandor is also in favour of it. We are both worried about you. There are rumours in town that you don't want to work for the party. That you refuse to sponsor anything with your name. That you draw back from everything. I know very well that this is not true. That you are fighting the enemy in your own way, as a guerrilla, though the party demands that you should obey orders like any soldier. There is nothing more suitable to dispel this misunderstanding than to undertake the editing of this anthology. This is why Sandor and I thought that we would ask you to edit this anti-cler . . .'

'Excuse me for interrupting,' I said in a voice so aggressive that it surprised me. 'Before coming down to brass tacks I should like to ask you something that has nothing to do with the subject in question. Do you remember our first meeting in Paris eleven years ago? We were so young then that it never occurred to us that one day we too would have to die. When we fell in love we went around telling everyone about it. We made no separate peace, either with social conventions or with the world. Do you remember that morning when you came up to my room at the hotel and I was sitting on my bed naked?'

'Of course I remember,' Bandi replied hesitatingly, but his face was alight with pleasure.

'And what happened then?'

'What do you mean, "what happened"? We walked down to the Seine and quarrelled.'

'That was a few days later. But what happened on that particular day?'

'I sat in an armchair. I told you that I had loved you even before meeting you. I said you too were a member of the great family of left-wing intellectuals. But you protested.'

'And what did I do after asking you to sit down?'

'You rose from the bed.'

'And?'

'I don't know.'

'I went to the wardrobe.'

'And you took out a bottle of wine,' said Bandi, his ears turning red. He rang the bell for the janitor to order black coffee, but I protested. I sent the janitor to fetch three bottles of Balaton wine from the pub and when Bandi wanted to pay I told him that I was going away to Czechoslovakia within forty-eight hours at government expense, so had plenty of money; besides, it gave me pleasure to take leave in style.

'Why all this leave-taking when you are coming back in three weeks?'

'In our days one never knows when one is seeing someone for the last time. This is why I like to play at saying goodbye for ever. Besides, I don't like the family drink of the intellectuals, black coffee. I belong to another family.'

'To which family?' Bandi asked absentmindedly, then suddenly looked at me attentively. Whenever we had been in danger of our lives, at the time of our flight through France, when we were pressed against the lance-shaped railings of the Bayonne customs house, on the ship which sank after we had got off it, in the internment camp of Ain Chok, or in Marrakesh during the slaughter we witnessed in the streets, there would always be a vertical scarlet line across Bandi's eyeball. Now I saw it again, more conspicuous than ever. Haraszti stopped walking up and down in his room and stood in the door. Although Bandi was gazing down at me from behind his desk like a judge at a criminal, I felt suddenly relieved. They are afraid! I thought. More afraid than I am, because they have to expend all their energies on hiding their fear from others and from themselves. They are so afraid that they daren't even shut the door between them.

'To what family do you belong?' Havas asked again, as if he were questioning me in some official matter. But his voice shook.

'To the family of writers, my dear boy,' I replied. The insult seemed to reassure him, although he blushed. Then, calm and collected as I had never seen him before, he said that I had nothing to worry about, that I must not pay attention to the malicious gossip spread about me. If I edited the anthology I should automatically clear myself. And the idea that we might never meet again was, of course, utterly ridiculous. Unless I intended to escape from Czechoslovakia to West Germany. However, that was something he would never believe of me.

'You are doing me a great honour, my friend, by assuming that I am the only one who may disappear. In a communist country accidents may happen to anyone. It's not only I who may be arrested but you too, or Uncle Sandor, or all three of us.'

'These jokes are in very bad taste, comrade Faludy!' Haraszti snapped at me from the door. 'But tell me,' he continued in an entirely different tone of voice, 'on what do you base your supposition?'

'On rumour-mongering and counter-revolutionary gossip,' Havas answered for me.

'On the circumstance,' I said, 'that you and Bandi are old communists – Hungarian communists, not Muscovites – and are only partisans but not servants of power. On the circumstance that Bandi and I have lived abroad, are therefore suspect, and in addition, prefer Dante to Surkov. On the circumstance that all three of us are fundamentally honest men; that is, men who must be wiped out.'

I waited for a moment to let them have their say, but they were silent. Bandi was staring before him angrily, while Haraszti came forward as if hypnotized and sat down in the armchair under the window.

'Therefore,' I said, 'I was wrong when I spoke of parting. According to every probability we shall meet again. If not in prison then under the scaffold.'

I was filled with a kind of happiness for having, at last, uttered something essential. Bandi gazed at me with a distorted grin frozen on his face, while Haraszti clasped his knee in both hands and whipped the tip of his elegant shoe.

'Courts of justice have always committed mistakes,' he said in a slightly schoolmasterish voice. 'Not even a communist society is proof against such mistakes. At least not in the first years of its existence. There have also always been Jagodas, imperialist agents penetrating our state security organizations and causing inexpressible harm. It is only natural that such scoundrels should cast their eye upon the best, the most loyal comrades. Let us assume for the sake of argument that I am arrested; even that would be further evidence of the strength of communism against which the imperialists have to apply such desperate weapons. I can assure you that even in prison I should remain true to the sacred cause of communism . . . Both with my life and with my death I should attempt to prove that justice is on our . . .'

When the commissionaire entered he fell suddenly silent.

'You would get a royalty of ten per cent of the retail price of each copy for the editing of the anthology,' Bandi threw himself into the gap heroically, 'two forints a line for the poems you translate yourself and for prose text . . .'

'What shall we drink to?' Haraszti asked when the commissionaire had left the room. Apparently he didn't feel like continuing with his oration.

'To the anthology,' Bandi suggested.

'I don't even know what anthology you are talking about,' I lied. 'Therefore, let us drink instead to the memory of the predecessor and spiritual forerunner of our good friend Sandor Haraszti: Peregrinus Proteus.'

'All right,' Haraszti agreed unsuspectingly. 'But who, exactly, was Peregrinus Proteus?'

'To Peregrinus Proteus, then,' I said raising my glass. It distressed me a little that the barbs of my attack had turned against Haraszti who, at this moment, was much more attractive to me than Bandi. But then I told myself. Six of one, half a dozen of the other; that if the Russians captured not only our bodies but also our minds it was thanks to this great family of left-wing intellectuals to which these two misbegotten writers belonged.

'Peregrinus,' I explained, imitating Haraszti's didactic style, 'lived in the days of Marcus Aurelius and was head of a fanatical religious sect. Somewhere around 910, *ab Urbe condita,* he announced that in the presence of his disciples, friends and the celebrating public he would jump into a fire on the edge of a forest near Corinth. He would jump into a fire and burn himself alive to prove, with this act, the existence of God.'

'What is the causal interdependence between the existence of God and being burned alive?'

'That question was raised at the time by several decadent contemporary philosophers and *bourgeois* writers who, because of their class background, had failed to recognize the world-redeeming ideology. Among these was Lucian, who joined the long procession to the forest near Corinth. He went, however, not to watch Peregrinus jump into the fire but to dissuade him from it. He explained to Peregrinus that though mankind could only benefit from getting rid of such an ox, his own humanistic attitude compelled him to intervene. God exists or does not exist independent of anyone jumping into a fire: thus, Peregrinus's suicide would prove nothing but his own boundless stupidity.

'Peregrinus would probably have permitted himself to be convinced by Lucian had he still been in a position to do so. However, his disciples had already dug a deep ditch and lit a fire in it because they were afraid that, should he climb on to the usual kind of pyre he might change his mind at the last moment and get down again. After all it was he who had instilled into his disciples the world-saving ideology . . .' I continued slowly, watching the teacher of Hungarian communists sipping his wine and sitting motionless in his armchair.

'It was he who had explained to them that no sacrifice was too great for the sacred cause, not even death. Therefore, he had no reason to be surprised when his pupils took him at his word. But the ordinary people, whom the prophet had wanted to feed on ideology instead of on bread and meat, had always looked upon him with suspicion. They were glad to be given at least a circus performance instead of bread.'

'And what happened then?'

'To Peregrinus Proteus?' I asked. 'What could have happened? His disciples pushed him into the fire and he burned alive. Lucian, however, as befits a thinker, walked away in peace and wrote a book about Peregrinus.'

A rather painful silence ensued. Havas gave me a mildly reproachful look because I had offended against the prevailing etiquette by talking about something which it was bad form to mention. Haraszti made no reply, but compressed his finely chiselled lips and, inclining his head to one side, gazed into the air.

The silence was broken by Bandi. He threw a conspiratorial glance at Haraszti who, however, failed to react, then suddenly began to speak about the anthology. In this way he indicated that he considered all I had said null and void. He explained that the task for which they had picked me was beautiful indeed. Then he delivered a long lecture about clericalism being the most dangerous enemy of the people's democracy, and how we must fight against the priests on every front. After the persecution suffered by the clergy in the last two years, after the Mindszenty trial and, last but not least, after my story abut Peregrinus, this seemed not only out of place but utterly crazy. Bandi noticed this too, but made all the greater efforts to whip himself into the necessary frame of mind. At times he looked at me as if he were expecting an answer but I kept silent, concentrating on pouring out more wine, which greatly embarrassed him. Finally he declared that it would put me into a very favourable position politically if I agreed to become the editor of this Rakosi-inspired anthology.

'Never,' I said.

'But you have hated the clerics all your life!' Bandi screamed at me. 'It was you who translated Florian Geyer's song into Hungarian! If reaction came to power again they would tear you to pieces as they would us!'

'I won't be blackmailed,' I answered.

'So you fight in the same harness with clerics and landowners?'

'This is not a political question.'

'What then?'

'A question of taste. One doesn't write against those who are being persecuted and who cannot defend themselves,' I replied, rising from my chair. I poured the last drops from the three bottles into the three glasses and handed each his glass. I notice that Haraszti was looking at me with warm appreciation and that, as always when we were in danger of our lives, the front of Bandi's shirt was wet with perspiration. I had intended to shoot a few more arrows at them before I left but somehow the condition they were in mollified me and I raised my glass.

'To whom do we drink?' Haraszti asked resignedly.

'To your health. To the three of us. To the fact that though we belong to different families our thoughts are identical. To the circumstance that although we speak differently we think the same. To the knowledge that although we sleep in different beds we have the same dreams!'

I nodded to Bandi and made a deep bow to my Peregrinus as he sat motionless in his armchair, then I hurried from the room lest I express the thoughts that were in my mind. The wine, drunk on an empty stomach, mounted to my head; on the staircase I did not quite know whether I should laugh or cry, but when I stopped outside the front door in the burning noon sunlight and felt its beams penetrating the two corners of my frontal bone like two hot, golden hypodermic needles, I knew that I too wasn't far from going mad.

PART FOUR

Arrest

When the green-painted iron door of cell No. 48 fell to behind me I drew a deep breath of relief. I felt a cool breeze behind my forehead and a delicious tingle in my gullet, as if an invisible abscess had burst open in my body. My situation gave no cause for cheerfulness. I too, like so many of my friends and enemies, had now disappeared down the AVO drain. The charge against me confronted me with the alternative of the gallows or life imprisonment, and my cheeks were still burning with the fever caused by the shock of my arrest nearly three days earlier.

I was in a windowless, underground cell surrounded on three sides by a corridor, on the fourth by the lift shaft. As I began walking up and down the slippery concrete floor, midges flew into my face. Opposite the door an inscription, printed in capital letters, showed through the mirror-smooth new whitewash: GOD HAVE MERCY ON ME, and, below it the name of a notoriously atheist Member of Parliament who had disappeared a year ago. When they locked the door behind me I decided that I would revive old memories: Amar's kashba, the view of Bermuda, or Telegraph Hill in San Francisco. On no account would I examine my state of mind, so as not to go mad.

But was this idyllic mood and the slight tingling in my loins not already a sign of madness? I sat down on my bunk and established that my knee reflexes were absolutely normal. Then I repeated to myself the forty-eight states of America, the formula of the cubic content of the sphere, the date of the Treaty of Westphalia, the names of the Roman Emperors from Augustus to Marcus Aurelius and the inscription on the grave of the two hundred fallen at Thermopylae:

'Ω ξεῖν', ᾆγγειλον Λαχεδαιμονίοις ότι τῇδε
χείμεθα τοῖς χείνων ρήμαδι πειθόμενοι.

The dystich made me feel definitely sentimental. I was almost reassured by the results when it suddenly occurred to me that all this was no proof. As long as I was alone in my cell, that is alone in the world, the definition of reason and madness depended on my arbitration. It was quite possible, for instance, that though mad, I was perfectly correct in remembering that the envoys pledged themselves to observe the Treaty of Westphalia at Osnabrück, on the twenty-fourth of October, 1648, or it was equally possible that the cubic content of the sphere was a figment of my sick imagination and that no such geometrical figure as a sphere existed. Perhaps even the tiny, invisible midges I could feel on my face did not exist. Finally, it was conceivable that the name of the first Roman Emperor was September, and that I was playing a crazy game with myself when I called him Octavianus Augustus.

This experiment having proved useless, I decided to investigate the causes of my serene attitude. Three days before, when they arrested me, I immediately felt relaxed. This sensation of ease became apparent simultaneously with the petrifying amazement of the arrest, and played second fiddle, so to speak, from the very first moment. I had been on my way to Czechoslovakia to spend my holiday in the mountains at government expense. On the Hungarian–Czech border two detectives had taken me off the train and driven me back to Budapest in a police car. They had told me reassuringly that they were taking me to 60 Andrassy Street to be questioned as a witness, and that I would be home by morning. I nodded at this transparent but kindly lie and wrapped myself in silence. I thought of the sleepless nights when I had still been waiting for my arrest; the arguments of formal logic according to which it was impossible that they should arrest me because I had done nothing; and my feelings telling me that in spite of all logic I would be arrested. At last it had happened. I felt like someone floating, relieved, above his own body a few minutes after death, looking down disdainfully, with the haughtiness of a young spirit, at his corpse and at the fear of death he had once experienced. I offered my detectives a packet of American cigarettes. They reached for it greedily and gave each other a look heavy with significance. Then I kept my eyes on the road: the blue-black poplars, the yellow village churches, the hares jumping about madly, blinded by the headlights.

I was led into a large, ground-floor cell at the Secret Police Headquarters at 60 Andrassy Street. A young sergeant with fever-spots on his face sat in a cane chair at the door.

'Give me everything you have on you,' he whispered. For a second I stood undecided in this atmosphere of sweat, blood and human excrement, then I put down before him on the table my money, my lighter and my watch. When his eyes fell on my Parker pen he threw me a respectful glance and slipped it with a quick movement into his pocket.

'I shall write down on this envelope what you had on you,' he said, girding the silver-studded belt I had brought with me from Arizona around his own middle. 'So you can't make me responsible for your stuff!'

While he wrote I looked about the room. At one end, in a sort of alcove, some ten people were sleeping on a platform, men and women, helter-skelter. About the same number of people were sitting on chairs turned towards the wall, their heads bent forward, at a distance of two yards from each other. These were all men, like the four standing in the corners. Those had their noses pressed against the wall and their knees were trembling; their trousers were wet. One man was lying on the ground in a puddle of blood, saliva and urine. He was tied up from his shoulders to his knees, like a mummy, and lay with his face pressed to the cement floor so that I saw only his fat, ham-coloured nape with three somewhat oblique wrinkles filled with perspiration. It seemed to me as if I had seen that nape in Parliament some years ago.

And I had seen not only that nape, but the whole scene. I recalled a film based on a piece of trashy literature which had been made in three or four variations since my boyhood. It was about a sadistic physician in whose house several people disappeared. The hero of the film, although he had been suspicious from the first, fell into the trap. The physician's servants grabbed him and dragged him down to the mysterious cellar. This scene, here, was the one in which the camera moved over the motionless collection of Dracula's victims. The four men in the corner stood as if they had been frozen into an ice-block. The mummy on the floor survived by drinking his own urine. The men sitting on chairs had been bewitched before their blood had been sucked from their bodies; only God knew how many weeks or months they had been sitting like that. At this scene, in which the clumsy artificiality of the scenario clashed with the brutal realism of the staging, a sigh of horror and wild laughter had risen from the audience. That was how I felt now. From the very beginning I had known that something absurd would happen; not only in the police car that had brought me here or during the past few years; I had known it when I left America, I had known it at the air-base in Kodiak and in Africa, on the day we escaped from Paris, and even on the evening of the day Freud died, when we dined at Fontainebleau with Lorsy and Bandi. And I had not been the only one to guess it: Bandi and Lorsy and Professor Vambéry had known it, as well as my American friends, the liberals, the fellow-travellers and the communists; they had guessed it as I had guessed it. I knew that there was a mysterious building in every communist state where terror was manufactured, but I had never pictured to myself what really happened in those cellars. And had I, overcoming my laziness and cowardice, permitted my imagination to conjure up this picture, I should have rejected it as a perverted and unreal figment of my imagination. Even now, when it was there before my eyes, I still could not admit its reality and, like the audience at that awful film, I was half horrified, half amused. It was all too senseless, illogical and horrible to be real; and far too ridiculous to be really horrible.

I spent thirty-six hours in that common cell. Most of the time I was sitting on one of the chairs turned to the wall. Only the snoring of the sleepers and the endless babbling of the mummy broke the silence. Of the four men standing in the corner three collapsed from time to time. The sergeant threw a bucketful of water on them, stood them on their feet and slapped their faces. The fourth did not collapse once. He must have been standing for only one or two days. The babbling of the mummy consisted of four or five sentences. Sometimes he cried with deep conviction: 'I am a Member of Parliament. My immunity has not been suspended and I have committed no crime.' Then, a few hours later he complained that he had been kept tied up for ten days, although according to the law nobody could be detained for more than twenty-four hours; or he demanded that a lawyer be sent to see him and that his family be told of his whereabouts. Every time he began to speak the warder hurried over and began to kick his nape and his ears, but he went on talking.

The second morning I was led across the yard to the main building. In the corridor, close to a door, they told me to stand quietly with my face against the wall. While I was waiting, I pictured to myself my last free days with a painful, almost unbelievable exactitude: my discussion with Bandi Havas and Haraszti at the Athenaeum; our passage on the ferry-boat last Sunday when the nose of the boat divided the surface of the lake into a blue half and a green half; and I felt again the perfume of the coffee that had been put down before us at the espresso where Suzy and I had talked that last afternoon, three days ago. I had been standing there for two hours or more when I heard an agreeable, ringing voice from behind the door:

'Let that fascist come in!'

A captain was standing behind the desk: an attractive, elegant young man with fair hair, a narrow waist and almost classical features.

'Soon,' he said gaily, winking at me, '*you will feel the weight of your behind on your neck*.'

He was quoting a line from a Villon poem in my translation. 'Sit down,' he continued kindly, then fished out from his desk drawer a typewritten page and a rubber truncheon. 'You know me, don't you? No? Well, I was there at your Villon recital at the Academy of Music two months ago. I talked to you in the interval.'

For a while he stared into my face with obvious pleasure.

'Your name?'

While he typed out my data he looked with enchantment at his own hands, illuminated by the sunlight streaming in through the upper window. Nacreous, silver half-moons shone on his nails, but their ends were yellowish, thick and rough.

'Do you know why you have been brought in here?' he asked threateningly.

I shrugged my shoulders.

'It doesn't matter,' he continued tolerantly. 'It's enough if we know. Read this.'

He handed me the typewritten page. It began by my admitting that I had committed serious crimes against the Hungarian working people and the laws of the people's republic in that:

first: I was an agent of the American secret service;

second: I had organized an armed uprising for the overthrow of the people's republic;

third: as a right-wing social democrat I had carried out various sabotage actions;

fourth: I maintained close relations with the head of the Hungarian Trotskyists, Pal Justus, and various Trotskyist circles abroad;

fifth: after Justus's arrest I had become the head of the Hungarian Trotskyists;

sixth: I had written fascist articles in *Népszava*;

seventh: I was friendly with people of a clerical or reactionary attitude, made imperialist propaganda in my conversations and hated the Hungarian people above all.

Then the paper said that I was making this confession of my free will, without compulsion, to relieve my conscience. A few lines below, in another type, came an *eighth*, according to which, fearing arrest, I had taken a train to Czechoslovakia with the intention of going on from there to Western Germany and reporting to the American secret service.

'Will you sign?'

'There isn't a word of truth in it,' I replied.

The captain picked up his rubber truncheon and swung it.

'We shall see,' he said. 'We too have our arguments. They convinced Rajk. They convinced Pal Justus. They convinced Zoltan Horvath. They'll convince you too.'

'Each of the eight accusations is false. According to number one,

I am an American spy. Where, when and why did I spy? What armament factory, barracks or industrial works have I visited? What secrets have I learned? To whom have I handed over the espionage report? And why should I have done all this? For fun, instead of writing poetry? For ambition, to gain fame and to be included in the *Illustrated World History of Spies*? Or have I been hired as a spy by the late Franklin D. Roosevelt, postpaid and free of charge in order to . . .'

'Now stop this,' the captain interrupted me, pretending to suppress a yawn. 'I didn't have you brought here to listen to your lectures. Answer me: Will you or won't you sign the confession?'

He got up, walked over behind my chair and began to tickle my nape with his rubber truncheon.

'What happens if I don't?'

'We'll stop playing around and will beat you until you do. And if that doesn't help and if we don't kill you by mistake, we'll send for that Suzanne Szegö. And your mother. We'll beat the shit out of them. But don't build on that. You won't see them. You'll only hear their screams from the next room.'

'I can't think if you stand there behind me,' I said and looked up into his face. He looked back, his pupils expanded.

'Don't think. Sign,' he said lightly but went back to his chair.

'Give me time to think it over.'

'Are you mad? Two months to think it over and a roast duck every day?'

'No. Five minutes to think and a cigarette.'

I sat back in my chair: the brutal force of the smoke hit me in the chest. My questioner looked absentmindedly at his wrist-watch. Obviously most people who came up before him refused to sign. After all each of us – even the arrested communists – were used to thinking according to Roman Law and could not immediately accept that these people could do with us as they pleased – and do it regardless of whether we signed or not. I had to accept that they could kill me or not, as they liked. There was no point in not signing. There was no point in signing after two months of torture. Zinoviev signed, Bucharin signed, Rajk signed, Pal Justus signed, Zoltan Horvath signed, all of them after having tried desperately to convince their jailers of their innocence – something our jailers must have known.

'Give me your pen!'

The captain was so surprised that he raised both hands in the air.

'In eleven copies,' he said greedily and gave me his pen. Then, helpfully, he blew on my signatures until they dried, so as not to spoil the documents.

A little while after I had been taken down to the cellar, I at last discovered the real cause of my mysterious happiness. I was happy simply because I was in jail. Every particle of my body protested against the admission that I should feel happier in the most frightful building of the country, in a windowless, underground cell fitted with three wooden planks instead of a bed and a two-hundred-watt electric bulb ablaze above the door, than I had been in a society outside which I detested but in which I enjoyed until the last minute the love of Suzy, the shape of the clouds, my walks in the reedbanks at Dunaharaszti and the smell of wine. And yet, this was what was making me feel well: that at last I was where, in a communist state, I ought to be. No matter what injustice or stupidity my jailers committed, they had put me finally in the place where I belonged and in a position worthy of me. They had put an end to the shameful situation in which, more than once, I had been compelled to keep silent when I should have raised my voice, or to praise that which I loathed. But, leaving those lofty principles aside, my jailers had saved me from an everyday life in which I had to give up my writing, my friends, all human relationships, my habits, including that of thinking, all in order to make place for fear, insecurity, helplessness and humiliation. When they locked the cell door behind me I suddenly regained my freedom: the right and the unlimited opportunity to think.

My objections to acknowledging the liberation of my conscience went deep. True, I considered materialist philosophy, particularly as the communists interpreted it, to be obsolete rubbish left over from the Age of Enlightenment; but still, I refused to believe that its contrary should be true and that a relieved conscience alone could create in me agreeable, almost erotic physical reactions. Three days ago, I was still called 'comrade' and did not protest against it; I had to go to party meetings because there was no way to avoid them; thus I had not been able to sever certain elusive ties binding me to the system. I had tried to behave as decently as possible, in the given conditions, without endangering myself. I did not behave badly, but I had given no proof of moral courage; not only because it would have been utterly useless, but also because my views on moral courage were rather unorthodox: I regarded political and human honesty as a pose which I had assumed since my early days mainly to impress myself and my biographers. This was the main reason why I was astonished at being so happy only because my conscience had less to be ashamed of than it had a week earlier. It seemed almost incomprehensible that conscientious and moral factors should affect me so deeply, should dominate my whole body, so to speak.

The idyllic feeling still persisted after I had undressed and spread my clothes carefully on the three boards of the bunk to lie on. I closed my eyes and imagined that I was sleeping in a baroque garden, or rather in a garden on a stage, probably at a performance of a comedy by Lope de Vega: the electric bulb was the morning sun, the green cell door the garden gate and the whispers of the jailers in the corridor those of the prompter. But as soon as I fell asleep I saw the flat-nosed, gorilla-like monster at the Criminal Records Office to whom I had been led earlier that day, and the fat, limping AVO man, the bath-master, whom I had also visited and who stood in trunks and a gunbelt before the old stove into which he was feeding books by André Gide, Ernest Hemingway and Panait Istrati. The water from the tap in my dream was ice cold or scalding hot, as it had been that morning, and I imagined that they had taken me to the police station in Hell where the Monster of Düsseldorf keeps the records and Jack the Ripper is the chief. Later, American planes began to circle above my head. My American paratrooper buddies were coming to rescue me. Although they jumped out above the Danube, the west wind was so strong that they came down exactly on the roof of 60 Andrassy Street, above which other triumphant planes were circling. When I woke with a start I suddenly remembered that I was next to the lift-shaft. It must have been ten o'clock: the AVO men were arriving for the night shift, to bring out the rubber truncheons from the desk drawers and the clients from the underground cells. But was it really the lift I had heard? I closed my eyes and concentrated on Truman's planes.

To my great relief I was not questioned again during the next fortnight. On my first morning in the cell I was already able to see that something in it had changed. The whitewashed wall had lost its smoothness and become patterned with damp spots, shadows and cracks. Soon the latter combined to form easily discernible, permanent frescoes, sketches and signs. On a level with the bunk I discovered the elegant arch of the Golden Gate Bridge and close to it the outlines of the British lion. At eye-level, in the middle of another wall, a wintry landscape with trees showed through the whitewash. Only after careful examination did I discover that it was not a landscape at all but a multiple scaffold with the victims hanging from its arms like grapes – the kind seen on the execution-hills of medieval towns.

On the end wall, where the atheist Member of Parliament had written his GOD HAVE MERCY ON ME, four apocalyptic horses were drawing a coach towards the large, vertical, zigzag crack. Behind the coach, to the left, I thought I could read the letters MMIR. I soon decided that the moist crack running from south to north on the wall-map was the River Rhine; but who were the travellers in the coach? Aristocrats escaping from the French Revolution? After a morning of hard thinking I came to the conclusion that the letters MMIR stood where Paris lay on the map and could consequently mean nothing else but the initials of *Maximilien Marie Isidore de Robespierre.* So the passengers in the coach were girondists fleeing not from the revolution but from Robespierre's reign of terror, and their coach had got stuck in the mud of the road. The myrmidons would catch up with them and drag them back to the Conciergerie.

I was annoyed that it had taken me so long to solve it. When I was first brought down to the cellar and the iron door closed behind me, pressing out the air with a sibilant whisper, and when the rusty bolt was shot into place, the two sounds had reminded me of the two syllables of the word *gi-ronde*. And when I caught sight of the bare bunk I remembered Vambéry's last words in New York harbour and suddenly everything I ever knew about the Gironde had come back to me. Among the girondists André Chénier and Mme Roland were closest to my heart: the image I drew to myself of the latter was so sharp that I could see the powder spilling from her wig and could almost smell her perfume. But what I was thinking about was not the similarity of our fates but the differences between them. Robespierre – however much I disliked him as a puritan who did not go to the café for his amusement but played billiards with human heads – was at least a man, attractive, witty, within his own narrow logic consistent; his followers adored him and he believed in what he was doing. My baldheaded jailer, on the other hand, was nothing but one of Stalin's henchmen, ugly, dull, unoriginal and a cynic behind his mask of a jovial grocer. He knew in his head, resting on two fat-rolls instead of a neck, that he was hated by the entire country and despised by his Russian master. And this was why André Chénier was allowed to write poems in prison, and why I in the communist Conciergerie was given no paper and pen; this was why they would kill me in secret and kick my body into the lime-pit.

The tumbril taking the condemned to the Place de Grève, from which they could call to their friends and relatives and even proclaim their opinions, seemed to me a triumphal car taking its passengers straight to the Pantheon. The fact that I would not be able to assure Suzy and posterity of my innocence was as dreadful to me as the idea of my execution. From some of my opinions and remarks – when, for instance, I had said that while Stalin assured the workers of his great love for them three times in every speech he made, Truman's America paid them three times more wages without prattle – Suzy might conclude that I had been an imperialistic agent, although I had only stated a fact. What I said after the Rajk trial might justify her in thinking that I had been one of Rajk's accomplices, although I had protested only because he had been hanged for invented crimes and not for his real ones.

In my earlier behaviour she might find psychological evidence for all the eight charges against me and should she still not be quite certain of my guilt, she would come to believe in it in time, after listening to friends and acquaintances, reading about it in the papers and hearing my confession from my own lips at the trial. And in the end I would believe it myself. In a year, only my accusers, tormentors and judges would know that I was innocent.

I was also concerned about the opinion of posterity. My friends might not need to be convinced, but they would die and the new generation would inherit neither their beliefs nor their experiences. Everything depended on the lifespan of the régime. True, it was not much stronger than a house built of cards, but a house that would not collapse by itself. It needed a kick or a breeze to bring it down, and as far as this kick or breeze was concerned I had nothing to hope from the knees or lungs of Western politicians. At Yalta, they had entrusted our lives to Stalin's care; two years ago, they had encouraged us to stand up for our convictions and resist communist expansion; now, they were assuring us of their sympathies over the radio.

It seemed hopeless and childishly naïve to struggle any more against the enemy's forces, but I tried my best. Every time I was taken to the WC the warder stood in the open door watching my every move. It took infinite cunning to secrete a piece of toilet paper and take it back to my cell. Under the bunk, between two bricks, I discovered a deep crevice; this was where I intended to hide a message. Twenty or fifty years hence, after the fall of the régime, this building would be torn down like the Bastille, but before it vanished they would pass every particle of dust through a sieve to see whether the one-time inmates had left any messages.

During the past two years I had diligently perused the better known prison diaries of Hungarian history and anything dealing with the imprisonment of our national heroes. I had little difficulty, therefore, in laying my hands on writing material. I tore out a few bristles from the broom the warder brought in the morning for me to sweep the wet floor of the cell. For a while I used my gum as an inkwell, and when it dried up I tore open my finger on the iron legs of the bunk and took blood from there whenever I needed it.

I had to keep my message short. I WAS INNOCENT sounded cheap and unconvincing; besides, my intention was not to let the world know that I was the victim of a miscarriage of law; I insisted on informing the world that there was no law at all. THE NAZIS BOIL SOAP, THE COMMUNISTS TERROR FROM THEIR OPPONENTS sounded pedantic and affected. And it was only half true, since the communists boiled terror from the body of Rajk, who was not an opponent, and, anyway, it might well be that my case would never come up for trial, the documents would be burned, my name never again mentioned, so that they would not even distil terror from my body; they had brought me here without any reason and would liquidate me for no purpose. I WAS KILLED BY THE CYNICAL INQUISITORS AND IMPOSTORS OF AN IRRATIONAL STATE POWER sounded much better, but it needed a whole volume of explanation, a volume I would have no time to write. ARTHUR KOESTLER WAS RIGHT was a tempting solution, but this formula suggested that I discovered it only here, in jail, which was untrue. Besides, I rejected any comparison between Rubashov and myself. Still, after a number of variations this was the one I chose, with the addition I WAS GUILTLESS and a postscript of two lyrical words for Suzy.

I used up ten or fifteen drops of blood for every letter, to make certain it would show on the paper for a few decades. I was busy on the last word of the postscript when the door of the cell flew open. The warder must have been watching me through the Judas-hole; he tore the paper from my hand, slapped my face and declared that my investigator would make sure I was punished. Five minutes later he returned with a rubber truncheon and ordered me to open my trousers and put my scrotum on the iron bed-head. For a second I wavered and cold sweat broke out on my forehead. At that moment inhuman screams broke out on the opposite side of the corridor. This was the first sound I had heard from my fellow prisoners since I was locked in the cell, except for the spasmodic coughing of the man in the cell opposite mine. This sound came from far away, at least five cells down the corridor. Anxiety was making my ear-drums throb and I felt as if hot water were streaming into my ears. Because of this I did not understand the words, although they were undoubtedly coherent. At the first scream the warder ran from my cell and locked the door on me. In the next second I was leaning against the door, listening to the sounds outside.

'Long live Stalin! Long live Stalin! I love our dear comrade Rakosi!'

In the pauses between the thuds of the rubber truncheon the 'Long live Stalin! Long live Stalin! I love our dear comrade Rakosi!' rose six more times, ever more strongly, ever more enthusiastically. Then I heard a splitting sound as if they had broken the victim's jaw along with his teeth. Then absolute silence, as if both victim and torturers had been buried alive under sand.

I felt that I knew that voice. I knew everybody in that cellar. The social democratic politicians, ministers, under-secretaries, generals, police chiefs, university professors and deputies who were here partly because they refused to sell their party to the communists, partly because they had not refused. But which of them would acclaim Stalin? This stupid trick, this fun-fair barker's humbug would never have occurred to the old trade union leaders, nor to Istvan Ries, Minister of Justice, nor even to Arpad Szakasits, President of the Republic, weak and cowardly but entirely without baseness or cunning. If anyone, only György Marosan would be capable of it; but the voice was not Marosan's voice.

I stood by the door for a long time, listening for the steps of the AVO men. Two hours later the same warder who had made me undo my trousers opened the door and pointed to a dixie full of meatballs. 'Pick it up and eat, you rotten plutocrat,' he said. For hours I kept pacing the cell, two and a half steps up, two and a half steps down, afraid that he might return with the rubber truncheon; but he did not show up.

After having spent a fortnight in my cell I was led before a pink-cheeked, fat-lipped, slightly bald major who was waiting for me at the window of his room, resting his backside on the sill and raising himself on tiptoe to seem taller. During the interrogation he threw back his head and with a lock of hair hanging over his forehead, his eyes bulging and his arms crossed over his chest, he bustled up and down the room, triumphant in his likeness to Bonaparte on the bridge at Lodi. As there was no name-plate on his desk I christened him Napoleon the Grocer.

The questions he asked me were so confusing that on this first day I couldn't make out what he wanted from me and I felt that he did not know it either. On the second day he ordered me to write my autobiography in at least thirty pages; Two days later, when I had finished, he read it carefully, then declared that if what I had written were true I should be decorated and not imprisoned. Then he called me Orwell's dirtiest disciple and spat into my eyes. During the following two days he made me tell him about every love-affair I had ever had, down to the smallest detail. It seemed as though he were simply passing the time of day until they had finished searching my room and collecting data and evidence against me.

During the following week, after he had made me write two more autobiographies, had torn them up and flung them in my face, I at last discovered what he wanted. I understood from certain remarks he made that they had not searched my room, knew nothing about my past activities and, what is more, were not even interested in them. They wanted nothing but that I should furnish, or to be more exact, invent, the proofs supporting the eight false charges against me. I had to realize that the AVO were not investigating, not examining, not proving and not reading. According to communist logic the very fact that they omitted to search my room, although they were accusing me of preparing an armed uprising, demonstrated that they were preparing to stage a show-trial. My remaining doubts were dispelled by Napoleon himself who, reminding me that I was a poet – a man of imagination – encouraged me to write a 'really beautiful and credible confession'. He said that if I refused he would have me taken to the cellar and beaten so thoroughly that they would have to take me out of the building in a dustbin. However, apart from a few slaps, he did not hurt me.

Finally he declared that we would write my biography in co-authorship. He sat down to the typewriter and I dictated. But when he handed me each finished page it turned out that he had typed something entirely different from what I had said. At first I would argue for hours concerning an expression; when, for instance, instead of putting down that my father was a university professor he typed 'As far as my father's profession is concerned, I come from a rich *bourgeois* family.' When I protested, he declared that nobody was responsible for his background and offered to delete the word 'rich'. 'Write,' I insisted, 'that my father was a college professor, because that is what he was.' But the Grocer refused to mention my father's profession; perhaps he feared that it might make a favourable impression on the audience at the trial.

He also omitted that I had studied philosophy, that I had been condemned *in contumnaciam* to eight years of prison for my anti-Nazi poems, that all my books had been burned by the Hungarian fascists, that I had been invited to America by Roosevelt and that I was secretary of the Free Hungary Movement. Thus I realized that truth had absolutely no place in this concoction. The only purpose of trials such as mine was to justify the politics of the communist party by a practical demonstration, or rather, like a biblical parable. The defendant had to be of *bourgeois* origin, he had to be a former lackey of the Horthy régime, he had to be a traitor to the working class from the cradle and, at the same time, a pro-Westerner, an egg-head and an admirer of Churchill, Hitler, Mussolini and Tito at one go. Since there was no real human being suited to their purpose, the AVO, willy-nilly, had to invent such beings.

As time went on I became more and more bored with the whole procedure. I watched the shadows of the guards walking up and down in front of the building, reflected on the white ceiling above the window hung with thick curtains, so that the interrogator had to shout at me repeatedly before I heard his question. My creased suit, dirty shirt and unshaven face made me self-conscious, the hard bunk hurt my back and I was nervous because since the Grocer had tried to blackmail me with cigarettes I had stopped smoking. But I was even more annoyed by the dullness and lack of drama in the interrogation; by the fact that the accusations were as stupid as I had expected them to be and the procedure even clumsier. I thought with a certain envy of my communist comrades in misfortune who were probably trying to defend themselves and convince their interrogators of their innocence. They were at least fighting for something, while

I knew beyond doubt that fighting was foolish. By some means or other they would extract from me the confession they wanted to have and I knew that the text of the confession was absolutely unconnected with whether they would hang me or not, because that was decided long before my arrest and if not, it depended on their whim.

A few days earlier, however, I had still cherished a few illusions, if not about communist justice, at least about its executants whom, remembering Ivanov and O'Brien, I had imagined to be much superior to this; probably because Koestler and Orwell had based their characters on the communist old guard, and had also observed the literary convention that they should be opponents worthy of their heroes. My Grocer, unfortunately, didn't even satisfy the requirements of a penny-dreadful. What incensed me most was not that he had no idea of geography, spelling, syntax or history but that although he was bustling up and down like mad and constantly falling into his Napoleonic poses, and although he showed more than a necessary interest in my person, he was even more bored with my case than I was myself. I was convinced that he had received detailed instructions as to what I was to confess, so that naturally he was bored; and the main reason I loathed him was not because he could eventually have me hanged but because I was compelled to converse with him.

On the second day of our joint biography-writing my fury exploded. We were discussing events in 1938–39 and the Grocer summarized my reasons for emigrating as follows: 'I could not resist my cosmopolitan nature, my unrestrained ambition and my yearning for money, therefore I travelled to Paris to contact various diversionary elements and became a member of Laszlo Fényes's Trotskyist group . . .'

I told the Grocer that Fényes had been a socialist, not a Trotskyite. I warned him that this passage was so stupid, so obviously AVO-inspired and drafted that not only foreign journalists but even the most loyal and idiotic party member could not believe it at the trial.

'Then you can say it without worrying. It involves no risk,' the major replied with a loud yawn. 'Besides, what difference does it make to poor Fényes whether we call him a socialist or a Trotskyist?'

We argued for a long time. I had learned during my interrogation that the Grocer divided humanity into two main categories: those who were already dead, or arrested or hanged; and those who were still free – that is, who had still to be arrested and hanged. He spoke leniently about the dead 'who chose liberty and escaped from us to the graveyards'; but when speaking about the prisoners in the cells below us there was even a certain fatherly warmth in his voice. He discussed them as a farmer would his livestock, which he must feed, which he must keep clean and which, when necessary, he must castrate, or, rather sadly, send to the slaughterhouse. Of the other category, those still unarrested, he spoke with a hatred that almost made him foam at the mouth. He called Imre Komor, the editor of *Népszava*, 'an old Trotskyite horse-thief'; said about a famous writer, who, in order to avoid dealing with the present took the subjects of his novels from history, that 'he is disguising himself as a carrion beetle although he is a scorpion'; and, when talking about one of the best actresses of the country, added, 'we shall bring her in as soon as we have room in the cellar, and we'll make that harlot drink her own urine'. I learned a great deal from the remarks he let drop, which often permitted me to guess what was going on outside and who had been brought in during the last few days. There was always a certain gentleness in his voice when he spoke of them.

We were still arguing about Fényes and my emigration when, unexpectedly, he asked:

'And when did you become acquainted with poor Bandi?'

'What Bandi?'

'Poor Bandi Havas, of course.'

Suddenly I was overcome with nausea and almost fell from my chair. I closed my eyes quickly to avoid watching Napoleon's pleasure at the effect of his words. I had been seeking the owner of the voice cheering Stalin on an entirely wrong track, among the social democrats, and that was why I had come to the false conclusion that he was an unfortunate impostor who could invent no better trick. But now I knew that the lunatic who had cried for Stalin could have been no one but Bandi Havas.

I went on sitting there with my eyes closed, trying to think. When Bandi was brought in he probably did not believe, as I did, that he had fallen into the murderers' trap. He probably believed that after a short and friendly conversation which would convince his comrades of his innocence, they would let him go. Perhaps this was how other communists thought, too, at the moment of their arrest. But what happens to a believer who discovers in prison that the priests of his church are cynics, his inquisitors heretics, his executioners pagans? He is faced with an appalling alternative: either he relinquishes his faith, or he sacrifices his sanity. Obviously the majority will defend themselves against going mad and will betray the faith that has betrayed them, so that the false accusation of heresy finally becomes true; not because the believer accepts the accusations brought against him as true, but because he discovers that his accusers know it to be false. After so much self-humiliation and cowardice, Bandi had made an insane, but still a manly and impressive gesture, and had chosen the other solution. He had thrown himself overboard so as not to have to sacrifice his faith and his party; he had chosen to believe his accusers when they said he was guilty, perhaps he even thought them right to beat and torture him. He admitted to heresy not only by signing a prefabricated confession, but by handing over his soul to the party's judgement. He protected his faith by recognizing sins he had never committed. He must have been the only person in the building who could sincerely wish Stalin and Rakosi a long life. Yes, he is the hero of our age – I thought. The hero of our age in the sense Lorsy and I had prophesied at Fontainebleau, ten years ago, on the day of Poland's fourth dismembering. I had been arrested by my enemies, he by his comrades; my doom was self-evident, uninteresting and rather ridiculous, because I had voluntarily gone through a door which could not be opened from inside; but Bandi had always been inside this closed room, his doom was tragic and characteristic of our age, belonging to the very essence of its history. The shedding of my blood was only a private affair, and a very common one at that, but the shedding of Bandi's blood cried to heaven.

I was still sitting there, with my eyes closed, feeling my temples swelling with torment like two large blisters, my throat and windpipe flattened out like paper cylinders under a heavy fist, my toes curling back tensely under my foot till they stuck in a hole in my shoe. When

I opened my eyes the Grocer was standing by the window, his arms crossed on his chest, a triumphant, watchful smile on his lips.

'I can see,' he said, 'that you don't want to denounce your friend Bandi. And you don't have to. Havas has admitted everything. He even betrayed your spy-contacts and those of Uncle Sandor Haraszti. He confessed that you three had worked together on the restoration of capitalism, Uncle Sandor in the service of Tito, he in the service of the British, and you in the service of the Americans. Learn from your friend's example and make a full confession. Admit everything,' he concluded, pointing his finger towards the dirty wall where Felix Edmundovich Dzerdzinski's black beard looked trim and well cared for under the glass protecting the old-fashioned oleograph.

During the following weeks Napoleon the Grocer extorted a detailed confession from me in which I admitted that I had gone to France to join Laszlo Fényes's Trotskyite group and to engage in anti-Soviet activity while working on the post-war restoration of capitalism. Then he handed me over to a plain-clothed AVO investigator who called himself an American specialist and made me describe how, with Vambéry, other arch-reactionaries, and the imperialists and fascists of America, I had engaged in subversive activity and had joined the OSS, America's espionage organization. From his questions I concluded that they were preparing a Trotskyist spy-trial of which I should be one of the principal accused. I therefore did my best to invent details of a kind to make foreign journalists guess what was going on. I told my interrogator, for instance, that I had been recruited for the Office of Strategic Services by two American agents: Captain Edgar Allan Poe and Major Walt Whitman, describing the two men in great detail. In case one of the investigators or the judge might discover my purpose I invented a third American agent, the club-footed Z. E. Bubbel – an anagram of Belzebub – whom I intended to unmask only at the trial. I talked at length about the wild orgies we had staged at the New York headquarters of the OSS from where – after we had got drunk to the gills on Coca-Cola – I had been carted home by Belzebub himself. When my interrogator asked me for the New York address of the OSS headquarters I was unable to answer, because I had never been there, so suggested that he should look it up in the New York telephone directory; upon which he gave me a beating and made me stand for two days and three nights with my nose pressed to the wall. By then he had put the address into my confession.

One evening during the interrogation, which usually lasted until ten p.m., I was just about to invent the instructions with which I had been sent home to Hungary by the American espionage organization, when my interrogator was called from the room. On his return he summoned a guard to remove me. The guard did not take me back to the cellar but put me in a car and drove me to another yard in the huge AVO headquarters. I was then made to walk down many steps into a deep cellar where I was put in a cell. Only then did I realize how elegant my former quarters had been. Here the bunk was mouldy and there was half an inch of water on the floor. There was no ventilation and a constant gasping rattle came from the next cell. The guard warned me that I was not allowed to sit down during the day and would be taken out to the lavatory only once every twenty-four hours. Should they catch me giving way to my needs in the cell they would make me drink my own water for a week instead of supper.

The next day I expected them to fetch me for interrogation, but nothing happened. It was the same on the following day, the next week and all the following weeks. At first I thought that they had discovered the lies in my confession and were punishing me for having tried to fool them, but I soon had to discard that idea. Had I been right they would probably have beaten me, bur they would not have interrupted the questioning. Perhaps they had sent me down here to put me to the usual tortures: but when day after day went by without anything of the sort taking place, I discarded that idea too. It was silly to seek for reasons in this completely irrational set-up. The most probable answer was that my interrogator had received new instructions, or that a new, more important prisoner had been put in my old cell.

This question did not preoccupy me for long, and I soon gave up guessing. On the second of those forty-two days, while I walked up and down in my cell like a pendulum, it flashed through my mind that I was in a privileged position. To hold mass a priest needs an altar and an altar-boy; to follow his bent a craftsman needs tools, a painter his brushes, a minister his desk, a worker his machine. I was the only man in this cellar who had in his head everything he required for his profession. The mere thought of being able to make poems filled me with a swaggering happiness that made me walk up and down with a smile on my lips. I felt that I was fooling my jailers and, at the same time, forgetting my miserable situation. At times it crossed my mind that the AVO had arrested me without cause and therefore, according to its own logic, it would have to hang me; for what else could they do with me? Every time I pictured my execution, my knees gave way, I stopped in my tracks and began to watch the rings forming in the half inch of water that had collected on the floor of my cell. In the next second, however, I shrugged my shoulders haughtily and forgot all about it. The poems on which I was working were more interesting to me than the problem of whether or not they world hang me.

This was not because I had become accustomed to the fear of death since I had been in prison, but because I had never become accustomed to it in all my life. At the age of nine or ten, almost every night, whenever I remembered that I should die, I would jump out of bed, switch on the light, or bite my pillow in utter despair. When my classmates in the first grade in grammar school were throwing paper pellets at each other I would think: this is how deadly bacilli fly around me, and one day one of them will hit me. When I heard words like *humanity*, *fate* or *life*, I saw hosts of men running with bare breasts towards machine-guns that mowed them down, generation after generation. If on some border the customs officer inquired about my destination, a graveyard emerged before my eyes. Whenever I lay back on my bed or took a sunbath at the swimming pool I always remembered that one day I would lie in the ground in this very same position. It was never the proximity of death that I feared, but its inevitability. Having always been conscious of deadly danger, even in the safest situation, and having always trembled at the thought of death with the greatest cowardice, I could not experience much greater fear at any moment of my life.

Until then I had never thought that it was possible to make a poem without pen and paper, but apparently they did not belong to the essence of poetry, not even to the ceremony of poem-making. Homer probably created his epic before writing was invented in Greece. I imagined him walking along the sea-shore or in a garden (I had to discard the legend of his blindness, for a blind man would never speak about an 'oily, wine-dark sea') reciting to himself his hexameters. There was no reason why I shouldn't do the same. The tinyness and semi-obscurity of the cell constricted my imagination and thereby caused it to explode. Forgotten scenes from my childhood and youth filled my mind; the world outside came to life again, and seemed more clear-cut to me than ever before: it had petrified into a somewhat dramatic stage-setting, complete with actors. It seemed to me as if one minute after my arrest the whole world had been declared a historic monument: all movement, all change had ceased; my friends had turned to stone in the position in which I had last seen them. I was standing in a huge picture gallery and I read hundreds of frescoes into the whitewashed walls of my cell.

My only problem was to memorize my poems. On the first day I thought up only twenty lines, but gradually I increased it to an average of fifty lines a day. I repeated each line twenty times, and all the previous lines three times in succession. By evening I had always forgotten the whole poem but the next morning I knew it without mistake. My preoccupation changed even the subjective length of a day: to me the time from six o'clock in the morning when the guard appeared with the soup until between nine and ten in the evening when he collected the dixie, never seemed longer than three-quarters of an hour. Thus, I completely forgot the present and the future and even came to disregard the noises seeping into my cell; except the brief howling to be heard once or twice a week, usually late in the evening that ended in a short, strangled death-rattle. The howl was always preceded by the guards dragging something mute and lifeless, probably an unconscious or drugged man, along the corridor, and by the sound of a body dropped into a bath filled with liquid. The basin must have been somewhere at the end of the corridor, behind a cell door. Five or six seconds after the howl I could smell acid, but whether it was hydrochloric acid or sulphuric acid I was never sure. I supposed that the victim, become useless to the AVO either because he had already signed a confession or because he refused to make one, was beaten half dead and then thrown into the bath of acid. For a few minutes I would stand petrified in my cell, but immediately afterwards I would find rhymes more beautiful and metaphors more unexpected than had ever occurred to me before.

In a month's time I could whisper to myself a whole volume of poems. I devoted the first of them to my father's memory, or rather, to the memory of our life-long quarrel. When I emigrated to Paris we were on bad terms and I addressed my letters to my mother whenever I wrote. Back in Budapest, I found only his grave. This was how our long feud, lasting over fifteen years, had ended. And yet, it was from him that I had inherited an essential part of my being: my cheerfulness, my patience, my interest in philosophy and art, my intense but never immoderate enjoyment of the pleasures of life, my fear of death, my yearning for travel and adventure. In his youth he had been an assistant teacher at the University of Johannesburg – perhaps even he did not know how he ever got there. The outbreak of the First World War found him in Switzerland, the Second in Italy. Both countries would have been glad to offer him asylum but he returned home, although he, like me, was only attached to Hungary, but did not like to live there.

Our differences began when I was still in grammar school. He always listened to my arguments, though he never considered them important. He said – and in this he was right – that several hundred chemical engineers were living in the country and with the exception of one or two they all earned a very decent living. At the same time, there were hundreds of poets and with the exception of one or two they were all starving. At the university they would give me a degree that would be recognized throughout the world. But I could not obtain a degree in poetry, and who could guarantee that my poems would meet with success, no matter how extraordinary they were? Poetry, beautiful as it might be, was but a violet vapour, intangible and difficult to define, nothing on which to build a life.

He liked to talk to me in the conservatory, among his test tubes, in a white coat, his arms crossed on his chest. He raised one of his eyebrows and watched me with tenderness. With his olive complexion, silver hair and domed forehead he resembled at times a famous gipsy musician, at times Einstein, then again Karl Marx. I would tremble with fury. It was not that I had doubted his benevolence. I knew that in his youth he too had wanted to be a writer. I had found some of his poems in his desk drawer, hidden under business correspondence. Some had been written during the First World War when he was serving in the Balkans as a first lieutenant in the Austro-Hungarian Army. A few of these poems were addressed to a pretty landlady in Cetinje, a big, hefty woman who threw out the more obnoxious guests with her own strong hands and with whom my father drank thick Thracian red wines under the setting sun until their tongues stuck to their palates. It made me particularly angry that my father should try to dissuade me from doing something that he himself had tried. I also knew that he pursued his profession, in which he was known throughout Europe as an expert, with the ambition and zeal of an alchemist, but not with love. When he was alone in the flat he locked himself in his room and played the violin. Sometimes I watched him through the keyhole: he stood on the bear-skin by the window, next to the piano. He clasped the violin to him with hand and chin, like some coveted prey. His face would still be alight with joy when, later, he left the room.

One of the most exalting moments of my life was when, while my father was praising the real and positive world of Mendeleyev's ninety-two elements and speaking with disdain of the violet vapour of poetry, the retorts – filled with the violet vapour of mercury – exploded behind him with a powerful noise, overthrew the Bunsen burners and broke some of the conservatory's windows. While my father was busy putting out the small fires I walked quietly away with the triumphant realization that even the ninety-two elements – of which I doubted not only the number and succession but also the very existence – had come to my aid.

After the explosion, though I was tactful enough not to laugh about it, the conflict between us was never bridged. Later, when he found out that instead of studying chemistry I was attending lectures in philosophy, history and medicine, or sitting peacefully in the university library, there were rather noisy scenes, though my father was a mild man. Subsequently, when in spite of my youth I became a well-known poet in my country, he spoke proudly of me to the others but never revoked his former opinion to my face, I never expected my father to apologize to me. All I expected of him was to congratulate me just once, between the two of us, on my success. He, however, could not resign himself to it – presumably in my own interest. If he could now see me in prison he would probably assure me, with an aching heart, that had I become a chemical engineer this would never have happened to me. Perhaps he would have been right. I should probably hold a university chair, I should be a member of the party, my students would loathe me and I would loathe myself. Even if they were to hang me, my choice had been the right one.

The apartment house in which my parents had lived until the middle of the 'thirties received a direct hit in 1944. By the time I returned to Budapest even the ruins had been cleared away. But I still pictured my father in his old study, floating in space four floors up, like a fragment of a disintegrated heavenly body. And this is how I described him in my poem: standing on the bear-skin next to the piano, turning his back on the desk and the bookcase with the busts of Heraclitos and Democritus on its top and the chemical and philosophical books on its shelves – the former now obsolete, the latter out of fashion. He stood there as he used to do, in his creased, loose, spotted black suit but not without some elegance, with his short legs, protruding stomach and huge, strong chest – looking like a big violin. And I listened to his playing behind the door, hovering, as he did, in space. Then, cautiously, I tried the door. To my surprise it was open. 'Why don't we make friends, Daddy?' I asked. But he pretended not to notice me. And I dared not hold out my hand to him because it is bad form to hold out your hand to your father even if he is dead.

The next poem was addressed to Rustem Vambéry. While at liberty I had dared to think of him only at night. At such times I accompanied him along the road to annihilation. I saw his skin turn purple, become bloated and begin to rot; I saw his swollen fingers spread out in the coffin; he could no longer hold his fountain-pen to write letters like strings of pearls; I saw filthy puddles fill the sockets that once embraced his wise, ironical eyes. His nails had fallen off and lay beside him like ten pale shells.

This is what the first eight lines of the poem dealt with. Then I went on to describe the atmosphere of our conversations in his room on the twelfth floor at the Hotel Van Cortland. I listened with only half an ear when, sometimes, he mentioned Roman Law. The law, he said, could be compared to an old-fashioned, uncomfortable, dirty though rather massive building, its corridors walked by vain and haughty judges, and money-hungry, noisy lawyers. But if someone were to bore a hole in the wall of this building, all the filth of the gutter would stream in until we were submerged to the lips. It was not by chance that Voltaire chose to rehabilitate the memory of Calas or that Zola fought with such unwavering energy for the not very attractive Captain Dreyfus. They knew exactly what follows every time society tolerates even one innocent man's condemnation.

There was a third poem to be written, the one to Suzy. That poem must be true, whatever the future might hold. If they hanged me the poem must be different from the one I should write if they did not hang me, and it must also fit Suzy's attitude – which was unknown to me. I was no longer worried about our argument, about the red handbag which turned into a white handbag at the patty's command. I knew that Suzy would sooner or later discard the communist fanaticism that she had assumed precisely in self-defence against communism. The question was only: when?

I was afraid that my arrest – however much it hurt her – would not be enough to open Suzanne's eyes. Not that I suspected her of reacting like people in general. In general people behaved about their arrested friends in a way exactly opposite to that in which they behaved about the dead, of whom it is usual to remember only the virtues; of the arrested they refused to remember anything but their bad habits and bad deeds, partly to rid themselves of inevitable pangs of conscience, partly to reject all moral obligation to stand up for them. Suzanne would never sink so low; the trouble was that she might regard my arrest as a misunderstanding, as a judicial error, and so might reconcile, at least temporarily, the sorrow felt over my loss with her faith in the party.

Suzanne had been driven into the communist party by her indignation against social injustice, by her father's richness, by her rebellion against her parents, by her benevolence, her humanity and her historical and philosophical ignorance. Like everyone who joined the party for moral reasons, she gave up moral scruples as soon as she had joined. It was obvious that those moral scruples, silenced for a while, would sooner or later kill her faith in communism and would bring order to the emotional chaos which that faith had engendered in her. I was afraid, however, that this would take a long time.

Strangely enough I came to this conclusion from the fact that Suzanne had never studied Greek and had taken Latin only for a short time, as a non-compulsory subject. In the course of the last few years I had noticed that knowledge of classical tongues and of the humanities existed in an inverse ratio with the penetration of communist ideas, which may have been why communists hastened to abolish the teaching of Latin in the grammar schools. Not one of my forty classmates had remained communists; those who had joined were disappointed within a few weeks or months. The most devoted, stubborn and biased supporters of the régime were middle-class people or intellectuals who had not studied Latin, while most of the communist writers or journalists occupying key positions had gone to technical schools, like Bandi Havas.

I felt that it was the things I had learned in the Latin, Greek and history classes of my school that formed the stumbling-block on which communism foundered. Whenever I read the works or listened to the speeches of the ideologists or politicians of the régime, the precise rules of Latin grammar and style warned me that the subjects did not correspond to the predicates, that the tenses were incorrectly used and that the text was impure. Not only formally impure, but also in its essence, because the writer, or speaker, was lying – lying consciously – and was in addition bored with his own lies. The little I had learned in logic, correct and incorrect deduction, immunized me against the arguments, slogans, promises, predictions and statistics of the communists. The entire Graeco-Roman world rose up against their pompous, dull and bilious life, from their nurseries hung with Stalin's portraits to their colourless and profane funerals, at which their corpses served merely as a pretext for the party secretary to attack Harry Truman in the funeral oration – all through their days steeped in intrigue, wasted in joylessness, in reckless hysteria or neurotic sham calm, without sincerity, sensuousness, walks, revelry and freedom: yes, the entire Graeco-Roman world rose up against them, the blue and serene skies of Homer, Marcus Aurelius's wisdom, the idylls of Theocritus, the sepulchres of the Diphilon cemetery of Athens, Catullus's erotics, the philosophers walking in the Stoa Poikile; everything that had been thought, done, written or said in the antique world, including the pornographic frescoes and curses preserved on the walls of Pompeii.

I was immunized against the outlook of the Bolsheviks by the philosophical school which they called simply 'the lackeys of Athens's *bourgeoisie*'. Among others, Aristotle, who, as an idealist and a natural scientist, refuted by his mere being the thought of a philosophy which the communists tried to present as a continuous wrestling match between idealism and materialism. But above all I could never forget Socrates, at whom my classmates and I so often laughed because he stopped in the market-place of Athens to discuss questions of ethics with the fishwives. We had also found comic the ceremoniousness with which he arranged his death. And yet in the people's democracy I considered him my patron saint, principally because it was from him that I learned that man can identify himself with the laws of his country and its official moral outlook only if the *daimon* inhabiting him approves.

I supposed that the intellectuals who had never learned Latin and Greek, and Suzy too, would have to realize this one day. They, like Suzy, were indifferent to Christianity, so that neither classical education nor Christian ethics protected them from communism in which they sought an *ersatz* religion. On the surface, they obtained this substitute in an almost perfect form: seminars to take the place of religious education and party meetings to take the place of mass, the rigorous fasts of the five-year plan-loan and the shortage of food to take the place of Lent, demonstration instead of procession, public self-criticism instead of confession, and instead of Abraham's bosom the promise of an earthly paradise, the constantly retreating mirage of which was painted on the horizon before the ragged armies marching across the desert.

These, however, were but appearances. Essentially the church is an eternal antithesis of the party, and in the end everyone who unconsciously seeks the church in the party must be disappointed. Not because philosophy cannot prove the eventual incorrectness of the church's dogma while it can prove the incorrectness of the communist dogma, but because the ethics of the Christian religion are to a great extent identical with the categorical imperative, and thus the observance of the dogma fills the conscience of the faithful with serenity even if they rebel against the church, while the Socratic *daimon* must inevitably say 'No' to the changing slogans of the communist state religion; the more loyally the faithful serve the ideals of communism, in fact, the more inevitably do those ideals afflict them with inner conflict and nervous disorder.

Such thoughts preceded my poem to Suzanne. As in most of the others, I was unable and did not even try to incorporate the thoughts that had initiated the poem; they furnished, at the most, the basic mood. I spoke, in the first place, about our love and the images I associated with it, not the Rajk affair or other political events, but the lakes, the reed-banks, the hidden dales of Hungary, the freshly excavated Bronze-Age grave in which the two pink skeletons lay with their knees drawn up like embryos in their mother's womb; I described our cross-country wanderings, the heavy wines we drank in little inns, hidden among the reeds, the way we sat in the car, at night, at level crossings in the forest, until the lamps of the locomotive appeared like the sharp, deep-set eyes of an old man; and the Latin, even Provençal hills of Transdanubia where we sat in vineyards looking down on the poplars in the valley, like the pillars of a blown-up bridge.

I pictured these things not for the sake of accuracy, but mainly to bind Suzanne to our love with the help of the entire Hungarian landscape. I spoke of the possibility that I might, one day, return and we might meet again, perhaps in a few years, perhaps in two or three decades, when my eyes would be as deep in their sockets as the locomotive lamps at night in a forest, at the level crossings. I spoke also of the possibility of my death and of Suzanne marrying someone else. Whatever happened, I swore humble, merciless and eternal fidelity; that I would conceal myself in frosted glass and mirrors, wrap myself in mist and in dreams, playing hide-and-seek with them; that I should accompany her and her husband when they went boating, the water reflecting me and my dislocated neck; that I should be there in the bloom of every grape, sit between them at the table and in bed, drinking to them with the heavy wine of my memories becoming ever clearer, ever sweeter; that I should hound their ageing, shapeless bodies with mine that would remain light, ethereal and young. Then, with a final chord that might have been a late nuptial song or a message from beyond the grave, I finished. Immediately I felt a rare happiness; happiness about the richness of the images, the sound, the sharpness of the vision; the rare happiness I felt when I had written a poem which would probably survive me. But this thought made me hesitate, since for the time being I was the only existing manuscript of my poem and we were bound together; it could not survive me without my survival.

One morning I was led up before the American expert whom I hadn't seen for six weeks. I thought he would continue the interrogation, but instead he asked me what I thought about Roosevelt and whether the elevators ever broke down in the New York skyscrapers? The next morning he inquired about Arab women and when he learned that they shaved their pubic hair he became so interested that I had to keep to the subject until midnight. Our conversations went on during the entire week, and I began to hope that my affairs had taken a favourable turn – because of the confusion, lack of co-ordination and organization characteristic of the AVO one could never be certain of anything. The interrogator never again mentioned the Trotskyist trial of which I was to be one of the principal defendants; and at the same time he let fall that I had 'wasted his time', and that I 'seemed to have friends everywhere'. It appeared possible that perhaps no charges would be preferred and that they might even let me go free.

The next Monday I was taken into a large cellar room. An ugly little lieutenant with a walrus moustache was sitting behind the desk in his shirt-sleeves and knickerbockers, engaged in pulling on with great difficulty a pair of beautiful, shining riding boots. I was painfully impressed by the circumstance that from a captain I had been demoted to a lieutenant, and also by the fact that we were in a cellar. It seemed obvious to me that this was the place where people were tortured.

'What are you staring at?' he shouted at me when he had finished pulling on the boots. 'What is going on in that rotten mind of yours? That I am a guttersnipe? What? Well, take it from me that I am as much of a freedom-fighter as yourself!'

He got up from behind the desk, approached me and began waving his fist in front of my face without, however, coming very close. Instead, he stalked me from the side, from behind, like a hyena.

'Or is it your poems you are so proud of? I could write poems like yours any time I wanted to. But I don't!'

That was how it went on the whole morning. In the afternoon he brought a heavy file out from his safe. He said it contained the evidence they had collected against me. The sight of it – at least a thousand pages – sent a cold shiver down my spine, but when he lifted it a few times to demonstrate its weight I reassured myself that the file was probably a sheaf of blank paper.

The first few hundred pages were denunciations. Puss-in-Boots read them with emphasis but did not betray the names of the denouncers. I found it, however, easy to guess who they were. Most of them came from Almassi, the librarian of *Népszava*. Usually he had been forced to invent, to lie or at least to distort. He was probably paid for each report separately. Here and there, however, when he had succeeded in solving some of my insinuations which I had thought him too stupid to understand he had written the truth. Thus, for instance, I had once used the word *televisor* in front of him. It never occurred to me that the AVO had made him read Orwell's book and that, consequently, he would discover that I too had read it.

On the second day we were still busy with Almassi's reports. Then came other denunciations. A short memorandum was sent in by György Maté, party secretary of the Writers Association. Puss-in-Boots gave it to me to read. 'In the course of the screening,' it said,

'I established that Faludy is an imperialist agent. Request urgent measures. Maté.'

'This is what I would call *prima facie* evidence,' I said, and yawned.

'You won't be bored for long, my friend,' Puss-in-Boots exclaimed in an offended tone and brought out a fat copy-book. It was Györgyi Vandori's diary, some of which had been used in evidence in the Rajk trial. And, indeed, I was no longer bored but only angry with myself for ever having talked at all with this hysterical blue-stocking; for having comforted her and seen her home when nobody dared to approach her; for having begged her again and again to burn her diary in which, according to her own admission, she had put down all the political secrets she knew and every private political conversation she had witnessed.

The first entry dealing with me was in May, 1946: 'I saw Faludy at the social-democratic headquarters. He has just returned from America. He is very haughty and looks at everyone down his nose. I talked to him for two minutes. I feel sure he is an agent of the Americans. How charming he is! It may be useful to be friends with him.' There were also remarks like: 'Faludy denies being a Trotskyist. But I feel this is only a front.' Before her arrest she wrote: 'Until now Faludy avoided me but now, suddenly, he has softened. Perhaps he loves me, after all. Or is it only solidarity because he too is a Trotskyist?' Then again: 'Faludy saw me home today, almost to my door. He too hates the régime. We were followed by detectives. Were they watching me or him?' And finally: 'Faludy advised me today to burn my diary. Sooner or later the henchmen of the AVO will drag us all over the hot coals. I find his anxiety ridiculous. Burn you, my dear diary? Never!'

When I remarked that the diary of a silly goose cannot seriously be considered evidence, Puss-in-Boots declared angrily that the diary had played a very important role in the Rajk trial and besides, I should see how right I had been when I called the employees of the State Security Police 'henchmen'. As far as my Trotskyism was concerned, he had decisive evidence in these files and tomorrow he would rub my nose in them.

When I was led before him the next morning there was no file on his desk. Instead the room was filled with the aroma of American cigarettes. The suitcase with which I had set out towards Czechoslovakia and from which he had taken the American cigarettes lay open next to the desk. Before him on the desk lay my little red notebook, which he began to read. Suddenly I felt a wave of panic engulf me because I remembered that on the fifth or the seventh page I had recklessly written, three years ago, and then forgotten:

Since I live among these I have come to love capitalism
Fictis causis innocentes, etc.
Savonarola – Calvin – Robespierre – Stalin
The grandchildren will all be idiots
Let these beasts explode with fury that there is still a Roman living among them
Rakosi's head: an ostrich-egg (rotten!!!) sticking out of the Hungarian swamp
The new Trinity: Father Marx (the Creator, antediluvian beard); Lenin, his Only-Begotten Son; Stalin, the Holy Ghost (descended upon the world on tongues of flame).

I could guess what a beating I should get if he ever read it. Fortunately he was still on the first page, where I had noted down the rhyme schemes of the last six lines of the sonnet.

'You'll give us the solution of this code, never fear, or we'll beat the shit out of you,' he screamed. He jumped up from his chair and pushed the notebook under my nose. 'What does this mean?'

'These are the forty different rhyme schemes of the tercettes of the sonnet,' I replied.

'Are you trying to fool me?' shouted Puss-in-Boots, kicking me in the side.

'This fifteen-line column,' I went on imperturbably, 'contains the three-rhyme variation. Here you see: *aba-bcc*: this is what Shakespeare preferred. I myself prefer the more unusual *aba-cbc*, the resigned *abc-bac*, or the melancholy *abc-bca*. These here are the two-rhyme variations: for three *a* and three *b*; for four *a* and two *b*; and for two *a* and four *b*. For instance, the heavy and baroque *aaa-bbb*, the playful, rococo *aab-abb*, the elegant *aab-aab* and the attractive *aba-bba*. I never have written a sonnet with these two rhymes.'

'And now you never will,' Puss-in-Boots said with a sigh. 'And what kind of a rhyme is this anyway? Can you give me an example for *abb-aab*? Or for *aba-bbb*?'

Until noon I explained with unflagging zeal the rhymes of the sonnet, so that he would read no further in the notebook. I was surprised by his interest in poetry but somehow it filled me with foreboding. During the two hours he took off for lunch, when I had to wait for him with my nose pressed to the wall, I was again and again bathed in perspiration. However, he returned in an excellent mood, put my notebook back in the file and declared that my lecture on sonnet rhymes was very interesting. To show his gratitude, he fished out one of my American cigarettes, broke it in two and threw me half.

Then he rose, opened his safe and brought out a folder almost as fat as the one containing the denunciations against me. I felt the blood mount to my head. The tips of my fingers tingled and went numb. Now comes the final catastrophe, the main accusation which has not yet been mentioned.

Puss-in-Boots took the folder and brought it over to my side. He was bending forward, as usual, his eyes on his gleaming boots, but instead of weighing the folder on his palm to show me how heavy it was, he held it close to his knees, limply, not triumphantly.

'I'd like to ask you a favour, Comrade Faludy. I have a nephew who writes poems. Would you read them? I am very interested in your criticism.'

'Your job is to murder me, not to make me read poems,' I replied insolently. 'But all right. Give them here.'

I was taken to a new, clean cell. The guard brought me dinner, then maize, grapes, and cakes and black coffee to end with. I received the same fare following day, Sunday. It would have been surprising had Puss-in-Boots been a good poet but I was spared that surprise. There were some seventy poems in the folder, mostly lyrical, but one of them a three-thousand-line epic. They emanated the characteristic smell of dilettantism, so that after reading a few lines I gave up and put the folder under my head as a pillow.

On Monday morning, contrary to AVO custom, Puss-in-Boots motioned me politely to take a seat when I entered. 'Well, how did you like the poems?' he asked excitedly.

For a few minutes, I watched him writhing. After all, I was master of the situation, though only for a short time. 'Does your nephew have some trade or profession? I mean, apart from writing poems?'

'Of course he has,' Puss-in-Boots straightened up proudly.

'That's good news,' I nodded. And then, very clearly and in great detail, I explained to him the aim and meaning of poetry. He listened to it as to a revelation, in the vain hope that he might learn something from it. Then I got down to his poems and took them completely apart, proving to him that he didn't even know Hungarian. I asked him to tell his nephew, as tactfully as possible, that he was writing decadent, rotten, reactionary poems of Western orientation. I begged him solemnly to forgive his nephew, but to try and lead him back to normality with a strong hand. He would never, under any circumstances, become a poet, and a communist society must fight with every means at its disposal against such dilettantism.

I had decided to tell him the truth while still in my cell, because apart from any utilitarian consideration I hated dilettantes even worse than AVO men. Now that I had told him frankly what I thought of his poems I felt almost happy; what must happen, must happen. Puss-in-Boots, however, switched the conversation to another subject, but he was obviously at a loss, not quite knowing what to do. First he read me a few new denunciations and then, with a studied gesture, he ordered me to name my espionage contacts abroad. Did I know Allan Dulles? Rankovich? And what about Zilliacus, the notorious agent of the British Intelligence? When I declared that it was ridiculous to call Zilliacus an agent of the British Intelligence, he boxed my ears until I saw stars. It annoyed me intensely to suffer these blows for the sake of an incorrigibly pro-Soviet British Member of Parliament who could perhaps still be saved – but perhaps not – if it were he who were receiving them. Puss-in-Boots soon stopped hitting me and declared that my not having met Allan Dulles, Rankovich or

Zilliacus would not save me from the gallows. Then, earlier than usual, he sent me back to my cell.

At dinner time three AVO guards came in. All three were handsome, young, bright and looked more intelligent than the rest. One brought a dixie full of stew and macaroni, the other a small table with paper and a pencil on it, the third a glass of wine and a few cigarettes. They surrounded me and looked into my face with curiosity and cheerfulness.

'This is your supper,' one of them explained. 'You can write to your family if you wish. If you want to sleep you can have a pillow. But no sleeping pills. It is now eight twenty-three p.m. At five in the morning you will be taken to the concentration prison, there to be hanged. At five thirty.'

They stood waiting for my reply.

'Well, have you nothing to say?' the youngest asked with an uncertain smile.

They went out but every few minutes one of them looked through the Judas-hole. My first coherent thought was that I still had eight and a half hours left. I should apportion the last thirty minutes separately, on the way. Naturally, I must first try to make up my mind whether they were really going to hang me, whether there would be a reprieve at the last minute or whether the whole thing was a joke. These AVO guards looked like impostors – but then, why shouldn't henchmen look like impostors? There was no point in trying to sleep. I was not going to write a letter, either. I was certain that it would never reach the person to whom I had written it.

Even if I tried to convince myself that I would not be hanged, I still had to face a horrible night. It seemed easier to accept the thought that they would hang me at five thirty. In that case, I could write a beautiful poem during the night; it would make the time pass quickly, and I was not going to wet my trousers in front of the three impostors. This was the simplest, apparently the bravest, but deep down the most cowardly solution. To eat up the stew quickly but save the wine for later, as a reward if the poem turned out well. The poem must be long, at least three times the fifty-line *pensum* I had given myself for every day, so I should have to hurry.

I already knew what I was going to write about the moment the three impostors left my cell. My grandfather's house in northern Hungary emerged before my eyes, and the pine-covered mountain opposite. Whenever I was in trouble I thought of this house: in the train at Juvissy, on the ship when we left Bayonne, at the massacre in Marrakesh, during attacks of malaria without quinine, on the way to New York with fish-poisoning, in the US Army at – there was no time for enumeration. I always knew that I would return to this house; I knew it from the time I was seven and was put to bed in the guest room at Christmas and noticed the light of the stove. This happened after my grandmother had come in, tall and thin, with a dish filled with oranges and candied fruits. She sat down on my bed and fed me the fruit bit by bit, because there too I was the favourite, as I was the favourite at my parents' house, at Vambéry's house and presumably even here at the AVO's house.

But what was it about the light? I could write my poem safely in treble rhymes; when one is about to be hanged one can think of an abundance of treble rhymes. My grandmother took the lamp with her when she left and the light streaming from the open door of the stove (the fragrance of pines! should I write about that?) danced on my eiderdown and painted my fists carmine. It was an unquiet, frightening light, not because it danced but because it occurred to me that I too would return to this house in the shape of an unquiet, frightening light. It was not later that I thought of this, when I should gladly have returned to that house in search of happiness though I had not been really happy there, but at the time, at seven years old, when I first watched the dancing flames of the stove.

Since then everyone who had lived there and whom I had met in that house had died; I was the last to die. Laszlo Fényes lay in a New York cemetery. My grandparents departed, as they should, in old age. My aunt who had rested in the roof-garden among the red carnations, with a volume of Nietzsche in her hand, the pages of which were ruffled by the wind, not by her, had cut her throat; my sister had been shot into the Danube by the Hungarian Nazis, my aunt and my uncle had been gassed. I should wave to my mother when I soared up. She did not belong to my father's family and was still alive eight hundred yards from my cell. I should wave to her from the air.

My grandfather too had always talked about light when he stood before me in the mill, holding his pipe like a fishing rod. He said that he would ride a beam of light after he died and fly in space at a speed of three hundred thousand kilometres per second. He must sit on a pretty long beam for he lived eighty-three years, the film of his life was eighty-three light-years long. My sister rode behind him, crossing rhombus-shaped star mists, rhombus-shaped like the splintering ice of the Danube; directly behind her rode my father, my aunt, my uncle and now came I! What else could happen, after all? Eiderdowns of mist on which the light of giant suns dance; the smell of pine-resin and gin, my fist is covered in carmine enamel and there is a red stripe around my neck where the dancing flames light it up, but who cares! Beautiful Milky Ways come and go, henceforth I shall wear a high collar, one can allow oneself such luxury after being hanged and walking among comets. The remaining problem is where to hold the family reunion. In some lovely place perhaps, to congratulate ourselves and each other on this wonderful century? There is an excellent roof terrace on Aldebaran. Since I met Amar as-Salahiya I have loved stars with Arab names, but grandfather is all for Sirius.

When the three AVO men came to get me I guessed at once that the journey was not to take place. They did not tie me up nor did they break the bones in my arms as is prescribed by Soviet etiquette before hanging, but took me to the washroom, to face the aluminium mirror.

'Now look at yourself! At your neck, idiot!'

At first I did not see what they were laughing about. Only when I raised myself on tiptoe and bent close to the mirror did I notice that all round my throat there was a red line, the imaginary mark of the rope.

Then I was taken to the lieutenant in command of the guards who handed me a document according to which, in consequence of my lawless actions inimical to the state, and in the interest of the security of the people's republic, I was going to be interned for . . . .
. . . . years.

'What are all these dots for?' I asked.

'Twenty-five dots, meaning twenty-five years, if you live that long,' he laughed.

A long line of men was standing in the yard, their noses to the wall. Behind them AVO guards were walking up and down, warning them in a blood-curdling tone not to turn around or look sideways. I glanced at my neighbour. It was the red-headed young man who, four years ago, had asked me at social democratic headquarters whether I had come home from America to be hanged. He had at least two weeks' growth of beard but the red welts of blows peeped through the red bristle like cart-tracks. When he noticed me he gave me a warm smile, then began to snigger. The long-haired young man in the bloody shirt next to him seemed familiar, I must have seen him in the social democratic party, or in Parliament, or somewhere. He too was laughing, his entire body was shaking with it. Suddenly I too began to laugh, and even after the guard had kicked me in the bottom, I continued laughing, wheezing, panting, bent double with laughter, shrieking with it, until they pushed us all up the steps of the Black Maria. Even there, bloody, ragged, half-starved as we were, we laughed so hard that tears were streaming down our cheeks, and we fell, helter-skelter, spent and exhausted on the floor of the lorry.

A few hours later we were herded into a hermetically isolated cell at the Kistarcsa concentration camp, the so-called 'screening department'. This was where prisoners were usually kept for a couple of weeks before being transferred to the camp proper. We therefore spent our days in happy expectation in a small, narrow room with double-decker bunks along the walls and almost no space between them. There were fifteen of us in the room and, having nothing else to do, we talked all day long in the permanent semi-darkness behind whitewashed window-panes. The two fat ones among us floated between the lower and upper bunks with the lazy ease of big fat carp, careful not to get caught in the writhing arms of an octopus: the flailing, restless limbs of thirteen people. Only the top pane of the window was not covered with whitewash. Through it I could look out at a watch-tower built back in 1944 when several thousand Jewish intellectuals had been tortured here by the Hungarian Nazis, and at the broad crown of a beech tree which was slowly but systematically shedding its copper-coloured leaves.

Fourteen of us were newcomers, with bloody shirts and red welts on our faces. The only old inhabitant of the cell, and the owner of the only straw mattress, was a tall man who greeted us with a friendly smile, although he immediately remarked that he had been there for a year and had seen hundreds of prisoners come and go. His yellowish-brown, wrinkled face resembled a gigantic raisin; he wore an eyeglass in his right eye and when he talked – sometimes even when he didn't – he made circular movements with the narrow lips of his toothless mouth like a ruminating cow. Though he seemed pretty old to me, his back was as straight as if he had swallowed a rod, and he moved with an elegant, affectedly casual ease. Each evening he put his trousers under his mattress to keep the crease as sharp and straight as though they had just been brought home from the tailor's. In the mornings he greeted each of us individually with a deep bow and a friendly good morning, tied his pink tie with the white polka-dots in front of the window, watching his reflection, pulled a horrible-looking, smelly rag from his pocket, rubbed his shoes until they shone, and then sat down to clean his nails.

His name, he said, was Kenedy. He talked with elegant gestures and in well-rounded, somewhat involved sentences. Having spent a great deal of time in prison, he gave us advice with paternal benevolence. One of his noteworthy suggestions was that, as soon as we were transferred to the camp proper, we should find ourselves boyfriends. 'If you don't heed my advice,' he explained seriously, 'I am afraid your sweet and gentle souls will suffer atrociously from vain yearnings for mesdames your wives.' The course to follow – he said – was to select our lovers from the lower classes, if possible, partly because then we would have someone to clean our clothes and make our beds – no occupations for a gentleman – and partly because, being used for manual labour and consequently properly fed by the AVO, they would be in a condition to oblige us whenever we felt like it.

Yet Kenedy was not a pushing sort of fellow; he preferred silence to talk. When one of us told the story of his arrest he would listen devotedly, chewing his long, empty cigarette-holder and swinging his crossed ankles as gentlemen used to do in the drawing-room when, pulling on their pipes, they listened to their friends telling amusing anecdotes. To him these stories took the place of an evening at the theatre, the cinema, the café; they were his social life, his books, and thus, though they were usually far too long, he listened with rapt attention, great enjoyment and endless patience. His joy was especially great when he came upon someone who had been arrested for espionage. With sharp little comments he derided the AVO methods of investigation, making fun of the investigators' inexperience in matters of espionage – though on other subjects he refrained from criticism, from prudence – and besides, interrupting the speaker was a breach of etiquette.

Peter Arok – a corpulent man of about forty, general manager of the Hungarian Nitrogen Works whom I knew by sight from social democratic party headquarters – summed up the story of his arrest in a single sentence.

'They arrested me,' he said, 'because I have sold the blueprints of the factory's machine installations to the British Intelligence.'

With a sudden, ruminating movement of his lips Kenedy dropped his eyeglass – always a sign of surprise with him – which fell straight into the right breast pocket of his white-dotted pink shirt, a pocket created for this very purpose. Until lunch, when he ceremoniously donned his jacket, he always sat in his shirt-sleeves.

'Parbleu!' he exclaimed. 'Do you mean to say, my young friend, that you, general manager of the works, were not aware of the facts that all the machines had been supplied and fitted in 1946 by a Manchester factory? So that if – let us suppose it for a moment – if the British Intelligence had really been interested in the blueprints they could, at any time, have obtained them from Manchester?'

'Don't be silly, of course I knew it,' Arok replied, blushing as if he were ashamed of the idiotic charge on which he had been arrested.

For a while Kenedy swung his ankles in silence, then he returned his eyeglass to his eye and declared that though he had worked for the British Intelligence for twenty-five years, the state had never been able to prove it. And now he was going to be released.

'And I owe it all to you, my dear young friends!' he cried, throwing us kisses like a ballerina. 'The real spy makes hay when these amateurs are locking up people like you!'

Seeing that we gave little credit to his words he delivered an exhaustive lecture on the art of espionage. As we were all utterly unfamiliar with the subject we suspected him of making fools of us and told him so. To prove himself, Kenedy then asked us to give him a description of our AVO investigators, so that he could tell us who they were. One of my cellmates described his investigator, whose name he had learned by chance, and immediately Kenedy came up with the right name, and the man's rank and age. On another occasion he told us the manpower of the Soviet occupation army in Hungary, where the units were stationed throughout the country and what arms they carried. He also told us at length about a mysterious punitive camp established by the AVO somewhere in the Matra mountains, near Recsk. According to him the prisoners in this camp worked sixteen hours a day, including Sunday, were never allowed to sit down, not even when eating, and were tortured in various ways until they died. When, the summer before, an inmate by the name of Dobo had escaped from the camp his entire family was arrested and brought to Kistarcsa in retribution.

Kenedy's stories served only to increase our suspicion. He had told us himself that he had been locked in this room, known as 'subdivision for spies and imperialist agents' for a year and the events he had just described had taken place only a few months before. When we expressed our doubts he shrugged his shoulders and declared that he didn't give a damn whether we considered him a fool or a liar, we would in time find out for ourselves that he was right.

One evening, when I joined him for a little private conversation, he confessed to me that he had never been happier than he was in this cell. Formerly, when he took a train to establish the condition of the concrete road running parallel with the railway, estimating from it the size and number of the Soviet tanks using it, and then dined on rabbit stew in some provincial town, he would look at the bottle of wine before him, the pretty woman sitting opposite who would share his bed for the night, and he would see not the bottle and not the woman but the loop of a rope dancing above them in the blue smoke of his cigarette. Here, at last, he felt secure. And in addition, he had the company of most distinguished people. Pity that there were so many Jews among them.

Sometimes he invited me to sit on his straw mattress and told me news of the Korean war, or of the latest wave of terror to engulf the country. On other occasions he told me about the secret political trials then going on. He could tell me all I wanted to know about prison conditions in Hungary and how justice was being meted out: for example, that Vladimir Farkas – son of Mihaly Farkas, Minister of Defence and one of the heads of the AVO – amused himself by urinating into the mouths of prisoners after first knocking out their teeth. He told me that in the death-row of the Budapest Central Prison the prisoners' daily fare consisted of half a pint of black coffee and a piece of bread, so that many died of starvation before they could be executed. As the bread was distributed in the evening, their torment was increased by the problem when to eat it. If they ate it in the evening they would have to suffer unbearable pangs of hunger all through the following day. If they left it for the next morning they might never be able to eat it because the AVO henchmen came for their victims in the middle of the night. He told me that at the prison of Vacz there were three times as many prisoners as there was room for, so that from time to time a few dozen prisoners sentenced to fifteen or twenty years were ordered to come, with their effects, to the prison office as if they were to be transferred to another institution. When someone was hanged, the prison doctor, too lazy to unbutton the victim's shirt, would tear it open over the left breast so that he could place his stethoscope over the heart. The shirts were then laundered and issued to other prisoners when they received a change of underwear. Strangely enough, the number of torn shirts always coincided with the number of 'transferred prisoners'.

Kenedy's stories made me shudder although I hoped that he was lying or acting as an *agent provocateur.* Yet there were always details – the problem of the bread, the torn shirts – that in my opinion neither Kenedy nor anyone else could have invented. Once he noticed my horror and immediately declared that he would now lead me from these sombre landscapes and show me more cheerful prospects. And so he did. He talked in great detail and with obvious pleasure about the amorous life of the prison governor, and on another occasion conducted me on a symbolic tour around the camp and acquainted me with our surroundings. In our corridor – he explained – there were nine cells; nine like the circles of Dante's Hell. The first, called the cell of *lèse majesté*, housed those who – however improbable this might sound – had indeed committed something: at least a small offence against the unwritten laws of society, good manners and good taste. For instance those who had spat on Rakosi's portrait, had sung chauvinistic songs when drunk, were or had been unable to prevent their dog from lifting his leg at the corner of a Soviet Memorial.

The next cell was that of the economic or bathtub absconders. Bathtub absconders were people arrested by the AVO in their bathtub on a Sunday morning, on suspicion of wanting to abscond. Economic absconders were those arrested for economic reasons; for the sake, that is, of their prosperous shops or desirable flats. The third cell was called the cell of the saboteurs, such as the engineer who had objected when the great planners decided to pipe the natural gas from Hungarian oilfields to Budapest and was therefore accused of sabotaging the capital's heating system; and the other engineer who had not objected when the great planners decided to pipe the natural gas from Hungarian oilfields to Budapest and was therefore accused of permitting the oilfields to run dry for lack of pressure.

The fourth cell was known as the salon of the two hundred prime ministers. Here lived the pub or café habitués, usually old-age pensioners, who met more often than the authorities considered necessary and were therefore accused of conspiring against the government. Some had been arrested because they amused themselves by setting up new governments on paper and distributing the ministries among each other. There were fortune-tellers who read a change of régime in their client's palm or in the cards, and spiritualists who called up notoriously reactionary spirits like Franz-Joseph, Bismarck or Napoleon III. At one time the cell housed two retired professors of Greek who met every morning in a public park and, feeling perfectly safe, abused the system in Plato's language. Unfortunately neither noticed that one morning they were overheard by Imre Waldapfel, Professor of classical philology at the Budapest University, who immediately denounced them. Later, they were transferred to the camp proper, where they died of starvation.

The fifth cell was the so-called isolator. Here were those who knew something that nobody else must learn. As they were not even allowed to go to the WC, Kenedy knew nothing about them. The next three cells, including ours, were for spies and imperialist agents, one for light-weights, one for middle-weights, one for heavy-weights. The light-weights were the prisoners who learned from the AVO that they had had 'connections with the OSS' but hadn't the faintest notion what OSS meant; middle-weights were men with relatives in the USA who had emigrated twenty or forty years ago – men, that is, with 'foreign espionage connections'; we were heavy-weights, because we had spent many a holiday abroad as children, some of us had attended foreign universities or served in a Western army or, which was even worse, had corresponded with our friends abroad.

The last cell in the row was the Greek cell. When he had been brought here over a year ago – said Kenedy – the inmates of that cell had talked and laughed all day and in the evenings sang the *Internationale* and communist songs in a language he did not understand. One day Lieutenant Toth, the local head of the Internment Department, asked him whether he knew English, which he naturally denied, and then, whether he spoke Italian. This he dared not deny because his *curriculum vitae* contained the fact that at the end of the First World War, he had been taken prisoner of war in Italy. The lieutenant then led him into the next cell, where he was received by a dozen dark-haired, oily, fattish and gay young men. Two immediately began to question him in broken Italian as to when their training would at last begin and why the lieutenant was so angry with them?

Kenedy soon found out that all twelve of them were Greeks living in London, who had come to the Continent to fight in General Markos's communist guerrilla armies against the Greek government. The Bulgarian Legation in London gave them Bulgarian visas and they were told that they would be given guerrilla training in Hungary. At the railway station in Prague there was a solemn reception in their honour, with flowers, music, a buffet and a copy of Stalin's short biography for each. At the Hungarian border they were loaded on lorries and brought straight here, where 'the military discipline was rather severe, though they had no cause to complain'.

Lieutenant Toth then instructed Kenedy to tell them that they were all imperialist agents whom the British secret service had sent to Greece. Hearing the words 'imperialist agent', the Greeks shook their fists, made slicing movements under their chins to show that they would cut the necks of the Greek monarcho-fascists, then bade Kenedy ask the lieutenant to give them guns and let them fight. Kenedy did his best to explain to them where they were, but they wouldn't believe him. For days afterwards he listened to their laughter in the next cell, then gradually they fell silent. One night one of them hanged himself on the window, but the towel broke. The next day the AVO men beat the whole lot to a bloody pulp and chained their wrists and ankles together. After that the Greeks were silent and stopped singing the *Internationale.*

Five of the fifteen men in our cell formed a special group. Although they usually kept their voices down, sometimes loud arguments broke out between them so that in a few days I had learned a great deal about their lives and their arrests. Two of them – two tall, athletic men – represented two opposed proletarian types. Tahy was a young, attractive worker, whom a sculptor of the Rodin school would gladly have modelled with a hammer in his hand. The other, Breuer, with his huge eyes, giant nose and strong jaw, was the kind of cringing but impudent ragamuffin who had enough heart to be careful, when stealing a pram, not to hurt the baby when tipping it out. Although he was at least forty years old, his quick movements, friendly smile and smart replies lent him a youthful and boyish charm.

The spiritual leader of this group was called Lencsés. The thick lenses of his spectacles robbed his eyes of all expression, while his round, frustrated, wilted, slightly embryonic face reflected both greedy curiosity and desperate boredom. Like many dogmatic communists he had a slightly crooked, transparent, waxy nose with dry, pink nostrils. The other intellectual of the group, Reinitz, was a pasty-faced, naïve, benevolent, officious and silly technician, who had obviously had his face deformed at birth by the gynaecologist's forceps. His nose deviated towards the corner of his mouth and lay flat against his cheek, so that even from the front he looked as if he were in profile, while the three-cornered tip of his ear pointed backwards, like that of a running hare. The fifth member of the group, Fritzi Meltzer, was a good-looking, fair young man – handsome in a vulgar way, without classic charm or style – who behaved very quietly and modestly. Except that in the mornings he would stand on his bunk completely naked, as if it gave him pleasure to show his body. He stood with his back to the whitewashed window, screwed his head round and gazed, enthralled, at the hazy reflection of his curved, pink buttocks, then turned round and inspected his scrotal sack, smooth and mighty like that of a bull. Then, slowly and reluctantly, with melancholy glances at his body, as if he were wrapping up his treasures to take to the pawnshop, he pulled on his tiny silk drawers.

From their conversation I soon learned that during the war Tahy, Breuer, Lencsés and Reinitz had belonged to the same communist group. This faction, so often mentioned and condemned in brochures dealing with the history of the Hungarian communist party, was called the Demény faction and had fought with courage for communist principles. When, during the war, the Hungarian communist party was dissolved on orders from Moscow, Demény, the leader of the group, had opposed the liquidation of the party while Lencsés had unconditionally approved the Moscow decision. The other three members of the faction shared Lencsés's views and broke away.

Soon afterwards Demény was arrested by the Horthy police, and was sentenced to fifteen years' hard labour for his communist activities. When the Red Army marched into Hungary, Demény was released – but only for a few days. The communists had not forgotten that he had once disobeyed Moscow's orders and sentenced him to another fifteen years in jail on the charge that he had been a spy of the Horthy police.

The four former Dményists had remained loyal members of the communist party and their circle had soon been joined by the white-collar worker Meltzer. But as time passed they had begun to talk more and more often about the good old days when a man had been in permanent danger of being hanged for his communist convictions. They began to loathe the present, when the reward of loyalty was a high office, a private villa and a car. They began to speak with affection of their former chief, Demény, and none of them objected – not even Lencsés their spiritual leader – when Tahy married his old flame, Demény's daughter.

Tahy, Breuer, Lencsés and Reinitz, with Tahy's wife and her mother, Mrs Demény, were all arrested simultaneously. AVO investigators read back to them conversations they had held in their homes, from which it was easy to deduce that Meltzer had denounced them. Therefore they were all the more surprised when, arrived at Kistarcsa, they found Meltzer in the cell with them.

On the first evening they held a rather stormy session. Lencsés explained at great length – as he always did – that in the case of ordinary, insignificant members, the party never took petty mistakes very seriously. Consequently, if they had been arrested for such relatively unimportant gossip, the party must have been keeping an eye on them, which it would only do if it considered them prominent members. They had been thrown into prison as an educational measure, in order to rid them once and for all of the remnants of the past – their damnable *bourgeois* mentality – so that later they could serve the great cause of socialism in posts more important than those they had hitherto occupied. They had every reason to be grateful to the party.

The lecture was repeatedly interrupted by Tahy, who declared emphatically that the months spent in the cellars of Andrassy Street must have robbed Lencsés of his senses. He asked his friend whether he regarded the blows he had received as part of the socialist education or only as an introduction to it? Lencsés replied angrily and was enthusiastically seconded by Reinitz. When they had calmed down, Lencsés began talking about the Meltzer affair.

There was no doubt – he said – that they had all offended against the party. They had criticized it, often laughed at its measures and judged them from the low point of view of *bourgeois* objectivism.He must admit – he went on – that he himself was the guiltiest of the lot, but the others had also sinned, especially Tahy, who had married the daughter of one of the party's enemies; a girl, who, quite naturally, could not divorce herself from her father's ideas. If Meltzer had denounced them, he had only been doing his proletarian duty. He must also have confessed his own share in the guilt or else he would not be here with them. Tahy again interrupted to say that Meltzer was a dirty scoundrel and that his arrest only went to show that the AVO locked up its own spies when it no longer needed them. Finally Lencsés put the Meltzer affair to the vote. With two votes against Tahy's one – Breuer abstained – they decided to invite Meltzer to join them and permit him to take part in their discussions as a full member.

The next day Lencsés informed us that until our socialist re-education began he would conduct a Leninist seminar, nightly, after the lights were put out. That evening, after having swallowed the dinner – a few spoons of millet-mush – the inhabitants of the cell prepared themselves with despair for the seminar. Peter Arok, director of the Hungarian Nitrogen Works, plugged his ears with two small rags – remnants of the lining of his pocket. Professor György Sarospataky, one of Hungary's foremost scientists – a powerfully built man with blazing brown eyes, well-padded cheeks, a broad, bushy, soot-black moustache with friendly, twirled ends, and an oval chin with a small, deep depression in the lower centre – turned towards the wall with the atavistic resignation peculiar to a people so often imprisoned as patriots, tied to the whipping post as peasants, burned at the stake as Protestants and enslaved as rebels. Kenedy, the master spy, retreated to the most distant corner of his straw mattress to watch subsequent events like a ferret from his lair.

'We shall speak about the problems of Leninism,' announced Lencsés in a loud voice. He sat on the edge of his bunk directly below me. Looking down between the boards I could see him lording it over his subjects, who squatted side by side at his feet. But Lencsés's first words were interrupted by my neighbour, the red-headed young man, Janos Garamvölgyi who, four years ago, had asked me on the stairway of the social democratic headquarters whether I had come home from America to be hanged by the communists.

'The only advantage of imprisonment,' he called down to Lencsés, 'is that we no longer have to listen to communist crap. Leave us in peace with your Leninist rubbish, you idiot!'

For a moment Lencsés was struck dumb.

'We shall speak about the problems of Leninism,' he repeated, but in a considerably more subdued voice.

'The first problem you should discuss is when to slaughter starving workers, as they did at Kronstadt,' suggested Garamvölgyi.

Lencsés did not reply, but he began talking in whispers so that we could not hear a word of what he said. A few minutes later the door was flung open and someone put on the light. Lieutenant Toth, the local head of the AVO's Internment Department, stood in the door. He was a tall, thin, long-legged man whom we had met when he had come to inspect our cell. According to Kenedy he had been one of the pillars of the arrow-cross movement five years ago at Esztergom. He had joined the communist party the day the Red Army marched into Hungary. A short, squat sergeant was standing behind him.

'What is going on here?' the lieutenant turned to Lencsés.

'I am conducting a seminar . . .'

'Get off that bunk and stand to attention when you speak to the lieutenant,' the sergeant screamed at him, 'and take off those glasses!'

'. . . on the problems of Leninism, sir.'

'Haven't you had enough of politics, you dirty traitor to the working class?'

'But, lieutenant, I only . . .'

'I have always known Lencsés as a man of leftist convictions,' murmured Reinitz, coming shyly to Lencsés's defence.

'Shut your trap!' the sergeant yelled at him.

'All right,' the lieutenant said quietly, 'come out, you two.'

For several minutes we listened to the dull thuds of heavy blows outside in the corridor, then Reinitz came flying in through the door. He was soon followed by Lencsés with blood streaming from his mouth, his nose, his ears. Then the light went out.

With admirable self-discipline Lencsés refrained from moaning.

'It seems,' he said uncertainly, after reaching his bunk, 'that our state security organs find it somewhat premature that we should discuss Marxism–Leninism in such mixed company. They also regard it as a provocation that I, who have sinned against party discipline, should conduct a seminar. Are you all here? The fact is that I ran against the wall in the corridor and cannot see very clearly. Where is Meltzer?'

Garamvölgyi, who was lying next to me, cleared his throat resoundingly. Indeed, Meltzer was nowhere near Lencsés's bunk but he was not in his own either. When Lencsés, who grasped the situation before I did, said 'Goodnight, comrades, goodnight, Mr Meltzer' – Meltzer began to giggle. His giggles came from Kenedy's bed, from the cell's only straw mattress, from under the cell's only blanket, which they had pulled up so high that not even the crowns of their heads showed.

Although I quickly made the acquaintance of all my cellmates, my closest friends became the three boys whom I had already noticed when standing in the yard at the Secret Police Headquarters and who I had known in the social democratic party. Their pleasure at having me with them was truly moving. On the first night, after the others had gone to sleep, I talked with them until dawn in a mood of excited happiness, and they claimed that if they were allowed to spend their imprisonment in my company their life would be more colourful than if they were at a foreign university.

All three – Garamvölgyi, Gabori and Egri – had been followers of Pal Justus, the ideologist of the social democratic party, who used to send his poems to me for publication and who was sentenced to life imprisonment at the Rajk trial. They had been arrested for being Justus's disciples. A year had passed since the Master's arrest, but they were still under his spiritual spell. Some of their attitudes had changed considerably, but none of them had yet escaped from Justus's magic circle. They agreed that even the most degenerate variant of Marxism was still preferable to any political alternative, and they clung to it even in prison.

Garamvölgyi, with his reddish, fair hair and his round, bespectacled, expressionless face, looked like a young German mathematics teacher facing his pupils for the first time and trying to appear indifferent to hide his embarrassment. But in Garamvölgyi's case embarrassment was only an appearance. Until the parties merged he was employed by the social democratic headquarters: he was regarded as our best and most reliable disorganizer. In the days of the coalition government, when the communists were still trying to win followers by talking about national unity, the social democratic party sent Garamvölgyi to various youth meetings. Wherever he raised his voice, immediate scandal ensued and the communists lost an opportunity to make propaganda speeches. Once he attended a lecture delivered by Jozsef Révai, who was exalting people's democracy as the most advanced and perfect form of socialism. When, after concluding his speech, he asked whether there were any questions, Garamvölgyi rose and declared that he fully agreed with everything Révai had said and had only one question to ask: if all Révai had said was true, why did the Soviet Union still adhere to the obsolete, dictatorial practices of bolshevism? Révai was so surprised by the question (and perhaps so frightened by its implication, that he had offended against the Soviet Union) that he turned pale and gaped like a fish on dry land. After that he gave orders that all young men with red hair and freckles should be kept off the premises when he was speaking.

Gabori looked like a lively, red jack-in-the-box, or perhaps the devil himself when, dressed as a commercial traveller, he entered the railway carriage in Thomas Mann's *Doctor Faustus*. In 1944, he made the acquaintance of a few Gestapo prisons and torture chambers, later of Dachau; since then he had been in various occupations, was artisan, merchant, commercial traveller, employee of the cultural department of the social democratic party and finally one of the heads of the state wine-export enterprise. His investigator had also been a commercial traveller before he entered the services of the AVO and Gabori was quick to notice it. To make matters less painful for both of them Gabori offered his investigator a gentleman's agreement. In exchange for two packets of cigarettes a day he would confess anything, as long as it didn't involve anyone else and did not land him on the scaffold.

Egri's questioning had been more stormy. He had left the social democratic party for the communist party out of opportunism, and had been rewarded by the communists first with a good position, then with arrest and the accusation of having defrauded the Bulgarian people's republic. What had happened was this: in 1948, when a severe shortage of black pepper threatened throughout the world, Egri, then general manager of the paprika-marketing enterprise, bought up the entire Bulgarian paprika output and sold it together with the Hungarian surplus, not as paprika, but mixed with crushed grain, as black pepper substitute, for approximately three times the price of paprika. With this manipulation he earned the Hungarian state several million dollars profit – but at the same time defrauded the Bulgarian people's republic of twelve million dollars.

'Yes,' Egri concluded his story, 'I did defraud Bulgaria.'

It was obvious that he was deeply sorry for what he had done. Gabori tried to comfort him by saying that had he offered that sum to Bulgaria he would have been arrested for defrauding the Hungarian people's republic. Gabori presumably hoped to impress his friend with his arguments, but Egri only sighed.

Thus, though the three boys held different views, in all essential questions they agreed with their arrested, perhaps already murdered, Master. Garamvölgyi's childish day-dreams culminated in a messianistic utopia in which, through some miracle, the Trotskyists of the world would one day seize power and put everything right that the forceful stupidity of the Stalinists and the tepid soft-headedness of the social democrats had spoiled. Gabori still hoped that the Platonic idea of Marxism would one day triumph over its unfortunate practice, while Egri conceded only that Soviet practice was mistakenly interpreted in Hungary.

The trouble lay not in what these boys thought but in their way of thinking. In spite of their really impressive erudition they were unable to think in other than Marxist categories or speak in other than Marxist terms. They seemed not to know any other language, and therefore there was little hope that they would rid themselves of their political ideas. These clung to them like once beautiful and elegant, but now torn and filthy clothes that they would gladly have taken off had they known what to put on instead. They were afraid that if they discarded the familiar set of ideas they would, willy-nilly, become reactionaries, and the thought of living without an ideology, depending on their own mental resources, scared them horribly.

I saw no point in starting political arguments and frightening them off. Besides, to attack their political convictions with political arguments would be to accept the convictions as a basis. I had always denied that human beings, or even their thinking, are determined by political categories. I knew that in a political prison my attitude would not make me very popular, but I resolved to remain true to my views rather than end up by re-creating in my own mind the intellectual prison of the people's democracy.

After I had learned everything I wanted to know about the opinions and the life-stories of my friends I led the conversation into other channels. I told them at length about my wanderings in Africa and America, with the secret intention of undermining the thin political crust on which they stood. At other times I made excursions into history, particularly the history of the fifteenth century when mankind rid itself of a universal ideology which, though it knew the answer to every question (the false answer, of course), wrapped thinking in a shell as thick as the eggshell holding a chick. Taking courage from the success of my lectures I decided one morning, after breakfast slops, to discuss Constantine the Great and the hereticisms of his age; the subject was well suited to the occasion and gave me an opportunity to belabour both Stalin and his opposition within the party. I began by telling them that Constantine the Great had everyone murdered who could have written a truthful biography of him, and that thus we had to make do with the biography written by Eusebius of Caesarea. This biography tells us nothing except eulogies; we learn nothing of the Emperor's deeds and even less of the motives behind those deeds. His brilliance, his truly impressive depravity, his redoubtable political purposiveness and the stubbornness with which he established his monolithic rule by every means, using even Christianity, are all lost in the empty apologies and nauseating flattery of this hypocritical historian.

'We have nothing but psychological factors and guesses to go on,' I said, and suddenly I felt in my throat the cramp of two weeks' starvation, together with the melancholy and humiliating taste of watery mush. 'Let me remind you of Constantine's statue standing before the Basilica San Giovanni in Lateran. Even the statues changed in those days of Byzantine tyranny. Instead of immortalizing the emperors with statues a little more than life size, they made them colossal. The requirement that the statue resemble its model was discarded. Enlargement and idealization prescribed by the rules of bureaucracy were the order of the day, and artistic quality was replaced by the rarity and costliness of the material.

'I don't know where Constantine's statue was made and where it originally stood, but I know that the statue of his son, Constantine II, was set up everywhere in his life-time, among other places in front of the Achilleon in Alexandria. He looked down from there, eight metres tall, with a fleshy and genial face (although in reality he was skinny and neurotic), his narrow lips smiling benignly upon the surging crowds. Spies and informers prowled about the statue and those abusing the tyrant were immediately incarcerated in dungeons dug under the base of the monument. Still, they were unable to prevent pagans, Catholics, gnostics and Jews from besmearing the statue with tar and paint, or throwing camel- and ass-dung at it, not to speak of the Arians who hated him even more than the others because, though an Arian emperor, he demanded to be adored as a deity.

'I must tell you, however, that in those days it was not only the statues whose eyes were devoid of the promising light of intelligence, not only the marble and bronze napes and hips which grew fleshy and ungraceful. Living people were just as bad. The sculptors were not so far from being realistic or, to be more exact, Arian-realistic. Even their contemporaries noticed this. A famous geographer, for instance, wrote that though he did not know why, the proportions of the human body seemed to have become distorted, more freaks were born than ever before and even the expressions of normal children were more stupid than in the past. What is more, food and wine lost their taste, and instead of being a shining, heavenly wheel, the sun looked down from the skies like the sweating bottom of an old harlot. When approaching Sicily by ship, Etna appeared smaller and less shapely than before, and the water of the sea more colourless and smelly than . . .'

Here I had to stop because a warder entered our cell and told us that with the exception of Kenedy we were to collect our things and stand in line in the corridor. We prepared in a fever of happy excitement, because we knew that as soon as we were settled in the camp proper we would be allowed to write to our families, who had not heard from us since our disappearance. And we were leaving our airless cell for the huge blocks of the camp, our small circle for the larger, more interesting and certainly also more secure community of prisoners.

'Pinch me, George, am I awake or am I dreaming?' Egri pushed me in the side twelve hours later, in a mood much more cheerful than our situation warranted. We were squatting side by side on the floor of a locked freight car, dressed in discarded army uniforms, so tired that we would certainly have collapsed had not our spines been supported, like those of heretics bound to stakes, by the stripes of red lead painted on the backs of our trousers and jackets, still smelly but already stone-hard. My cell-mates and the fifty men locked in with us at Gödöllö station were already asleep, except for two who kept vigil, like Egri and me, watching over the dreams of the others. One was a young man whose mystical smile conflicted strangely with the sharp look in his eyes and who reminded me of a youth by Antonello da Messina, though at first glance his face looked more vulgar than beautiful. Next to him sat a narrow-faced man with a nose like a carrot, who watched his companion with devoted, adoring eyes.

In the yard of the Kistarcsa camp I had already noticed with surprise how much thinner, paler, but at the same time calmer and more dignified these old prisoners were than my companions. It was not just the effect of their hair being long, like that of medieval knights, nor of the disfiguring blows which some of us, particularly Lencsés and Reinitz, had received the previous night. My companions and I could have been taken for ordinary criminals, while the others walked up and down the yard like the livid, bloodless ghosts of martyrs. When we climbed into the freight car and the two groups squatted down facing each other, Lencsés whispered in my ear that these people were certainly fascists. Egri wondered whether we were permitted to talk to them. The question, humbly put and clumsily formulated, was entirely neutral. Had I said no he would have taken my answer for an order and obeyed it, and he would have done the same if I had answered yes. But I remained silent, though I knew that Egri would misunderstand my silence.

When the train began rolling the old prisoners whispered among themselves, then threw us a few indifferent, quick glances. They probably thought that we were reds. Later we all lay down, but not a single word had been exchanged between the two groups. Even though we were crowded together in a very narrow space and most of the sleepers threw themselves about in their sleep, there remained a clearly discernible dividing line as though between two hostile camps; across this dividing line only the young man with the face like an Antonello da Messina and I exchanged a few conspiratorial glances.

I knew this locked freight car, crowded with unfortunate people on their way to an unknown destination, from so many books and stories told by friends that I almost felt at home in it. Obviously, I thought, no one can escape his fate; the experience from which I had fled to America had now caught up with me. This experience was probably the preordained lot of everyone born in this century – and born Hungarian – just as the stake had been in the sixteenth century, and the pyramids of skulls raised by the Mongols in the main squares of the towns in the thirteenth century. Our train, eight or ten freight cars with similar loads, its passenger car, the locomotive and the bumpers, crammed with AVO men armed to the teeth, rolled along the only direct railway to the Soviet Union. Egri's cheerful mood was no better justified than his request that I should pinch him.

'To pinch your arm and wake you,' I said cautiously, 'I should have to be Sancho Panza and you the Knight of the Sorrowful Countenance, while as it is, I am by nature Don Quixote and you, if you will forgive me for saying so, with your practical thinking and your closeness to the realities of this world, are my armour-bearer, more faithful than any Sancho Panza. In order to wake you, it is your realism that I should need. As it is I can only repeat what I have said before: we have been projected into the unreal world of a picaresque romance where those whom you still insist on regarding as well-meaning windmills are in reality evil and merciless wizards. And these galley-slaves dragged away to some forced labour camp are not thieves, bandits or highwaymen, as one would expect, but innocent and noble knights. Our situation is so completely lacking in reality that I am often led to doubt my own perception, but you don't seem to have realized it yet.

'Will anyone ever believe our story when we tell it? And if no one will believe us, why should we tell it? However, it is no use worrying about that, because it is highly probable that we shall never live to tell our story. Both Lieutenant Toth and Major Prinz have given us their word that we shall be released after three months of forced labour. And now our train is on its way to the Soviet Union.'

Suddenly the train came to a stop. My eyes met those of the Antonello da Messina youth. The carrot-nosed man sitting next to him opened his lips.

'We are standing in the station of Hatvan, at platform 3.'

'You asked me to pinch you,' I said in the sudden silence. 'But what is the use of waking you? As I see it you intend to follow the example of Mr Goyadkin who regarded everyday reality as a continuous nightmare, and believed only in his nightly dreams. I could invent no more agreeable escape from prison.'

Egri shook his head.

'Then perhaps you have escaped into the opposite extreme. You find it ridiculous that everyone here should play the role of a heroic fighter for freedom. Perhaps they are doing it because it is a noble and rewarding role, or perhaps because it gives them the moral strength to put up with their lot. Yet the fact that someone plays Coriolanus on the stage doesn't make him Coriolanus in life. I know it only too well. I, for instance, did not return from America to fight against the communists but to enjoy Hungarian democracy, and when I saw that a reign of terror was approaching I remained not because I was brave, but because I was curious. I am afraid our companions are in the same boat. Either they observed events with indifference or passive disgust, or they were in favour of it until they were arrested. But the circumstance that the spy-hysteria of the system constantly demands new victims, or that someone's position is coveted by someone else, turns no one into a freedom fighter.

'We would be freedom fighters only if the AVO's accusations against us were true. Since they are untrue, our companions are in a rather delicate situation and are behaving inconsistently. On the one hand they haughtily refute the AVO's accusations – on the other they play themselves up as freedom fighters. They obviously hope that history, which will find a great scarcity of heroes in our age, will be merciful to them and accept their pretence as reality. I understand your motives in refusing to delude yourself and choosing the other way out by confessing to the imaginary crimes of which you are accused. As the only genuine criminal among all these mock-criminals you can thus walk proudly and endure the just sentence meted out to you with great patience and fortitude of mind.'

Egri gave me a scared look with his small mouse-eyes. He had a round, fleshy face, strong and broad – almost a peasant face – but as I looked at his profile under the rim of his cap in the dancing light of the paraffin lamp, he resembled, with the pointed outline of his wax-white nose, a frightened little boy. Obviously he had not fully grasped the meaning of my words and was now making ready to think them over carefully. This reassured me, for I was sure that Egri would do his utmost to face the truth without reservations and, having faced it, would act accordingly. Had he lived in the past century when the dividing line between the white of morality and the black of evil was sharp and unmistakable he would never have committed the stupidities for which, a while ago, I had still been angry with him. In 1947 he had resigned from the social democratic party and joined the communists, disowned his friends and played the role of a good communist with so much conviction that in the end he convinced himself. Unfortunately he was a slow thinker and could not keep pace with events. He acted hastily, unthinkingly, and then adjusted his ideas to his actions. He was like a toy train which, when it is derailed, runs into a table-leg or the wall, but when it is put back on its lines, rolls on without a hitch.

In the meantime the train had begun to move. Carrot-nose listened with bated breath to the clicking of the points, then, his eyes closed, as if he were pronouncing a magic prophecy, he said:

'We are not going to the "Glorious", but up a branch line into the Matra mountains.'

The little station in which we stood bore the name of Recsk. The trees on the hillside opposite appeared as near as if Great Birnam wood had come to meet us. The late autumn morning was surprisingly mild, vapoury, dusty and grimy. When the AVO men removed the chains from the freight cars, the prisoners, about five hundred of us, climbed down. A tall, one-legged man with a crooked nose, and supported by two crutches, dismissed his helpers and stood to attention like a soldier; only his thick, fair hair fluttered in the breeze as he gazed with sharp eyes into the distance like a general before a battle. A queer little man, who also had to be helped down, stood for a while as if uncertain what to do next, then suddenly squatted down on all fours. Even the young were yellow with exhaustion and leaned with rattling teeth against the side of the wagon.

Some two hundred AVO men and soldiers were standing round us, their submachine-guns pointing at us. In the background were lorries and four tanks. In the middle of the ring, where Lieutenant Toth and Major Prinz were standing expectantly as if waiting for a reception committee that never came, there was a swarm of AVO men. It was almost unbelievable that this was not a film company on location, shooting a film about the Gestapo dragging off Hungarian or Polish patriots to a concentration camp during the last war. The whole thing seemed unauthentic, not like the film itself, but like a rehearsal; something was wrong, some factor of realism was missing, either around me or in me. For a second I remembered last night's conversation. Perhaps I was indeed Don Quixote, who saw noble knights in galley-slaves?

At that moment a squat and sweating lieutenant broke his way through the ring of power, accompanied by a few plain-clothes detectives. He passed us, panting with haste, and cried from afar:

'There you are! I didn't expect you till seven . . . And who are these? Didn't I tell you that I wanted healthy, strong young men? What am

I to do with these cripples? Half of them will kick the bucket before we even reach the camp!'

At this point he stumbled over the feet of the little red-nosed man on all fours.

'Stand up, can't you! What's your name, where are you from, old swine?'

Slowly, comfortably, the little man straightened up and turned uncomprehending, limpid eyes on the lieutenant.

'Don't you understand? When were you born?'

'At manuring time.'

'An idiot! An idiot!' the lieutenant repeated with a theatrical gesture of utter desolation.

While the lieutenant conferred in low tones with Prinz and Toth, the Antonello da Messina-faced young man informed me that the camp was about ten miles from the station, up in the mountains. He said we ought to do our best to be at the head of the procession and must not allow ourselves to be hurried because of the old men and the cripples. If, on the way, we should be fired at, we must run straight at the machine-guns to give the others time to scatter. The squat little lieutenant was the camp commander, and was called Schwartz. He had formerly been a shyster lawyer at Salgotarjan. The detective with the beret, standing behind him, had, only five years ago, been an arrow-cross informer.

'How do you know all this?'

'From my neighbour.'

'And where does your neighbour get it?'

'From his neighbour. You'll soon learn that in prison everyone knows everything.'

'And who is the little man on all fours?'

'Uncle Endre Horvath. He was brought in two weeks ago. He was chairman of the social democratic party organization in a Budapest suburb. He is an iron founder . . . Paralysis,' he added. 'I pray for him every night.'

I told him my name, whereupon he embraced me and begged the Holy Virgin to bless me. He introduced himself as Istvan Todi, professional soldier, and expressed his delight at meeting a real socialist at last.

The camp commander ordered us to stand four in a line with our backs to the freight cars, then pointed to a tall, elderly man.

'You there! Step out! Take the lead and order a right turn!'

The man's chin trembled, then he cupped his palms in front of his mouth: 'Boys! At my command all right turn!'

'He doesn't know the first thing about commanding, the old moron,' said the shyster lawyer in a melancholy voice, shaking his head. 'What was your profession?'

'Chief of Staff of the Hungarian First Army.'

I took my place in the first line at Todi's side. Each of us selected an old man as our neighbour so that we could adjust our steps to theirs. Immediately behind us came our bodyguards: Egri, Gabori, Garamvölgyi and, Ajtai, the railwayman from Hatvan who, during the night, had established the direction of the train from the clicking of the points. When we reached the main road the AVO men began shouting at staff colonel Kéri to speed up, but he paid no attention to them. Then one of them pressed the barrel of his submachine-gun into his side and another, with a gaping mouth full of aluminium teeth, slapped his face. The colonel ignored them. He glanced back to see whether we were following and turned contemptuous eyes at the tanks creeping back and forth in the field beside the road.

We were advancing along a copper-red farm road towards wooded, rocky, blue-green, gothic regions. The landscape seemed familiar, as if I had been here before in childhood and later, when in my dreams I revisited the scenes of my youth. There had been no rain for weeks or months, the dust rising from under our heavy steps settled on the roof of my mouth; and I felt as if the skin at the corners of my eyes was drying up and breaking open like the arid, autumnal soil under my feet. Before us a heavy, yellowish-grey cloud rose higher and higher above the mountains as if we were approaching the Great Wall of China. The most interesting feature of this rain cloud was its absolutely straight edge with a small protrusion in the middle. I had the impression that I had already seen a threatening rain-wall like this somewhere, sometime; then too I had advanced towards it along a narrow, zigzagged path until I came so close that I was almost engulfed by its dark, forward-thrown shadow. But where had it been? I couldn't remember the place; all I knew was that even then I had been threatened by some danger and that the protrusion of the cloud had looked like a dragon's open mouth ready to swallow the burning disc of the sun, while now it was like the bust of a woman, raising its head high towards the sun. From the end of the line we heard shouts and curses, the AVO men beating those who could not keep up. We slowed our pace still more.

'Are you an unbeliever?' Todi turned to me.

'No.'

'So,' he looked at me eagerly, 'you believe in God?'

'I don't. But, lacking evidence, I have suspended judgement.'

'Then look at the evidence,' he exclaimed triumphantly, pointing to the cloud.

The cloud represented the Holy Virgin holding the Child in her arms. It was not a likeness, but the actual thing. I was disinclined to believe my senses and submitted the sight to thorough scrutiny. The child was standing in his mother's lap, raising one hand and putting the other lightly on his hip. The next moment, when the sun reached a point exactly behind the Virgin, a halo appeared round her head and shoulders – not a golden halo but an ethereal, silvery one.

'Let us consider this a favourable sign,' said the small and delicate professor whom I was supporting and who, since we had heard the thuds of the gun-butts, had been resting his head in the crook of my arm as though in a nest. 'But let us not expect a miracle. I must confess that I am badly frightened. In this century the need for a miracle has been almost permanent and yet, unfortunately, none has occurred. Besides,' he continued, 'in medieval paintings they usually represented the Holy Virgin standing on the sickle of the moon. For she is akin to Diana, the virgin goddess, who transforms Apollo's golden aureole into a silvery moon-ring before our very eyes.'

'That's right,' Todi replied, 'she is a mild, virginal and merciful goddess, comforter of all *which are persecuted for righteousness' sake*. But I object to your comparing the Holy Virgin with pagan Diana.'

'Your namesake,' the old professor said with a delicate movement of his wrist, 'your namesake and example, Jacopone da Todi, would have given the same reply seven hundred years ago. And yet I must protest against your applying to us the tenth verse of the fifth chapter of the Gospel according to St Matthew . . . I revere justice too much to dare hold myself its depositary . . . At least that is what my great masters, Renan and Berthelot, taught me . . . Furthermore I believe that in your truly enviable faith you place the Holy Virgin on a pedestal perhaps not too high, but certainly too lonely, when you forget her forerunners. The Virgin Queen of Heaven with her only-begotten Son in her arms,' he continued, panting, 'has meant different things in the course of centuries . . .'

'What else?' Todi turned to me.

'For instance the Virgin Queen of Heaven, Isis, with her only-begotten Son Horus.'

'Stop that chatter,' Kunéry, a former army officer, shouted at us from the third row. 'In an hour's time we shall all be dead and you can find nothing better to talk about than Isis . . .'

I turned back and the sight of the young officer filled me with desperate anger. It was not that the subject of our talk had been particularly important to me. It was difficult enough to keep up a conversation while marching with parched throats, and yet I had felt that this talk, our somewhat snobbish, absurd and pathetic attachment to spiritual life, was less an intellectual necessity than a physical urge: an animal reaction of the will to live, without which I would surely perish.

'Each according to his needs, my dear colleague,' I said to the officer. 'There are men, think only of Hindenburg, Voroshilov, Ludendorff, Mackensen, Franchet d'Espérey, Pétain, Budjonni or Horthy – who were supported to the ultimate frontiers of human life by the joint forces of healthy military living and stupidity. Allow us to attempt to survive the life before us in our own way.'

At this moment the camp commander's car stopped immediately in front of us. The shyster lawyer climbed from his seat and came running towards us.

'At Mauthausen,' Gabori said in a loud voice as he passed us, 'the SS beat us in exactly the same way. Later, when the Americans came, we caught a few of them and . . .'

'Fascists! fascists! fascists!' the camp commmander roared, beside himself with rage, wiping his sweating forehead with a large red handkerchief.

However, this time it was not us he meant, but his own men.

'You sit down and rest!' he shouted at us.

We sat down under an acacia tree. The small leaves of the tree hung ochre-yellow and limp as if cut out of satin. The great rain cloud loomed directly above us but the contours of the Holy Virgin were no longer visible.

Soon a few lorries arrived to pick up the old men and the cripples. Then the commander ordered Kéri to get the procession going, but at a comfortable pace.

'This is not a fascist army!' he exclaimed proudly, pointing to his men.

'The dirty Jew,' murmured the AVO man with the pointed nose and the gaping mouth. He was standing next to us on the side of the road with one of his comrades.

As we approached the camp I noticed that the barbed-wire fence, following a cleared strip of woodland, ran up the two sides of a huge mountain. The fact that the camp's territory included a whole, forest-covered mountain made me almost happy. Once within the fence we advanced for a while among apple and wild pear trees; a friendly little cottage stood on the side of the hill with seven plum trees in front of it; a little further on stood a towering, lonely oak, and a few miles up we saw, outside the fence, a hunting lodge on the edge of the forest, like the house of Little Red Riding Hood's grandmother in the fairy tale.

The road was covered with freshly broken, movingly beautiful, pale blue andesite rock. Between the stones, here and there, I saw round or oval, filmy patches of scarlet, as if poppy petals had been trodden into them.

'Blood, blood and blood,' the professor woke me from my idyllic day-dream. Only then did I notice that prisoners were working not far from the road, in dirty old army uniforms like the ones we were wearing. Behind them AVO men with submachine-guns were sitting comfortably in the grass.

I looked closer to see whether Bandi Havas was among them, but saw only Péter Casplar, former chairman of the trade union council, who was sharpening the end of a telegraph pole and who greeted me with a resigned flick of the hand.

We reached a long, narrow clearing and were told to sit down on our overcoats. A deep, rapid streamlet wound its way along the edge of the clearing; its water was transparent and violet-coloured, as though indelible pencils had been dipped in it. On its bed I saw the sharp contours of a motionless vegetation: green and rust-coloured grasses and algae showing no sign of organic life. A metallic smell rose from the water as if the plants had just been galvanized.

Opposite, on the other edge of the clearing, stood a few gigantic beeches, at least two hundred years old. Their trunks reminded me of the feet of prehistoric reptiles. The clearing ran up the steep slope of the mountain. Lemon-yellow acacias were followed by oaks with orange and rust-coloured foliage, like huge catafalques on which the wreaths are already wilting; then came pines and among them stones and rocks, their sharp outlines softened by the fresh and poisonous green of thick moss.

Suddenly I knew whence that *déjà vu* feeling I was experiencing came. I had indeed been here before, in my fledgling days. Three of my classmates and I had decided to climb Hungary's highest mountain, the Kékes. We had set out on a Saturday, in the autumn, had got off the train at Recsk and had come up this very same road, along the stream. I could still remember these huge beeches and it was then that their resemblance to the feet of reptiles had first occurred to me. That was twenty-five years ago.

When the order came to strip ourselves completely, empty our pockets and put the contents on the ground, I obeyed automatically. I smuggled my few cigarettes and Suzy's little embroidered handkerchief that had, by chance, remained with me, back into my trousers pocket. All in all we must have had some three thousand five hundred pockets. I hoped that they would not take the trouble to search them all.

Some of us undressed with extreme slowness as if to gain time. In the deadly silence the old professor turned to me:

'When do we dig the graves?'

'Digging is unnecessary,' I replied, 'there is the bed of the stream.'

However, I soon saw that, at least for the time being, we did not have to fear the worst. There were only four AVO men with us, four submachine-guns. We were five hundred and it would have required a platoon to massacre us.

The yellow, heavy rain cloud had now spread over the entire horizon. The air was so still that I could not even feel the smell of the forest. The gaping AVO man, whom we had in the meantime given the nickname of Dentures because of his numerous aluminium teeth, was walking slowly up and down the line. Behind him walked a red-faced cattle merchant, with a blanket in his hand in which he collected from his fellow-prisoners all pocket knives and handkerchiefs, wrist-watches, lighters, cigarette cases, toothbrushes, soap, pipes, identification papers, internment orders and court sentences. Although he was completely naked and couldn't stop his teeth from chattering, he walked with a swagger. He was obviously very proud of being entrusted with so important a task.

A yellow-faced, emaciated old man was holding on desperately to a catheter. He must, not long ago, have been very fat, for the skin of his belly gathered in huge wrinkles, like a leather bag.

'What is this?' Dentures asked in a low voice, pulling the catheter from the old man's hand.

'A catheter.'

'You mean you can't hear without it? I don't believe you.'

'Sir, I have an enlarged prostate and without this I cannot urinate.'

At this minute we became aware of loud singing from the direction of the forest. A platoon of soldiers emerged from the wood about three hundred yards away. They were singing at the top of their voices as they advanced towards us with fixed bayonets, swinging their arms in the Russian manner:

. . . you're the richest, loveliest of countries,
all your people know that they are free!

Petrified, we all stared at the approaching soldiers. Sweat broke out on my forehead, drenched my brows and dripped into my eyes.

Fountains broke under my arms and ran down to my elbows pressed to my side. *Animula vagula blandula, hospes comesque corporis* – I repeated to myself quickly, and bent my head. Is there no better way to spend the last moments of my life? I asked myself while my eyes ran down the colonnade of thighs and legs. From under the wrinkled leather-bag of the old army doctor's belly an orange-coloured, forked jet of water trickled in so miserable an arch that it hit the inside of his thighs and ran down between his trembling knees.

'You can piss all right, you old scoundrel, if you want to!' Dentures exclaimed cheerfully, and flung the catheter into the stream.

Five minutes later, when the song of the soldiers rose up from down in the valley, Dentures ordered us to dress.

And then the rain came down. Our toothbrushes and family photographs, pocket-books and documents were burning with a fierce yellow flame on the edge of the forest. The red-faced cattle merchant, who was already dressed, stood by the bonfire and whenever the AVO men looked away, stuffed a pipe or a cigarette holder into his pocket.

By the time I had pulled on my trousers it was pouring so thick and fast that the more distant, colourful trees and the mountains had disappeared as though behind a curtain and only the clearing and the angry green of the mossy rocks was still visible. A small, self-contained hell with a sulphur-yellow, sizzling fire in the centre.

PART FIVE

The Forced-Labour Camp

When, ten minutes after the first search, I learned from the old inhabitants of the camp what I had already guessed – that we were not allowed to write to our families, could receive no letters, parcels or visitors and that no books, no newspapers, no paper, pencil or pen were available – I experienced only a moment of acute anxiety which soon softened into a chronic, tame melancholy.

It became evident very quickly that the information I had received from Kenedy at the Kistarcsa screening camp was true in every detail, although according to the two hundred social democrats who had been here since early summer and had built the camp, the treatment had lately improved. The guard huts built in the crowns of the ancient oaks and approached by rope ladder had been taken down, the beatings we received were but a pale imitation of those given before and the blows which had deafened many of the inmates had been discontinued. Unlike the first inmates, we were permitted to sit on the ground while we were eating, but we were not too eager to soak our behinds in the muddy, slippery clay. We consumed the half pint of barley-coffee we received for breakfast, the soup and vegetable we got for lunch and the vegetable served us as dinner standing on the hillside in front of the camp kitchen, where the cauldrons and cooks were protected against the rain by corrugated sheet-iron mounted on four posts. We poured the hot soup down our throats, spooned out the vegetable (automatically counting the little pieces of horse meat put in it three times a week) and then Gabori, Egri, Garamvölgyi and I squatted down side by side. Egri broke a cigarette in three equal parts – Garamvölgyi did not smoke but drew his cigarettes, to give them to us – then asked someone for a light. While we smoked I told them about Africa, California or Paris and they listened eagerly, enthralled, not caring about the rain running in rivulets from their hair into the collars of their jackets.

The rain fell for two months, exactly until Christmas morning. Sometimes it rained without pause for twenty-four hours, sometimes only during the day or during the night, but there were mornings when the sky cleared and overclouded again ten or twenty times. By the afternoon of the second day our overcoats were wet through and they never dried out again. At first we tried to dry them in the barracks by the large brick stove, but there was only one stove and there were a hundred and fifty overcoats. If we spread them over the stove they caught fire, and we were far too exhausted to hold them up. A few days later, when the shoulder pads of our jackets were wet through from the muddy logs we carried and even our shirts were dripping with water, we gave up the struggle against the rain.

It was much more difficult to get used to wet boots. Often we were unable to pull them off in the evening and had to sleep in them, at other times the sticky mud tore them off our feet when we most needed their protection. In the evening all eight hundred of us had to stand up in the shape of a chessboard on the hillside while the commander and his men watched us from the hilltop. AVO men ran up and down between our ranks with their electric torches, but sometimes it took hours before they had counted us to their satisfaction. It was not that they were slow – they wanted to get it over as soon as possible and go down to the village afterwards – but they were not very strong on figures and the more they hurried the more mistakes they made. After the counting they dismissed us and we stumbled down the steep hillside in the dark, falling over logs and tree stumps, crossed the stream bed and climbed up the other side towards our barracks with a pale, blinking light above the door. The AVO men ran after us, beat and kicked those falling behind and herded us into the building, closing the heavy door with the iron cross-bars. If someone lost a boot he could hope to find it only in the morning. They protruded from the slimy clay like old discarded stove-pipes and were filled ankle-deep with water. We never troubled to empty them but simply stepped into them.

Strangely enough not one of us cursed the rain or even worried about it. It enabled us to wash our hands and faces in the morning – no other provision had been made for our hygiene – and when it rained the AVO kept to their huts, leaving us alone, while our *kapos* whom, as in Soviet labour camps, we called *nachalniki*, sat around their camp fires. And the rain had another, much less tangible, advantage. It accentuated the narrow, drab and inescapable limits of our existence, saving us from vain and painful dreams by cutting off the far too beautiful view and hiding the two highest peaks of the country, the Kékes and the Galyatetö with their luxurious hotels, where I was to have spent the summer with Suzy. The cold, swampy forest was a décor befitting our primitive way of life and the atmosphere in which we lived. Even those less well-versed in thinking out things for themselves were aware of this aspect of the weather and were duly grateful to the ever-present rain clouds that shrouded our existence of doubtful value and even more doubtful length into a wet and monotonous mist. Thus, every single day seemed to last two months while in our memory two months lived on as a single, endless day.

One afternoon I was holding one end of a saw while Egri held the other, pulling it back and forth across the trunk of a wild cherry tree as in a slow-motion picture. I was looking at the sawdust that accumulated in a small cone beside the trunk of the tree. When it was approximately an inch high, a raindrop landed on its point so that now it looked like a white volcano with a mountain lake in its crater. I knew that subsequent raindrops would wash away my little volcano, so I turned away to escape witnessing its destruction, keeping my eye on the four or five blood-red leaves clinging desperately to a twig of a blackberry bush.

Gabori stood a little behind us, cutting a wedge in the trunk of the tree we were to fell next. His main job, however, was to watch out for AVO men. At first we noticed them in the still dense wood only when it was too late. The dilemma seemed insoluble. We never got enough food to work at the rate they demanded, but if they caught us squatting or just standing idle, they beat us up and threw us into the dungeon, where the water stood knee-high, and starved us for three or four days. When Egri and I were sawing wood in the clearing, we used to cut into the log and then, turning the saw with its edge up, would save energy by pulling it back and forth in the same groove for three or four hours. But when we were felling trees immediately along the footpath we could not use this method.

Fortunately our senses became simultaneously refined and dulled with miraculous rapidity. My face, hands, feet were soon anaesthetized by the continuous humidity, and my shoulders and back became indifferent to the weight and roughness of the heavy logs. My sense of touch was virtually extinct. As to my sight, I limited it intentionally, as did my companions. I walked and stood with my head bowed, my shoulders sagging and never straightened out except at night, after the light was put out and we sat talking on the edge of our bunks. I was very careful never to gaze around me in a wide circle like a lighthouse. I had discovered that an AVO man or *nachalnik*, even if his back was towards me, would turn around automatically at the flash of a lighthouse. My sense of smell and my hearing, on the other hand, had considerably sharpened, particularly my sense of smell. During the second week at Recsk I found out that though I never saw an AVO man until he was about five metres from me, I could smell him from a hundred metres. My fellow prisoners were of the opinion that the AVO must have arrested the owner of a perfumery in one of the nearby towns and have kept the perfumes for themselves. We usually worked on the northern slope of the mountain, our guards coming up from the valley below, and the north wind often helped us smell them from afar. As time went on, their smell of perfume became stronger and stronger, as if they were drenching themselves in scent every morning. It was the same with the kitchen: we knew from a distance of five hundred metres whether we would get cabbage, peas, lentils, potatoes or beans for dinner, though sometimes smell-hallucination confounded the stench of the boiled beans with the fragrance of boiled ham that was certainly not being cooked. The plundering of a perfumery seemed so convincing an explanation of the AVO smell that at first I too was inclined to believe it. It was weeks before I realized the truth. It was not perfume we smelled on our guards; they never used scent. As we never washed and possessed no soap, it was the smell of scented toilet soap that we believed to be perfume.

This refined sense of smell was of great advantage to us. The creaking of the saws, the snapping of the felled trees and the swishing of the axes prevented us from relying on our hearing, so we were thrown back on our sense of smell like hunted animals. The duty of AVO-smelling was undertaken by one man in each small group. This time Gabori was the 'smeller', Egri and I, squatting on the ground steeped in the vinegar-odour of the injured cherry tree, were useless.

Garamvölgyi did not belong to our work-group. To the undisguised envy of the entire camp he was chosen to herd the guards' pigs. He owed this job to a very attractive young AVO guard – whom among ourselves we called the Fair Murderer – to whom, with a good deal of psychopathological tact, he had told a few anecdotes about the Emperor Heliogabalus. One of these anecdotes was that the young Caesar had ordered the boys with the biggest penises from all provinces to be brought to Rome; when he grew tired of them he had their sex organs cut off and personally fed them to the wolves of the Capitol. The job had two advantages: one, that Janos had absolutely nothing to do; two, that he himself could eat the leavings destined for the pigs. In the mornings, when he drove the pigs out to feed on acorns, he would come our way, to give us each a handful of raw maize, which we then chewed all day as if it were some hard candy.

He stood before us in his clean, long and elegant overcoat, with his tortoise-shell-rimmed glasses, his arms crossed on his chest like the swineherd of a rococo pastoral play. He told us that we would all soon go to hell, but I paid little attention to his warning. In the evenings I was ready to listen patiently to all complaints and did my best to comfort my companions, but during the day, in the soap-bubble of rain, vapour and mist, I drew back deep into my coat and my skin. There was no opportunity for long conversations and for the time being I still concentrated all my attention on economizing my strength and spending as little energy as possible. Besides, at such times I felt the need to be alone with myself – though surrounded by friends – and instead of talking to float like a bubble amidst dreams, phantasmagoria and hazy impressions in an utterly relaxed spiritual attitude.

It soon became clear to me that I owed both my physical and spiritual resistance chiefly to this way of behaving, which was partly yogi-like, partly monkish and partly schizophrenic. I paid no attention to the rain running down my spine, did not mind the lack of washing facilities and gave no thought to thirst, drinking only from the stream when, every second or third day, we worked near it. My physical suffering was thus much less than I should have expected. It seemed to me that I was acclimatized, that I had become used to, or rather, was sufficiently degraded for the camp; that disagreeable impressions stopped at the surface of my body and never penetrated my epidermis; that, though they crossed the threshold of my consciousness, they never reached the pain-threshold. The most interesting experience was furnished by a sudden toothache. Outside in the world, this toothache would have tormented me for two or three days before I made up my mind to have the tooth pulled. Here I tolerated the pain like a cave-dweller in the Stone Age who knew no dentist or pain-killer. I slept well and although I was conscious of the pain during the day I did not really feel it. It was as if someone close to me were complaining of toothache.

My day-dreams embraced the widest variety of subjects, some themes returned every hour, others I carefully avoided; the problems of my captivity and future, for instance, and memories from my past life. Mostly I restricted myself to the intensive but cool observation of the surrounding flora, as if I were attending a lecture in natural history. What preoccupied me most was the change of colour of the leaves. I watched them day after day as they were transformed from the blue-green and blood-red of the late October into golden and lemon-yellow, and finally into tar-black, the leaves of each tree differently and at a different time, until at last they merged on the ground in a dark chestnut-coloured carpet. But even on the ground they behaved differently. Some leaves, like those of the plane-tree, fell down flat like soldiers shot in battle; the leaves of the oak swelled and blistered like the skin on top of some thick, bubbling liquid; the leaves of the wild chestnut tree immediately disintegrated and were held together only by their veins, like a rotting catch by an old fishing net. The leaves of the wild cherry and the beech tree rolled up like the wrapping of a cigar and their example was followed by most of the other leaves. The small cylinders tossed and turned until at last they found the appropriate spot in which to decay in this forest mass-grave. Long-legged, egg-shaped insects played hide-and-seek in their tunnels, and scarlet bugs with two ugly black spots on their backs.

I had several favourites, for instance the water-spiders that scattered when my bearded face appeared in the mirror of the stream, and threw tiny rings with their running feet; or the completely bare hawthorn bushes offering their red berries in gnarled claws turned downwards, and reminding me of the hands of Lady Macbeth. Then there were the huge silver grapes of rain-drops hanging from the twigs until our axe cut into the tree. But it was the few golden-yellow leaves I loved best, which by some trick of fate still clung to the snow-white, straight branch of a birch. I admired this sight four times a day: in the morning when we arrived, when we knocked off for lunch, when we returned from the kitchen-tent and in the evening when we left the place where we worked. Those leaves on the birch branch were like a golden bracelet on the arm of a skeleton – though I found this image too sentimental to mention to my friends. Gabori, who was so concerned about my physical and spiritual welfare that he watched every one of my movements, looked up several times at the birch tree without, obviously, guessing what I saw there.

This dispassionate and amusing observation of nature did not, however, last long; a few weeks later we were all overwhelmed by the terrible sight of the forest's destruction. While we were cutting out only a few trees here and there, we noticed nothing, nor did I take too much to heart the withering and death of small plants. After all, I had always known that the glorious fulfilment of spring and summer was followed by death. But everyone mourned the final destruction of the forest. We knew that Hungary had few forests and that this was the oldest and most beautiful. Even during the first few weeks we had been saddened by its defilement. The moss, which we used as toilet paper, disappeared and the rocks beneath it looked like revolting lepers; our feet wore away the grass, and the clearings turned into lakes of mud; we ate the beautiful red berries of the briar bushes to assuage our hunger for vitamins and tore up the ferns to suck their slender, white roots that were sweet as saccharine. Whenever we worked near juniper bushes I filled my pockets with their berries. As long as the stock lasted I gave my friends three berries each morning to clean their teeth with. Hours later I could still feel their taste, but by then it was like the taste of my first glass of gin drunk in my grandfather's inn with Laszlo Fényes before we set out to visit Simon Pan.

Real despair took hold of us only when the death of the forest became evident after we had cleared a good part of the mountain-side for a quarry. One morning our *nachalnik*, an old Stakhanovite by the name of Kreybig who had been arrested because he wanted to leave his job at a state factory and go to work in another state factory where they offered him more pay, sent us up to the mountain top, just below the peak. We owed this wonderful job – wonderful because nobody could follow us up the eighty-five-degree slope – to Gabori who, the night before, had related to Kreybig how, on the day of the Americans' arrival, he had, with his two hands, hanged his *kapo* in the German concentration camp of Dachau. We had to cut down a few oak trees, but these oaks up at the top were entirely different from those we had felled below in the valley. They were ancient, crooked, hollow, gnarled and distorted; some grew from cracks in the rock, long and slim, with their sides flattened; the cross-section of another resembled a three-pointed star; with a third it was impossible to establish whether it was two trees in a close embrace, or one tree split in two at the base. When we reached the top it was still raining mildly but the valley opening before us showed us the terrible havoc we had wrought in the forest.

Later the rain cloud descended and the sky sparkled bright blue above our heads. Immediately above us an eagle circled. As we felled the trees we had to hold on to rocks and bushes with one hand. When one snapped we crawled rapidly away. Sometimes, after we had sawn through the trunk, the tree remained standing, or leaned back a little against the rock, like an old man against the head-rest of his armchair. At other times it crashed, taking its roots and the huge rocks embedded in the roots along with it. It rolled over and over down the slope into the deep valley with loud, painful sighs ending in a death-rattle, like the sighs of a suicide throwing himself from a mist-enwrapped bridge into a galloping stream. While Garamvölgyi explained why we would soon perish, I thought of this suicidal fall of uprooted oaks.

Then, without any transition, I thought of Suzy. This occurred twenty or thirty times a day without causing particular emotional upheaval or compelling me to delve into my memories. Just as the Portarini girl who walked in the streets of Florence, who often laughed, who perspired in the summer, who ate and drank, who chattered and quietly panted in her sleep when the torches fixed to iron rings had burned down to ashes, had almost no connection with the idealized Beatrice deprived not only of her physical functions but also her physical existence and transformed into a wraith by Dante – so Suzy also had transformed herself into a transcendent and cool ghost since my arrival in Recsk. My vision of her was inexact and ethereal, awakening no greater pain than the image, had I conjured it up, of Diane de Poitiers, Poppea Sabina or Roxane. But it was not of some historical figure she reminded me; it was rather of a girl in a Botticelli painting or in the pink and blue tapestries in the Cluny Museum – not one particular girl, but the abstract image of a girl. She was insubstantial, coldly brilliant, like a vision but an every-day vision that no longer surprised or moved. I thought of her as if she had been dead a long, long time; a dead girl once very dear. Yet, I knew all the time that I was playing a cunning game, that I was looking at the negative of her image, because in reality it was I, not she, who was dead.

Suddenly I became conscious of Garamvölgyi's bored but triumphant nasal voice:

'The camp commander has promised the *nachalniki* that he will set them free as soon as they have liquidated us to the last man. In addition, Gyurka Nadaban told me that the lime pit has been dug two metres deep, twenty metres long and six point one metres wide. This makes two hundred and forty-four cubic metres, half the space for the bodies, the other half for the lime cover. This means one hundred and twenty-two cubic metres for the bodies. Nadaban said one can figure six and a half bodies per cubic metre, one hundred and twenty-two times six and a half makes exactly seven hundred and ninety-three, the number of inmates including Nadaban and the *nachalniki*. Clear? In addition the date of Robespierre's rule of terror was one thousand seven hundred and ninety-thr . . .'

Janos stopped and stood as though petrified, leaning on his shepherd's staff, gazing after the pigs that had disappeared in the forest as if he were still seeing them with his mind's eye. The so-called masterminer, a noncommissioned AVO officer in civilian clothes, had appeared at the bottom of the footpath. He was called Andras Toth and came from Egerszolat, a few kilometres from Recsk. According to fellow-prisoners who came from the same village he had been, six years ago, head of the local arrow-cross party and had, with his henchmen, dug up the Jewish cemetery to look for jewellery – which he didn't find. He was an ugly little man with a tiny head, a pointed, red nose, and when he wasn't about we always called him the Gravedigger.

Although he attacked anyone whose face he disliked with his cudgel, and changed his victims at random, he was the only AVO man nobody feared. We had no need of our sense of smell to foresee his coming: whether he came in the morning or in the afternoon he was always drunk: noisy, singing, cursing, spitting drunk. We recognized him from afar by his clothing. He wore a green, narrow-brimmed hat with a tuft of chamois-hair, a short, pearl-grey overcoat, butter-coloured riding breeches, purple- and blue-checked Scottish socks, white leather gloves and cherry-coloured boots. Yet we had to regard his attire as being in the best of taste because we recognized the various pieces as coming from the wardrobes of our fellow-prisoners, Counts Jozsef Somsich, Péter Zichy and Gyula Ambrozy, while the lining of the short overcoat bore the proud escutcheon of the marquess Alfréd Pallavicini.

He approached with a great display of geniality, explaining that we had been done a great honour by being permitted to open up the largest quarry of the entire country. On the day of the official opening we should all be released.

'You can bet on it if I say so,' he repeated in his hoarse voice, keeping his eyes on the ground. 'Until then, work honestly. Outside, they have again introduced bread rationing. You get half a kilo free every day. The whole country is envious of you. Who else can afford to spend his days in the most beautiful health resort of the Matra?'

He watched us from the corner of his bloodshot eyes. The smell of alcohol radiating from him was rather agreeable, invisible stalls loaded with slightly fermenting fruit were swimming around me in the air. From the inner pocket of his overcoat, above the Pallavicini arms, protruded the party's daily paper.

'Our country is more beautiful every day,' he said, pointing with his stick towards the peak of Mount Kékes rising above the lookout towers and the barbed-wire fence. 'Do you see that big tower there, Gabori? The tower they are building on Kékes? Do you know what it is? What it is for?'

'The national watch-tower, Mr Master-miner. It is from there the secret police will watch the Hungarian cemeteries.'

'Idiot. A meteorological station,' the Gravedigger replied angrily. 'And do you know, Gabori, what they watch from a meteorological station?'

'Meteors, of course.'

'Hahaha! But look,' he pushed the point of his stick into the muddy clay, 'this mountain, on which we stand, is many hundred years old. Perhaps even a thousand. Who knows? True? What are you laughing at, Gabori, you stupid animal? Do you want to make me angry? A rotten *bourgeois* lad like you ought to show more interest in science. Particularly genealogy.'

'Not genealogy, Mr Master-miner. Gynaecology.'

'What do I care! But do you know what it is?'

'Sure. The science with the help of which treasures are dug up from the ground, even from a Jewish cemetery.'

The master-miner gave a loud, animal roar. I could not understand Gabori's purpose in provoking the drunkard. Some ten of our fellow-prisoners, who were carrying heavy logs, stopped and watched the scene curiously. The Gravedigger lifted his truncheon, Gabori started to run and the Gravedigger went in pursuit, but in his muddled state he became confused among the logs and tree stumps. Gabori turned back, came up behind him and tripped him. The next moment they were rolling in the slimy mud, fighting and cursing. A few minutes later Gabori returned to us, red in the face but very cheerful, which again I couldn't understand because, though he was pretty drunk, the master-miner had given him a good beating.

Garamvölgyi went on with his lecture on our liquidation and I bent, vexed, over my saw. He had discussed this question several times, always in the same nasal voice, but we refused to argue, because arguments wouldn't have led anywhere. From this Janos drew the conclusion that we were hiding our heads in the sand and refusing to face reality.

I tried to re-create my dreamy mood without, however, losing sight of the practical side of things – for instance that the tree we were felling should fall awkwardly and break to smithereens on a sharp-crested rock. If the tree remained whole the paymaster sergeant would sell it to the cabinet-makers of the region, the AVO would get drunk on the money and would have their fun with us when they returned from the village. Whenever we cut valuable timber we tried to damage it, and if there was no simple way of doing so, we sawed it up and hid it. We set up the wood-piles in the deepest mud so that they would rot, or in places where the stream would wash them away; we gathered the cut branches in such a way that nobody could disentangle them, and hid the cornel-wood from which the shafts of the stone-breaking hammers were made, under these piles. It was not only we who acted like this. Everyone in the camp engaged in systematic sabotage without discussing it. Only in the evening, when with quick movements we nicked our axes on the rocks, did we exchange conspiratorial glances.

I ought to have despaired at the insignificance of our efforts. What little damage we did was to the state, and that didn't interest the AVO in the least. By nicking our axes and working slowly we could, at the most, delay but could certainly not prevent the opening of the quarry and the very difficult work of stone-breaking waiting for us. This, however, occurred to me but rarely. What I saw before me in a light as brilliant as that surrounding Suzy, was the collapse of the mine. This apocalyptic vision was not a mere wish-dream but an idea based on very real foundations. I knew the plan of the mine, knew how it was conceived and knew the development to be expected.

I had known Karoly Sarkany, Professor of Geology at Budapest University, before the war. He was anti-Nazi and never made a secret of his opinions, but was saved from persecution at that time by his international reputation. He hated the communists just as much, but got into no trouble with them for some time, until they consulted him about their plan for an underground railway in Budapest. This was a Russian-sponsored military project, and therefore could not be criticized. The line was to be built fifty yards below the surface. When Sarkany pointed out that in sandy soil it was dangerous to run a line at such a depth, he was arrested the same night.

In the summer Professor Sarkany was brought to Recsk. According to the old prisoners, he arrived in a beautiful Russian car, wearing handcuffs and very cheerful. He was in excellent condition and told the prisoners that he was using his own typewriter in his cell, had all the scientific books of his library at his disposal and received all letters addressed to him from abroad in which he was asked for geological advice. With the advice he gave he earned approximately six to eight hundred dollars a month. With one per cent of his earnings he was allowed to buy himself cigarettes and sweets, the rest went to the state as payment for the use of his own typewriter and books, for board, lodging and protection.

During the forty-eight hours spent at Recsk he thoroughly examined the mountain, had a few trial borings made and then, in the presence of some twenty prisoners, the camp commander and a few AVO men he summed up his observations and handed over the draft-blueprint of the future quarry. While he was explaining his plans he glanced expectantly at his old friend, Gabor Alapy, former engineer officer in the army. The camp commander approved Sarkany's plan and Sarkany walked back, handcuffed and cheerful, to the waiting Pobeda.

The Zerge was a tent-shaped mountain. The side on which we

worked was very steep, whereas the opposite side descended in a series of ridges. Sarkany advised that the quarry should be cut into the steep side, to a depth reaching almost to the core of the mountain. His purpose in devising this plan was unmistakable. Had he really wanted to open a quarry he would have chosen the gentle slope of the mountain. As it was, the weight of the giant peak would press down more and more heavily on the clayey northern slope, rich in springs and thus less resistant the more deeply we cut into the mountainside. One day there would be a landslide.

As I bent over my saw – Garamvölgyi was still talking in his montonous, nasal voice – I saw the bare andesite pillars of the mountain top crashing down on the quarry which, at this moment, was still covered with wood and grass. I saw the power-house cracked open like an egg-shell by the heavy machinery inside, saw it slide and tumble over the edge of the lower level, saw the rope become slack and the buckets plough up the concrete road. I saw the remaining trees bend in all directions like the bristles of an old toothbrush, and the barbed-wire fence sag like a fishing net hung out to dry while in other places it tensed to breaking point, emitting a falsetto buzzing.

This vision was highly enjoyable but it did nor solve our problems. I remembered the anarchist Souvarine from Zola's *Germinal*; this was how he too imagined the destruction of the mine when he dislocated the props in the shaft, dreaming of the destruction of society as a whole as he set out in the night. I could hardly cherish such hopes. In a society like ours sabotage was a great emotional satisfaction but from the point of view of the system it was almost negligible. The system was supported by the state police force and by nothing else; and if one day, every mine in the country blew up simultaneously, this, as far as the system was concerned, would be a useful phenomenon, not a harmful one. Terror produces sabotage; the sabotage produces more terror. This adds new fuel to the three-phase motor of the state apparatus of which terror is the ignition, economic disaster the necessary pressure and sabotage the petrol.

'Look out! She's falling!' yelled Gabori, and Garamvölgyi jumped forward to shield me and pushed the tree with all his might in the opposite direction. A minute later the cherry with its snow-white cross-section and its orange ring immediately under the bark lay dead at our feet. From the sound of its falling we knew that it had broken to pieces on the rocks.

When we moved on to the next tree Janos came closer. He must have noticed that we were not interested in his conversation because he changed the subject.

'It has always been my dream to go into a pastry-shop and order six pieces of chocolate cake at once,' he said and the corners of his mouth curved downwards. There was self-mockery in his face, but under the assumed cynicism the little boy in him was near to tears. 'But I never had enough money to eat more than one or two. And now I shall never eat chocolate cake again. Never. Not even one slice.'

He looked at me and I read reproach in his eyes. Perhaps because I had seen so much in this life and had had the opportunity to eat so many slices of chocolate cake. How many? During my student years and in America – during twice five years – I ate two slices of cake each day. This added up to seven thousand two hundred slices – six hundred whole cakes. If I calculated that a cake is about ten centimetres high, this gave a cake-tower twelve storeys high. At the bottom were the heavier cakes: caramel, chocolate, nut; then came the fruit and rum cakes, and finally the feather-light chestnut-creams and vanilla cakes with whipped cream. In this respect I had nothing to reproach myself with; I had eaten all the cakes that were coming to me.

Unfortunately, it was somewhat different where women were concerned. Only the night before Gabori had told me about Eva Balogh, the very pretty girl employed by the cultural department of the social democratic party, who used to be my official guide when I went to the provinces to lecture. When she had come back to the office one Monday morning, Gabori related, she had cried and thrown tantrums and complained to everyone that 'again nothing has happened!' I had liked Eva Balogh, but I had thought it was her job to accompany me, and that it was my poems she had favoured, not me. Then there was that beautiful woman in her polka-dotted skirt, the wife of an engineer, with whom I had flirted so outrageously on New Year's Eve, 1948. Three days later she came to see me at the editorial offices, my room-mate disappeared with a knowing smile on his face and she perched on my desk and spread her wide, polka-dotted skirt over my manuscripts. We agreed that I would telephone her in a few days, but the liquidation of the social democratic party intervened and the taste of life was so bitter in my mouth that I did not ring her. And all the other opportunties I had missed! Suddenly the faces of at least four dozen women appeared before my eyes. Usually I had not even noticed their advances because I had been convinced that they admired me only for my poems and I would have felt it immodest to ask them to extend their admiration to my person as well. No use crying over spilt milk! Now it was too late.

While I mused, Egri scolded Garamvölgyi for dreaming about six slices of cake instead of looking for a way to send messages to our families by one of the AVO guards. His wife had received no news of him for five months now, and what about Janika's mother? Besides, to hell with cakes! Why wasn't he clever enough to snitch a sausage from the AVO kitchen when he went for the slops in the afternoon? Garamvölgyi replied that the guards always walked in twos to control each other, and if Egri had no other wish than to be beaten to death he could try sending a message himself. With that he distributed some of the pigs' maize and departed, offended.

When we had felled the next tree and stopped for a moment to get some rest I remarked that this business of sending messages was hopeless. The AVO guards were well paid, they informed on each other, and our isolation was almost complete. However, we might try the contrary and obtain some information as to what was going on outside. The best thing, of course, would be to lay our hands on a newspaper.

'The party's daily, for instance?' asked Gabori innocently.

'Of course. Half a page anyway, or even a quarter of a page. We could figure out a great deal from it.'

'There is a whole newspaper in my trousers pocket,' declared Gabori proudly. 'In the evening I shall try to sit behind you and read it to you. I daren't bring it out here. Do you want a cigarette? I mean a whole cigarette, not a third?'

He brought out from his pocket an almost full packet of cigarettes and a pencil.

'I felt a bottle of brandy in the Gravedigger's hip pocket while we were fighting, but there was no time to get that too.'

'And the prognosis?' I asked the physician. Had I been able to speak aloud, my question would have had an accent of curiosity; after all I was asking for a medical opinion and the least I could do was to show interest. But I had to whisper. We were sitting on his bunk with our heads drawn into our shoulders, surrounded in the twilight by exhausted men drying their feet, talking in low voices or listening to our words openly or covertly. My whispering sounded excited even to my own ears, although I was absolutely calm and had no doubt about the answer I would get.

Doctor Acs was the living image of Imre Komor. The same narrow, delicate face, high cheekbones and elegantly receding forehead with two flat protuberances over the temples, like those one sees on the muscular bellies of young boys on either side of the navel. I knew only that he had been chief bacteriologist in a smart Budapest sanatorium and was now imprisoned for the second time: first, in 1944, for hiding Jews, and now for hiding nuns, although he came from an old Protestant family, was a convinced atheist and disliked both Jews and nuns. His basic nature was identical with Komor's, who fought for the rights of workers and peasants although he detested them; but because Doctor Acs struggled against each case of injustice individually and practically, he bore his fate without resignation and self-justification, while Komor, having invited the oppressed and persecuted to rebellion, moved over to the side of the oppressors and persecutors.

'And the prognosis?' I repeated.

Instead of replying Doctor Acs offered me the top of his dixie with a few slices of carefully toasted bread on it – the wildest extravagance according to the conventions of Recsk hospitality. Then he lit a cigarette, threw back his head and let out the smoke through his nostrils. I looked at his beautiful, expressive mouth, the lips lightly but hermetically closed as if chiselled. Where had I seen lips like those? Komor's, of course, but where else? On one of the Egyptian Pharaohs, but not in a granite statue, it was of sand-stone, I could still remember the granules. It must have been Amenophis III or IV. Suddenly I felt a flea-bite in the centre of my navel and shuddered with pain. I was used to the fleas pulsating and streaming in my armpits and between my buttocks but this bite was unexpected. I should catch it, but by the time my fingers found the spot the flea would be gone. Yes, it must have been the lips of Amenophis IV; he was the only ruler of the eighteenth dynasty interested in social and intellectual reforms.

'The prognosis is simple as a slap in the face. If we take as a basis the present rations, with the working and psychological conditions, everyone in this camp will starve to death within a year. Except, naturally, those who do no work. Some of the young boys may hold out for two or three years. But within twelve months ninety-five per cent of the inmates will be dead as doornails. All of them, I tell you. All. And twelve months is the utmost limit. We shall begin to have casualties in six months; in nine months people will die like flies in the autumn. You can take this literally, because in nine months it will be autumn.

'I am sorry that my prognosis is not more favourable, Gyurka, but there it is. I am a biologist and I know how long the human body can survive, working twelve to fourteen hours a day on two thousand two hundred calories, without animal protein and sugar. Sugar is not so important because the organism produces sufficient sugar from starches; but meat, oil, milk and eggs are irreplaceable. The little meat and oil we get are practically useless. Here you have the general picture. Are you interested in details?'

'Of course. But first, answer me one question. You said a little while ago that you have performed two appendectomies in the shed. While you were operating, the chaff from the loft floated down into the patient's open abdomen. You had no penicillin. Both recovered in a miraculously short time. Yes, and you had no gauze, you bandaged them with torn underpants. Let me ask you: don't you think that you over-estimate the alleged rules of biology? Aren't you forgetting that unknown factor, the resistance of the spirit and the adaptability of the human body? After all, Simeon the Stylite lived for forty years on top of a pillar in the desert near Aphroditopolis, eating nothing but barley boiled in water. He never washed except when the rain bathed him, just like us. I do not believe that his diet or his living conditions were better than ours.'

'But the psychological conditions were considerably better,' Doctor Acs smiled. 'He believed in God, not in Harry Truman. I do not deny, however, that our body adapts itself to conditions. There are hardly any colds or cases of pneumonia here, although the appearance of such illnesses would seem natural. The tubercular and those with stomach ulcers may recover, thanks to the food and the climate, before they die of starvation. But, please believe me, had there been a particle of animal excrement on the chaff falling into the patient's abdominal cavity during the operation he would have contracted peritonitis and died. Only immunity or vaccination can protect us against typhus bacteria and only food can save us from starvation. Those whose nourishment is below the minimum subsistence level must sooner or later die. This is a law; neither spiritual fortitude nor physical toughness can exempt you from it. However, we can distinguish certain definite categories within these general rules, the various types of quickly and slowly starving people. Powerful bodies like that one for instance,' he pointed to Joska Borostobi squatting on his bunk and carving a cigarette holder from a briar root with the help of a nail and a sliver of glass, 'go much more rapidly than for instance Gabori with his fifty-five kilos. I don't believe Gabori has lost more than two or three kilos while Borostobi, who weighed a hundred and ten, cannot now be over ninety. But there are considerable differences even between people of the same physical structure. Not every organism utilizes even the two thousand two hundred calories we get. Take the leguminous plants that form approximately one-third of our nourishment. Somebody may love beans or lentils but his intestines pay no attention to this preference and assimilate only fifty, or twenty per cent of the lentils, while someone else who swallows the same food with disgust may utilize it completely. The spiritual attitude – how deeply someone can sleep under the given conditions, how economically he deals with his energy at work, whether he is in a constant panic while idling, or phlegmatic like you – is important but not sufficiently so. It means another two or four weeks of life.'

He looked at me fleetingly, while with a characteristic movement – again reminding me of Komor – he smoothed down his hair with the back of his hand, but the movement lacked its usual calm, and that embarrassed him.

'Your chances,' he said almost angrily, 'are a little better than average. You will go sometime after about half of the others. However, they have given me a surprisingly large quantity of dextrose with the medical supplies. Approximately eighty-eight thousand calories. With this quantity the life of a couple of people – people who are important to the nation – can be prolonged for one or two months, perhaps even longer . . .'

Again he smoothed down his hair but this time he looked, embarrassed, at the middle button of my jacket. I made a movement of protest.

'Under such conditions there is no point in prolonging life, as you know very well. What sense is there in my living two months longer?'

'It is my duty, as a physician, to prolong life. Whenever I perform an appendix or gallstone operation successfully I only lengthen a life. It is always death who kicks the final, decisive goal; all the doctor can do is to equalize while the game still lasts.'

'This is quibbling.'

'But what if something happens during those two months? If conditions improve, if you are exchanged for Nazim Hikmet, or if a revolution breaks out in the Soviet . . .'

'Roll call!' someone shouted from outside. We rose from our places slowly, we had been told that very day that henceforth roll call would be held in the barracks. This made life considerably easier. It meant that we could eat our supper in the barracks, take off our boots and, instead of standing for hours on the snow-covered hillside, could wait here, leaning against the bunks, wearing our favourite footwear, wooden clogs. When searching the barracks the AVO always took everything from us, but they did not seem to mind the clogs that our fellow-prisoners made for us in the carpenter's shop. I loved them most in the evening when we invited guests to our bunks. It was part of our etiquette that, after knocking on the side of the bunk, the guests slipped out of their clogs and climbed in while the clogs stood side by side at the foot of the bunk like cars before a brightly lit villa somewhere in the West.

The space between the rows of bunks was three metres wide, which gave hardly enough room for all hundred and fifty of us to stand. Gabori warned us beforehand not to talk to each other while we were waiting, because we were surrounded by curious ears. Since our *nachalniki* had moved from the barracks into the pretty, one-storey building we had had to build for them and where they were two to a room, they had organized a dangerous network of spies in the barracks. As the spies were given lighter work, or received an extra dixieful of food, they quickly increased in numbers and, to retain their privileged position, often reported conversations we never had. It would have been wisest to stop talking altogether, but my friends and I considered this a voluntary relinquishing of our last freedom which 'under the given conditions would be useless and would only precipitate things . . .' By 'given conditions' we meant slow starvation, and by 'things' death itself, but we regarded these words as improper and avoided using them.

With whom should I talk to shorten the long period of waiting? The beans I had eaten half an hour earlier hurt my stomach as if someone had boxed me in the solar plexus and left his fist there. Every time I breathed I felt in my throat the sharp smell of the weeds cooked with the beans. After Doctor Acs's words I craved light chatter, but Gabori, Egri and Garamvölgyi who stood near me were out, and so were my two neighbours, Pali Musza and Toni Vojacsek.

Musza stood with his hands crossed on his stomach, his head slightly bowed and a beatific smile on his porcelain-white, smooth, childish face. Presumably he was praying or meditating; if I spoke to him he would answer at once and pretend I had not interrupted him, because he regarded ostentatious prayer as a great sin. He was almost a child. Two years earlier he had wanted to enter a religious order but the church authorities had refused him because they considered him too stupid. Musza then went to work, but with his earnings he bought Bibles which he distributed at railway stations among the travellers. For this he was arrested. At night he walked about in the barracks barefoot, noiseless. He gave a large part of his bread and rations to those who asked for it. I soon discovered that those who asked were usually spies, informers, and the thieves who robbed the haversacks of their neighbours. I sent Gabori to Musza to tell him to give his food not to scoundrels but to the old and sick, like Porpak with his serious heart condition or the paralytic Uncle Horvath. Gabori returned from this mission shaking his head.

'Well, what did he say?' I inquired.

'He does not consider himself called upon to determine who is a scoundrel and who isn't,' Gabori replied. 'He will go on giving to those who ask for it.'

Since then my admiration and regard for Musza had grown continually. Although this feeling was mutual we never talked to each other; neither of us saw much purpose in such talks. He showed respect for, but no interest in, my stories, my philosophy, my witticisms; exactly as I reacted to his prayers.

With my other neighbour, Toni Vojacsek, I had even less to talk about, although I did nor share my companions' disdain for Toni. His face, though pink-cheeked and pimply, resembled Musza's as though they were brothers: brothers of whom one had become a monk and the other had fallen into depravity but had preserved, even in his depravity, an original animal innocence. Toni boasted to everyone about having been a safe-breaker, not as if he were particularly proud of it, but only as if he, too, wanted to have something to boast about. Turning innocent blue eyes on his interlocutor he would explain that there were still a good many safes in Budapest waiting for him. He would tell at length where these safes stood, how he intended to fool the police patrol and disconnect the alarm, and how thick a wall he would have to dig through. Many of the political prisoners found it humiliating that we had to share our daily life with ordinary criminals, but Toni met his fate with resignation and his attitude to us was a mixture of esteem and contempt: he regarded us as madmen who had sacrificed our lives for a hopeless and incomprehensible cause.

He never understood – and didn't particularly care – why he was shut up with us. They had caught him entering a Budapest textile factory with intent to rob. He had tried this branch of the profession only for fun. One should always stick to one's speciality, as he often said. When they arrested him he was convinced that he wouldn't get more than a month, but to his surprise he was accused of sabotage. The length of cloth he had tried to steal was destined for the Soviet Union. There was nothing he could say in his defence but that he was of proletarian origin. He was sentenced to fifteen years' imprisonment because, according to the verdict, he had executed the robbery at the instigation of the American embassy to destroy friendly relations between Hungary and the Soviet Union.

Toni had described the safes waiting to be broken into so often that it was beginning to bore me. In addition he admired and trusted me to such an extent that he asked me every time we talked: 'Tell me, brother George, will I ever be a free man again? Say yes; you are the only one I believe.' He would look at me with such entreaty in his innocent blue eyes that in spite of my conviction to the contrary, I promised him again and again that he would soon be free to break into all the rich safes waiting for him. However, I should not have liked to repeat this encouragement as publicly.

So I decided to talk to North-Eastern Inrush. It was a good moment to have the names of the various cloud formations, the cyclone and anticyclone, wind-speeds, and such explained to me. I had neglected this side of my education and I could have found no more suitable teacher among the nine million inhabitants of Hungary than North-Eastern Inrush.

He was standing in the first line, next to Egri. He was a kind, mild man with a huge head and a powerful chin which covered his neck and part of his chest. He was also the smallest inhabitant of the camp, almost a dwarf. His real name was Géza Toth – Uncle Géza as we called him – and he had been one of the heads of the Meteorological Institute. He owed his arrest to the fact that in the meteorological report edited by him he had promised, one day 'soft Western breezes' and on the next had foretold an 'inrush of icy cold air from the North-East, the direction of the Soviet Union'. The next day he was arrested by the AVO 'because of imperialist propaganda smuggled into a meteorological report, espionage activity and vilification of the Soviet Union.' Staff Colonel Valér Czebe, who had worked in Military Intelligence and was arrested two days after Uncle Géza, told us that on the day in question a Soviet division had arrived in Hungary simultaneously with the 'inrush of icy air' and this coincidence had caused Uncle Géza's doom. We took good care never to mention this coincidence to the old man for fear it might drive him to despair.

North-Eastern Inrush bore his fate with admirable calm. Climatically the Matra region is Hungary's most interesting spot, with unexpected cloud penetrations and other meteorological phenomena that delighted him. The inadequate nourishment sufficed for his tiny body, he loved work and found every trade absorbing. In the forest he looked like a leprechaun, or one of the seven dwarfs come to life, wielding some giant tool, a saw or an axe, while throwing sharp glances at the clouds. He was continually busy even in the barracks, making a shelf above his bunk, smoothing it with sand-paper and painting it green. He collected all sorts of objects, which he arranged on his shelf in order – as he used to say – 'to feel at home'. Only at night did he sometimes sit on his bunk with his heavy head in his hands. Once I asked him what he was meditating about. He told me that he had left his wife in an extremely expensive five-room apartment. He had no doubt that his friends gave his wife sufficient money to pay the rent, but how, if they let him go in five or ten years, would he pay them back?

Three months earlier, on our first evenings in Recsk, our conversations had been restricted to a few minutes after the lights were put out, and of my three listeners two would soon fall asleep. Only Garamvölgyi would stay awake, having fed copiously on slops. Kunéry, the former officer who had tried to pick a quarrel with us on the way up because of the Goddess Isis, protested loudly that we were disturbing him, and others warned us benevolently against trying to maintain our intellectual interest. And yet, strangely enough, the number of my listeners grew so rapidly that I had to submit the newcomers to a severe screening. The other unexpected phenomenon was that in spite of the increasing lapses of memory caused by slow but constant loss of physical strength, our intellectual thirst was growing so that we always talked for at least an hour. When it became known that they were doing the same in the other barracks, our example was followed by many.

Except for myself, the prisoners had completely lost interest in the story of each other's arrests. Only new arrivals were asked to tell their stories, briefly, as part of the ceremony of introduction, and we stuck to this custom because it was severely forbidden. The AVO explained that telling our stories was equivalent to the betrayal of state secrets and punishable by an extra fifteen years' imprisonment, and anyway, if we persisted, they would simply beat us to a pulp.

The largest groups were the social democrats – usually old trade-union men, strike leaders, who could not get used to having to serve the interests of the state instead of those of the working class; former army officers who had gone over to the Russians in 1944 and believed that they would be able to organize an independent Hungarian army; the leading men of the different parties whom the communists had asked in 1945 to organize local smallholder or social democratic cells and who, three years later, had been arrested for having done so; *kulaks*, who were made to disappear in order that their lands might be expropriated, and poor peasants who were appointed *kulaks*, so that when the real thing was lacking they in turn could be made to disappear; so-called undisciplined workers from large factories who were arrested in order to frighten their fellow-workers; and *élite* workers who were arrested to frighten their fellow-workers even more. Then there were smaller groups – for instance, almost all the officers from sea-going ships, arrested for espionage; peasants and artisans of Serbian extraction from the environment of Pécs who had participated in the banquet given by Rakosi when Tito visited Hungary, arrested for high treason; and some thirty men from the village of Battonya, from the notary to the swineherd, arrested for conspiracy against the state. What had happened in Battonya was that the schoolmaster was a member of an anti-communist movement called Sword and Cross. In order to obtain funds for the movement he had made the parents of his pupils buy from him stamps with a sword and a cross on them, and the parents, not knowing what they were buying but unwilling to antagonize the teacher, had complied. One night the

AVO surrounded the village and searched every house. They arrested everyone in whose house they found one of the sword and cross stamps – and if someone confessed to a stamp collection they arrested him anyway, without a search.

There were, however, cases that didn't fit into any category but were interesting in themselves – for instance that of Gyula Fazekas, veterinary surgeon from Paks. He had been arrested by the AVO and interrogated about alleged friends whose names he had never heard. They beat and tortured him for three whole weeks. Then, one night, an AVO colonel came into his cell and told him that, unfortunately, they had made a mistake and it was not he but another Gyula Fazekas they were looking for. However, in the state he was in it was impossible to set him free. This he must understand. So he was sent to Recsk.

A big, strong peasant by the name of Macza had served in the Foreign Legion and had later opened a pub in Oran. He made his pile and in 1947 decided to return to Hungary and buy his parents some land. He was cautious, however, and arriving in Paris asked the redheaded Councillor of the Hungarian Legation whether it was safe for him to go home. The Councillor (in whom I could not help but recognize Bandi Havas) assured him that he would be received with open arms and that he would be very happy in socialist Hungary. Macza was arrested at the frontier as a French spy and robbed of the ten million francs he had on him. For three years he was kept in utter isolation at the Kistarcsa camp so that neither his parents nor his wife, who had remained in Oran, knew what had happened to him.

Ajtai – the carrot-nosed young man who had travelled in the same freight-car with me and had told us from the clicking of the switches where we were – had been a railwayman in Hatvan. In 1949 there was a demonstration in Hatvan in favour of Cardinal Mindszenty who was already in prison. Ajtai and his brother, also a railwayman, got back to Hatvan a few hours after the demonstration, and were arrested at the station. They were accused of having participated in the demonstration. Both men showed their papers which proved that they had just returned from a fourteen-hour journey to the other end of the country. 'Then it was your harlot wives who participated in the demonstration,' the AVO man said. 'We are both unmarried.' 'Never mind,' replied the lieutenant, 'now you will remain unmarried for good.'

Engineer Hugo Koch was appointed by Rakosi himself as general manager of the nationalized Meinl colonial produce stores. One day his chauffeur Galba was driving him along the Gödöllö highway. As they reached the worst hairpin bend of the country, three huge cars, coming from the opposite direction on the wrong side of the road, stopped directly before them. The second car disgorged Rakosi in person. When he recognized Koch he embraced him, begged him to excuse his retinue for their irregular driving, sent his regards to Mrs Koch and climbed back into the car. The first car, then the second, drove away, but the third remained. From it descended four AVO men who arrested both Koch and his driver Galba. They were taken not to AVO headquarters but to the court of law where both were accused of planning an attempt on Rakosi's life. Koch, however, was permitted to hire a lawyer. After talking to his client the lawyer went to see Rakosi at party headquarters. On hearing the story Rakosi turned purple with fury, thanked the lawyer for warning him and promised that his client would be free within two hours. Five minutes later, as the lawyer was leaving the building, he too was arrested and taken to Kistarcsa. Koch was tried by a fat, pink-faced judge called Rigo who, to everybody's surprise, brought a verdict of not guilty. When Koch and his driver left the court building they were again arrested by the AVO. At Kistarcsa Koch met his lawyer, who remained there while Koch and Galba were brought to Recsk. They lived in the barracks next to ours and slept side by side. The judge Rigo, on the other hand, slept next to North-Eastern Inrush, directly below me.

Gabor Szarka, commercial attaché at Ankara, did excellent work at his post. The summer before, shortly after he had closed a very important business deal between the two countries, he was called home. His Turkish friends advised him to embezzle the money and remain in Turkey but he, though he was rather scared, returned to Hungary. To his surprise he was awarded high government distinction, offered a four-week holiday at an exclusive resort at government expense and then given orders to return to his post. However, at the Hungarian border he was taken off the train. The AVO lieutenant who arrested him kept calling him a treacherous swine and an absconder, whereupon Szarka showed him his diplomatic passport and letter of credit.

'If you dare refer to these again I'll make you eat them!' the lieutenant shouted.

'It took me two hours to eat them,' Szarka concluded his story. 'I never knew how difficult it was to eat a passport.'

Janos Cseri, a peasant lad of twenty, was arrested at the pub. His friends, with whom he was having a few drinks, sang old, forbidden soldier songs, like: 'I am Miklos Horthy's soldier . . .' etc. Cseri wasn't aware of this because he was lying under the table, dead drunk. His friends were taken to the local police station, given a good beating and released, but Cseri was sent up to Budapest to the AVO. His internment order, that he always carried on his person, was a masterpiece. 'Janos Cseri was arrested in a pub together with his friends who were singing anti-democratic songs. Although it was proven that, owing to the high degree of his intoxication, Cseri did not participate in the singing, it can be presumed that had he been sober he would have done so. On the basis of the above I intern Cseri for six months for state security reasons. Lieutenant-Colonel Marton Karolyi.' Beneath, the date: December, 1948. That was exactly two years ago.

Gyula Mauthner had worked in the country's largest factory, the Weiss Manfred Works at Csepel, and was, on the side, a spy of the local AVO. The summer before, the AVO told him to write down the names and addresses of social democratic workers and employees who were known for their anti-communist sentiments. Mauthner put down the names of the twenty-four people he disliked most (regardless of their party affiliation) and at the bottom of the list signed his own name. The Csepel AVO branch made him put the list in an envelope and sent it on to the Budapest AVO. Three days later a prison van stopped before his house; when he climbed in he saw that the twenty-four men he had denounced were already there. All twenty-five of them landed at Recsk. The twenty-four amused themselves night after night by wrapping Mauthner in a blanket and giving him a good hiding. After a while Mauthner confessed what he had done. Surprisingly, instead of beating him to a pulp, the ironfounders took pity on him and henceforth left him alone.

Ferenc Wittipp was a design engineer at a factory making precision instruments. One summer afternoon, as he was on his way home, he was pushed into a car and taken to Andrassy Street. When they told him with what sabotage action he was charged he smiled with relief. The Soviet Union had ordered gun sights from his factory. They had enclosed a design. Wittipp had examined the design and observed that there were a few obvious errors in it. He corrected the errors, informed his superiors of the corrections and, at the same time, informed the Ministry in Moscow, which replied in a letter dripping with gratitude. His investigator, to whom he explained what had happened, nodded. This, precisely, was the sabotage. He should have manufactured the gun sights according to the design sent from Moscow. Did it never occur to him, the investigator asked, that perhaps the Soviet Union had planned to send those guns to one of the people's democracies, to Hungary, let us say? Wittipp was struck dumb by this question. There, now I've got you – the investigator had triumphed. You corrected that design because you knew the guns were intended for the Hungarian army and you were in contact with a conspiracy of army officers who planned to attack the Soviet Union. This is why it was so important to you that the guns should shoot straight.

Professor György Sarospataky, the scientist, with his broad, bushy, soot-black moustache, who had been in the same cell with me at Kistarcsa, was sent to a biological congress at Bucharest. The Czechoslovakian delegate said that in Southern Slovakia there was a plague of scale insects. He blamed the Horthy régime which, when during the war Southern Slovakia was temporarily Hungarian, had badly neglected the care of orchards. In his reply Professor Sarospataky declared that the Hungarians had taken over the Southern Slovakian orchards in a very neglected state in 1938, and to this effect he quoted the official statistical data of the Czechoslovak Statistical Bureau from 1937. He added, however, that there was not much point in digging up past mistakes; it was much more important that close co-operation be established between the two neighbouring states because if one neglected insect extermination, the orchards of the other also suffered. On this they all agreed. The following afternoon, however, he was taken off the train at Biharkeresztes, at the Roumanian–Hungarian border. An AVO sergeant informed him that he was under arrest because he had arranged a chauvinistic scandal at the congress, in order to sabotage international co-operation.

Titus Banvölgyi, a lanky, pink-faced, freckled, angry and cranky lawyer, had been interned in 1946 for various fascist crimes he had never committed. The AVO confiscated his excellent library and his beautiful art treasures, and threw his wife and small children out of his apartment. His communist judge friends left no stone unturned to get him freed – for instance, they held a regular trial in his case, hearing over one hundred witnesses, and found him not guilty. And when it became evident that not even the Hungarian communists could help him, they turned to the Soviet Embassy and had him released from Kistarcsa. During the first week of his return to civil life, Banvölgyi found out who had his library, who shared in his art treasures and which AVO officer had taken the flat from his wife. Then he sent a petition to the Supreme Court, asking for the restitution of his books, art treasures and apartment, damages for the thirty-two months of internment he had suffered and a set of false teeth to replace the real ones that had been knocked out of his head. A few days later he was taken away in a curtained car by detectives who began to kick and hit him as soon as he was in the car. An hour later he was thrown, half dead, into our train to Recsk. Unlike the other prisoners Banvölgyi was constantly harping on his grievances.

'And what would you do, Titus, if they released you again?' his fellow-prisoners asked him.

'I would immediately send a petition to the Supreme Court,' he lisped with his toothless mouth. During his one week of freedom he had had his remaining teeth pulled, but was arrested before he could pick up his plate from the dentist.

Marton Dobrai had been a faithful communist, had held a high position in a bank and was, in addition, a party functionary. One evening, at the time of the Rajk trial, two detectives searched his flat. They were looking for foreign currency, cut open the chairs and mattresses with a razor but found nothing.

'Never mind, we'll take you in anyway,' they told him and, instead of taking him by car, as was usual, they put him on a streetcar like an ordinary thief. At Széna Square, where they had to change to another line, Dobrai escaped from the detectives in the crowd. He spent the night at the house of a friend and in the morning he set out towards the Austrian border. He was arrested and taken to 60 Andrassy Street. The interrogator asked him what had caused him, a man of excellent position, of high party function, with a villa and a car, to try to abscond? Dobrai explained that he was driven to this step by his unlawful arrest. There was nothing left for him to do but to try and get away. His interrogator then asked him to describe the two detectives who had searched his house, and when he was given the description broke into merry laughter. They had been false detectives.

Most of these stories, of course, harmed not only the AVO's prestige but our own as well, and this was probably why my fellow prisoners kept them brief and rarely mentioned them again. To put up with our fate, the work, the filth, the prospect of starvation, it was absolutely necessary that we should be able to look upon ourselves as tragic heroes, but the reasons and circumstances of our arrests prevented us from doing so. The moronic AVO officer who sincerely believed that the *hand of the enemy could be detected everywhere*, even in a meteorological report, shifted the cheap absurdity of his utter stupidity on to the victim whom he arrested. The initials of the social democrats arrested on the same day – from Otto Beöthy, Parliament librarian, and Péter Csaplar, chairman of the trade-union council, to Egri, myself, Garamvölgyi and Gabori – ranged without irregularity from A to G, so we could not even pretend that we had been arrested because of our acts. It was obvious that the AVO had simply lifted out a batch of names from an alphabetical file.

At the same time we felt that we were pretty ridiculous ourselves. Until the day of our arrests ninety-five per cent of us had not been declared enemies of the régime. Most of us had regarded it as something like a storm that would, in time, abate, while others, who at first had believed in it enthusiastically, had waited with fading illusions. Looking back on it, our former life did not seem very heroic either. All of us had had to find some sort of a *modus vivendi* with the régime. Those who were arrested earlier despised us because everyone regarded collaboration with the régime as discrediting after he himself had been arrested. We became ridiculous in our own eyes because we had tolerated, even supported, the régime which laid the traps in which it caught us.

Though I found most of the stories revolting and humiliating I went on collecting them fanatically, the way one clings to a fixed idea which one knows that it is unreal. In my student years I used to hop out into the hall on one foot to fetch the mail, expecting that I might be rewarded for this effort by a letter from my beloved of the moment asking me to a rendezvous. Often I walked in the street, stepping carefully on every second paving stone because I imagined this would bring me luck, although I knew very well that luck had nothing to do with paving stones. This was how I collected the stories: hopelessly, yet with a very real and exact purpose. 'When I go back to the West,' I thought, 'and try to describe my experiences, I shall meet with almost insurmountable difficulties.' I knew very well that the things I was going through were unimaginable, improbable or even suspect to people in the West because they were irrational. And the Westerner's love of comfort, lack of imagination, horror of moral indignation – his determination to protect his inner peace and put his conscience to sleep – would act against his crediting my story. I remembered that five years ago, in New York, I too would have doubted the veracity of such a book or at least I would have believed the allegations to be exaggerated. Even now, living the experience I hoped one day to describe, I constantly doubted its reality. If I believed in anything, it was in these stories; or rather, I stopped disbelieving them after I had heard the first few. At the tenth, twentieth, I saw that they not only characterized the régime but were utterly uninventable, because to invent them would have required Aeschylus's psychological insight, Shakespeare's imagination and Maupassant's art of story-telling. I thought that these stories would be the main proofs of my book's authenticity – and this saddened me considerably because until now I always judged books by artistic value and not by authenticity.

The roll call was over. I took off my jacket and trousers and sat on my bunk, waiting for the lights to be put out. The serious conversation had to wait until darkness; now we stuck to lighter subjects. Gabori, Egri and Garamvölgyi had settled down round me; our two somewhat more distant neighbours, Ödön Berzsenyi and Florian Wrangel, reclined on their mattresses and listened with interest to what we were saying. With his delicate, oval face, his melancholy, narrow, greying moustache and his strong nose, Berzsenyi called to my mind the Hungarian noblemen of the past century who, after 1825, stood up for the rights of the common people and in more than one case gave their lives for their serfs, but who would never have imagined shaking hands with them. With his reticence, good manners, wit, well-concealed haughtiness, generosity, liberal views and conservative habits, all of which made him as different from his Horthy-general father as it made him like his more distant ancestors, he was, from the very first moment, close to my heart. My friends had some difficulty overcoming their distrust of him.

Florian Wrangel's ancestors had belonged to the guild of honey-cake and candle-makers in the township of Esztergom ever since, a thousand years ago, the first Hungarian king made Esztergom his seat and invited German artisans into the country. When he spoke he lowered his eyes and, apart from his slowly writhing lips, the only bit of his body that moved were his big toes, calling attention to the pointed, thick and yellow nails, like the claws of a vulture. He was twenty-five or twenty-six but there was nothing young about him except his beautiful eyes. With his powerful, square forehead and powerful, square jaw, his terrifying nose in the depths of which scarlet flash-bulbs pulsated as if he were wearing his tonsils in his nostrils, he looked exactly like a film villain. An ideal villain, of course, because he was far too clever and far too demoniac to suit Hollywood. But had he lived a few centuries earlier and had there been a film industry then, he would have been the star of the studio owned by the Borgia family, in which Sigismondo Malatesta was the producer and Hieronymus Bosch van der Aachen painted the sets.

Florian was equally versed in pastry-making, strategy, archaeology, astrology and magic. He prepared our horoscopes in his head and could talk just as instructively about whether at Cannae, in 216 BC, the Romans or the Carthagians stood with their backs to the sea, as he could about the general customs of the second Roman *legio auxiliaris* stationed in Hungary, or about Kepler's famous horoscope – printed in book form – that foretold Wallenstein's death to the hour, even to the minute, many years before the warlord's murder.

My acquaintances warned me over and over again that Florian was one of the most dangerous informers in the camp. I had always suspected it but did not fear him. His attachment to me – a perverted and penetrating mixture of intellectual hunger, humility, subconscious homosexuality and frantic adoration – was so strong that I knew he would sell his own mother before he betrayed me. Though he showed the authorities a cermonious obedience, whenever he caught sight of me he broke all the rules and began to tell me the story of his life. Berzsenyi, who had spent two years in the same cell with him at Kistarcsa, told me that of Florian's espionage stories not a word was true. Wrangel had been arrested by Lieutenant Toth – also from Esztergom – out of vengeance because he had seduced the beautiful prostitute who supported Toth. But when Florian saw that everyone had a story, he too invented one for himself – a story which grew more terrible every time he told it.

Now Florian was telling us how, immediately after the declaration of war, in December, 1941, he had sent espionage reports to the Americans on his radio transmitter. I figured out that at the time he could not have been over sixteen, and glanced questioningly at Berzsenyi. He glanced back at me with a melancholy look that seemed disproportionate. I knew he was terribly tired of Florian's stories, but there must have been another reason. Perhaps he was hurt because I had never asked him for his own story, though we had lived side by side for over three months. I thought I was being tactful, but he may have read a lack of interest in my silence. So now I touched Wrangel's shoulder and asked him kindly to stop talking, he could go on with it next time. Then I turned to Berzsenyi and told him how sorry I was never to have heard the story of his arrest, and how I had felt I should wait with this question until we became friendly enough for him not to regard it as an intrusion.

Berzsenyi sat up on the mattress and his expression changed. He began to speak, without introduction or transition, calmly and smoothly, like someone who had prepared and rehearsed his story carefully, many times, waiting for an opportunity to tell it. Every sentence was well rounded and delivered with a great economy of words.

'I was a lieutenant in the Hungarian army,' he began, giving me a friendly smile. 'In the summer of 1943 our battalion surrendered to the Russians in the bend of the River Don. Officers, men, all of them. I was taken to a Russian prisoner-of-war camp but only for three days. On the third day I was summoned to the camp commander. Two Soviet soldiers pushed me into a car and we drove on and on and on. We drove for almost a week and then, one day, stopped before a huge building. I was led into a great hall with a pink marble floor. From there I was led into a room also decorated with pink marble. A pink marble bench ran along the four walls and a rococo chandelier hung from the ceiling. A powerful, deep-chested woman entered the room carrying a tray piled high with salmon, caviare and ham sandwiches. She put it down in front of me and gave me a friendly pat. "Go on, eat, *batyushka*," she said, "you won't see food again!" "Where am I?" I inquired, my mouth full of caviare. "Where? At the Moscow headquarters of the NKVD," the fat woman replied readily, and winked at me.'

'Speak louder!' Judge Rigo whispered from the bunk below and, to give his request more weight, he kicked our mattress.

'Not long after that I was taken up to the room of a Soviet Colonel. He asked me to sit down, offered me a cigar and vodka, then asked for my personal data. Name? Ödön Berzsenyi. Profession? Lawyer. Address? Budapest, District IV, 4 Kigyo Street, Apartment 1. Rank? Lieutenant. Mother's name? Born where, etc., etc. The Colonel put down everything I said, then he looked up and said:

'"We shall release you immediately if you relieve your conscience and admit what we know anyway. Confess that you are Major Schultze, the notorious German agent."

'"But Colonel,' I replied indignantly, "I don't know a word of German! Here are my papers: I am Ödön Berzsenyi, lawyer, from Budapest. In the Don bend our entire battalion surrendered . . ."

'"Confess that you are Major Schultze, the notorious German agent."

'"I am Ödön Berzsenyi, lawyer, from Budapest."

'"Take him away," the Colonel ordered.

'The next day I was again taken before the Colonel. This time he offered me neither cigar nor vodka but made me sit down before he asked: "Who are you?"

'"Ödön Berzsenyi, lawyer, Budapest, District IV, 4 Kigyo Street," I replied.

'"Confess that you are Major Schultze, the notorious German agent!"

'"I am Ödön Berzsenyi . . ." I tried again.

'"Take him away!" the Colonel cried.

'On the next day there was neither cigar nor vodka, and he did not offer me a chair.

'"Who are you?" he asked me, so curiously that it might have been the first time.

'"Ödön Berzsenyi, lawyer, Budapest, 4 Kigyo Street, Apartment one . . ."

'"This is your last opportunity. Confess that you are Major Schultze, the notorious German agent."

'"Why don't you stop this idiocy?" I asked angrily.

'"Take him away!" the Colonel yelled. Two of his men loaded me into a lorry and we drove and drove and drove. After a few days we arrived at the prison in Archangel. They led me into the right wing of the prison, along a corridor from which eighteen cells opened on one side, eighteen on the other, and at the end of the corridor they pushed me into cell No. 37. The next morning . . .'

At that moment the bolt on the barrack door was pushed open and a voice called my name:

'Faludy!'

I pulled on my trousers, stepped quickly into my boots and smiled at my friends, who sat petrified on their bunks. When someone was denounced by an informer it was usually at this hour, before the lights were put out, that he was called out and beaten up, kicked around and made to crawl in the mud. Two weeks before, Porpak, the old and sick former police colonel, had been beaten so badly that he became deaf in his left ear. I wondered who had informed on me. Perhaps I over-estimated Florian's attachment to me?

I tried to appear calm and unconcerned while I walked out between the two rows of bunks. Outside, the dog-sergeant was standing, resting his back against the barrack wall. We called him dog-sergeant because he had arrived in the freight-car bringing the police dogs, though he had nothing to do with them. He was a smiling, fair-haired young man, the only AVO man who never hurt anyone.

'Are you Faludy?' he asked in a whisper. 'Come closer. Closer still.'

His breath smelled of goulash, wine and cigarettes. He had been drinking red wine, not white. I too leaned my back against the wall. The fur of his cap tickled my forehead. 'How can he hit me standing so close?' I asked myself.

'We had a Villon recital at the camp headquarters this evening. Did you write those poems?'

'Yes,' I replied, rather uncertainly, as if I had not really adapted Villon's poems myself, but had only always pretended to have done so.

'I've brought you your royalties,' the dog-sergeant said, handing me an apple – a red Jonathan apple so big that I could hardly put it in the pocket of my blouse.

'The poems were beautiful. Eat that apple. And if someone asks you why I called you out, tell them I slapped your face. Goodnight.'

It was dark in the barracks when I got back, but when I climbed on to my mattress a light beam from the watch-tower's searchlight fell directly on my friends through the small, barred window near the ceiling. Egri offered me a whole cigarette, as was usual on such occasions. Garamvölgyi was lying on his stomach, twitching convulsively, Florian was crying soundlessly, Gabori was sitting up straight, his hands balled into fists, and Berzsenyi lay still with his arm over his eyes. Though I was glad that I had not been beaten I was also a little ashamed of it because all my friends – with the exception of Garamvölgyi – had undergone very severe beatings. At first they wouldn't believe my story but the evidence of the apple convinced them in the end. We cut it into six equal parts with Gabori's sharp knife made from a large nail, and then I asked Berzsenyi to go on with his story.

'I was telling you,' Berzsenyi began in a shaky voice, as if the wonderful sweetness and aroma of the apple slice had gone to his head, 'I was telling you how they led me along the corridor of the Archangel prison. There were eighteen cells with even numbers on one side, eighteen with uneven numbers on the other, and at the end there was a cell bearing the number 37, and this is where they put me. The next morning I was taken to the office, where I was received by a female NKVD lieutenant. She asked me for my personal data. I told her I was Ödön Berzsenyi, lawyer, Budapest, District IV, Kigyo Street, lieutenant, battle on the Don, etc., etc. The young lieutenant looked at me:

'"Confess that you are Major Schultze, the notorious German Agent . . ."

'I denied the unfounded accusation, as usual, and as usual was led back to my cell. Let me make it brief. This went on for three and a half years, every morning at half past nine. Every single day I assured the lady – who was, by the way, very pretty – that I was Ödön Berzsenyi, lawyer, from Budapest, and every single day she ordered me to confess that I was Major Schultze, the notorious German agent. It was enough to drive the sanest man crazy. That I did not go mad was due to the fact that every single evening – also on Sundays – exactly at eight o'clock, two guards took me to the flat of the pretty lieutenant, where I spent the night in the most delightful manner. At six in the morning I was taken back to my cell and at nine thirty I was taken before the lady who, in her official capacity, tried with great zeal to convince me that I was not Ödön Berzsenyi, but Major Schultze, the notorious German agent.

'After three and a half years, on a cold December night in 1946, my pretty lieutenant – whom in the meantime I had taught to speak Hungarian – spoke to me thus:

'"Listen, my darling Ödön. I have to go to Vienna on official business but on the way I shall stop off at Budapest and try to do something for you. Give me the address of your family and I shall obtain papers to prove that you are indeed Ödön Berzsenyi and not Major Schultze, the notorious German agent."

'You could have knocked me down with a feather – had I not been in bed – I was so surprised.

'"Then you know that I am Ödön Berzsenyi?" I asked her.

'"Of course, I know. That's why I want to get you released."

'"Won't you get into trouble, for helping to free the man they believe to be Schultze?" I asked her anxiously. I must confess, I didn't want anything to happen to my pretty lieutenant.

'"Don't be silly, darling," she laughed. "Did you notice those eighteen cells on the right and eighteen on the left? Well, each of them holds a Schultze. We have thirty-six Schultzes and you are the thirty-seventh. If we let you go we shall still have thirty-six."

'The next day my lieutenant left for Vienna and for the next three months I was questioned by a sergeant every morning at nine thirty. Then my lieutenant returned – with my papers. I was immediately released. On the last night I visited her a free man. Towards morning my pretty lieutenant became sentimental.

'"Look, darling, why do you want to go back to that dirty, poor, ruined Budapest? Isn't it better for you here, in Archangel? I have a lovely room, there is even a water tap in it . . ."

'I felt as if a chasm had opened at my feet. I mumbled something about my poor, sick, old father whom I wanted to see once more and finally we agreed that I would return. In the meantime she would obtain Soviet citizenship for me and we would live happily ever after . . . At least this is what I promised,' Berzsenyi added with some melancholy.

At this moment the lights went on again and we heard the bolt being pushed aside.

'Go on, it's only the store-keeper,' Gabori reassured Berzsenyi.

It was usually at this time that the store-keeper corporal appeared to select men for night-work. Usually he asked Istvan Todi, the prisoner responsible for order in the barracks, to appoint the men and Todi always chose the informers and the ordinary criminals, so we had nothing to fear.

'When I said goodbye to my lieutenant at the railway station,' Berzsenyi continued a little nervously, because of the light and the repeated interruptions, 'I cried real tears, which surprised even me. The trip from Archangel to Moscow took four days, that from Moscow to Ungvar two days, but the last thirty kilometres took six weeks.'

The corporal entered the barracks and without speaking to Todi, looked along the bunks.

'You, come along!' he pointed to three young men.

'On the Hungarian border I was arrested,' Berzsenyi said while we were all watching the corporal. 'They accused me of being Schultze, the notorious German agent . . .'

'. . . and you,' the corporal pointed at me. Then he looked at Berzsenyi, who immediately reached for his trousers.

'You stay where you are, Uncle,' said the corporal.

In spite of the fact that I was completely exhausted (strangely enough, our tiredness was much more difficult to bear during the hours of rest than at work) the corporal's choice gave me a certain amount of pleasure. The reason was vanity. The peasant corporal was looking for young men, the three he had selected were all under twenty. In the daytime, as an instinctive protection against the guards, the weather and hunger, I moved slowly, with sagging shoulders and bowed head, swinging the weight of my body from one foot to the other with deliberation, to seem older and weaker than I really was because, although the peasant lads who made up the majority of the AVO guards had been taught in party schools to hate the enemy, they had learned at home and in the village school that age should be respected. Only in the evening, after the lights were put out, did I straighten up and move freely as before. The corporal must have caught me out and this was why he thought me younger than Berzsenyi who was, in fact, a few years younger than I.

My joy increased when I found that we were going to the railway station of Recsk to unload coal. My companions were glad because they hoped to be able to collect cigarette butts and I because I hoped to see people in the village. I was yearning for the sight of people, particularly children. However, we were all disappointed. As soon as we had climbed into the lorry it began to rain, which spoilt the butts and drove people into their houses though it was only about eight thirty. I got a whiff of smoked bacon as we drove through the village, and breathed deeply of the smell of freshly baked bread. Then we reached the station and the sturdy little locomotive at the head of the freight train reminded me of my travels.

I was standing in one of the freight cars shovelling coal into a lorry. An AVO guard squatted in a corner of the car. As I started work he lit a cigarette, drew on it three times, then threw the almost whole cigarette on the ground at my feet. I did not pick it up. Already on our first day in Recsk my friends and I had decided that we would not permit ourselves to be humiliated. We were strengthened in our resolution by an empty filing card we had found one day on the dustheap. It was headed PERSONAL DATA OF PRISONER; and over the last two columns was printed: 'Does he smoke?' and 'Can he be bribed with cigarettes?'

The guard looked at me uncomprehendingly, then went on humming to himself. It seemed that my outing would end without anything interesting happening to me when suddenly a peasant appeared from behind the tracks. He noticed me immediately because I was standing under an arc lamp in the softly falling rain. When he came close he stopped and shook his fist at me:

'Now you've got what you deserved, you damned *kulak*!'

On the way back, under the tarpaulin, my companions laughed heartily about my adventure and kept calling me *kulak*. I laughed with them but inside, for the first time since my arrest, I felt real despair. I had borne my fate calmly, coolly, almost painlessly, more as a spectator than as a victim; but now I felt my strength deserting me.

We all hoped that the West had not forgotten us and that, one day, they would come and save us. We did not wonder when that would be – we knew it would not be too late – but each of us had a different vision of how it would occur. Garamvölgyi believed that the Americans would drop a detachment of marines in the field below the camp;

the marines would massacre the AVO guards in a few minutes, hang the camp commander, the political officer and the three detectives on the points of the star above the gate, and would carry us all off in aeroplanes. I dreamed that in the pale grey mist of early morning, American tanks would come rolling down the mountainside, flattening the barbed-wire fence. By then our guards would have run away and from one of the tanks a former army buddy would call my name. The staff officer among us thought that General Anders's army would land in Poland, supported by the British, and would rout the Russians from Poland and all the way down to Albania. Mennyhért Boka, a former Christian Party deputy, dreamed about a tiny aeroplane motor that the Americans would invent, so tiny that one could simply strap it to one's chest, extend one's arms and fly. They would drop such motors by parachute and we would all be in Vienna within twenty minutes; then Stalin would have to spread an iron net over Russia and the satellite countries all the way from Kamchatka to the Elbe. We played with these dreams as one plays with the idea of what fun one would have if one were invisible. Mennyhért Boka imagined that we would land in the Stephans Platz and there divide into two groups. The socialists would go to a café and the Catholics to church. Garamvölgyi planned to visit Trotsky's grave in Mexico City, and I dreamed about taking a flat in San Francisco, on Telegraph Hill.

These day-dreams were our only luxury, a mild drug or a glass of excellent wine before going to bed. Our moral attitude and emotional balance, however, were maintained by the circle of friends we collected. I have never had so many devoted, faithful and selfless friends, and even though our careers, professions, education, philosophy and political principles may have been fundamentally different, our moral outlooks were as similar as if our attitude were determined not by individual consciousness but by a common categorical imperative.

This phenomenon was less surprising to the other inhabitants of the camp than it was to myself who had belonged, both before and after my emigration, to a radical, democratic and socialist intellectual *élite* swimming against the tide – against the feudal and fascist tendencies of the majority – and who now found myself part of a national unity in which I had to sacrifice nothing of my original ideas. And this national unity did not stop at the fence of the camp. The regulars manning the watch-towers often threw us quick, conspiratorial glances when, in the course of our work, we approached the barbed-wire fence. We believed that this solidarity embraced the entire country and was valid not only for the present but also for the distant future. Should I perish, my fellow-prisoners would carry the memory of my name to every village of the country; and should we all perish, there would be a memorial above the collapsed mine bearing all our names. This was the most a man who had never aspired to being a hero could hope for.

This was why I felt such despair after the peasant had abused me at the railway. To be taken for a rich peasant in spite of my long, oval face and delicate, long hands was humiliating enough, but the perspective opened before me by those fists shaken at a political prisoner was simply terrifying. I had taken it for granted that our people would come out of the Soviet occupation as unscathed as it had once come out from the hundred and fifty years of the Turkish occupation. It would straighten its spine and except for a few Russian loanwords nothing would be left to remind us that they had been there. The five-pointed stars would be taken down and destroyed within an hour, as the crescent moons were once destroyed; the land would be distributed among the peasants as the lands of the pashas and beys had been distributed, and the communist teachings would leave no mark because no one had believed them anyway. The behaviour of the peasant and the use of the word *kulak* warned me of another possibility: that in ten or twenty years the communists could produce an entirely different new generation. This generation would use more or less the same words as mine, but these words would stand for entirely different ideas, or no ideas at all. Of Plato they would know only what the Soviet philosophical dictionary has to say about him: 'a hireling of the Athenian *bourgeoisie*', and they would know nothing of his works. The conditions they would call happiness and freedom would be, to me, equivalent to unhappiness and slavery. And that meant I would have lived in vain: the ideas of my kind and my generation would have been burnt in their witch's kitchen together with our dictionaries and encyclopedias, exactly as Orwell described it.

When the guard switched on the light and let us into the barracks four men were standing behind the door, among them North-Eastern Inrush and the hussar captain Tamas Purgly. The latter threw himself on his knees before the guard.

'Dear inspector, sir,' he begged, 'let me out to the outhouse, I can stand it no longer.' His frightening black moustache wobbled up and down like that of a capricorn beetle. His moustache was the great passion of his life, apart from eating. He used boot-blacking on it and twirled it and curled it whenever he had a moment's time.

'The hell I will!' the warder shouted and locked the door from the outside.

'Scoundrel!' hissed Purgly, sitting down quickly on the threshold. Only Porpak remained standing, a lanky old man who had a heart disease, a purple face, forget-me-not-blue eyes, a gaping baby mouth and a huge snub nose, and who moved like a ballet master. During the Horthy régime he had been a colonel in the police. His conspicuous appearance attracted the AVO lads as honey attracts bears and he received more kicks and slaps in a day than the rest of us in a week.

'Why scoundrels?' he asked Purgly, fidgeting as he stood. 'Six years ago I would have done the same to them.'

The lights went out. The barracks had settled down for the night and only a few were still awake: Istvan Todi, who squatted at a certain distance from the stove looking into the fire, Paul Musza, who walked up and down barefoot, his hands clasped on his stomach, his head bowed in meditation, and four men who were doing something around the stove, from where a strong smell of game came floating.

One of them was a red-faced cattle-merchant, the other a frighteningly dissipated-looking man called Zsoffka who every night tormented his old bunk-neighbour until the latter gave him his cigarettes and the little bread he had saved. About the third man, a certain Szanto, who was six feet tall and had a freckled moon-face, we knew only that he had been an AVO investigator at Miskolc whose greatest pleasure was to make the women whom he questioned sit on a hot stove. The cause for his arrest was that he did not share the loot with his buddies. These three were ostracized by everyone in the camp. The fourth man was even more disgusting. The colour of his slimy-brown, pock-marked face reminded one of the tobacco juice in a filthy cigarette holder, and his granite-coloured, swollen lips over black teeth were like the gate of hell: not Dante's passionate and noisy inferno but a puritanical hell which devours its mute victims in haughty silence. I had noticed him on the first morning and had asked him who he was. His name was Jamnitzki and he had been director, producer and owner of the flea-circus in the Budapest Luna Park. He was arrested because he had seduced the wife of the party secretary of the Light Entertainment National Enterprise – a pastime which he regarded as light entertainment but not so the party secretary.

At first I wouldn't believe him, but when he told me how he kept his fleas in a flat glass container to make them lose the habit of jumping and how he fabricated the tiny coaches they drew from gold thread, I remembered that when I had last visited Luna Park before the war I had seen these rococo coaches, and Jamnitzki's face came back to me. He had a cheap but amusing sense of humour and therefore, though he was despised by everyone, the barracks forgave him his friends and his minor squealings. He never informed on important, political affairs, or so he repeatedly assured us. When his victims were beaten up, he sat with them, confessed that he had told on them and comforted them with a few good jokes.

That afternoon he and his friends had been working together in the forest and had discovered a squirrel. At Jamnitzki's suggestion they felled the neighbouring trees and then brought down the squirrel with a well-aimed stone. Informers were also hungry – though not quite as hungry as we were. They obtained salt from the cook, and some bacon – probably in return for information – and were now engaged in preparing a meal. The skinny, reddish-brown, miserable body of the squirrel lay in a dixie on top of the stove among slivers of bacon and a few juniper-berries used for seasoning. As I went closer the smell of food hit me sharply in the face as if they were cooking venison, not a squirrel. My palate tingled but at the same time nausea was creeping up my throat. The light streaming from the open door of the stove cut a mauve tunnel into the darkness of the barracks. The four rascals stood at the entrance of that tunnel like four thieves about to quarrel over the loot. Further back, in the semi-darkness of the tunnel, squatted Todi with his hands in his lap, like a godly hermit impervious to temptation.

I stopped immediately behind Todi. Suddenly a wild, animal desire to taste that meat shook my entire body. 'If I speak to them,' I thought, 'they will feel honoured and offer me a piece of meat. At least a leg! But then, tomorrow, the whole camp will know that I humiliated myself before these informers. This is the time to show how strong you are, George.' Until then I had played the hero, however hungry I was. When Garamvölgyi had brought us a whole dixie full of slop under his coat Gabori and I had declared that we wouldn't touch it. A week earlier Helvetius, the cook, had entered the barracks with some leftover soup and had beckoned to me to come and get it. It was wonderful, thick soup from the bottom of the cauldron, at least four hundred calories! 'Give it to someone else,' I had said loudly, for the whole barracks to hear, though I was faint with hunger. And I had felt that this refusal gave me four thousand calories of self-confidence. Only where snails were concerned did I know no pride. The entire camp was collecting snails for me, and this was not regarded as greediness, on the contrary, everyone admired me for it: oh, this gourmet who got into the habit of eating snails in France and won't do without them even at Recsk! When I was given a snail I had to control myself not to swallow those thirty grammes of animal protein on the spot. I put it in my pocket for twenty-four hours until it had discharged its bowel, and then threw it into a hot soup or vegetable stew, but never into my morning coffee, however much I felt like doing so.

I put my hand on Todi's shoulder.

'It is ready, we can take it out,' said Jamnitzki.

Todi looked up at me with his burning eyes and grasped my hand.

'The Holy Virgin,' he said, 'promised me that we would all be free by Easter.'

I remained silent though he was obviously waiting for a reply. He

– I said to myself – doesn't smell the squirrel, perhaps he does not even see it. But for me this squirrel is the whole world. If I eat some of it that means the end of my prestige not only in the eyes of my companions but also in my own. First to be called a *kulak*, and then this! I would have nothing left to hold me up but would collapse like a folding rule. This squirrel is the sea-water of the shipwrecked sailor, if he partakes of it he dies. What can I win? A quarter of a squirrel, one hundred calories at the most. But even if they offered me not a quarter of a squirrel but four hundred squirrels . . .

I felt as if a strong hand were trying to disconnect my brain, the way one disconnects the electric current in one's home before going off on a holiday. If the hand succeeded I would throw myself on that squirrel with bared teeth and bloodshot eyes. Fortunately at this moment the guard opened the door of the barracks.

'Do you have a daughter, old man?' he asked one of the men waiting at the door, the mild, rotund and erudite Béla Solymos, the only member of the Upper House who had, at the time, voted against declaring war on the Soviet Union. The guard's voice was kind and he sounded really interested.

'I have an adopted daughter,' the old gentleman replied.

'What is her name?'

'Clara,' Solymos answered, smiling.

The guard hesitated a moment.

'You see,' Todi whispered in my ear, 'there are still decent men even in the AVO. He is bringing a message.'

'In that case,' the guard said, 'tell me how you f— your Clara?'

For a few seconds there was absolute silence.

'Well, will you or won't you tell me?'

'No.'

'If you don't, you won't go to the outhouse. Well?'

'No.'

'If you change your mind you can knock on the door,' the guard said, and went out.

The four rascals were standing around the stove eating the squirrel. The violence of temptation weakened to a point where I was again able to speak. Paul Musza walked by noiselessly and when he reached the end of the barracks, he turned back. I raised my hand and stopped him.

'What is your opinion on squirrel eating, Paul?'

'St John the Baptist ate locusts. Why shouldn't the son of man eat squirrel if he is hungry? I wish there were a hundred squirrels for each of us every day.'

I smiled and in a moment forgot the entire squirrel problem. Then I sat down on the ground next to Todi and watched the huge shadows thrown by the legs of the four rascals that crossed like the supporting pillars of a bridge in construction. Suddenly I heard Purgly's grating, throaty voice from the corner.

'I am surprised at you, my dear Uncle Béla. You are a gentleman and therefore it is your duty to consider your friends. We have no intention of shitting in our pants because your false modesty or whatever it is prevents you . . .'

'Speak for yourself, captain, not for me . . .' North-Eastern Inrush interrupted.

'And I am simply amazed at your impertinence!' cried Porpak. 'I am surprised, Tamas, that with views like yours you could serve with the hussars. Or rather, I am not surprised. At forty you were still only a captain, though you are a relative of Horthy's. That in itself explains . . .'

His words were swallowed up by the barking of the police dogs. The guards were changed and from the neighbouring barracks the men were let out to the outhouse. Todi rose. It was time to go to sleep.

I undressed, kneeling between Egri's and Gabori's legs. Only Garamvölgyi was still awake, or had been awakened by the barking of the dogs. He raised himself on his elbow and looked out of the small window.

'The daily circus performance,' he said as I crept up to him.

Some twenty AVO guards were standing under the window in the strong light of the searchlights directed at them from the watch-tower. It took a few minutes until my eyes got used to the blaze, and I could distinguish what was going on down there. Our fellow-prisoners were crawling in the mud on all fours with their bottoms bared, one behind the other. First came Uncle Géza Toth, then Porpak, Purgly and finally Solymos. Each had to push his nose into the bottom of the one in front of him, with the exception of Uncle Toth, who raised his head desperately into the air like a turtle when it comes to a wall and does not know what to do.

'Keep going, scoundrels, keep going, murderers! Purgly, push your moustache into Porpak's arse!' shouted the captain of the guards, a short, bigheaded little man with a crooked back whom we called Gnome. His voice was hoarse with excitement and pleasure. 'Solymos! You can get up and go to the outhouse! But first tell us how you f— your wife! Do you hear me? Answer!'

'I hear you but I won't answer!' croaked Solymos from between Purgly's buttocks which looked like two dirty, wrinkled handkerchiefs hanging from a nail.

While I watched the scene from the corner of the window thoughts that I registered with shame chased each other in my mind. First: that my bowels were functioning faultlessly, consequently nothing like this could happen to me. Second: that my sleep was so healthy and deep that I usually never heard the barking of the dogs except in my dreams. Thirdly: why was I looking out of the window? From sadism or because I wanted to write about it all one day? To answer the last question I would have to make up my mind whether I still believed that I would survive. Or can one be simply curious – curious without a trace of moral indignation?

'Awful!' I whispered in Garamvölgyi's ear.

'It goes on every night.'

'Every night?' I asked, unbelieving.

'Yes, every night. Not only here but in every camp of the country and in every camp of nine other countries from the Elbe to Indo-China, what is more, not for the last three months but ever since 1945, and in the Soviet Union for seventeen years more. And it will still go on when we have been under the ground for a long, long time.'

The guards fell on the four men, beat them, kicked them, pushed their faces into the mud. Suddenly I felt as if I were watching some horrible performance from a comfortable box. I crept back to my place, lay down and stuck my fingers in my ears. However, when

Porpak began to sing a well-known drinking song at the top of his voice, I could not help hearing.

Red wine, red wine, I've been drinking red wine
My shining star, my darling.
Now where are my feet, oh where, oh where?

The guards laughed so hard their sides were almost splitting. Porpak was standing in the middle of a long, narrow, slippery plank which bridged the stream. One of the guards put his foot on one end of the plank and made it jump up and down, but the sick man, lit up by the searchlights, straightened his back and, his mouth foaming, sang on, balancing himself with theatrical movements:

Now where are my feet, oh where, oh where?
But the girls still love me, the girls are here,
My shining star, my darling.

'Look,' Garamvölgyi whispered, 'he is like the leading man of a musical comedy. Or a troubadour who came back an old man from the Holy Land to sing under the window of his beloved. Or he could be the Romeo of a travelling company. Or perhaps Henry IV of the Holy Roman Empire under Canossa. The sleet goes very well with the scenery and in the tower not the guards but Countess Mathilda is having a high old time with Pope Gregory VII . . .'

'All right, I've had enough world history for today,' I whispered furiously and lay down.

The singing soon stopped, Garamvölgyi fell asleep and after a little while the four old men were herded back into the barracks. Garamvölgyi ground his teeth in his sleep, Egri groaned and I was still awake. Musza was still walking up and down in his bare feet. Every time he passed my bunk I heard him murmur something. I could distinguish a few Latin and Hungarian words. After a while I realized that he was repeating the Lord's Prayer again and again, mixing Hungarian words with his faulty Latin.

'*. . . et ne nosin in tentacione, my good Lord . . .*'

The more desperately I tried to fall asleep the less I succeeded. My fingers contracted convulsively into fists, my left leg grew numb and only the burning pain in my thigh reassured me that it was still attached to my body.

'*. . . sicut dimittimus debitoribus omnibus* AVO *guards, nam tuum est . . .*'

At any other time Musza's prayer would have moved me but now it only increased my fury. I decided to ask him whether he truly believed that such weapons – prayer and incantation – were of any use in the fight against Evil? I was about to get up and ask him when I suddenly realized that we had no other weapon. This, unexpectedly, calmed me down and I fell asleep.

We were climbing up the steep mountainside without hurry in a long, single line. Half to the left, beyond the deep valley, we were greeted, as we were every morning, by a Japanese water-colour: the grey of the snowy, wooded mountain range with its blue and black dots. To the right, at a few yards from us, bare hawthorn bushes followed the snow-covered path. Between the gnarled twigs the setting moon appeared white and round. At my every step it leaped up and down as if a hawthorn bush's long hands were playing basket-ball with it. Above my head the still mountains and the dancing moon were bridged by an unbelievably limpid early morning sky with a few large but already blinking stars.

Almost at every step I raised my head to admire the sky. The enthralling change of colours we had watched in the autumn was repeated in every season, though in a specific way. In the winter the beech trees were the most beautiful of all, because their crowns put forth swelling buds as early as January, making the tree look like a large pink puff. In May we sniffed all day long at the strong smell of acacia brought by the breeze from the opposite hillside. In summer we concentrated on mushrooms – not the edible ones which we devoured by the dozen whenever the guards looked away, but the much less utilitarian toadstools which, with their mad colours and odd shapes, fitted so perfectly into the half-crazy fairy-tale world of our imaginations.

In the meantime our conversations were gaining a growing hold on us. We were all losing weight and strength but while the solitary, taciturn and friendless among us lay on their bunks in the evening full of despair, gazing with dull eyes at the beams of the ceiling, we sat on our mattresses to talk like well-balanced, cheerful ghosts round an imaginary chimney. We could no longer restrict our conversations to the hours after dark. Towards spring, while for weeks we were carrying stones down from the mountain and up to the commander's hill where we were building a house of culture for the AVO, or in the summer when seven of us were harnessed to a cart like horses to carry stones to the double serpentine lead linking the gate of the camp to the quarry according to Professor Sarkany's plans, we talked almost all day. And when I had to cart sand alone or was working in a spot so exposed that we couldn't talk because of the proximity of the *nachalniki*, I would ponder our conversation of the night before, or wonder what subject to discuss next. When the sun shone or we had beans for dinner I could usually think logically; but when it rained, or when I had no cigarettes, or when the fermented sauerkraut we had for dinner ran bubbling through my bowels, I would weave loose associations around my themes and my thoughts went round and round it in widening circles. The weakening of my body was accompanied by the highly agreeable phenomena of weightlessness and spiritualization, so that my fate, my misery, my tormentors and my work seemed at first secondary, later irrelevant, negligible, and then, slowly, almost imaginary. Time was filled with problems of history, aesthetics and philosophy, with our conversations, with the phenomena of nature, so there was none left for anything else and the days flew as though Nausicaa and her girls were playing ball with the golden apple of the sun and the silver apple of the moon beyond the illuminated edges of the horizon.

Thus, between the two poles of our life, one of which we called (after Knut Hamsun) spiritual fornication with nature, and the other of which was the Magic Mountain world of our conversations, we skipped the plane between, which we defined as the 'Zolaesque component'. The everyday life of the camp was so monotonous, anyway, that it was not worth noticing, and we banned everything connected with the camp from our conversations. Only in the morning, when, panting, we climbed the steep hillside, would I recapitulate the more important events.

Apart from a few changes in our way of life and in the AVO personnel we noted only two significant events – and even the change in our way of life was only relative, consisting of the fact that water had been laid on to the camp so that washrooms and water closets were built in the barracks, and there were punishment cells instead of a cave. On the other hand we had to listen all night to the wailing of the people put in short chains for punishment. They built a kitchen and a hospital for us, but in the new kitchen they cooked the same old beans, potatoes and cabbage, while in the hospital the prisoner-doctors lacked even the most important medicines and instruments and had no authority to keep the sick in bed. Neither did it make much difference that the lieutenant commanding the camp was replaced by a captain, and the anti-Semitic, thieving political officer, a gentleman, by an arrogant and sadistic Jew.

The first of the two important events was the non-occurrence of an expected series of happenings. Almost a year had gone by since Doctor Acs's prognosis, and according to him ninety-five per cent of the camp's population should by now lie buried in the lime-pit where my friends and I sometimes squatted to talk and where Florian Wrangel prepared his horoscopes. No one had yet died of starvation. The death rate was surprisingly low. The old man with the catheter died of cancer; old Porpak had a heart attack one night while singing in the middle of the plank and fell dead into the streamlet; an electrician called Janke was shot dead by an AVO guard when, on the orders of another guard, he was running towards the barbed-wire fence to fix a telephone line; one of my fellow-prisoners was crushed by a rock weighing several tons while working in the quarry, and another went out of his mind and died soon after being taken to the prison hospital. As the population of the camp had risen in the meantime, with the arrival of a new trainload of prisoners from Kistarcsa, to thirteen hundred, the death rate was less than four per thousand in fifteen months: which, according to the optimists, insured our lives for another hundred years.

The other really noteworthy event took place on May 20, 1951, when eight prisoners escaped. Previously, when discussing the question, we had all agreed that it was impossible to escape from Recsk. Our barracks were surrounded by a double barbed-wire fence, and between the two barbed-wire fences extended a ploughed strip of no-man's-land five metres wide. Beyond the fence stood watch-towers, forty metres apart. The camp as a whole was again surrounded by a double barbed-wire fence with watch-towers all round it. When, in the evening, we marched from the larger corral into the smaller, the guards remained in the outer watch-towers until the roll call was over and we were safely locked in. In the morning the procedure was the same, only in reverse. After roll call, when we marched out into the larger corral, the guards were permitted to leave their places in the inner watch-towers. To disarm the guards and break out, as people so often do in films, seemed utterly hopeless. In the camp the guards carried revolvers, adding submachine-guns only when they took a party of prisoners outside the barbed-wire enclosure to cut wood in the forest or to work at the spring which supplied the camp's water. But even had we laid hands on three or four submachine-guns and thirty or forty revolvers, escape would still have been impossible because the guards in the watch-towers followed our movements closely and would have mowed us down with their machine-guns, and the guards at the gate would have turned on us the flame-throwers waiting there for just such an opportunity.

So the plan elaborated by Gyula Michnai, a tall young cadet with a high, white forehead and thin blond hair, was all the more brilliant. In the carpenter's shop he carved himself a machine-gun from wood, fitting pieces of tin where steel should have shown. Then, one Sunday morning, he went to the tailor's and the shoemaker's which were run by men who were in on his plan, and where the guards had their suits pressed and their boots mended, and dressed himself from head to foot in AVO uniform. Then, pulling the AVO cap down over his eyes, and herding seven of his friends, including the heads of the tailor's shop and the shoemaker's shop, he walked to the gate. There he commanded the soldiers guarding the gate to let them out. The soldiers opened the gate but one of the conspirators took fright and refused to go on. Michnai kicked him in the small of his back with such force that he flew several metres beyond the gate, thus establishing his identity beyond any eventual doubt, and the eight men disappeared in the woods. Under their prison clothes they were all wearing navy blue overalls, the kind worn by workers, and they had agreed in advance that they would not go home, but would scatter at once in eight directions, but all heading north in an attempt to reach the Czechoslovak frontier before night. There they were to turn towards the West and try to reach Austria.

They chose a Sunday because on weekdays there was always a roll call at noon, before we got our dinner, while on Sundays we worked until three or four o'clock and were counted only before being locked in for the night. When the political officer – a tall grocer's assistant from Sajoszentpéter – discovered the flight at five in the afternoon, nine hours after it occurred, he delivered a short, nervous lecture in the barracks, saying that we had shown ourselves unworthy of socialist re-education and the good will of the AVO and would now get a taste of the fist of the working class. Later the barracks were searched and those who possessed overalls received a few blows. The guard Dentures discovered the green shelf North-Eastern Inrush had made for himself, on which he kept his dixie, a few crusts in a dirty handkerchief, empty shoe-polish boxes and a few once beautiful but now wrinkled wild chestnuts, tore it off the wall and hit North-Eastern Inrush over the head with it. However, he gave him back the shoe-polish box in which he kept his tobacco. We had to strip to the skin and, as usual, the pockets of the old prisoners yielded a wide variety of completely needless objects. They could not get used to possessing nothing but their clothes and their dixie, and would collect whatever they could find: coloured pebbles, bits of wire, boot-nails, empty match-boxes, and berries. The AVO guards slapped them about a bit and took away these valuable possessions, but we knew the old men would immediately begin collecting again, as they always did. Finally the guards left and we were locked in again.

We climbed up on the upper bunks and looked out towards the hillside opposite where, in the damask-blue of the May afternoon an AVO battalion was advancing with armoured cars. We were madly excited, beside ourselves with joy, laughing into our mattresses so as not to be heard by the guards outside. We received no dinner and no supper, but cigarette smoke filled the barrack and we talked and talked until late into the night.

Our joy fed on several sources. First, we were happy that eight of our fellow-prisoners (with whom we completely identified ourselves, so much so that we felt almost as brave as they) had succeeded in fooling the AVO with all its security measures, severity, power, flame-throwers, machine-guns and barbed-wire fences. Their act turned the secret police, so proud of its system of isolation and the terror it created through the entire country, into a lot of clowns. It did occur to me that they might kill us all during the night but I felt not a trace of fear. It was strange to discover that my hate for the AVO was stronger than my love of life.

Another cause of joy was that we knew the escape would cost the camp commander, the political officer and his three detectives their jobs. Some of us hoped that they would be put into our barracks as prisoners the same night. Others thought they would be sent to the Yugoslav border, which was equivalent to a death sentence. We all hoped that at least one of the escapees would reach Vienna and from there go on to Germany. The four hundred kilometres to Vienna would take eight to ten days on foot, and within two weeks he would inform the West over the radio and in newspapers of what was going on at Recsk. Michnai knew the names of the thirteen hundred prisoners by heart. It seemed probable that the Hungarian government would issue a statement that it was all a pack of lies, that there were no internment camps in Hungary and consequently no punitive camp at Recsk, but we were certain that simultaneously they would improve the food and the treatment as they usually did in such cases. And from our comrade's broadcast our friends and relatives would learn that we were still alive.

For a few days we were restricted to barracks and the doors were opened only when the food was brought in. From time to time half a dozen AVO guards would come in and beat us up, or would make us lie on our bunks and jump about on our chests. But they could not kill our joy. Our only complaint was that our cigarettes ran out. Szuha, a taciturn provincial public notary with a head like a lion, held out longest, because he had exchanged his bread ration for cigarettes. His neighbours warned him that he would die of starvation, but he told them to mind their own business and went on smoking furiously. For a day or two we got smokes by cutting our cigarette holders in two lengthwise and smoking the nicotine-juice smeared on paper. Then we scraped off the inside of the cigarette holder with pieces of glass and smoked that.

A few days later we were again driven out to work. There was no improvement in our food and we received more blows and kicks than before. Soon, as was to be expected, they replaced the camp commander, the political officer and the three detectives. One day, in the summer, we were assembled in the square between the barracks and were officially informed that seven of the escapees had been recaptured and that Michnai had been shot dead by the frontier guards on the Austrian border. We did not believe a word of this, but still found it rather disturbing. The summer went by and then the autumn; we were rapidly losing weight and strength, but nothing happened. We rarely mentioned Michnai although we thought of him often, and our hopes, though waning, were not yet dead. We imagined that he had gone to work for peasants in Czechoslovakia, a few weeks here, a few weeks there, getting closer and closer to the Austrian border. Someone remembered him talking about his student days and how he had once spent an entire summer camping in a forest near the Danube, hiding in the bushes, hitting stray geese over the head with a volume of Gibbon and baking them in clay. This was how we saw him now: in the summer hidden in the reed-banks of the Danube, in the autumn hiding in fragrant lofts, fed and loved by peasant girls who passed him on from village to village, always towards the West.

Since water had been laid on in the camp our supply of information had become continuous and we no longer needed Gabori's heroic and romantic methods in order to learn something about the world outside. The sewer discharged into a trench within the fence and the trench led into the stream. The AVO made Knocke, the almost completely deaf and one-legged former army major – whom they considered useless for any other kind of work – stand at the mouth of the sewer and watch the refuse coming out. He took no notice of the rubbish or of the soft, bright yellow excrement of the prisoners, but when he saw a fat, brown sausage coming along, obviously the product of an AVO guard – he shifted his weight on to his good leg and used his crutch to fish out the quarter- or half-page of *Szabad Nép* that swam behind it. He dried the loot under his mattress and on the following morning put it in my pocket. In the evening I read it behind Florian Wrangel's broad back and returned the ragged bits of paper to the old man. He himself never read these pieces of newspaper because, he yelled in the stentorian tones of the deaf – the Americans were idiots and the Russians murderers. He used the paper to roll cigarettes.

I never found anything relating to Michnai. One day, as we were marching back from work, we caught sight in the dusk of seven men, chained together, on the hill where the commander's house stood. A few minutes later a sergeant called Mongol came into the barracks and asked for volunteers to beat the captured escapees to death. 'These scoundrels are responsible for your situation!' he said. 'You would have been released long ago if they hadn't run away!' Nobody stepped forward. Then Mongol walked up to the tall, yellow-haired former army major Laszlo Téti who, with his hooked nose and abrupt gestures, reminded one of a Roman centurion. When Téti declared that he would rather be beaten to death than do the beating Mongol kicked him in the groin. While he was looking for other victims, an AVO officer called to him that they already had the required number of volunteers.

Some fifteen people were walking towards the hill, mostly *nachalniki*. One of them was Dezsö Tamas, the chief *nachalnik* He was a middle-sized man with rusty hair and a few lonely freckles in the corners of his eyes who had grown a large, soft belly while we had thinned to skeletons. Another was our new *nachalnik*, a large, handsome smuggler who loathed me and had several times made the AVO guards beat me up because I had 'destructive conversations' with my friends in the evenings, instead of telling them about my tramp of a wife. Another was the head cook Lepcses, a squat butcher with a blond moustache, who at dawn, when we were marching out bent double with exhaustion, liked to stand in the kitchen entrance with a whole cigarette in his mouth watching us and the morning star overhead, with an ironic half-smile. In one hand he would hold a dixie full of strong black coffee and with his other he would delve deeply into a ten-pound bag of sugar – the daily ration of thirteen hundred prisoners.

'So you're the ones,' the lieutenant said contemptuously, and spat on the ground at their feet. The fifteen, however, stood undismayed, then set out along the muddy path to the hill-top, shaking their fists, giggling and encouraging each other. In the twilight we could still discern the seven prisoners waiting motionless, their heads bowed, under the giant oak. An hour later the *nachalniki* returned and towards midnight we watched the Black Maria standing in the focus of search-lights and the seven prisoners helping each other to climb in. They were in a pitiful state – but alive.

On the hillside next morning instead of swearing and grumbling as usual, we pointed appreciative fingers at the hoary trees and the full moon, or just sighed. Amidst all this beauty we forgot the more important and more practical blessings – that there was no wind and almost no frost.

Further up, at mining level, a new delight awaited us. Three hitherto undiscerned snow-capped sugar-loaves shone bright above the panorama framed by the Gömör–Szepes ore-mountains. For the last fifteen months we had climbed up here every single day but we had never yet seen a trace of these peaks. We soon agreed that one was the High Tatra, another the Iglo Alps. What the third might be nobody knew.

'Like the three hills in the Hungarian coat of arms,' said Egri as we stood waiting outside the toolshed.

'Not on your life!' protested Elek Pokomandy, professor of history, who wore a red-and-white checked tea-towel round his neck for warmth. 'The hills in the Hungarian coat of arms are green and joined together. These are white and separate . . .'

'I'll separate your heads from your shoulders!' piped a squeaky voice down behind the line. The sergeant's presence was no surprise, our noses had been aware of him ever since we had left the enclosure. We knew without turning that it was Dentures, because the stench of rancid hair-oil mixed with the cheap scent he used distinguished him from his colleagues.

'Allot them their jobs, Talian,' the squeaky voice went on, 'and then get a move on, you bastards!'

We fell silent. The stone-breakers picked up their sledgehammers, the hewers their chipping hammers and the loaders their forks. Egri, I and about ten others were given no tools. The cloud of scent receded. Dentures must have gone into the hut to sit by the stove.

The foreman paired me up with Egri: our job was to carry stone to the breakers. We were both glad of the assignment because while we were carrying the stone it was safe to talk, and we had to load up on the edge of the mining level, behind a large heap of stone, where we could rest at every turn for a minute or two. We regarded this job as a gift of God, 'the most agreeable pastime in the most painful situation', as Egri used to say.

'Let's decide now what we shall talk about,' begged Egri as we took hold of the shafts of the stretcher and set out towards the stone pile. He liked to make plans and always insisted that we stick to them. I often made fun of him because of it, for in this intellectual planned economy I discerned a remnant of Egri's communist training, the belief that man's spiritual requirements can be determined with the same exactitude as his physical requirements, and that these spiritual requirements are independent of man himself, of the opportunity and the momentary mood.

'What would you like to talk about?' I asked him politely. I almost asked him 'How many syllables of poetry, in your opinion, is one man's daily requirement?' but I liked Egri very much and had no intention of hurting his feelings.

'Begin where you left off last night, when you were quoting the words of the Barbarian king from Plato's *Charmides*, that certain conversations cure the soul. Then talk about Africa, the African summer . . . Have you read Aragon's book, *Communist Man*? Yes?

Absolute rubbish, wasn't it? He says that communists represent a higher morality . . . Talk about that too, it's good for a laugh . . . Then you could continue with a subject you once mentioned. The women in fiction with whom you have been in love . . .'

We put the stretcher down in the snow and looked around. It would have been difficult to imagine a spot more ideal than our loading place for the day. On one side, in a half-circle, there was the rock wall, in front of us a huge pile of rock, and on the other side the precipice. It was impossible for the guards to keep an eye on us. I knelt down in the snow and suddenly realized how exhausted, how terribly weak I was. Egri remained upright, his bull-neck thrust forward, his smile triumphant.

We loaded the stretcher with big chunks of rock and started back.

'Let's begin,' said Egri behind me. 'After all we have only two hours.'

'What do you mean, two hours. We have twelve.'

'Everything is relative,' Egri declared pompously. 'Last night Zoli Nyeste lectured us on the relativity of time. If you sit in a spaceship that advances at the speed of light towards a fixed star, your heartbeats will slow down and so will your watch. Four years later you turn back and in eight years you are back on earth. But on earth twenty thousand years have gone by in the meantime and you have aged only by eight years.'

We advanced with the gait of drunken sailors on the uneven, rocky ground but knew that we could not fall because our heavy load nailed us to the ground as if we were walking on soles of lead. When we unloaded near the breakers I turned back to Egri.

'All right, but what is the connection with the length of the workday?'

'Time is relative not only objectively, but also subjectively. If they had put me on this job with anyone else for a partner, the day would be forty-eight hours long. With you it is only two hours long. Now what about Plato?'

We threw down the stretcher and knelt by it. A few yards away a curiously shaped andesite rock rose from the snow like a heavy, monumental desk, the desk of the boss. As if some giant had kicked it askew it looked, from the side, like a regular rhombus, but its surface was square and smooth. I thought of Michnai searching the snow-covered underbrush for hazelnuts. He finds a handful but they are all hollow and he throws them angrily away. I was in no mood to talk about Plato, Egri must have misunderstood me the night before as he also misunderstood the general purpose of our talks. In this respect he dived from his former materialism, straight into the transcendental: I insisted on conversation in order to preserve a certain degree of human dignity while we were slowly starving to death; Egri, on the other hand, believed that our conversation would save us from starving to death.

'I would rather talk about the women in literature with whom I was in love,' I said. 'I feel weak and in the mood for day-dreams.'

I let Egri take the front shafts of the stretcher and took the rear ones myself. The man doing the talking always walked behind. During our first trip I talked about Grushenka in *The Brothers Karamazov.* We unloaded quickly and hurried back to our loading place because close to the breakers the *nachalnik* Talian was driving a group of twenty prisoners who were putting down rails for the miners' trucks. Behind the pile I spoke about Gyton in *Trimalchio's Feast.* On our third trip the sun rose from behind the mountains and when we got back behind our heap a lovely surprise was awaiting us: a lizard, sunning itself on the blue surface of the desk-shaped rock. We loved these beautiful, lazy, yellow and black lizards that appeared once in a while in the quarry. We never tired of watching the strange, slow movement as they lifted one forepaw into the air and then simply forgot it there. At such times their foot reminded one of the tiny helpless hand of a baby.

A few more turns and I was out of fiction heroines. I went on talking, though, about Botticelli's Venus, Nefertiti from the Cairo museum and the unforgettable Aphrodite of Kyrene, all of whom I loved.

'Do you ever add a head to Aphrodite or a body to Nefertiti in your imagination?' asked Egri.

'Never,' I replied with deep conviction.

Every time we returned to our loading site we noticed with pleasure that our lizard was still there, sunning itself on the blue stone. We counted the trips, as usual, and after the twelfth took a long rest. When we set out with the sixteenth load we came upon an unexpected, astonishing sight. It seemed as if the prisoners working on mining level had suddenly all been turned to stone. The breakers sat motionless with their hammers raised, the loaders and railworkers stood petrified, all gazing towards the edge of the mining level. The only moving thing in the whole tableau was the lion-headed notary, Szuha, who exchanged his bread ration for cigarettes. He was walking calmly, deliberately through the deep snow towards the forest.

'Szuha! Where are you going? Don't you know you are not allowed to leave your place of work? Come back here or I'll kick your bloody arse!' shouted Talian, beside himself with rage. His big hands were balled into fists but he made no move to follow the notary.

But Szuha paid no attention to him. He walked on, leaving a straight track behind him in the snow, and somehow his movements no longer had any resemblance to ours. Even his head was held high, not bowed like that of the other prisoners. This is how, when still free, he must have walked on winter Sunday mornings going to church or to the pub: with calm dignity, taking deep breaths from the clean, fresh air, thrusting the point of his boots into the snow as if he were trying its thickness or hardness. He took perhaps twenty more steps and then, without a sound, he collapsed.

In a second Talian was at his side.

'Trying to fool me, are you, old peasant exploiter? You won't get away with it!' he screamed, kicking the notary in the side. When the latter did not move he gazed down at him wonderingly, then lifted the inert body on to his shoulder and carried him back to the others.

'Musza, Czebe, Todi, Jonas!' he yelled. 'Take this bastard down to the infirmary. Report to the sergeant-major that he collapsed. What are you staring at? Get a move on! And you,' he turned to the others, 'what are you waiting for? You keep moaning all day long and feel sorry for yourselves, but not one of you has kicked the bucket! Not one, not one . . .' he screamed, looking at us with angry, reproachful eyes.

We made seven turns without saying a word; took no rest and forgot even our lizard. When we stopped beside Pokomandy with our eighth load, the professor of history raised his arm, which meant that we should wait a minute, he wanted to talk to us.

'The boys are back,' he whispered. 'Acs said Szuha is beyond help. Defatigation.'

'What the heck is defatigation?' asked Egri.

'Death by starvation. But communist etiquette forbids us to call anything by its name.'

For a while we worked in silence, but finally Egri gave voice to the opinion that if Szuha died, it was his own fault. He who exchanges his bread for cigarettes, dies. We do not exchange our bread for cigarettes, consequently we shall not die. After this syllogism he suggested that we light a cigarette at the next turn, at the fire Talian had built for himself. This was the only legal means of stopping work for a moment, the only excuse the AVO tolerated. We had to urinate with the shafts of the stretcher in our hands and its rope around our neck, like horses, and if we received permission to defecate we had to climb down the slope and squat on a pole laid over a trench on the edge of the forest where an AVO man by the name of Dücskö hid among the trees watching our behinds to make sure we hadn't come down merely for a rest. If he caught someone cheating he would kick his bottom black and blue.

The half cigarette put me in a better mood and on the way back I recalled some of my forgotten loves: Diane de Poitiers and the fair Lucrezia Borgia as she looked in the fresco on the wall of Pope Alexander VI's room at the Castle of St Angelo; Baudelaire's great love, the courtesan Madame de Sabatier, Titian's Diana, Giorgione's Venus, Furini's Magdalen . . . The lizard was still there, relaxing in the sun. We knelt down in the inch-thick snow and I continued my day-dreaming. I had been talking happily for about fifteen minutes when I was suddenly struck by the idea that as far as I was concerned, these imaginary women were no more attainable than living ones – that I was but a ghost at a lovers' tryst. I weighed scarcely ninety pounds, my ribs stuck out like an old, neglected garden fence on which my heart drummed wildly, like a desperate fist. Eight weeks or ten, and we would all be dead.

'That's all,' I said curtly. 'These are the portraits I once loved.'

The sunshine, however, was far too beautiful, the lizard flicked out its long, narrow tongue, the clay beneath the snow clung tenderly to our knees and Egri did not understand my sudden change of mood.

'All right,' he said, 'then talk about Aragon's book. What was it that moron said about the superior morality of the communists?'

'What did he say?' I thought automatically. I closed my eyes and suddenly Aragon's face emerged before me as I had seen it twelve years before in Paris. It was a rather attractive face and I felt an overwhelming desire to make it look squarely at the truth. What shall I tell him if we meet again? Won't it be time wasted to talk to him at all? But my feelings were too violent, my imagination too extravagant, to stick to one subject for long. Suddenly, behind Aragon's features I saw the Place de la Concorde, cars going round and round the fountain, girls, foreigners sitting in taxis, hurrying students with books under their arms and again the cars going round and round the Concorde, regardless of whether I was alive or dead. Behind my closed lids my eyes embraced the Place de la Concorde, focusing on the Obelisk, and all the while I felt the unusually warm December sun on my face like the pressure of a light hand. And then I caught a whiff of patchouli, as sharp and cruel as if I had stuck my nose into a bottle of ammonia.

My eyes flew open and I met Egri's horrified glance. It was too late. Dentures was advancing towards us along the quarry face. He dug his pink, pointed nose into the air and gaped at us with his rounded lips. Although I was badly frightened I suddenly recalled where I had seen this medieval face before. It was in the paintings of Dutch masters. He looked like one of the Roman soldiers under the Cross. Not one of the evil-faces, throwing dice for Christ's cape, but one gaping in the background, bored and indifferent.

He was swinging a hatchet in his hand but didn't say anything. This, as we knew, was a dangerous sign. If only he would shout! If only he would abuse us! But no. This meant that he would kick us in the belly, beat us to a pulp, kick us again. In our terror we forgot to rise. Yet we knew that staying on our knees would only incense him further.

He was almost upon us when, suddenly, he caught sight of the lizard. He came to a halt before the desk-shaped blue rock, about two yards from where we were still kneeling in the snow. He had his profile towards us so that we could watch his face breaking into a wide, happy grin. It was obvious that he had never seen a lizard before. He gazed at it avidly, curiously and with evident satisfaction.

Spellbound by this unexpected development we remained on our knees. We were exhausted and, besides, we knew that Dentures could take in only one phenomenon at a time, two were too much for him. Either he watched the lizard and we were safe, or he abandoned the lizard and it was too late anyway.

The sergeant gaped at the lizard enthralled, his open lips trembling. His usually stiff, straight back relaxed; he bent slightly forward and his beautifully cut greatcoat was furrowed into deep wrinkles around the shoulder-blades. I was strangely moved. Until that moment I had never discovered a single human trait in the man. He had seemed an indifferent brute; and there he was now, bending over the lizard like a scientist over his microscope. He is acquainting himself with the phenomena of the world – I thought to myself – even if only with an animal; but this attention, this deep absorption, may be the forerunner of thinking.

Suddenly the sergeant raised his hatchet and with a flick of the wrist – his lips still extended in a wide, enchanted smile – he cut off the animal's right foot. A scarlet half-sphere appeared in the opening of the wound, became elliptical and began to swing softly to and fro like a soap-bubble. Then it burst and the blood gushed forth like red oil-paint pressed from a tube. The lizard turned its head and examined its mutilated limb curiously, uncomprehendingly.

I felt Egri's shoulder go tense. What could I do to stop him? If he hurled himself at the sergeant it wouldn't help much if I threw myself between them. Egri was ten times as strong as I.

'Don't die for a lizard!' I whispered in a voice so low that he could not possibly have heard me. Perhaps it was better so, for hadn't we both long ago come to the conclusion that one would rather die for a lizard than for an ideal. Besides, the wounding of the lizard moved me more deeply than Szuha's death, and I was certain that Egri shared my feeling. Thus it was not the words that mattered. I concentrated all my energy on the movement of my lips, I willed him to understand that his life was at stake. He stared at me for a moment, then his body relaxed.

Dentures gaped at the bleeding animal for a few minutes then raised his hatchet for the second time. He swung it not from the wrist but from the elbow and with a single, expert blow severed the animal's left foot. The tiny paw flew off the blue rock in a wide arc and dug a small hole in the snow immediately before us. The lizard dropped its head on the rock as if it were giving up the hopeless struggle.

The moment it collapsed Dentures straightened up and the three deep creases in the back of his coat smoothed out without leaving a trace. He turned to us and looked at us for a moment with unseeing eyes. We did nor move. Our knees ate deep into the soft clay like the nose of a blown-up tank. Time enough to rise – I told myself – when he starts yelling. Then he would strike me or, if he liked, kick me down the slope. I might break my arms or legs and lie on my back for six weeks at the infirmary. This prospect was so pleasing that I forgot everything else and gazed absentmindedly into the snow that clung like a collar of frilly white lace to our knees.

The sergeant, however, did not yell. He turned his back on us and walked towards the quarry face where, in the blue-tinged shadow, the snow was harder and deeper. He stooped and with both palms began to sweep the snow into a neat pile between his straddled feet. From the heap he moulded a beautiful, big snowball. When it was finished he lifted the almost perfect sphere in both hands and gaped at it in awe. Then he turned, aimed carefully and with a startled expression on his face threw the snowball at me. Then he smiled a charming, boyish smile because the ball hit the exact spot he had aimed at, it no more than brushed my shoulder then flew on, in a wide arc, towards the precipice.

We were still on our knees when Dentures turned and walked

away along the quarry face. He described a complete half-circle of approximately twenty yards' radius, approaching us again from the other side, walking on the very edge of the precipice. He advanced with rapid, springy steps on the uneven ground. Behind his waist the mountain chains of northern Hungary were etched sharply, clearly, into the limpid air. The gun-holster wobbling at his side seemed to be sledging up and down the hills and slopes of the Gömör–Szepes ore-mountains, the dull, grey metal of the butt peeping out from under the leather flap. He walked on the edge of the precipice with his profile towards us. But behind that profile there were no more mountains: the vibrating, resigned blue of the winter sky served as a background to his face. His pointed, pink nose sniffed the air, his mouth, as always, was gaping. He appeared an allegorical figure, eating and swallowing, swallowing and eating the blue sky not only symbolically but in fact. For a second the white peak of the High Tatra flashed between his platinum-coloured teeth like a mound of vanilla ice-cream, then he had swallowed that too and walked on towards the guard-hut to fry himself some bacon for lunch.

On that day dusk was like dawn: above the thinned-out forest the sky enveloped us like an egg-shaped rather than a spherical cupola made of translucent blue crystal. Our working day was over and we were marching down the slope with heavy logs on our shoulders to be cut up into firewood and sold by the guards. The two men walking before me argued about the way to make egg-nog. Musilla, a tiny, elderly social democratic office worker, insisted that he used to put the eggs into the alcohol, shell and all. His wife had suffered from tuberculosis and the doctors advised him to give her as much calcium as possible.

'So I gave her egg-nog,' Musilla explained. 'There were the shells of twenty-four eggs in every litre of it.'

'You are nuts, Musilla,' said Uncle Torma, an old welder whom the AVO had arrested because he had asked, at a party meeting, whether this was already socialism or whether it would become even worse. 'You never made egg-nog at home, you went to the pub and bought a bottle.'

'I swear to you that I made it myself. I washed a dozen eggs and put them in alcohol, where they dissolved, then . . .'

'Calcium doesn't dissolve in alcohol.'

'Why shouldn't it? I bet you it does. If I lose I'll pay you the day we get out of here.'

'But not in egg-nog!' Uncle Torma laughed. 'I refuse to drink that slop. Let's make it ten litres of Balaton white wine.'

I fell back. I hated egg-nog as much as Uncle Torma but now I would have lapped it up. Not only my stomach, but my whole body craved food. I saw myself sticking ten fingers into the sticky egg-nog, then my foot, which left a round, squelchy print in it as if I had stepped in wet sand. Egg-nog was flowing on top of Mount Kékes where, in the wake of the setting sun, yellow puddles collected among the trees. Resin – like egg-nog – hung from the hollow of a pine tree I passed.

Wrangel and Berzsenyi, whom I overtook to get some intelligent conversation, were on the same subject, discussing questions we usually dismissed contemptuously, under the heading, 'take a fire-proof dish'. Fortunately they were not exchanging recipes.

'When I get home,' Wrangel was saying with feeling, 'I shall ask my mother to prepare my favourite dish, risotto à la Milanese. Forty pounds of it, in a bucket . . .'

'Disgusting,' Berzsenyi exclaimed. 'I am all for quality foods. The first evening out I shall invite three of my friends. I shall buy eight woodcocks, put them in pairs into the bellies of four partridges, into two pheasants, the two pheasants into a hare, roll the hare in strips of bacon and bake it. I shall serve stewed quince with it and Chablis. But first there will be a cheese soufflé . . .'

Poor Berzsenyi, I thought, has no idea that there is neither Chablis, nor woodcock, nor partridge, nor pheasant to be had outside; if he is lucky he will get a couple of hares. I fell back again because I heard Egri's voice behind me. He was arguing in a rather arrogant manner with a young man by the name of Fürst whom he despised as he despised everyone who had lost his religion but still held on to theology.

'Try to live without an ideology,' he shouted at him, 'perhaps you will succeed. And if you are not interested in what Faludy has to say about the Platonic idea, you have only to remain on your bunk at night.'

'But I am interested!' replied Fürst in melancholy tones. 'The trouble is only that I find him to be a reactionary. I myself am a materialist.'

'What do you mean by that?'

'I am ashamed to tell you, but as far as I am concerned, a dixie full of sticky, dirty boiled beans in my belly means more than all of Plato's ideas.'

'All right,' Egri said, 'but in that case, be consistent.'

'What do you mean?'

'Inform the sergeant that we are having reactionary conversations in the evenings and ask for your reward: a dish of beans. Be materialistic to the end, brother!'

I was about to intervene on Fürst's behalf – he was gazing at Egri with stricken eyes – but Egri took pity on him and began to explain that our nightly discussions had only one purpose: to save us from becoming like animals.

'Besides,' he added, again in an arrogant voice, 'it is silly of you to belittle our conversations. These conversations immunize us against typhoid and pneumonia. This, naturally, is something you will never understand because your brain is paralysed by ideology. Believe me, you and your materialism will soon be buried in a lime-pit and we shall still be talking over your grave.'

I was again about to intervene, but we had reached the wood-pile at the inner gate where we had to unload our logs, and I lost them in the crowd. It was not so much that I wanted to defend Fürst; what was more important to me was to rebuke Egri for his demagogy, because I felt in a way responsible for his arrogance. True, I had quoted the Barbarian king's words from Plato's *Charmides*: 'certain conversations cure the soul', but I had never said that conversation protected the body against typhoid bacilli.

At the entrance to the barracks I came upon Joska Borostobi, a county official, who, if Doctor Acs was right, would be one of the first victims of starvation in spite of his strong, large body. He was one of the most intelligent members of our nightly discussions whom

I liked particularly because he always spoke briefly but to the point. Whenever we wanted to go to sleep he begged us to talk a little longer and came out with new, exciting subjects.

'I should like to talk to you alone, George,' he said, drawing me to the barrack wall. I looked into his face. It appeared calm, as always, but it seemed to me that his calm was self-imposed, artificial. It had changed within the last twenty-four hours, but I could not have explained what the change was. His gaily pointed moustache, his provincial pink cheeks were the same, but his jaws seemed stiffer than usual when he spoke and the light in his eyes, instead of radiating from the centre of his pupil, seemed diffused all over his eyeball.

He said that he liked me and had always been deeply interested in our nightly conversations. His sentences were much more elaborate than usual and so was my reply. While we talked I looked around me. On the other side of the stream, about a hundred and fifty yards away, forty or fifty people were waiting by the infirmary for medical attention. Most of them sat in the snow, some leaned their sagging shoulders against the wall. In front of the barracks five men were washing themselves from head to foot in the snow. Usually I was the sixth and I could hardly wait to take my place among them. I lifted my nose, and tried to guess from the smells coming from the kitchen what we would have for supper. At noon it had been cabbage, worth no more than three hundred calories. If only they gave us noodles or beans!

Meanwhile Borostobi was speaking solemnly. 'George,' he said, 'I have decided not to take part in the conversations any more. Last night, while you were talking about the Platonic ideas, I suddenly realized that I had lost interest in intellectual matters. Don't blame me, blame circumstances . . . I think that in future I shall sleep more and think less. I shall live the life of the algae. At least until things improve,' he added uncertainly.

I looked at him quickly and suddenly it occurred to me that this man was close to death; Not for physical reasons – there Doctor Acs was wrong – but because he had resigned himself to the thought of death. I was tempted to call him a coward but I remembered that a few minutes ago I had wanted to rebuke Egri for his transcendentalism and lo, I was in the same boat with him. Borostobi stood quietly, obviously waiting for me to talk him out of his decision but I hardly noticed him. Was it true that he who would not talk about Plato had to die? Did reciting Keats's poems immunize one against bacilli?

Borostobi disappeared and the evening star shone bright above the barracks. I must be going mad – I thought – and went in for my wash-basin. This time, however, even the icy water failed to refresh me.

It was the night for clean shirts. Every sixth man was given six clean shirts to distribute, and I was one of them. Usually my friends could hardly wait for their clean shirt but now they lay apathetically and I too was far too tired to move. We had dehydrated potatoes – nylon potatoes, as we called them – for supper which, according to the experts, contained no more than three hundred and forty calories. We were almost desperate, most of all Garamvölgyi who had only recently lost his job as swineherd when two of his pigs died of starvation. It was fortunate that the Blond Murderer, supreme master of the pigs, had been a waiter before entering the political police, so that he simply dismissed Garamvölgyi instead of punishing him for depriving the pigs of their slop. Thus Garamvölgyi had only made the acquaintance of hunger during the last weeks and it made him hysterical. In addition he was beside himself with rage because 'his sex thoughts were deserting him and he was beginning to feel like a capon'. We others had become used to this state of affairs long ago.

I lay for a while without moving; the overcoats hanging from the beams threw large shadows in the poor light from the single, weak bulb. Looking out from under half-closed lids it seemed to me as if Death by Starvation in person were sitting on the opposite bunk with its large, domed baby-head and its legs crossed, like a Buddha. I thought I should get off my bunk and try to change Borostobi's mind for him; it was my duty, but then I recalled five lines from Rilke:

. . . Denn Engel kommen nicht zu solchen Betern
und Nächte werden nicht um solche gross.
Die Sich-Verlierenden lässt alles los
und sie sind preisgegeben von den Vätern
und ausgeschlossen aus der Mütter Schoss.

and I just let it go. Hunger was gnawing at my stomach and creeping up my gullet. The dirty, ragged overcoats hanging from the beams brought to my mind the retreat of the Grande Armée in Russia. The uniform of Napoleon's soldiers was red and blue, not khaki like ours, but perhaps after crossing the Berezina they too lost colour. Risotto à la Milanese and Arrigo Beyle, Milanese, I repeated to myself. Why did Stendhal, born in Grenoble, demand that this lie be written on his tombstone? And why was I thinking of Stendhal? Probably because he too wore an overcoat like this when following Napoleon's army on its retreat from Moscow. What did he do? Did he comfort the soldiers? Not at all! He washed in snow-water every day, just like me, and made notes. He didn't care who died or why, he cared just as little about his own fate, he was interested only to make his notes for his book, nothing else.

Suddenly Pali Jonas's smooth, intelligent face appeared by my bunk. He had just returned from the infirmary and had talked to Doctor Acs. Szuha was dead and in the morning an army surgeon had arrived from Vac, the medical superintendent of the camp and of the Vac prison. Acs had shown him the body and appealed to his conscience. The colonel had shrugged his shoulders and replied that he couldn't prescribe sausages for the prisoners. Why didn't Doctor Acs ask Churchill for help?

Jonas's words woke me up from my apathy. I sat up and looked around. Garamvölgyi was squatting at my feet gazing, as if hypnotized, at the shirts under my elbow. Egri had brought out from his pocket a huge piece of paper. It was part of a cement-bag and he could have been put in short chains for stealing it. Not even the AVO could obtain cement from the factory until it returned the large paper bags in which it was delivered. We regarded cement-paper as even more valuable than real cigarette paper, because it tasted good and burned slowly. Wrangel was just coming in with a full dixie in his hand which he placed on the shelf above his bunk. He had received it in the shed behind the kitchen, obviously in exchange for information. Perhaps a week earlier he had confessed to me one night that in his fear of starvation he had turned into an informer but would never inform on me. I told him that he must not count on me as a witness for the defence in his trial, and that I wouldn't move a finger to save him from being hanged. He said he knew it. A few minutes later, when I was already half asleep, I felt him kissing my hand and wetting it with his tears. I shuddered with disgust but was too tired to draw away my hand.

I looked at the shirts: there was one white and five coloured, and one of these was obviously torn. When I lifted the white shirt, Garamvölgyi threw me a pleading look. I handed it to him and he held it in his arms like a mother holds a baby. Then, while the others put their shirts under their heads, he examined his. When he noticed that one cuff of the white raw silk shirt was missing his mouth turned bitter and when he discovered two small holes in the shoulder he flung it down furiously. Then he gazed unmovingly and admiringly at the pink shirt with white polka-dots that I kept for myself. He didn't know it was torn.

'What are you looking at, Janika?'

'You gave me the worst of the lot again.'

'Let's change,' I offered.

'Would you really do that for me? You know how vain I am where shirts are concerned.'

When he noticed that I hesitated for a second, he raised his hand.

'Well, will you or won't you?'

'Of course,' I said, throwing the shirt in his lap.

'You are very good to me, I shall never forget this,' he exclaimed gratefully. He crawled back to his bunk and tried to put on the clean shirt. When he noticed the tear he shuddered with fury but said nothing. He flung down the shirt, crawled back to my bunk and looked at me with hostile eyes.

'I would never have believed this of you, George,' he said at last.

'What?'

'That you would make me accept a torn shirt to get the beautiful white one yourself.'

'I didn't make you take it. You wanted it.'

'I am young and inexperienced. You should be ashamed of yourself for cheating a young boy!'

'We can remedy the situation very easily. Let's change again.'

'Are you joking?' he asked suspiciously. 'Or would you really give it back?'

'Here, take it!' I said with a side-glance at Gabori and Berzsenyi, who had been watching the scene. Then I inspected the shirt that was to be mine. I suddenly realized that the pink shirt with the white polka-dots, with a pocket on the right side, had once belonged to Kenedy – he had the pocket specially made for his eye-glass. On the left side there was a long tear – the tear always made by the prison doctor when he ripped open the shirt of a hanged man in order to put his stethoscope on his heart.

An hour later some twelve men were sitting around me on our straw mattresses in the dark. For a year and a half we had not missed a single evening but now we were so tired that if Szuha had not died we would never have had the energy to sit up. We were prompted not only by the fear of death but also by rebelliousness, as if this were a protest meeting which gave us the opportunity to boast of our courage. As I sat between the kneeling, squatting, sitting friends I remembered Roman sarcophagi with the relief of the deceased on their side, sitting up on his death-bed to have a last talk with his friends and family about his life, his principles and experiences before reclining on the wrinkled sheet wet with perspiration to abandon himself to the sly vision of non-existence. I said nothing because my mind was full of Kenedy. Now that I knew he had been hanged his surrealistic personality had suddenly become very real to me. I thought that he had played at being a spy, had made a game of it, stupidly, shortsightedly, until at last he was believed and hanged.

Our conversation was rather slow in hitting its stride. Gabori related an argument with a French industrialist when he was last in Paris.

'The idiot believed that his workers would be better off if the communists took over in France, and that he himself would be appointed to some important post out of gratitude because he had given them financial support. I told him that once the communists seized power in France his workers would be much worse off and he himself would be hanged. Do you know what he said? He laughed in my face.'

'Why didn't you bring him here?' said Uncle Bandi Horvath, the paralytic old man who was already half dead, from the lower bunk. In the mornings his neighbours helped him to dress, at night he urinated into our boots – never into his own – but in his clear moments he often hit the nail on the head with biting remarks. At times he talked to us about his past life, how he had knocked his wife about – she was twenty years older than he – whenever he found a speck of dust on the carpet, and what fun he had scaring young lovers among the trees of Budapest parks. His rheumy blue eyes twinkled gaily and he seasoned his tales with the most revolting obscenities. When we were working in the forest Garamvölgyi often kicked him in the bottom to make him shut up.

Our conversation became suddenly livelier. Egri declared that the strongest weapon of the communists, against which Western culture, richness and humanism were powerless, was the fact that the West didn't know them. Zoltan Sztaray, a young sociologist, spoke about the frustrations of the Western – in the first place French and Italian – intellectuals and about the suicidal neurosis of Western culture. Zoltan Vér, a tall, pale journalist with a cocky moustache who resembled Cyrano de Bergerac's brothers-in-arms from Gascony and who had already spent five years in various concentration camps, said that it was up to me to defend the West against these unjust accusations. However, I refused to comply.

Wrangel, whom I had noticed earlier sneaking out to the outhouse with his dixieful of potatoes to eat it in peace, was back on his bunk on Egri's other side, with his eyes closed and his face a deadly white. From time to time old judge Rigó, who was a little deaf, called up to us from the lower bunk to speak louder.

Egri, Gabori and eight more men were sitting round me in a narrow circle and two more kneeled at my ankles, motionless. While we others put our heads together and whispered, as if we were engaged in preparing a revolt, the two at my feet were like two marble statues, two kneeling guardian angels watching over us in the dark, never moving, not even when the beams of the searchlight, sweeping the window, lit them up for a moment, a sparkling white.

One of them, a young student of philosophy called Elemér Földvary, looked, with the unbroken line of his forehead and nose, his tiny mouth and bird eyes, like a beautiful, ancient Greek Antinuos. In the day-time he worked on the andesite-pillars of the quarry face, hanging from the mountain peak on a twenty-metre rope and cramming two or three dozen Greek words I had written down for him on a piece of paper the night before. During our evening conversation he was mostly silent because, though he considered the subjects intellectually refreshing, he found them trivial and preferred to talk to me alone about mysticism, Gnosis, Plotinus or Persian literature.

The other kneeler, Helvetius, had once worked in a slaughterhouse. Compared to Földvary he seemed a veritable colossus with a small, charming head on his athlete's body, salmon-coloured, sensual lips, a freckled snub nose and a hundred coal-black curls around his smooth, snow-white forehead. We were certain that he was the only honest one among the cooks, who were usually given this job because they were informers. The AVO would never have put up with him if he hadn't been so immensely strong. When we were unloading the lorries bringing our rations he walked up and down the steps with two 120-kilogramme sacks on his shoulders, or picked up 12–15-metre logs, heavy with mud, that even six of us could not move, to throw them into the lorry. He too was always silent when we talked, but every once in a while – with my consent – he would pick me up and carry me to his bunk, where I had to explain to him what we had been talking about or, as a special treat, recite one or two of my poems. When I finished he would carry me back to my place.

Apart from Egri and Gabori these two were my favourite friends, but I think I liked the beautiful butcher best. One of the reasons for this was that while with the others intellectual conversations were a combination of routine and protection against adverse circumstances, Helvetius's intellectual curiosity was spontaneous, elementary and eruptive like a volcanic outbreak. At last I had met Cashel Biron's *alter ego.* I have always liked Shaw's book and it did not detract from my appreciation that I had always considered its hero an improbable, artificial figure – until I met Helvetius. Last but not least it pleased me that my fellow-prisoners misunderstood my visits to Helvetius's bunk, regarding them as erotic excursions. They not only envied me but invested me in their imagination with superhuman energies. It impressed them that someone who encouraged and entertained his listeners for twelve hours a day like a radio station, and arranged brains-trust meetings in the evenings, should spend his nights with an aggressively, challengingly handsome butcher-boy – and all this on the threshold of death by starvation. My young friend was flattered by the suspicion and in a way nurtured it. Whenever I visited him in his bunk he pressed his pale face, reminding me of a pale blue patch of colour in an impressionist painting, with pink, slightly parted, frightened lips, to my cheek and gazed at me with enchanted eyes. Contrary to the accepted custom of the camp, which demanded that the host give the longer half of a broken cigarette to his guest, Helvetius would share a whole one with me while the gigantic muscles of his arm ran down my shoulder and hip like streams.

My friends were still discussing Western intellectuals, but their target now was the *New Statesman* and Zilliacus. Paul Jonas, former leader of the university students, squatting at my thigh, confessed that not so long ago he too had belonged to that category of left-wing intellectuals who served the idea with the altruistic notion that though it might eliminate them, it would, in the end, bring happiness to mankind. To comfort him Sztaray remarked that the left-wing intellectual and the amateur-suicide playing at politics was a characteristic type of our age, whereupon Garamvölgyi told the story of the Duke of Orléans, Philip Égalité, who represented the same type at the time of the French Revolution. He too woke from his day-dreams only when he was in the tumbril taking him to the guillotine.

Our conversation shifted to the Encylopaedists, then to Rousseau and de la Mettrie's mechanical materialism. Berzsenyi, raising himself on his elbow behind Gabori, declared that it was the latter we had to thank for state-imposed vulgar materialism. Jonas protested fiercely. True, the system preached dialectical and historical materialism but what it practised was the most radical idealism. The communist state-ideal cannot even be compared to the state-ideal of enlightened absolutism because it is transcendental and without a trace of utilitarianism. The state pays no attention whatsoever to the material welfare and happiness of its subjects. It restricts itself to the spreading of the communist state religion the way the orthodox Caliphs spread Mohammedanism. The individual farmer produces more than the *kolkhoz*, but the idealist state would rather starve its citizens than renounce winning the soul of the peasants. Ever since 1948 the state had been busy ridding the public administration, ministries, factories and enterprises of all experts and appointing shoe-makers in place of the managers, salesmen in the place of hospital directors, charwomen in the place of the tradesmen. The state didn't care if the factories produced waste, if the goods produced rotted in warehouses, if the sick died like flies, so long as the functionaries lived happily in a mystical spiritual community with the communist ideal. Or, at least, pretended to do so.

'The Platonic idea of the communist state,' Jonas continued, 'hovers high above the obsolete experiments at *étatism* and looks down upon the welfare stare as a blessed soul from the Garden of Eden looks down on the copper coins dropped here on earth, into the hat of a blind beggar. And the central committee, representing the communist state idea, is a Platonic idea of the various councils of ministers and praesidia, the ideal of state wisdom, almost a deity representing absolute truth, and incarnating in its own womb the Dalai Lama. It sets before its citizens further, though much more limited Platonic ideas, just as it has its own obligatory Platonic ideas concerning everyday life, science, and all the arts.'

'I can't hear you!' grumbled the judge below us, and to give his discontent emphasis, he kicked my straw mattress with all his might.

'Before the grave-digger, for instance,' Jonas explained mildly, 'the state set the Platonic idea of the grave-digger. The communist grave-digger works in socialist emulation, he has no time to joke, as in *Hamlet*, and has long ago sold Yorick's skull for a packet of tobacco. His main ambition is to win the title of "foremost grave-digger of the people's democracy". In his time off he doesn't sit in a pub or chase women, he breaks his head about how to make funerals cheaper and faster. While digging a grave he thinks of the Party.

'The police chief has his eye on the Platonic idea of a police chief. His duty is not to rid society of robbers and murderers because these endanger only the lives of citizens, but not that of the state. The communist police chief must arrest imperialist agents and saboteurs, and if there aren't any he has to create them in order to justify the Platonic idea of the state which cannot exist for a moment without more and more proofs of imperialist aggression and the sharpening of the class struggle. In the same way the writers were given Fadejev as an example – or rather not the true Fadejev, who drinks himself into oblivion day after day to silence his pangs of conscience, but the Platonic idea of Fadejev: that is, of a writer who ignores reality because the chasm between the ideal and its realization is so deep that obligatory idealism cannot possibly take any notice of it. Instead of reality, the writer has to portray its Platonic idea, that is a society which knows no intellectual or spiritual conflict, which has eliminated unhappiness, railway accidents, cancer, the fear of death, drought and egotism. He has to depict an ideal, quasi-paradisal society in which all asocial instincts have ceded their place to the passionate love of work, and sex is replaced by the orgies of the party meetings.

'The Platonic idea set before the painters is the carefully drawn daub. The state has determined the Platonic idea of a correctly dressed, loyal party member, of morals, fashion and female beauty. The criteria of female beauty are: a modest, imbecile smile, a greasy nape, and short, fat hands. The breasts should be like the buffers of a cattle-wagon and the bottom must not be smaller than two twenty-pound water-melons. But this must never be talked about because the idealist society is more hypocritical than the *petite bourgeoisie* of Victorian England . . .'

We were exhausted and would gladly have gone to sleep, but not one of us betrayed this desire. We were still waiting for something. Perhaps for our two fellow-prisoners who had been taken away for questioning and had not yet returned; perhaps for some unexpected event. We went on arguing about the Platonic idea; some of my friends denied its existence; only Joska Varga, who had studied philosophy and theology, insisted that such a thing really existed. Gabori declared, for instance, that the chair preceded the Platonic idea of the chair, and it was the same with beauty. The idea of beauty was different in Knossos and different again in Athens, just as our idea of beauty differs from that of the Zulu.

'This,' I interrupted him, 'is no evidence against the Platonic idea of beauty. All it proves is that the idea of beauty changes according to the era and the country.'

Gabori replied that ideal beauty was nothing but a social convention. A society agrees on what its members will regard as beautiful. We have a few dozen female blueprints – basic types, put together from the features of film stars, fashion models, magazine illustrations, the covers of trashy books and the portraits of fashionable painters. Film and stage, post-cards and books, friends and acquaintances, posters and the dummies in shop-windows, all proclaim these types to be the modern ideal, and we submit to this mass-hypnosis and consent to regard the women who most resemble these blueprints as beautiful.

'How fortunate that we are not always in a position to do so,' I said. 'Let us suppose that two hundred men are sitting in a restaurant, each by himself. Suddenly a beautiful woman enters. Not a cliché-beauty, but, let us say, Botticelli's Primavera. Her shoulders pointed; the contours of her lips disagreeably sharp; her nose too long, her forehead higher than necessary. Separately each of her features is ugly, but the whole creates an impression of absolute loveliness. In fact her beauty is irregular, unforeseeable, unimagined, an unbearably exciting beauty.' I looked at Helvetius, illuminated for a moment by the searchlight.

'The two hundred men,' I continued, 'will exclaim with one voice: what a beautiful woman! And yet they have not conspired to find her beautiful. And the more unexpected, the more extraordinary the woman, the more she will please them. It seems to me that the ideal of beauty is not merely a social convention but also a Platonic idea: a Platonic idea living in us.'

'Do you mean to say that you believe in *a priori* ideas?' asked Gabori with some surprise.

'I have always believed in them but I haven't dared say so for years, not even in prison,' I replied triumphantly; and suddenly I felt as light as if I had just slaughtered the dragon and were sitting on the red carpet of its blood, surrounded by lovely virgins whom I had saved, playing, like a juggler, with the dragon's seven heads.

'When I was little,' I continued, 'my mother had two friends who used to visit her. One had dark, wiry hair, a square face, high cheekbones and a swarthy skin like an Abyssinian princess, and was ugly. The other had soft lips, a pointed little nose, pink cheeks and white skin; she was as beautiful as the most beautiful rococo lady on a snuffbox. When the ugly one came into my room I screamed and kicked until she fled; but when my mother's pretty friend came in I smiled and began to cry only when she left. I was then six months old, or so my mother says, and knew nothing about social convention, not even the convention of speech. Thus, it seems that the Platonic idea of beauty lived in me long before I learned the word "beauty". And I don't want to limit myself to this one Platonic idea. I believe that the other Platonic ideas, the moral laws and the categorical imperative . . .'

'They are bringing someone,' Garamvölgyi interrupted from the window.

I looked out. A prisoner was being led down from the hill where the commander's house stood. He looked like Michnai who, I had hoped, was already in Vienna. I broke into goose pimples and felt the hair rise on my nape. Only when they reached the lamp by the guard-hut did I notice that there were two of them, a short man following behind the tall one: our two fellow-prisoners were being returned to the barracks. At the same moment I heard the baying of hounds approaching from another direction, and it seemed to me that they were hoarser than usual.

My friend and I slipped quickly under our blankets. We lay down as we were, there was no time for the others to return to their bunks. If the guards looked into the barracks they might beat us up, or set the hounds on us or, worse, report us to Lieutenant Laszlo Nagy, the political officer, whose greatest pleasure was to discover indications of conspiracy. About a month ago he had sent four of our fellow-prisoners to Budapest because he found them near the fence. Allegedly two had been hanged for attempted rebellion.

Helvetius was the only one who was not afraid. He climbed down and started towards the door to find out what was going on. We watched, hardly breathing, as the doors were unlocked from the outside and our two fellow-prisoners were pushed in. The next second we heard wild shouts of fear and surprise. 'Hold on, mine has got loose!' – 'Don't shoot, idiot, can't you see me standing in your way?' 'This blasted animal has gone crazy!' Then they began to laugh like mad. The barrack was filled with an unexplainable, rumbling noise, as if a windstorm bad entered the door to sweep along the bunks. Then the door was locked and everything was quiet.

'This is a day of animals, George,' said Egri in the silence. 'In the morning the lizard, and now these . . .'

I didn't know what he was talking about, but the next moment Helvetius appeared on my bunk carrying the huge, white dog which he used to feed in the kitchens.

'Three of them are here,' he announced triumphantly. 'They have deserted to us.'

Opposite, on the lower bunk, I suddenly discovered the black-and-white striped hound that scared me to death every time I saw it. It was working its way up the narrow triangle between, the legs of Uncle Péter Csaplar, bus-driver, and Kalman Kéri, staff colonel. It chose Uncle Péter until the old man, mumbling in his sleep, put his arm about the dog's neck. The bitch, brought to me by Helvetius, settled down without a sound behind my back.

'The argument is closed,' I said and placed my head on the wonderful, living pillow. 'We can consider it as proved that even dogs have their Platonic ideas.'

'About what?' Garamvölgyi asked mildly.

'About man,' replied the paralytic Uncle Horvath from the lower bunk.

Joska Borostobi, the kind, handsome county official, died exactly one week after he told me that he would no longer participate in our discussions. He collapsed at work, whereupon his *nachalnik*, Géza Junasz, member of the Hungarian national football team (who had been arrested because he lodged with an alleged Trotskyist) hit him until he bled. Later they took him to the infirmary but Doctor Acs refused to give us any information about him. After the lights were put out Garamvölgyi told me to look out of the window. Two AVO men were coming down the hill towards the hospital, each carrying a mattress. A few minutes later they came out again but now they each held one end of the two mattresses that had been tied together. The sight was unexpected because the AVO men never carried anything heavy; at the same time we couldn't understand why it was necessary to lug two mattresses about in the middle of the night. As they advanced along the ridge of the hill, about a hundred metres away from us and lit by the lights illuminating the double barbed-wire fence, we suddenly noticed a large, coconut-shaped object slip from between the mattresses. The two men stopped, deliberated for a moment, then turned the mattresses around so that the bottom was on top. Then I could clearly distinguish Borostobi's lifeless head sticking out from between the mattresses before, finally, it slid back between them.

We could not quite understand the necessity for such discretion, but we were no longer surprised at Borostobi's death. Four men had died during the last week under similar conditions, while a young engineer, Szeremley, was crushed by a rock weighing several tons. When the rock began to slide his neighbours called out to warn him. They said that Szeremley looked up at the rock, and although he could have jumped to safety, remained where he was, bending his head in resignation. On the following Saturday, in the square between the barracks where they announced the names of those sentenced to solitary or other punishment, the officer added a sentence to the usual speech. He declared that Szuha, Borostobi and the others 'had been sent up to Budapest to a prison hospital for treatment'. About half the men sentenced to solitary confinement received their punishment because they had talked about the deaths and complained loudly about the low calorie content of our food. At this time the AVO spread through their informers a rumour that the Americans had landed in Albania and Yugoslavia and were approaching the Hungarian border. This was done to calm us. The simple souls who believed the story were certain that we would be liberated within a week. They lived in constant euphoria, made plans for the future and in the meantime, comforting themselves with the thought that it wouldn't last long now, went on breaking stone, carrying heavy loads, pushing the tumbrils. They literally worked themselves to death. Three of the four dead belonged to this category.

The false news, followed every two days by other rumours (rebellion in Warsaw, attempt on Rakosi's life, Chinese-Soviet conflict), was invented by the AVO to give us new hope, while punishments became daily more severe, to strengthen discipline. The AVO was obviously afraid that we might rebel and get ourselves mown down by machine-guns, rather than obey communist etiquette and die quietly without fuss. Their twofold precautions had very real justification: we had seriously been considering rebelling before we died of hunger, and killing a few of our tormentors before we ourselves were slaughtered. The AVO probably got wind of the plans which we were now too weak to carry out. Meanwhile those who were still strong – *nachalniki*, informers, cooks – were waiting impatiently for us to die, most of them believing that after we had perished the AVO would release them.

My friends and I felt it our duty to expose the rumours and to convince our fellow-prisoners that it was better to do some quiet sabotage and to work more slowly instead of losing their heads with joy and engaging in senseless feats. Our task was difficult and of doubtful value. We were working from the premise that some miracle would happen to prevent our death, but at the same time we were almost certain that death would soon come, and that our efforts were only prolonging our own suffering and that of our fellow-prisoners. In my own case, strangely enough, it was Borostobi's death which generated the necessary energies. When I saw that dead head lolling from between the sandwiched mattresses I was suddenly overcome by fierce pangs of conscience. I blamed myself for not having tried to change his mind when, a week earlier, he had announced that he had lost interest in our discussion of Platonic ideas and would henceforth live a vegetable life. I had been wrong in applying my principle of never interfering in other people's lives, because this time it was death, not life, which had demanded interference. I had disobeyed a distinct, though incomprehensible, order from my categorical imperative to speak up – an order which had been clear, even though logic and reason protested against telling dying men that we would not die.

My task and that of my friends was also highly involved. In the mornings, when before we marched out to work I sought out my acquaintances as they stood with chattering teeth in the square between the barracks, they would usually greet me with the request: 'Say something comforting, George, it doesn't have to be true!' Attempts to disprove the false but comforting rumours circulating in the camp were thus made almost impossible by the fact that the prisoners were determined to believe them. Not only the simple souls, but the intellectual *élite* as well, such as Ödön Berzsenyi, would read into such scraps of newspaper as they could lay hands on, not what was in them, but what they wanted to see in them. One morning Berzsenyi handed me half a page from a newspaper, saying that it contained good news: the Yugoslavs had attacked Bulgaria with British support. I read the article, which dealt with a Yugoslav–Bulgarian border incident. There was not a word about the British in it. I mentioned this to Berzsenyi, who grew angry and said that I didn't know how to read a newspaper.

While checking exaggeratedly optimistic false rumours, we had to be careful not to drive our companions into despair: lethargy – as in Borostobi's case – led to the same result: early death. The news that Churchill had become Prime Minister was more catastrophic in its consequences than any of the false rumours spread by the AVO. Until then the political prisoners had put their faith in the American people and in the new President to be elected. They held a poor opinion of Truman and spoke of Roosevelt with something akin to hatred. 'It is not Stalin or Rakosi who are responsible for our fate, but Roosevelt,' they used to say. But everyone, including the simple peasants, was familiar with Churchill's wartime role and knew what he had said in his speech at Fulton. When it became known, one evening, that he was again Prime Minister, the younger among us turned somersaults on their bunks and old peasants distributed their last cigarettes. Nine out of ten believed firmly that our captivity would be over within a few months. The next morning the mountainside resounded with the blows of pick-axes and the miners' trucks rolled downwards at a frightening speed. Within the next forty-eight hours seven people had been taken to the infirmary, and four of them died immediately.

We did all we could to disprove the news. I did not even try to explain that it was not in Churchill's power to liberate us and that, in the present situation, England could undertake no independent political action. No one would have believed me. I tried instead to persuade them that the British general election was not due for another year, that for the time being there was a Labour majority and that Churchill's premiership was a false rumour spread, obviously, by the AVO. Three days later, when I had more or less succeeded in calming the general hysteria, Knocke fished a piece of newpaper from the sewer from which, to my great surprise, I learned that Churchill had indeed become Prime Minister. I immediately destroyed the paper and continued to refute the rumour with the greatest energy.

While depriving our fellow-prisoners of such harmful illusions we had to supply them with other, less feverish, long-term dreams. I could easily have invented a dozen but I had no wish to become a central figure and therefore I turned to the religious Pista Todi for help. I approached him cautiously, tactfully, because however deep our mutual affection and admiration, I was afraid my request would offend him and turn him into an enemy. What I hinted was that we were in urgent need of the Holy Virgin, who ought to put in an appearance, if possible that same evening, if not, the next day. I suggested that she should inform him that our food would soon be improved and that a year from now, around Christmas, the régime would collapse of its own accord, without bloodshed, and that we should all celebrate the New Year at home with our families.

I watched his reaction closely as he sat on the floor before the stove with a perturbed look in his eyes. But instead of jumping at me, he pulled me to him and embraced me. The next morning the whole camp was buzzing with the news that the Holy Virgin had appeared to Todi in the radiant circle thrown by the open door of the stove, announcing that we would all be back home next Christmas. Everyone was deeply moved, including the atheists, who were as ready as anyone to take their part of the divine mercy. Though the majority still trusted Churchill more than they did the Holy Virgin, the effect of the apparition surpassed my boldest expectations. Only the two most devoted Catholics in the camp, Musza and a teacher of mathematics called Kertész, seemed disappointed. Particularly Kertész, who was more militant than Musza and who not only covered his ears when he heard the AVO men swear, but went up to them and warned them of the danger of eternal damnation. These two men were disappointed because two days earlier, on Christmas Eve, the AVO had come into our barracks to search it. They had made us all strip, had searched our clothes, had emptied the straw from the mattresses, torn the festive pine-branches from the wall, taken down North-Eastern Inrush's shelf again and hit him over the head with it, confiscating his rock crystals, shoe-shine boxes and other toys, and had then built a fire in the middle of the square of the Bibles, New Testaments and Jewish prayerbooks they had found, and had solemnly burned that in the presence of the camp commander. Musza and Kertész had watched the scene from the window of the outhouse, praying to the Holy Virgin to come to our aid. And lo, the Holy Virgin had ignored their prayers and had appeared to Todi.

The appearance of the Holy Virgin marked the beginning of sabotage actions the scope and cunning of which amazed even me, who was considered chief expert in feverish loafing, the feigning of work and destruction. On the lower level of the quarry, groups of four hewed the rock, loaded it into miners' trucks and emptied it down the slope. Each group of four had to mine and load at least twelve trucks a day. An AVO guard sat near the rail with a notebook in his hand in which he put down which group's truck passed by him. Any group loading and unloading less than twelve trucks was locked up and received one slice of bread a day instead of half a pound, or was made to work all day and sit in short chains all night so that they became weaker and weaker, and less and less able to fulfil their quota. Gabori's trick was not to empty the truck on the slope but to push it back again along the elliptical rail, thus passing several times before the guard with the same truckload. This system was very dangerous, partly because the guard could easily, have noticed the absence of the noise made by the rock being tipped out, partly because it required a superhuman effort to push the heavy truck back up the slope.

On the day after the apparition the camp settled down to a long period of resistance. Istvan B. Racz, former deputy, a young peasant lad who was leader of the young generation of smallholders, invented a method adopted within minutes by all the thirty-five trucking groups: some hundred and forty men. They wired large roots – feather-weight as compared to the andesite rock – in the bottom of the trucks so that what looked like a full load of the usual two thousand eight hundred kilogrammes really only amounted to two or three hundred kilogrammes of rock. In this way it was child's play to push the unemptied trucks back up the slope. The groups' work was reduced to one-tenth and they spent their time listening to staff colonel Valér Czebe, who could whistle entire operas for them.

The only decent *nachalnik*, a social democratic engineer called Janos Lund, a mild six-foot-six giant, worked with his group on top of the mountain. They were cutting rock along a two-hundred-and-fifty metre front, right on the edge of the precipice, from where it tumbled down to land at the foot of the mountain. When they reached the triangulation point Lund decided that the construction which marked it would have to go down the precipice with the rock. There was no other fixed point by which the amount of rock cut could be measured, so Lund was ordered to drive a pole into the ground ten metres behind the old triangulation point, to act as a new one.

When he was digging up the wooden construction which marked the original triangulation point, Lund found a bronze Maria-medal buried, probably, when it was put up. He was not a religious man, but still he felt there must be some connection between the appearance of the Holy Virgin and the finding of this Patrona Hungariae medal. While trying to solve this mystery he hit upon a wonderful idea. He told his men to work without haste and leave the rest to him. That evening, when the norm-controller arrived to check up on how much rock had been cut during the day, he congratulated Lund: the brigade had cut two hundred and fifty metres. This was because Lund had discovered that if he moved the new triangulation point nearer the edge of the precipice each day, it looked as though great progress had been made. He had no reason to fear that he would be found out. Not even the foremost mining engineers of the country could have calculated or even estimated the weight of hewn rock piling up at the foot of the mountain, and not even a new geodesic measurement of northern Hungary could have proved that he had cheated.

Lund's discovery helped not only his brigade but all the prisoners working on the quarry front, among them the men dangling from the top on ropes ten or twenty metres long, hewing steps into the quarry wall. The beautiful boy with the Antinuos face told me of Lund's trick that same evening and asked for twice his usual Greek lesson because now he had more time to study. He said that Lund, a very modest person, was inordinately proud of his idea and compared himself to Archimedes because, contrary to Archimedes who said, 'Give me a fixed point to stand on and I shall move the earth from its orbit', he had removed the fixed point and brought everything to a standstill.

We hoped that by slowing down work at the quarry and on the road-building we could at least arrest our further deterioration if not gain new strength. This, however, did not affect the forty or fifty elderly men who suffered so badly from the cold and the wet that there was little hope for their survival. One evening I was visited on my bunk by a very intelligent man with soft eyes and hard features, György Korda, formerly a captain in the so-called economic police. Korda told me that the chief *nachalnik*, Dezsö Tamas, and his deputy, Sandor Jeges, had offered him the job of *nachalnik*. He was the third to be interviewed, because two other former police officers had rejected the offer – as a result of the appearance of the Holy Virgin. Korda's information did not surprise me. A year ago the AVO had selected the *nachalniki* from among the 'un-real social democrats' (which was what we called the careerists who joined the party in 1945, to distinguish them from the old – that is the 'real' – social democrats); these were later replaced by lumpen-proletarians and lumpen-intellectuals who pretended that they had remained good communists even in prison; while lately – perhaps from professional solidarity – the posts of *nachalniki* were generally given to policemen – not Horthy police, but those who had served in the 'democratic police'.

Korda told me that he had accepted the offer, but could still resign if I disapproved. He had decided to form a brigade of the older men and thus to save them. His plan was ready and he had already discussed it with Illésfalvy, who was working in the AVO store-house and who had promised to throw the wooden pegs supplied by the main AVO stores into the fire. We knew that the shoemaker's shop was still making Sunday boots for the AVO staff – although the camp commander had prohibited it after Michnai's escape. The head of the shoemaker's shop had informed Dentures that very day that they could make no more boots if they were given no pegs; Korda, on the other hand, had told Dentures that there would be plenty of pegs if he was permitted to organize the old men into a brigade which would manufacture treenails in a covered shed among the woodpiles. Korda planned to deliver a few handfuls to the shoemaker's shop every evening and throw the rest into the fire. Neither the camp commander nor the political officer need know anything about the arrangement. Though the plan sounded somewhat naïve, Korda was certain that it would come off. And if the wooden pegs business folded up he would invent something else.

The reason why Korda told me his plans in detail was that he wanted me to use my name and prestige to win for him not only an acquittal but a *summa cum laude* forgiveness for his communist past and for having been a captain in the notorious economic police. I gave him my word that I would do so on condition that the old men survived without exception.

I did not have much confidence in Korda's undertaking, but soon learned that he was executing his plan with exemplary courage and coolness. In the mornings, when we left the camp for our places of work, Korda led his brigade in the direction of the quarry, because it would have been dangerous to remain behind, seeing that the commander and the political officer were always snooping about to catch idlers. On the way to the mine the old men disappeared as if the earth had swallowed them up. They stole back, one by one, to the shed among the woodpiles behind the barracks and sat there all day around a fire. It was Korda who obtained the charcoal – so that there should be no smoke – from the charcoal-burners working in the depths of the forest. The calorie-value of their diet sufficed for this way of life, and the old people soon began to show signs of recovery. This solution of the problem was welcomed by the entire camp because the constant – though justified – complaints of the older men had been driving us to despair.

The first weeks of January, therefore, passed in relative calm. Because of the slower tempo of the work and the universal, quiet confidence created by the appearance of the Holy Virgin, nobody died of starvation. I often thought of Michnai and still hoped that he had reached his destination. At the same time I was affected by the atmosphere in the camp and almost came to believe that I myself had seen the Holy Virgin, instead of having conjured her up. At least I was almost convinced that she had indeed appeared to Todi above the embers and, by some strange coincidence, had announced the very things I had suggested – or perhaps prophesied. And in addition to the easier work and the heavenly vision there was another reward for our renewed strength and determination to resist: the dogs.

We often talked about what we would do to the AVO if conditions changed. Only twenty or thirty of our comrades insisted that they must be hanged to the last man or imprisoned in exactly the same conditions as ourselves. My friends, myself and the Catholics, Pali Musza, Kertész and Pista Todi, declared that we had no wish to live in a society that maintained prisons like this, no matter who was in them. If we did as the communists did we would, willy-nilly, become identical with them. The judges and lawyers – Rigo, Banvölgyi, Berzsenyi – said that according to the penal code, any independent Hungarian court would sentence to death thousands and thousands of AVO men, high party functionaries and party secretaries for murder and complicity in murder, and that even communist law would support the sentences on the basis of the paragraphs dealing with the unlawful torturing of individuals and entire classes of people. However, we all agreed that the law must not be applied. At the beginning of the century the feudal régime had suppressed the agrarian-socialists and social democrats with brutality and machine-gun fire; then the 1919 dictatorship of the proletariat had introduced a Red Terror, to be followed by the Horthy régime, and a White Terror; then came the blood baths of the arrow-cross and the Gestapo in 1944, and finally the present situation. The vendetta must be stopped once and for all.

In this we were united; but none of us had any idea as to what to do with the guilty. In principle we were all for forgiveness, but in practice the idea of living under the same roof with these people in a decent society appeared impossible. Finally we had agreed that the best solution would be to deport them, with their families, to the Soviet Union – although, since a complete change of régime in Hungary implied a complete change in the Soviet Union, it seemed heartless to wish them on a democratic Russia. The fate of the dogs, however, changed our attitude. We did not discuss it, but a few days later Egri informed me that I had been talking about AVO murderers in my sleep, and planning to strangle Stalin – in English, which made things even worse. Paul Musza, who was known for his boundless tolerance, was pacing the barracks in his bare feet, shaking his fists and calling to the Almighty to mete out justice.

On the morning after they escaped into our barracks we wanted to take the dogs to work with us, but, obeying their instincts, they crawled under the bunks. After we had left the camp the AVO guards ordered the cooks to remain in the kitchen and keep away from the windows. Then – as Helvetius related – they coaxed the dogs out into the yard and began to shoot at them. They did not aim at the head but at the hind legs, obviously to revenge the desertion. When we returned from work, the whole camp was drenched in blood. The black-and-white-striped mastiff which had spent the night on Uncle Csaplar's bunk escaped, wounded, to a spot between the two barbed-wire fences and was still alive the next morning.

My large white bitch escaped to the shed behind the kitchen, where it was nursed by Helvetius. He called over one of the doctors from the infirmary, who extracted the bullets from the dog's legs and thighs and bandaged them. At noon, when Helvetius and the other cooks brought the kettles out to the work-sites, he laid the dog in an empty kettle. He carried the animal to the charcoal-burners' furnace where two reliable fellow-prisoners were working: Palffy-Muhoray and Lajos Dalnoki Miklos, son of the prime minister of the 1945 democratic Hungarian government. They hid the animal in a woodpile and Helvetius visited it every day, bringing bones and half of the AVO guard's goulash. I always looked in on the dog whenever I could. She lay motionless in the dark and, according to the charcoal-burners, never came out into the open. I squatted down by her, seeing nothing but her luminous eyes and feeling her chin on my hand. She never made a sound except when she smelled a guard. Then she began to growl, persistently, monotonously, but not louder than the humming of a bee.

In the middle of January our situation again began to deteriorate. The *nachalniki* must have noticed something, because they were constantly on the look-out for sabotage, though in vain. In their fury they sicked the AVO guards on us every time they caught us resting or talking. The guards – when they were alone, and particularly those of peasant origin – shrugged their shoulders and snapped at the *nachalnik*: 'Don't you see he's finished?' However, when they came in twos, they vied with each other in brutality. One morning, for instance, when I was loading logs in the forest, a young AVO guard with a face like Lord Byron's dropped a whole bar of chocolate at my feet; but the same afternoon, when he was accompanied by another guard, Mongol, he hit me, at Talian's request, with such force that I fainted and discovered only later that he had knocked out two of my teeth.

In the third week of January one of us was collapsing every day, usually around a quarter to twelve, immediately before the cooks arrived with the cauldron, when we heard the distant sound of church bells from the village in the valley. Those who collapsed usually died the same afternoon or during the night. They were all middle-aged, well-built, once strong men: workers, clerks, peasants. There was not one intellectual among them. The fact that our once so feverishly debated theory had proved correct no longer interested us. Even the materialists recognized by now that it was the spirit which fed the body with the last drops of the *vis vitalis*, but even the idealists had to recognize that though, by some miracle, we had been the guests of Christ, the feast was now over.

Although I had lost approximately one quarter of my weight, which had remained unchanged at sixty-six kilogrammes since my student days, I felt relatively strong, above all spiritually. Therefore I thought it my duty to devote my energies to comforting and entertaining my fellow-prisoners, even if my friends repeatedly warned me to be careful. But what was the use of being careful? It became increasingly clear to me that death by starvation would catch up with me in six to eight weeks, and if our food were unexpectedly improved, or the prisoners were released, I, who could write of my experience, would be the last man of all the thirteen hundred that they would let go.

In spite of this I still had some confidence left in my habitual luck, which had so far preserved me from being beaten or kicked to death. However, even luck deserted me. The blows received from Byron-face were only a prelude to what was to follow. The next day eight of us were carrying a heavy tree-trunk ten metres long down to the camp from the forest near the quarry. On the uneven slope the full weight of the trunk bore down now on four, then on two of us, so that they were sighing and cursing uninterruptedly.

'Imagine that you are carrying Stalin's coffin,' I said to comfort them. 'It will immediately feel lighter.'

I noticed too late that a *nachalnik*, György Kerekes, was standing behind me on the side of the path. Kerekes had been a communist party functionary when they arrested him; he said he had committed grave mistakes, though nobody believed him. He often explained that if he had the opportunity to send a message to his wife he would beg her to tell their son that his father was a scoundrel and that he must learn to hate him. At first, when he drove them to greater and greater achievements with double portions of food and extra cigarettes, the young members of his brigade had been devoted to him. But when the men no longer possessed the strength required of them he accused them of sabotage and had them locked up. When, exhausted with hunger and from sitting in short chains, they returned to work, he demanded that they perform their previous quota. He repeated this process two or three times until his men were reduced to skeletons.

Kerekes was not as stupid as my *nachalnik*, Talian, who denounced us every five minutes and exasperated the AVO with his oily flattery and ceaseless, hysterical tantrums. Kerekes approached the AVO guards not more than once or twice a day, asking for their help in whispers, because, he said, he could no longer bear to listen to the slandering of our socialist society, or to watch the sabotage. If they didn't help him he would be obliged to go to the camp commander. The implied threat scared the guards and they did what he asked, locking up the alleged culprit or beating him senseless on the spot. At such times Kerekes stood by with his arms crossed on his chest and turned away his head, though his muddy eyes were alight.

The previous week I had had a quarrel with him. An AVO colonel from Budapest had held an inspection in the square between the barracks. I was standing next to Gabori and immediately before us stood the *nachalniki* and the camp commander. After the inspection the colonel addressed us briefly. 'I have now seen for myself that you are all right. Or has anyone a complaint to make?' he asked, reaching for his revolver. 'Well, that's that, then,' he concluded with satisfaction, and trod deliberately on Gabori's boot in the toe of which there was a palm-sized hole. Gabori waved a cheerful goodbye with his big toe and the colonel turned away nervously. After the inspection Kerekes demanded that Gabori be punished because he had attacked the AVO's prestige and had tried to make the camp a laughing stock. This time, however, nobody listened to him.

Two days later, as I was coming back from visiting the sick dog, I met Kerekes in the forest. He stopped me and addressed me as 'comrade', against which I vehemently protested. Kerekes swallowed the insult and then begged me to help him re-educate my destructive friends, in the first place Gabori. It was his duty as a communist to attempt this almost hopeless task.

I felt myself going green with fury.

'You are not a communist,' I replied. 'An honest communist who attempts to preserve his faith even in prison must necessarily go mad. You are neither mad nor a communist. When you were brought here you saw at once that the physical effort demanded of the prisoners was too much for you, so like Richard III you resolved to become a villain. If you get out of here you will continue playing the communist to get yourself a good job and make others work. It is a comprehensible attitude but it has nothing to do with communist ideology.'

He watched me from under his straight brows and did not interrupt. I noticed for the first time that he was slightly hunchbacked, which had brought Richard III to my mind. He was so completely unprepared for my words that he began to stammer and defend himself. I remarked that he was not the only one to have attended lectures on psychology at the university, and went on my way. When, a few days later, he overheard my remark about Stalin's coffin it was easy to guess what was to come.

The same evening, as I was about to go into the barracks, two giant, red-faced AVO guards whom I had never seen before stood in my way. They led me behind the building. Both were at least a head taller than I and I stood between their broad, square shoulders like a football on the starting line. They began to hit me expertly, without emotion, pushing me back and forth between them. I tried to behave like a ball, to transform myself into kinetic energy and fly from one to the other without resistance. In the end they pushed me a few times in the chest and back, then they let me go. My friends were busy playing bridge with hand-painted cards made of old cardboard boxes and had not noticed my absence.

Two days later I had another misadventure. The guards must have cracked one of my ribs, because I felt a deep, stabbing pain at every breath and could hardly walk. In the morning, in the quarry, I simply kneeled down behind a small pile of rock. There was no *nachalnik* around. Some ten of my fellow-prisoners stood in a circle round me, begging me to recite a poem I had written to Suzy. This poem was very popular and although some hundred men knew it by heart they always liked to hear me recite it.

I was coming to the lines:

> *. . . And when I die I will speak from my grave,*
> *Standing in its pit to send you my eternal love.*

I will send you the sound of my vanished footsteps
Sandalled in the fallen leaves of autumn . . .

when a boulder began falling from the crest of the mountain where Lund and his men were working. Usually no rubble fell on the spot where we were, but this time a round stone, the size of a child's head, fell on the pile behind which I was kneeling, ricocheted and hit me squarely in the forehead. I was immediately covered in blood. My companions led me to Doctor Bede, who was on duty in the quarry and who put iodine on the wound. With this I considered the problem solved.

The next morning I felt faint, feverish and sick Doctor Acs, who inspected the barracks before the inmates went to work, told me that I had concussion. This, however, did not suffice to keep me in bed, even less to take me to hospital. But when he noticed an egg-sized boil on my neck to which I had paid no attention his face cleared.

'With this,' he said, 'they will let you into the infirmary.'

About thirty of us stood in line outside, waiting for the camp commander to appear. He sent the first, a peasant called Csibraki, suffering from sciatica, who had been crawling on all fours for a week, to join his working party. He did the same with another peasant suffering from cirrhosis of the liver. In Mutor's case he hesitated. Mutor had a brain tumour and the entire camp knew it. At night, when he got up to go to the outhouse, he often knocked his head against the upper bunk in the dark and the bump woke us all. We watched his loping, unbalanced gait with horror but what horrified us even more was the circumstance that his name, Mutor, was an anagram of his disease, *tumor*.

'All right, you can stay behind,' the camp commander conceded. With the others he was more lenient and with the exception of two cases of sciatica and a serious case of coronary thrombosis he herded the others – who suffered from visible diseases, mostly boils on the neck, the knee or the hip-joint, into the infirmary. I was the last. He looked with horror at my neck. 'Go in there and have yourself treated,' he said.

Doctor Acs pointed out my bed, then took me into his consulting room and put me on his own bed so that he could talk to me while he was treating the others. But first he repeated the offer he had made me a year ago concerning glucose. When I again refused he said we would talk about it later and called in the first patient. During the treatment he told me that he had constructed an electric instrument to cure sciatica which the AVO, because it was an invisible disease, regarded as malingering. When the patient left he inspected my boil and said he would open it as soon as the staff sergeant arrived. He had plenty of chloroform and every minute of unconsciousness was a precious gift. I begged him not to wait because I might talk under chloroform and abuse the communists as I did in my sleep. He laughed and declared that he had operated on many an AVO guard and officer in the presence of the sergeant and they all sent Rakosi to the devil under the anaesthetic. The staff sergeant had never read Freud and didn't take anything said at such times seriously. Besides, he was interested only in the operation and in nothing else.

'A sadist?'

'No. Or rather, only within the civilized, Galenian limits, like myself.'

Acs stood at the window, framed by the black-green, ghostly pines of the distant forest, and looked at me beseechingly. His face was lead-grey and thinner than was warranted by the work he was doing. It was rumoured in the camp that he was a morphine addict, but even if that had been true, his trouble was his conscience. A year before he and Count Janos Hoyos, both working in the infirmary, had been the most popular men of the camp. 'At least our hospital is headed by two just men,' my friends used to say. Very soon, however, Hoyos told the camp commander that he refused to work in the hospital if he was not supplied with penicillin and insulin. He was put in chains and sent to Budapest. We never heard of him again. Acs became chief physician in his place. At first Acs portioned out the medicines at his disposal equally and was hated because the small quantities didn't do anyone any good. During the last few months he had changed his method, trying to save the *élite* of the camp, and making himself even more bitterly hated by the others. When, in the morning, he visited the barracks, people reminded him of medical ethics and spat in his face. Acs suffered terribly from all this. That was why he had constructed his electric instrument, which, he hoped, would prove his goodwill. When he saw me come into the infirmary his whole face lit up. Now, at last, he could open his heart to someone.

'This is what happens to those who accept any kind of post under the communists,' he said suddenly. 'Look at me, George. All night long I walk up and down in this room. I agreed to become head of the infirmary because I had to agree. I am the most experienced of the five physicians in the camp, if someone has to shoulder the responsibility it is best that it should be me. At least, that's what I told myself. But there's no excuse for a physician who doesn't notice what subconscious waters feed the roots of his rhetoric. I accepted this post because I was afraid to work, the blows and the thing we call, so euphemistically, "fatigue". Fear won't save me,' he said, pointing to the green-black pines, straight as cypresses, in the distance, 'because death will catch up with me anyway.'

He could not continue because Robert Gati, obviously tired of waiting outside, came into the consulting room. Acs looked at him angrily, but then kneeled down to take off the plaster from his broken leg. Gati – a short, delicate young man with sagging shoulders – had once worked on the party's official daily, *Szabad Nép*. They arrested him on the Czechoslovak–German border when he was trying to escape to the West. The prisoners hated him; they alleged that shortly before his arrest he had written a report on the Vac penitentiary in which he complained that the political prisoners had it too good there. Gati behaved modestly and was mostly silent. When I first talked to him while we were carrying stone together, he told me that in 1949 he had come to the conclusions that Rakosi, Gerö and Farkas were rascals. Within forty-eight hours he was on the Czech border, because he felt that he must enlighten the West without a moment's delay. His childish simplicity moved me deeply and I suggested to my friends that we invite him to join our nightly conversations. They, however, protested because they said Gati smelled like a communist.

'Well,' Acs asked him while cutting the plaster, 'are you still devoted to your one-time comrades?'

'I was never devoted to them,' Gati replied quietly. 'All I did was declare that not every communist is a scoundrel. There are honest men among them.'

'For instance?'

'For instance Sandor Haraszti, Géza Losonczy, Miklos Gimes . . . and I could name at least half a dozen on *Szabad Nép*.'

'Try to stand up,' Acs commanded.

'Besides,' Gati continued, 'I never approved of what was going on here. The members of the Hungarian communist leadership are cynics and criminals. They compromised the cause of communism,' he added, walking a few steps with his face distorted with pain but without complaint. 'I am deeply convinced that it is different in the Soviet Union. It is simply unthinkable that such prison conditions should prevail there.'

'Stop spinning!' I moaned, resting my swimming head on Acs's straw pillow. 'Rakosi does exactly what Stalin tells him to do. Our treatment here, the layout of the camp, and even the number of barbs in the barbed-wire fence are copied from the Soviet example. Besides, I find that both from the point of view of theoretical and practical bolshevism this camp is perfection itself. It is a miniature edition of the communist society of the future.'

The AVO sergeant appeared before I could develop my theme. I woke, some time later, on bed No. 13 in the common ward. One of twelve other patients, a man whose name nobody knew, lay unconscious on his bed. His dixie, still half full of beans, and his bread were on his bedside table. His neighbour, an informer by the name of Deak, had raised himself on his elbow and was watching the movement of the blanket over the dying man's chest. His hand was hovering above the dixie and the bread, ready to swoop down as soon as the man had drawn his last breath. The others waited for me to open my eyes and then begged me to tell them about America.

I began to tell them the story of my captivity on Ellis Island. While I talked I took my temperature, which was above 104°. A few minutes later I felt sick and staggered out into the bathroom. I leaned my head against the barred window and looked out on the still, black-green pine trees. The shadow of death – I thought.

When I returned to my bed, Deak was still in the same position, his hand extended towards the food. Around four o'clock we were honoured by a visit from Hans Arse, accompanied by Doctor Acs. I had never seen this man before but knew him well by description. Nobody knew his real name but his nickname was known in prisons all over Hungary. He was the medical colonel from Vacz who tore open the shirts of the hanged to put his stethoscope on their hearts. Every two weeks he came to Recsk to inspect the infirmary. He was a middle-aged, puny little man with an old-fashioned, black leather medical bag under his arm.

He came directly to my bed.

'This malingerer has been lying here for months!' he shouted at Doctor Acs. 'How long, do you think, I will tolerate it?'

'*Habet concussionem cerebris, collega excellentissime* . . .'

'Stop gassing,' the colonel interrupted. 'And you, get dressed and go back to work right away!' he yelled at me.

He remained standing beside my bed and waited until I had dressed. Deak took advantage of the opportunity and devoured the dying man's bread. Acs bent his head. It seemed to me as if red, linoleum-like spots were dancing up and down his lead-grey face; but perhaps it was only my feverish imagination. When I stepped out of the infirmary and began walking up the mountain slope in the icy wind, I felt considerably better.

Three days later, one Saturday afternoon when at roll-call they read out the names of those who had earned punishment, mine was included. I was to be locked up at night for two weeks and spend two hours each night in short chains. Garamvölgyi's name came immediately after mine. Two days before, coming back from work – we had been working at different places – we were glad to have an opportunity to talk but, just inside the barbed-wire fence, we came face to face with the Gravedigger. He was sitting, dead drunk, on the side of the ditch and shook his fist at us.

'I saw you,' he screamed. 'I saw you playing cards in the bushes instead of working . . .'

'But, sir . . .' Garamvölgyi tried to explain. 'Faludy was not . . .'

'Shut your face, carrot-top!' the Gravedigger yelled. 'That Faludy, he is a decent fellow, but this one here,' and he pointed at me, 'this one here is a scoundrel! I'll show him, never fear!'

But it is possible that I had my own carelessness to thank. Wrangel had warned me that Deak had denounced me for imperialist propaganda while in the infirmary, and denounced Doctor Acs for having kept me there though there was nothing wrong. Before Hans Arse's arrival I had been telling my fellow-patients about the weeks spent on Ellis Island. I had come at Roosevelt's invitation, but without a regular visa, and he had omitted to inform the immigration authorities, who decided to make a case of it, arrested my wife and myself on board ship and took us to Ellis Island. Here a square-faced and disagreeable judge declared that the United States had no need for Hungarian poets and therefore sentenced us to deportation. My friends left no stone unturned to get me out. 'Roosevelt's guest on Ellis Island,' screamed the newspaper headlines. After Dorothy Thompson's extremely outspoken article on this subject, the judge who had sentenced me apologized in the name of the United States and personally put me and my wife on a ship taking us into New York harbour.

I told my fellow-patients about the days spent on Ellis Island. During the day we sat around, in comfortable armchairs, in a huge room, reading, playing table tennis, listening to the radio. The authorities ordered all the Hungarian newspapers for me, and from a public telephone box I could talk with my friends in New York. In the dining-room we sat around beautifully laid tables and had a choice of American, French, Chinese and Jewish dishes. Every afternoon I received visits from my friends . . . It never occurred to me that I was giving Deak, who was busy devouring his dead neighbours's bread, plenty of material for denunciation with which to earn himself more bread.

However, there was no time for speculation. A few minutes later we were standing in line, with our blankets under our arms, before the door of the prison within the prison. Mongol – a slant-eyed, pale-faced, hysterical and vain young guard – led the twelve of us sentenced to short chains to an empty cell and locked the door on us. There was so little room that we couldn't sit down. Doctor Acs squatted in a corner with his back against the wall. His face was stiff and grey like the cheap, synthetic marble used, in the last century, for kitchen cupboards and stairs. He could not have been more humiliated. The night before, he had tried out his home-made electric instrument on Csibraki, a peasant suffering from sciatica. The screams of the patient were heard even in the most distant barracks. He was so badly burned that the cartilage between two of his vertebrae fell literally to pieces. Acs, who was usually sober, cold and precise and despised nothing more than his colleagues' love of quackery, seemed to have been carried away by a strange *furor operationis*; when the guards finally freed the patient from his hands the unfortunate man was dying. At the morning inspection several of the prisoners called Acs a 'murderer' and they looked at each other in amazement when he was given only three days in the cell. It did not even occur to them that it was not for Csibraki's death that Acs had been sentenced, but for keeping me in the infirmary on allegedly false pretences.

Uncle Horvath was sitting behind me on the floor. In the morning we had been shifting woodpiles from one place to another. The paralytic old man had crawled around on all fours, building miniature woodpiles in the middle of the road from tiny twigs. Sub-lieutenant Laszlo Nagy, the political officer, had asked him harshly what he was doing. 'I am amusing myself,' the old man replied, and crawled away in the mud. The long-legged sub-lieutenant asked the sergeant guarding us whether the old man was being impertinent, and the sergeant assured him that Horvath wouldn't even recognize his own wife any longer.

'Do you know who I am, Horvath?' the sub-lieutenant asked.

Horvath raised his watery blue eyes and examined the features of the one-time grocer's assistant.

'Sure, I know. You are that damned kike who wouldn't even leave the dying alone.'

The sub-lieutenant stared at him as if he couldn't believe his ears and then, shaking his fists hysterically, he ran away.

Dani Kis, who was standing next to me with his arms crossed on his chest, was the first to be called out. I had always liked the look of this young man. With his jet-black hair and moustache, his strong nose and almond-shaped eyes he was the very image of the Hungarian peasant of the lowlands. This was how I had always imagined György Dozsa, leader of the 1514 Hungarian peasant insurrection, whom the nobles – though he was a nobleman himself – fried on a white-hot iron throne and then made his lieutenants eat his living flesh. One of the informers had denounced Dani Kis and he was sentenced to short chains on the grounds that he had exchanged his bread for cigarettes. Everybody in the camp knew that Dani did not smoke.

Through the door I could hear Mongol ordering him to put as much wood on the fire as the stove would take. When he called me out Dani was sitting in chains close to the blazing iron stove in the polygonal room from which the corridors and the cells opened. I was led into a small cell where the guard tied my wrists to my ankles. When he had finished with me he went to fetch Doctor Acs. He made the doctor sit on the floor and put his two hands between his ankles. Then he jumped on the extended hands and tied the wrists to the ankles in such a way that the rope cut deep into the flesh. Acs didn't even wince. There was no room left for Garamvölgyi in the cell, so Mongol tied him up in the corridor, lifted him by his collar and his red hair and plumped him down on the broad shelf built into the cell-wall for that purpose.

When he had locked the door on us I pulled out both hands from the loops of the rope and straightened my back. I did not know whether I owed my freedom of movement to my narrow hands or to Mongol's goodwill. I at once offered to loosen the bonds of my friends, but Acs refused, saying that he had deserved this punishment and would bear it like a man – if he could still be called a man – and Garamvölgyi refused because he was afraid the guard might come in and catch him. He wanted me to put back my hands too and, out of solidarity, I complied though the loose rope hardly bothered me at all. A few minutes later Garamvölgyi began to moan and soon he was howling like a dog at the moon. Acs tried to explain to him that if he concentrated on his position and thought of nothing else, his suffering would soon become unbearable, but if he occupied his mind with other thoughts the two hours would soon be over. Besides, he ought to be grateful to the pain because it made him forget hunger and exhaustion.

'I can't stand it!' Garamvölgyi sobbed, gnashing his teeth.

Apart from the slight itching in my wrist when I leaned back, I was filled with peaceful indifference. After all, I could free my hands any time I wanted. If I couldn't, I would probably also suffer – I thought – but as it was, only the suffering of the others turned this cell into a torture chamber. I freed my hands again and listened to the moans and cries. A conversation was going on immediately outside our door between the guard and Kertész, the bigoted mathematics professor who, whenever he heard an AVO man swearing, warned him of the hell fire awaiting him. The guards thought he was slightly mad and liked to have their joke with him.

'Tonight I'll teach you to swear, you son of a bitch!' announced Mongol.

'Thank you, sergeant, sir, but I don't swear.'

'And why not?'

'I am a Catholic, sir. My faith forbids me to swear.'

'Do you like rats, Kertész?'

'I don't, sir. I am frightened of them.'

'Well, if you won't swear I'll shut you into the dark cell, and that's full of them.'

'Don't do that, sergeant, please!'

'Then swear. Now!'

'What shall I swear?'

'I'll give you something easy,' Mongol said after some deliberation. 'It won't take you long to get it out. Say after me: That the tin-Christ of Buda put his scabrous pr—— into your arse!'

For a few seconds there was complete silence.

'Will you say it, or won't you? If not, it's the rats for you!'

A door banged in the corridor and Garamvölgi, who had forgotten his pain listening to the conversation, began to howl again:

'I can't stand this any longer! Sergeant, shoot me like a dog!'

'I should be ashamed to act as you do,' I said quietly.

'Let's try and distract his attention,' suggested Acs. 'A few days ago you said, George, that this camp was the symbol of the ideal communist society. Would you explain why you said that?'

'Even an idiot would know why,' said Garamvölgi. 'But never mind. Go on, tell us, George.'

'We have been given the job of opening up a quarry,' I began, closing my eyes and realizing suddenly how great an effort it was for me to talk fluently. 'We have been given the job of opening up a quarry,' I repeated. 'We all know that it will collapse before the job is accomplished and that we shall all perish. Just as outside communism will collapse before it is accomplished, but our contemporaries will all perish before it collapses, Here, as outside, the authorities are not interested in production, they use work to keep us busy, and turn us into weak, tormented, mentally degenerate wretches. The only difference is that here they are doing it more openly, more violently and more rapidly than outside. Here the conditioning to communism is carried out with the help of a handful of beans – more practically and realistically than outside. Outside, they still tolerate family ties and separate apartments and permit a man to have two suits of clothes. Here, where communism has almost been reached, handkerchiefs, books, newspapers and watches are no longer required. Even the right to spread rumours has been taken away from us, as it is in Orwell's book, because even subversive action has become a state monopoly. The iron curtain is replaced with a barbed-wire fence, but within it the monolithic power has no need to fear Western competition. So here it can throw culture, science, propaganda on the dust-heap and needs to make no effort to win us for communism. Outside, they would reach this stage only if communism became victorious throughout the entire world.

'At the same time, they have also attained the final stage of communism as far as the psychological effect is concerned. There are signs of it outside, too, but here we have perfection. They have gained absolute power over our bodies by violence, cunning, threats and a network of informers, and they can do with us what they please. But at the same time they have taught us to think. Their moral effect is like nitric acid separating the gold from the filth. Because of it scoundrels become even worse scoundrels, rotten to the core, but the gold of honour remains unchanged, or rather, receives an added sheen. He who extends even his little finger to them must inevitably . . .'

'Well,' Acs turned to Garamvölgyi. 'Do you still feel the pain?'

For a reply Garamvölgyi began to scream and simultaneously we heard a cell door open on the opposite side of the corridor.

'You can come out, Kertész,' we heard Mongol's voice. 'I told you that your mottled-arsed Holy Virgin would not protect you from the rats! Say it.'

'What shall I say?'

'The tin-Christ of Buda.'

'On my responsibility I won't.'

'On whose responsibility, then?'

'On yours, sir!'

'Shut up, you idiot! What do you mean, on my responsibility?'

'I mean that you will have to answer for it, sir, before God and men.'

'The hell I will! You can say it on Faludy's responsibility or Doctor Acs's.'

'I can't do that, sir. They are not answerable for the fact that the powers above compel me to swear. If I have to commit a sin, then I must throw the responsibility upon the godless authority that . . .'

'Swear on your own responsibility, Kertész! You won't! Then back to the rats . . .'

When the door slammed, Garamvölgyi moaned again.

'Perhaps you should go on with your explanation,' Acs suggested.

'No, don't . . .' wailed Garamvölgyi.

'Then what shall I talk about?'

'Nothing.'

Suddenly I had a saving idea.

'What about enumerating the English kings . . . and then perhaps the caliphs, and after the caliphs from Childebert to Vincent Auriol?'

Garamvölgyi swallowed the bait. Ten minutes later he was in full swing:

'. . . after the Omayads came the Abbasid . . . first Abdul Abbas who ordered the blood-bath of Damascus, from 750 . . . from 754 the founder of Baghdad, al-Mansur, from 775 . . .'

On the other side of the corridor Mongol opened the door again.

'. . . the firstborn son of Caliph Muhammad al-Mahdi was killed by his brother, Haroun al-Raschid, from 786 . . . then came his two sons, al-Amin and al-Mamun . . .'

'Did the rats bite you, Kertész?'

'They did, yes, they did . . .'

'Did you like it?'

'It was dreadful, sergeant, sir, dreadful . . .'

'Then say it after me and don't gape there like a duck! That the tin-Christ of Buda stick into your arse his scabrous . . .'

'Yes, sir. That the tin-devil of Buda stick into your arse his . . .'

'I'll tear you to pieces, you shit! Not into me, into you!'

'That the tin-devil of . . .'

'Christ!'

'Devil!'

'Christ! Christ! Christ!'

'No! Devil!'

'How dare you contradict me! Get inside!'

We heard Mongol's slow, uncertain steps as he went back to his small desk by the stove. Suddenly I noticed a strong, penetrating smell.

'Burning textile,' Acs said. He had already been sniffing the air for a few moments.

'Henry II until 1559 . . .' Garamvölgyi declared triumphantly. 'The Capet dynasty died out with three brothers and so did the Valois with Henry II's three sons, Francis II, Charles IX and . . .'

Suddenly we heard Uncle Horvath's deep voice above the chorus of moans.

'Come here, son, take these strings off me . . . it isn't nice to play such jokes on an old man . . . you hear me, sergeant, you lout!'

'Where are you, Horvath?' asked Mongol, who had forgotten into which cell he had locked Horvath.

'Here!'

'Where?'

'In hell!' mumbled Uncle Horvath in the cell next to ours.

The sergeant must have taken the rope off him because the old man thanked him loudly while Mongol tried in vain to shut him up.

'Bring me a bottle of wine and some salted almonds,' the old man ordered as the guard left his cell and locked the door.

The smell of burning fabric became more and more unbearable. Garamvölgyi noticed nothing. He had reached the Third Republic.

'. . . . was shot down by an anarchist in 1894 . . . a year later Casimir Perrier resigned . . . the sixth, Félix Faure, had a beautiful, long beard. He liked to tie it, at night, to his mistress's long hair. One night, when he died while copulating, the poor woman was so completely entangled with the corpse that they had to be cut apart, while in the morning, at the Élysées . . .'

'I can't hear you. Louder!' Mongol encouraged Kertész.

'That the tin-devil of Buda put his scabrous penis . . .' Kertész sighed.

'What's that, penis?' Mongol shouted. 'How dare you use such bigoted expressions?'

'That the tin-devil of Buda put his scabrous . . . his scabrous . . .'

'Get it out!'

'His scabrous penis. *Vulgo;* pr—'

'What is *vulgo*, Kertész?'

'Sergeant, sergeant!' Acs yelled excitedly. 'I smell burning flesh!'

'Shut up or I'll step on your balls, old quack!' shouted Mongol. 'Yesterday you burned one of your fellow-prisoners to death and you dare open your mouth? What is *vulgo*, Kertész?'

A moment later, however, he came into the cell and untied Acs and myself. Outside, leaning against the white-hot iron stove, sat Dani Kis in short chains. He was conscious and gazed at us, nodding his tired head. His limbs were so tightly bound that they must have been completely numbed, so that he was oblivious to the pain and to his situation. On his right arm and thigh the fabric of his suit, the lining and his shirt were smouldering like shells on top of the glowing stove. I was nauseated by the smell of burning human flesh.

With a quick movement Acs tore Dani away from the stove. Mongol pushed me into the common cell, and then, a few minutes later, Acs, who told me that Dani had been taken to the infirmary.

His arm and thigh had burned to the bone. If he survived he would remain a cripple for life.

At dawn we tottered back, exhausted, to our barracks with our blankets on our shoulders. Uncle Horvath fell back near the pit where, according to the engineers, there was room for thirteen hundred corpses, with the necessary covering of lime. I went back for the old man. The stream, swelled by the heavy rains, had overflowed into the pit, transforming it into a small, round lake. Uncle Horvath was standing on the bank watching the surface of the lake with his head bowed, a beautiful, serene smile on his lips. It was quite obvious that he didn't know where he was. He was humming a melody from the last act of the musical *Janos Vitéz.* This musical is based on a folk legend about a shepherd boy who comes to fairyland in search of his dead bride. He stands by the Lake of Life and, to bring back his loved one, throws a rose into the blue water. Uncle Horvath was singing the shepherd's song:

Blue lake, limpid lake, lake in which all life is created . . .

The blows, the concussion and two weeks of nightly punishment-cell wore me out completely. I was still in possession of my mental capacities but I doubted whether I could hold on to them for long. I was rapidly losing strength and my will-power was almost gone. The first morning, on my return from the cell, I found a slice of bread in the pocket of my overcoat. Only Helvetius or Egri could have put it there. I decided to investigate after work and return the bread to its rightful owner. However, the temptation was too strong and I devoured it on the spot. On another occasion I noticed that Robert Gati, who, to do me a favour, had fetched my supper along with his, was transferring half of his own portion into my dixie. When I protested, Gati declared that he was a very small eater and his condition was far better than mine, so he was not giving me anything but was only levelling. I didn't have enough energy left to spoon back the food into his dixie but the next day, when he offered to fetch my dinner, I refused and went for it myself.

In the first week of February only two of our fellow-prisoners died of starvation but in the second week the number of victims began to increase rapidly; one, two, or even three a day. The older prisoners were still whittling pegs under Korda's watchful eyes and their condition had considerably improved; so had that of Lund's brigade, since by moving the marking pole he had almost completely freed them from work. Most of those who succumbed were middle-aged, between thirty-eight and fifty-two. After a few weeks we could always tell in advance, from their complexion and their somnambulistic walk, who was going to die within the next two or three days. As none of us possessed a mirror Egri and I inspected each other's faces every morning, after having made a sacred pledge to tell each other the truth. I feared that Egri would not have the courage to tell me, so I also made the same arrangement with Helvetius who, I thought, was too naïve not to betray the truth by his expression. Of our circle of friends no one, with the exception of Borostobi, had yet succumbed: though we had a feeling that the island on which we were standing would soon be inundated by the flood.

We were building a road several kilometres below the camp, to lead from the railway station to the quarry. We were working on the upper half of the road; the lower, we heard, was being built by the inmates of another camp recently set up near Recsk. Each morning, accompanied by a large number of guards, we walked several miles along muddy or snowy ridges to our place of work. Once there, we had to move the several hundred metres of barbed-wire entanglement that surrounded us, and, in addition to wounding our hands, we tore our already ragged clothes. Talian, our *nachalnik*, made us take off our overcoats because – he said – the weight of them made us even more lazy. We lacked the strength to warm ourselves with work and thus almost froze to death in the icy wind blowing on the northern mountain slope.

I and some of my comrades who were beginning to show signs of complete exhaustion were usually made to do the heaviest jobs. The stronger ones paved the road, on their knees, while we had to carry stones in so-called racing-barrows with boards attached to their sides so that they took a load sixty per cent heavier than usual. The idea had been Dezsö Tamas's, the chief kapo. We found the load excessive, so three of our fellow-prisoners – all former navvies – went to the political officer to complain. They told him that the shape, size and capacity of barrows had been moulded by the experience of thousands of years throughout the world. The former grocer's assistant replied that in the Soviet Union they had introduced double-decker barrows because socialist man is more resistant than any other type of man. Their complaint proved only that they were reactionary blackguards who had no place in the new world. Then he sent them to solitary confinement.

At times the *nachalnik* made me stand in the ditch at the side of the road to dig. The work itself was not too bad, but after a while I was unable to straddle the ditch and had to stand up to my knees in the icy water, which completely filled my boots. In the mornings, while we were waiting for the guards under the hoary trees by the gate, Egri invited me to dinner and told me in detail about the delicacies he was going to offer me. At other times I invited him to dinner. But on the way to the road work we no longer talked. As soon as I picked up the shaft of the barrow or took my place in the ditch I started wool-gathering. I dreamed mostly about my childhood friends, our games, my grandfather's house and mill, and the morning passed with incredible speed, never seeming longer than fifteen or twenty minutes. During our lunch break I sat with Egri or Földvary on the roadside, huddled together, silent. The afternoon again seemed no more than an hour. Only when we were marching back to camp along the rough, uneven hillside did I suddenly feel sweat break out over my whole body with fear that I might not be able to walk all the way back.

My situation, however, was unbearable only when the guard called 'the SS' stood near me. According to fellow-prisoners who had been in Dachau, this guard had worked there a short eight years before. He was a real giant with a long, red nose, a livid face, a short, strong neck and protruding shoulder blades. He stood among the bushes with his arms crossed and never spoke a word to anyone. When Talian reported someone to him he called the culprit with a hardly visible movement of his forefinger, took him by the neck, knocked his head repeatedly against the barbed wire of the barrier, then, still without a sound, kicked him far out from among the bushes.

Once Talian caught me as I was standing still in the ditch. He pointed to the stump of an oak tree where the road was to continue and told me that unless I dug it out within three hours he would take me to the inspector. He meant the SS, who pretended to hear nothing. Three hours would have been sufficient to dig out the stump had the soil not been frozen and had I been given the necessary tools. But I had no saw, no shovel, and the pick-axe was too heavy for me to lift. I felt certain that I would not survive a beating by the SS. A moment later Egri was at my side and in a short while he had dug out half of the stump. The SS stood up to the waist in the underbrush, never looking towards us. When Egri was called away the boy with the Antinuos face took his place. I protested violently; he was just as exhausted as I. But he begged me with boyish charm to let him try.

'Give me ten minutes,' he said. 'I still owe you for the lessons in philosophy.'

In fifteen minutes he had dug out the stump from the ground. When Talian returned he gaped, unbelieving, at the empty hole and looked questioningly towards the SS. But the inspector held his head haughtily averted and kept silent.

Next morning, when Egri looked at my face his eyes seemed strange for a fraction of a moment. Helvetius assured me that I looked much better than the day before, but I became suspicious and followed him into the washroom. The scene I came upon was so amusing that I could hardly refrain from laughing aloud. Egri was standing in a corner, his head bent, his arms hanging lifeless by his side. Big tears were running down his face. The attractive butcher boy was swearing in whispers, hitting the wall with his clenched fists. Suddenly I felt as light as if I were already a ghost. I stole in on tiptoe and smiled at them.

'Don't be shocked,' I said. 'I have always respected other people's sorrow but I find it extremely funny that you should weep for me like two professional mourners . . .'

But I stumbled and was suddenly so weak that I gasped for breath.

I put my arm round Helvetius's neck, kissed him on the cheek and drew Egri to me. So we stood for a moment until I regained my strength.

At the barrack door I ran into a former naval officer, Frici Kopilarcsik, in the softly falling snow. He pushed a packet of cigarettes into my pocket, while Brigadier Lund stuffed a portion of bread in the other. While we were lining up for roll call, someone smuggled two packets of tobacco into the cuff of my overcoat, so that I had more tobacco and bread than anyone in camp. For a moment I wondered which was the more moving: human solidarity or the fact that I would soon be dead. Then I forgot everything and escaped into daydreams.

This time Talian assigned me and two of my fellow-prisoners to the lightest jobs: I had to shovel the snow from the already finished section of the road. This section was surrounded not by an entanglement but by an ordinary barbed-wire fence, and there were watch-towers along it manned by benevolent, or at least indifferent regulars. My companions worked on a distant part of the road so that I walked alone in the billowing snow moulded into hills and vales by the wind. The guard in the watch-tower threw down a box of matches so that I could light up quite often. I noticed that I had eaten both my bread portions only when my fingers encountered nothing but a few crumbs in the bottom of my pocket. My stomach was full, but somehow my entire body remained just as hungry as it had been before. I noted this, however, without attaching great importance to it and returned to my dreams.

I saw my grandfather's house at Zsolna, the flat-roofed yellow house with the pub in the front. Snow was falling in the square, a sleigh was standing before the door, the guests beat the clinging snowflakes from their boots and overcoats and in the sparkling cold both men and horses blew gin-scented steam from their noses. Then I was in the sleigh. I saw Laszlo Fényes wrapped in his black cape and myself at his side, huddling close to the warmth emanating from his body. We were on our way to Hatarujfalu, to Simon Pan's house. I heard the sharp tingling of the bells, the thud of the horses' hoofs, as we flew across the wooden bridge over the River Vag. Then the picture changed. Stinging, icy snowflakes were dancing madly in the sharp wind over the graveyard on the bank of the River Hudson. Six men were carrying Laszlo Fényes's coffin; behind it Rustem Vambéry, and Paul Kéri in black, and myself in American army uniform. We kept our heads bent because – grown men that we were – we were ashamed of our tears. But all the time I was only a spectator, I saw myself from the outside, as a stranger, as if my soul were ready to go on its separate way and I were practising the parting with my body.

Later the weather grew milder and the wind abated. I was trying to recall one of Andersen's tales, the Ice-Princess, but I remembered only the icy wind that had made me shiver at the time, after reading the story. How much I once loved Andersen's cool, intellectual imagination! The moving picture rolled on. Eva, the young actress, love of my student days in Vienna, was walking at my side in the deep snow. The fog that had settled over the landscape was so dense that I had to hold on to her hand so as not to lose her. From the pine forest covering the mountainside up to the alpine plateau only a few dark green, threatening shadows loomed in the fog. The shadows of death – I thought now. I had the same thought nineteen years ago, on the day of Hitler's ascent to power, the day we were walking up that alpine plateau. On the next square of film I was kissing Valy among the ruins of the Acquincum amphitheatre. I was suddenly deeply moved; I forgot her hysterical outbursts and remembered only what an honest, selfless, diligent and loving wife she had been, and how beautiful. Then I was walking with Suzy in the Municipal Park on Stalin's seventieth birthday. She had just come from Party school and I had a poem against Stalin in my pocket which I had written the same afternoon and now dared not show her. A torchlit procession was coming along György Dozsa Avenue in Constantine the Great's honour – we saw it from among the trees. Suzy looked on happily – and I shivered. Not because of the procession, but because the heavy boots were treading on our love. Suddenly I realized that the double portion of bread had not remained without effect: my dreams were becoming increasingly rational.

The snow-storm broke after lunch. Again I saw myself skating as a child, on the ice of the artificial lake in Budapest. On the other side the muddy snowpile had frozen into bumpy little mountains of ice at the foot of the dark, mysterious, low arch of a wooden bridge. There were no lamps there and no one ever went there to skate. I closed my eyes and sped, full speed, into the darkness. On the next square of film I saw one of the favourite poets of my youth, François Villon, whose poems I had so successfully translated into Hungarian. He too was walking in the snow. He had been condemned to death and then exiled from Paris and was now wandering towards Meung along the banks of the Loire. His pocket, like mine, was filled with fleas instead of bread. But had the snow ever stood so deep on the Orléans highway? Not in our days; but in the Middle Ages the winters were colder than today. I wondered why? Was it possible that the Gulf Stream had made itself felt only after the discovery of America? Then I saw the beautiful, fair Ulla Winblad driving her gig at a crazy speed towards a pub on the seashore. At her side Bellmann, the poet, with a bottle of *aqua vitae* between his knees, the way Lorsy used to hold a wine bottle. Was there an era more beautiful than the Swedish rococo? The ice over Lake Melar split with a noise like the uncorking of a bottle of champagne. After dinner the pony stood in the snow outside the pub, while Ulla lay fully naked on the bed upstairs, covering with her beautiful hand the only part of the body a rococo lady is ashamed of on such occasions: her face. The poet was leaning out of the window to close the shutters. His eyes met those of the jealous pony and the pony stamped its feet in impotent rage. Then I saw Michnai of the high forehead, treading the deep snow on his way to Vienna. He disappeared, then reappeared again between the tall heaps of snow with huge, white-painted radio-microphones hovering above his head like lilies of the valley.

And now, I thought to myself, I shall fling down the shovel and start walking, like Szuha, the notary. My knees are trembling and the bottle of *aqua vitae* slips from my hands. Why hold on to life? I am only tormenting myself. I see Stalin standing before a giant refrigerator, his hand on its handle. This is where he puts his victims after kicking them in the face and spitting on them. How many million in that refrigerator? Am I in it too? Objectively they have already refrigerated me; subjectively, however, I am just being frozen.

Suddenly my vision turned inwards; I no longer saw myself from the outside. It was I, myself, who was wandering in his ragged prison uniform in the sparkling sunshine along the snow-covered highway, climbing upwards, always upwards. Hundreds of woolly clouds hovered about me and, behind the clouds, angels with submachine-guns. Funny that I hadn't realized it till now. I am dead. I died a moment ago, Friday afternoon. The Neighbour promised that I would be admitted to Heaven this very day.

I was so delighted with the idea that I opened my eyes. The sun had indeed broken through the clouds. I tried to dominate my vision and give it at least some reality. Ten minutes ago I died on the Cross and Christ has promised me that I will be admitted to Heaven. It is to Heaven this new road leads, like every terrestrial road, not to Rome, though at times through Rome. There is nothing surprising in its being bordered by barbed-wire fences and guarded by soldiers: it is probably very crowded sometimes. It is prohibited to leave the road, everyone is obliged to follow its curve, no suicidal short-cuts across the snow!

When I reached the Gate of Heaven I beat it with my fists. I knew that I had landed myself in a pretty difficult situation. The Great Neighbour would not arrive for another forty days, first he went down to Hell to free my friends, Socrates and Plato, and then he would spend a few more weeks on Earth. I had only his oral promise to repeat, no document to prove it. I hoped that St Peter would credit my words but suddenly it occurred to me that even Peter had twenty more years to spend on Earth as an Apostle and would arrive only in Nero's days, while now Tiberius was Emperor. And Heaven was empty, like the summer resorts in winter: I was the first guest.

What are the angels doing at such times? They were probably spring-cleaning. I was about to turn away, certain that no one would open the Gate when suddenly I saw Bandi Havas stepping out from the gatekeeper's lodge. My heart leaped with joy.

'Have you become an angel, Bandi?' I asked.

'Don't be impertinent,' he replied coolly. 'True, at the time of the

Great Rebellion I sided with Lucifer, but later I made a public self-criticism and was forgiven. I was fired from the office but got this job as a gatekeeper. So as to be under constant surveillance . . .' he finished, blushing.

'And your thoughts, dear friend? Are they always loyal?' I asked with murderous irony.

He looked at me out of bloodshot eyes and wiped his sweating forehead. But he made no reply. I asked him to open the gate for me but he shook his head.

'You were a social democrat,' he said with unconcealed hostility. 'You need a document to get in here.'

'Then give me something to eat, at least. I haven't had anything for three days.'

'The party's eyes see everything,' he said, looking severely at a point near my navel. 'You have three portions of bread in your belly. Sorry.'

He backed slowly towards the lodge.

'The party is omniscient and omnipotent,' he mumbled. 'It smokes out the heretics and excludes the unbelievers from the Celestial Empire.'

He turned his back on me and entered the lodge. Only in the last second did I notice that a stump was protruding from his jacket between his shoulder blades. They have cut off his wings; that is what he had been trying to hide from me.

I sighed deeply, stuck my shovel into the snow and sat down. I was just thinking that I would starve to death there, before the Gate of Heaven, when Egri clapped me on the shoulder.

'We thought you had escaped from us,' he said, and blushed because he realized the double meaning of what he had said.

They were all waiting for me in the dusk. The brigadiers shouted and we were on our way back to the camp. Egri and Földvary took my arms and someone was pushing me from behind with his palm on my back. All I had to do was move my legs like a rag-doll. In the square between the barracks Helvetius took over and while he was leading me to my bunk he told how a huge consignment of food had arrived during the day. Beginning with the day before yesterday our bread ration was to be six hundred grammes instead of four hundred and the arrears would be distributed immediately. Our oil ration would be doubled and instead of roasted barley we would, henceforth, be given real coffee with milk. In addition there would be bacon and jam every day and also other measures were expected.

'This means that Michnai got through,' I said, collapsing on my bunk. But while I went through the daily, automatic motions of exhaustion I realized that I was cheating because I was no longer exhausted at all.

'Tonight I shall tell you about the Swedish Rococo,' I cried after Helvetius.

During the next hour they distributed food every ten minutes. The bread arrears for the previous two days, our dinner, a bunch of onions for everyone, three times twenty grammes of bacon, jam, and the bacon ration for the next day. North-Eastern Inrush put the jam into his shoe-shine box and hung the strips of bacon on the beams. Several men followed his example, to insure themselves against the next period of starvation. When Egri arrived with our bacon rations he looked at me questioningly.

'Eat up everything immediately,' I ordered and stuck the bacon in my mouth.

Later the political officer came in to deliver a short speech. The destructive elements who believed that the régime intended to exterminate us were mistaken – he declared. The building of socialism demanded many sacrifices, there was no food even outside. Still, they had improved our food and if we did good work there would be further concessions. While he talked he looked now at Todi, now at myself, as if he were trying to convince us. We were sitting on our bunks with our legs crossed and looked through him. I kept my eyes on his larynx, which was quite an effort. Here and there people were sobbing.

The next day Acs ordered several of us to remain in the barracks on the grounds that we were too weak to work. We sat around the stove all day long, creating wonderful delicacies: pease-pudding on toast with jam on top and such like. Sunday, for the first time in a year and a half, they gave us a day off. Towards evening it was rumoured that Michnai was in Munich and had spoken over Radio Free Europe. He was said to have broadcast almost the complete list of the inhabitants of the camp, named the informers and *nachalniki* and given the names of the camp commander and the detectives. He had spoken with admiration about Todi and me without, however, giving any details, which was very wise of him.

Due to Acs's kindness I also spent the following days in the barracks. Wednesday night, unexpectedly, because hitherto we were allowed to shower only on Sunday, we were ordered to line up before the bath house.

'Cyclon B,' said Fürst, who had returned from Auschwitz in 1945.

'They wouldn't dare,' replied Toni Rainprecht, former smallholder county lieutenant, with an arrogant smile that made him look like a naughty old cardinal.

Gabori, who since his days at Dachau never permitted himself to be dragged into anything blindfolded, went to investigate and returned with the reassuring information that Hans Arse was in the shower room, there was no danger.

And, indeed, the colonel was standing inside the door of the shower room with his small Zeppelin-shaped medical bag hanging on a nail behind him. As we filed slowly by he pinched and kneaded our bottoms like a housewife when buying a goose. My friends explained that this was how medical examinations were conducted in the Soviet Union. The Russian physicians established three categories according to the hardness of the bottom: the first category was those fit for work, the second those fit for light work, the third those who must no longer be made to work because they would die in a few days anyway.

When my turn came Hans Arse pinched my bottom and although I turned away my face in disgust, he recognized me.

'Well, young man,' he asked kindly, 'have you recovered from your concussion?'

To my surprise he put me in the second category, but Acs, who was standing next to him with the list of names, put a Roman three after my name. Hans Arse, by the way, gave proof of some liberalism in his interpretation of the Soviet method, in that he established not three but four categories.

Those in category four were moved to a separate barracks the next day. They were allowed to stay away from work for several weeks. I was assigned to a very light job but even the others were no longer driven as hard as before. Since our food had been improved there was not a single death. Soon a new political officer arrived in the camp and the camp commander was replaced by a major. The new camp commander introduced the eight-hour work day, gave us Sunday off and limited the power of the *nachalniki*. As a result he was called the Good Major and the former camp commander the Bad Captain. Gabori, however, declared that the AVO officers had not changed but had only had new orders; that our 'bad captain' was now a 'good captain' in another prison and our 'good major' had until recently been a 'bad major' elsewhere.

I studied Knocke's newspaper rags even more thoroughly than before to find out the cause of the changes. But there was no explanation in the papers during the first half if 1952; not a single sign this side or beyond the Iron Curtain that would have explained the new situation. I had nothing else to fall back on other than my theory that Michnai had succeeded and was now in the West. But then why had it taken him so long?

The following, rather bearable period of my captivity was soon over. One afternoon, towards the middle of the summer, we were working on the hill near the punishment cells. We were building new hanging gardens, several hundred metres long, in front of the staff headquarters. The AVO officers loved flowers, particularly the detectives coming down from Budapest who stopped by for an hour or two to question one or another of the prisoners, usually in connection with some new victim. Before they left they would send a prisoner to the chief gardener, Professor György Sarospataky, asking for ten or twelve dozen roses. Sometimes the detectives were accompanied by an MVD officer. The Russians always went down personally for the flowers and asked the professor politely for 'a pound of roses', or 'two pounds of lilies'. In exchange they handed him a few long-tipped and extremely smelly Russian cigarettes.

We too got our cigarettes from AVO officers, usually several packets. Our men usually came to the Matra mountains at week-ends, and invariably questioned Egri or Gabori. Never me. After half an hour of desultory conversation they asked my friends, off-hand, if they knew this or that poem of mine. They offered a packet of cigarettes for a written copy of the poem. Usually they asked for my poem to Suzy or some other non-political poem written at 60 Andrassy Street – they didn't know about the political ones. Gabori would reply, without moving a muscle in his face, that he did not know my poems, nor was he acquainted with me. Thereupon the officer would offer two packets of cigarettes, then three, four, five. At five Gabori gave in, for our small circle was provided for. I was very glad that there were so many poetry-loving AVO officers. Until then I had believed that the fate of my poems written in prison depended on whether we survived or not; now I knew that if no one else, at least my murderers would see to it that my work outlived me.

On that very warm summer afternoon I was working on one of the flower beds with Antinuos at my side. Or rather, I stuck my hoe into the soft ground and moved my arms as if I were working while I spoke about the mystical Persian poets. I was just about to begin on Mewlana Djelaleddin Rumi when I suddenly noticed that the pure perfume of yellow carnations blooming before the punishment cells – a perfume that I felt not to much in my nose as on my palate, like the memory of some delicacy seasoned with clove – was defiled by the odour of cheap scent. We smelled the AVO guard before he saw us, but as he was coming out from one of the guard's barracks he might have been watching us for quite some time.

The guard was a puny, tiny little man with grey-green, blinking eyes, hanging, red cheeks and a wrinkled forehead, so that he looked like a premature baby or an old, old woman although he couldn't have been over twenty. In the camp he was know as Little He-Devil. He took me to the punishment cells, pushed me into a dark one and put on the light. He followed me in, gave me a good beating, then departed. I thought they would let me out in the evening, for it had become a custom for the AVO guards to beat the prisoners in the punishment cells. One of the reasons for this was that the Good Major did not like his men to do their beating in the open; another, that the guards were dressed in warm woollen clothes and preferred to do such jobs in a cool place.

I remained in the dark cell for two whole weeks. The warders didn't hurt me but twice a day Little He-Devil would appear and beat me until I bled. He beat me standing on tiptoe, his tongue protruding from between his rotten teeth. Each time he asked me my profession, the name of my mother, the day of my birth and the reason for my arrest. To the last question I always gave a noncommittal answer. On the eighth day my shirt was so stiff with blood that it felt like sailcloth and I wondered all day how I could get rid of Little He-Devil.

When he appeared on the morning of the ninth day I knew what I would do. After the first two dozen slaps he stopped, as usual, to get his second wind.

'Why are you here?' he screeched.

'Because I had a love affair with an old Catholic bishop.'

He-Devil's mouth fell open with amazement.

'How old was he?'

'Ninety-three,' I replied without moving a muscle.

'And where did you f—?'

'On the main altar, at midnight,' I said, smiling, and closed my eyes as if I were remembering indescribable delights. But all the time I was watching He-Devil from under my half-closed lids. He almost crossed himself with fright, backed away, blinked at me suspiciously and left the cell. He even forgot to put out the light. When he failed to return the next day I felt sure that the exorcism had been successful, and I began to dance with joy. As a matter of fact, I had been dreaming of solitary confinement for quite a while but I had never told my friends for fear that it might hurt their feelings. For two years I had never been alone, and I yearned to write poems, which was impossible in the barracks.

A few days later Mongol took me to a smaller cell where Lieutenant Toth was waiting for me, standing in a corner. Or rather, he was not standing: he leaned his back against the angle of the wall, pushed the back of his bent head into the ceiling, straddled his long legs and reached out his snaky arms towards me. He looked at me like a large spider waiting for his victim in the corner of his web. I stood resigned; I knew that he could take hold of me without moving.

I noticed his extremely strong smell of toilet water only when, instead of starting on the terrible beating I expected, he addressed me with a short speech:

'We have found out,' he said, caressing his beautifully shaven, smooth, bluish face with the palm of his right hand, 'that there are, in this camp, a few notorious scoundrels who disturb the peace of the place, organize sabotage, disparage the State Security Organization and constantly spread false rumours. There aren't many of them. To mention only two: there is Todi and there is you. Two fascists! We were patient. Very patient. We hoped you would come to your senses. But you didn't. You have only yourself to blame, Faludy. I'll make a quiet man of you, a very quiet one, never fear. I shall dispatch you to a place you wouldn't find on the map!'

He fell silent. I felt utterly bored. What can this man do to me if he doesn't even hit me? What power does he have over me, if any?

'Do I bore you?' the lieutenant asked suddenly. 'Answer me. I give you my word of honour that I won't hurt you. Well, do I bore you?'

'To death, lieutenant, sir.'

Mongol led me into a standard cell, number 12. I counted seven horizontal and seven vertical bars on the whitewashed window – that is, sixty-four squares. There was a rusty, empty, three-gallon can in one corner and fleas swarmed in the dust covering the floor. I felt immediately as if my legs had been sprinkled with curry, for I was barefoot. The bunk, five smooth boards laid side by side, was about twenty centimetres above the ground and took up exactly half of the cell. Three heavy beams ran across the ceiling with cobwebs hanging from them. After inspecting the cell I decided that I was feeling wonderful and that I would begin working on my poems the next day. The guard opened the door, pushed in my boots and Lieutenant Toth threw into my lap a small pillow filled with straw.

'Here, you stinking fascist, now you have nothing to complain of,' he said disdainfully.

At noon I heard the cook, accompanied by the guard, go from cell to cell and put down a full dixie before each door.

'You don't leave anything here,' said the guard as they reached my right-hand neighbour. 'Nor here.'

This happened every morning and every noon. Only in the evening did I get something to eat: a dixieful of mush and a piece of bread. Not more that four hundred to four hundred and fifty calories. But I had been in pretty good condition when they brought me in – in the last few months I had regained approximately two-thirds of the weight lost, and so had most of the others. This was due to the improved food, and also to the nationalization of the Globus canning works, or rather to the consequences of the nationalization. The Globus works were manufacturing cooked foods in glass jars for domestic consumption. A considerable part of these foods got spoiled and were withdrawn from circulation to be used – as we learned from our comrades who had returned from Budapest prison hospitals – as food for prisoners. Each day every prisoner was given a half-litre jar of pigs' liver in rice, beef goulash or some other delicacy. The cooks always brought twice as many bottles as there were prisoners, because some of them were completely inedible. We cheated by dividing the contents of a spoiled jar into two jars and adding water, so that when we returned it to the cook, we got two good jars in exchange for an inedible one.

I figured that in my present condition I could survive on four hundred to four hundred and fifty calories a day for eight or ten weeks. Looking at the window I thought that the sixty-four squares symbolized the remaining sixty-four days of my life. From then on I calculated time not in months and days, but in window-squares, and established in the morning that I had reached square number so-and-so of row so-and-so. The prospect of death did not frighten me as it used to, instead of despairing I trembled with fury, disgust and hatred. Between the bombing of Juvissy, the blowing up of the *Château de Boncourt* and the period of starvation last February, I had escaped death twenty-two times. I hoped that I would again escape it and could no longer create in myself the internal tension befitting the dramatic occasion. On the other hand, I loathed the AVO for its lack of imagination; instead of inventing something new, it conjured up again the well-known spirit of starvation. I was careful to limit my movements to the minimum and decided to devote all my attention to poetry.

I used the first three days to get used to my hard bunk, familiarize, myself with the daily routine of the punishment cells and find out who my neighbours were. My sharpened senses – the sense of smell and hearing – were a great help. My eyes were of little use here. Standing on tiptoe on my bunk I reached only the lowest row of squares but I couldn't see through the whitewashed glass. True, very soon I discovered a pinpoint hole in the whitewash through which, when the sun shone, a tiny beam penetrated to paint a slowly advancing ochre-yellow circle on the opposite wall. Looking out through the tiny hole I could see only a clay slope. The path ran on the crest of the slope, some ten metres from where I was. In my hermetically closed cell I could smell the fragrance of carnations blooming on the other side of the building, I knew when the lilies were in full bloom and distinguished the perfume of petunias. In the morning, at about five o'clock, I woke when the cook stepped on to the bridge leading across the stream to the cells, about a hundred metres from my bunk. I smelled the coffee the others had for breakfast and knew, at noon, whether they were getting liver in rice or beef goulash. This smell of food at noon was so strong and tormenting that I had to stop working on my poem.

Very soon I learned to recognize the guards on the corridor by their smell, their whisper and the way they walked. There were always two on duty and they were relieved at noon: first Mongol and the Stable-boy, then the Gnome and the Nut. I knew the Stable-boy by the rancid body odour that filled the corridor when he was on duty. He was an unusually tall, middle-aged man with a crooked back. When he asked something I had to repeat my answer twice or three times while he listened attentively, his dirty-blue, suspicious eyes never leaving my face, or his hand the butt of his gun. He never slept, never put out the light in the cell when he was on duty every fourth night, but walked up and down the corridor and looked in every few minutes through the spy-hole to make sure I hadn't escaped.

Mongol gave me a benevolent smile when I appeared. When I had been sentenced to spend two weeks in short chains, he had chained me up only on the first day and even then very loosely. After that he put me in a cell with a straw mattress on the floor and let me sleep until dawn. The Gnome, with his hump, his dilated pupils, his long hair worn *à la bohème*, and his intellectual attitude reminded one of the Hunchback of Notre-Dame or a sixteenth-century Inquisitor from some Spanish provincial town. When he was on duty he liked to stand around in one cell or another and hold long, moralizing monologues, telling us that we should bear our punishment with humility and be grateful to the AVO, the fist of the proletariat, for the patience and benevolence it showed us in spite of our crimes. When he reached this point we had to nod – if we missed he would punch and kick us. Once, when, afraid of the kicks, I began praising the AVO's generosity, he looked at me with indescribable disdain and stalked from the cell. He came even on the days when he was off duty and could have been chasing the girls in the village.

The Nut didn't look different from any attractive, red-cheeked peasant lad, and yet it was he who caused most of the trouble with his incalculable moods. In the mornings and evenings, at a certain time, we were led to the wc for three minutes each. When the Nut was on duty he would usually walk along the corridor and shout into every cell: 'There's no shitting today!' This was all the more painful as we got no water to drink except from the jug standing in the WC. At other times, when I reached for my dixie on the floor outside my cell door he would send it flying with a well-aimed kick. But it also happened that he made the cook give everyone double rations. When on duty he visited every cell after 'lights out' and slapped the prisoners around. Mongol did the same but he always left me and my right-hand neighbour out. The Stable-boy hit only those who had offended against discipline.

We could talk to the guards only in whispers, yet I could follow a conversation from a distance of five or six cells. In this way I had soon discovered that my right-hand neighbour was Todi. In the cell opposite there were two people, both, to judge from their speech, peasant lads, whom I did not know. From the lectures the Gnome delivered in their cell I knew that they had gone on hunger strike. In the first days Doctor Acs came every morning and every night to feed them artificially after the guards had beaten them half unconscious, and later they were put on starvation diet. Next to them came the cell of the informer Gergely Deak, who had denounced me for carrying on imperialist propaganda when I was telling my fellow-prisoners in the infirmary the story of my days on Ellis Island. I did not know why he was there, but I knew that the guards gave him extra pieces of bread and a straw mattress to sleep on. My left-hand neighbour was the eccentric lawyer called Titus Banvölgyi, whom the AVO arrested because, returning from internment, he had demanded the restitution of his flat, his library and art treasures. He had been in the punishment cells for several months because of an occurrence for which the entire camp envied him.

When the political officer went away on holiday, Banvölgyi had asked to speak to his deputy. The deputy was a notorious moron. Banvölgyi declared that he wanted to divorce his wife. He asked the sergeant to forward his request to the authorities. A few weeks later he was taken to Budapest, to his great pleasure straight to the law court. Here he not only saw, but also talked to his wife whom he idolized, while the judge decreed the divorce. When Banvölgyi returned and the political officer heard about the affair he was livid with fury, and sent Titus to the cells. I often listened while he lectured the guards on prison regulations and demanded decent treatment. They beat him instead, but the next day he began again.

Although I tried to pay as little attention as possible to my physical condition, I grew so weak after the first two weeks of starvation diet that I thought I would not last sixty-four squares. At roll call my knees shook so badly that I could hardly stand. One Sunday night, when the Stable-boy handed me my bread ration for the day, he smeared the spoonful of plum jam – my dinner – over my shaved head. After he had left I had a crying fit, but later, sitting on my bunk, scratching the jam off my head and sucking it from under my nails, I told myself that I deserved all I got for having left America. When I sat or lay down my body ached all over. The flesh had literally disappeared from my bones and I felt as if I were sitting on broken glass. After a few days I had to stop writing poems and began to conjure up in my mind the American landscapes I had known: the junction of the Allegheny and Monongahela Rivers at Pittsburgh, trout-fishing of an evening in the streams of Pennsylvania, the Golden Gate Bridge at San Francisco shrouded in mist, the muddy, grey banks of the Big Snake River, where I used to wander with my army buddies, the airfield at Kodiak, my Eskimo friends and the top hat on the totem-pole, or Washington which I visited with Vambéry to complain about American political dilettantism to some official in the State Department. If only I could once again voice such complaints in Washington!

On the fourteenth day of my starvation I woke one morning to the realization that a new cook was bringing the food. His steps on the wooden bridge were lighter, fresher, almost happy. When, some ten metres from my door, he began putting down the dixies, I was certain it must be Helvetius. In my excitement I pressed my mouth, my nose, my entire body against the heavy cell door. As he passed my cell he brushed the door with his shoulder. On the way back he repeated the performance. A moment later I caught the smell of linseed oil. Now I was sure. The last day before my incarceration Helvetius had stolen a bottle of linseed oil from the engine-house and had put some on my hair as well as on his. The smell accompanied me to the cells but on the Thursday following my conversation with Lieutenant Toth, they had shaved my head. The barber came once a week, every Thursday, and he was the only fellow-prisoner I saw. He went with a small, three-legged stool from cell to cell and while he was shaving us the guard stood in the open door watching. We could communicate only by signs. I gave him a gay smile, which meant that he was to tell my friends outside that I was well, and he caressed my nape, which meant that they were thinking of me.

At noon, when Helvetius arrived with the dinner, he again brushed my door with his shoulder. On the way back he stopped for a moment and leaned against my door. The board separating us was only two or three centimetres thick so that I listened enchanted to his light, boyish breathing. He probably wanted to inform me that he knew where I was. In the evening, at last, he brought food for me too. He distributed the dixies quickly, noisily, but put down Todi's and mine with slow care. When he departed and the guard opened the door I lifted the dixie in both hands to see whether there was a message scratched on it. There wasn't, but when I had swallowed the thin pease pudding it contained I discovered a piece of bacon at the bottom. It was attached to two tiny hooks soldered on to the inside of the dixie. I figured that the bacon must have been twelve decagrammes, the daily portion of six men, eight hundred and forty calories. This, added to the mush and the bread, made a thousand two hundred and ninety calories. On this I could last for a year. I wondered whether Todi had also received bacon. Two hours later, when three guards were busy working over Banvölgyi, I had my answer. Todi made use of the opportunity to communicate with me in Morse signals:

'Hahaha! Hihihi!'

My joy lasted exactly two months. During that time I spent most of my days thinking up poems and I found a remedy for my only discomfort: that I could never wash. In the mornings I brought some water with me from the WC in my mouth and with it I rubbed myself down from head to foot. The portion of bacon in my dixie became larger every day, more and more people must have banded together to feed me and Todi. One evening Pali Musza was brought in and put in the cell next to Banvölgyi's. He was evidently on full food because the next morning I found half a kilogramme of bread in the wc. I left half of it for Todi and concealed the rest in my trousers. The next morning there were two pieces of bread on top of the bowl, one for Todi, one for me.

Early in October I was visited one evening by Lieutenant Toth.

'What's this? You are still alive?' he asked, surprised. 'How do you do it?'

For a while he looked at me curiously, then he shrugged his shoulders and walked out.

He must have guessed what was going on because, though Helvetius continued to bring the food, the dixies were distributed by the guard, helped by the informer Deak. In addition, from then on Todi and I were the first to be let into the wc and thus there was no more bread. In theory, my daily ration was again down to four hundred and fifty calories, but only in theory.

The guards – with the exception of the Gnome – were used to us by now. This was evident not only from their attitude to me but also by the way they treated Banvölgyi. When he explained to them the rights of a *detained person* – not having been sentenced, he did not consider himself a prisoner – the guards giggled and joked with him. When the prisoners were beaten, they left the three of us alone and concentrated their attention on the newcomers. They began to regard us as old pieces of furniture, or rather, as domestic animals for whom it was their duty to provide. In the evenings when we were waiting behind our doors for the food, I did indeed feel like a pig waiting in his sty for the slops. The guard usually told Deak to put more food in our dixies and a larger piece of bread into our hands when the door was opened. They did this instinctively, without pity or complicity, the way a farmer will feed his cattle.

But even so that food alone would not have sufficed to keep me going and I decided to employ every trick to acquire more of it. One day at noon I smelled Stable-boy distributing pigs' liver in rice among the prisoners. I was suddenly convinced that I would go mad if I couldn't have some. I pressed my body against the door of my cell and when Stable-boy approached I began to hypnotize him through the planks. 'You dirty animal, you beast,' I cursed soundlessly, 'you handful of snot without will, you stupid henchman, obey my will! Remember what your schoolmaster told you thirty years ago about good deeds! Remember that here, behind this door, you have a Hungarian poet whose name will be remembered long after dogs lift their legs against your caved-in tombstone. Give me food, miserable sinner! Obey my will! Feel an irresistible urge to put down a full dixie before my door! Give! Give! Now!'

I put so much effort into conveying my will to him that I almost collapsed with exhaustion. A few minutes later, as he was coming back, I repeated the whole performance.

A moment later I heard the welcome clatter of the dixie on the floor.

'All right, you. Take it in!' he cried. In my excitement I didn't even hear him open the door. There was a kilogramme of pigs' liver in rice in my dixie. I ate half and poured the other half into my pocket for the next day.

I repeated this game every fourth day when Stable-boy was on duty. Once, however, when the door opened I found myself facing the Nut. As I reached for the dixie he kicked my hand.

'Leave it there!' he ordered. 'You move too slowly. You are not hungry.'

'I am hungry all right,' I replied, looking down sadly on the full dixie – 'but this pittance wouldn't fill the belly of a mouse . . .'

'What? Could you eat two of these?'

'Ten.'

'Repeat what you said.'

'I said I could eat ten!'

'All right,' the Nut nodded. 'You can take it in. But I am taking you at your word. And if you don't eat up at least half of what you said – do you see this iron rod? Well, I shall beat your balls with it until they burst. Understood?'

On the fourth day, at noon, the Nut took me to an empty, dark cell. A few minutes later he took me back to my own and locked the door on me. Ten dixies were standing on my bunk side by side, in all, twenty-six pounds of rice.

I started with a well-prepared plan. I stepped out of my wide boots and poured a dixie of rice into each. Then I stepped back into the warm rice. It felt wonderful, because the weather had turned cold. Then I folded my trouser legs into my boots, as I always wore them. Next, I distributed the contents of dixies three and four into the other six dixies and ate up five and six without effort. I was eating away on number seven when the Nut returned, with a thick iron rod in his hand. When he saw the six empty dixies he gazed open-mouthed at my stomach. Then he searched my pockets, disturbed the thick layer of dust on the ground, looked under the bunk, inspected the three-gallon can in the corner, and finally called in his fellow-guard, the Gnome.

'This bastard here has gobbled up seven kilogrammes of rice in half an hour,' he said admiringly.

'He'll bust his guts!' the Gnome replied happily and walked out again.

'Now you will believe me,' I turned to the Nut, 'if I tell you that outside I used to eat a whole fattened goose for dinner and drink four gallons of wine with it.'

'Sure,' the Nut said and shivered. Then he reached for the still full dixies.

'Leave those!' I cried, throwing myself on the dixies as if I wanted to defend them with my body. 'I want to eat them!'

'Don't you want to leave some for your neighbour?' the Nut asked, pointing towards Todi's cell.

'All right,' I replied after some hesitation.

A few minutes later Todi, who had listened to the whole scene, knocked a cheerful message on the wall.

'Hahaha! Hahaha!'

Until late in the evening the Gnome came in every half-hour to inspect me as if I were his bride.

'Well, aren't you swelling up yet?' he inquired. Seeing that I wasn't he departed with a long nose.

Having turned two of the guards into my serfs, paying tithes in bread and rice, my self-confidence increased to a ridiculous degree. Soon I won over the Mongol too by writing four- and eight-line poems into the albums of his peasant girl sweethearts.

The enslavement of the Gnome presented great difficulties and I should never have succeeded had chance not come to my aid. One winter morning he asked me whether I should be willing to scrub the wc floor. This was regarded as a favour. I gladly agreed because it gave me an opportunity to wash myself at last – after five months – in the bucket used for scrubbing. I looked out through the window at the snow-covered pine trees, then went down on my knees and began to wash the seat of the bowl. But the brush slipped from my stiff fingers and fell in, to be carried away by the stream.

When the Gnome noticed what had happened he took me to the guard room. He made me stand close to the table and sat down behind it to write his report with maddening slowness.

'The notorious György Faludy has accomplished a sabotage action by throwing the wc brush into the bowl to endanger the hygiene of the camp and spread the plague . . .'

He looked up at me repeatedly to see whether I could read what he was writing and stuck his left hand into his trousers pocket to move it slowly up and down for an unmistakable purpose. It occurred to me to put him to a test. I made use of my particular gift, namely that I can break into tears whenever I wish. I closed my eyes and visualized my funeral. I saw Suzy standing by my grave, blonde, emaciated, clad in deep black. There were no orphans: for that I was too late getting out of jail.

'I request that the above-mentioned György Faludy be punished either by corporal punishment or by further withholding of food rations . . .'

Heavy tears were running down my cheeks. The Gnome turned his face towards the small window beside his desk and the misty pane reflected his lewd grin. His hand moved faster and faster, his breath came in gasps and his tongue stuck out from between his lips. When he had finished he led me back to my cell but on the way he pushed half a loaf of bread under my arm.

The third day he came back to my cell, called me a dirty capitalist and swore that he would starve me to death. All the time he was waiting to see whether I could cry. I was in no mood to play and he left, disappointed. Forty-eight hours later he would have visited me again had he not been prevented by an unexpected occurrence. I succeeded in talking to one of my friends which, though it was of little practical use, I considered a great moral victory because it wounded the AVO in its most vulnerable point. The camp authorities made a point of it that the inhabitants of the camp and of the cells should not be able to communicate. When we spoke to our guards we had to say our names in whispers and we were led to the wc one at a time. I could never fathom the purpose of this secrecy as we all knew who was in the cells and so did the inhabitants of the camp. A year ago, when a fellow-prisoner called Dénes tried to smuggle in a note through a cell window, the guards beat his head with iron rods until his brain was injured. He was taken to a Budapest prison hospital and never returned.

On a November morning when the Gnome was on duty I suddenly distinguished the voice of Robert Gati, the communist journalist.

'I beg to report that I have come to whitewash the walls of the corridor!' he announced in a loud voice. I heard the Gnome take him to the middle of the corridor and stay there while Robert quickly but haphazardly worked away on the wall. The whole thing seemed highly suspicious to me. We had eight masons and two house-painters in the camp, old professionals, and Robert was certainly not one of them. As most of the work to be done was in the living quarters of the AVO guards, they wanted no amateurs. It seemed impossible that Robert should have been advanced to the rank of a house-painter since I was shut up. The only imaginable answer was that he had escaped from his place of work and grabbed an unguarded pail of paint and a brush in order to get near me. This boldness was amazing but just like him.

An hour later the Gnome had grown tired of standing around and had retired to his office. The next moment Gati was at the spy-hole of my cell.

'Hallo, George, it's me, Gati!'

During the next few moments he pushed a huge quantity of bread, cut into strips, through the spy-hole, talking unceasingly as he did so.

'You have lost weight, but not too much . . . we are all relatively all right . . . they don't drive us too hard . . . we talk a lot . . . André Gide has died . . . terror in the country is unchanged . . . democracy is consolidated in West Germany . . . this is good news . . . the Korean war is still on . . . and the other good news: Eisenhower has been elected president . . . everyone hopes that this will improve our situation . . .'

A few hours later when the Gnome emerged from his office, Deak, the informer, called him to his door and told the guard that the house-painter had talked at great length with the inmate of one of the cells opposite his. He didn't know what, the only word he heard was West Germany. The Gnome questioned first Banvölgyi, then Todi. Although they must have heard every word of our conversation and both knew who the culprit was, I had nothing to fear from them. The Gnome left me until last because it was me he suspected least. In the end he declared that we would get no food and would stand with our noses to the wall until we confessed. An hour later the eight house-painters were in one of the cells at the end of the corridor but they must have had alibis because after a good beating the Gnome let them go. We stood four days and four nights, then the Gnome pretended to have forgotten the whole affair. He must have realized that his superiors would hold him responsible for having permitted the house-painter to work in the corridor without being guarded.

Early in December they stopped starving us and we all received full rations. I threw all my ingenuity into fighting the cold in order to go on with my work. I put several kilogrammes of dust into my boots, threw my overcoat over my head and stood all day in the tepid tent of my own breath. I thought up forty or fifty lines each day and after each new rhyme repeated three times all the lines I had done that day. In the morning I started out by recalling all my poems of the previous days. I was working on a carefully planned volume where the sequence was very important and this presented an extra difficulty. I hoped that my fellow-prisoners would learn the poems by heart and those who survived would take them out with them into the world, but I couldn't expect them to learn the table of contents as well. After long deliberation I decided to start each poem with a letter of the alphabet, in exact order from A to Z, and thus the table of contents would be clear, even should I be dead.

The days passed far too quickly. As I had no blanket I undressed each evening to the skin, filled the pockets of my clothes with dust, put my underclothes under me and the rest on top of me. I pulled up my knees to my chin so that I was completely covered and stuck the sleeves of my overcoat into each other. Thus a C-shaped pipe conducted the warm air I expelled down to my navel and I felt as if I were in a centrally heated tent. My face was burning with the excitement of working on a poem, and after the lights were put out I could always do twelve or sixteen more lines. By March I had almost completed the volume. However, my invention of fuelless central heating made me even prouder.

Towards the end of the year, but particularly in the new year, the AVO men visited my cell more and more often. They gave me all kinds of tasks: to draw and cut out large letters in red cardboard, and the numbers 7 and 3. From this I concluded that they were preparing for Stalin's seventy-third birthday. At other times they made me fill in questionnaires. They said I was to answer questions like: what books do the prisoners read? – do the prisoners like to listen to the wireless? – what are the prisoners' psychological problems? – using my imagination to the full. These were questionnaires sent out by UNESCO. Mostly, however, they came to listen to my stories. Towards the middle of January, by the time I had accustomed them to listen to my lectures, I declared that henceforth I would talk only in the evenings. I had two reasons for this: first, that the repeated visits interrupted me in my work, second, because it was usually in the evening, after the lights were out, that they amused themselves by beating up my fellow-prisoners. I hoped to put an end to that practice. However, they accepted my ultimatum only after a few days' hesitation. Each knew that the others also came to my cell, but now there had to be open complicity, because none of them could conceal these sessions from the other guards on duty.

Usually they came to fetch me after roll call. They took me to the guard room, one took his place on the bed, the other by the stove. I stood by the window so as not to get too warm and talked until both became sleepy. Then one would take me back to my cell and return to the guard room to sleep – and there would be no beatings that day. I didn't have an easy time with them. Of my experiences they appreciated only my African adventures, but they delighted in the stories of Boccaccio, *The Arabian Nights*, Rabelais, Marguerite of Navarre and Brantôme. Surprisingly enough they were fond of poems. Not lyrical poems like Verlaine's or my own, but epic poems: the works of Janos Arany for instance and François Villon's ballads, which I had to recite again and again as the weeks went by. I was even more successful with the work of a few secondary, nineteenth-century poets, in the first place two poems I had been made to learn by heart in school though they revolted me. One was *The Polish Captive* by a poet called Csengey, telling how the proud Tsar wanted a Polish captive to recite a verse of congratulation on his birthday. The captive refused and told his captors that his name was Koscziusko, upon which the Tsar and his nobles blushed with shame. The other was a poem by Reviczky, entitled *Death of Pan*. In this the poet elaborates on a story by Aulus Gellius. At the time of Christ's death on the Cross the pilot of a Roman galley, called Thamus, heard mysterious voices in the night on his way from Greece to Italy. The voice commanded him to tell Emperor Tiberius in Rome that the ancient gods were dead. Thamus refused to believe the heavenly voice. The next day, however, as the galley passed near the Cape of Palodes, he heard from the shore the cries of the naiads, nymphs and fauns: 'The Great Pan is dead! Great Pan is dead!' They liked this poem so much that I had to recite it almost every night.

Early in March the Mongol came to fetch me at the usual time. When I stepped out into the corridor I saw, to my amazement, that my fellow-prisoners were already lined up along the wall, pale and shivering with cold. I was told to stand beside Todi. The next moment the two guards threw themselves on us and beat us and kicked us with such force that blood was spurting in all directions. When they came to the end of the line, they started again at the beginning. They repeated this performance once more, then kicked us into our cells. In the darkness I wondered what the cause of their fury could be. Had war broken out? But then, as Recsk was on the air route between Kiev and Budapest, I should have heard the planes.

The next morning I heard Egri's voice from the top of the slope outside my window, ten metres away. He spoke considerably louder than usual.

'Do you know Reviczky's famous poem, *Pan's Death*, Tony?'

'Who is Reviczky? I never heard of him,' answered Tony Rainprecht. Then I listened to their departing steps.

The dialogue was obviously meant to attract my attention. Rainprecht had been County Lieutenant, he was a university graduate and one of the most erudite men in camp. It was impossible that he shouldn't have known who Reviczky was, or shouldn't have been able to recite the poem by heart; just as impossible as for an Oxford don not to have heard of Robert Southey's *Blenheim*.

Five minutes later they were back again.

'How did that famous Reviczky line go?' asked Rainprecht in his agreeable, nasal voice.

'The great Khan is dead! The great Khan is dead!' recited. Egri enthusiastically, in a voice that made the sixty-four window-squares tremble.

On the third day, towards noon, someone knocked on the door of my cell. I was so surprised that I forgot to answer. Never had anything like that happened to me before. Mongol greeted me with a loud 'Good morning' and let in the barber with the three-legged stool.

'The Caucasian bandit has at last departed from our midst!' he cried, and embraced me.

I put my finger to my lips in warning and looked fearfully at the door where the guard usually stood, but there was no guard there.

'To hell with them!' the barber laughed and handed me a cigarette. 'Yesterday Dentures went from one barracks to another begging the prisoners to forgive him. We hear that on the day of Stalin's death a quarter of a million people went in procession in Budapest under red banners with a black veil tied to them. They covered their faces with their hankies and laughed themselves sick. The camp commander has completely lost his head. The guard in the towers has been doubled. But they are looking outwards, not inwards. Do you know why?'

'No.'

'To see whether the Americans are coming. Well, in a day of two they'll be here.'

'Do you seriously believe this?'

'Why? Do you think Eisenhower is an idiot?'

'Not in the least!' I protested fearfully.

'Well, wasn't it he who liberated Western Europe seven years ago?'

'Yes.'

'Then why shouldn't he liberate Eastern Europe now? He could advance all the way to the Urals without firing a single shot. Why then shouldn't he come?'

He searched his pockets for a match, and when he didn't find one he called out into the corridor:

'Be a good fellow, sergeant, give us a light, will you?'

This time the Gnome came in and lit my cigarette for me. The first in nine months. I leaned my back against the wall of the cell and inhaled deeply while the barber was shaving my chin tenderly. Before he left he begged me not to forget him when I was a minister.

The next day we were all released from the punishment cells.

On September 17, 1953, there were only twenty-one of us left in the camp. Or rather, twenty, because the barber stayed only to give us all a good shave before we left. We were sitting on the ground in front of the barracks in the warm September sunshine. But only eighteen. The remaining two were sitting on the white-painted bench in front of the cells between the political officer and an AVO major with a tab on his collar that showed he was an attorney. When the wind blew our way we could pick up a word or two of their conversation. The major was explaining something, asking, begging, threatening, then begging again. The man sitting next to him was Uncle Magyarits, once pilot of a ship on the Danube, a West German citizen arrested, contrary to international law, in the Budapest port. He declared that he hated life in a people's democracy worse than he hated jail and therefore refused to leave the camp unless they gave their word to deport him to his country. The other man was Menyhért Boka, former Christian party deputy, who had, two months before, submitted to the AVO a memorandum addressed to Matyas Rakosi in which he declared that the day was approaching when all the leading communists, Rakosi first, would be lynched by the people. As a good Christian he could not condone such a thing and therefore he suggested that Rakosi should resign and cede power to certain Christian party politicians, among them Boka himself. They would then hold democratic elections and guarantee a transition without bloodshed. Neither Rakosi nor the others would be hurt: on the contrary, they would receive good pensions.

The major talked now to one, now to the other. He said that if Magyarits would remain in Hungary and Boka would revoke his memorandum he would set them both free immediately. The old pilot, with his self-made pipe between his teeth, laughed into the major's face. Boka only shrugged his shoulders.

⋆

The past six months had been considerably less idyllic. On the March morning when I was released from the cells, my friends had carried me up to the mountain in a veritable triumphal procession. There were no AVO guards around and the *nachalniki* kept their eyes on the landscape. We talked all day and reached for our pickaxes only when the talk began to bore us. We broke, on the average, fifty kilogrammes of rock; the norm was two cubic metres, which is five thousand six hundred kilogrammes. The most enjoyable sight, however, was the crack only fifty centimetres wide but unfathomably deep between the mining level and the mountain, signalling that very soon the entire plateau would crumble.

Ten days later, as was to be expected, they recalled the camp commander, the Good Major. His place was taken by a lieutenant-colonel, formerly a shoemaker, an insignificant little busybody whom we called Victor Emmanuel. A short time after they began again to drive us, beat us and, at the suggestion of the chief *nachalnik*, Dezsö Tamas, they set up a so-called corrective brigade. This brigade consisted of the hundred and fifty most dangerous subversives of the camp, that is, the most intelligent and the ten most cunning informers. We were marched out before daybreak and returned to the camp only after sunset, after all the others had been herded in, and we had to crawl from the mountain to the camp gate on our bellies. We were bossed by the two most cruel *nachalniki*, Kerekes and Talian, we received no cigarettes and our daily rations were considerably lowered. Egri – who to his shame and heart-ache was left out of this brigade – put a packet of tobacco under a certain bush each evening, with the important news and messages written on it and as we crawled by, Gabori slipped it into his pocket. We were breaking stone in the quarry under strict AVO supervision. Victor Emmanuel often came to look at us, accompanied by the new political officer, a young, grinning fellow called Istvan Florian who was not even able to pronounce the world 'imperialist' correctly. Victor Emmanuel always did me the honour of speaking to me directly.

'I am sorry for you, my poor boy,' he used to whisper sadly, nervously rubbing his hands while I stood before him, naked to the waist. Then he would pat my neck.

'I must go,' he would say, 'I don't want the political officer to catch me talking to you.' Then he would sink his nails into my flesh until blood ran down my back.

At the end of April Egri sent us the following message on the pack of tobacco: 'Eisenhower's speech caused all to piss in their pants. Great improvement expected soon.' The next day, at dinner time, when Kerekes came into the barracks to order the cook, as usual, to spoon off the thin layer of frozen fat from the surface of the soup and send it back to the kitchen, Dentures began to shout at him and called him a dirty swine. The next day we noticed a passive, incomprehensible nervousness among our guards but we could not even guess at the reason. Only in the evening, when no one was beaten up after roll call, did we realize that there hadn't been a single blow all day. It was obvious that the guards had received very strict orders not to touch us, because they wandered among us sadly, their heads bent, and were so jumpy that we almost felt sorry for them.

One morning, early in June, the mountain lurched forward to such an extent that the concrete pillars of the engine house standing on the edge of the mining level slanted. Three days later the steam engine slid from the engine house through a beautiful round hole it punched in the wall and fell over the precipice. The rope-way carrying the stone to the railway line eight or ten kilometres away slackened so that the tubs were lying on the new road. On the 20th of June we received the following message on the pack of tobacco: 'East German workers rebelled. Hardware store of widowed Mrs Joseph Stalin bankrupt.' The same evening a lorry full of fruit arrived at the camp; we hadn't seen cherries for three years.

The next morning we were led to the trench that, according to our engineers, was to hold all our dead bodies. Here Victor Emmanuel addressed us:

'I want you to be as happy as possible in the short time you still have to spend here. Therefore I should like you to transform this ditch into a swimming pool and enjoy the pleasures of the summer. I have already ordered the diving board.'

We went to work on the swimming pool, while two of us watched the sky for the American planes. This time even I believed they were coming. The same evening they disbanded the corrective brigade and henceforth treated us like anyone else. The next day – twenty-four hours later – we learned that Imre Nagy was the new Prime Minister. We read about it in the newspapers the AVO guards left lying on top of the woodpile, on the threshold of the toolshed and in other conspicuous places.

Two days later I was fetched for questioning. A young, handsome lieutenant who had just arrived from Budapest received me.

'I have gone through your file, Faludy, and read the confessions you made three years ago. You are a naughty boy, Faludy,' he said, looking at me attentively but cheerfully. 'Yes, you are a very naughty boy. You lied to the State Security Organization, you deliberately misled us. Don't you know that this is a punishable offence? Or did you sign this rubbish under physical or psychological compulsion? In that case, you must revoke your confession. Right now. And at the same time you are supposed to give me the names of the person or persons who forced you to make a false confession incriminating yourself. We shall proceed against these imperialist saboteurs who have wormed their way into the officer corps of the AVO with the merciless severity of the . . .'

I stopped him by raising my hand.

'I am not in a position to denounce AVO officers while I am still in the hands of the AVO. I am, however, ready to revoke all my confessions.'

'You are a smart fellow, Faludy,' the lieutenant said and pushed a document before me according to the printed text of which I revoked my confessions made under duress but could not, try as hard as I might, remember who extracted those confessions from me.

When I returned the setting sun was peering forth from among the slender trees of the Kékes Mountain. I stopped in the middle of the hanging gardens and looked down upon the swimming pool in which some of my fellow-prisoners were soaking their feet. A cool wind was blowing and I shivered because, for the first time, I realized that I was soon going to be released. Suddenly I felt a hand on my shoulder.

'Won't the boys catch cold, Georgie?' asked Victor Emmanuel solicitously.

*

From the middle of the month the inmates of the camp were released in groups of ten, twenty, fifty a day. The first to go were the safe-breakers, ordinary criminals, smugglers, and then came the politically indifferent elements. Later only four or five people left every day and then nobody. One night a hundred and twenty of our comrades were taken by lorry to Kistarcsa with the explanation that this would speed up administrative procedure and with the promise that they would soon be released. Among them were Todi, Gati, numerous Catholics and former communists: approximately two-thirds of the camp's *élite*. The selection and removal made us all suspicious. We had read in the press that Imre Nagy had decreed the immediate and complete liquidation of the internment camps. One night the AVO picked out the eight so-called Titoists of the camp and they disappeared without trace.

In the middle of August, when the discharging of prisoners was accelerated, our fellow-prisoners returning from Budapest prison hospitals told us that the hundred and twenty who had been taken to Kistarcsa had again been tried for the same alleged crimes, found guilty and thrown back in jail. They also related that the treatment had improved in the other Hungarian prisons but that nobody had been released. Other news they had for me was that Bandi Havas, who had gone insane at 60 Andrassy Street, had been beaten to death a year ago by AVO guards at the Vacz penitentiary.

Under such circumstances I waited nervously, anxiously, for the barber. I had often imagined my release in the years past but always in a different form. I had dreamed of a triumphant mood, of looking at the world through bars of tears. Instead I felt fear, disgust and, even worse, apathy. I wasn't even certain whether I would be released or not. After the transfer of the hundred and twenty men to Kistarcsa our numbers decreased from day to day but there were still twenty-five or thirty men who looked at each other questioningly after a new group departed, because none of them was ever included. These men, or rather eighteen of them, were now waiting to be shaved. These men were the public figures, parliamentary deputies and leading intellectuals of the camp; the very men who opposed the régime more uncompromisingly than the average in their deeds as well as in their thoughts. The selection was extraordinarily clever of the AVO, which usually showed little sense for fine distinctions. The experience of forty months and hundreds of reports from their informers had made them realize at last that their greatest enemies were not the men who spat on Rakosi's picture but those who talked about history and philosophy in their free time.

It seemed probable that they would try us again or simply stick us into some other prison. But there were even more depressing possibilities. The week before, after a group of twenty prisoners had left and Gabori and I were burning straw mattresses on top of the hill, he had called my attention to a familiar sound shortly after the group of twenty had marched out through the gate on its way towards the railway station of Recsk. We heard machine-gun fire from the valley, approximately two or three kilometres away. The next day we listened again. Again a group of twenty marched out by the gate towards noon, waving cheerfully to us who were standing among the burning mattresses in the ashes of which we were baking potatoes. We almost believed that we had had hallucinations the day before, when suddenly the machine-gun fire began again. I could clearly distinguish the sound of three machine-guns, each firing thirty to forty rounds. I figured that fifteen or sixteen must be dead, three or four wounded and one untouched.

'The wounded are finished off with a pistol,' Gabori murmured. 'But we are too far off to hear the shot.'

We decided not to say anything to our comrades, but in the evening it turned out that they too had heard the machine-gun fire and had drawn the same conclusions. I argued that it was unlikely that the AVO would go to the trouble of writing letters of discharge, provide everyone with civilian clothes and hand them their fares, only to shoot them dead a few kilometres below the camp. It would be much simpler to lock us in and set the barracks on fire. Gabori declared that I had spent too much time in the West to understand this kind of logic. This complicated and cowardly method of committing murder was absolutely characteristic of the secret police.

There were also other disturbing rumours in the camp. According to some the peasants of the community of Recsk received the released prisoners with enmity and beat them bloody with hoes and scythes. They refused another group free passage through the village so that the unfortunate men had to return to the gate from where, however, the guard chased them away. We heard that the AVO had explained to the peasants that we were the former land-owners who now wanted to take the land back from them. Remembering my adventure at the railway station two and a half years ago, this appeared probable and so did the news that the miners had prevented prisoners, all 'former exploiters, counts, landlords and capitalists', from boarding the train at Recsk, so that they had to start out on the hundred and forty kilometres to Budapest on foot. According to another rumour the inhabitants of Recsk hated us because 'we had brought the AVO hordes upon them'. The AVO officers and guards spent their time off in the village terrorizing everybody, chasing the peasants from the pub and driving the locals to distraction with their carousing and excesses. Dentures and two of his buddies had, in the course of two years, raped every girl in the village whose father was a well-to-do peasant. If one of them happened to be a virgin, he whipped her afterwards for having bloodied his dress trousers.

Behind this layer of fluctuating anxiety there was another, permanent and deep. What if I were not taken to another prison, not machine-gunned, not beaten to death in the village. What was the world I would have to face in a few hours like? After Beria's liquidation and the East German uprising my friends predicted the fall of the régime. They thought it was impossible that the West should not take advantage of the situation, the acute palace revolt, the obvious weakness of the enemy, and would force the Soviet Union out at least from Germany, Czechoslovakia and Hungary. At first I shared their views but when, six months after Stalin's death, nothing had happened, I gave up hope. At that point my friends began to expect that the régime would collapse by itself or at least that the structure of dictatorship would be loosened; but I thought that if the structure of dictatorship were loosened the régime would have to collapse, so that therefore there was no hope of any loosening.

The nearer the moment of liberation came the more frightened I was. Was my mother still alive? Was Suzy waiting for me? Would my friends have the courage to talk to me? Would I have a place to sleep at night? Would I get a job as a worker or a night watchman? These questions, however, were only secondary. Formerly, when I had thought of my release, I had pictured myself in a free society. It had never even occurred to me that I should be released by a people's democracy. True, I might perhaps sleep in a soft bed, see Suzy again, have matches in my pocket; there would be curtains at my window and I would not starve to death. Yet, instead of a triumph, this liberation seemed to me a defeat. I should again lose the intellectual freedom I had enjoyed behind the barbed-wire fences. Here I had the opportunity to be brave and honest. Outside, if only because of my family, I would not have that opportunity. Here I had cherished the illusion that, once released, I should be able to write my experiences; that my return from America and my adventures afterwards had not, in fact, been in vain. Outside, where a flat could be searched at any moment, it would be impossible to put down my experiences on paper and my unwritten memories would weigh me down like the fear of a new arrest. In here the solitude of the cell had taught us all to think, our knowledge of human nature had increased, our senses had become refined. We all believed that we had become more intelligent, more sensitive, more honest than before – while outside we would find a society that had stupefied, corrupted and desensitized its members. Formerly, in the people's democracy, and here in prison I had always felt like a researcher who had renounced for a certain time the pleasures of life and had descended in a steel globe to the bottom of the sea to observe the life of the deep-water monsters, who would one day report his scientific experiences objectively and exactly, though without concealing his horror of them. Now, shortly before my release, I felt as if my steel globe had broken away from the chains securing it and would never be pulled up again. I would have enough air and food to last me until I died but I should never have the opportunity to report my findings. I should have to live in the globe until I died, observing the polyps, sharks and algae about which I knew everything there was to know, until I went mad with boredom and disgust. I had thought I should be covered with glory, whether I got out alive or finished in the lime-pit. But now I would have to exist, neither dead nor alive, in an alien world.

After having been shaved we climbed up towards the warehouse on top of the hill. Gabori and I helped Mutor, our poor comrade with the brain tumor, who couldn't walk straight. Each was given a suit of old clothes and a pair of shoes with holes in the soles. I alone was given back my suitcase which contained the somewhat bloody, somewhat mouldy, but still very elegant Burberry suit in which I had been arrested. For some mysterious reason the AVO had put a seal on the suitcase and the sergeant had always respected it. Not so the prisoners. In the course of the years the *nachalniki* had stolen my shirts, my bathing trunks and my handkerchiefs,, Then, when it became known that we would be released, a reverse process took place: my friends smuggled their own things into my suitcase until it was full of objects I would have to return. I discovered in it Musza's prayer books, a few beautifully engraved pipes and North-Eastern Inrush's twenty portions of bacon, that he had saved so as not to starve to death outside.

At the door of the staff headquarters we were met by the attorney who had talked to Boka and Magyarits. We were told to go past him slowly and he repeated the same words to each of us:

'In the name of the Hungarian People's Republic I ask your forgiveness for the injustice, the wrong and indignity you were made to suffer . . .'

A few weeks ago he had shaken hands with everyone, now he only nodded.

In the assembly hall of staff headquarters the political officer, the camp commander, two detectives, the Gnome and Dentures, and a few AVO guards were standing at the head of a long table. They seemed excited and sad. The political officer gave everyone a painful grin, then looked away and began to drum on the windowpane. Victor Emmanuel hung his head and the two detectives stood by like two undertakers. First, I was amazed. I had seen these creatures in many moods but never yet sad. Then it occurred to me that they were mourning the camp; their beautiful camp.

The next phase of the procedure was unexpected. As soon as the attorney had begged our forgiveness in the name of the people's republic, Florian, the political officer, handed us each a judge's order placing us under police surveillance. And then – befitting the solemn occasion – he warned us that the law promised six to ten years' imprisonment should we drop but one word about the circumstances, place, or reasons for our imprisonment. He would advise us to report anyone who asked insistent questions and to tell our families that we had been on a study trip in the Soviet Union. Then with a conventional 'Here, son', Victor Emmanuel handed us our letters of discharge.

During the political officer's speech I had already felt a cool breeze on my neck; as if I had suddenly grown, my head floated near the ceiling and while my heartbeats reverberated on my eardrums I heard loud, melodious birdsong. A slight nausea mounted in my throat and the pitiful figures, petrified in strange positions behind the table, looked like gangsters in a waxworks museum. I sped by them, unseeing, like a visitor carried up by an escalator.

At the gate I turned back once more while the guard inspected our papers. The barracks stood dark and deserted in the basin under the strong autumn sunshine. Between the pillars of the ruined rope-way tubs lay upside down on the road to the quarry. Around the AVO quarters, too, it was as if life had stopped. Menyhért Boka was sitting, legs crossed, on the white bench in front of the cells, listening, obviously bored, to the attorney's impassioned harangue.

When, at about a hundred metres from the gate, we reached a dip and the fence of the camp disappeared from view, Mutor, whom Gabori and I had led along by the arms, drew his arms from ours.

'Thank you,' he said. 'I don't need help.'

'But we are skirting a ravine, idiot!' cried Gabori.

'Oh, I thought you knew I was pretending . . .' said Mutor, blushing. 'I have no tumour on the brain. You understand, don't you . . .?' and he walked on quickly, surely, a man we never knew.

The barber wondered whether we should not skirt the village where they might beat us to death. As I remembered it, the road led straight through the village and the mountainside on both sides was too steep to climb. Besides, the railway station lay just inside the village. Pista B. Racz, a former smallholder deputy, himself a peasant lad, ridiculed our fears. He promised to be the first to enter Recsk.

After approximately thirty minutes of walking, after a sharp curve in the road that lay between a steep mountainside and a ravine, we found ourselves face to face with an AVO detachment lying in the ditch behind three machine-guns. They aimed their guns at us. Mutor moved to the edge of the road to throw himself, if necessary, into the underbrush. Gabori took me by the hand.

'Be a man,' he murmured to himself in an offended voice.

I slipped my other hand under B. Racz's arm.

'Let's talk,' I said, 'or at least pretend we are talking. *Justum ac tenacem propositi virum nec civium ardor prave jubentium* . . . Whether we survive this or not, we can congratulate each other on the beautiful century into which we were born. *Justum ac tena—*'

'I can see only ricocheted bullets on the ground,' said Sandor Visnyei, former social democratic deputy, behind me. 'When we were retreating from Kiev I saw bullets like these lying in the streets of the Stanislav ghetto. But the road and the pavement were also covered with locks of hair and spilled brains. Here I see nothing of the kind, so there is no reason to be nervous.'

From the forest we heard the feverish cooing of a wild pigeon. I looked at the ground at my feet and the light dust stirred up by my shoe. When we reached the AVO men they laughed in our faces and, after we passed, fired a round of shots into the opposite mountainside. Then they dismantled their machine-guns, picked them up and set out towards the camp. But first they turned back and waved us a cheerful goodbye.

Once they had disappeared beyond the bend in the road we almost collapsed on the roadside. We gazed at the grey-pink, bare rock-wall of the Zerge, and felt as if we had just stopped work after ten hours of loading and unloading.

'Well,' said the former social democratic deputy, when we rose to go on, 'let us now say adieu to this socialist re-education camp where so many of our comrades perished and where we have suffered so much.'

'And where we had many a good laugh . . .' Gabori murmured in my ear.

An hour later we stole into the village, heads bent, hearts full of anxiety. Pista Racz walked some fifty steps ahead of us, squat and calm. The first house of the village was like all village houses: there were a few slender fruit trees in its garden, between them lacy cabbage-heads and pumpkins on their creepers. The whitewash was snow-white. The ground under the eaves bore the traces of last night's storm; the rain had formed small ditches and tiny clayey craters. A large, eiderdown-shaped cloud sat round and comfortable on the chimney. It was a house that looked as if a loving couple had built it for themselves in spring and were walking around on tiptoe behind the tiny windows among pitchers of milk, in the fragrance of freshly baked bread.

As I was thinking this a girl between eight and ten years old came running out of the house, her long, golden plaits flying behind her. She put down a large woven basket in the middle of the road, full of pale-pink, tender-skinned grapes. When we reached it her grandfather emerged, a long, skinny, barefoot peasant with greenish-yellow hair and moustache, almost like a Russian peasant straight out of Tolstoi. He shook hands with all of us. When the barber opened his mouth to say something he put a finger in front of his lips.

'We know everything,' he said. 'Everything.'

Then he took nineteen large slices of bread from his knapsack, put a pinch of salt from his pocket on each and – according to the ancient custom of hospitality – offered us one each with a slight bow. He must have been watching for us and seen us coming down the slope. In the meantime the little girl had sped back into the garden and was staring at us with round, blue eyes, from behind the fence.